"In this monograph, a revised edition of his award-winning doctoral thesis, David Rudolph presents a comprehensive treatment of a much-debated passage in First Corinthians where Paul seems to relativize his Jewish identity (1 Cor 9:19–23). Far from supporting a traditional portrait of a Torah-free Paul, Rudolph argues that the position of the self-identified Apostle to the Gentiles builds on the similar strategy of Jesus to practice commensality with all, sinners and righteous alike, as he tries to win all—ordinary Jews, strict Jews, and Gentile sinners—for Christ. This is a major contribution to Pauline research, which locates Paul firmly within Judaism. It is essential reading for all students of Paul as well as for those interested in the relationship between the Jesus movement and other forms of Judaism."
—**ANDERS RUNESSON**, Professor of New Testament, University of Oslo

"Traditionally, 1 Corinthians 9:19–23 has been one of the key texts for proving that Paul refuted Judaism and converted to Christianity. David Rudolph's masterful analysis of the passage shows, however, that it is fully possible to understand Paul from a completely Jewish perspective, allowing for a fully Jewish, even Torah-observant, Paul. This highly persuasive study is an important breakthrough in the process of creating a paradigm shift within Pauline studies, resulting in a historically more accurate picture of the Apostle."
—**MAGNUS ZETTERHOLM**, Associate Professor of New Testament Studies, Lund University

"Rudolph at the minimum destabilizes well-established positions through thorough and intelligent engagement with a range of evidence, both from the Pauline epistles and the wider New Testament as well as from a range of ancient Jewish sources. While focusing upon a very specific text, Rudolph's monograph in fact touches upon a welter of significant issues relevant to New Testament scholars and scholars of ancient Judaism. His stimulating book deserves a wide readership."
—**JAMES CARLETON-PAGET**, Senior Lecturer in New Testament Studies, University of Cambridge

"In *A Jew to the Jews*, David Rudolph convincingly undermines the traditional interpretation of 1 Corinthians 9 that depicts Paul as abandoning Jewish law observance when amongst Gentiles, but keeping it strategically amongst Jews. Rudolph shows how historically unlikely, not to mention how morally and theologically problematic, such a reading is. This book is a welcome addition to a growing body of literature that reads Paul within Judaism, not against it."
—**MATTHEW THIESSEN**, Associate Professor of New Testament, McMaster University

"One of the most controverted issues in contemporary theology and biblical studies is Paul's relation to the Law. Was he starting a new religion that broke with Torah-based Judaism? David Rudolph makes a careful and persuasive argument that sheds new light on Paul, the early Jesus-movement, and the meaning of Israel for Christians. This book is a must-read for every scholar, pastor, and layperson interested in these critical subjects."
—**GERALD McDERMOTT**, Anglican Chair of Divinity, Beeson Divinity School

"In David Rudolph's capable hands the Apostle Paul comes to life as a Torah-observant Jew, not only in the Book of Acts but also in the letters of Paul. Advocates and critics of this perspective will profit not only from Rudolph's patient critique of the prevailing interpretation of 1 Corinthians 9:19–23 but also from the remarkably fruitful interaction with Jewish sources that characterizes his own exegesis. Highly recommended for everyone interested in situating

Paul in (relation to) Judaism and reassessing their image(s) of the Paul of the letters and the Paul of Acts."

—**WAYNE COPPINS**, Associate Professor of Religion, The University of Georgia

"Many have viewed Paul with suspicion, as an opportunist who made himself 'all things to all people' in order to lure as many as possible into Christianity. Paul's motto could imply that he took his Jewishness rather casually, no longer considering himself to be 'under the Law.' David Rudolph perspicaciously argues against this perception of Paul's Jewishness, presenting us with a compelling portrait of the Jewish apostle who could adapt to varying cultural contexts all the while upholding the Torah. His illuminating analysis of 1 Corinthians 9:19–23 will challenge Jew and Christian alike to embrace Paul as a Jew who remained wholeheartedly a Jew."

—**ISAAC W. OLIVER**, Assistant Professor of Religious Studies,
   Bradley University

"*A Jew to the Jews* by David J. Rudolph is a great scholarly work on the meaningful and difficult passage of 1 Corinthians 9:19–23. The book is written with a clear, approachable language, which should be understandable even for those who are not experts in Pauline exegesis. The plethora of literature and scholarly views confronted by the author are aptly summarized and categorized in a fair and honest manner. ... Every scholar and student exploring 1 Corinthians, the issue of Paul's Jewishness, and his missionary strategy, should get familiar with this publication."

—**MARCIN KOWALSKI**, Faculty of Theology, The John Paul II Catholic
   University of Lublin

"Rudolph has succeeded in his primary goal to shake loose the consensus reading from its place of uncontested primacy and has provided a compelling alternative reading of Paul that is worth serious consideration. However, reader beware: Rudolph's Paul has the potential to revolutionize the field."

—**JOEL WILLITTS**, Professor of Biblical and Theological Studies, North
   Park University

"Did Paul the apostle remain Torah-observant after his experience on the Damascus Road and his confession of the Lord Jesus the Messiah? Traditional readings of 1 Corinthians 9:19–23 have consistently answered this question with a resounding negative. In his enlightening study of 1 Corinthians 9:19–23, however, David Rudolph presents a decisive case against traditional interpretations of this passage and opens the door afresh to the possibility of a Torah-observant Apostle Paul. This study is expertly researched, and Rudolph's fresh exegesis provides a promising pathway into the Jewish landscape of Pauline theology."

—**JUSTIN K. HARDIN**, Associate Professor of Biblical and Theological
   Studies, Palm Beach Atlantic University

"Rudolph's study is masterful, an argumentative tour de force that requires serious engagement by those contending that Jewish identity is no longer relevant for Jews 'in Christ.' It will most likely be looked at as a seminal work among New Testament scholars engaged in post-supersessionist interpretation."

—**J. BRIAN TUCKER**, Professor of New Testament,
   Moody Theological Seminary

"If only we could pause the presses until every Pauline student seriously interacts with David Rudolph's masterful work on 1 Corinthians 9. This passage has served far too long as a convenient and over-used interpretive key to Pauline theology and David Rudolph offers a sobering challenge to the dominant paradigm. With careful exegesis and an irenic spirit, he peals back layers of misunderstanding and replaces them with a more satisfying perspective of a first-century, Jewish Paul who models his life and ministry after Jesus. This book really is a must read for anyone interested in Pauline studies."
—**CHRIS MILLER**, Senior Professor of Biblical Studies, Cedarville University

"Traditionally used to prove that Paul was anything but a Torah-observant Jew, 1 Corinthians 9:19–23 ('To those under the law I became as one under the law, though I myself am not under the law. . . . To those without the law I became as one without the law . . .') is exposed in this book to a brilliant, thought-provoking analysis which shows, instead, that Paul simply aimed at following Jesus' example of adaptation with respect to commensality. As Jesus had become all things to all people through eating with ordinary Jews, Pharisees, and sinners, this book argues, Paul's purpose was to became 'all things to all people' through eating with ordinary Jews, strict Jews (those 'under the law'), and Gentile sinners; additionally, by affirming that he himself was 'not under the law,' he meant that he no longer viewed Pharisaic (or other strict sectarian) halakhah, which is not the same as the law in general, as a final authority. David Rudolph examines carefully and consistently the history of the interpretation of this key Pauline passage and adds new important arguments to those put forward by P. Tomson, M. Nanos, and M. Kinzer against its traditional reading. Widely acclaimed since its publication in 2011, this new edition will certainly help this landmark study of the post-supersessionary reading of Paul to reach even more readers."
—**CARLOS A. SEGOVIA**, Lecturer in Quranic and Islamic Studies, Saint Louis University, Madrid

"Rudolph's overall thesis is persuasive and compelling, particularly in light of his thoughtful analysis of Paul's 'calling' language in 1 Corinthians 7:17–24, where he persuasively demonstrates that Paul intended Jewish Christians to continue following Jewish law, while Gentile Christians need not adopt these precepts. Each was to remain 'called' in the state they were in. Rudolph argues that this provides the lens through which we should understand Paul's own relationship to Jewish law. . . . [O]verall this work is cogent and provides a good corrective to the mainstream of scholarship on 1 Corinthians 9:19–23, though it may actually be Rudolph's discussion of 1 Corinthians 7:17–24 that proves the most fruitful for future research."
—**MEIRA Z. KENSKY**, Joseph E. McCabe Associate Professor of Religion, Coe College

"This study of Paul's practice of personal adaptation is a model of careful, disciplined, and insightful exegesis. Rudolph's methodological rigor and temperate tone lead us step by step to a conclusion with far-reaching theological implications: contrary to traditional readings of 1 Corinthians 9, nothing in this biblical text prevents us from viewing Paul as a faithful, Torah-observant Jew."
—**MARK S. KINZER**, President Emeritus, Messianic Jewish Theological Institute

A Jew to the Jews

A Jew to the Jews

Jewish Contours of Pauline Flexibility in 1 Corinthians 9:19–23

Second Edition
With a New Appendix

David J. Rudolph

Foreword by Richard Bauckham

☙PICKWICK *Publications* · Eugene, Oregon

A JEW TO THE JEWS
Jewish Contours of Pauline Flexibility in 1 Corinthians 9:19–23. Second Edition

Copyright © 2016 David J. Rudolph. All rights reserved. Except for brief quotations in critical publications or reviews, no part of this book may be reproduced in any manner without prior written permission from the publisher. Write: Permissions, Wipf and Stock Publishers, 199 W. 8th Ave., Suite 3, Eugene, OR 97401.

First edition published in 2011 by Mohr Siebeck GmbH & Co., KG, Postfach 2040, 72010 Tübingen, Germany. First US edition published by Cascade Books under license from Mohr Siebeck, 2016.

Pickwick Publications
An Imprint of Wipf and Stock Publishers
199 W. 8th Ave., Suite 3
Eugene, OR 97401

www.wipfandstock.com

PAPERBACK ISBN: 978-1-4982-9616-8
HARDCOVER ISBN: 978-1-4982-9618-2
EBOOK ISBN: 978-1-4982-9617-5

Cataloguing-in-Publication data:

Names: Rudolph, David J. | Bauckham, Richard (foreword writer)

Title: A Jew to the Jews : Jewish contours of Pauline flexibility in 1 Corinthians 9:19–23. Second edition / David J. Rudolph, with a foreword by Richard Bauckham

Description: Eugene, OR: Cascade Books, 2016 | Includes bibliographical references and index

Identifiers: ISBN 978-1-4982-9616-8 (paperback) | ISBN 978-1-4982-9618-2 (hardcover) | ISBN 978-1-4982-9617-5 (ebook) | XIV + 296 pages

Subjects: LCSH: Bible. Corinthians, 1st—Criticism, interpretation, etc. | Jews in the New Testament | Gentiles in the New Testament | Paul, the Apostle, Saint

Classification: BS2675.52 R836 2016 (print) | BS2675.52 (ebook)

Manufactured in the U.S.A.

Cover Image "Theological Debate" (1888) by Eduard Frankfort

For Harumi

Table of Contents

Foreword by Richard Bauckham ... xv

Preface ... xvii

Chapter 1: Introduction ... 1

1.1 The Case for the Traditional View ... 2
    1.1.1 Intertextual Argument ... 3
    1.1.2 Contextual Argument ... 10
    1.1.3 Textual Argument ... 11
1.2 The Inadequacy of the Traditional View ... 12
1.3 The Need for Reassessment ... 13
1.4 Aim and Method ... 18
1.5 Overview of the Argument ... 19

Part I: A Reassessment of the Traditional View of 1 Cor 9:19–23

Chapter 2: Intertextual Issues: Understanding Paul's Jewishness in Relation to Being in Christ ... 23

2.1 Text Group A: Jewishness Is Inconsequential in Christ ... 23
    2.1.1 Timothy's Circumcision: An Example of Paul Treating Jewish Identity as a Matter of Expediency (Acts 16:3) ... 23
    2.1.2 Erasure Language ... 27
        2.1.2.1 Circumcision Is Nothing (1 Cor 7:19; Gal 5:6; 6:15) ... 28
        2.1.2.2 No Longer Jew or Greek (Gal 3:28) ... 30
    2.1.3 Third Entity Language (1 Cor 10:32) ... 33
    2.1.4 "Weak in Faith" Language (Rom 14) ... 35
    2.1.5 "Former Way of Life" and "Rubbish" Language (Gal 1:13; Phil 3:8) ... 44
    2.1.6 "Live Like a Gentile and Not Like a Jew" Language (Gal 2:14) ... 46
2.2 Text Group B: Jewishness Is a Calling in Christ ... 53
    2.2.1 Paul's Testimony About His Torah Observance (Acts 21:17–26) ... 53
        2.2.1.1 Paul Was a Torah-Observant Jew ... 54
        2.2.1.2 Paul Lapsed in His Faith ... 59
        2.2.1.3 James Tricked Paul ... 60
        2.2.1.4 James and Paul Fooled the Naïve Jewish Converts ... 62
        2.2.1.5 Paul Was Inconsistent ... 63

2.2.1.6 Luke's Account in Acts 21:17–26 Is a Pious Fraud	64
2.2.1.7 Paul Became as One Under the Law to Win Those Under the Law	67
2.2.2 Circumcision and Foreskin Language	73
2.2.3 Jewish "Calling" Language (1 Cor 7:17–24)	75
2.3 Summary and Conclusion	88

Chapter 3: Contextual Issues: Paul's Stance on Food Offered to Idols (1 Cor 8:1–11:1) — 90

3.1 Overview of the Exegetical Problem	90
3.1.1 Is 1 Cor 8:1–11:1 a Compositional Unity?	90
3.1.2 Did Paul Address Two Factions That Diverged Over the Issue of Idol-Food?	91
3.1.3 Did Paul Forbid Eating Idol-Food on Some Occasions but Not Others?	93
3.1.4 What Is the Relationship Between Paul's Stance on Idol-Food and the Apostolic Decree (Acts 15:1–16:5; 21:25)?	97
3.2 The Jewishness of Paul's View	101
3.3 The Function of 1 Cor 9	107
3.4 Summary and Conclusion	108

Chapter 4: Textual Issues: Variations on the Setting and Language of 1 Cor 9:19–23 — 110

4.1 Greco-Roman Thought	110
4.1.1 Servile Flatterer	110
4.1.2 Antisthenes' Odysseus	111
4.1.3 Enslaved Leader *Topos*	112
4.1.4 Political Commonplaces About the Factionalist and the Non-Partisan	112
4.1.5 Epicurean Psychagogic Technique	113
4.1.6 Sophistic Deception to Deceive the Deceived	114
4.1.7 A Synthetic View	114
4.2 Jewish Thought	115
4.2.1 Jews Associating With Jews	116
4.2.1.1 Pharisees Living as Priests	116
4.2.1.2 Pharisaic Accommodation to Mainstream Jews	119
4.2.1.3 The Limits of Pharisaic Accommodation and Jesus' Association With Sinners	120
4.2.1.4 Standards of Table-Fellowship at Qumran and in Pharisee Homes	123
4.2.2 Jews Associating With Gentiles	125
4.2.2.1 Evidence That Some Jews Did Not Eat With Gentiles	125
4.2.2.2 Evidence That Some Jews Ate With Gentiles	127
4.2.3 Jewish Outreach	130
4.2.3.1 Henry Chadwick and Philo's *QG* 4.69	131
The Text of *QG* 4.69	132
Jewish Missionary-Apologetic Activity in *QG* 4.69?	134
4.2.3.2 David Daube and Jewish Missionary-Apologetic Background	135

	Recent Scholarship on Jewish Missionary-Apologetic Activity in the First Century	136
	Matt 23:15 and Proselytizing Pharisees	137
4.2.4	The Ideal Guest and Host	142
4.3 Gospel Traditions		147
4.4 Variations on the Language of 1 Cor 9:19–23		149
4.4.1 "Free" (ἐλεύθερος)		150
4.4.2 "I Became as" (ἐγενόμην . . . ὡς)		151
4.4.3 "Under the Law" (ὑπὸ νόμον)		153
4.4.4 "Without the Law" (ἄνομος)		159
4.4.5 "Though I Am Not Without the Law of God" (μὴ ὢν ἄνομος θεοῦ)		160
4.4.6 "In Christ's Law" (ἔννομος Χριστοῦ)		163
4.4.7 "Win" (κερδήσω)		165
4.4.8 "Weak" (ἀσθενεῖς)		167
4.5 Summary and Conclusion		169

Part II: A Proposed Interpretation of 1 Cor 9:19–23

Chapter 5: Imitating Christ's Accommodation and Open Table-Fellowship — 173

5.1 The Exegetical Context of 1 Cor 9:19–23	173
5.2 "Interchange" in Paul's Letters	176
5.3 Paul's Knowledge of Jesus Tradition	179
5.4 Jesus as "All Things to All People" in the Gospels	180
5.4.1 A Slave of All	181
5.4.2 Eating With Sinners, Pharisees and Ordinary Jews	181
5.4.3 Paul's Awareness of Jesus' Example of Adaptation	182
5.4.4 Jesus' Rule of Adaptation	183
5.4.5 Paul's Awareness of Jesus' Rule of Adaptation	187
5.5 Paul as "All Things to All People"	190
5.5.1 "I Became as"	191
5.5.2 "I Became as One Under the Law"	194
5.5.2.1 The Reason for Paul's Use of the Term "Under the Law" in 1 Cor 9:20	196
5.5.2.2 The Meaning of the Restrictive Clause "Though I Myself Am Not Under the Law"	201
5.5.3 "I Became as a Jew"	202
5.5.4 "I Became as One Without the Law (Though I Am Not Without the Law of God but Am in Christ's Law)"	204
5.5.5 "I Became Weak"	208

Chapter 6: Conclusion and Implications	**209**
Appendix: Five Years Later: New and Notable Publications	213
Bibliography	219
Index of Ancient Sources	264
Index of Modern Authors	281
Subject Index	288

Foreword

Did Paul, the apostle to the Gentiles, remain a Torah-observant Jew? I have long thought he probably did, though, of course, this is not the same as thinking that he continued to observe the Pharisaic halakhah that had previously governed his conduct. But I have also long been puzzled by 1 Corinthians 9:20–21. These verses are puzzling whether or not one thinks Paul continued to observe Torah. If, as most scholars have thought, Paul means that he observed Torah when he was with Jews but not when he was with Gentiles, how could that possibly work in practice? Did he expect Jews to think he was always Torah-observant? The Jews with whom he spent time in Corinth would know very well that he broke the rules when he was with Gentiles? So how could that help him to "win" them for Christ? And can we really suppose Paul adopted a form of deception as a key missionary tactic?

In this important book David Rudolph succeeds in showing how unsatisfactory the most common interpretations of these verses are. But the questions certainly do not end there. If Paul continued to practice Torah in the company of Gentiles as well as Jews, how could he say that he was "not under the law"? Rudolph's fresh and refreshing approach to these verses, which focuses on table fellowship and the kinds of accommodation a good guest would make at the table of a host, is illuminating and, to my mind, very persuasive. Particularly interesting is Rudolph's suggestion that Paul's practice of table fellowship with different groups of people was based on Jesus' practice of table fellowship with all sorts of Jews. This coheres with recent tendencies to see Paul as more dependent on the traditions about Jesus than has conventionally been thought. It gives strong and contextually relevant content to the exhortation with which Paul closes this section of 1 Corinthians: "Be imitators of me as I am of Christ" (11:1).

Some questions remain. Rudolph thinks that, at dinner with Gentile hosts, Paul would have eaten meat from the meat market in Corinth, much as he advises his readers to do in 10:25–28. But what if the meat had not been drained of blood in the way the Torah required? What if Paul was served pork? I am inclined to think he may have availed himself of the principle that, where commandments conflict, one must overrule the other. The standard example is: Should you circumcise your son on the eighth day if the eighth day is a Sabbath? In that instance no Jew could avoid disobeying one of the commandments in order to obey the other. Jesus deployed this principle in the parable of the Good Samaritan, implying that the commandment to love the neighbour, in such a context, should overrule the requirement that priests avoid corpse-impurity. Might not Paul, in some such way, have thought he was permitted to eat meat with blood in it?

The larger question, of course, is Paul's Judaism. It scarcely needs any longer to be argued that Paul's theology is thoroughly Jewish. But did he still think of himself as a Jew or did his new identity in Christ supersede his membership of Israel? Did the church as he understood it comprise Jews and Gentiles, each still identifiable as such, or was it composed of ex-Jews and ex-Gentiles, now indistinguishably Christians? There is much in Paul to suggest the former, but Jewish identity was inseparable from practice of the Mosaic law. A truly Jewish Paul must be a Torah-observant Paul. Rudolph's argument for such a Paul is a key piece in what seems to me to look like an increasingly plausible argument: that in the early Christian movement generally it was taken for granted that Jewish Christians would continue to observe Torah, as Jesus did – and in the way Jesus did. The arguments about Torah-observance were concerned with Gentiles, not Jews.

As is not uncommon in Pauline studies, the exegesis of a few verses has wide-ranging implications. David Rudolph's thesis is important for Messianic Jews today and for the way Paul is regarded in Jewish-Christian dialogue. It is not for Gentile Christians to tell Jewish Christians how they should relate to the Torah, but all of us who want to understand Paul and his role in the early Christian movement need to grapple with the issues Rudolph explores in this significant study.

Richard Bauckham
Cambridge

Preface

This monograph is an updated version of the doctoral thesis that I completed at Cambridge University in 2007 and that won the Franz Delitzsch Prize from the Freie Theologische Akademie. Since I put down my pen, a number of important books and articles have been published on Paul and Judaism, and I am pleased to have the opportunity to interact with some of these sources in the present work. I have also included an Appendix to the Second Edition that points up new and notable publications from 2011–16.

The writing of this monograph would not have been possible without the generous support of many people, first and foremost my Doktorvater Prof. Markus Bockmuehl. In addition to guiding the course of my research, Prof. Bockmuehl saw to it that my Cambridge experience included seminars, cultural events, participation in the Grantchester Meadows Group of Ph.D. students that met fortnightly at his house and visits to the Christian catacombs in Rome among other day trips. Prof. Bockmuehl regularly extended hospitality to me as well as to my family during the course of my doctoral studies and I am forever grateful for these happy times.

I am also indebted to the erudite Prof. William Horbury and Dr. Peter Head for their supervisions and wise counsel, as well as to my examiners, Prof. Richard Bauckham and Dr. James Carleton Paget, who carefully reviewed the thesis and encouraged me to publish it. Special thanks should go to the Hebrew, Jewish and Early Christian Studies Seminar at Cambridge and the Oxford-Cambridge New Testament Conference (2005) for providing me with an opportunity to discuss my research with colleagues working in the field of Second Temple Judaism and Christian origins. I am particularly grateful for comments received from Prof. Graham Stanton and Prof. Morna Hooker.

The community of scholars at Tyndale House, Cambridge, warmly welcomed me into their company and I benefited greatly from their insights. I am especially thankful to these friends whose constant encouragement and *koinonia* made my season in Cambridge a magical time. These tall pillars and mighty hammers included Wayne Coppins, Sarah Hall, Todd Wilson, Joel Willitts, Justin Hardin, Charles Anderson, John Yates, Stephen Witmer, Jonathan Moo, Bill Barker, Joel Lawrence, Barry Danylak, Poul Guttesen, Chris Vlachos, Caryn Reeder, Dr. Elizabeth Magba and Dr. David Instone-Brewer.

Many of the ideas contained in this monograph were borne out of extended conversations with these extraordinary people.

Of all my dialogue partners, I particularly want to thank Wayne Coppins for the hundreds of hours we spent together in the Selwyn College Dining Hall discussing Paul and Judaism. Wayne pressed me to question every assumption and to go deeper with every argument. A special word of appreciation goes to my friend Jane Heath who read through the thesis and gave me sixteen pages of invaluable comments in the weeks leading up to submission. I am also grateful to Todd Wilson, Charles Anderson, Dr. Mark Kinzer, Kent Meads, David Kindred, Hana Rudolph, Elisa Rudolph, Yahnatan Lasko and Dr. J. Brian Tucker, who took time out of their busy schedules to carefully review the work.

The completion of the thesis would not have been possible without scholarship assistance from the British Government, Cambridge University and Selwyn College. The Divinity Faculty's Peregrine-Maitland Studentship for Postgraduate Research on the Relationship between Judaism and Christianity was especially helpful during my final year of study in England. I am also grateful to the Union of Messianic Jewish Congregations, Prof. Dan Juster, Rabbi Carl Kinbar and Dr. Jeff Feinberg for their scholarship assistance and enthusiastic support. I would also like to thank Prof. Jörg Frey at Mohr Siebeck who accepted the monograph for publication in the WUNT 2 series as well as Dr. Henning Ziebritzki and Tanja Mix for their guidance in preparing the final manuscript. I am also indebted to Dr. Robin Parry and Mike Surber at Pickwick Publications who helped make possible the Second Edition.

A warm word of appreciation goes to my parents Carol Ann Rudolph, Michael Rudolph, Marie Rudolph, Morimitsu Kondo and Teruko Kondo, whose continual encouragement helped me to run the race to win the prize.

Friday evenings at 14 Merton Street in Newnham, Cambridge, were always filled with *Shabbat* peace, guests at our table, Hebrew blessings and *zemirot* (Jewish hymns), beginning with the *Eshet Chayil*, "A wife of noble character who can find? Far beyond pearls is her value. Her husband's heart relies on her and he shall lack no fortune" (Prov 31:10–11). My wife Harumi believed in the importance of my Ph.D. studies and joyfully sacrificed much so that I could be a full-time student from 1999–2005. Without her companionship, encouragement and devotion to the Lord, I would have never completed this research project. "Many women have done excellently, but you my darling surpass them all" (Prov 31:29). Finally, I am grateful to my three wonderful daughters, Hana, Elisa and Miryam, who followed me to England and back so that I could live out my dream.

Chapter 1

Introduction

On the basis of Rom 9:1–4, it seems fair to say that Paul loved Jews as his own people. As for Paul's Jewish identity in a cultural sense, some things evident to us (e.g., his use of Jewish tradition and methods of interpretation) and no doubt many ordinary things hidden from our gaze continued to be part of Paul's Jewish identity after his call and remained dear to him. But one thing that most Jews prized as central to their cultural identity – specifically, the way of life specified by the Law – is no longer a defining mark of Paul's identity. For proof one has only to look at Phil 3:2–11, where he says that he now counts his former Jewish identity in the Law as "garbage" because of the superior value of knowing Christ; and 1 Cor 9:19–23, where he describes his missionary strategy of becoming "all things to all people".[1]

In his essay "Did Paul Value Ethnicity?" Charles Cosgrove describes Paul as a faithful Jew, a pious Jew, a Jew's Jew but not a Jew who considered himself under the jurisdiction of Mosaic law, at least with respect to distinctively Jewish commandments. In other words, Paul was not a "Torah-observant Jew".[2] One of two decisive passages that Cosgrove cites as "proof" of Paul's break from "the way of life specified by the Law" is 1 Cor 9:19–23. Here Paul states plainly, "To the Jews I became as a Jew, in order to win Jews. To those under the law I became as one under the law (though I myself am not under the law) so that I might win those under the law. To those without the law I became as one without the law…" (1 Cor 9:20–21). Cosgrove echoes the consensus of

---

[1] Charles H. Cosgrove, "Did Paul Value Ethnicity?" *The Catholic Biblical Quarterly* 68:2 (2006): 289.

[2] The term "Torah-observant Jew" is used in this study to refer to Jews who seek to observe God's commandments in the law of Moses. Three nuances are implied by my usage of the expression: (1) A sense of obligation with respect to observing the law; (2) A distinction between Jews who practise Judaism primarily as a response to election/calling/covenant (Torah observance) and Jews who practise Judaism primarily for other reasons (e.g. cultural expression, contextualization for mission); and (3) A recognition that Torah observance includes distinctively Jewish commandments. While the term "law observant" could communicate these nuances, this is not always the case in New Testament scholarship. For example, Bruce W. Longenecker, "Contours of Covenant Theology in the Post-Conversion Paul", in *The Road from Damascus: The Impact of Paul's Conversion on His Life, Thought, and Ministry* (ed. Richard N. Longenecker; Grand Rapids: Eerdmans, 1997), 140, suggests that "Paul saw nothing wrong with nomistic observance in and of itself, for Jewish Christians could still be law-observant if they so desired". Longenecker, like many scholars (e.g. Olufẹmi Adeyẹmi, "The New Covenant Torah in Jeremiah and the Law of Christ in Paul" [Ph.D. diss., Dallas Theological Seminary, 2005], 186), overlooks the fact that "law" by definition is obligatory.

New Testament scholarship when he refers to this text as evidence that Paul burst the bounds of first-century Judaism. How else could the expression "I myself am not under the law" be interpreted? Heikki Räisänen puts it bluntly, "1 Cor 9.20f. is absolutely incompatible with the theory of an observant Paul".[3] But is the "occasional conformity to Jewish law" interpretation of 1 Cor 9:19–23 as irrefutable as commentators make it out to be? And if it can be refuted, how might one understand 1 Cor 9:19–23 as the discourse of a Torah-observant Jew? This is the central query of this monograph.

1.1 The Case for the Traditional View

Pauline scholars give three rationales for why 1 Cor 9:19–23 rules out the possibility of a Torah-observant Paul. The first rationale is an *intertextual* argument: 1 Cor 9:19–23 is part of a group of texts in the Pauline corpus and Acts that depict Paul's Jewishness as erased or inconsequential in Christ. The second rationale is a *contextual* argument: 1 Cor 9:19–23 is consonant with Paul's permissive stance on idol-food in 1 Cor 8 and 10, which was a radical break from Judaism. The third rationale is a *textual* argument based on 1 Cor 9:19–23: Paul's nomistic language in 1 Cor 9:19–23 demonstrates that he did not consider himself to be under the jurisdiction of Mosaic law. Together these three rationales form a cogent case that the writer of 1 Cor 9:19–23 was not a Torah-observant Jew.

Below I will briefly unpack the logic behind each of these rationales and in so doing introduce the state of research (which will be discussed in more detail in chapters 2–4). More space will be devoted to the first rationale (the intertextual argument) in order to highlight the assertion it makes, based on 1 Cor 9:20a, that Paul no longer considered himself to be a Jew.[4] The first rationale underscores the significance of this study, for if the "occasional conformity" reading of 1 Cor 9:19–23 is found to be weaker than assumed, and a reasonable interpretation of the passage exists that does not preclude the possibility of a Torah-observant Paul, then the far-reaching assertion that Paul no longer considered himself to be a Jew would need to be reassessed.

---

[3] Heikki Räisänen, *Paul and the Law* (2d ed.; Tübingen: Mohr Siebeck, 1987), 75 n. 171.

[4] Some scholars who argue for an erasure reading of 1 Cor 9:19–23 suggest, on the basis of other Pauline texts, that Paul considered himself to be a Jew on some level. E.g. James D. G. Dunn, "The Jew Paul and His Meaning for Israel", in *A Shadow of Glory: Reading the New Testament after the Holocaust* (ed. Tod Linafelt; New York: Routledge, 2002), 201–15. It is often unclear whether the exegete is inconsistent or if he/she views Paul as inconsistent. Moreover, the term "Jew" is rarely defined in these studies. For the purpose of this section, I am concerned only with how these exegetes interpret 1 Cor 9:19–23 and why. I discuss Paul's definition of the term "Jew" in 2.1.1, 2.1.3, 2.2.2, 2.2.3 and 5.5.3.

1.1.1 Intertextual Argument: 1 Cor 9:19–23 is part of a group of texts in the Pauline corpus and Acts that depict Paul's Jewishness as erased or inconsequential in Christ

The following is a sample of contemporary scholars who have articulated the first rationale. Direct quotations have been used where possible, rather than paraphrase, to underscore the homogeneity of the argument.

Peter Richardson and Paul Gooch (1978)

Richardson and Gooch contend on the basis of 1 Cor 9:20 that Paul no longer considered himself a Jew, "Paul says that to certain Jews he became a Jew, which suggests (in *ginomai* and *hōs*) that he was not a Jew. But he was, wasn't he?"[5] Several pages later, they explain, "For him, Judaism was superseded, not merely altered in certain ways; he hardly regarded himself as a Jew legitimately . . . His freedom from all people and systems opens up for him a new identity 'in Christ'. He is really a Jew no longer".[6]

In support of their view, Richardson and Gooch build an intertextual case based on Rom 14, Gal 2:15 and other passages. With respect to Gal 2:15, they note that Paul rebuked Peter for continuing to live as a Jew:

The only place where Paul calls himself a Jew is in Galatians 2:15, but there he is arguing with Peter that although they are Jews by birth they ought not to continue to live like Jews now that they are Christians.[7]

In a follow-up study of 1 Cor 9:19–23, Gooch reaffirms his earlier view:

By defining himself only as Christ's slave, Paul cuts himself free from other identities. This means, I think, that he no longer regards himself as a Jew. That is crucial: by disclaiming his former life Paul may justify behaviour that otherwise would indeed be inconsistent.[8]

E. P. Sanders (1983)

Sanders proposes that the only time Paul lived as a Jew was when he was in Jerusalem surrounded by Jews. Outside of Jerusalem, Paul consistently lived like a Gentile and expected other Jesus-believing Jews to do the same. Sanders points to Gal 2:11–14 as evidence of this, "The Antioch incident would seem to show that, if Jews were present, Paul would expect them not to observe the Jewish dietary laws".[9] Paul's stance in Rom 14:1–6, that days and

---

[5] Peter Richardson and Paul W. Gooch, "Accommodation Ethics", *Tyndale Bulletin* 29 (1978): 96.

[6] Richardson and Gooch, "Accommodation Ethics", 107, 111.

[7] Richardson and Gooch, "Accommodation Ethics", 111.

[8] Richardson and Gooch, "Accommodation Ethics", 137–38.

[9] E. P. Sanders, *Paul, the Law, and the Jewish People* (Philadelphia: Fortress, 1983), 177.

food were matters of personal conscience, was theory. In reality, "the factors which separated Jews from Greeks must be given up by the Jews".[10]

Sanders leads into his discussion of 1 Cor 9:19–23 by noting that explicit third entity language is found in 1 Cor 10:32, "Give no offence to Jews or to Greeks or to the church of God".[11] Paul's all things to all people behaviour was an expression of his ecclesiology, "Nevertheless, in very important ways the church was, in Paul's view and even more in his practice, a third entity".[12]

The three categories in 1 Cor 10:32 are mutually exclusive in Sanders's view. Paul considered himself a member of the third entity ("the church") and a former Jew. To support this argument, Sanders steps outside of the Corinthian correspondence. He reminds the reader that "in Gal. 1:13 Paul can speak of 'his former life in Judaism'. Does he not reveal here that there is a sense in which he is no longer fully described by the appellation 'Jew' or 'Israelite'?"[13]

Sanders then turns to Gal 3:28. Paul regarded members of the church as "neither Jewish nor Greek" (Gal 3:28), but a third entity. Paul "viewed the movement of which he was a part as aiming toward a 'new creation' which would not be merely one group among others, but which would transcend and replace the old humanity, which consisted of circumcised and uncircumcised".[14] Members of this transcendent group adhered to the rule given in Gal 6:15, "For neither circumcision nor uncircumcision is anything; but a new creation is everything!"

How did Paul understand the relationship between this new creation association (the church) and the covenant people of God (Israel)? Sanders proposes that Paul's "thought is informed by the conception of 'true Israel' . . . there is substantial evidence that Paul considered Christians to be 'true Israel'".[15] What of the old Israel? In Sanders's view, Paul considered the inheritance transferred from the old Israel to the true Israel, "Paul thought that those who 'turned to the Lord' (2 Cor. 3:16) were the sole inheritors of the promises to Abraham".[16]

To sum up, Sanders contends that 1 Cor 9:19–23 precludes a Torah-observant Paul. 1 Cor 9:19–23 should be read in light of 1 Cor 10:32, the "third entity" text. From 1 Cor 10:32, Sanders builds an intertextual case using Gal 2:11–14, Rom 14:1–6, Gal 1:13, 3:28, and 6:15, among other passages. In the end, 1 Cor 9:19–23 is elucidated in light of Paul's overarching

---

[10] Sanders, *Paul, the Law, and the Jewish People*, 177–78.
[11] Sanders, *Paul, the Law, and the Jewish People*, 171–79.
[12] Sanders, *Paul, the Law, and the Jewish People*, 178–79.
[13] Sanders, *Paul, the Law, and the Jewish People*, 179, 188.
[14] Sanders, *Paul, the Law, and the Jewish People*, 173.
[15] Sanders, *Paul, the Law, and the Jewish People*, 173–74.
[16] Sanders, *Paul, the Law, and the Jewish People*, 175–76.

theology of transcendence and transference. Jewish identity and lifestyle are old realities superseded in Christ and the church. For Sanders, Paul's ecclesiology is central to understanding the meaning of 1 Cor 9:19–23.

D. A. Carson (1986)

Carson posits on the basis of 1 Cor 9:20 that Paul did not view himself as a Jew any longer. Evidently "in one sense Paul does not see himself as a Jew: rather, he *becomes* like a Jew in order to win Jews (1 Cor. 9.20)".[17] Paul's status as neither Jew nor Gentile enables him to conform to the law on occasion as a matter of expediency:

> Paul occupies a *third ground* and, so far as law is concerned, is prepared to move from that ground to become like a Jew or like a Gentile, because in his relationship to Torah he is neither one nor the other. This also explains why Paul could be charged with being antinomian by some of his contemporaries – because his understanding of God's redemptive purposes in history left Torah *qua* covenant superseded.[18]

Barbara Hall (1990)

Hall regards 1 Cor 9:19–23 as a form of the Gal 3:28 "baptismal formula". As the "baptismal formula" explicitly refers to "no longer Jew", 1 Cor 9:20 implicitly refers to the erasure of Jewish identity, "'What does it mean that Paul, a Jew, becomes as a Jew?' Paul can say that he became as a Jew because he has in mind the baptismal formula: The Christian is now neither Jew nor Greek, but a new creation".[19] Hall's analysis, which receives broad support in the scholarly literature on 1 Cor 9:19–23, does not simply maintain that 1 Cor 9:19–23 is informed by Gal 3:28 but that 1 Cor 9:19–23 is Gal 3:28 in a restated form. It is the same "baptismal formula". Paul emphasizes in 1 Cor 9:19–23 that the Corinthians are an eschatological community and that distinctions related to ethnicity have disappeared in the new creation:

> The use of the baptismal formula in the passage sets the idol-meat issue squarely in an eschatological context. The formula proclaims the reality of a new creation, the transformation of relationships . . . To say that neither circumcision nor uncircumcision counts is to claim that the distinction between them is gone in Christ . . . The eschatological community has come into existence.[20]

---

[17] D. A. Carson, "Pauline Inconsistency: Reflections on 1 Corinthians 9.19–23 and Galatians 2.11–14", *Churchman* 100:1 (1986): 12; cf. D. A. Carson, "Mystery and Fulfillment: Toward a More Comprehensive Paradigm of Paul's Understanding of the Old and the New", in *Justification and Variegated Nomism: The Paradoxes of Paul* (ed. D. A. Carson et al.; Tübingen: Mohr Siebeck, 2004), 2:402.

[18] Carson, "Pauline Inconsistency", 37; cf. Carson, "Mystery and Fulfillment", 403.

[19] Barbara Hall, "All Things to All People: A Study of 1 Corinthians 9:19–23", in *The Conversation Continues: Studies in Paul and John* (ed. Robert T. Fortna and Beverly R. Gaventa; Nashville: Abingdon, 1990), 146.

[20] Hall, "All Things to All People", 147–48.

Other passages that Hall cites to build her intertextual case for an erasure reading of 1 Cor 9:19–23 include 1 Cor 7:19, Gal 5:6 and 6:15.[21]

John Barclay (1995–1996)

Barclay portrays Paul as an "apostate" from Judaism based on 1 Cor 9:20–21 and related passages, including Gal 1:13–14, 2:11–14, 3:28, Phil 3:2–11 and Rom 2:25–29, 14:1–6, 14.[22] He approvingly quotes Barrett's interpretation of 1 Cor 9:19–23 that Paul no longer considered himself a Jew, "C. K. Barrett [1971:211] rightly comments on 1 Cor 9.20 that Paul 'could become a Jew only if, having been a Jew, he had ceased to be one and become something else. His Judaism was no longer of his very being, but a guise he could adopt or discard at will'".[23] In support of this reading, Barclay notes that Paul's Jewish opponents accused him of being a chameleon:

> The attempt to maintain his dual loyalties, to be, as he put it, "all things to everyone" (1 Cor 9.22) was bound to lead to charges of opportunism (Gal. 1:10) and to engender the special bitterness of a community who felt that one of its members was only masquerading as a Jew.[24]

James Dunn (1999)

Dunn submits, on the basis of 1 Cor 9:20–21, that Paul did not consider himself a Jew:

> What is striking here is the fact that Paul, even though himself ethnically a Jew, can speak of becoming "as a Jew". To become as a Jew is obviously to follow the patterns of conduct distinctive of Jews. In other words, Paul speaks as one who does not acknowledge "Jew" as his own given identity, or as an identity inalienable from his person . . . So we ask again: Did Paul think of himself as a Jew? The answer is evidently No, for the most part. Insofar as "Jew" was an ethnic identifier (and insofar as he was an ethnic Jew), Paul wished neither to be known as such nor to identify himself as such. Insofar as "Jew" denoted a lifestyle, a commitment to the ancestral customs of the Jews, Paul wished neither to exercise such a commitment nor to insist that other Jews be true to their ethnic-religious identity.[25]

Dunn supports this interpretation of 1 Cor 9:19–23 by pointing to Gal 1:13–14, 2:14–15, 3:28, 5:6, 6:15, Phil 3:5–8, 1 Cor 7:19, 2 Cor 11:22, Rom 2:25–

---

[21] Hall, "All Things to All People", 148.

[22] John M. G. Barclay, "Deviance and Apostasy: Some applications of deviance theory to first-century Judaism and Christianity", in *Modelling Early Christianity: Social-Scientific Studies of the New Testament in its Context* (ed. Philip F. Esler; London: Routledge, 1995), 122–23; John M. G. Barclay, "Paul Among Diaspora Jews: Anomaly or Apostate?" *Journal for the Study of the New Testament* 60 (1995): 103, 113; John M. G. Barclay, *Jews in the Mediterranean Diaspora: From Alexander to Trajan (323 BCE – 117 CE)* (Berkeley: University of California Press, 1996), 384–86.

[23] Barclay, "Deviance and Apostasy", 114 n. 44.

[24] Barclay, "Deviance and Apostasy", 117.

[25] James D. G. Dunn, "Who Did Paul Think He Was? A Study of Jewish-Christian Identity", *New Testament Studies* 45 (1999): 182.

29, 11:1, 14:14, 20, Acts 21:39, 22:3, and Mark 7:18–23, among other New Testament passages.

Daniel Rode (2002)

Rode posits in his exegetical study of 1 Cor 9:19–23 – "El Modelo de Adaptación de Pablo Según 1 Corintios 9:19–23" – that Paul transcended his identity as a Jew in the Gal 3:28 sense:

> Why did Paul need to show himself "as a Jew" if he indeed was a Jew? The declaration that to the Jews he became "as a Jew" is notable since it shows how radically he conceived of the demand for Christ, and this position forced him to transcend all cultural allegiance, "To relate to Jews as a fellow Jew (cf. Acts 21:17–26) is for Paul now seen as an act of accommodation!"[26]... The apostle occupies a third entity perspective, which transcends ethnicity. Above all things, he is a Christian more than a Jew; thus, becoming a cross-cultural missionary ... he knew that in Christ "there is no longer Jew or Greek, there is no longer slave or free, there is no longer male and female; for all of you are one in Christ Jesus" (Gal 3:28) ... he was above all these differences.[27]

David Horrell (2005)

Horrell looks to 1 Cor 9:20 as evidence that Paul considered his Jewish identity "displaced" and "dissolved" in Christ:[28]

> The evidence from Paul's letters indicate that for Paul himself a new and defining identity ἐν Χριστῷ implies a radical transformation of his Jewish identity and practice (1 Cor 9:20; Gal 2:15–20; 4:12; Phil 3:8, etc.). Similarly, Paul is clear that the identity distinction between Jewish and Gentile Christians, the circumcised and the uncircumcised, is now "nothing" (οὐδέν) since both are part of God's new creation in Christ (1 Cor 7:19; Gal 5:6; 6:15).[29]

The Greek text of 1 Cor 9:20 ("I became *as a Jew* [ὡς Ἰουδαῖος] ... I myself am *not under the law* [ὑπὸ νόμον]") is quoted by Horrell as proof that Paul was no longer a "law-abiding Jew".[30] Further attestation that Paul viewed his Jewishness as dissolved in Christ is that "Paul speaks of his 'former life in

---

[26] Richard B. Hays, *First Corinthians* (Louisville: John Knox, 1997), 153.

[27] Daniel Rode, "El Modelo de Adaptación de Pablo Según 1 Corintios 9:19–23", in *Pensar la Iglesia Hoy: Hacia una Eclesiología Adventista, Estudios teológicos presentados durante el IV Simposio Bíblico-Teológico Sudamericano en honor a Raoul Dederen* (ed. Gerald A. Klingbeil et al.; Libertador San Martín, Entre Ríos: Editorial Universidad Adventista del Plata, 2002), 337–38.

[28] David G. Horrell, "'No Longer Jew or Greek': Paul's Corporate Christology and the Construction of Christian Community", in *Christology, Controversy and Community: New Testament Essays in Honour of David R. Catchpole* (ed. David G. Horrell and Christopher M. Tuckett; Leiden: Brill, 2000), 333.

[29] Horrell, "No Longer Jew or Greek", 343; cf. David G. Horrell, *Solidarity and Difference: A Contemporary Reading of Paul's Ethics* (London: T & T Clark International, 2005), 18, 260 n. 50.

[30] Horrell, "No Longer Jew or Greek", 334; Horrell, *Solidarity and Difference*, 18.

Judaism' (Gal 1:13–14)".[31] For Paul, the Jew/Gentile distinction is "obsolete", belongs to a "former era" and is "transcended by a new identity in Christ".[32] "In both Galatians and Colossians the declaration is that now 'there is no longer Jew and Greek'".[33] In Rom 14, Paul "stands on the 'Gentile' side of the division" in declaring that nothing is unclean (Rom 14:14a, 20). Thus, "Paul's convictions seem hardly to be those of a Torah-observant Jew, nor of one who urged that 'Jews and Gentiles should each stick to their respective ways of life'".[34] Paul has joined a third entity as indicated by the tripartite language in 1 Cor 10:32.[35] In 1 Cor 10:18 Paul implicitly refers to the church as spiritual Israel, even as in Gal 6:16 he apparently regards the Christian community as the Israel of God.[36]

Wolfgang Schrage (1995), Anthony Thiselton (2000), Roy Ciampa and Brian Rosner (2010)

The view that Paul regarded his Jewishness as erased or inconsequential in Christ, based on 1 Cor 9:19–23, is a commonplace in contemporary New Testament scholarship. In addition to the exegetes mentioned above who make this intertextual case and link it to 1 Cor 9:20, several critical commentators will be noted to round off this section. Schrage interprets 1 Cor 9:20 in light of Gal 3:28 and depicts Paul as no longer a Jew. Through freedom in Christ, Paul became "as a Jew" to win Jews:

> Paul does not simply become a Jew or heathen but like a Jew and like a heathen . . . We see that in Ἰουδαίοις ὡς Ἰουδαῖος. For how can Paul who has been born a Jew (cf. Gal 2:15 Ἡμεῖς φύσει Ἰουδαῖοι) *become* a Jew only now? It is not a coincidence that there is missing a μὴ ὢν Ἰουδαῖος in analogy to the following two examples. But can't he only become something that in a certain way he has not been lately? Indeed this is true because in Christ we have neither Jew nor Greek (Gal 3:28; cf. 1 Cor 12:13). Paul is, even as a born Jew, not simply a Jew any longer but he is becoming one in order to win Jews. We see here that the γίνομαι ὡς is not simply a natural identification but the thing that comes from ἐλευθερία and moves into δουλοῦν ἐμαυτόν. It is a movement set in motion by freedom to the other thing which comes from love, to put oneself next to the other.[37]

Thiselton writes, "The phrases ὡς Ἰουδαῖος and ὡς ὑπὸ νόμον are especially revealing of Paul's theology of the new creation . . . (cf. Gal 2:15; 3:28; and 1

---

[31] Horrell, "No Longer Jew or Greek", 334; Horrell, *Solidarity and Difference*, 18.
[32] Horrell, "No Longer Jew or Greek", 322.
[33] Horrell, "No Longer Jew or Greek", 327.
[34] Horrell, "No Longer Jew or Greek", 340; Horrell, *Solidarity and Difference*, 15–19.
[35] Horrell, "No Longer Jew or Greek", 341; Horrell, *Solidarity and Difference*, 259.
[36] Horrell, "No Longer Jew or Greek", 341; Horrell, *Solidarity and Difference*, 19.
[37] Wolfgang Schrage, *Der erste Brief an die Korinther* (Neukirchen-Vluyn: Neukirchener Verlag and Benziger Verlag, 1995), 2:340.

Cor 12:13)".[38] Quoting this statement, Ciampa and Rosner underscore that Paul no longer identified as a practising Jew in a covenantal sense, "Although Paul is a Jew in terms of his ethnicity and heritage, he no longer understands himself to be part of Judaism, and would not consider himself a Jew if that word is defined by those who understand their relationship with God to be based on their adherence to the Mosaic covenant".[39]

1 Cor 9:19–23 and Luke's Portrait of Paul

In the same way that 1 Cor 9:19–23 is often connected to Pauline texts that emphasize the erasure of Jewish identity (e.g. Gal 2:14, 3:28; 1 Cor 7:19; Rom 14), 1 Cor 9:19–23 is also commonly related to Lukan texts that depict Paul as a Torah-observant Jew.[40] Commentaries on Acts and 1 Corinthians often make this correlation. The vast majority of 1 Corinthians and Acts commentators identify Acts 16:3 and Acts 21:17–26 as instances of Paul applying his 1 Cor 9:20 principle of adaptation in a Jewish setting. Leon Morris, for example, comments on 1 Cor 9:20, "But in approaching Jews he conformed to practices that would enable him to win *those under the law*. The sort of thing in mind is his circumcision of Timothy (Acts 16:1–3) and his joining in Jewish 'purification rites' (Acts 21:23–26)".[41]

The correspondence between 1 Cor 9:19–23 and Paul's nomistic practices in Acts would seem to be self-evident. Acts 16:3 explicitly states that Paul circumcised Timothy "on account of the Jews". Paul apparently viewed circumcision as a matter of expediency and circumcised Timothy to please the Jews of Derbe and Lystra in order to win them to Christ. In Acts 21:17–26, Paul followed James' advice to undergo ritual purification in the temple and thereby make it possible for four Nazirites to offer sacrifices in the temple in keeping with their vows. Paul presumably agreed to this in order to conciliate the Jews in Jerusalem who were "zealous for the law" and concerned that he was teaching Jews not to circumcise their children or live according to the customs of the fathers. It seems clear from both of these examples in Acts that Paul does not practise Jewish ritual as a response to commandment, but as an expedient. For the apostle, Torah observance was a matter of indifference.

---

[38] Anthony C. Thiselton, *The First Epistle to the Corinthians: A Commentary on the Greek Text* (Grand Rapids: Eerdmans, 2000), 702.

[39] Roy E. Ciampa and Brian S. Rosner, *The First Letter to the Corinthians* (Grand Rapids: Eerdmans, 2010), 425–26.

[40] The only ostensible examples of Paul participating in distinctively Jewish practice (or helping others to participate in distinctively Jewish practice) are in Luke's portrayal of Paul (e.g. Acts 16:3, 18:18; 21:17–26). The historical reliability of Acts 21:17–26 will be discussed in 2.2.1.6.

[41] Leon Morris, *The First Epistle of Paul to the Corinthians: An Introduction and Commentary* (Leicester: InterVarsity, 1985), 136.

1.1.2 Contextual Argument: 1 Cor 9:19–23 is consonant with Paul's permissive stance on idol food in 1 Cor 8 and 10, which was a radical break from Judaism

The second rationale for the traditional case posits that Paul did not regard idol-food as forbidden for Jesus-believers, a perspective in conflict with the Torah-observant life. The 1 Cor 8:1–11:1 pericope was prompted by a query that Paul received from the Corinthians concerning idol-food (Περὶ δὲ τῶν εἰδωλοθύτων [1 Cor 8:1; cf. 7:1]). Because Jews regarded idol-food as forbidden food, Paul's response to the query provides the exegete with something of a barometer of his Jewish convictions. If Paul's stance on idol-food was permissive, it stands to reason that he was not a Torah-observant Jew. What was Paul's stance? The modern consensus interpretation of 1 Cor 8 and 10 is that Paul was indifferent to idol-food. Since an idol was nothing, idol-food was also nothing (1 Cor 8:4–8; 10:19–20). Idol-food was not spiritually contaminated or dangerous as 'the weak' thought (1 Cor 8:7–8). There was nothing wrong with eating it. However, because eating idol-food in a temple might cause the weak to stumble, Paul counselled the strong to renounce their ἐξουσία (1 Cor 8:9–12).

Though Paul prohibited the eating of idol-food in a temple, he permitted the Corinthians to eat freely from the meat market, "Eat whatever is sold in the meat market without raising any question on the ground of conscience" (1 Cor 10:25). They could also eat freely in the homes of polytheistic Gentiles. Only if they were explicitly informed that the food before them had been offered to idols were they to refrain from eating it. Declining in this situation was not because idol-food was dangerous, but because of the other person's conscience, "If an unbeliever invites you to a meal and you are disposed to go, eat whatever is set before you without raising any question on the ground of conscience. But if someone says to you, 'This has been offered in sacrifice', then do not eat it, out of consideration for the one who informed you, and for the sake of conscience, I mean the other's conscience, not your own" (1 Cor 10:27–29).

Most commentators agree that Paul's approach to idol-food burst the bounds of Judaism. C. K. Barrett remarks that "Paul is nowhere more un-Jewish than in this μηδὲν ἀνακρίνοντες ['without raising questions', 1 Cor 10:27]".[42] Gordon Fee describes Paul as an "absolutely liberal" Jew who goes "quite over against his own Jewish tradition".[43] Dunn sums up the standard view, "The usual understanding of Paul's advice in the matter is that it disregarded traditional Jewish sensibilities: the Paul who counselled the Corinthians not to raise questions (*mēden anakrinontes*) about the source of the

---

[42] C. K. Barrett, "Things Sacrificed to Idols", *New Testament Studies* 11 (1965): 49.

[43] Gordon D. Fee, *The First Epistle to the Corinthians* (Grand Rapids: Eerdmans, 1987), 360 n. 10.

meat served (10.25, 27) was no longer governed by the characteristically Jewish antipathy to idolatry so fundamental to Jewish identity. The issue of Christian liberty and desirability for Christians to maintain social involvement and responsibilities (10.23–30) had taken precedent. The parallel with Romans 14 seems to settle the issue".[44]

Since Paul's stance on idol-food in 1 Cor 8 and 10 appears to contravene normative standards of Second Temple Judaism, and since 1 Cor 9:19–23 occurs in the middle of the 1 Cor 8–10 pericope, it is concluded that 1 Cor 9:19–23 was not written by a Torah-observant Jew.

1.1.3 Textual Argument: The nomistic language in 1 Cor 9:19–23 demonstrates that Paul did not consider himself to be under the jurisdiction of Mosaic law

The third rationale for the traditional case contends that Paul's statement in 1 Cor 9:20b ("*I myself am not under the law*") is an explicit renunciation of Mosaic law. Almost all contemporary studies of the passage maintain that "not under the law" means *not under the authority of Mosaic law*. C. K. Barrett provides a succinct explanation of the expression, "To be a Jew is to be under the law and thereby related to God in legal terms. Paul is no longer related to God in this way; at the most he may pretend to be so related. He is not under the law; he behaves as if he were under the law. The law here means the law of Moses; but if this is repudiated by an *a fortiori* argument all less important and directly divine laws are repudiated. Paul is now related to God through Jesus Christ (cf. 1.30), and no room is left for law".[45] Paul's statement in 1 Cor 9:20a ("To the Jews I *became as a Jew*") adds to the case that Paul no longer considered himself a Torah-observant Jew (1.1.1).

That Paul only occasionally conformed to Jewish law is indicated by 1 Cor 9:21, "To those without the law *I became as one without the law* . . . so that I might win those without the law". Paul became as a Gentile (one who was without the law) when he was with Gentiles. What does this mean practically? The consensus view is that Paul did not observe distinctively Jewish practices when he was with Gentiles. Paul's statement that he is "in Christ's law" (1 Cor 9:21) also leaves the impression that Paul did not remain Torah observant. While commentators vary in their interpretation of "in Christ's law", almost all concur that it does not include distinctively Jewish commandments. Seyoon Kim takes this a step further and argues that being "in Christ's law" includes embracing the teaching of Jesus that all foods are now clean, "This line of reasoning suggests that Paul not only sees 'the law of Christ' as emphasizing the love command but also dispensing with the food/purity rules of

---

[44] James D. G. Dunn, *The Theology of Paul the Apostle* (Grand Rapids: Eerdmans, 1998), 702.

[45] C. K. Barrett, *A Commentary on The First Epistle to the Corinthians* (London: A & C Black, 1971), 212.

the law of Moses. With 'the law of Christ' Paul refers to Jesus' setting aside the food/purity rules as well as his stressing the love command. Only so could Paul, guided by 'the law of Christ', accommodate himself to the Gentiles 'as one outside the law', that is, ignoring the food/purity regulations of the law of Moses. This conclusion points to Jesus' ruling about food/purity in Mark 7:15/Matt 15:11, the *mashal* saying of Jesus whose intent Mark correctly interprets: 'Thus he declared all foods clean' (Mark 7:19)".[46]

Taken together, the nomistic language in 1 Cor 9:20–21 suggests that Paul did not consider himself a Torah-observant Jew. He explicitly states that he is not under the law, that he sometimes lives as one without the law and that he upholds another law ("Christ's law") that, in the view of some scholars, not only excludes distinctively Jewish commandments but is based on Jesus' repudiation of the Mosaic food/purity regulations.

1.2 The Inadequacy of the Traditional View

Despite the apparent strength of the argument surveyed in 1.1, there are underlying weaknesses. A few of these weaknesses will be pointed out below; others will be commented on in the course of the investigation. The most obvious problem is that the traditional portrayal of Paul as all things to all people is not historically realistic. It does not fit the first-century socio-historical context or what is known of Paul's character. There are multiple problems:

1. Paul could not have been "all things to all people" all the time as the standard interpretation maintains. When Paul is viewed in his historical setting, it is apparent that he was often around Jews and Gentiles together, thus restricting his ability to be "all things to all people".[47]
2. The standard interpretation portrays Jews as simpletons. It implies that Jews did not notice that Paul observed Jewish law only when he was around them. More likely, however, the Jewish community knew how Paul lived. According to Luke, Paul's congregation in Corinth met in a house that was next door to the synagogue (Acts 18:7).[48]
3. It is doubtful that Paul employed such a foolhardy strategy. Once his inconsistency with respect to basic Torah commandments became known, it would have caused to "stumble" the very people he was trying to "win".

---

[46] Seyoon Kim, "Imitatio Christi (1 Corinthians 11:1): How Paul Imitates Jesus Christ in Dealing with Idol Food (1 Corinthians 8–10)", *Bulletin for Biblical Research* 13:2 (2003): 203; Cf. Fee, *The First Epistle to the Corinthians*, 490 n. 70; Horrell, *Solidarity and Difference*, 177.

[47] Sanders, *Paul, the Law, and the Jewish People*, 177–86; Gerhard Ebeling, *The Truth of the Gospel: An Exposition of Galatians* (trans. David Green; Philadelphia: Fortress, 1985), 115.

[48] Bart J. Koet, "As Close to the Synagogue as Can Be: Paul in Corinth (Acts 18.1–18)", in *The Corinthian Correspondence* (ed. R. Bieringer; Leuven: Leuven University Press, 1996), 409.

His behaviour would have been seen as unprincipled and devious, thus bringing his message into disrepute. Was Paul so lacking in common sense? As Wilfred Knox put it, "Obviously no Jew would be in the smallest degree influenced by the fact that he observed the Law when it suited his purpose to do so; obedience to the Law was a lifelong matter".[49] Francis Watson concurs, "Occasional conformity to the law is entirely alien to the Jewish way of life, and could never have helped him to 'win those under the law'".[50] Even today, Jewish writers describe Paul as a proponent of 'trickery',[51] 'deceit'[52] and 'pious fraud'[53] based on the traditional explanation of 1 Cor 9:19–23. By contrast, Paul claimed to be one who did not "practise cunning" when he proclaimed the gospel of God (2 Cor 4:1–2; cf. 1 Thess 2:3). Surely, there is something missing here!

4. Proponents of the traditional view of 1 Cor 9:19–23 do not typically respond at length to Pauline or Lukan texts that appear to be at variance with the view that Paul was only occasionally Torah observant (e.g. Acts 21:17–26; Gal 5:3; 1 Cor 7:17–24). 1 Cor 9:19–23 is used as a hermeneutical starting point or hermeneutical centre; "problem" texts are expected to come into alignment with 1 Cor 9:19–23. There is no overriding reason, however, to maintain this presupposition. One could just as easily argue that 1 Cor 9:19–23 should come into alignment with Paul's "rule in all the churches" in 1 Cor 7:17–20 that Jews are to remain Jews and not live as Gentiles.

1.3 The Need for Reassessment

Only three studies of noticeable length in contemporary scholarship have attempted a reassessment of the case that 1 Cor 9:19–23 precludes a Torah-observant Paul. One is Peter Tomson's *Paul and the Jewish Law* (1990), of which the last eight pages are devoted to 1 Cor 9:19–23. Tomson's approach to the "all things to all people" passage is a text-critical argument. He proposes omitting ὡς ("as") in 1 Cor 9:20a, based on several late manuscripts, and translating the phrase: "I was born the Jews a Jew".[54] Tomson's study

---

[49] Wilfred L. Knox, *St. Paul and the Church of Jerusalem* (Cambridge: Cambridge University Press, 1925), 122 n. 54.

[50] Francis Watson, *Paul, Judaism and the Gentiles: A Sociological Approach* (Cambridge: Cambridge University Press, 1986), 29.

[51] Beth Moshe, *Judaism's Truth Answers the Missionaries* (New York: Bloch, 1987), 212.

[52] Gerald Sigal, *The Jews and the Christian Missionary: A Jewish Response to Missionary Christianity* (New York: Ktav, 1981), 272.

[53] Michael Drazin, *Their Hollow Inheritance: A Comprehensive Refutation of Christian Missionaries* (Safed: G. M. Publications, 1990), 18.

[54] Peter J. Tomson, *Paul and the Jewish Law: Halakha in the Letters of the Apostle to the Gentiles* (Minneapolis: Fortress, 1990), 276–77.

also recommends omitting the restrictive clause μὴ ὢν αὐτὸς ὑπὸ νόμον ("though I myself am not under the law") based on "late manuscripts, including the majority of Greek minuscules which all follow one main tradition".[55]

While Tomson's text-critical argument was a helpful reminder to re-examine variant readings of 1 Cor 9:19–23, it lacked the necessary weight to convince most scholars. The widespread rejection of Tomson's approach ironically had the reverse effect from the one Tomson hoped for. Rather than causing scholars to reconsider the traditional interpretation of 1 Cor 9:19–23, the seemingly extreme lengths to which Tomson went to make his argument only reinforced the impression that 1 Cor 9:19–23 precludes a Torah-observant Paul. Sentiments to this effect are found in dozens of books and articles that reference 1 Cor 9:19–23. For example, Kim writes:

> Tomson's interpretation of the crucial text of 9:19–23 is very revealing. Against the overwhelming manuscript evidence, he, first of all, seeks to eliminate the ὡς before Ἰουδαῖος as well as the phrase μὴ ὢν αὐτὸς ὑπὸ νόμον in v. 20 (pp. 276–79) . . . It is amazing to see the extent to which Tomson's presupposition of Paul as a law-observant Jew pushes him to go in distorting the Pauline statements about the law.[56]

Horrell similarly remarks, "It is telling that Tomson must delete a number of these Pauline statements, on the basis of weak textual evidence, since they conflict with the picture of Paul he presents".[57] While Tomson's treatment of 1 Cor 8 and 10 has been well received by many scholars, I am not aware of any who have adopted his text-critical argument for interpreting 1 Cor 9:19–23.

A second reassessment of the traditional interpretation of 1 Cor 9:19–23 is Mark Nanos's 2009 essay "Paul's Relationship to Torah in Light of His Strategy 'to Become Everything to Everyone' (1 Corinthians 9:19–23)".[58] Nanos

---

[55] Tomson, *Paul and the Jewish Law*, 277.

[56] Kim, "Imitatio Christi (1 Corinthians 11:1)", 212–13.

[57] Horrell, *Solidarity and Difference*, 18.

[58] Mark D. Nanos, "Paul's Relationship to Torah in Light of His Strategy 'to Become Everything to Everyone' (1 Corinthians 9:19–23)", in *New Perspectives on Paul and the Jews* (ed. Reimund Bieringer and Didier Pollefeyt; Leuven: Peeters, forthcoming). Paper presented at the New Perspectives on Paul and the Jews: Interdisciplinary Academic Seminar, Katholieke Universiteit, Leuven, Belgium, 14–15 September 2009. Cited 26 December 2010. Online: http://www.marknanos.com/1Cor9-Leuven-9-4-09.pdf. Below I reference page numbers from the online version (rev. 9-4-09) but quote from an updated version that Mark Nanos kindly sent me (rev. 1-13-10). See his earlier discussions of 1 Cor 9:19–23 in Mark D. Nanos, "Paul and Judaism: Why Not Paul's Judaism?" *Paul Unbound: Other Perspectives on the Apostle* (ed. Mark D. Given; Peabody: Hendrickson, 2010), 120–23; Mark D. Nanos, "The *Polytheist* Identity of the 'Weak', and Paul's Strategy to 'Gain' Them: A New Reading of 1 Corinthians 8:1–11:1", in *Paul: Jew, Greek, and Roman* (ed. Stanley Porter; Leiden: Brill, 2008), 179–210; Mark D. Nanos, "A Torah-Observant Paul? What Difference Could It Make for Christian/Jewish Relations Today?" (paper presented at the Christian Scholars Group on Christian-Jewish Relations, 4–6 June 2005), 33–39.

argues that 1 Cor 9:19–23 refers to Paul's "rhetorical adaptability" (in the manner of Socrates or Antisthenes' Odysseus) and not to "'conduct' or 'lifestyle adaptability'".[59]

> Such "rhetorical adaptability" consists of varying one's speech to different audiences: reasoning from their premises, but not imitating their conduct in other ways . . . This behavior arises when one seeks to express views in vocabulary and by way of models and examples that are calculated to persuade. One thus works from the audiences' premises or world-views, even though seeking to lead them to a conclusion that is based on another set of premises or world-views. Teachers normally seek to relate to students in this way. It is highly useful for making a persuasive argument in any context, especially in philosophical or religious debates, including recruitment and discipleship, as well as for apologetical purposes. That is just how Socrates approached his interlocutors, starting from their premises in a way calculated to lead them step by step to conclusions they had not foreseen and might otherwise be unwilling to accept . . . I propose Paul's self-description here [1 Cor 9:19–23] refers entirely to his evangelistic tactic of rhetorical adaptability, and did not include the adoption of conduct representing his various audiences' convictional propositions, but not his own. He could undertake this argumentative tactic as a Jew faithfully observing Torah, even when speaking to lawless Jews, Jews upholding different halakhic standards, and non-Jews of any stripe. Thus Paul's behavior can be described as free of the duplicitous conduct which serves as the basis for the charges of moral dishonesty, inconsistency, and so on, that arise logically from the prevailing views.[60]

Nanos points to Acts 17 as an example of Paul "becoming" (i.e. reasoning) as a Jew to the Jews and as an idolater to idolaters.[61] In the history of interpretation of 1 Cor 9:19–23, many commentators have argued that Paul's "all things to all people" principle *included* rhetorical adaptability as evidenced by Acts 17 and other texts.[62] However, Nanos uniquely contends that lifestyle adaptability is *not in view at all* in 1 Cor 9:19–23 and that the text therefore does not preclude a Torah observant Paul.[63]

Nanos's essay makes an important contribution by showing how presuppositions of Paulinism – "privileging of gentleness, freedom from Torah and Jewish identity"[64] – inform the traditional reading of 1 Cor 9:19–23 and *ipso facto* validate a hyper-literal interpretation of the text. Nanos is also correct that Paul's accommodation language in 1 Cor 9:19–23 can have a range of meaning and there is no reason to exclude rhetorical adaptability. However, there are a number of reasons in my view to interpret 1 Cor 9:19–23 as *including* some element of lifestyle adaptability:

---

[59] Nanos, "Paul's Relationship to Torah in Light of His Strategy", 11, 17, 25–28.
[60] Nanos, "Paul's Relationship to Torah in Light of His Strategy", 16–18.
[61] Nanos, "Paul's Relationship to Torah in Light of His Strategy", 28–33.
[62] See Henry Chadwick's seminal essay, "'All Things to All Men' (I Cor IX.22)", *New Testament Studies* 1 (1955): 261–75, and 4.1 below.
[63] Nanos, "Paul's Relationship to Torah in Light of His Strategy", 18 n. 42, 26–27.
[64] Nanos, "Paul's Relationship to Torah in Light of His Strategy", 3.

1. As Mark Given has demonstrated, the expression ἐγενόμην . . . ὡς, in both literal and figurative contexts, refers to "concrete, observable changes".⁶⁵
2. Paul's repeated use of nomistic language in 1 Cor 9:20 ("I became as one under the law . . . I became as one without the law [though I am not without the law of God but am in Christ's law]") would seem to indicate that lifestyle is in view. The second restrictive clause ("though I am not without the law of God") likely points back to "the commandments of God" in 1 Cor 7:19,⁶⁶ and suggests that Paul's conduct in relation to the ἄνομος could be misunderstood. The restrictive clause is Paul's way of saying, "Do not misunderstand the nature of my close association with these people. I remain law observant".⁶⁷
3. 1 Cor 9:27 ("but I punish my body and enslave it"; cf. v. 19 "slave to all") reinforces the impression that Paul is speaking about lifestyle adaptability in the previous verses.
4. 1 Cor 10:32–33 ("Give no offence to Jews or to Greeks or to the church of God, just as I try to please everyone in everything, not seeking my own advantage, but that of many, so that they may be saved") is a recapitulation of 1 Cor 9:19–23. The language of trying to "please everyone in everything" presumably includes lifestyle adaptability (cf. 1 Cor 7:32–34; 9:1–18; 2 Cor 5:9).⁶⁸ Moreover, the following verse, 1 Cor 11:1 ("Be imitators of me as I am of Christ"), points back to Paul's *imitatio Christi* ethic in 1 Cor 8–10 and 9:19–23.⁶⁹
5. The 1 Cor 8–10 context focuses on food-related accommodation. There are more than twenty-five references to food and commensality in the pericope.⁷⁰ Also, in 1 Cor 10:27b, Paul appears to echo Jesus' rule of adaptation with respect to being a guest in another's home ("eat what is set before you" [cf. Luke 10:8]). This is lifestyle adaptability.⁷¹
6. A compelling case can be made that Paul applies his 1 Cor 9:19–23 principle of accommodation to the "strong" in relation to the "weak" in Rom 14–15.⁷² Here Paul emphasizes lifestyle adaptability, not rhetorical adaptability.

---

⁶⁵ Mark D. Given, *Paul's True Rhetoric: Ambiguity, Cunning, and Deception in Greece and Rome* (Harrisburg: Trinity Press International, 2001), 109. See 4.4.2 below.

⁶⁶ Frank Thielman, *Paul and the Law: A Contextual Approach* (Downers Grove: InterVarsity, 1994), 104; cf. 101. See 2.2.3 and 4.4.5 below.

⁶⁷ See 4.4.5 below.

⁶⁸ Also Rom 15:1–3, "We who are strong ought to put up with the failings of the weak, and not to please ourselves. Each of us must please our neighbor for the good purpose of building up the neighbor. For Christ did not please himself".

⁶⁹ See 4.3, 5.1 and 5.3 below.

⁷⁰ See 5.5.1 below.

⁷¹ See 5.4.4, 5.4.5 and 5.5.4 below.

⁷² Carl N. Toney, *Paul's Inclusive Ethic: Resolving Community Conflicts and Promoting Mission in Romans 14–15* (Tübingen: Mohr Siebeck, 2008), 189–90, 205. See 2.1.4 below.

7. As I propose in chapter 5 of this monograph, Paul's accommodation language in 1 Cor 9:19–23 likely refers to halakhic adaptability in different table-fellowship contexts, with ordinary Jews, strict Jews and Gentiles.[73] This interpretation does not portray Paul as duplicitous and therefore mitigates the need for an exclusively "rhetorical" reading of 1 Cor 9:19–23.[74]

A third study that challenges the consensus view is Mark Kinzer's *Postmissionary Messianic Judaism* (2005); three pages are devoted to 1 Cor 9:19–23. Kinzer argues that ὑπὸ νόμον ("under the law") in 1 Cor 9:20 refers to Jews who relate to God in a pre-New Covenant way, "The term has more to do with status than with observing particular behavioural norms".[75] Kinzer superimposes his interpretation of ὑπὸ νόμον in Gal 3:23–26/4:4–5 onto 1 Cor 9:20. Should it be assumed, however, that the meaning of ὑπὸ νόμον in Galatians is the same as in 1 Corinthians? And what of Rom 6:14–15? In addition to not fully addressing this intertextual question, Kinzer offers no interaction with the context of 1 Cor 8:1–11:1. Moreover, the problem of repetition that results from his interpretation of ὑπὸ νόμον in 1 Cor 9:20 is not resolved. Why would Paul mention the same group twice in 1 Cor 9:20? Quoting Markus Bockmuehl, Kinzer raises the possibility that Paul's accommodation language in 1 Cor 9:19–23 may reflect halakhic flexibility but he does not elaborate on what this might mean exegetically or practically.

It may be reasonably concluded that contemporary scholarship lacks a full-scale reassessment of the traditional view that 1 Cor 9:19–23 precludes a Torah-observant Paul. The lack of such a reassessment has resulted in a fairly one-sided debate over the meaning of the passage in the scholarly literature. A more critical engagement is in order, especially given that 1 Cor 9:19–23 is crucial for understanding how Paul understood the relationship between his Jewishness and his being in Christ.

---

[73] See 5.5 below.

[74] J. Brian Tucker, "'Beyond the New Perspective on Paul' and the Evangelical New Testament Scholar: Is Paul Torah-Observant in 1 Corinthians 9.20–21?" (paper presented at the annual meeting of the Evangelical Theological Society, New Orleans, 20 November 2009), 6–7, argues that Nanos overstates the case for a rhetorical reading of 1 Cor 9:19–23, "First, in 1 Corinthians 1–4 Paul appears to be somewhat opposed to this type of rhetorically-based complex form of argumentation or communication. How would a finely developed rhetorical strategy described in 1 Cor. 9.19–23 relate to e.g. 1 Cor. 2.1–5 ['I did not come with superior eloquence ... My conversation and my preaching were not with persuasive words ...'] or the earlier context of 1.18–25? ... I would suggest an approach to 1 Cor 9.19–23 that understands Paul, following Rudolph and Tomson, as having a relaxed halakah with regard to the idolatrous intentions of gentiles". See my discussion of Greco-Roman *topoi* in 4.1 below.

[75] Mark S. Kinzer, *Postmissionary Messianic Judaism: Redefining Christian Engagement with the Jewish People* (Grand Rapids: Brazos, 2005), 86.

1.4 Aim and Method

In chapters 2–5, the objective is not to prove that Paul was a Torah-observant Jew (this is beyond the scope of this study and perhaps the available evidence). Rather, the primary aim is to demonstrate that scholars overstate their case when they use 1 Cor 9:19–23 as incontrovertible evidence that Paul was not Torah observant. Such overstatement is demonstrated by pointing out holes in the traditional reading, a task which takes up the bulk of the monograph. A secondary aim is to show how one might understand 1 Cor 9:19–23 as the discourse of a Torah-observant Jew.

In order to fulfil the primary aim of the monograph, the three rationales given for why 1 Cor 9:19–23 precludes a Torah-observant Paul must be reassessed. This is done in Part I (chapters 2–4). Part II (chapter 5) puts forward a fresh interpretation of 1 Cor 9:19–23. The organization of the monograph is as follows:

PART I

Chapter 2	Reassessment of Rationale 1 (Intertextual Argument)
Chapter 3	Reassessment of Rationale 2 (Contextual Argument)
Chapter 4	Reassessment of Rationale 3 (Textual Argument)

PART II

Chapter 5	A Proposed Interpretation of 1 Cor 9:19–23

It is important to point out that even if one does not accept my proposed interpretation of 1 Cor 9:19–23 in chapter 5, the primary thrust of the monograph – the reassessment of the traditional view in chapters 2, 3 and 4 – still stands. The argument in Part I that 1 Cor 9:19–23 does not preclude a Torah-observant Paul is the larger and more important part of the monograph. By demonstrating that the three rationales which underpin the traditional view do not stand up under close scrutiny, I destabilise the consensus reading and open the door for scholars to take a fresh look at 1 Cor 9:19–23. This is a significant contribution to New Testament studies because 1 Cor 9:19–23 is used by many scholars as a hermeneutical lens for understanding Paul. It is a paradigm-shaping text.

1 Cor 9:19–23 may be compared to the hub of a wheel that is connected to many spokes. These spokes represent various biblical and theological issues. Because of the eclectic nature of the arguments that make up the traditional reading of 1 Cor 9:19–23, it is necessary to use more than one method of exegesis to address the standard interpretation and present a counter case. In chapter 2, examination of the intertextual argument will for the most part employ conventional historical-critical methods of exegesis. At the same time, in dealing with Lukan texts (e.g. Acts 16:3 and 21:17–26), historical-literary criticism is also utilized. Since chapters 3–5 are mainly an attempt to under-

stand the historical setting behind the language of 1 Cor 8:1–11:1 (with particular focus on analogues to the pericope in Greco-Roman *topoi* and Jewish literature, including gospel tradition), conventional historical-critical methods of exegesis will suffice.

1.5 Overview of the Argument

The primary aim of the monograph is to demonstrate that scholars overstate their case when they maintain that 1 Cor 9:19–23 is incompatible with a Torah-observant Paul. A secondary aim is to show how one might understand 1 Cor 9:19–23 as the words of a law-abiding Jew.

The study is divided into two parts following the introduction. Part I (chapters 2–4) addresses the intertextual, contextual and textual case for the traditional reading. Weaknesses are pointed out and alternative approaches are considered. Part II (chapter 5) brings the data together and shows how 1 Cor 9:19–23 can be read as the discourse of a Jew who remained within the bounds of pluriform Second Temple Judaism.

The exegetical case in Part II centres on interpreting 1 Cor 9:19–23 in light of Paul's recapitulation in 1 Cor 10:32–11:1, which concludes with the statement, "Be imitators of me, as I am of Christ". Given the food-related/hospitality context of 1 Cor 8–10, and Paul's reference to dominical sayings that point back to Jesus' example and rule of adaptation (1 Cor 9:14; 10:27/Luke 10:7–8), it is argued that 1 Cor 9:19–23 reflects Paul's imitation of Christ's accommodation and open table-fellowship (Mark 2:15–17; Matt 9:10–13; 11:19; Luke 5:29–32; 7:34–36).

As Jesus became all things to all people through eating with ordinary Jews, Pharisees and sinners, Paul became "all things to all people" through eating with ordinary Jews, strict Jews (those "under the law") and Gentile sinners. The restrictive clause in 1 Cor 9:21 ("not without the law of God") should be interpreted in light of Paul's rule in 1 Cor 7:17–20 that Jesus-believing Jews are to remain practising Jews. Upholding Christ's halakhah with respect to table-fellowship with sinners is what Paul meant by being "in the law of Christ" (1 Cor 9:21).

Part I

A Reassessment of the Traditional View of 1 Cor 9:19–23

Chapter 2

Intertextual Issues: Understanding Paul's Jewishness in Relation to Being in Christ

This chapter addresses the first rationale given for why 1 Cor 9:19–23 precludes a Torah-observant Paul: 1 Cor 9:19–23 is part of a group of texts in the Pauline corpus and Acts that depict Paul's Jewishness as erased or inconsequential in Christ. Since it is not possible to respond to every text used to support the traditional interpretation of 1 Cor 9:19–23, ten of the most commonly cited have been selected and divided into six distinct intertextual arguments (Text Group A). After responding to this intertextual case, three texts (Acts 21:17–26; Gal 5:3; 1 Cor 7:17–24) are considered that lend support to the possibility that 1 Cor 9:19–23 was written by a Torah-observant Jew (Text Group B). The aim is to demonstrate that the intertextual argument behind the traditional view is not irrefutable and that a coherent exegetical case can be made that 1 Cor 9:19–23 does not preclude a Torah-observant Paul.

2.1 Text Group A: Jewishness Is Inconsequential in Christ

2.1.1 Timothy's Circumcision: An Example of Paul Treating Jewish Identity as a Matter of Expediency (Acts 16:3)

The standard interpretation of Acts 16:1–3 is that Paul circumcised Timothy for missiological reasons.[1] From Paul's perspective, the circumcision was op-

---

[1] New Testament scholarship is divided on the question of the historical reliability of Acts in general and Luke's portrait of Paul in particular. It is beyond the scope of this study to rehearse the reasons for this. For a survey of the issues, see C. K. Barrett, *The Acts of the Apostles* II (Edinburgh: T & T Clark, 1998), xxxiii–lxii, and Gerd Lüdemann, *Early Christianity according to the Traditions in Acts: A Commentary* (London: SCM, 1989), 1–18. I concur with Hemer that the evidence needs to be examined on a case by case basis; dismissing the whole on the grounds that it is a "secondary" source is less than fully critical scholarship, "It is a recurring motif of contemporary scholarship to stress that the evidence of the Epistles is 'primary' for Paul, and that of Acts 'secondary'. Paul's own evidence is intrinsically 'superior'. The trustworthiness of Acts is thus made the subject of a value judgment upon comparative, rather than internal, grounds. The use and the non-use of Acts as a source are treated like transitional or skeptical poles, where a partial, or eclectic, or qualified, or subordinate, use is made to seem the scholarly mean. The designation of Acts as 'secondary' is formally valid,

tional, a matter of expediency and for the primary purpose of furthering the gospel. It was in order to make Timothy an acceptable Jew to win Jews.[2] Some commentators will add that it was justified on cultural grounds since Timothy's mother was Jewish.[3] What most exegetes agree on is that Paul was indifferent to circumcision as a sign of the covenant.[4]

The major problem with the standard interpretation of Acts 16:3 is that it is at variance with the literary context. Luke places the account of Timothy's circumcision between the convening of the Jerusalem Council in Acts 15 (which debated the question of circumcision for Gentile believers) and the delivering of the consular letter by Paul and Timothy in Acts 16:4–5.[5] The Jerusalem apostles and elders ruled that "believers of Gentile origin" (ἀδελφοῖς τοῖς ἐξ ἐθνῶν) were exempt from the requirement of circumcision (Acts 15:23).[6] Significantly, the letter gives no indication that Jesus-believing Jews are exempt from covenantal responsibilities. As F. Scott Spencer points out, "The representatives at the Jerusalem conference – including Paul – agreed only to release *Gentile* believers from the obligation of circumcision; the possibility of nullifying this covenantal duty for Jewish disciples was never

---

but this does not answer the separate question of its trustworthiness as a source. Is Acts, 'secondary' as it is, trustworthy or not? 'Primary' sources themselves are not exempt from error either, and certainly not from *Tendenz*. Until we re-examine the evidence specifically, the range of possible options remains open" (Colin J. Hemer, *The Book of Acts in the Setting of Hellenistic History* [ed. Conrad H. Gempf; Tübingen: Mohr Siebeck, 1989], 15; cf. 1–29, 312–64). For the purposes of this monograph, it is not necessary to offer a definitive judgment on the historical reliability of Acts. Nevertheless, because of the prominent attention given to Acts 21:17–26 in this chapter, I make a preliminary attempt in 2.2.1.6 to persuade the reader that Luke's account of this episode is arguably (though not uncontroversially) consistent with the available historical evidence. Moreover, I contend that even if Luke's portrait of Paul is considered tendentious, it is nonetheless "the earliest *Wirkungsgeschichte* of Paul's life and teachings with respect to Torah observance. This is how the cultural and practical 'footprint' of Paul's person impressed itself on a Gentile Christian author within living memory of less than a generation of Paul's death" (Markus Bockmuehl, personal correspondence, 3 June 2006). While my case is strengthened if Luke's presentation of Paul in Acts is historically reliable, it does not depend on this conclusion.

[2] Ben Witherington III, *The Acts of the Apostles: A Socio-Rhetorical Commentary* (Grand Rapids: Eerdmans, 1998), 476–77.

[3] James D. G. Dunn, *The Acts of the Apostles* (Valley Forge: Trinity Press International, 1996), 216.

[4] F. F. Bruce, *The Book of the Acts* (Grand Rapids: Eerdmans, 1988), 304.

[5] The assumption here is that Luke has written a carefully constructed narrative, "But if we allow that Luke's account has a narrative logic (an assumption which any writer deserves before he is shown to have been an illogical eclectic), then his explanation of Paul's action must be viewed against the background of the Jerusalem conference and its decisions" (Irina Levinskaya, *The Book of Acts in Its Diaspora Setting* [vol. 1 of *The Book of Acts in Its First Century Setting*; ed. Bruce W. Winter; Grand Rapids: Eerdmans, 1996], 14–15).

[6] That all Gentile believers are in view is indicated in Acts 21:25.

considered".[7] If the Jerusalem leadership had viewed circumcision as optional for Jews, there would have been no point debating the question of exemption for Gentiles or delivering a letter specifically addressed to Gentiles. "If it was no longer obligatory for Jews, how could it possibly become so for others?"[8] That Luke placed the account of Paul's circumcision of Timothy immediately after the council decision, and amid the delivering of the consular letter, suggests that Paul did not regard Timothy as a Gentile, but a Jew who should have been circumcised "on the eighth day" (Luke 1:59; Acts 7:8; Phil 3:5).

The standard interpretation of Acts 16:3 has multiple problems in light of the literary context: First, if Paul considered Timothy a Gentile, then Paul's actions would have been counter to his convictions expressed in Galatians that Gentiles should remain uncircumcised. Second, it is a stretch to think that Paul advocated surgical operations to facilitate cross-cultural evangelism, as Luther and other commentators maintain ("Timothy's circumcision was a minor surgical operation carried out for a practical purpose").[9] Third, circumcising a Gentile would have been ill timed and would have sent the wrong message to the Gentiles who were receiving the apostolic decree that exempted them from circumcision, "Is it likely that Luke would show Paul choosing to do this [deliver the decree] while accompanied by a companion who was a walking contradiction of the very thing that the decree said?"[10] Fourth, the view that Paul regarded Timothy's circumcision as a matter of indifference is historically unrealistic. Luke implies that Timothy's circumcision would become public knowledge and that Timothy would be more acceptable to the Jewish community as a result of his circumcision. But would not people ask Timothy questions about why he decided to be circumcised after all these years? If he told the truth, that he became a Jew (or normalized his status as a Jew) for evangelistic reasons, and not for covenantal reasons, it would have caused to stumble the very people Paul and Timothy were trying to win. Paul and Timothy would have been viewed as devious and as having misused a

---

[7] F. Scott Spencer, *Acts* (Sheffield: Sheffield Academic Press, 1997), 159. Acts 15:10–11 may mean that Jews are "saved through the grace of the Lord Jesus" and not by Torah observance according to the standards of Pharisaic halakhah (see 5.5.2.1). It does not follow from this statement that Peter considered Jews exempt from their covenant responsibilities stipulated in the law or that he considered these covenant responsibilities necessary for salvation. He may have viewed them as commandments of God for Jews, the observance of which did not have a bearing on salvation. Similarly, the apostolic decree lists a number of ritual "requirements" (ἐπάναγκες) for Gentile believers (Acts 15:28–29) but there is no indication that they are necessary for salvation.

[8] Michael Wyschogrod, *Abraham's Promise: Judaism and Jewish-Christian Relations* (ed. R. Kendall Soulen; Grand Rapids: Eerdmans, 2004), 194.

[9] Bruce, *The Book of the Acts*, 304.

[10] Christopher Bryan, "A Further Look at Acts 16:1–3", *Journal of Biblical Literature* 107 (1988): 293.

covenant symbol. Were they so lacking in common sense as to think that circumcision for the wrong reason would have impressed people? The traditional interpretation of Acts 16:3 wrongly assumes that Jews at this time did not ask questions. They were simpletons.

More historically realistic is the interpretation of Acts 16:3 proposed in this study: Paul considered Timothy a Jew on the basis of matrilineal descent.[11] Timothy identified as a Jew and lived as a Jew (Acts 16:1; cf. 2 Tim 1:5; 3:15). The young man was uncircumcised probably because his Gentile father had not permitted it. Now the circumstances were different and Timothy desired to fulfil his covenant responsibilities.[12] Paul thus circumcised Timothy to *confirm* a pre-existing covenantal identity. Bornkamm concurs that circumcision was not a matter of indifference for Paul; it had religious-covenantal meaning.[13] Significantly, Paul's actions would have also implemented the im-

---

[11] See Maren R. Niehoff, "Jewish Identity and Jewish Mothers: Who Was a Jew According to Philo?" *The Studia Philonica Annual* 11 (1999): 31–54; Bryan, "A Further Look at Acts 16:1–3", 294; Peter J. Tomson, *"If this be from Heaven...": Jesus and the New Testament Authors in their Relationship to Judaism* (Sheffield: Sheffield Academic Press, 2001), 222. "If there was no authority to impose uniformity, there was also no incentive to suppress variety. Opinions might vary wildly between one community and another on crucial questions of Jewish status such as the validity of conversions and the status of the offspring of mixed marriages" (Martin Goodman, "Jews and Judaism in the Mediterranean Diaspora in the Late-Roman Period: The Limitations of Evidence", in *Ancient Judaism in its Hellenistic Context* [ed. Carol Bakhos; Leiden: Brill, 2005], 185). Cf. Martin Goodman, "Identity and Authority in Ancient Judaism", *Judaism* 39:2 (1990): 192–201; Martin Goodman, *Who Was a Jew?* (Oxford: Oxford Centre for Postgraduate Hebrew Studies, 1989), 11–12. In response to Shaye Cohen's objection that no pre-mishnaic text supports the matrilineal principle with "the only possible exception of Acts 16:1–3" ("Was Timothy Jewish [Acts 16:1–3]? Patristic Exegesis, Rabbinic Law, and Matrilineal Descent", *Journal of Biblical Literature* 105:2 [1986]: 267), it may be argued that single attestation is enough to make the above case. See Levinskaya, *The Book of Acts in Its Diaspora Setting*, 16–17. Against this historical backdrop, Paul may have regarded Timothy as a Jew whose identity was ambiguous and in need of clarification. In support of the ambiguous identity argument, it is notable that Luke does not identify Timothy as a Jew or Gentile. He refers to him as "the son of a Jewish woman who was a believer; but his father was a Greek" (Acts 16:1).

[12] "That the father was no longer living is a reasonable conjecture. A few MSS (1838 gig p) take it into account by speaking of the mother as a widow" (Ernst Haenchen, *The Acts of the Apostles: A Commentary* [trans. Bernard Noble and Gerald Shinn; Oxford: Basil Blackwell, 1971], 479 n. 1).

[13] Bornkamm and others arrive at the same narrative reading of Acts 16:3 but call into question the historical reliability of Luke's account, "Above all, however, it must have been impossible for Paul, especially after the agreements made at the Apostolic Council, to consider circumcision as a ceremony irrelevant to faith and missionary activity. He could scarcely do such a thing for the sake of the Jews for whom circumcision meant more than that. Nor could he do it for the sake of his gospel, for it was precisely with regard to this question that there was a head-on collision between his gospel and the Jewish and Judaizing understanding of salvation. We are, therefore, forced to contest the accuracy of the remark in

plication of the Jerusalem council decision, that Jews should be circumcised in keeping with the "covenant of circumcision" (Acts 7:8; Gen 17:9–14).[14] There is no evidence in the literary context that Paul regarded circumcision as a Jewish cultural expression detached from its first-century meaning as a sign of the covenant. A covenant-keeping motive would also explain Paul's approval of Timothy's circumcision but not Titus'. One was a Jew and the other a Greek (Gal 2:3).[15]

From a literary perspective, Paul's circumcision of Timothy also informs the reader in advance that the later accusations levelled against Paul, that he taught Diaspora Jews not to circumcise their sons (Acts 21:21), are false:

> What better way for Luke to lay the ground for the reader's, so to speak, "knowing" that Paul did not teach Jews to leave their children uncircumcised than by showing Paul, immediately after the episode of the Apostolic Decree, himself *insisting* on maintaining circumcision where appropriate?[16]

The literary context suggests that Luke's explanatory statement ("because of the Jews who were in those places") does not mean that the *act of circumcision* was an expedient, but that the *timing of the circumcision* was an expedient. I contend that the passage be interpreted: "and he took him and had him circumcised [at that time] because of the Jews who were in those places". Paul thought that the optimum time for Timothy to be circumcised (in order to confirm his covenant identity as a Jew) was prior to visiting his home region. The covenant-keeping motive for circumcision would have been *well received* by the Lystra Jewish community and would have opened hearts to Paul's message.

2.1.2 Erasure Language

Paul makes three statements that are often taken by proponents of the traditional reading of 1 Cor 9:19–23 to be synopses of his view that Jewish iden-

---

Acts 16:3 and to explain it in terms of the well-known tendency of Luke to prove Paul's loyalty to the law, in the face of arguments to the contrary" (Günther Bornkamm, "The Missionary Stance of Paul in 1 Corinthians 9 and in Acts", in *Studies in Luke-Acts* [ed. Leander E. Keck and J. Louis Martyn; Nashville: Abingdon, 1966], 203). See 2.2.1.6 below.

[14] Luke refers to Jesus-believing Jews as the "circumcised" (περιτομῆς) in Acts 10:45 and 11:2.

[15] The assumption here is that Timothy and Titus were two different people. Some call this assumption into question. See Richard G. Fellows, "Was Titus Timothy?" *Journal for the Study of the New Testament* 81 (2001): 33–58.

[16] Bryan, "A Further Look at Acts 16:1–3", 293. Cf. Barrett, *The Acts of the Apostles*, 2:762; Chris A. Miller, "The Relationship of Jewish and Gentile Believers to the Law between A.D. 30 and 70 in the Scripture" (Ph.D. diss., Dallas Theological Seminary, 1994), 133–34.

tity is relativised to the point of indifference in Christ. The similar language suggests to some scholars that they are variations of a slogan:[17]

Circumcision is nothing, and uncircumcision is *nothing* (ἡ περιτομὴ οὐδέν ἐστιν καὶ ἡ ἀκροβυστία οὐδέν ἐστιν); but obeying the commandments of God is everything (1 Cor 7:19)

For in Christ Jesus neither circumcision nor uncircumcision counts for anything (ἐν γὰρ Χριστῷ Ἰησοῦ οὔτε περιτομή τι ἰσχύει οὔτε ἀκροβυστία); the only thing that counts is faith working through love (Gal 5:6)

For neither circumcision nor uncircumcision is anything (οὔτε γὰρ περιτομή τί ἐστιν οὔτε ἀκροβυστία); but a new creation is everything! (Gal 6:15)

When the above texts are combined with Gal 3:28 ("There is no longer Jew or Greek [οὐκ ἔνι Ἰουδαῖος οὐδὲ Ἕλλην] . . . for all of you are one in Christ Jesus") and 2 Cor 5:17 ("So if anyone is in Christ, there is a new creation: everything old has passed away; see, everything has become new!"), it becomes evident to many exegetes that Jewish identity, for Paul, was not only "totally irrelevant",[18] but also erased in Christ, "Paul understood himself in a significant sense to be a former Jew".[19] For Boyarin, Christian universalism, of the kind described in these passages, precludes Jewish particularity.

2.1.2.1 Circumcision Is Nothing (1 Cor 7:19; Gal 5:6; 6:15)

Did Paul consider circumcision to be a matter of indifference, as 1 Cor 7:19, Gal 5:6 and 6:15 seem to indicate? Horrell assumes that "nothing" or "not anything" points to unimportance.[20] But given the context, Paul is more likely saying that οὐδέν is "related strictly to salvation",[21] that is, "neither circumcision nor the lack of circumcision has ultimate bearing on salvation".[22] With respect to status before God and eschatological blessing, being Jewish or Gentile is irrelevant.

---

[17] James D. G. Dunn, "Neither Circumcision nor Uncircumcision, but . . . (Gal 5.2–12; 6.12–16; cf. 1 Cor 7.17–20)", in *La Foi Agissant par L'amour (Galates 4,12 – 6,16)* (Rome: Benedictina, 1996), 80–81.

[18] F. F. Bruce, *The Epistle to the Galatians: A Commentary on the Greek Text* (Grand Rapids: Eerdmans, 1982), 273, 232.

[19] J. Louis Martyn, *Galatians: A New Translation with Introduction and Commentary* (New York: Doubleday, 1997), 382 n. 265. See Andreas Lindemann, *Der Erste Korintherbrief* (Tübingen: Mohr Siebeck, 2000), 212; Daniel Boyarin, *A Radical Jew: Paul and the Politics of Identity* (Berkeley: University of California Press, 1994), 85.

[20] Horrell, "No Longer Jew or Greek", 343; Horrell, *Solidarity and Difference*, 18, 260 n. 50.

[21] Hans Conzelmann, *A Commentary on the First Epistle to the Corinthians* (trans. J. W. Leitch; Philadelphia: Fortress, 1975), 126.

[22] Raymond F. Collins, *First Corinthians* (Collegeville: Liturgical, 1999), 284. Also Peter J. Tomson, "Paul's Jewish Background in View of His Law Teaching in 1 Cor 7", in *Paul and the Mosaic Law* (ed. James D. G. Dunn; Grand Rapids: Eerdmans, 2001), 266; Thiselton, *The First Epistle to the Corinthians*, 550.

I contend that Paul uses hyperbole in these passages to stress that being "in Christ" is *more important than* being Jewish.[23] This means that being Jewish could still be very important to Paul.[24] He is simply relativising A to B. In support of this possibility, there are several occasions when Paul uses "nothing" (οὐδέν) or "not anything" (οὔτε . . . τι) language in a clearly hyperbolic way. First, with respect to the work of planting the Corinthian congregation, Paul describes himself as nothing compared to the Lord:

> What then is Apollos? What is Paul? Servants through whom you came to believe, as the Lord assigned to each. I planted, Apollos watered, but God gave the growth. So neither the one who plants nor the one who waters is anything (οὔτε . . . ἐστίν τι οὔτε), but only God who gives the growth (1 Cor 3:5–7).

Are Paul and Apollos truly nothing? Did they really do no work of any significance? On the contrary, their work was vital to the establishment of the Corinthian congregation. But *relative to* what God did, the miracle of changing lives, their work was nothing. Similarly, Paul writes in 2 Cor 12:11, "I am not at all inferior to these super-apostles, even though I am nothing (οὐδέν εἰμι)". Again, was Paul – the apostle to the Gentiles – truly "nothing"? Or is he saying that, *relative to* the Lord, he is nothing, even as *relative to* the super-apostles he is something?

Another example of Paul relativising two important works of God is 2 Cor 3:6–11. Here Paul contrasts the glory of Moses' ministry with the ministry of the Spirit. Though God performed miracles through Moses' ministry that were unparalleled in history, Paul refers to Moses' ministry as having no glory now, for "what once had splendour has come to have no splendour at all, because of the splendour that surpasses it". It all pales in comparison. Moreover, three times Paul uses a *kal vachomer* (*a fortiori*) argument to compare old covenant and new covenant experiences of the presence and power of God (vv. 8, 9, 11). *Both* are truly glorious revelations of the God of Israel, but one is more glorious than the other. To emphasize the "surpassing glory", Paul uses language that downplays the Sinai revelation. But it is wrong to mistake this as trivialization of the old covenant glory.[25] It is instead a rhetorical device intended to highlight the greater glory. He refers to something

---

[23] Cf. Caroline Johnson Hodge, *If Sons, Then Heirs: A Study of Kinship and Ethnicity in the Letters of Paul* (Oxford: Oxford University Press, 2007), 131–34; Christopher Zoccali, *Whom God Has Called: The Relationship of Church and Israel in Pauline Interpretation, 1920 to the Present* (Eugene: Pickwick, 2010), 129.

[24] Wayne A. Meeks, "The Christian Proteus", in *The Writings of St. Paul: A Norton Critical Edition* (ed. Wayne A. Meeks; New York: W. W. Nortan & Co., 1972), 442; William S. Campbell, "The Crucible of Christian Identity: Paul Between Synagogue and State", The British New Testament Conference, Birmingham, 2003.

[25] Scott Hafemann, *Paul, Moses, and the History of Israel: The Letter/Spirit Contrast and the Argument from Scripture in 2 Corinthians 3* (Tübingen: Mohr Siebeck, 1995), 321–27.

genuinely important to emphasize what is *even more important*. It is likely that Paul used the same rhetorical device when he referred to circumcision and uncircumcision as "nothing".

Second, Paul's manner of expression (οὐδέν . . . ἀλλά and οὔτε . . . τι . . . ἀλλά) in 1 Cor 7:19, Gal 5:6 and 6:15 is consistent with the Jewish idiom of dialectic negation in which the "'not . . . but . . .' antithesis need not be understood as an 'either . . . or', but rather with the force of 'more important than'".[26] Consider, for example, how the prophet Hosea makes the same kind of hyperbolic-comparison statement when he speaks in the name of the Lord, "For I desire steadfast love and not sacrifice, the knowledge of God rather than burnt offerings" (Hos 6:6). Sacrifices were important, for the Lord commanded them, but "steadfast love" was *even more important*. To emphasize this, the Lord states that he does *not* desire sacrifice. The negative statement should be taken as hyperbole; it is a Hebrew rhetorical device. A variation of this is found in the *Letter of Aristeas* 234. See also Mark 2:17 and 7:15.[27]

Third, Paul's anti-circumcision language (directed at Gentiles) in Galatians can be understood as upholding Jew-Gentile distinction rather than collapsing it, "Circumcising Gentiles would have made Jews and Gentiles all the same. Paul's vehement rejection of circumcision demonstrates his commitment to maintaining Jews and Gentiles as different and distinct, and militates strongly against seeing Paul's goal as creating human homogeneity".[28]

2.1.2.2 No Longer Jew or Greek (Gal 3:28)

In the traditional intertextual interpretation of 1 Cor 9:19–23, Gal 3:28 is thought to indicate that Paul considered Jewishness erased in Christ.[29] But examined more closely, there are numerous holes in this argument. First, the Gal 3 context has more to do with the justification of Jesus-believing Jews and Gentiles in Christ and the community formed by these believers than the

---

[26] James D. G. Dunn, *Jesus, Paul and the Law: Studies in Mark and Galatians* (Louisville: Westminster/John Knox, 1990), 51. Cf. E. P. Sanders, *Jesus and Judaism* (Philadelphia: Fortress, 1985), 260–64; Roger P. Booth, *Jesus and the Laws of Purity: Tradition History and Legal History in Mark 7* (Sheffield: Sheffield Academic Press, 1986), 69–70; Jonathan Klawans, *Impurity and Sin in Ancient Judaism* (Oxford: Oxford University Press, 2000), 147.

[27] Klawans, *Impurity and Sin in Ancient Judaism*, 147.

[28] Paula Fredriksen, "Judaizing the Nations: The Ritual Demands of Paul's Gospel", *New Testament Studies* 56 (2010): 249–50. Also Pamela Eisenbaum, "Paul as the New Abraham", in *Paul and Politics: Ekklesia, Israel, Imperium, Interpretation* (ed. Richard A. Horsley; Harrisburg: Trinity Press International, 2000), 518; Mark D. Nanos, *The Mystery of Romans: The Jewish Context of Paul's Letter* (Minneapolis: Fortress, 1996), 116 n. 84; Dunn, "The Jew Paul and His Meaning for Israel", 209; Dunn, "Who Did Paul Think He Was?" 189–90; Dunn, "Neither Circumcision nor Uncircumcision", 82.

[29] Cf. 1 Cor 12:13; Col 3:11. See Douglas A. Campbell, *The Quest for Paul's Gospel: A Suggested Strategy* (London: T & T Clark, 2005), 97, 101–102, 104; Boyarin, *A Radical Jew*, 19–23; Martyn, *Galatians*, 376–77; Cosgrove, *Elusive Israel*, 279.

elimination of Jewish and Gentile identity in the present age. Gal 3:28 should be taken as "denying the presumed significance of fundamental Jewish and Gentile identity markers for inheritance of the eschatological blessings and membership in the people of God".[30] Paul makes the same point in Rom 10:10–12, "For one believes with the heart and so is justified and one confesses with the mouth and so is saved . . . For there is no distinction between Jew and Greek".

Second, Paul states in Gal 3:28b that "there is no longer male and female". But is the male-female distinction erased in Christ? On the contrary, Paul distinguishes between men and women in his congregations (1 Cor 11:1–16; 14:34; Eph 5:22–24; Col 3:18; 1 Tim 2:12).[31] The created order with respect to "male and female" (Gen 1:27–28) is not overturned in Christ.[32] This raises an important question: if in Paul's thought the third pair (male and female) is not erased, why should it be concluded that the first pair (Jew and Greek) is erased?[33]

Third, the NA[27] text of Gal 3:28 includes the word εἷς ("one").[34] The NRSV accordingly translates verse 28b "for all of you are one in Christ Jesus". What is this oneness? Boyarin interprets it as a "universal human essence" where all distinction is eradicated.[35] But where is the direct evidence for this? If "male and female" in Gal 3:28 alludes to Gen 1:27–28, perhaps

---

[30] Judith M. Gundry-Volf, "Beyond Difference? Paul's Vision of a New Humanity in Galatians 3.28", in *Gospel and Gender: A Trinitarian Engagement with being Male and Female in Christ* (ed. Douglas A. Campbell; London: T & T Clark, 2003), 18–19. Also Pamela Eisenbaum, "Is Paul the Father of Misogyny and Antisemitism?" *Cross Currents* 50:4 (2000–01): 515; Troy W. Martin, "The Covenant of Circumcision (Genesis 17:9–14) and the Situational Antitheses in Galatians 3:28", *Journal of Biblical Literature* 122:1 (2003): 121.

[31] See James R. Beck and Craig L. Blomberg, eds., *Two Views on Women in Ministry* (Grand Rapids: Zondervan, 2001), for egalitarian and complementarian interpretations of these passages.

[32] "This phrase is awkward in both Greek and English because of the switch from the disjunctive 'neither/nor' to the conjunctive 'and'. Because of this mismatching and the fact that Paul does not normally use the words 'male' (*arsen*) and 'female' (*thelu*), it seems that the last clause constitutes a not-so-subtle allusion to God's creation of the first human beings in Genesis 1" (Eisenbaum, "Is Paul the Father of Misogyny and Antisemitism?" 519). Cf. Pauline Nigh Hogan, *"No Longer Male and Female": Interpreting Galatians 3.28 in Early Christianity* (London: T & T Clark, 2008), 28–29, 195; Boyarin, *A Radical Jew*, 24, 181, 186.

[33] Mark D. Nanos, *The Irony of Galatians: Paul's Letter in First-Century Context* (Minneapolis: Fortress, 2002), 99. Paul regards both pairs as natural distinctions, "In Gal. 2:15, Paul refers to himself as a Jew '*by birth* and not a Gentile sinner'. The phrase 'by birth' (*phusei*) can also be translated 'by nature' and is the same expression Paul uses in 1 Corinthians 11 (v. 14) to validate first-century hairstyles. Paul believes Jews and Gentiles, like men and women, are fundamentally different kinds of people" (Eisenbaum, "Is Paul the Father of Misogyny and Antisemitism?" 516).

[34] P[46] omits εἷς.

[35] Boyarin, *A Radical Jew*, 7.

"one in Christ Jesus" is not unlike the בשר אחד ("one flesh") between male and female in Gen 2:24.[36] Here אחד describes a composite unity (two that are distinct but one). Might Paul have been thinking of a Genesis 2 אחד-like unity in Gal 3:28?[37] The argument adds to the case that the relationship between Jew and Gentile in Galatians 3:28 is one of "unity with distinction", not sameness.

Fourth, Paul refers to Jews and Gentiles (Greeks) in his letters.[38] To Peter, who withdrew from eating with Jesus-believing "Gentiles" (Gal 2:12), he says, "You are a Jew" (Gal 2:14). The writer of Colossians 4:10–11 refers to Aristarchus, Mark and Justus as "the only ones of the circumcision among my co-workers for the kingdom of God". By contrast, Titus is a "Greek" (Gal 2:3). In Romans 11:13, Paul writes, "Now I am speaking to you Gentiles" (cf. Rom 4:11–12). All of this suggests that, for Paul, the Jew-Gentile distinction is preserved, not erased in Christ.[39] "He accepts, and even insists on retaining, the differences as ethnic-identity markers at the same time as he strips them of soteriological significance . . . 'there is neither Jew nor Greek' is not about erasure of differences but revalorization of differences".[40]

To sum up section 2.1.2, 1 Cor 7:19, Gal 5:6 and 6:15 refer to Jewishness being relativised in Christ. With respect to status before God and eschatological blessing, being Jewish or Gentile is irrelevant. This does not mean, however, that Jewishness is unimportant to Paul, for everything is relativised in Christ. The use of hyperbole is consistent with the Jewish idiom of dialectic negation and does not trivialize circumcision or the circumcised life but revalorizes it. Paul's hyperbole indirectly attests to the importance of circumcision even as he positively equates "Jews" with "circumcision". His anti-circumcision polemic needs to be understood as a response to pressure placed on Gentiles to become Jews in order to receive eschatological blessing, which would have collapsed Jew-Gentile distinction. Concerning Gal 3:28, the justification context, the correspondence between the first and third pair, the semantic range of εἷς, and Paul's reference to "Jews" and "Gentiles" in his let-

---

[36] Gundry-Volf, "Beyond Difference?" 31–34; cf. Richard W. Hove, *Equality in Christ? Galatians 3:28 and the Gender Dispute* (Wheaton: Crossway, 1999), 69–76, 107–109.

[37] Eisenbaum, "Is Paul the Father of Misogyny and Antisemitism?" 520–21.

[38] See Christopher D. Stanley, "'Neither Jew Nor Greek': Ethnic Conflict in Graeco-Roman Society", *Journal for the Study of the New Testament* 64 (1996): 101–24, for a discussion of the term "Greeks".

[39] Denise K. Buell, *Why This New Race: Ethnic Reasoning in Early Christianity* (New York: Columbia University Press, 2005), 76; Denise K. Buell and Caroline Johnson Hodge, "The Politics of Interpretation: The Rhetoric of Race and Ethnicity in Paul", *Journal of Biblical Literature* 123:2 (2004): 247–50; Kathy Ehrensperger, *Paul and the Dynamics of Power: Communication and Interaction in the Early Christ-Movement* (London: T & T Clark, 2007), 192–93.

[40] Gundry-Volf, "Beyond Difference?" 21. Also Hodge, *If Sons, Then Heirs*, 126–31.

ters, are all nodal points that, when pressed, reveal the weakness of the erasure reading of the passage.

2.1.3 Third Entity Language (1 Cor 10:32)

E. P. Sanders interprets 1 Cor 10:32 ("Give no offence to Jews or to Greeks or to the church of God") in light of the *Kerygma Petri*[41] and the *Apology of Aristides*.[42] He then draws the inference that Paul regarded himself as part of a third entity, the church, and left his Jewish identity behind.[43] Consistent with this line of argumentation, J. Louis Martyn and Joel Marcus make use of the expression "former Jews" and "former Gentiles" to describe members of the church.[44]

---

[41] Clement, *Strom.* 6.5.41.

[42] Aristides, *Apol.* 2.1. See Judith Lieu, *Neither Jew Nor Gentile? Constructing Early Christianity* (London: T & T Clark, 2002), 55–56; Judith Lieu, *Image and Reality: The Jews in the World of the Christians in the Second Century* (Edinburgh: T & T Clark, 1996), 164–69; David F. Wright, "A Race Apart? Jews, Gentiles, Christians", *Bibliotheca Sacra* 160 (April–June 2003): 131–41; Adolf von Harnack, *The Expansion of Christianity in the First Three Centuries* (trans. James Moffatt; New York: Putnam's Sons, 1904), 301–309.

[43] Sanders, *Paul, the Law, and the Jewish People*, 173–75. Cf. Love L. Sechrest, *A Former Jew: Paul and the Dialectics of Race* (London: T & T Clark International, 2009), 156, 161. It is notable that Sechrest does not discuss Paul's rule in all the churches (1 Cor 7:17–24) that Christ-believing Jews are to remain Jews. See David J. Rudolph, "Paul's 'Rule in All the Churches' (1 Cor 7:17–24) and Torah-Defined Ecclesiological Variegation", *Studies in Christian-Jewish Relations* 5 (2010): 1–23. Also 2.2.3 below.

[44] Martyn, *Galatians,* 382; Joel Marcus, "The Circumcision and the Uncircumcision in Rome", *New Testament Studies* 35 (1989): 68. Cf. the KJV translation of Eph 2:11a, "Wherefore remember, that ye being in time past Gentiles in the flesh". Most English translations follow the RSV, "Therefore remember that at one time you Gentiles in the flesh". What is the "one new humanity" in Eph 2:15? Andrew T. Lincoln, "The Church and Israel in Ephesians 2", *The Catholic Biblical Quarterly* 49 (1987): 613–14, 616, considers it "all believers" who form "a new, third entity, a third race". That is, the "one new humanity in place of the two" (Eph 2:15 NRSV). Markus Barth, *Ephesians: Introduction, Translation, and Commentary on Chapters 1–3* (Garden City: Doubleday, 1974), 309–110, challenges this interpretation, "The new man is 'one . . . out of the two' . . . the new creation is not an annihilation or replacement of the first creation but the glorification of God's work . . . this man consists of two, that is, of Jews and Gentiles . . .Their historic distinction remains true and recognized even within their communion . . . The members of the church are not so equalized, leveled down, or straitjacketed in a uniform as to form a *genus tertium* that would be different from both Jews and Gentiles". When Eph 2:15 states, "He has abolished the law with its commandments and ordinances", the writer may have in mind expansions of the law, fence-like ordinances that produce enmity and division between Jew and Gentile. See Barth, *Ephesians,* 290–91; William S. Campbell, *Paul's Gospel in an Intercultural Context* (New York: Peter Lang, 1992), 110–16; William Rader, *The Church and Racial Hostility: A History of Interpretation of Ephesians 2:11–22* (Tübingen: Mohr Siebeck, 1978), 27, 33, 222–34; Kinzer, *Postmissionary Messianic Judaism*, 165–71; Zoccali, *Whom God Has Called*, 165 n. 46; Michael J. Vlach, *The Church as a Replacement of Israel: An Analysis of Supersessionism* (Frankfurt am Main:

An underlying presupposition of the third entity ecclesiology is the existence of hermetically sealed boundaries between Jews, Gentiles and members of the church; no overlap is possible.

While the third entity reading has the advantage of being clearly defined, the viability of the model is significantly weakened by Pauline references to Jesus-believing Jews as "Jews" and Jesus-believing Gentiles as "Gentiles" (1 Cor 1:22, 24; 12:13; Gal 2:3, 12, 14; Rom 11:13; Eph 2:11; Col 4:10–11; Acts 21:39; 22:3). He does not speak of them as "former Jews" and "former Gentiles". Moreover, there is no direct evidence that the third entity in 1 Cor 10:32 is independent of Jews and Gentiles. It is just as possible, if not more likely given the context, that Paul viewed the third entity as a body of Jews and Gentiles who believed in Jesus.[45] The overlap between the first two categories could be depicted in the following manner:

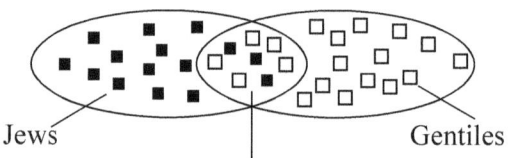

Church of Jesus-Believing Jews and Gentiles

Viewed in this way, Paul would have seen himself as part of the first category ("Jews") and the third category ("the church of God"). Soulen describes this alternative (unity with distinction) model in the following way:

Traditionally, the church has understood itself as a spiritual fellowship in which the carnal distinction between Jew and Gentile no longer applies. The church has declared itself a third

---

Peter Lang, 2009), 181–83; Ronald E. Diprose, *Israel and the Church: The Origin and Effects of Replacement Theology* (Rome: Istituto Biblico Evangelico Italiano, 2004), 44–47.

[45] "The verse could be understood as referring to those outside the Christ-movement with regard to the first two [Jews, Greeks] and to those within with regard to the final group [the church of God]. Or, more likely one could understand καί assensively, rendering the verse, 'Jews and Greeks, even those belonging to the ἐκκλησία'. In that case, Paul is describing those within the ἐκκλησία in the context of their continuing ethnic identities" (J. Brian Tucker, *You Belong to Christ: Paul and the Formation of Social Identity in 1 Corinthians 1–4* [Eugene: Pickwick, 2010], 81). See J. Brian Tucker, "The Continuation of Gentile Identity in Christ" (paper presented at the annual meeting of the Society of Biblical Literature, Special Session on Intercultural Interaction and Identity Formation in Pauline Tradition, Atlanta, 20 November 2010), 1–21; "The Church does not represent so much a *tertium genus* over against Jews and Gentiles as a third group, distinguishable from the rest of Jews and Gentiles, that might take offence at an individual's behaviour. As 1:24 (cf. 12:13) shows, the Church itself is composed of, and called out from (οἱ κλητοί), *Ioudaioi* and *Hellenes*; it cannot be contrasted starkly with them" (Peter Richardson, *Israel in the Apostolic Church* [Cambridge: Cambridge University Press, 1969], 123).

and final "race" that transcends and replaces the difference between Israel and the nations . . . The proper therapy for this misunderstanding is a recovery of the church's basic character as a table fellowship of those who are – and remain – different. The distinction between Jew and Gentile, being intrinsic to God's work as the Consummator of creation, is not erased but realized in a new way in the sphere of the church.[46]

2.1.4 "Weak in Faith" Language (Rom 14)

The traditional intertextual case for the "occasional conformity" reading of 1 Cor 9:19–23 interprets the spiritually "weak" in Rom 14 as Jesus-believing Jews and Gentiles who maintain Jewish dietary and calendar distinctions. "'Weak' is a pejorative term applied to *Christians deficient in their faith,* and the 'weaknesses of the weak' were the result of their failure to realize the full measure of their freedom in Christ from the practices of the Law, as contrasted with the 'strong', who along with Paul, have learned to 'trust God completely and without qualification'".[47] Jewish life motivated by covenant responsibility or divine commandment is thus portrayed as a sign of spiritual immaturity.

Romans 14 can certainly be interpreted in this way. But given that a main point of the text is that Jesus-believers should not "look down on" or "judge" or "put a stumbling block or hindrance in the way of another" (14:3–4, 10, 13), there is reason to question this interpretation. Is not "weak" condescending language?[48] Would this not have been a stumbling block to the very people Paul was standing up for? Surely, there is something missing here.[49]

An alternative way of interpreting the passage is that the weak were not simply Jews and Gentiles who maintained Jewish dietary and calendar dis-

---

[46] R. Kendall Soulen, *The God of Israel and Christian Theology* (Minneapolis: Fortress, 1996), 169–70. Cf. William S. Campbell, "'I Laid the Foundation': Paul the Architect of Christian Identity?" (paper presented at the annual Society of Biblical Literature International Meeting, Cambridge, July 2003), 10.

[47] Nanos, *The Mystery of Romans*, 88.

[48] ". . . in my view such a paternalistic attitude cannot be in tune with the 'imitation of Christ' Paul advocates elsewhere (1 Cor. 4.16–17; 11.1). It also is hardly in tune with the 'welcoming of Christ', the example Christ-followers are admonished to follow in their 'welcoming of each other' (Rom. 15.7). Most significantly, it would require that eventually Jews in Christ would have to give up their identity as Jews and accommodate to the Gentiles' way of life in Christ, obliterating differences and rendering the Gentile way of life, that is, a particular way of life, the norm for being in Christ" (Kathy Ehrensperger, "'Called to be Saints' – The Identity-Shaping Dimension of Paul's Priestly Discourse in Romans", in *Reading Paul in Context: Explorations in Identity Formation: Essays in Honour of William S. Campbell* [ed. Kathy Ehrensperger and J. Brian Tucker; London: T & T Clark International, 2010], 92); cf. Ehrensperger, *Paul and the Dynamics of Power*, 137–54; Paula Fredriksen, "Paul, Purity and the *Ekklesia* of the Gentiles", in *The Beginnings of Christianity: A Collection of Articles* (Jerusalem: Yad Ben-Zvi, 2005), 215–17.

[49] David J. Rudolph, "Messianic Jews and Christian Theology: Restoring an Historical Voice to the Contemporary Discussion", *Pro Ecclesia* 14:1 (2005): 63.

tinctions; they were individuals who were "over-sensitive" about issues related to Torah observance.⁵⁰ A sign of their weakness was that they easily stumbled in their faith, even to the point of eschatological ruin (note ἀπόλλυμι in Rom 14:15).⁵¹

Paul indicates in Rom 14:2, 21 that the weak had concerns about meat and wine. Moreover, his reference to "impure" (κοινός) and "clean" (καθαρός) food in Rom 14:14, 20 suggests that these were Torah-related concerns. But since wine is not prohibited in Mosaic law, what was the problem? It may be reasonably assumed that the weak were concerned about Gentile contact with meat and wine. The weak worried that the wine and meat in question had been tainted by idolatry or unintentionally mixed with unclean foods:

> Apart from the ingredients, uncleanness could also be incurred through food preparation . . . Watson, Ziesler, and others suggest a variation on this theme. They conclude that some Jews practiced "safe eating" through abstinence. The Jews could not trust the level of truth in advertising when the gentile butcher claimed that the meat was free of uncleanness. They avoided contact with meat altogether, rather than risk contamination.⁵²

In his *NTS* article on the use of κοινός in Acts 10:14–15 and 11:8–18, Clinton Wahlen makes a convincing case that first-century Jews were not only concerned about the Torah's clean/unclean dietary distinctions; they were also concerned about κοινός. This category of defilement, not mentioned in the law of Moses, was the result of clean food being in close proximity to unclean food (as in Peter's Acts 10 vision; cf. 1 Macc 1.47, 62 and 4 Macc 7.6 with 4 Macc 6.15).⁵³ Colin House refers to this perceived contamination as "defile-

---

⁵⁰ Tomson, *Paul and the Jewish Law*, 244–45.

⁵¹ Nanos, *Mystery*, 85-165, argues that the weak are non-Christian Jews. For a response, see A. Andrew Das, *Solving the Romans Debate* (Minneapolis: Fortress, 2007), 116-48.

⁵² Gary Steven Shogren, "'Is the kingdom of God about eating and drinking or isn't it?' (Romans 14:17)", *Novum Testamentum* 42:3 (2000): 246–47. "The avoidance of wine could possibly be linked with Jewish avoidance of Gentile wine which we know from other sources, even if it is not entirely clear precisely why it was avoided. In general terms, Jewish avoidance of Gentile wine seems to have been linked with idolatry, again an issue at the heart of table fellowship between Jews and non-Jews. The avoidance of Gentile wine on the assumption that it is idolatrous appears to be assumed in the following example: 'These things belonging to gentiles are prohibited, and the prohibition affecting them extends to deriving any benefit from them at all: wine, vinegar of gentiles which to begin with was wine . . . (*m. 'Abod. Zar.* 2.3)'" (James G. Crossley, *The New Testament and Jewish Law: A Guide for the Perplexed* [London: T & T Clark International, 2010], 109).

⁵³ Bruce, *The Book of the Acts*, 206 n. 18, remarks, "Peter might no doubt have slaughtered and eaten one of the 'clean' animals; but he was scandalized by the unholy mixture of clean animals with unclean". Clinton Wahlen, "Peter's Vision and Conflicting Definitions of Purity", *New Testament Studies* 51 (2005): 514–15, agrees, "The sight of unclean animals intermingling with the clean seems to have convinced Peter that the clean animals should be treated as κοινά or 'common', that is as potentially defiled and hence unacceptable as food . . . Peter comes to the conclusion that no one is to be labelled 'potentially defiled' or 'unclean'". Cf.

ment by association".⁵⁴ Wahlen calls it "potentially defiled food" or "doubtfully pure food" (an allusion to the Mishnaic tractate דמאי "Doubtful"]).⁵⁵ It is likely that Jesus-believers in Rome were overly concerned about clean food becoming *defiled by association* (κοινός) at communal meals. Vegetables apparently did not pose the same risk in their view and the weak were content to eat only vegetables (Rom 14:2),⁵⁶ action that Paul considered extreme and unnecessary. The level of concern for scrupulous food preparation and unintentional mixtures (which may have risen to crisis level proportions in their thinking) was excessive from Paul's perspective and a reflection of misplaced spiritual priorities (Rom 14:17). Paul was aware of their pastoral needs and he knew that this outlook was not healthy.

A second explanation for why Paul considered this group to be "weak in faith" is that they viewed "impurity (of food) and holiness (of days) as objective ontological categories".⁵⁷ Contrary to Paul who regarded nothing as "impure *in itself*" (οὐδὲν κοινὸν δι' ἑαυτοῦ [Rom 14:14]), the weak maintained that food could be "*intrinsically* impure" and that Sabbaths, festivals and fast

---

Colin House, "Defilement by Association: Some Insights from the Usage of ΚΟΙΝΟ'Σ/-ΚΟΙΝΟ'Ω in Acts 10 and 11", *Andrews University Seminary Studies* 21 (1983): 149.

⁵⁴ House, "Defilement by Association", 147. See Witherington, *The Acts of the Apostles*, 350.

⁵⁵ Wahlen, "Peter's Vision and Conflicting Definitions of Purity", 512–13.

⁵⁶ Cf. Josephus, *Life* 14; Shogren, "'Is the kingdom of God about eating and drinking or isn't it?' (Romans 14:17)", 248–51; "Finally, some Jews were *generally* unwilling to eat pagan food, even when there might be no legal objection to it. Some, if they had to eat Gentile food, would eat only vegetables and drink only water; some would eat nothing cooked at all. That is, some Diaspora Jews responded to the pagan environment, full of idolatry and sexual immorality (from their perspective), by cutting themselves off from too much contact with Gentiles . . . Other Jews, it must be emphasized, participated in numerous aspects of pagan culture, such as the theatre and games, quite cheerfully . . . These people may have felt less queasy about Gentile food" (E. P. Sanders, *Judaism: Practice and Belief, 63 BCE – 66 CE* [Philadelphia: Trinity Press International, 1992], 216).

⁵⁷ Kinzer, *Postmissionary Messianic Judaism*, 77. Ehrensperger, "Called to Be Saints", 106, notes that in Rom 14:14, 20 Paul is not "stating something revolutionary or breathtaking that is foreign to Jewish tradition". Rather, he is communicating a Jewish concept, "'Everything is indeed pure' refers to Jewish perceptions of purity and impurity as non-ontological categories, but as God's ordinances, his Torah for his people. A tradition attributed to Jochanan ben Zakkai formulates: 'In your life, it is not the corpse that defiles . . . and not the water that cleanses . . . it is the ordinance of the King of all Kings'. Read in this context, Paul quite unspectacularly merely states what is the Jewish perception in this matter: the Jewish food laws of course are regulations related to God's covenant with the people Israel. That 'the earth is the Lord's and all that is in it' (Ps. 25.1) is not questioned in any way by the setting of the laws that regulate which parts of God's creation are at the disposition of the people Israel. The impure animals are impure for the covenant people, as is emphasized in an almost mantra-like manner in Leviticus 11: 'it is unclean/impure for you' (11.4, 5, 6, 7); 'they are unclean for you' (11.8); 'they are untouchable for you' (11.10–11, 12, 23) etc. As with other purity regulations, these apply to the covenant partner Israel and not to the nations". See also Yechiel Tzvi Lichtenstein, *Römerbrief* (Leipzig, 1898), on Rom 14:14.

days could be "*inherently* more holy" than other days. There is no explicit indication in the Pentateuch, however, that pork or shellfish is *intrinsically* impure (κοινός) or unclean (ἀκάθαρτος); uncleanness of food seems to be imputed by the word of God.[58] Consider that bread with yeast in it is forbidden during the festival of unleavened bread but eaten during the rest of the year (Exod 12:14–20). The substance of the food does not change, only its designation as forbidden or permitted for Israel. Paul's approach in Rom 14 is consistent with the *peshat* (plain) reading of Mosaic law concerning forbidden food. The apostle's rejection of impurity as an objective ontological category is also consistent with Hillelite-Pharisaic halakhah.[59] In his doctoral study on intention and theology in the disputes between Beit Shammai and Beit Hillel, Eric Ottenheijm found that "The Hillelite rationalized halakhic logic presupposes that impurity is not an external, objective force . . . Hillelite logic remained heavily disputed and it was only with R. Akiva's refined concept of intention and deed, that the human will as the *locus halakhicus* with regards to purity was accepted".[60] Ottenheijm adds that in Mark 7:14–15 (Matt 15:10–11), Jesus "agrees with the Hillelite Pharisees in the negation of the inherent power or the merely physical quality of ritual impurity".[61] In Rom 14, Paul may allude to Jesus' Hillelite teaching to support his stance on food-related disputes in Rome, "*I know and am persuaded in the Lord Jesus* that nothing is impure (κοινός) in itself" (Rom 14:14).

As a contemporary example of how Torah-observant Jews can differ radically in their view of what makes a food defiled, consider the issue of accidental mixtures between clean and unclean food (m. Ḥul. 7; b. Ḥul. 96–100; Shulchan Aruch/Tur, Yoreh De'ah 109; 99.5). Among traditional (Torah-observant) Jews who have not studied at yeshiva (rabbinical academy), pork is sometimes treated as a radioactive substance. If their food comes into contact with pork, the knee-jerk reaction is to discard the food because it is contaminated. The mindset behind this mentality is that pork is unclean in itself. It has some physical or spiritual property that contaminates.

A well-educated ultra-Orthodox Jew, however, one who has attended yeshiva and studied Jewish law, knows that pork is not unclean in itself. It has been assigned an unclean status. Thus, if the ultra-Orthodox Jew's kosher food comes into contact with pork, there is a legal remedy – nullify the pork!

---

[58] "Purity is not intrinsic; it is imputed" (Nanos, *The Mystery of Romans*, 199–200).

[59] Bruce Chilton, "The Purity of the Kingdom as Conveyed in Jesus' Meals", in *Society of Biblical Literature 1992 Seminar Papers* (ed. Eugene H. Lovering; Atlanta: Scholars, 1992), 485–86.

[60] Eric Ottenheijm, "Impurity Between Intention and Deed: Purity Disputes in First Century Judaism and in the New Testament", in *Purity and Holiness: The Heritage of Leviticus* (ed. M. J. H. M. Poorthuis and J. Schwartz; Leiden: Brill, 2000), 132, 143.

[61] Ottenheijm, "Impurity Between Intention and Deed", 146. Cf. Yair Furstenberg, "Defilement Penetrating the Body: A New Understanding of Contamination in Mark 7.15", *New Testament Studies* 54 (2008): 176–200.

Ultra-Orthodox Jews understand that nullification of unclean foods is a fundamental aspect of maintaining a kosher kitchen.

There are two ways to nullify unclean foods: *bitul b'rov* (nullification in a majority)[62] and *bitul b'shishim* (nullification in a ratio of sixty).[63] If pork accidentally falls into the ultra-Orthodox Jew's kosher food and the pork constitutes the minority of the food, then under the principle of *bitul b'rov*, the pork may be legally nullified and the food eaten:

> In the opinion of most *Poskim* [legal decisors, heads of yeshivot and members of rabbinic courts], when a non-kosher food becomes *batel* [nullified], the mixture may be eaten even by the most scrupulous. Indeed, some authorities soundly censure one who hesitates to eat the mixture, as this shows a heretical reservation about the effectiveness of *bitul* [nullification].[64]

What if the accidental mixture with pork results in the ultra-Orthodox Jew's food tasting like pork? In this case, the whole mixture changes its status to unclean under the principle of *taam k'ikar* and is now prohibited. If the ratio of clean food to pork is 60:1, however, then the pork and its taste in the mixture is legally nullified through *bitul b'shishim*, and the entire mixture is ruled clean to eat.

How can an ultra-Orthodox Jew in good conscience eat food that contains pieces of pork and tastes like pork? He can do this in good conscience because he does not believe that pork is unclean in itself. A food is unclean because it has been legally designated unclean, whether by God or rabbinic authority (cf. *Pesiq. Rab. Kah.* 4.7). The ultra-Orthodox Jewish approach is coherent when one considers the extreme difficulty of keeping clean food separate from agents of uncleanness. What of unclean smells and residues that are transferred by touch? The more scrupulous one becomes, the more one sees mixtures. Thus, an Orthodox Jew who does not have a yeshiva education may experience revulsion at seeing his food mixed with pork and throw it out thinking it is corrupted in toto. The *ultra*-Orthodox Jew handles it with legal precision and may determine that the food in its entirety is clean to eat. The irony is that it is the stricter Jew who eats the pork.

Returning to Rom 14, many exegetes assume that Paul's teaching in Rom 14:14 – "nothing is impure (κοινός) in itself; but it is impure (κοινόν) for anyone who thinks it impure (κοινόν)" – is a reflection of the apostle's emancipated view of the Lev 11 food laws. From this perspective, the "weak in faith" are Torah-observant and Paul is not. I contend, however, that Paul's training in Pharisaic halakhah led him to ask critical questions about accidental mixtures that the weak in Rome did not ask. Paul is echoing a Pharisaic understanding that no food is impure (κοινός) or unclean (ἀκάθαρτος) in es-

---

[62] *Bitul b'rov* applies to cold, dry foods.

[63] *Bitul b'shishim* applies to foods that are blended or cooked together.

[64] Binyomin Forst, *The Laws of Kashrus: A Comprehensive Exposition of Their Underlying Concepts and Applications* (Brooklyn: Mesorah, 2004), 52–53.

sence; it is the halakhic designation of it as "impure" or "unclean" that makes it impure or unclean.[65] I am not arguing that Paul observed a proto-rabbinic *bitul* halakhah comparable to what is found in Mishnah and Talmud. The Pharisees, I maintain, asked some of the same questions that the later rabbis asked about accidental mixtures, and they arrived at a similar conclusion: there were circumstances when clean food could be eaten after accidental contact with the unclean even as small bits of unclean food could be eaten. Sanders affirms that this was the case:

> The Pharisees moderated the biblical law in two ways: First, they eliminated the smallest of the swarming things (gnats, midges, mites and the like) by specifying that bits of carcass smaller than a lentil did not render foodstuff impure. Because of this decision, I shall use the term "fly-impurity" to describe the pharisaic interpretation of the law on dead swarming things. The second and more important decision was that moisture did not count unless a human *intended* the foodstuff to be wet. This step was supported by exegesis. According to Lev. 11.37f. a seed becomes impure when a forbidden carcass falls on it only if water *was put* on the seed. The verb *yutan* clearly implies "put by human intention". They then applied this verb not only to seeds, but to all foodstuff. Thus the law became much easier to observe, since its application was determined by human intention.[66]

Paul would have been familiar with the intricacies of Pharisaic halakhah that enabled the nullification of accidental mixtures. He would have also understood that it was impossible to avoid all accidental mixtures.

While Pharisaic halakhah exempted the gnat, it is notable that some Pharisees, who were particularly scrupulous about purity issues, went beyond the halakhah and attempted to strain out gnats and other small insects from their foods – "You strain out a gnat but swallow a camel!" (Matt 23:24):

> Jesus portrays here [Matt 23:24] Pharisees more scrupulous than Pharisaic legal rulings required. If a fly fell into one's drink, they might hope to strain it out before it died, lest it contaminate the drink (cf. Lev 11:34). But Pharisaic legal experts decided that any organism smaller than a lentil (such as a gnat) was exempt (Sanders 1990:32).[67]

Paul probably viewed the reaction of the weak in Rome to be comparable to overscrupulous Pharisees that he knew. He understood that even Pharisaic halakhah did not require such stringency.

It may be reasonably assumed that most Jesus-believing Gentiles in Rome, out of sensitivity, brought food to communal meals that conformed to the Lev

---

[65] Daniel R. Schwartz, "Someone who considers something to be impure – for him it is impure" (Rom 14:14): Good Manners or Law?" (paper presented at the International Symposium "Paul in His Jewish Matrix", Pontifical Gregorian University and Pontifical Biblical Institute, Rome, 21 May 2009), 1–23.

[66] E. P. Sanders, *Jewish Law from Jesus to the Mishnah: Five Studies* (London: SCM, 1990), 32–33. Cf. Jordan D. Rosenblum, *Food and Identity in Early Rabbinic Judaism* (Cambridge: Cambridge University Press, 2010), 177–78.

[67] Craig S. Keener, *A Commentary on the Gospel of Matthew* (Grand Rapids: Eerdmans, 1999), 552.

11 dietary laws. The weak, however, were concerned about accidental contact with defiling sources or defilement through association (κοινός). One could imagine that some of the Gentiles who were less familiar with the Torah unwittingly brought levitically unclean food to the communal meals and placed it side-by-side with clean food on the table. The weak were distraught and outraged over this; some may have even left the table-fellowship over it. For them, accidental mixtures were repulsive because they naively viewed such food to be innately defiled and thus spiritually dangerous.

Contrary to the standard reading of Rom 14, Paul did not equate being strong in faith with having an indifference view of the Lev 11 dietary laws. Rather, it is proposed that he considered the strong in faith to be those who did not have scruples about eating κοινός, i.e. food that was *potentially* defiled by association or of an *indeterminate* status due to accidental mixture. Paul knew that κοινός was not prohibited in the Torah but a later expansion of the law. He treated it as one of the customs of the fathers, not as a binding matter of God's law. Thus Paul can say in Rom 14:14 that "nothing is impure (κοινός) *in itself*; but it is impure (κοινός) for anyone who thinks it impure (κοινός)". This is not a rejection of the Torah's dietary laws but a minimizing of the importance of κοινός.

The strong in faith among Jesus-believing Jews and Gentiles were those who did not raise questions of conscience about κοινός. They understood that defilement by association was an expansion of the law and not integral to the law itself. Their approach was to be discriminating in what they ate. At communal meals, they could eat clean food and avoid the unclean (if unwittingly brought) without being shaken or flustered. They did not stumble at the thought of accidental mixtures because they understood that accidental mixtures were ultimately unavoidable in real life, even for the scrupulous. They knew that accidental mixtures did not result in spiritual harm. When Rom 14 is read in this way, Paul's teaching does not undermine law observance for Jews but directs law observance so that Mosaic law is prioritized over traditional interpretations and expansions of the law, an approach consistent with Jesus' halakhah (Mark 7:1–15; Matt 15:1–20; see Rom 14:14 "I know and am persuaded in the Lord Jesus that . . .").[68]

How is Rom 14:20 ("Everything is indeed clean [καθαρά]") to be understood? Since a guiding principle of the apostle to the Gentiles (Rom 11:13) was that Gentiles did not need to become Jews in order to be members of the people of God, it is possible that Paul had Gentiles specifically in mind when he made this statement. If impurity and uncleanness were *intrinsic* to food, then Gentiles would need to observe Israel's dietary laws and be concerned about ritual purity. If uncleanness was *imputed by the word of God for Jews alone*, however, and Gentiles were exempt from these laws (Acts 15), then

---

[68] "You abandon the commandment of God and hold to human tradition" (Mark 7:8).

food could be simultaneously unclean for Jews and clean for Gentiles. Rom 14:20 may articulate Paul's halakhah for Gentiles.[69] For Jesus-believing Gentiles, everything was indeed clean:

> . . . the addressees in this passage are Gentiles. Thus what Paul formulates here is not a general statement about the perception of food, but a specific statement addressed to specific people in a specific context. Food laws are part of the rules that regulate ritual purity for those under the covenant. Non-adherence to these laws does not render Gentiles impure or sinners, because they are irrelevant for them from a Jewish perspective. The division of animals according to purity categories is thus irrelevant for Gentiles. "For them" the food laws do not apply. Thus, "for them" all food is pure. Paul, in addressing non-Jews, is arguing in a Levitical vein here. The pure/impure categorization of animals and the admonition to observe these laws is addressed to the covenant people, that is, these animals are impure "for you" – the addressees of Leviticus. It follows they are not impure for non-Jews, who are addressed here by Paul, thus, for them, everything is pure.[70]

Another plausible interpretation, given a context of Jews and Gentiles, is that Paul is still focusing on defilement by association (κοινός). He has in mind the kinds of foods that the Jesus-believers in Rome ate when they came together for table-fellowship and he assumed that all of the food ("everything")[71] on the table was indeed clean by Lev 11 standards. The Gentiles, out

---

[69] Kinzer, *Postmissionary Messianic Judaism*, 81–82; Tomson, *Paul and the Jewish Law*, 244.

[70] Ehrensperger, "Called to Be Saints", 106–107. "An additional consideration is that Mark wrote his gospel 10–20 years after Paul's epistle to the Romans had been circulated. Early Patristic sources suggest that he wrote it from Rome and that his audience was the same community that Paul addressed – the Roman church. This presents the likelihood that Mark was familiar with Paul's epistle to the Romans and his halakhah on Gentiles and food. It is possible that Mark was influenced by this epistle in the construction of his editorial comment in verse 19b. Amid numerous Markan-Pauline parallels, the similarity of Mark 7:19b and Romans 14:20 stands out . . . While direct influence cannot be proven, the textual affinity and Roman audience make it a reasonable hypothesis that Mark has taken Pauline halakhah (specifically for Gentile Christians) and rooted it in Jesus' teaching in Mark 7 . . . It has been demonstrated so far that Mark's parenthetical statement in verse 19b was directed at a Gentile Christian audience and may have served as a theological justification for the Jerusalem Council decision that exempted Gentile Christians from the Leviticus 11 dietary laws. Pauline halakhic influence is also plausible. All of this suggests that verse 19b is most accurately read: 'Thus he declared all foods clean [for Gentile believers]'" (David J. Rudolph, "Jesus and the Food Laws: A Reassessment of Mark 7:19b", *Evangelical Quarterly* 74:4 [2002]: 304–305).

[71] Πάντα in Rom 14:2, 20 need not imply that Paul eats everything. See James G. Crossley, *The Date of Mark's Gospel: Insights from the Law in Earliest Christianity* (London: T & T Clark, 2004), 192; M. Casey, *Aramaic Sources of Mark's Gospel* (Cambridge: Cambridge University Press, 1998), 159–62. Paul is speaking of "food" (βρώματος; Rom 14:20a). But what is "food"? C. E. B. Cranfield, *A Critical and Exegetical Commentary on The Epistle to the Romans* (Edinburgh: T & T Clark, 1979), 2:723, maintains that Paul has in mind "the resources of the created world which are available and appropriate for human consumption". If Cranfield is correct, πάντα in Rom 14:2, 20 may exclude those "things" that God did not give human beings for food (e.g. blood, what has been sacrificed to idols and the flesh of strangled animals – Gen 9:3–4; Acts 15:20, 29 – note the absence of βρώματος in the

of sensitivity to their Jewish brothers and sisters, were generally not bringing pork or shellfish to the common meals. Rom 14:20 may simply be Paul's affirmation to the strong that the weak are incorrect in their outlook that the meals are unclean by association; "nothing within the parameters of 'clean' food should be thought of as being made 'common [κοινός]'".[72] Nevertheless, the strong should do what they can to avoid causing the weak to fall. Thus, Paul writes in the following verse that "it is good not to eat meat or drink wine [food and drink that the weak considered potentially defiled by association] or do anything that makes your brother or sister stumble" (Rom 14:21).[73]

To conclude, there is no reason to assume on the basis of Rom 14 that Paul considered Jesus-believing Jews "weak in faith" because they observed Jewish dietary and calendar commandments.[74] The possibility should be allowed

---

apostolic decree). Jews and Gentiles had different definitions of βρώματος based on their perceptions of what God permitted them to eat. In Rom 14:2, πάντα could simply refer to everything that was set on the table at the congregation in Rome. It could also be an allusion to those foods in particular that the weak did not eat (e.g. meat and wine).

[72] House, "Defilement by Association", 153.

[73] "Paul adapts the argument of 1 Cor 8–10 when he writes Rom 14–15. In both letters he encourages compromise between the strong and weak for the sake of unifying the communities. In 1 Cor 8–10 Paul asks the strong to avoid eating idol-food (1 Cor 8:7–13; 10:14–22, 28–29) while he asks the weak to allow eating food from the market and to allow eating with unbelieving Gentiles (1 Cor 10:25–27). In Rom 14–15 the strong are asked to follow the practices of the weak during community gatherings (Rom 14:13–23), while the weak are asked to allow the strong to follow their own convictions in private settings (Rom 14:4–12). Although Paul's advice is intended for both groups, in both letters Paul places the primary responsibility upon the strong to give up their rights for the benefit of the weak. He encourages the strong to avoid behavior that causes the weak to 'stumble' . . . In both letters, Paul presents himself (Rom 14:13–23; 1 Cor 9:1–23; 11:1) and Christ (Rom 15:3, 7–9a; 1 Cor 11:1) as models of adaptive behavior to emulate. He expects this advice to accomplish similar objectives in both letters. Paul asks the strong to base their actions on glorifying God (Rom 15:7; 1 Cor 10:31) and for the building up of others within the community . . . Just as Paul's model of adaptation and compromise is not limited to internal relationships in 1 Cor 8–10, so Paul also broadens these concerns in Rom 14–15. In both letters, Paul sees internal unity being integral to an outward mission. In 1 Cor 8–10 Paul attempts to end disputes over idol-food so that the Corinthians can reach out to unbelieving Gentiles. Paul explains that adapting to the practices of others should lead to the salvation of others (1 Cor 9:19–23; 10:28–11:1). In Rom 14–15, Paul attempts to end disputes so that the Romans can join his mission to reaching out to both unbelieving Jews and Gentiles (Rom 15:9b–12; cf. 11:11–15). Paul highlights the outward mission in 1 Cor 9:19–23; 10:28–11:1 and in Rom 15:7–13. In both letters, Paul encourages the community to look beyond itself to God's wider mission of salvation . . . Rom 14–15 is written for a new context where Paul applies the principle from 1 Cor 8–10 of becoming 'all things to all people'" (Toney, *Paul's Inclusive Ethic*, 189–90, 205).

[74] "In the reading proposed here, it is evident that Paul does not in principle 'undermine the law', or even declare part of the law, as related to food, to be irrelevant in Christ. Paul rather argues within the parameters of Jewish reasoning. He is talking about the realm in which those who are in Christ now live, that is, the realm of a holy community. The food

that the strong were those who viewed uncleanness as imputed by the word of God (in accordance with biblical law) and did not stumble at the thought of accidental mixtures. They were able to eat clean food on the table and avoid the unclean (if accidentally brought). Other Jesus-believers viewed uncleanness as innate and the eating of accidental mixtures as spiritually harmful. They rejected everything on the table except vegetables. As one trained in Pharisaic halakhah, and having a nuanced understanding of the issues surrounding accidental mixtures, Paul viewed the discriminating (like himself) as strong in faith and the non-discriminating as weak in faith.

2.1.5 "Former Way of Life" and "Rubbish" Language (Gal 1:13; Phil 3:8)

Paul's reference to his "former way of life in Judaism" in Gal 1:13 is sometimes taken by proponents of the traditional reading of 1 Cor 9:19–23 to mean that Paul was no longer Torah observant. Stanley Porter, for example, interprets the passage to suggest that Paul abandoned the "beliefs and practices that characterized Judaism as a whole".[75] The assumption here is that Paul converted from Judaism to Christianity, leaving behind his Jewish way of life. Dunn, however, reminds the exegete that, in the mid-first century, Christianity had not yet become a separate and distinct religion from Judaism. Paul understood his religious identity in Jewish sectarian terms:

> Paul wrote Galatians 1.13–14 with a backward glance to his life "within Judaism", but his was a conversion not from one religion (Judaism) to another (Christianity), but rather from one "sect" within the diversity of Second Temple Judaism to another.[76]

There is no reason to conclude that Paul's "former way of life in Judaism" refers to "common Judaism";[77] the expression could just as well refer to a right wing form of Pharisaic Judaism ("For you have heard of my former life in Judaism, *how I persecuted the church of God violently and tried to destroy it*" [Gal 1:13 ESV]).[78] Paul's previous way of life was characterized by sepa-

---

laws, and purity laws more generally, have something to do with this realm, but in different ways for Jews and Gentiles. It certainly does not imply that Paul denies the validity of food laws in Christ . . . Significantly, Paul does not call the covenant obligations for Jews *adiaphora*; to the contrary, they are inviolable in Christ . . . The particular identities of Jews and Gentiles in Christ are not a threat to holiness and to peace, joy and harmony within the community; they are rather presupposed. Holiness is living in diversity and, as such, constitutes nevertheless the 'universal' identity-shaping category for both Jews and Gentiles in Christ" (Ehrensperger, "Called to Be Saints", 104–105).

[75] Stanley E. Porter, "Was Paul a Good Jew? Fundamental Issues in a Current Debate", in *Christian-Jewish Relations Through the Centuries* (ed. Stanley E. Porter and Brook W. R. Pearson; Sheffield: Sheffield Academic Press, 2000), 170–73.

[76] Dunn, "The Jew Paul and His Meaning for Israel", 204. Cf. Dunn, *The Theology of Paul the Apostle*, 259; Dunn, "Who Did Paul Think He Was?" 179.

[77] Sanders, *Judaism: Practice and Belief,* 45–314.

[78] Zoccali, *Whom God Has Called*, 127.

ration from sinners (Jewish and Gentile) and punctilious concern for Pharisaic interpretations and expansions of the law (Gal 1:14; Phil 3:5; Acts 22:3). This was matched by a sense of "righteousness . . . that comes from the law" (Phil 3:9) and a Phinehas-like zeal to "act with violence against those he perceived to be in breach of the law" (cf. Acts 8:1; 9:1–3).[79] Paul left behind this right wing form of Pharisaic Judaism when he joined the "sect" known as "the Way" or "the Nazarenes" (Acts 9:2; 19:23; 24:5, 14, 22; 28:22). Viewed in this way, there is no reason to conclude from Gal 1:13–14 that Paul stopped living as a Jew according to the normative standards of common Judaism or even that he stopped identifying as a Pharisee.[80] It should also be pointed out that ποτε in Gal 1:13 does not preclude continuity ("You have heard, no doubt, of my *earlier life in Judaism*" [Gal 1:13 NRSV]). The *Revised English Bible* overstates the evidence for discontinuity when it renders the verse, "You have heard what my manner of life was *when I was still a practising Jew*".

Phil 3:8 is also interpreted by many commentators as a reference to Paul leaving behind his Jewish identity. After Paul describes his Jewish background and zeal for the law in verses 5–6 – "circumcised on the eighth day, a member of the people of Israel, of the tribe of Benjamin, a Hebrew born of Hebrews; as to the law, a Pharisee; as to zeal, a persecutor of the church; as to righteousness under the law, blameless" – the apostle goes on to indicate that he regards all of this as "rubbish" (v. 8: σκύβαλα). The context, however, should not be missed. First, Paul acknowledges that his Jewishness resulted in "gains" (Phil 3:7). Second, it is not only Jewishness that Paul considers "loss" upon gaining Christ. He regards "everything as loss" (πάντα ζημίαν εἶναι). Presumably, this included the Scriptures, the covenants, the promises, his mother and father, friendships, etc. Everything is relativised in Christ.

As noted above (1.2.1), Paul at times refers to something genuinely important to emphasize what is *even more important* (1 Cor 3:5–7; 2 Cor 3:6–11; 12:11). Dunn would seem to be correct in his analysis that the same rhetorical device is being employed here, "The sharpness of the contrast is not so much to denigrate what he had previously counted as gain, as to enhance to the highest degree the value he now attributes to Christ, to the knowledge of Christ, and to the prospect of gaining Christ".[81] By referring to his Jewishness

---

[79] James D. G. Dunn, "Philippians 3.2–14 and the New Perspective on Paul", in *The New Perspective on Paul: Collected Essays* (Tübingen: Mohr Siebeck, 2005), 472.

[80] Mark D. Nanos, "Rethinking the 'Paul and Judaism' Paradigm" (paper presented at the Yale Post-Grad Seminar, New Haven, 3 March 2005), 14; Nanos, "A Torah-Observant Paul?" 16–20.

[81] Dunn, "Philippians 3.2–14 and the New Perspective on Paul", 475. "Paul is not making an absolute statement on the value or lack of value of Judaism *per se*. Rather he is evaluating in comparison to knowing Christ (Phil. 3:8). He would count everything as loss from this perspective. It is not just Jewish flesh or boasting that he includes but boasting in anything,

as "rubbish", Paul indirectly points up the importance of Jewishness (cf. Rom 3:1–2; 9:4–5; 11:29) and the surpassing greatness of knowing Christ.

2.1.6 "Live Like a Gentile and Not Like a Jew" Language (Gal 2:14)

In Gal 2:11–14, Paul rebukes Cephas for "hypocrisy". According to Paul, Cephas ate with Gentiles before certain men came from James. But after they arrived, he "drew back and kept himself separate for fear of the circumcision faction" (Gal 2:12). Paul confronted Cephas, "If you, though a Jew, live like a Gentile and not like a Jew, how can you compel the Gentiles to live like Jews?" The implication of Gal 2:11–14, according to many commentators, is that Cephas had stopped living as a Jew.[82] In Christian freedom, Cephas had been living like a Gentile and eating unclean food with the Gentiles. But when certain men came from James, Cephas reverted to his former Torah-observant way of life and refused to eat unclean food.[83] This resulted in him no longer eating with Gentiles. Paul corrected Cephas for returning to Judaism.

This interpretation rests on a number of tendentious assumptions. First, it assumes that the reason Cephas "drew back and kept himself separate" (Gal 2:12) was that he was under pressure to avoid eating unclean food.[84] A second

---

gentile or Jewish i.e. all things . . . Thus I might assert that health, wealth, home and family are of no significance compared with being in Christ, but that would not mean that I do not attribute great and lasting value to these in and by themselves" (William S. Campbell, "Covenant, Creation and Transformation in Paul" [paper presented at the Interdisciplinary Academic Seminar on "New Perspectives on Paul and the Jews", Katholieke Universiteit Leuven, 14–15 September 2009], 4–5). Cf. William S. Campbell, "I Rate All Things as Loss: Paul's Puzzling Accounting System: Judaism as Loss or the Reevaluation of All Things in Christ", in *Celebrating Paul: Festschrift in Honor of J. A. Fitzmyer and J. Murphy-O'Connor* (ed. Peter Spitaler; Washington, D.C.: Catholic Biblical Association of America, forthcoming); Zoccali, *Whom God Has Called*, 127–29.

[82] See Justin Taylor, "The Jerusalem Decrees (Acts 15.20, 29 and 21.25) and the Incident at Antioch (Gal 2.11–14)", *New Testament Studies* 46 (2000): 380; Horrell, "No Longer Jew or Greek", 335.

[83] R. Y. K. Fung, *The Epistle to the Galatians* (Grand Rapids: Eerdmans, 1988), 110–11; H. D. Betz, *Galatians: A Commentary on Paul's Letter to the Churches of Galatia* (Philadelphia: Fortress, 1979), 104, 108. For a response to Betz, see Mark D. Nanos, *The Galatians Debate: Contemporary Issues in Rhetorical and Historical Interpretation* (ed. Mark D. Nanos; Peabody: Hendrickson, 2002), 294–95.

[84] Some exegetes argue that ritual purity and idol-food concerns were at issue. See Magnus Zetterholm, "Purity and Anger: Gentiles and Idolatry in Antioch", *Interdisciplinary Journal of Research on Religion* 1 (2005): 4f; Michelle Slee, *The Church in Antioch in the First Century CE: Communion and Conflict* (London: Sheffield, 2003), 28; Philip F. Esler, *Galatians: New Testament Readings* (London: Routledge, 1998), 93–116; Philip F. Esler, *Community and Gospel in Luke-Acts: The Social and Political Motivations of Lucan Theology* (Cambridge: Cambridge University Press, 1987), 71–109. Also Magnus Zetterholm, *The Formation of Christianity in Antioch: A Social-Scientific Approach to the Separation Between Judaism and Christianity* (London: Routledge, 2003), 134–35, for a synopsis of other reasons.

assumption often made by commentators is that Cephas knew that Israel's dietary laws had been abolished. This contention is usually based on Mark 7:19b and Luke's account of Peter's vision in Acts 10. A third assumption is that Paul viewed the law as a matter of indifference (as Gentiles did) and he expected Peter to adopt the same outlook.[85] Sam Williams puts it bluntly, "In effect, then, Paul was insisting that Cephas and Barnabas and the other Christian Jews make themselves Gentiles. When the oneness of God's new inclusive Israel was at stake, Paul would have *everyone* be Gentile!"[86] Horrell concurs, "He and Peter no longer live like Jews (Ἰουδαϊκῶς) but like Gentiles (ἐθνικῶς, Gal. 2.14)".[87] Each of these assumptions will be examined below.

To begin with, the text does not state that Cephas ate unclean food or was concerned about others seeing him eat unclean food. Rather, the text focuses on Peter's association with Gentiles. He ate "with the Gentiles" but after the men from James arrived he "kept himself separate" (Gal 2:12). The focus is on men, not the menu.[88] To put it another way, the problem was "not the food but the company".[89]

On the second assumption, there is no indication in Gal 2 that Peter considered Israel's dietary laws abolished. The often cited texts, Mark 7 and Acts 10–11 (Luke's account of Peter's vision), can be read in a way counter to the traditional view:

1. I have explained elsewhere how Jesus' parable in Mark 7:14–19a, and Mark's editorial comment in 7:19b, uphold the validity of the Torah's ritual purity system. Prioritization, not abrogation, is the aim of Jesus' teaching. Mark 7:19b is best understood as a matter of Gentile halakhic application and not an apocalyptic pronouncement that all foods are now clean.[90]

---

[85] Oskar Skarsaune, "Jewish Believers in Jesus in Antiquity", *Mishkan* 42 (2005): 48.

[86] Sam K. Williams, *Galatians* (Nashville: Abingdon, 1997), 60. Also Cosgrove, "Did Paul Value Ethnicity?" 280; Eckhard J. Schnabel, *Early Christian Mission* (Downers Grove: InterVarsity, 2004), 2:957–58; Ebeling, *The Truth of the Gospel*, 118; Betz, *Galatians*, 112.

[87] Horrell, *Solidarity and Difference*, 18.

[88] Zetterholm, "Purity and Anger", 1–20; Richard Bauckham, "James, Peter, and the Gentiles", in *The Missions of James, Peter, and Paul: Tensions in Early Christianity* (ed. Bruce Chilton and Craig Evans; Leiden: Brill, 2005), 125.

[89] Markus Bockmuehl, *Jewish Law in Gentile Churches: Halakhah and the Beginning of Christian Public Ethics* (Edinburgh: T & T, 2000), 73; Pierre-Antoine Bernheim, *James, Brother of Jesus* (trans. J. Bowden. London: SCM, 1997), 177. Nanos, *The Galatians Debate*, 301, proposes a middle position, "It was not the fact that Peter ate *with* Gentiles that was at dispute but *the way* that he ate with *these* Gentiles". Gentile guests were being treated as though they were proselytes at communal meals. Cf. Hodge, *If Sons, Then Heirs*, 121–22.

[90] Rudolph, "Jesus and the Food Laws", 291–311; Crossley, *The Date of Mark's Gospel*, 183–205; James Crossley, "Mark 7.1–23: Revisiting the Question of 'All Foods Clean'", in *Torah in the New Testament: Papers Delivered at the Manchester-Lausanne Seminar of June 2008* (ed. Michael Tait and Peter Oakes; London: T & T Clark International, 2009), 8–20;

2. Three times Peter rejects Jesus' instruction to kill and eat impure (κοινόν) and unclean (ἀκάθαρτον) animals (Acts 10:14–16). This implies that Peter had never received such a teaching or example from Jesus.[91]
3. The meaning of the vision was not immediately clear to Peter. He was "greatly puzzled about what to make of the vision" (Acts 10:17). When Peter saw the vision, he did not understand it to mean that Israel's dietary laws had been abolished.
4. What was the meaning of the vision? The vision concerned men, not the menu.[92] When Peter arrived at Cornelius' house, he interpreted the meaning of the vision: The impure (κοινόν) and unclean (ἀκάθαρτον) animals symbolized impure (κοινόν) and unclean (ἀκάθαρτον) people (a likely reference to God-fearers and pagans respectively).[93] In keeping with Jewish "taboo" (ἀθέμιτος [Acts 10:28], not νόμος),[94] Peter had considered non-Jews impure and unclean and avoided contact with them. But through the vision, God informed Peter that he was no longer to view Gentiles in this way, "God has shown me that *I should not call anyone impure* (κοινόν) *or unclean* (ἀκάθαρτον). So when I was sent for, I came without objection . . . I truly understand that God shows no partiality, but in every nation anyone who fears him and does what is right is acceptable to him" (Acts 10:28–29, 34–35). It is important to note that Peter's decision to associate with Gentiles did not overturn biblical law. Mosaic law does not prohibit Jews from associating with Gentiles. Peter's perspective that Jews should

---

Martin Pickup, "Matthew's and Mark's Pharisees", in *In Quest of the Historical Pharisees* (ed. Jacob Neusner and Bruce D. Chilton; Waco: Baylor University Press, 2007), 85–86.

[91] Heikki Räisänen, *Jesus, Paul and Torah: Collected Essays* (trans. David E. Orton; Sheffield: JSOT, 1992), 144. Matthew 15:15 describes Peter as present on the occasion of Jesus' *mashal* (cf. Mark 7:1–23).

[92] Zetterholm, "Purity and Anger", 8; Kinzer, *Postmissionary Messianic Judaism*, 68–71; Chris A. Miller, "Did Peter's Vision in Acts 10 Pertain to Men or the Menu?" *Bibliotheca Sacra* 159 (2002): 317; Miller, "The Relationship of Jewish and Gentile Believers to the Law between A.D. 30 and 70 in the Scripture", 92; Peter S. Zaas, "The (Double) Vision of the Divine Picnic (Acts 10:1–11:18): The History of New Testament Kashrut III", in *Jewish Law Association Studies IX: The London Conference Volume* (ed. E. A. Goldman; Atlanta: Scholars, 1997), 296; Joseph B. Tyson, "The Gentile Mission and the Authority of Scripture in Acts", *New Testament Studies* 33 (1987): 628; Martin Dibelius, *Studies in the Acts of the Apostles* (London: SCM, 1956), 118.

[93] Wahlen, "Peter's Vision and Conflicting Definitions of Purity", 515; House, "Defilement by Association", 149.

[94] Bruce, *The Book of the Acts*, 209 n. 34; Zaas, "The (Double) Vision of the Divine Picnic (Acts 10:1–11:18)", 300. *Pace* Bauckham, "James, Peter, and the Gentiles", 107–109, who prefers the translation "unlawful".

not visit or eat with Gentiles because they are impure (κοινόν) or unclean (ἀκάθαρτον) is a traditional expansion of the law.[95]

5. Peter reiterated the symbolic meaning of the vision to the "circumcised believers" in Jerusalem. After he recounted the vision, his response to it, and the Lord's admonition – "What God has made clean (ἐκαθάρισεν), you must not call profane (κοίνου)" (Acts 11:9) – Peter explains that the vision concerned men, "The Spirit told me to go with them and *not to make a distinction between them and us*" (Acts 11:12). At the Jerusalem Council, Peter once again alludes to the symbolic meaning of the vision. The Gentile-believers are clean, for "in cleansing [καθαρίσας] their hearts by faith *he has made no distinction between them and us*" (Acts 15:9). The vision concerned men, not the menu.

6. No indication exists in Acts that Peter understood the vision literally.[96] There is no example of him eating unclean food or encouraging other Jesus-believing Jews to eat unclean food.

7. The Jerusalem Council decision in Acts 15 centred on the question of whether Jesus-believing *Gentiles* were exempt from Mosaic law. If the Torah's dietary laws had been abrogated as early as Acts 10, and Jesus-believing Jews were now exempt from the requirements of Mosaic law, there would be no reason to debate whether the law was binding on Jesus-believing Gentiles. Acts 15 implies that Peter's vision in Acts 10 concerned men, not the menu (cf. Acts 15:9). The apostolic decree was only addressed to "Gentile believers" and clarified the "requirements" (including certain minimal food restrictions) that were incumbent upon the "Gentile believers" (Acts 15:19–20, 23). The presupposition throughout Acts 15 is that Jesus-believing Jews like Peter (who was present at the Jerusalem council) continue to observe Mosaic law.

The third assumption – that Paul consistently lived as a Gentile and expected Peter to do the same – is contradicted by the standard interpretation of 1 Cor 9:19–23 that Paul sometimes lived like a Jew. But if Paul "occasionally conformed to Jewish law" to win others, how could he correct Peter for doing what appears to be the same thing?[97] One may reply that an important differ-

---

[95] Hannah K. Harrington, *The Purity Texts* (London: T & T Clark, 2004), 112; Christine E. Hayes, *Gentile Impurities and Jewish Identities: Intermarriage and Conversion from the Bible to the Talmud* (Oxford: Oxford University Press, 2002), 19–44.

[96] Tomson, *"If this be from Heaven . . .",* 231–32; Barnabas Lindars, "All Foods Clean: Thoughts on Jesus and the Law", in *Law and Religion: Essays on the Place of the Law in Israel and Early Christianity* (ed. Barnabas Lindars; Cambridge: James Clarke, 1988), 67.

[97] See John McHugh, "Galatians 2:11–14: Was Peter Right?" in *Paulus und das antike Judentum* (ed. Martin Hengel and Ulrich Heckel; Tübingen: Mohr Siebeck, 1991), 320–22; Peter Richardson, "Pauline Consistency in 1 Cor 9:19–23 and Gal 2:11–14", *New Testament Studies* 26 (1980): 347–62; Maurice F. Wiles, *The Divine Apostle: The Interpretation of St. Paul's Epistles in the Early Church* (Cambridge: Cambridge University Press, 1967), 19, 22, 71.

ence between Peter and Paul was that Paul's inconsistency did not compromise the gospel but Peter's "hypocrisy" did. But how did Peter's behaviour compromise the gospel? What does it mean to "compromise the gospel"? And why did Paul's practice of becoming all things to all people not compromise the gospel?

Given the questionable assumptions behind the traditional interpretation of Gal 2:14, there is reason to consider an alternative explanation of Paul's words, "If you, though a Jew, *live like a Gentile and not like a Jew*, how can you compel the Gentiles to live like Jews?" When one steps back from the text and views Paul and Cephas in light of their respective Jewish backgrounds, a fresh way of interpreting the text emerges.

Paul was reared as a Pharisee, and it may be reasonably assumed that in various ways he continued to identify as a Pharisee. Luke describes him saying (in the present tense), "I am a Pharisee, a son of Pharisees" (Acts 23:6) on an occasion when it was rhetorically advantageous to identify as a Pharisee. Leading up to Gal 2, Paul refers to his Pharisaic upbringing and *contrasts himself with less strict Jews*, "I advanced in Judaism beyond many among my people of the same age, for I was far more zealous for the traditions of my ancestors" (Gal 1:14). In Gal 2:15, immediately after the passage in question, Paul uses language that one would expect of a Pharisee, "We ourselves are Jews by birth and not *Gentile sinners*".

By contrast, Cephas did not grow up in a Jewish sect known for strict observance of the customs of the fathers. Luke portrays Peter as a faithful Jew, one who carefully avoided unclean food and close association with Gentiles on account of Jewish mores (Acts 10:14, 28); but there is no indication that Peter was scrupulous about ritual purity and tithing of foods like the Pharisees. In fact, Luke describes Peter as an "ordinary" man (Acts 4:13). The gospel writers portray Peter and the other disciples as indifferent to ritual handwashing before meals and untroubled by close association with sinners. The Pharisees, on the other hand, are depicted as particularly focused on these areas. The disciples, including Peter, are thus rebuked by the Pharisees for their lack of attention to strict standards of ritual purity in relation to food and people (Mark 7:1–5; Matt 15:1–2; Luke 5:30, 33).

Pharisees sometimes looked down on ordinary Jews like Peter (John 7:49). Qumran Jews could be even more condescending. To deviate from the sectarian calendar was to be guilty of "forgetting the feasts of the covenant and walking in the feasts of the Gentiles, after their errors and after their ignorance" (*Jub.* 6.35; cf. *Sol.* 1.8). From the standpoint of a strict sectarian Jew, an ordinary Jew like Peter could easily be viewed as one who lived like a Gentile and not like a Jew. As Dunn points out, "these are relative terms . . . for one

Jew to accuse another Jew of 'living like a Gentile' was wholly of a piece with the language of intra-Jewish sectarian polemic".[98]

A reasonable alternative to the standard interpretation of Gal 2:14 is that Paul was echoing the language of the individuals from James who accused Peter of "living like a Gentile" because he ate *with Gentiles*.[99] As James Crossley has argued, this interpretation need not imply that Peter ate unclean food:

> Paul apparently rhetorically adopts their speech, "live like a gentile". Thus Galatians 2.14 can be paraphrased: "Before, you agreed to live and eat as a Jew together with the gentiles, and although some call that 'living like a gentile', why do you now separate and wish to eat with them only if they become Jews?" Paul is not urging Peter to join him again in a "non-Jewish way of life" but rather he urges "for a Jewish life which does not force gentiles to judaize" ... These two differing opinions are echoed in Judaism from at least the Second Temple period through rabbinical literature.[100]

Alternatively, it is possible that in Gal 2:14 Paul speaks as a Pharisee to Cephas and intentionally belittles Cephas' Jewishness to help him recognize his hypocrisy and repent. This argument is supported by the present active participle ὑπάρχων with the present active indicative ζῇς in Gal 2:14. According to Paul, Peter *presently* (after having withdrawn from the Gentiles) lives like a Gentile.[101] The focus is on the present, *not* the past. Paul is essentially saying, "Peter, from my Pharisaic perspective, you *are* like these Gentiles. Compared to the Jews I grew up with, you have a low to non-existent standard of ritual purity. You are acting hypocritically by compelling Gentiles to become Jews (through your act of separation) when you know very well that the Lord has accepted them as Gentiles (Acts 10:28–29, 34–35; 11:12; 15:9)". In this scenario, Paul is not necessarily saying that Cephas has violated biblical dietary laws, etc. As Sanders notes, the language is polemical hyperbole:

> Paul's statement that Peter had been "living like a Gentile" (Gal 2:14) was exaggerated. He probably had not been doing anything as drastic as eating pork, shellfish, or hare. Exaggeration on this point fits perfectly since the charge that Peter was "forcing Gentiles to live like Jews" in the same verse goes beyond the story as he tells it. Paul very often used extreme or

---

[98] James D. G. Dunn, *The Epistle to the Galatians* (Peabody: Hendrickson, 1993), 127–28; cf. James D. G. Dunn, "Echoes of Intra-Jewish Polemic in Paul's Letter to the Galatians", in *The New Perspective on Paul: Collected Essays* (Tübingen: Mohr Siebeck, 2005), 224–31.

[99] Bauckham, "James, Peter, and the Gentiles", 125; Dunn, *The Epistle to the Galatians*, 128; Dunn, "Echoes of Intra-Jewish Polemic in Paul's Letter to the Galatians", 231.

[100] Crossley, *The Date of Mark's Gospel*, 152.

[101] Dunn, "Echoes of Intra-Jewish Polemic in Paul's Letter to the Galatians", 229–30; Nanos, *The Galatians Debate*, 313.

hyperbolic language to polarize a situation, to make it black and white, and this seems to me to be the best explanation of the term "live like a Gentile" in Gal 2:14.[102]

Paul is reminding Cephas that his Jewish upbringing, education and standard of Jewish living are all minimal, below par, even *Gentile-like*, by Pharisaic standards.

Intra-Jewish sectarian polemic of this kind abounds in modern times. As an illustration, the Orthodox rabbis of Prague, members of the "Great Court", wrote in 1819 that Jews who attended Reform synagogues were "neither Jews nor Christians" because they prayed in a language other than Hebrew and played the organ on the Sabbath.[103] Rabbi Moses Schick (1807–1879) in a responsum to Rabbi A. S. Binyamin of Pressburg wrote concerning the status of Reform rabbis (most of whom continued to observe Jewish dietary laws, festivals, etc.), "They are not Jews, but are worse than non-Jews . . . Since they are like complete gentiles, their daughters and sons are prohibited for us . . . Since we have made it clear that their legal status is like that of the gentiles, it is prohibited to worship in their houses of worship".[104] Similar intra-Jewish barbs are found in Chaim Potok's *The Chosen*. Here the Hasidic rabbi, Reb Saunders, describes Jewish Zionists (including the Orthodox Jew David Malter, a Talmudic scholar at a local yeshiva) as "Jewish goyim" who are not "true Jews":

> "The land of Abraham, Isaac, and Jacob should be built by Jewish goyim [Gentiles], by contaminated men?" Reb Saunders shouted again. "Never! Not while I live! . . . Why do you think I brought my people from Russia to America and not to Eretz Yisroel? Because it is better to live in a land of true goyim than to live in a land of Jewish goyim! Who says we should build Eretz Yisroel, uh? I'll tell you who says it! Apikorsim say it! Jewish goyim say it! True Jews do not say such a thing!"[105]

All of this is rhetorically effective intra-Jewish language used by strict Torah-observant Jews to posture themselves in relation to less strict Torah-observant Jews. Put-downs such as "Gentiles", "Goyim", "like complete gentiles", "not Jews" and "not true Jews" do not reflect reality. Insiders know that the "Jewish Goyim" in question are Torah-observant Jews who keep Mosaic law. The intra-Jewish posturing, however, can easily be mistaken by outsiders to mean that the "Jewish goyim" in question have abandoned Torah lifestyle and are

---

[102] Sanders, *The Conversation Continues*, 186–87. Also Dunn, "Echoes of Intra-Jewish Polemic in Paul's Letter to the Galatians", 231. See Carol J. Schlueter, *Filling up the Measure: Polemical Hyperbole in 1 Thessalonians 2.14–16* (Sheffield: JSOT Press, 1994), 124–63, for other examples of polemical hyperbole.

[103] Alexander Guttmann, *The Struggle over Reform in Rabbinic Literature* (New York: The World Union for Progressive Judaism, 1977), 216; *Eleh Divre Haberit*, resp. 17.

[104] Guttmann, *The Struggle over Reform in Rabbinic Literature*, 273–74; *Orach Chayim*, resp. 305.

[105] Chaim Potok, *The Chosen* (New York: Ballantine, 1967), 198.

now eating unkosher food, etc. Such a misunderstanding may have occurred in the history of interpretation of Gal 2:14. When read by outsiders to the world of pluriform Second Temple Judaism, Paul's comments are easily thought to mean that Peter was not a Torah-observant Jew and that he was eating unclean food with Gentiles when in fact there is no direct evidence in Gal 2 or elsewhere to support this assertion. There is ample evidence, however, that Jews could eat with Gentiles without necessarily eating unclean food. This will be shown in 4.2.2.

2.2 Text Group B: Jewishness Is a Calling in Christ

2.2.1 Paul's Testimony About His Torah Observance (Acts 21:17–26)

The case that 1 Cor 9:19–23 does not preclude a Torah-observant Paul is supported by Acts 21:17–26, arguably the most explicit statement in the New Testament that Paul remained a Torah-observant Jew. In Luke's portrayal of Paul's last journey to Jerusalem, the apostle faces myriads of strict Torah-observant Jews who were informed that Paul instructed Jesus-believing Jews in the Diaspora to: (1) Abandon Moses (ἀποστασίαν . . . ἀπὸ Μωϋσέως); (2) Not circumcise (μὴ περιτέμνειν) theirs sons; and (3) Not observe the customs (μηδὲ τοῖς ἔθεσιν περιπατεῖν).

James develops a plan to demonstrate to the myriads of Torah-observant Jews that: (1) The rumour concerning Paul is *false* ("there is nothing in what they have been told about you" [v. 24b]); and (2) That Paul is as Torah observant as they are ("that you yourself *also* live in observance of the law" [v. 24c ESV]). Note the negative and positive side of the testimony. James' plan is for Paul to enter the temple, to purify himself with four men who are under a Nazirite vow (the ceremony involved the men being sprinkled with water mixed with the ashes of a red heifer offering [Num 19:12]), and for Paul to pay for the sacrifices connected with the vow (vv. 23–24). Without objection, Paul follows James' plan. He purifies himself with the four men. Then he informs the temple priest when the days of purification would be over and sacrifices would be offered for each of them (v. 26).[106]

---

[106] Some have suggested that Paul was completing a Nazirite vow in Jerusalem (Acts 18:18). See Volker Stolle, *Der Zeuge als Angeklagter: Untersuchungen zum Paulusbild des Lukas. Beiträge zur Wissenschaft vom Alten und Neuen Testament* (Stuttgart: W. Kohlhammer, 1973), 76–77; Dunn, *The Acts of the Apostles*, 246; Jacob Neusner, "Vow-Taking, the Nazirites, and the Law: Does James' Advice to Paul Accord with Halakhah?" in *James the Just and Christian Origins* (ed. Bruce Chilton and Craig A. Evans; Leiden: Brill, 1999), 81. Others maintain that Paul purchased sacrifices only for the four and that he joined them in the ritual purification ceremony. Cf. H. Strack and P. Billerbeck, *Kommentar zum Neuen Testament aus Talmud and Midrash* (München: C. H. Beck, 1924), 2:757–58; Stuart D. Chepey,

2.2.1.1 Paul Was a Torah-Observant Jew

Acts 21:17–26 is particularly relevant to this study because it describes Paul participating in Jewish practice (ritual purification in the temple, paying for fellow Jews to fulfil their Torah responsibilities) *and* provides a clear reason for this practice: to dispel the false rumour and to demonstrate that he is a Torah-observant Jew. The following eight points represent the affirmative case that Paul is portrayed by Luke as Torah observant:

1. James maintains that Paul "observes the law" (φυλάσσων τὸν νόμον [Acts 21:24]). The language (in the present active tense) refers to careful observance of the law as a whole (Gal 6:13; Rom 2:26):

   Many NT occurrences of φυλάσσω speak of *observing* the law or commandments (used thus also in the LXX). The basic idea of "keeping a law, etc. from being broken" (BAGD s.v. 1.f) yields the meaning *observe, follow, keep*. Initially this refers to observance of the Torah, the law as a whole (νόμον: Acts 7:53; 21:24; Gal 6:13), the commandments (ἐντολάς: Mark 10:19; Matt 19:17; Luke 18:20), or individual provisions among them (δικαιώματα: Rom 2:26). In the Synoptics as in Acts and Paul this usage is linked with criticism of Jewish observance of the law (a significant exception is Acts 21:24, where Paul is presented as being in agreement with the Jewish Christians).[107]

   φυλάσσω. . . serves esp. to express the divinely required attitude of man to the divine covenant, Ex. 19:5 etc., and to the cultic statutes, laws, commandments, admonitions and warnings; in this sense it becomes a tt. [*terminus technicus*] in the legal traditions from Ex. to Dt.[108]

   φυλάσσω. . . to continue to keep a law or commandment from being broken.[109]

   Covenant imagery – zealous for the law, Moses, circumcision, Nazirites, ritual purification, temple, sacrifice, Pentecost season (when the law was given [Acts 20:16]) – saturates the Acts 21 pericope and adds to the covenant-keeping connotation of φυλάσσων τὸν νόμον.

2. The καί in ἀλλὰ στοιχεῖς καὶ αὐτός (Acts 21:24) is emphatic,[110] as in the ESV ("*you yourself also* [καί] *live* in observance of the law"), and

---

"Nazirites in Acts and Late Second Temple Judaism: Was Luke Confused?" (M.Phil. thesis, University of Oxford, 2000), 67. Purification was necessary to enter the temple (Josephus, *Ant.* 12.145; *J. W.* 1.229) and concluded the Nazirite vow. See Roy E. Gane, "The Function of the Nazirite's Concluding Purification Offering", in *Perspectives on Purity and Purification in the Bible* (ed. Baruch J. Schwartz et al.; London: T & T Clark International, 2008), 9–17. Each Nazirite required a burnt offering (a year old male lamb without defect), a sin offering (a one year ewe lamb without defect) and a fellowship offering (a ram without defect), together with their respective grain offerings and drink offerings and a basket of unleavened bread (Num 6:13–15).

[107] Kratz, "φυλάσσω", *EDNT* 1993:3:442.
[108] Bertram, "φυλάσσω", *TDNT* 1981:9:237.
[109] BDAG 2000:1068; cf. Johannes P. Louw and Eugene A. Nida, eds., *Greek-English Lexicon of the New Testament Based on Semantic Domains* (New York: United Bible Societies, 1989), 1:468.

identifies Paul with the antecedent – the thousands of Jesus-believing Jews in Jerusalem who are "zealous for the law".[111] Paul's identification with his Torah observant brethren is also vividly expressed in the picture of him leading the four Nazirites (the most zealous of the zealous) into the temple ("Then *Paul took the men . . .* he entered the temple *with them*" [v. 26]). Here Paul is numbered among the "zealous for the law".[112] James' point is that Paul, whom Luke describes as "a Pharisee, a son of Pharisees" in the present tense (Acts 23:6), continues to "observe the law" like the "zealous for the law".[113]

3. The use of στοιχεῖς in Acts 21:24 (cf. Rom 4:12; Gal 5:25) suggests a consistency of lifestyle.[114] It can be variously translated: "live in" (ESV, NET), "living in" (NIV), "live" (RSV), "way of life" (NJB), "living as a

---

[110] Mikeal C. Parsons and Martin M. Culy, *Acts: A Handbook on the Greek Text* (Waco: Baylor University Press, 2003), 412, note, "The conjunction is emphatic ('you *also*')". See Max Zerwick and Mary Grosvenor, *A Grammatical Analysis of the Greek New Testament* (Rome: Editrice Pontificio Istituto Biblico, 1996), 427; F. Blass et al., *A Greek Grammar of the New Testament and Other Early Christian Literature* (Chicago: The University of Chicago Press, 1961), 146.277.3. Most English Bible translations leave the καί in Acts 21:24 untranslated; exceptions include the NRSV, ESV, NJB, NASB, ASV, KJV. Cf. John 7:10.

[111] "Consistent with its ancient roots, 'zeal' in Second Temple Judaism had to do with an impassioned defense of the covenant by observance of the Law" (Vincent M. Smiles, "The Concept of 'Zeal' in Second-Temple Judaism and Paul's Critique of It in Romans 10:2", *The Catholic Biblical Quarterly* 2 [April 2002]: 298). Also Torrey Seland, "Saul of Tarsus and Early Zealotism: Reading Gal 1,13–14 in Light of Philo's Writings", *Biblica* 83 (2002): 461–62.

[112] Stuart D. Chepey, *Nazirites in Late Second Temple Judaism: A Survey of Ancient Jewish Writings, the New Testament, Archaeological Evidence, and Other Writings from Late Antiquity* (Leiden: Brill, 2005), 174.

[113] See Jacob Jervell, *The Unknown Paul: Essays on Luke-Acts and Early Christian History* (Minneapolis: Augsburg, 1984), 71; Jacob Jervell, *Luke and the People of God: A New Look at Luke-Acts* (Minneapolis: Augsburg, 1972), 159, 163, 169; Jacob Jervell, *The Theology of the Acts of the Apostles* (Cambridge: Cambridge University Press, 1996), 14; David B. Gowler, *Host, Guest, Enemy and Friend: Portraits of the Pharisees in Luke and Acts* (New York: Peter Lang, 1991), 288; W. D. Davies, *Paul and Rabbinic Judaism: Some Rabbinic Elements in Pauline Theology* (Philadelphia: Fortress, 1980), 70. Cf. Acts 26:5. Here "the RSV is probably correct in translating the aorist ἔζησα by 'I have lived', instead of by the past tense as in AV, RV, NEB. Not merely would there have been little point in stressing to King Agrippa what he had done, if he no longer did it, but in addition it hardly brings out the force of the καὶ νῦν that follows, which implies not a contradiction but rather an intensification" (H. L. Ellison, "Paul and the Law – 'All Things to All Men'", in *Apostolic History and the Gospel: Biblical and Historical Essays Presented to F. F. Bruce on his 60th Birthday* [ed. W. Ward Gasque and Ralph P. Martin; Grand Rapids: Eerdmans, 1970], 199). Jack Sanders, *The Jews in Luke-Acts* (Philadelphia: Fortress, 1987), 100, claims that in referring to himself as a Pharisee "Paul is just playing a trick on his audience". Sanders, however, provides no direct evidence from Acts to support his claim.

[114] Miller, "The Relationship of Jewish and Gentile Believers to the Law between A.D. 30 and 70 in the Scripture", 141–42.

constant" (Wms), "order your life in" (Ber), "walk orderly" (NASB), "walkest" (KJV).

4. The Nazirite imagery in Acts 21 is significant. Bart Koet argues that Paul, by serving as a benefactor of the four Jesus-believing Nazirites, "associates himself with their lawabidingness" given that a "Nazir is a paragon of lawabidingness".[115] The Nazirite vow was a special act of consecration; a way of expressing one's piety above and beyond the requirements of Mosaic law (Num 6:1–21). In this regard, Paul's apparent Nazirite vow mentioned in passing in Acts 18:18 (outside of Jerusalem) confirms James' view of Paul in Acts 21, for it indicates that Paul is "even more than lawabiding, he is doing more than what is strictly necessary".[116]

5. James anticipates Paul's concern that such a public demonstration may be misinterpreted by Gentile believers to mean that they too should be Torah observant. James reassures Paul that the Gentile believers will not misunderstand because "as for the Gentiles who have become believers, we have sent a letter with our judgment that they should abstain from what has been sacrificed to idols and from blood and from what is strangled and from fornication" (Acts 21:25). Here James points back to the Acts 15 Jerusalem Council decision that exempted Jesus-believing Gentiles from most of the distinctively Jewish requirements of the Torah, "James parallels the necessity of Jews keeping the law with the necessity of Gentiles to keep the Apostolic decree (21:25)".[117] This is reinforced by Luke's use of φυλάσσω in Acts 16:4 (in reference to Gentile observance of the apostolic decree) and in Acts 21:24 (in reference to Paul's Torah observance).

---

[115] Bart J. Koet, "Why did Paul shave his hair (Acts 18, 18)? Nazirate and Temple in the book of Acts", in *The Centrality of Jerusalem: Historical Perspectives* (ed. M. Poorthuis and Ch. Safrai; Kampen: Kok Pharos, 1996), 139. Also Chepey, *Nazirites in Late Second Temple Judaism*, 273–74.

[116] Koet, "Why did Paul shave his hair (Acts 18, 18)?" 141; cf. Koet, "As Close to the Synagogue as Can Be", 415; Chepey, *Nazirites in Late Second Temple Judaism*, 159–74. Paul's vow (Acts 18:18) also seems to refute the accusation in Acts 18:13, "This man is persuading people to worship God in ways that are contrary to the law".

[117] Miller, "The Relationship of Jewish and Gentile Believers to the Law between A.D. 30 and 70 in the Scripture", 142. Cf. Richard Bauckham, "James and the Jerusalem Church", in *The Book of Acts in Its Palestinian Setting* (ed. Richard Bauckham; Carlisle: Paternoster, 1995), 475; Michael Wyschogrod, "Letter to a Friend", *Modern Theology* 2 (1995): 170; "V. 25 recalls the decision by the Apostolic Council (cf. esp. 15:20). This verse 'reveals the whole paragraph as a thought that, in the spirit of Luke's interest, is central: the differentiation between Jewish Christians and Gentile Christians with regard to Torah observance' (STEGEMANN, *Synagoge*, 177)" (Heiner Ganser-Kerperin, *Das Zeugnis des Tempels: Studien zur Bedeutung des Tempelmotivs im Lukanischen Doppelwerk* [Münster: Aschendorff, 2000], 275 n. 15).

Notably, Luke depicts Paul as delivering the decree to the Gentiles in Acts 15:22–16:4.[118]

6. James' stature in the early church was well known, "For Luke's readers James is an undisputed authority, an incontestable figure so well-known that it is unnecessary for Luke even to make the slightest mention of his credentials. Luke can count on his readers' accepting James' authority without objection".[119] Luke brings James into the narrative especially on those occasions where there is controversy and misunderstanding.[120] In Acts 21, "Luke depicts James as knowing both that the rumors are false and that Paul himself lives in obedience to the Law".[121]

7. Acts 21:17–26 is not simply an example of Paul participating in ritual purity and paying for sacrifices. Paul's actions were intended to *set the record straight* concerning his way of life with respect to the law of Moses. His statement of clarification was made in the temple courts, before myriads of strict Torah-observant Jews who understood the meaning of his actions.

8. Subsequent to Acts 21, Paul confirms on three occasions that he lived according to the standards of Jewish law and custom:

Confirmation 1: Paul's standard of faith and life is *the law* (24:14–18)
Confirmation 2: Paul has not violated *Jewish law* (25:8)
Confirmation 3: Paul has not violated *the customs of the fathers* (28:17)

From a narrative point of view, each of these confirmations point back to Acts 21:17–26.[122] One may ask what more Luke could have included in his narrative to express that Paul was a Torah-observant Jew. Acts is replete with statements that describe Paul as faithful to Jewish law and custom; statements to the contrary are consistently identified as false rumours.[123]

---

[118] Miller, "The Relationship of Jewish and Gentile Believers to the Law between A.D. 30 and 70 in the Scripture", 142. Also Margaret Diffenderfer, "Conditions of Membership in the People of God: A Study Based on Acts 15 and Other Relevant Passages in Acts" (Ph.D. diss., University of Durham, 1986), 266; cf. 93–100, 262, 263 n. 150.

[119] Jervell, *Luke and the People of God*, 187.

[120] Jervell, *Luke and the People of God*, 188, 196.

[121] Jervell, *Luke and the People of God*, 194.

[122] David L. Balch, "'... you teach all the Jews ... to forsake Moses, telling them not to ... observe the customs' (Acts 21:21; cf. 6:14)", in *SBL 1993 Seminar Papers* (ed. Eugene H. Lovering; Atlanta: Scholars, 1993), 370, 383.

[123] George P. Carras, "Observant Jews in the Story of Luke and Acts", in *The Unity of Luke-Acts* (ed. J. Verheyden; Leuven: Leuven University Press, 1999), 693–708. Some exegetes argue that Paul was a consistently practising Jew but not a Torah-observant Jew. W. L. Knox, *St. Paul and the Church of Jerusalem*, 100–103, 122 n. 54, held that Paul viewed the law as a "duty" because the Jewish mission required it. Adolf Schlatter, *The Church in the New Testament Period* (trans. Paul P. Levertoff; London: SPCK, 1955), 58–59, 207–208, similarly maintained that Paul regarded law observance as a "sacred call and duty" on account of the gospel.

How do proponents of the view that Paul was no longer a Torah-observant Jew respond to these eight points? Among commentators who argue for the historical reliability of Acts 21:17–26, most do not address these details. Typically 1 Cor 9:20 is cited as a proof-text to explain Paul's actions.[124]

---

[124] IN ACTS STUDIES: Paton J. Gloag, *A Critical and Exegetical Commentary on the Acts of the Apostles* (Minneapolis: Klock & Klock Christian, 1870), 2:279; H. A. W. Meyer, *The Acts of the Apostles* (Edinburgh: T & T Clark, 1877), 2:206; J. Rawson Lumby, *The Acts of the Apostles* (Cambridge: Cambridge University Press, 1904), 377; Kirsopp Lake and Henry J. Cadbury, *Acts of the Apostles: English Translation and Commentary* (ed. F. J. Foakes Jackson and Kirsopp Lake; London: MacMillan, 1931), 4:273; F. F. Bruce, *The Acts of the Apostles: The Greek Text with Introduction and Commentary* (Grand Rapids: Eerdmans, 1951), 392; Bruce, *The Book of the Acts*, 406; Richard N. Longenecker, "The Problem Practices of Acts", in *Paul: Apostle of Liberty* (New York: Harper & Row, 1964), 250–51; Walter Schmithals, *Paul and James* (London: SCM, 1965), 92; W. D. Davies, *The Gospel and the Land: Early Christianity and Jewish Territorial Doctrine* (Sheffield: JSOT, 1974), 192; W. D. Davies, *Jewish and Pauline Studies* (Philadelphia: Fortress, 1984), 238; I. Howard Marshall, *Acts* (Grand Rapids: Eerdmans, 1980), 346; Martin Hengel, *Acts and the History of Earliest Christianity* (Philadelphia: Fortress, 1980), 88; Martin Hengel, "The Attitude of Paul to the Law in the Unknown Years between Damascus and Antioch", in *Paul and the Mosaic Law* (ed. James D. G. Dunn; Grand Rapids: Eerdmans, 1996), 36; Jürgen Roloff, *Die Apostelgeschichte* (Göttingen: Vandenhoeck & Ruprecht, 1981), 314; R. Maddox, *The Purpose of Luke-Acts* (Edinburgh: T & T Clark, 1982), 39; S. G. Wilson, *Luke and the Law* (Cambridge: Cambridge University Press, 1983), 65, 67–68; Christopher Rowland, *Christian Origins* (London: SPCK, 1985), 217–18; Rudolf Pesch, *Die Apostelgeschichte* (Zürich: Benziger Verlag, 1986), 2:220; Räisänen, *Paul and the Law*, 74; Gerd Lüdemann, *Opposition to Paul in Jewish Christianity* (trans. M. Eugene Boring; Minneapolis: Fortress, 1989), 236; Brice L. Martin, *Christ and the Law in Paul* (Leiden: Brill, 1989), 147; John R. W. Stott, *The Message of Acts* (Downers Grove: InterVarsity, 1990), 342; Hemer, *The Book of Acts in the Setting of Hellenistic History*, 189; Craig C. Hill, *Hellenists and Hebrews: Reappraising Division within the Earliest Church* (Minneapolis: Fortress, 1992), 182; John B. Polhill, *Acts* (Nashville: Broadman, 1992), 448, 450; Moratio B. Hackett, *Commentary on Acts* (Grand Rapids: Kregel, 1992), 249; Thomas R. Schreiner, *The Law and Its Fulfillment: A Pauline Theology of Law* (Grand Rapids: Baker, 1993), 226; Roger Tomes, "Why Did Paul Get His Hair Cut? (Acts 18.18; 21.23–24)", in *Luke's Literary Achievement: Collected Essays* (ed. C. M. Tuckett; Sheffield: Sheffield Academic, 1995), 197; Dunn, *The Acts of the Apostles*, 285; Justin Taylor, *Commentaire Historique (Act 18,23–28,31)* (Paris: Librairie Lecoffre, 1996), 6:112; Jürgen Wehnert, *Die Reinheit des christlichen Gottesvolkes aus Juden und Heiden: Studien zum historischen und theologischen Hintergrund des sogenannten Apostoldekrets* (Göttingen: Vandenhoeck & Ruprecht, 1997), 102; Friedrich W. Horn, "Paulus, das Nasiräat und die Nasiräer", *Novum Testamentum* 2 (1997): 136; Joseph Fitzmyer, *The Acts of the Apostles* (New York: Doubleday, 1998), 692; Witherington, *The Acts of the Apostles*, 648, 651; Craig L. Blomberg, "The Christian and the Law of Moses", in *Witness to the Gospel: The Theology of Acts* (ed. I. Howard Marshall and David Peterson; Grand Rapids: Eerdmans, 1998), 411; Frank Thielman, *The Law in the New Testament: The Question of Continuity* (New York: Crossroad, 1999), 174; Stanley E. Porter, *Paul in Acts* (Peabody: Hendrickson, 2001), 182; Darrell L. Bock, *Acts* (Grand Rapids: Baker Academic, 2007), 644. IN 1 CORINTHIANS STUDIES: Charles J. Ellicott, *St. Paul's First Epistle to the Corinthians* (London: Longmans, Green, and Co., 1887), 167; H. A. W. Meyer, *Paul's First Epistle to the Corin-*

Among commentators who acknowledge a tension between the traditional discontinuity view of Paul and Acts 21:17–26, some offer a counter-narrative to explain Paul's actions: Paul lapsed in his faith, James tricked Paul, James and Paul fooled the naïve Jewish converts or Paul was inconsistent. Other exegetes concede, from a narrative perspective, the eight points listed above. They agree that Luke portrays Paul as a Torah-observant Jew. This conclusion, however, does not cause them to reassess the traditional view that Paul considered Mosaic law a matter of indifference or something he left behind. Rather, it compels them to reject the historical reliability of Acts or Acts 21:17–26 in particular. In other words, Acts is a pious fraud. In sections 2.2.1.2–2.2.1.7, these different approaches will be evaluated. The 1 Cor 9:20 explanation of Acts 21:17–26 will be discussed at the end.

2.2.1.2 Paul Lapsed in His Faith

One of the earliest attested explanations of Acts 21:17–26 is that Paul lapsed in his faith. Paul was weak and compromised his faith on several occasions because of "fear of the Jews" (Jerome, *Epist.* 112). Acts 21 was the worst of these episodes since he knowingly gave an impression of his teaching and lifestyle that was untrue. It was hypocrisy. Sacrificing in the temple was counter to everything Paul believed. From Jerome's perspective, Paul should

---

thians (trans. William P. Dickson and Frederick Crombie; Edinburgh: T & T Clark, 1892), 1:271; F. L. Godet, *Commentary on the First Epistle of St. Paul to the Corinthians* (trans. A. Cusin; Edinburgh: T & T Clark, 1898), 37; Archibald Robertson and Alfred Plummer, *A Critical and Exegetical Commentary on the First Epistle of St. Paul to the Corinthians* (Edinburgh: T & T Clark, 1914), 191; James Moffatt, *The First Epistle of Paul to the Corinthians* (London: Hodder and Stoughton, 1938), 122; Charles Hodge, *An Exposition of the First Epistle to the Corinthians* (Grand Rapids: Eerdmans, 1953), 164; F. W. Grosheide, *Commentary on the First Epistle to the Corinthians* (Grand Rapids: Eerdmans, 1953), 212; Bornkamm, "The Missionary Stance of Paul in 1 Corinthians 9 and in Acts", 202, 204–205; Barrett, *A Commentary on The First Epistle to the Corinthians*, 211; Richardson, "Pauline Consistency in 1 Cor 9:19–23 and Gal 2:11–14", 354; John N. Rietveld, "A Critical Examination of 1 Corinthians 9:19–23 as it Pertains to Paul's Missionary and Apologetic Strategy" (M.Th. thesis, Calvin Theological Seminary, 1983), 91–105; Morris, *The First Epistle of Paul to the Corinthians*, 136; David Prior, *The Message of 1 Corinthians: Life in the Local Church* (Leicester: InterVarsity, 1985), 160; Friedrich Lang, *Die Briefe an die Korinther* (Göttingen: Vandenhoeck & Ruprecht, 1986), 120; Fee, *The First Epistle to the Corinthians*, 428; Paul W. Gooch, *Partial Knowledge: Philosophical Studies in Paul* (Notre Dame: University of Notre Dame Press, 1987), 133, 139–40; S. J. Kistemaker, *1 Corinthians* (Grand Rapids: Baker, 1993), 305–306; Craig L. Blomberg, *1 Corinthians* (Grand Rapids: Zondervan, 1994), 184; Richard Krause, "All Things to All Men: Where is the Limit? An Exegetical Study of 1 Corinthians 9:19–23" (paper presented at the Metro North Pastoral Conference, Southeastern Wisconsin District of WELS, 20 March 1995), 2; Hays, *First Corinthians*, 153; Peter Back, *All Things to All Men: A Study of 1 Corinthians Chapter 9:19–23* (London: Red Sea Team International, 1999), 8–9; Thiselton, *The First Epistle to the Corinthians*, 702; Ciampa and Rosner, *The First Letter to the Corinthians*, 426.

have rejected the advice of James and the Jerusalem elders in Acts 21:24, explaining that the rumour about him was *true* and that he did teach Jesus-believing Jews not to observe the law of Moses any longer. Jerome rebuked Paul for his reversion:

> Paul, I must ask you again, why did you shave your head, why did you take part in the procession barefoot in accordance with the Jewish customs? Why did you offer sacrifices and allow victims to be slaughtered on your behalf in accordance with the law? No doubt you will answer that you did so to prevent the believers who had been Jews from being put off. So you pretended to be a Jew in order to bring the Jews over to your side, having learnt this kind of hypocrisy from James and the other elders.[125]

The positive evidence for a Torah-observant Paul in Acts 21:17–26 (from Luke's point of view) has already been presented in 2.2.1.1. An additional weakness in Jerome's case is the absence of any evidence in Acts that Paul lapsed. As Humphrey points out, Luke does not correct Paul or suggest he did anything wrong, "If Paul made a mistake in what he did with these four men, the New Testament does not reveal it as being a mistake. Peter made a mistake (Gal. 2:11), but the New Testament reveals it as a mistake so that students are not left to wonder. In the case of Paul in Acts 21, there is not a single hint that he erred. If Paul made a mistake, all the people who advised him about the event also made a mistake. They are not rebuked or understood as having erred".[126]

2.2.1.3 James Tricked Paul

A. J. Mattill argues that James' plan in Acts 21 was really an attempt to conspire against Paul. The Jerusalem leadership "decided against Paul in the question concerning Paul's attitude towards the Law" and agreed to draw "Paul into an ambush by luring him into the Temple".[127] James revoked the apostolic decree and refused Paul's collection in a symbolic rejection of the Gentile mission.[128] When Paul was being beaten and dragged from the tem-

---

[125] Jerome, *Epist.* 112; *FC* 12:353. By contrast, Augustine argued that Paul observed the law in honour of the "divine authority and the prophetic holiness of the sacraments" (*Epist.* 82).

[126] Alex Humphrey, "The Implications for Today of Paul's Conduct as Recorded in Acts 21:20–26" (M.Sc. thesis, Abilene Christian College, 1960), 91.

[127] Andrew J. Mattill, "The Purpose of Acts: Schneckenburger Reconsidered", in *Apostolic History and the Gospel* (ed. W. Ward Gasque and Ralph P. Martin; Grand Rapids: Eerdmans, 1970), 116. Cf. Sanders, *The Jews in Luke-Acts*, 284; Johannes Munck, *Paul and the Salvation of Mankind* (trans. F. Clarke; London: SCM, 1959), 240; S. G. F. Brandon, *The Fall of Jerusalem and the Christian Church* (London: SPCK, 1957), 135.

[128] Mattill, "The Purpose of Acts", 116. Luke's silence about the collection in Acts 21 does not have to imply that the Jerusalem leadership rejected the gift, "Another possibility, entailing a significantly different understanding of Luke's historiographical practice, is that the collection was accepted and Luke knew this, but did not choose to refer to the collection because it had no relevance to his own purposes in this narrative. Much of the discussion has

ple, the Jesus-believing Jews in Jerusalem stood by and took no action to help him. They gave him up in order to conciliate the Jews who did not believe in Jesus.[129] Luke saw all of this and committed that day to defend Paul against the misconceptions that led to his arrest.[130]

Stanley Porter also maintains a conspiracy theory following Mattill's reconstruction, "Mattill's proposal, to my mind, being a very plausible and convincing explanation of what happened in Jerusalem".[131] As such, Porter holds that James and the Jerusalem elders were "suspicious" of Paul.[132] It is reasonable to think that "Paul was in some way, if not directly lured into, at least not prevented from, stepping into a trap" in order to "put Paul in his place".[133] The accusations themselves may have been "manufactured by the Jerusalem leaders".[134] Porter sees this implied in the text itself, "Though the church leaders apparently rejoice, on closer examination it appears that they are in full agreement with a more strongly Pharisaical group in the Jerusalem church who wish to accuse Paul of encouraging Diaspora Jews to abandon the law of Moses".[135] Dunn suggests that James made no attempt to rescue Paul in the

---

proceeded on the assumption that, since the collection was very important to Paul and evidently central to his purpose in travelling to Jerusalem, Luke would certainly have referred to it if he knew it was accepted. But this is to confuse narrative and history by neglecting to consider Luke's purpose in this narrative. Since all historiography cannot but be selective, even the most stringent requirements of historical accuracy would not oblige Luke to clutter his narrative with material not relevant to the story he has decided to tell. It does not follow that, just because the collection was so important for Paul, it had to seem important to Luke from the perspective from which he was writing. Of course, if Luke's purpose were to portray harmony between Paul and the mother church in Jerusalem, the acceptance of the collection would be very relevant. But, although Luke does presume agreement between Paul and the Jerusalem church leaders, his purpose in this passage is not to make that point. Luke's purpose in Acts 21,18–30 would seem to be twofold: to explain how Paul came to be a prisoner charged with serious offences under Jewish Law, and at the same time to vindicate Paul against these charges by showing that, so far from incurring them, when Paul was seized in the Temple he was in the act of demonstrating his reverence for the Temple and his obedience to the Torah . . . Luke's silence about the collection probably implies, not that there was a problem about it, but that it played no significant part in the sequence of events that led to Paul's imprisonment" (Richard Bauckham, "The Final Meeting of James and Paul: Narrative and History in Acts 21, 18–26", in *Raconter, interpréter, annoncer: Parcours de Nouveau Testament: Mélanges offerts à Daniel Marguerat pour son 60e anniversaire* [ed. E. Steffek and Y. Bourquin; Geneva: Labor et Fides, 2003], 257–58).

[129] Mattill, "The Purpose of Acts", 116.
[130] Mattill, "The Purpose of Acts", 117. Also Blomberg, "The Christian and the Law of Moses", 413.
[131] Porter, *Paul in Acts*, 179.
[132] Porter, *Paul in Acts*, 178–79.
[133] Porter, *Paul in Acts*, 179.
[134] Porter, *Paul in Acts*, 182.
[135] Porter, *Paul in Acts*, 185.

temple, "It looks very much as though they washed their hands of Paul, left him to stew in his own juice".[136]

Mattill's and Porter's historical reconstruction is far-fetched. There is no direct evidence in Acts that the Jerusalem leadership opposed Paul or plotted to get rid of him during his final journey to Jerusalem. Bauckham calls it "absurd".[137]

> But it is very important to notice that the act the elders propose that Paul should undertake is an act of very public association with the Jerusalem church, to which the four nazirites belong. This decisively contradicts the idea that the proposal was devious, intended to expose Paul to lethal public hatred and in this way to dispose of the problem he presented for the Jerusalem church leaders. The action proposed could only benefit the Jerusalem church if it succeeded in clearing Paul's good name as a fully observant Jew. If it failed to do this, it would harm the church, by firmly associating the apostate Paul with the Jerusalem church. That, either in Luke's narrative or in historical actuality, James and the elders expected their advice to lead to Paul's lynching is inconceivable. Luke's narrative certainly makes no sense unless James and the elders genuinely believe that Paul keeps the law, as they say, and really expect him to be able to clear his name by following their advice.[138]

James' "advice shows confidence that Paul could in fact defy his unjustified reputation and prove himself Law-observant".[139] Moreover, while it is true that the elders would have known of the danger to Paul, "their advice was calculated to dispel the danger, not to increase it".[140] Finally, Bauckham argues that Dunn "concludes far too much from Luke's silence. James and his colleagues had not influence with either the chief priests or the Romans. Any attempt they made on Paul's behalf would surely have been unsuccessful. Luke's narrative, which naturally does not record everything that happened, had more important concerns than with actions of the Jerusalem elders which made no difference to the course of events".[141]

2.2.1.4 James and Paul Fooled the Naïve Jewish Converts

David Trobisch maintains that James and Paul colluded to deceive the Torah-observant Jesus-believing Jews in Jerusalem, "The two apostles devise a plan to fool the naïve Jewish converts . . . In order to create the impression that Paul lives in strict observance of the law, James advises Paul to participate in

---

[136] James D. G. Dunn, *Unity and Diversity in the New Testament* (London: SCM, 1977), 256.

[137] Bauckham, "James and the Jerusalem Church", 478.

[138] Bauckham, "The Final Meeting of James and Paul", 255.

[139] Bauckham, "James and the Jerusalem Church", 478. Also Bauckham, "The Final Meeting of James and Paul", 251, 253.

[140] Bauckham, "James and the Jerusalem Church", 478.

[141] Bauckham, "James and the Jerusalem Church", 478–79; cf. 479 n. 190. Also Bauckham, "The Final Meeting of James and Paul", 256–59.

the private ritual of Nazirite purification".[142] Once again, there is no direct evidence for the proposed interpretation.

2.2.1.5 Paul Was Inconsistent

Adolf von Harnack became an ardent proponent of the historicity of the book of Acts while conducting a source-critical study of the book between 1906–1911. The study, which was published in three volumes, included an extended treatment of Acts 21 in "The Attitude of the Apostle St Paul Towards Judaism and Jewish Christianity, According to the Last Chapters of the Acts".[143] Harnack stressed that Paul viewed ritual elements of Jewish law as still "in force for Jews by birth" in the New Covenant era.[144] They were not optional.

Harnack, however, argued that, while Paul could testify "with a clear conscience" in Acts 21 that he lived a law-observant life,[145] inwardly he wrestled with the implications of Christian freedom and equality in his communities (e.g. 1 Cor 6:12; Rom 10:12).[146] Paul was sincere but ambivalent, bound but free, in a state of personal conflict and "self-contradiction" over his theology.[147] The apostle was "swayed by contradictory thoughts and feelings" within.[148] Thus, he remained "inconsistent", and his theology reflected this "paradoxical" and "perplexing contradiction".[149]

Several scholars have followed Harnack's view, including F. J. Foakes Jackson and Kirsopp Lake. These scholars affirm the "binding character of the Law" in Pauline thought as expressed in Acts 21:17–26.[150] At the same time, they read Paul's letters as contradicting this premise. Citing Harnack's treatise, Jackson and Lake conclude that there is "illogicality inherent in his position",[151] not because Paul is deceptive but because he is working out ten-

---

[142] David Trobisch, *The First Edition of the New Testament* (Oxford: Oxford University Press, 2000), 83.

[143] Adolf von Harnack, *The Date of the Acts and of the Synoptic Gospels* (trans. J. R. Wilkinson; New York: Williams & Norgate, 1911), 67–89.

[144] Harnack, *The Date of the Acts and of the Synoptic Gospels*, 74.

[145] Harnack, *The Date of the Acts and of the Synoptic Gospels*, 75.

[146] Harnack, *The Date of the Acts and of the Synoptic Gospels*, 52, 49.

[147] Harnack, *The Date of the Acts and of the Synoptic Gospels*, 52; Adolf von Harnack, *The Acts of the Apostles* (trans. J. R. Wilkinson; New York: Williams & Norgate, 1909), 282–83.

[148] Harnack, *The Date of the Acts and of the Synoptic Gospels*, 53.

[149] Harnack, *The Date of the Acts and of the Synoptic Gospels*, 49, 63, 53.

[150] F. J. Foakes Jackson and Kirsopp Lake, "The Disciples in Jerusalem and the Rise of Gentile Christianity", in *The Beginnings of Christianity: The Acts of the Apostles* (ed. F. J. Foakes Jackson and Kirsopp Lake; London: MacMillan, 1939), 1:311; F. J. Foakes Jackson and Kirsopp Lake, "The General Presentation of Paul in Acts", in *The Beginnings of Christianity: The Acts of the Apostles* (ed. F. J. Foakes Jackson and Kirsopp Lake; London: MacMillan, 1922), 2:292 n. 1.

[151] Jackson and Lake, "The General Presentation of Paul in Acts", 2:291.

sions in his theology.¹⁵² Räisänan similarly concludes that "Paul's thought on the law is full of difficulties and inconsistencies".¹⁵³

Does Luke portray Paul as inconsistent on the matter of Torah observance for Jesus-believing Jews? In Acts 21:17–26, James does not address an ambivalent Paul. On the contrary, James is confident of Paul's orthodoxy and constancy (Acts 21:24). Second, Paul responds to James' plan speedily. The text gives little indication of hesitation or wavering.¹⁵⁴ Third, Acts 21 portrays Paul as a man of conviction and single-mindedness. When his disciples urge him (through the Spirit) not to go to Jerusalem, he continues on his way (Acts 21:4–5). When Paul receives a prophetic warning from Agabus that imprisonment awaits him in Jerusalem, he does not turn back (Acts 21:10–15). Paul's own entourage pleads with him not to go up to Jerusalem, but Paul is not swayed (Acts 21:12–13). Luke concludes the journey account by noting, "Since he would not be persuaded, we remained silent" (Acts 21:14). Paul is depicted as a man of conviction not prone to equivocation. Fourth, there is little evidence in Acts as a whole that Paul wrestled with the implications of "Christian freedom". Acts 15 portrays Paul as resolute on the issue of "Gentile" exemption from the law (Acts 15:1–2). He hand-delivers the apostolic decree as a statement of his support for Gentile freedom (Acts 16:4). At the same time, he circumcises Timothy (Acts 16:3) as a testimony that Jews should circumcise their sons, the unstated assumption of the Acts 15 Jerusalem Council decision. Subsequent to Acts 21, Paul confirms three times that his life and teachings are consistent with the Torah (Acts 24:14–18; 25:8; 28:17). Once he refers to himself in the present tense as a Pharisee (Acts 23:6).

2.2.1.6 Luke's Account in Acts 21:17–26 Is a Pious Fraud

F. C. Baur devoted a chapter of his book *Paul, the Apostle of Jesus Christ* to Acts 21. In this treatment, he refers to the various passages in Acts that describe Paul's support for circumcision, pilgrimage festivals and Nazirites.¹⁵⁵ Concerning the trajectory's climax in Acts 21:17–26, Baur asserts that Paul is "made to accommodate himself to Judaism in a way to which he could not have consented without utterly deserting his principles".¹⁵⁶ Paul's actions in Acts 21, against the backdrop of Galatians, are beyond the bounds of possibility:

---

[152] Jackson and Lake, "The General Presentation of Paul in Acts", 2:291.

[153] Räisänen, *Paul and the Law*, 264.

[154] Gilbert Bouwman, *Berufen zur Freiheit: Freiheit und Gesetz nach der Heiligen Schrift* (Düsseldorf: Patmos-Verlag, 1969), 92.

[155] F. C. Baur, *Paul, the Apostle of Jesus Christ, His Life and Work, His Epistles and His Doctrine: A Contribution to a Critical History of Primitive Christianity* (trans. Allan Menzies; London: Williams & Norgate, 1876), 1:195–215.

[156] Baur, *Paul, the Apostle of Jesus Christ*, 1:196, 198.

In his own Epistles he states in the frankest manner that he is an opponent of circumcision, and considers adherence to it to be quite inconsistent with the principles of his teaching. Here again we find the Epistle to the Galatians maintaining a consistent and irreconcilable contradiction to the Acts of the Apostles . . . With what appearance of truth could he then come before the Jews with the statement, "In all that you have heard of me there is not a particle of truth. I am an adherent and an observer of the law as well as you!" Would this have been a less contemptible ὑπόκρισις than that which the Apostle himself so unreservedly condemned in Peter? It is impossible that the Apostle should have resolved on such a course of action on the grounds given by the author of the Acts; and if the motive disappears from which a certain course of action is said to have proceeded, how doubtful does the action itself become![157]

Paul's statement in Acts 23:6 that he is a Pharisee (present tense) and his claims to be law observant and faithful to the customs (Acts 24:14–18; 25:8; 28:17) must also be erroneous in light of Galatians.[158] The historical Paul could not have spoken any of these statements.[159]

On the historical elements in Acts 21:17–26, Baur acknowledged that Paul travelled to Jerusalem to deliver a collection from the Gentile churches.[160] This can be established from Rom 15:25.[161] For Baur, however, the Paul of Galatians would not have purchased sacrifices for Jesus-believing Nazirites or participated in a ritual purification ceremony as a testimony of his Torah observance. Paul opposed all forms of Christian adherence to Jewish law.[162] On this mark, Acts 21 is fiction.[163]

In the twentieth century, Ernst Haenchen built on Baur's conceptualization of primitive Christianity and used redaction criticism to interpret Acts 21:17–26. For Haenchen, "Luke" lived in the sub-apostolic period, after the separation of Judaism and Christianity.[164] Because Luke was far removed from the historical Paul and the early church, he used late sources and a rich imagination to write his account. This explains why Luke's account of the four Nazirites in Jerusalem does not agree with the historical context. He confused his sources,[165] a view echoed by Conzelmann, Barrett, Tomes and Neusner. For Haenchen, Acts 21:17–26 is a prime example of historical fiction. The author would have the reader believe the impossible – that "Paul through the proposed action will prove himself a law-abiding Jew".[166]

---

[157] Baur, *Paul, the Apostle of Jesus Christ,* 1:200–201.

[158] Baur, *Paul, the Apostle of Jesus Christ,* 1:205–10, 213–14.

[159] Baur, *Paul, the Apostle of Jesus Christ,* 1:213.

[160] Baur, *Paul, the Apostle of Jesus Christ*, 1:196.

[161] Baur, *Paul, the Apostle of Jesus Christ,* 1:196.

[162] Baur, *Paul, the Apostle of Jesus Christ,* 1:196.

[163] F. C. Baur's approach to Acts 21 was adopted by Albert Schwegler, Eduard Zeller, Bruno Bauer and Franz Overbeck.

[164] Haenchen, *The Acts of the Apostles*, 116.

[165] Haenchen, *The Acts of the Apostles*, 610–11.

[166] Haenchen, *The Acts of the Apostles*, 610. Hans Conzelmann, *Acts of the Apostles* (trans. James Limburg, et al.; Philadelphia: Fortress, 1987), 180, who built on Haenchen's

In more recent times, Philip Esler has applied socio-redaction criticism to Acts 21:17–26 and concurs with Baur and Haenchen that Luke emphasizes the "apostle's total and uninterrupted fidelity to the Jewish law".[167] Luke responds to the charge of Paul's opposition to circumcision, temple and Torah by showing how Paul upheld each one of these Mosaic institutions:

> There can be little doubt that Luke wants his readers to conclude that the Jewish charges against Paul were false. How could Paul have preached against circumcision, implies Luke, when he circumcised Timothy? How could he have been opposed to the Temple when he came to Jerusalem with offerings for it? How could he have been against the law in general when, by both his words and his deeds, he continually upheld it? In this respect he is identical with other Jewish Christians in Acts, such as Ananias (22.12) and the thousands of Jewish Christians whom James describes as all zealously devoted to the law (21.20).[168]

Like other proponents of the pious fraud reading of Acts 21, Esler considers Luke's portrait a fabrication. The Paul of the epistles, the real Paul, was responsible for "renouncing the Levitical food laws" and permitted (if not encouraged indirectly) Jesus-believing Jews to abandon Jewish practice.[169] Historically, the Acts 21:21 accusations against Paul were accurate but Luke shaped the "sources and traditions at his disposal" to exonerate Paul.[170]

An investigation of the evidence for the historical reliability of Acts as a whole, or the "we-passages" in particular, is beyond the scope of this study. For this the reader should consult Hemer among others.[171] Some preliminary conclusions regarding the historical reliability of Acts 21:17–26, however, may be advanced. There is widespread agreement that Acts 21:17–26 includes some historical data; the question is how much. Support for the view that Acts 21:17–26 is of "great historical value" comes from an unexpected quarter, Gerd Lüdemann.

Few have given more attention to the historical-critical study of Acts 21:17–26 than Lüdemann in contemporary scholarship. Lüdemann concludes that the writer of Acts 21 used reliable traditions as source material for his narrative:

> *The Historical Reliability of the Source.* If we inquire concerning the historical reliability of the source, the answer must be unconditionally positive. The individual elements are confirmed as probable or at least possible by other reports independent of Acts 21 . . . Our analysis of the traditions underlying Acts 21 can then be summarized as follows: Luke uses a con-

---

redaction critical approach, arrived at the same conclusion, "The reader of Acts knows that these accusations are false. Paul has always been Torah observant" even though the "real facts were certainly otherwise". Cf. Richardson, "Pauline Consistency in 1 Cor 9:19–23 and Gal 2:11–14", 353–54.

[167] Esler, *Community and Gospel in Luke-Acts*, 125.
[168] Esler, *Community and Gospel in Luke-Acts*, 126.
[169] Esler, *Community and Gospel in Luke-Acts*, 128.
[170] Esler, *Community and Gospel in Luke-Acts*, 129.
[171] Hemer, *The Book of Acts in the Setting of Hellenistic History*, 1–29, 312–64.

nected source, which in fact does deal with Paul's last trip to Jerusalem and which is of great historical value.[172]

Stuart Chepey's 2005 published Oxford dissertation *Nazirites in Late Second Temple Judaism* also supports the historical reliability of Acts 21:17–26.[173] This finding is significant given that a key argument against the dependability of Acts 21:17–26 is Luke's portrayal of Naziritism.[174] Chepey argues that Luke's account is historically plausible:

> In summation, like Acts 18:18, Luke's information regarding Nazirite behaviour in 21.23–7a is historically plausible as it stands, and there is no basis for the rationale that Luke misconstrued his facts. The reference to the purification process of all five individuals, all due to corpse contamination and all taking place simultaneously, is easily conceivable given what is known about Nazirites in the period Luke composed his account. Moreover, there is no need to suppose that Luke considered Paul as having taken a mere seven-day Nazirate, nor that he completed a vow taken some time previously, nor that Luke confused his sources. In addition, Luke's narrative use of the Nazirite custom is sound. There is no reason to suppose Luke's use of Nazirites in Acts 21.23–4, namely as a means of portraying Paul as a pious, Law-minded Jew, stands out as odd either when comparing Luke's account with early rabbinic or other sources of the period. Not only would Nazirites have been thought of as pious individuals (in some cases), but by purifying himself along with four impure Nazirites and covering their costs to restart their avowed periods, Paul would have had a high chance of being seen participating and promoting Mosaic cult ritual and associating himself with Law-minded Jews.[175]

2.2.1.7 Paul Became as One Under the Law to Win Those Under the Law

Among exegetes who accept Acts 21:17–26 as historically plausible, most will contend that Paul accommodated to the Jesus-believing Jews in Jerusalem. The standard interpretation is that Paul entered the temple and participated in ritual purification. He purchased sacrifices. His actions, however, reflected his principle of adaptation described in 1 Cor 9:19–23. He became as a

---

[172] Lüdemann, *Opposition to Paul in Jewish Christianity*, 58–59; cf. Gerd Lüdemann, *Heretics: The Other Side of Early Christianity* (trans. John Bowden; Louisville: Westminster John Knox, 1996), 46–47.

[173] Chepey, *Nazirites in Late Second Temple Judaism*, 173–74.

[174] Haenchen, *The Acts of the Apostles*, 610–12; Neusner, "Vow-Taking, the Nazirites, and the Law", 81.

[175] Chepey, *Nazirites in Late Second Temple Judaism*, 173–74. He adds, "James' plot in the narrative is actually quite clever. Nazirites would have been a popular sight in the temple during Pentecost and easily noticed because of their appearance . . . By being present with such figures, Paul's action of purifying himself and paying for the four men to have haircuts and sacrifices offered to renew their vows would likely have been easily witnessed . . . That Paul's actions would have assured onlookers that he was a Jew well observant of Mosaic custom seems highly plausible". Cf. Chepey, "Nazirites in Acts and Late Second Temple Judaism", 66; Hilary Le Cornu with Joseph Shulam, *The Jewish Roots of Acts* (Jerusalem: Academon, 2003), 2:1183–192.

Jew to win the Jews. He became as one under the law to win those under the law. He became like the weak in faith to win the weak in faith.

There are several problems with this argument. First, how is it known that Paul's principle of adaptation (1 Cor 9:19–23) can be applied to this situation? In order to argue for its application, one has to establish the meaning of 1 Cor 9:19–23 and define its limitations. Acts commentators do not typically do this.

A second problem with the accommodation argument is that it does not explain all of the data. 1 Cor 9:19–23 is often used as a proof-text to explain Paul's actions. Exegetical issues that are in tension with the view that Paul was no longer Torah observant are often overlooked or sidestepped.

Third, by not defining the limits of Pauline flexibility, the accommodation argument effectively avoids dealing with the ethical implications of Paul's actions. Commentators rarely discuss the issue of perception: What is the purpose of James' plan? How did James perceive Paul's actions? How did the myriads of Torah-observant Jews perceive Paul's actions?

Perception is a critical factor in adjudicating whether a person has deceived another. Luke indicates that Paul's actions were for the purpose of denying the false rumour and confirming that he was a Torah-observant Jew. The apostle's actions were to be interpreted by everyone in this way, "*Thus all will know* (καὶ γνώσονται πάντες) that there is nothing in what they have been told about you, but that you yourself also live in observance of the law" (Acts 21:24). This was not an ambiguous situation (e.g. Paul in the synagogue on the Sabbath) where motivation and public perception could differ. Rather, it was a situation where Paul agreed to a plan to communicate through his actions a particular message about his teaching and way of life. Everything had been prearranged. He was setting the record straight before James and his opponents, and he was doing this in the Jerusalem temple among four Torah-observant Jews who were making vows to God. Paul was fully responsible for how his actions would be perceived in this situation.

Proponents of the accommodation argument sometimes describe Paul's actions as a "conciliatory gesture"[176] designed to *win* the law-observant Jewish Christians in Jerusalem to maturity in Christ.[177] From an ethical standpoint, however, using a reasonable person's standard, the accommodation argument presents a disturbing image of Paul. Here is a man who purportedly agreed to set the record straight publicly, in the holy temple, about his life and teachings, but it was all a pretence for a higher good (according to the accommodation argument). Trobisch's contention that James and Paul devised "a plan to

---

[176] Marshall, *Acts*, 346.
[177] Schmithals, *Paul and James*, 89–93; Richardson, "Pauline Consistency in 1 Cor 9:19–23 and Gal 2:11–14", 354; Roloff, *Die Apostelgeschichte*, 314; Wilson, *Luke and the Law*, 110; Hill, *Hellenists and Hebrews*, 182–83; Witherington, *The Acts of the Apostles*, 648; Porter, *Paul in Acts*, 177–78.

2.2 Text Group B: Jewishness Is a Calling in Christ

fool the naïve Jewish converts" was noted in 2.1.3. The accommodation argument would seem to suggest that Paul alone fooled the naïve Jewish converts for their own good. As Baur put it, such an action would have been "reprehensible hypocrisy".[178] Baur would seem to be correct.

Is the accommodation argument realistic? Since Paul rebuked Peter for ὑποκρίσει in Gal 2:13, would Paul have opened himself up to the same charge? Also, Paul would have certainly known that the Jerusalem community would continue to receive reports about his life and teachings after he left Jerusalem. Is it likely that Paul publicly set the record straight that he remained a Torah-observant Jew but that he gave no thought to the fact that his testimony would shortly thereafter be contradicted by his actions? Was Paul so facile? Was there a darker side to Paul?

How would Paul have justified putting on a pretence? While most exegetes do not address this question, the few who do generally respond with an ends-justifies-the-means argument. John Chrysostom uses the analogy of a doctor with his patient:

Do you see the advantage of deceit? And if any one were to reckon up all the tricks of physicians the list would run on to an indefinite length. And not only those who heal the body but those also who attend to the diseases of the soul may be found continually making use of this remedy . . . For great is the value of deceit, provided it be not introduced with a mischievous intention. In fact action of this kind ought not to be called deceit, but rather a kind of good management, cleverness and skill, capable of finding out ways where resources fail, and making up for the defects of the mind . . . And often it is necessary to deceive, and to do the greatest benefits by means of this device, whereas he who has gone by a straight course has done great mischief to the person whom he has not deceived.[179]

Chrysostom would have the reader believe that James and the Jerusalem congregation were spiritually sick and that Paul viewed himself as a good doctor who came to heal them by means of deception. However, Luke does not describe Paul as a doctor among the sick and weak in Jerusalem. Chrysostom's analogy, moreover, does not exonerate Paul but affirms that underlying the accommodation case is an ends-justifies-the-means argument. A significant weakness in Chrysostom's case is that Paul explicitly states in 2 Cor 4 that he does not minister in a deceptive way – "we refuse to practise cunning or to falsify God's word; but by the open statement of the truth we commend ourselves to the conscience of everyone in the sight of God" (2 Cor 4:2; cf. 12:16). In Rom 3:7–8, Paul rejects the principle that the ends justifies the means, "But if through my falsehood God's truthfulness abounds to his glory, why am I still being condemned as a sinner? And why not say (as some peo-

---

[178] Baur, *Paul, the Apostle of Jesus Christ*, 1:130.
[179] Chrysostom, *Sac.* 1.8 (*CPT* 1906:23–24; *NPNF* 9:38); cf. *Hom.* XXII on 1 Cor 9:13–14 (*BP* 2.263; *NPNF* 12:128).

ple slander us by saying that we say), 'Let us do evil so that good may come'? Their condemnation is deserved!"

F. F. Bruce defended Paul on the basis of a "higher consistency". The following quote by Bruce appears in numerous Acts commentaries as a quick and easy way of addressing Paul's seeming hypocrisy in Acts 21. In Bruce's view,

> the consistency which some would like to impose on Paul is that "foolish consistency" which R. W. Emerson describes as "the hobgoblin of little minds, adored by little statesmen and philosophers and divines". Those who deplore the absence of this consistency from Paul miss the higher consistency which aimed at bringing all the activities of his life and thought "into captivity to the obedience of Christ" (2 Cor 10:5) and at subordinating every other interest to the paramount interests of the gospel (1 Cor 9:23).[180]

But what is this higher consistency? Bruce is vague and does not elaborate. Could Paul do anything for the sake of Christ and the gospel? Were there no limits? Bruce is simply adding a rhetorical flourish to Chrysostom's argument. It sounds reasonable but it is ultimately an ends-justifies-the-means argument. Notably, in the end, Bruce was unable to reconcile his position with Luke's account and suggested that Acts 21:24 reflected James' "*naïveté*" concerning Paul's stance on the law.[181]

In 1968, C. K. Barrett argued that Paul assumed a Jewish "guise" before James and the Jerusalem congregation. For a higher purpose, Paul "pretended" that he was a law-abiding Jew:

> His Judaism was no longer of his very being, but a guise he could adopt or discard at will. His adoption of Judaism is illustrated in Acts xxi. 23–6: but Acts is scarcely aware of Paul's un-Jewishness . . . to be a Jew is to be under the law and thereby related to God in this way; at the most he may pretend to be so related.[182]

Three decades later, Barrett changed his position and asserted in his commentary on Acts (1998), that the accommodation argument was flawed. He came to realize that, in Acts 21, Paul was asked to clarify his beliefs so that all would know the truth about his life and teachings with respect to Jewish law. In this kind of situation, Barrett concluded that accommodation would be unethical because Paul would be suggesting something that was "not true". According to Barrett,

> the real question here is not whether on occasion Paul would do what Jews did: 1 Corinthians 9 proves conclusively that he was prepared to do this. The question is whether Paul was prepared to use a special occasion such as the one described [Acts 21:17–26] in order to suggest something that was not true, namely that he too (καὶ αὐτός, he just like the ardent Jews who

---

[180] Bruce, *The Book of the Acts*, 304.
[181] Bruce, *The Book of the Acts*, 406–407.
[182] Barrett, *A Commentary on The First Epistle to the Corinthians*, 211–12.

suspected his loyalty) was regularly observant of the Law as understood within Judaism. Readiness to do this is not covered by 1 Corinthians 9.[183]

As a contemporary analogy to the ethical question in Acts 21:17–26, consider more conservative theological seminaries in the United States that annually require faculty members to sign a statement of faith and conduct. Such statements are often intended to ensure that the seminary's faculty conforms to the doctrinal and ethical standards of the denomination it serves. Imagine if a professor of theology in one of these seminaries was accused of teaching and living in a way counter to the seminary's standards. Rumours about the professor spread throughout the denomination. In point of fact, the faculty member was in violation of the standards. Here is the question: At the annual review, would it be ethical for the professor to sign the statement of faith and conduct but privately reinterpret the language in a way that violated the intent of the document? Would it be ethical to sign the statement to conciliate the seminary's board of directors, or as an act of accommodation (for the sake of Christ and the gospel) to help the seminary grow to spiritual maturity by subverting its doctrinal and moral standards? Most people (certainly the seminaries!) would consider such conduct unethical. The bottom line is that the professor is given a formal opportunity to set the record straight about his controversial views and lifestyle. If the professor signs the document, he is telling the seminary that *he also* (cf. καὶ αὐτός in Acts 21:24) shares the school's religious convictions.

In an attempt to absolve Paul from the charge of hypocrisy, some accommodation proponents argue that James and the Jerusalem community were only concerned that Paul observed the law when he was with Jews. The Jesus-believing Jews in Israel did not mind if Paul violated the law when he was with Gentiles. Thus, Porter maintains that ἀλλὰ στοιχεῖς καὶ αὐτὸς φυλάσσων τὸν νόμον (v. 24) does not mean Paul "observes the law" consistently but that he "obeys the law when dealing with Jewish Christians".[184] Morton Smith writes that James' request "in Acts 21:23f. must have been in fact for a demonstration of occasional conformity".[185] D. A. Carson similarly proposes that "v. 24 may mean only that Paul is living in obedience to all the strictures of Torah *during his sojourn in Jerusalem*".[186] But where is the direct evidence that James and the Jerusalem congregation held such an emancipated approach to Jewish law? Would the "zealous for the law" have found this religiously indifferent outlook acceptable? Porter's view does not seem to

---

[183] Barrett, *The Acts of the Apostles*, 2:1013.
[184] Porter, *Paul in Acts*, 182.
[185] Morton Smith, "The Reason for the Persecution of Paul and the Obscurity of Acts", in *Studies in Mysticism and Religion Presented to Gershom G. Scholem on His Seventieth Birthday by Pupils, Colleagues and Friends* (Jerusalem: The Hebrew University, 1967), 266.
[186] Carson, "Pauline Inconsistency", 18.

be consistent with Luke's portrayal of the Jerusalem community or the wider *Sitz im Leben*. Mosaic law in Second Temple Judaism was considered a unity (Gal 5:3; Jas 2:10) and Jews were expected to keep the law whether in Jewish company or not:

> By definition, one does not keep the Law part of the time. If a Jew kept the Law while he was in the presence of Jews but abandoned the Law when with Gentiles he was not a keeper of the Law but a breaker of the Law. If this was not the case, none of the Jewish believers would have been convinced by Paul's actions. Consistency is a necessary component of the concept of keeping the Law.[187]

Consistency in keeping the law included Leviticus 11 dietary restrictions and lesser commandments (Matt 23:23; 5:17–20). As Räisänen points out, standards of law observance varied (strict, less strict, minimal, etc.) but a selective approach to the law was unthinkable:

> Christian expositors of Paul sometimes seem to assume that as long as some aspect of the law remains important to Paul, he cannot be charged with annulling it. But, for a Jew, to be *selective* about the Torah meant to disobey it, indeed to reject it.[188]

Bruce concedes that an indifference or optional approach to the law would have been considered "apostasy from Moses":

> For anyone who stayed by the letter and spirit of the law, Paul's regarding some of its requirements as matters of indifference, his treating as optional things that the law laid down as obligatory, must in itself have constituted "apostasy against Moses".[189]

Porter's interpretation of Acts 21:24 – Paul obeys the law when dealing with Jewish Christians [but not with Gentiles] – would seem to be a levelling down of Luke's portrait of Paul to make it conform to a certain reading of 1 Cor 9:19–23. There is no direct evidence for it in Acts 21. Moreover, since such a stance would have been unacceptable to the zealous for the law, it makes no sense to think that James wanted Paul to clarify this. If Paul privately interpreted his actions to mean that he observed the law *only when dealing with Jews* (i.e. to the Jews he became as a Jew), but he allowed James and everyone else to think something entirely different, then the implication of the accommodation argument once again is that Paul deceived the Jerusalem congregation.

To sum up, a cogent case can be made that Luke portrays Paul as a Torah-observant Jew in Acts 21:17–26. At least six different explanations have been

---

[187] Miller, "The Relationship of Jewish and Gentile Believers to the Law between A.D. 30 and 70 in the Scripture", 142.

[188] Räisänen, *Paul and the Law*, 71–72. Cf. Heikki Räisänen, "Galatians 2.16 and Paul's Break with Judaism", *New Testament Studies* 31 (1985): 549; E. P. Sanders, "On the Question of Fulfilling the Law in Paul and Rabbinic Judaism", in *Donum Gentilicum: New Testament Studies in Honour of David Daube* (ed. E. Bammel et al.; Oxford: Clarendon, 1978), 109f.

[189] Bruce, *The Book of the Acts*, 406.

put forward by scholars to explain why Acts 21:17–26 should not be interpreted in this way: Paul lapsed in his faith, James tricked Paul, James and Paul fooled the naïve Jewish converts, Paul was inconsistent, Luke's account is a pious fraud and Paul became as one under the law to win those under the law. A case has been made that each of these explanations fails to account for the details of the text unpacked in 2.2.1. While these counter-narratives are creative, there is no textual evidence to back up the assertions made. The explanations that "Paul was inconsistent" and "Acts 21:17–26 is a pious fraud" concede that Luke portrays Paul as a Torah-observant Jew in Acts 21. In response, arguments have been presented that Paul is consistent in Acts and that Acts 21:17–26 is based on reliable traditions.

2.2.2 Circumcision and Foreskin Language

Paul's division of humanity into circumcision and foreskin (Gal 2:7–9; 5:3; Rom 2:25–27; 3:30; 4:11–12; 15:8; Phil 3:3; cf. Eph 2:11; Col 3:11; 4:11)[190] supports the view that 1 Cor 9:19–23 does not preclude a Torah-observant Paul. The two categories suggest that Paul did not view being in Christ as collapsing Jew-Gentile distinction. What did Paul mean by circumcision and foreskin? Why didn't he say "Jew and Gentile"?

A constructive entry point into the issue is to examine the significance of circumcision in common Judaism. Consider, for example, that Philo places circumcision at the beginning of his discussion *On the Special Laws* (cf. 1 Macc 1.48, 60–61; 2.46; 2 Macc 6.10; Josephus, *Ant.* 13.257–58, 318; *Jub.* 15.25–34). Dunn explains that circumcision was a metonymy for the circumcised life:

> Circumcision was not merely a single act of law-keeping. It was the first act of full covenant membership and obligation. "Circumcision" could stand metonymically for a whole people precisely because it characterized a people's whole existence, a complete way of life. As Christians today speak of a "baptismal life", so we could speak of a "circumcision life".[191]

Tomson equates circumcision and foreskin with "being a law-abiding Jew or living as a gentile".[192] "Circumcision" is thus *pars-pro-toto* language for Jewish life as it relates to law, covenant and customs.[193] "As the Lord was one

---

[190] The distinction between Jew and Gentile in Christ is so fundamental in Paul's thought that he can speak of "the gospel of the foreskin" (τὸ εὐαγγέλιον τῆς ἀκροβυστίας) and "the [gospel] of the circumcised" (τῆς περιτομῆς) (Gal 2:7). Contra William O. Walker, "Galatians 2:7b–8 as a Non-Pauline Interpolation", *The Catholic Biblical Quarterly* 65:4 (2003): 580, who rejects Pauline authorship of these words.

[191] Dunn, "Neither Circumcision nor Uncircumcision", 86; cf. James D. G. Dunn, "What was the issue between Paul and 'Those of the Circumcision?'" in *Paulus und das antike Judentum* (ed. Martin Hengel and Ulrich Heckel; Tübingen: Mohr Siebeck, 1991), 297.

[192] Tomson, "Paul's Jewish Background in View of His Law Teaching in 1 Cor 7", 267.

[193] Cf. Acts 21:20–21.

God, as Israel was his people, so circumcision was the sign and seal of the covenant bond between God and his people ... Covenant, law, Jewish ethnic identity, circumcision were mutually interdependent categories, each inconceivable without the other".[194]

Rom 2:25 and Gal 5:3 confirm that Paul linked circumcision to being law observant. In Rom 2:25 – "Circumcision indeed is of value if you obey the law; but if you break the law, your circumcision (περιτομή) has become uncircumcision (ἀκροβυστία)"[195] – Paul describes circumcision as integrally related to Torah observance or Jewish identity, and lack of Torah observance is indicative of foreskin or Gentile identity (cf. Rom 4:11–12, 16). Circumcision is incomplete without the circumcised life:

> When Paul speaks of "being a Jew (Ἰουδαῖος ὑπάρχων)" or elaborates on its significance and implications as he does in Rom 2:17–29, he clearly has in mind an ethnic identity whose distinctive elements include Jewish parentage, male circumcision, Torah observance in its many dimensions, and a distinctive lifestyle that results from all of these.[196]

In Galatians 5:3, Paul makes the same point in more explicit language – "Once again I testify to every man who lets himself be circumcised (περιτεμνομένῳ) that he is obliged to obey the *entire law* (ὅλον τὸν νόμον)" – Paul uses circumcision here as *pars-pro-toto* language for keeping all of God's commandments. The apostle seems to uphold the Second Temple Jewish understanding that ritual circumcision initiates one into the covenant. Covenant responsibilities (detailed in the law) are binding on the circumcised one.[197] As Dunn puts it, "'the Jewish way of life' was a complete package".[198] Following this line of thought, Mitternacht contends that Galatians 5:3 should be read straight up as "whoever is circumcised (including Paul) is obligated to observe the whole law".[199] Paul's words appear to imply that he was living the circumcised life. Otherwise, his words would have had no force:

> If the Galatians did not know Paul as a Torah-observant Jew, then the rhetoric of 5:3 would have no bite: "I testify again to every man who receives circumcision that he is bound to keep

---

[194] Dunn, "What was the issue between Paul and 'Those of the Circumcision?'" 305.

[195] See Marcus, "The Circumcision and the Uncircumcision in Rome", 76.

[196] Carl R. Holladay, "Paul and His Predecessors in the Diaspora: Some Reflections on Ethnic Identity in the Fragmentary Hellenistic Jewish Authors", in *Early Christianity and Classical Culture: Comparative Studies in Honor of Abraham J. Malherbe* (ed. John T. Fitzgerald et al.; Leiden: Brill, 2003), 452.

[197] Shaye J. D. Cohen, *The Beginnings of Jewishness: Boundaries, Varieties, Uncertainties* (Berkeley: University of California Press, 1999), 218–19, 324–25.

[198] Dunn, "Neither Circumcision nor Uncircumcision", 88; cf. Matt 5:18–19; Jas 2:10.

[199] Dieter Mitternacht, "Foolish Galatians? – A Recipient-Oriented Assessment of Paul's Letter", in *The Galatians Debate: Contemporary Issues in Rhetorical and Historical Interpretation* (Peabody: Hendrickson, 2002), 409.

the whole law". Otherwise, they might simply respond, "but we want only what you have: Jewish identity, without obligation to observe 'the whole law'".[200]

2.2.3 Jewish "Calling" Language (1 Cor 7:17–24)[201]

In 1 Cor 7:17–24, Paul refers to his "rule in all the churches" that Jews are to remain Jews and Gentiles are to remain Gentiles.[202] Since this text describes "circumcision" and "foreskin" (metonymies for Jewish/Gentile identity and lifestyle)[203] as enduring *callings* and not merely temporary situations in life, it adds strength to the argument that 1 Cor 9:19–23 does not preclude a Torah-observant Paul.[204]

---

[200] Nanos, *The Galatians Debate*, 405. Also Nanos, "Rethinking the 'Paul and Judaism' Paradigm", 21; Mark D. Nanos, "Intruding 'Spies' and 'Pseudo-Brethren': The Jewish Intra-Group Politics of Paul's Jerusalem Meeting (Gal 2:1–10)", in *Paul and His Opponents* (ed. Stanley E. Porter; Leiden: Brill, 2005), 92; Bockmuehl, *Jewish Law in Gentile Churches*, 171.

[201] See Rudolph, "Paul's 'Rule in All the Churches' (1 Cor 7:17–24) and Torah-Defined Ecclesiological Variegation", 1–23, for a more extended discussion of the theological implications of this text.

[202] NRSV, ESV, RSV, NIV, NJB, REB, NLT, NCV, NIRV, CJB; "I make this rule (διατάσσομαι) in all the churches" (*BDAG* 2000:238). Cf. διατάσσω in 1 Cor 9:14; 16:1; 2 Tim 1:5; Luke 17:9–10; Acts 7:44; 18:2; 23:31; 24:23. See Schrage, *Der erste Brief an die Korinther*, 2:351; Conzelmann, *A Commentary on the First Epistle to the Corinthians*, 126; Adolf Schlatter, *Die Korintherbriefe* (Stuttgart: Calwer Berlag, 1950), 86. For a study of how 1 Cor 7:17–24 fits within the context of Paul's social vision in the letter, see J. Brian Tucker, *You Belong to Christ: Paul and the Formation of Social Identity in 1 Corinthians 1–4* (Eugene: Pickwick, 2010); Bruce Hansen, *"All of You Are One": The Social Vision of Gal 3.28, 1 Cor 12.13 and Col 3.11* (London: T & T Clark, 2010), 105–57.

[203] Discussed in 2.2.2 above. Paul's congregation in Corinth appears to have begun with a core of Jesus-believing Jews – Aquilla and Priscilla (Jews from Rome), as well as Crispus, the president of the synagogue (ἀρχισυνάγωγος) and his family (Acts 18:1–2, 8). See Richard G. Fellows, "Renaming in Paul's Churches: The Case of Crispus-Sosthenes Revisited", *Tyndale Bulletin* 56:2 (2005): 111–30. Lucius, Jason and Sosipater were also Jews (Rom 16:21). Luke notes that Paul stayed "next door (συνομοροῦσα) to the synagogue" with a God-fearing Gentile named Titius Justus (Acts 18:7). The term συνομοροῦσα means "was bordering on" or "having a common wall with". Perhaps the Jesus-believers in Corinth first met in this home next to the synagogue. "The fact that Luke shows that Paul remains spatially as near to the synagogue as possible is more or less a metaphor for his being as closely connected to the synagogue as can be and that thus Luke makes a point about Paul's desire for a continuing relation to Jews" (Koet, "As Close to the Synagogue as Can Be", 409). Paul's reference to Jews and Greeks (1 Cor 1:22–24; 9:20–21; 10:32; 12:13), circumcised and uncircumcised (1 Cor 7:17–20), Apollos (1 Cor 1:12; 3:4–5, 22; 4:6; 16:12; cf. Acts 18:24; 19:1), Cephas (1 Cor 1:12; 3:22; 9:5; 15:5; cf. Gal 2:7), Timothy (1 Cor 4:17; 16:10; cf. Acts 16:1–4), Passover (1 Cor 5:7), the people of Israel (1 Cor 10:18), the timing of the Jewish festival of Pentecost (1 Cor 16:8) and the gift to Jerusalem (1 Cor 16:3) all suggest that Paul's congregation in Corinth remained within the orbit of Jews and Judaism.

[204] William S. Campbell, "Perceptions of Compatibility between Christianity and Judaism in Pauline Interpretation", *Biblical Interpretation* 13:3 (2005): 307; Campbell, *Paul's Gospel in an Intercultural Context*, 106; Nanos, "A Torah-Observant Paul?" 31; Tomson, *Paul and*

A closer look at 1 Cor 7:17–24 should begin with the parallel verses – 1 Cor 7:17, 20 and 24:

v. 17 each one (ἑκάστῳ) should retain the place in life (περιπατείτω) that the Lord assigned to him and to which God has called him (κέκληκεν).

v. 20 Each one (ἕκαστος) should remain (μενέτω) in the situation/calling (κλήσει) which he was in when God called him (ἐκλήθη).

v. 24 each man (ἕκαστος), as responsible to God, should remain (μενέτω) in the situation God called him to (ἐκλήθη).

Verse 24 states: ἐν ᾧ ἐκλήθη . . . ἐν τούτῳ μενέτω (literally: "in what he was called, in this remain"). Here the "in what he was called" (NRSV "to which God called you") seems to refer to particular modes of life and not simply to "God's call to salvation".[205] This argument is strengthened when the parallel in verse 20 is examined: ἐν τῇ κλήσει ᾗ ἐκλήθη, ἐν ταύτῃ μενέτω (literally: "in the calling in which he/one was called, in this let him remain"). Most translators concede that v. 20 κλήσει refers to one's place in life when called (NRSV, ESV, NASB, REB, NET; cf. 1 Cor 1:26).[206] This would suggest by extension, on the basis of Paul's use of ἐκλήθη in vv. 20, 24, that the "situation" (κλήσει) in life is itself a calling.[207] This is how Augustine interpreted 1 Cor 7:17–20:

---

the Jewish Law, 272; Gregory W. Dawes, "'But if you can gain your freedom' (1 Corinthians 7:17–24)", *The Catholic Biblical Quarterly* 52 (1990): 684 n. 17.

[205] Some commentators maintain that Paul only uses call language to refer to God's call to salvation. However, Paul refers to his apostleship as a calling, "Paul, called to be an apostle (κλητὸς ἀπόστολος)" (1 Cor 1:1; cf. Rom 1:1). Here, "called" does not refer to a calling to salvation but a calling to a particular kind of service in God's kingdom. Later, in 1 Cor 12:4–5, 28–31, Paul identifies apostleship with "gifts" (χαρίσματα) and "services" (διακονιῶν) of God. Cf. Joseph A. Fitzmyer, *First Corinthians: A New Translation with Introduction and Commentary* (New Haven: Yale University Press, 2008), 307, "The verb *kalein* denotes not merely a 'call' to salvation or to Christianity, as in 1:9 (see NOTE there; also Gal 1:15; Rom 8:30; 9:24), but a call to it in a certain ethnic, legal, or social status, reiterated in vv. 20 and 24; with the same verb in vv. 18, 21–22".

[206] See Brad R. Braxton, *The Tyranny of Resolution: 1 Corinthians 7:17–24* (Atlanta: Society of Biblical Literature, 2000), 40f, for a survey of call language in 1 Corinthians.

[207] William F. Orr and James A. Walther, *1 Corinthians* (Garden City: Doubleday, 1976), 216; Jean Héring, *The First Epistle of Saint Paul to the Corinthians* (trans. A. W. Heathcote and P. J. Allcock; London: Epworth, 1962), 54–55. Cf. Fee, *The First Epistle to the Corinthians*, 310, "But the concern throughout is with their social situation *at the time* of that call, which is now to be seen as that which 'the Lord assigned to each' . . . Paul means that by calling a person within a given situation, that situation itself is taken up in the call and thus sanctified to him or her"; Ciampa and Rosner, *The First Letter to the Corinthians*, 309, note that in Paul's thought "my station in life is under the sovereign and gracious direction of God. He *assigned* it to me and *called* me to it . . . The Corinthian Christians' lot is part of their 'assignment' and 'calling'". Also Mark D. Nanos, "The Myth of the 'Law-Free' Paul Standing Between Christians and Jews", *Studies in Christian-Jewish Relations* 4 (2009): 3; Joel Wil-

"Was one called having been circumcised? Let him not become uncircumcised [1 Cor 7:18]", *that is, let him not live as if he had not been circumcised* . . . Because of the view which he expressed in the words: "Was one called having been circumcised? Let him not become uncircumcised. Was one called being uncircumcised? Let him not be circumcised [1 Cor 7:18]", *he actually conformed to obligations.*[208]

Alan Johnson notes that the NIV translation of 1 Cor 7:17–24 followed Luther and the reformers who considered the text evidence of the existence of "vocational" callings (i.e. callings to a particular way of life in the service of God).[209] Johnson, however, demurs that "calling" and "called" in 1 Cor 7:17–24 refers solely to one's *call to faith* in Christ:

---

litts, "Weighing the Words of Paul: How do we understand Paul's instructions today?" *The Covenant Companion* 3 (2009): 28–30. More cautious is W. A. Beardslee, *Human Achievement and Divine Vocation in the Message of Paul* (London: SCM, 1961), 63.

[208] Augustine, *Op. mon.* 11 (12) (trans. Muldowney [FC], italics mine). This is also how Rabbi Jacob Emden, a leading eighteenth century Torah scholar, interpreted 1 Cor 7:17–24 in *Seder Olam Rabbah Vezuta* (1757), "But truly even according to the writers of the Gospels, a Jew is not permitted to leave his Torah, for Paul wrote in his letter to the Galatians (Gal 5) 'I, Paul, say to you that if you receive circumcision, the Messiah will do you no good at all. You can take it from me that every man who receives circumcision is under obligation to keep the entire Torah'. Again because of this he admonished in a letter to the Corinthians (1 Cor 7) that the circumcised should not remove the marks of circumcision, nor should the uncircumcised circumcise themselves . . . You may therefore understand that Paul doesn't contradict himself because of his circumcision of Timothy, for the latter was the son of a Jewish mother and a Gentile father (Acts 16), and Paul was a scholar, an attendant of Rabban Gamaliel the Elder, well-versed in the laws of the Torah. He knew that the child of a Jewish mother is considered a full Jew, even if the father should be a Gentile, as is written in the Talmud and Codes. He therefore acted entirely in accordance with the Halakha by circumcising Timothy. This would be in line with his position that all should remain within their own faith (1 Cor 7). Timothy, born of a Jewish mother, had the law of a Jew, and had to be circumcised, just as he was enjoined to observe all commandments of the Torah . . . for all who are circumcised are bound by all the commandments . . . Certainly, therefore, there is no doubt that one who seeks truth will agree with our thesis, that the Nazarene and his Apostles never meant to abolish the Torah of Moses from one who was born a Jew. Likewise did Paul write in his letter to the Corinthians (1 Cor 7) that each should adhere to the faith in which each was called. They therefore acted in accordance with the Torah by forbidding circumcision to Gentiles, according to the Halakha, as it is forbidden to one who does not accept the yoke of the commandments" (Harvey Falk, "Rabbi Jacob Emden's Views on Christianity", *Journal of Ecumenical Studies* 19:1 [1982]: 107–109). Cf. Ernst F. Stroeter, "Does the Jew, in Christ, Cease to Be a Jew?" *Our Hope* 2:6 (December 1895): 129–134.

[209] "Vocation" is derived from the Latin *vocare* ("to call"). "This text [1 Cor 7:17–24] is fundamental to the Lutheran theology of vocation" (Gary D. Badcock, *The Way of Life: A Theology of Christian Vocation* [Grand Rapids: Eerdmans, 1998], 39); "Calvin interpreted 'vocation' in a way very similar to Luther's. God, he says, has appointed duties and a way of living for everyone, and these ways of living are 'vocations'" (Rupert Davies, "Vocation", in *A New Dictionary of Christian Theology* [ed. Alan Richardson and John Bowden; London: SCM, 1983], 602).

The NIV translation of verse 17 is unfortunate. Following Luther and other sixteenth-century reformers who understood "calling" and "called" throughout this passage as vocational or occupational callings, the NIV renders the text as *each one should retain the place in life that the Lord assigned to him to which God has called him.* Better is the TNIV: "each of you should live as a believer in whatever situation the Lord has assigned to you, just as God called you". The primary emphasis is on Christian behaviour that is appropriate to our call to faith in Christ in every situation of life in which we may find ourselves when we were called to salvation. On the other hand, that Paul also says *the Lord assigned* [to each] hints that as a secondary matter these life situations may also be thought of as in some sense divinely ordered . . . Verse 20 comes closest to Luther's sense of vocational calling.[210]

Though Johnson dismisses the "life situation" interpretation of "calling" in 1 Cor 7:17–24, he does pause to note that "these life situations [referred to in v. 17] may also be thought of as in some sense divinely ordered" and that v. 20 "comes closest to Luther's sense of vocational calling". Thiselton concurs with this assessment:

Yet in v. 20a τῇ κλήσει comes very close to the notion of a *calling* to a specific state or role. The very use of the phrase ἐμέρισεν ὁ κύριος in v. 17a should make us wary of claiming that Paul did *not* regard some prior role in society as a matter of divine vocation.[211]

Schrage similarly views κέκληκεν in verse 17 as a call to salvation and τῇ κλήσει in verse 20 as a reference to the situation and modality of the calling, the concrete condition of the calling.[212]

---

[210] Alan F. Johnson, *1 Corinthians* (Downers Grove: InterVarsity, 2004), 121.

[211] Thiselton, *The First Epistle to the Corinthians*, 549. "Thus despite the relativization of everything in Christ, the situation (the point of receipt of call – κλῆσις) in which one received the call to faith has a specific significance in Paul's ethics. This remains a vital factor in determining future conduct even in issues as significant as whether or not to accept or reject circumcision. One's situation may not be the decisive factor, but it is still significant. So circumcision or lack of it still plays a role in the ethical decisions of those in Christ . . . So even if, as some would hold, ethnic issues – Jew or Gentile – are not quite so pressing in Corinth as sexual matters, our discussion thus far confirms that for Pauline ethics, circumstances form part of the criteria for ethical decision in Christ . . . Whatever eschatological freedom Christ-followers may enjoy, this freedom is limited by one's situational starting point when called to faith, which Barth terms, 'the whole of the particularity, limitation and restriction in which every man meets the divine call and command' . . . The fact that Paul uses call/κλῆσις for the point of receipt of the call to faith indicates that he is in fact giving a Christological significance to the human status and condition at this crucial juncture. Those who are called must take into account and respect where they and others were when they were called . . . The force of Paul's theologizing must not be overlooked. Calling takes place at a particular time and place and that status remains a given, an essential component of one's ongoing identity in Christ, subject only to the Lordship of Christ" (William S. Campbell, *Paul and the Creation of Christian Identity* [Edinburgh: T & T Clark, 2006], 91–92).

[212] Schrage, *Der erste Brief an die Korinther*, 2:137–38. According to Schrage, Paul understood circumcision to have an *adiaphora* character in Christ (1 Cor 7:19; cf. Gal 5:6; 6:15). Cultic-ritual commandments were no longer binding (Gal 4:9) (*pace* Justin K. Hardin, *Galatians and the Imperial Cult: A Critical Analysis of the First-Century Social Context of*

To sum up, 1 Cor 7:20 links κλήσει ("situation"/ "calling") with ἐκλήθη ("called"). Verse 24 ἐν ᾧ ἐκλήθη ("in what he was called") points back to the antecedent (v. 20 κλήσει situation/calling) in the same way that v. 17 points toward it: "This situation, this setting-in-life in which the call of God has reached one, is now (by extension) itself described as a 'call' . . . it seems to be the only solution which respects the context".[213] For this reason, Conzelmann and others translate 1 Cor 7:20, "Each should remain in the call(ing) in which he was called".[214]

What situation-callings are in view in 1 Cor 7:17–24? Paul focuses on married/celibate and Jew/Gentile stations in life (slave/free will be taken up below). Luther argues in his *Kirchenpostille* that all godly spheres in life are divine callings to service,[215] but this would seem to go beyond what 1 Cor 7:17–24 states. Following Dawes, a medial view between the minimalist (Johnson) and maximalist (Luther) positions on 1 Cor 7:17–24 would seem to be in order.

Two intertextual arguments add to the cumulative case that Paul in 1 Cor 7:19–20 viewed "circumcision" (περιτομή) and "foreskin" (ἀκροβυστία) as God-ordained *callings*. First, the Jew/Gentile distinction reflects an historic calling; the Lord elected Israel to be his "treasured possession (סְגֻלָּה) out of all the peoples" (i.e. set apart in identity and manner of life). The Jewish nation was called to be a "kingdom of priests and a holy nation (ממלכת כהנים וגוי קדוש)" (Exod 19:5–6; Deut 7:6; 14:2; 26:18). This was Israel's service to God.[216]

Paul's Letter [Tübingen: Mohr Siebeck, 2008], 116–47). At the same time, Schrage understands 1 Cor 7:17–24 to mean that Jewish Christians should not become Gentile Christians and Gentile Christians should not make themselves Jewish Christians, "Weder sollen Judenchristen Heidenchristen werden noch Heidenchristen sich zu Judenchristen machen" (Schrage, *Der erste Brief an die Korinther*, 2:136).

[213] Dawes, "'But if you can gain your freedom' (1 Corinthians 7:17–24)", 684 n. 17.

[214] Conzelmann, *A Commentary on the First Epistle to the Corinthians*, 125. "Let each man continue in that calling in which he was called" (Barrett, *A Commentary on The First Epistle to the Corinthians*, 169); "Let each one remain in the calling in which he or she was called" (Collins, *First Corinthians*, 274); "Each in the calling in which he was called, in this let him remain" (Braxton, *The Tyranny of Resolution*, 8).

[215] Martin Luther (*WA* 10.1.1, 308). See Gustaf Wingren, *Luther on Vocation* (trans. Carl C. Rasmussen; Philadelphia: Muhlenberg, 1957), 1–7.

[216] Edward Breuer, "Vocation and Call as Individual and Communal Imperatives", in *Revisiting the Idea of Vocation: Theological Explorations* (Washington, D.C.: The Catholic University of America Press, 2004), 42–43. Israel was to be a servant nation that mediated the knowledge of God to the Gentiles (Exod 8:10; 9:14; 14:4, 18; 18:11; Deut 4:5–8; Isa 2:2–4; 41:8; 42:6; 43:10; 44:1–2, 8, 21; 49:3–6; 60:3; 61:6; 62:12; Zech 8:23; 14:16–21). In the Second Temple period, Exod 19:6 is attested in Peter's correspondence (1 Pet 2:9; cf. v. 5) and in Qumran literature (*4Q504*; cf. *4Q491*). Philo considers the Exod 19:6 calling fundamental to Israel's identity (*Abr.* 56, 98; cf. *Legat.* 3; *Mos.* 1.149; *Praem.* 114; *Spec.* 1.97, 168; *QE* 2.42) and compares the Jewish nation's role to a king's royal estate and to a priest who ministers on behalf of a city (*Plant.* 54–60; *Spec.* 2.163–67). See Martha Himmelfarb, *A Kingdom of*

Second, in Rom 11:29, Paul uses the term κλῆσις to refer to the "irrevocable calling" of the Jewish nation:

... but as regards election they [the Jewish people] are beloved, for the sake of their ancestors; for the gifts and the *calling* (κλῆσις) of God are *irrevocable* (Rom 11:28–29).[217]

When κλῆσις in 1 Cor 7:20 is interpreted in light of κλῆσις in Rom 11:29, the medial position put forward receives significant support. Noting the possible correlation between the Jewish κλῆσις in 1 Cor 7:20 and Israel's irrevocable κλῆσις in Rom 11:29, Adolf von Harnack held that Paul in 1 Cor 7:20 was encouraging Jesus-believing Jews to view their Jewishness as a divine calling.[218]

The notion of a "Jewish calling" finds further exegetical support in Paul's command to Jesus-believing Jews in 1 Cor 7:18: μὴ ἐπισπάσθω ("do not put on foreskin"/ metonymically: do not assimilate or Gentilise yourself).[219] The

---

Priests: Ancestry and Merit in Ancient Judaism (Philadelphia: University of Pennsylvania Press, 2006), 158–59; Peder Borgen, "Philo and the Jews in Alexandria", in *Ethnicity in Hellenistic Egypt* (ed. Per Bilde et al.; Aarhus: Aarhus University, 1992), 135; David Winston, "Philo's Ethical Theory", in *ANRW: Part 2, Principat, 21.1* (ed. H. Temporini and W. Haase; Berlin: De Gruyter, 1984), 398–99; Michael Bird, *Jesus and the Origins of the Gentile Mission* (London: T & T Clark International, 2007), 126–30; Stuart Dauermann, *The Rabbi as a Surrogate Priest* (Eugene: Pickwick, 2009), 21–40.

[217] See Joseph Sievers, "'God's Gifts and Call Are Irrevocable': The Reception of Romans 11:29 through the Centuries and Christian Jewish Relations", in *Reading Israel in Romans: Legitimacy and Plausibility of Divergent Interpretations* (ed. Cristina Grenholm and Daniel Patte; Harrisburg: Trinity Press International, 2000), 127–73.

[218] Harnack, *The Date of the Acts and of the Synoptic Gospels*, 47. Cranfield, *A Critical and Exegetical Commentary on The Epistle to the Romans*, 2:581, comments on Rom 11:29, "By ἡ κλῆσις here we may understand God's calling of Israel to be His special people, to stand in a special relation to Himself, and to fulfil a special function in history. Compare Paul's use of κλητός in connexion with his own call to be an apostle (I.I)". The pairing of "gifts" with "calling" in Rom 11:29 supports the case that κλῆσις is at least in part an election for service. The gifts mentioned in Rom 3:1–2 and 9:4–5 (commonly recognized as antecedents of τὰ χαρίσματα in Rom 11:29) enable Israel to fulfil its servant calling. They equip and empower the Jewish nation to be a kingdom of priests and a holy nation.

[219] "*Let him not undo his circumcision* . . . Paul is thinking of more than surgical operation, of one kind or another. The converted Jew continues to be a Jew, with his own appointed way of obedience" (Barrett, *A Commentary on The First Epistle to the Corinthians*, 68). A metonymic interpretation of μὴ ἐπισπάσθω is also adopted by Hays, *First Corinthians*, 122; Fee, *The First Epistle to the Corinthians*, 312 n. 27; Conzelmann, *A Commentary on the First Epistle to the Corinthians*, 126 n. 10; Gundry-Volf, "Beyond Difference?" 19. Contra Bruce W. Winter, *Seek the Welfare of the City: Christians as Benefactors and Citizens* (Grand Rapids: Eerdmans, 1994), 146–64, who argues that 1 Cor 7:20 refers to epispasm operations. Winter, however, offers no direct evidence that epispasm was common enough in the first century to warrant Paul making a "rule in all the churches" (v. 17) banning the operation. More recently, Braxton (*The Tyranny of Resolution*, 165–70) has argued for a non-metonymic reading of μὴ ἐπισπάσθω but with less evidence than Winter. It should be noted

language is a likely allusion to 1 Macc 1.11–15 where the expression "removed the marks of circumcision" is linked to dejudaisation and the adoption of Gentile customs that collapse Jew/Gentile distinction:

> In those days certain renegades came out from Israel and misled many, saying, "Let us go and make a covenant with the Gentiles around us, *for since we separated from them* many disasters have come upon us". This proposal pleased them, and some of the people eagerly went to the king, who authorized them to *observe the ordinances of the Gentiles*. So they built a gymnasium in Jerusalem, according to Gentile custom, *and removed the marks of circumcision* (καὶ ἐποίησαν ἑαυτοῖς ἀκροβυστίας), *and abandoned the holy covenant* (καὶ ἀπέστησαν ἀπὸ διαθήκης ἁγίας).

Notably, the clause "and removed the marks of circumcision" is immediately followed by the words "and abandoned the holy covenant" (1 Macc 1.15). The two are interrelated since circumcision (as noted in 2.2.2) is *pars-pro-toto* language for Jewish life as it relates to law, covenant and customs (see Gal 5:3; Rom 2:25; 4:11–12, 16; Acts 21:20–21).[220] Josephus' retelling of 1 Macc 1.11–15 brings out this interconnection. According to Josephus,

> they were desirous to leave the laws of their country, and the Jewish way of living according to them, and to follow the king's laws, and the Grecian way of living: wherefore they desired his permission to build them a Gymnasium at Jerusalem. And when he had given them leave *they also hid the circumcision of their genitals*, that even when they were naked they might appear to be Greeks. *Accordingly, they left off all the customs that belonged to their own country, and imitated the practices of the other nations.*[221]

Harnack viewed Paul's "rule in all the churches" (v. 17b) – μὴ ἐπισπάσθω (do not assimilate or Gentilise yourself) – as an imperatival instruction to "remain faithful to the customs and ordinances of the fathers".[222] Since the law was fundamental to Jewish identity,[223] Harnack held that, by implication, Paul encouraged Jesus-believing Jews to remain law observant. In Harnack's view,

---

that the metonymic and non-metonymic positions are not mutually exclusive. A metonymic interpretation of 1 Cor 7:20 would include epispasm among the diverse ways that Jews could assimilate into Gentile identity and lifestyle. Even if Winter and Braxton were correct, the underlying principle in the context of 1 Cor 7:17–24 would be the same: Jews should remain in their calling as Jews and not take on Gentile calling.

[220] Paul's inclusion of women under the categories of circumcised and foreskin (Gal 2:7–9; 5:3; Rom 2:25–27; 3:30; 4:9–12; 15:8; Phil 3:3; *cf.* Eph 2:11; Col 3:11; 4:11) adds to the case for a metonymic interpretation of 1 Cor 7:18. For a discussion of the covenant identity of Jewish females, see Shaye J. D. Cohen, *Why Aren't Jewish Women Circumcised? Gender and Covenant in Judaism* (Los Angeles: University of California Press, 2005), 111–42.

[221] Josephus, *Ant.* 12.240–41.

[222] Harnack, *The Date of the Acts and of the Synoptic Gospels*, 43.

[223] Holladay, "Paul and His Predecessors in the Diaspora", 456–57; Dunn, *Jesus, Paul and the Law*, 179–81, 221; Ellison, "Paul and the Law – 'All Things to All Men'", 196–98, 200.

the Jewish Christian is to keep the Law because in it is given the manner of life which God had willed *for him*. Hence *the whole Law* continues to exist as custom and ordinance for Jewish Christians.[224]

Harnack's interpretation of 1 Cor 7:18 and 20 is strengthened by Paul's use of nomistic language in 1 Cor 7:19 – "obeying the commandments of God" (τήρησις ἐντολῶν θεοῦ). Frank Thielman has shown that the expression "obeying the commandments of God" occurs in various forms throughout Second Temple Jewish literature and consistently means "keeping the law of Moses":

> The phrase "the commandments of God" is frequently used in the Jewish and Jewish Christian literature of Paul's time to refer to keeping the law of Moses. Late in the second century B.C., for example, the grandson of the Jewish scholar Ben Sira translated his grandfather's summary of the law this way: "Guard yourself in every act, for this also is the keeping of the commandments *[tērēsis entolōn]*" (Sirach 32:23). Similarly, Matthew translates Jesus' reply to the rich young man's question about how to obtain eternal life as "Keep the commandments" *(tērēson tas entolas)*, a clear reference to the law of Moses, as Jesus' list of commandments and summary of the first table of the law from Leviticus 19:18 demonstrate (Mt 19:17–19). Moreover, the Septuagint's translation of Ezra 9:4 uses the phrase "commandments of God" as a synonym for the law of Moses. The phrase Paul has chosen to refer to God's commandments, therefore is one that in his cultural context clearly referred to the Mosaic law.[225]

---

[224] Harnack, *The Date of the Acts and of the Synoptic Gospels*, 44. Harnack held that, in Paul's view, the promises of God to the Jewish nation were still valid (Rom 11:12–15, 25–27). Jesus-believing Jews were to live out Israel's call to be a priestly nation and serve as conduits of spiritual blessing to the Gentiles (Rom 15:27). Jews needed to remain law observant in order to fulfil Israel's eschatological calling: "for if the nation no longer observes its Law, then it is no longer the Jewish nation; and thus there is now no nation for which the special promise belonging to the Jewish nation can be fulfilled. Thus life in accordance with the Law must continue" (Harnack, *The Date of the Acts and of the Synoptic Gospels*, 51; cf. 46). Also Harnack, *The Acts of the Apostles*, 282, 288.

[225] Thielman, *Paul and the Law*, 101. Frank Thielman, "The Coherence of Paul's View of the Law: The Evidence of First Corinthians", *New Testament Studies* 38 (1992): 239, underscores that "the injunction to keep the commands of God, using the verb φυλάσσω with ἐντολή and a genitive noun or pronoun referring to God occurs forty-five times in the LXX". Ciampa and Rosner, *The First Letter to the Corinthians*, 310–12, note that Paul's use of the verb περιπατέω ("to walk") in 1 Cor 7:17 is a "thoroughly Jewish metaphor. In Judaism one was to 'walk', or conduct one's life, according to teachings of the Law of Moses. The exposition of the legal requirements of the Mosaic covenant were referred to as *halakah*, based on the Hebrew word 'to walk' *(halak)* . . . the terms 'keeping' and 'commands', point to Paul's meaning that what is paramount is observing the law of Moses. Apart from here in v. 19, the noun 'commandments' or 'commandment' is used thirteen times in Paul's letters. In the majority, ten times, it refers unambiguously to the Jewish law (Rom. 13:9; Eph. 2:15; 6:2; Tit. 1:14; and six times in Romans 7; the other three [1 Cor. 14:37; Col. 4:10; 1 Tim. 6:14] refer to Paul's own instructions). The verb 'to keep' can mean 'obey' in the New Testament and is used regularly with reference to keeping the law of Moses, namely, 'God's commandments' (Rev. 12:17; 14:12), the 'commandments' (of Moses; Matt. 19:17), 'the law of Moses' (Acts

Why does Paul emphasize "obeying the commandments of God" in the middle of elucidating his ecclesiastical rule that Jesus-believing Jews and Gentiles are to remain in their respective callings? A reasonable explanation would seem to be, as Harnack contends, that Jewish and Gentile believers in Jesus have different sets of commandments to keep. Raymond Collins points out that "'Keeping the commandments of God' is similar to the exhortation that the Corinthians conduct their lives in a way that is in accordance with their call from God (v. 17)".[226] To put it another way, since the κλήσει (calling) differed between Jew and Gentile (1 Cor 7:18–20), Paul likely held that God's commandments differed as well. This is how Peter Tomson interprets 1 Cor 7:19:

> Paul can only mean that gentiles should obey commandments also, although evidently not the same ones as Jews. He views gentiles as included in the perspective of the Creator which involves commandments for all. In other words: he envisages what elsewhere are called Noachian commandments . . . The saying would then imply that whether or not one is a Jew does not matter before God, but whether one performs the commandments incumbent upon one does: Jews the Jewish law, and gentiles the Noachian code – in the version to be propagated by Paul.[227]

> I conclude that the observance of distinct sets of commandments by Jewish and gentile Christians was the basic principle of Paul's missionary work, and he laid it down in the rule, "circumcision is nothing and the foreskin is nothing, but keeping God's commandments".[228]

Markus Bockmuehl arrives at the same conclusion in his book *Jewish Law in Gentile Churches*:

15:5), the Sabbath commandment (John 9:16), and 'the whole [Jewish] law' (Jas. 2:10). In this verse the related noun is used, which refers to 'persisting in obedience' (BDAG). Thielman is right to observe that 'keeping the commandments/laws' in Jewish and Christian literature regularly referred to obeying the Mosaic law (Sir. 29:1; 32:23; Wis. 6:18; Matt. 19:17; Josephus, *Antiquities* 8.120, 395; 17.159)". After making this observation, Ciampa and Rosner propose that 7:19a ("circumcision is nothing") reflects Paul's repudiation and replacement of the law of Moses. For a response, see 2.1.2.1 above.

[226] Collins, *First Corinthians*, 284. Cf. Niko Huttunen, *Paul and Epictetus on Law* (London: T & T Clark International, 2009), 28.

[227] Tomson, *Paul and the Jewish Law*, 271–72.

[228] Tomson, "Paul's Jewish Background in View of His Law Teaching in 1 Cor 7", 267–68. 1 Cor 7:17–27 may be viewed as Pauline halakhah, "A halakhically specific reading enables us to imagine Paul as violently protesting against forcing the law on non-Jewish believers, while still supposing Jewish believers to remain law-observant. In parallel to this specific reading, we are able to see that Paul's 'law theology' does not intend to do away with the law but to argue its distinctive value for Jews and for non-Jews. Yes, there is 'law theology' in Romans and Galatians, but its application is halakhically specific: it has distinct practical implications for Jews and for non-Jews. Both are justified by faith only – *therefore* non-Jews must not start observing the law and Jews must not stop doing so. Such is the message of Paul's 'ecclesiastical rule' in 1 Corinthians (7:17–20)" (Peter J. Tomson, "Halakhah in the New Testament: A Research Overview", in *The New Testament and Rabbinic Literature* [ed. Reimund Bieringer et al.; Leiden: Brill, 2010], 204–205).

The apostle himself in 1 Corinthians 7:17–20 makes clear that his "rule for all the churches" is for Jews to keep the Torah (indeed Gal 5:3, too, may mean they are obliged to do so) and for Gentiles to keep what pertains to them – and only that. In either case, what matters are the applicable commandments of God.[229]

This reading of 1 Cor 7:19, which is overlooked by most commentators, fits the 1 Cor 7:17-24 context and reflects the implications of the Jerusalem Council decision in Acts 15. I concur with Tomson and Bockmuehl, among others,[230] that verse 19 means as follows: with respect to status before God

---

[229] Bockmuehl, *Jewish Law in Gentile Churches*, 170–171.

[230] "When Paul states that 'circumcision is nothing and uncircumcision (the foreskin) is nothing', he does not mean that one's identity, whether Jewish or Gentile, is thus irrelevant to one's relationship with God. If there are different commandments for Jews and Gentiles, different roles and responsibilities assigned by God, then circumcision or uncircumcision make a great difference in one's relationship with God. What Paul means is that circumcision and Jewish identity do not elevate the Jew above the Gentile before God. There is a difference in role, but no hierarchy of status" (Kinzer, *Postmissionary Messianic Judaism*, 74); "Calling functions as a means of social cognition and serves as the foundation of the 'in Christ' social identity . . . in 1 Cor 7:18–20, calling continues to serve as that which re-orients social life. Ethnic identity is not opposed with reference to circumcision and uncircumcision, but is re-prioritized. This occurs as Paul teaches the community to stay in the social situation they were in when they began to follow Christ. He does not call the community to discontinue practices associated with their ethnic identity; he simply reminds them that what is foremost is 'keeping the commandments of God' (1 Cor 7:19; Gal 5:6; 6:15). Winter insightfully remarks that '[e]thnicity and social identity were the results of the providential oversight of God (7:18, 21, 23)'" (Tucker, *You Belong to Christ*, 80–81; cf. 9, 30, 65–66, 82–84, 125, 139–41, 157, 203, 232, 245); "Indeed, the fundamental conviction of Paul, and in my view the key to understanding his theological position on law and faith, is that all people must remain in the condition in which they were when they were called (1 Cor 7:17–20)" (Anders Runesson, "Inventing Christian Identity: Paul, Ignatius, and Theodosius I", in *Exploring Early Christian Identity* [ed. Bengt Holmberg; Tübingen: Mohr Siebeck, 2008], 80–81); "Paul nowhere suggests that *Jews* should reject their Torah observance, and in fact seems to assume that they would and should remain committed to it (1 Cor 7:17–20; cf. Gal 5:3; Acts 21:17–24)" (Douglas Harink, *Paul among the Postliberals: Pauline Theology Beyond Christendom and Modernity* [Grand Rapids: Brazos, 2003], 219); "Saul expected those of his converts who were Judahists to continue to practice Judaism and to respect its laws (1 Cor 7:19) and he expected the same of himself. Anything else would have been hypocritical: it was only the Gentile followers of Yeshua to whom the finite rules of Torah did not apply, at least not fully" (Donald H. Akenson, *Saint Saul: A Skeleton Key to the Historical Jesus* [Oxford: Oxford University Press, 2000], 252); "Paul observed the Law, and that in the pharisaic manner, throughout his life. In 1 Cor 7:18 he implies that obedience to it is his duty…" (Davies, *Paul and Rabbinic Judaism*, 70); "It is clear that Paul throughout his life continued to practice Judaism: and that he expected Jewish converts to do so, cf. 1 Cor 7:18…" (Knox, *St. Paul and the Church of Jerusalem*, 122 n. 54). See also Mark D. Nanos, "Paul and Judaism", in *Codex Pauli* (Rome: Società San Paolo, 2009), 54; Magnus Zetterholm, "Paul and the Missing Messiah", in *The Messiah in Early Judaism and Christianity* (ed. Magnus Zetterholm; Minneapolis: Fortress, 2007), 49–50; J. Brian Tucker, "The Continuation of Gentile Identity in Christ" (paper presented at the annual meeting of the Society of Biblical Literature, Atlanta, 20

and eschatological blessing, being Jewish or Gentile is irrelevant. What is important in God's eyes, what pleases him, is that Jews and Gentiles keep their respective commandments.[231]

Having presented an interpretation of 1 Cor 7:17–24 that supports the notion of a permanent "Jewish calling", and a "unity with distinction" understanding of the people of God (Gal 3:28; Acts 15), the objection may be anticipated that such a reading would then infer that being a slave is a lifelong calling and that one should remain in this calling (1 Cor 7:21).[232] A well thought out response to this argument is found in Gregory Dawes's *Catholic Biblical Quarterly* article "'But if you can gain your freedom' (1 Corinthians 7:17–24)".[233] Dawes proposes that 1 Cor 7:17–24 be understood in the context of Paul's discussion of marriage and celibacy in 1 Cor 7:1–39. It is contended that 1 Cor 7:17–24 functions as a *digressio* integral to Paul's argument, and that an analogy exists between pair 1 (circumcision and slavery) and pair 2 (marriage and celibacy). In support of this argument, Dawes notes the parallelism between v. 18 and v. 27:

1 Cor 7:18	1 Cor 7:27
Was anyone at the time of his call already circumcised?	Are you bound to a wife?
Let him not seek to remove the marks of circumcision μὴ ἐπισπάσθω	Do not seek to be free μὴ ζήτει λύσιν
Was anyone at the time of his call uncircumcised?	Are you free from a wife?
Let him not seek circumcision μὴ περιτεμνέσθω	Do not seek a wife μὴ ζήτει γυναῖκα

Dawes contends that in 1 Cor 7:17–24, circumcision and slavery function as illustrations to help Paul communicate his stance on marriage and celibacy. The Corinthians were questioning whether married life was compatible with the life of a Jesus-believer (1 Cor 7:1) and specifically whether a married person should remain married.[234] Paul responds by encouraging single people with sexual desire to marry (vv. 2–8); he commands the married to remain married even if married to an unbeliever (vv. 10–16). Marriage is good and

---

November 2010), 1–21; Gudrund Holtz, *Damit Gott sei alles in allem: Studien zum paulinischen und frühjüdischen Universalismus* (Berlin: de Gruyter, 2007), 247–50.

[231] See 2.1.2.1 for a discussion of 1 Cor 7:19a ("Circumcision is nothing").

[232] Because of the ellipsis at the end of v. 21 (μᾶλλον χρῆσαι), translators can add the word "slavery" (NAB) or "freedom" (NRSV). For a survey of the lexical and syntactical problems with the "remain in your slavery" view, and Bartchy's "third possibility", see David E. Garland, *1 Corinthians* (Grand Rapids: Baker Academic, 2003), 308–11; Dawes, "'But if you can gain your freedom' (1 Corinthians 7:17–24)", 689.

[233] Garland, *1 Corinthians*, 298–316, adopts Dawes's approach.

[234] In 1 Cor 7:1, Paul seems to restate the Corinthian view, "Now concerning the matters about which you wrote: 'It is well for a man not to touch a woman'".

has its advantages (vv. 2–6). Being single is also good and has its advantages (v. 7). It is wrong to think of celibacy as good and marriage as bad. Neither way of life is sin (1 Cor 7:28, 36–37). Both marriage and celibacy have the Lord's approval.

In order to emphasize that *both marriage and celibacy have the Lord's approval*, and that each should remain in their respective calling,[235] Paul reminds the Corinthians of "circumcision" and "foreskin", which are callings from the Lord. Jews are called to remain in their calling as Jews. Gentiles are called to remain in their calling as Gentiles. It is wrong to think of "circumcision" as good and "foreskin" as bad, or the reverse. Both have God's authorization and seal of approval. Both callings are consistent with the believing life. Jews *and* Gentiles have commandments to keep. "With respect to salvation no social situation is more advantageous than another".[236]

The point of the circumcision/foreskin illustration is that the Corinthians should adopt the same perspective toward marriage and celibacy (v. 27); each is a legitimate calling from God. The Corinthians should not think of celibacy as good and marriage as bad (see esp. vv. 17–27). Eschatological blessing is not contingent on marriage or celibacy.[237] More important than whether

---

[235] Since Paul permitted the single person to marry but not the married person to divorce, it may be reasonably assumed that Paul considered the single person's "calling" to be epistemologically less absolute until it was clarified through either marriage or an intentional decision to remain celibate. Natural desires may lead to the clarification of one's calling ("But if they are not practising self-control, they should marry" [v. 9]; "if his passions are strong . . . let him marry as he wishes" [v. 36]). Paul also recognizes that one's calling can be affected by circumstances beyond one's control (e.g. the death of a spouse [v. 39]).

[236] Collins, *First Corinthians*, 274.

[237] Does 1 Cor 7 reflect an imminent eschatology? There is a spectrum of views on Paul's eschatological expectations in 1 Corinthians. "As Deming and Wimbush urge, Paul's pragmatic pastoral criteria [e.g. his instruction in 1 Cor 11:2–16 that women should wear head-coverings] do not suggest a theology of eschatological imminence which depends on the conviction that the Pauline communities are the last generation" (Thiselton, *The First Epistle to the Corinthians*, 575). Garland, *1 Corinthians*, 328–29, concurs, "He is not talking about how little time is left but about how Christ's death and resurrection have changed how Christians should look at the time that is left. He is not recommending that one should take the short-term view of life, nor is he offering an interim ethic for the impending end-time tribulation. Instead, he understands the compressing of the time to mean that the future outcome of this world has become crystal clear . . . Fee comments (1987:339), 'Those who have a definite future and see it clearly live in the present with radically altered values as to what counts and what does not'. It requires them 'to rethink their existence'". Also David W. Kuck, "The Freedom of Being in the World 'As If Not' (1 Cor 7:29–31)", *Currents in Theology and Mission* 28:6 (2001): 585–93; Brian S. Rosner, *Paul, Scripture and Ethics: A Study of 1 Corinthians 5–7* (Grand Rapids: Baker, 1994), 161–63; Ciampa and Rosner, *The First Letter to the Corinthians*, 337–38. For my argument, however, the more important point is that even if one were to conclude that Paul expected an imminent return of the Messiah, it would still remain necessary not to overstate an eschatological motive for his instructions; Paul was also influ-

someone is married or celibate is whether they keep the commandments of God that apply to them:

> Paul wanted to assert (perhaps against those who, for super-spiritual reasons, wanted to dissolve their marriages) that what was important was not one's marital status, but rather one's Christian obedience – keeping God's commandments.[238]

But just because marriage and celibacy are both good, and matters of indifference with respect to eschatological blessing, does this mean that (for those without prior commitments) there is no advantage to choosing one over the other? Paul would have the Corinthians know that, while their affirmation of both celibacy *and* marriage in the community is essential, there are distinct advantages of celibacy over marriage for those who are not yet married and for those who are no longer married. What is the advantage of celibacy over marriage? Celibacy is a special "gift from God" (χάρισμα ἐκ θεοῦ) (1 Cor 7:7, 17). What is the purpose of this gift? Paul explains that a celibate per-

---

enced by christological and ecclesiological concerns, among others. Granting an imminent eschatology, the question would still remain, "How imminent? And what was the interim ethic Paul envisaged for Jesus-believers in Corinth?" Following this line of thought, a reasonable argument can be made based on Paul's "rule in all the churches" and the principle of divine callings (1 Cor 7:17–24) that Paul wanted his communities in the interim to reflect Torah-defined ecclesiological variegation. A related question is whether Paul viewed the church as a prolepsis of Israel and the nations in the eschaton. If this was the case, Paul's interim ethic could have been informed by Second Temple Jewish eschatological expectations that envisioned Jewish and Gentile identity continuing in the age to come. See Zetterholm, *The Formation of Christianity in Antioch*, 158; Bockmuehl, *Jewish Law in Gentile Churches*, 81; Nanos, *The Mystery of Romans*, 181–84; William Horbury, "Jerusalem in Pre-Pauline and Pauline Hope", in *Messianism Among Jews and Christians: Twelve Biblical and Historical Studies* (London: T & T Clark, 2003), 218, 223; William Horbury, "Land, Sanctuary and Worship", in *Early Christian Thought in its Jewish Context* (ed. John Barclay and John Sweet; Cambridge: Cambridge University Press, 1996), 221–22; Scott Hafemann, "Eschatology and Ethics: The Future of Israel and the Nations in Romans 15:1–13", *Tyndale Bulletin* 51 (2000): 174, 186, 190–91; Davies, *Jewish and Pauline Studies*, 139, 141; Douglas Harink, "Paul and Israel: An Apocalyptic Reading" (paper presented at the annual meeting of the Society of Biblical Literature, Philadelphia, November 2005), 1–26; Kinzer, *Postmissionary Messianic Judaism*, 151–79; John Howard Yoder, *The Jewish-Christian Schism Revisited* (ed. Michael G. Cartwright and Peter Ochs; Grand Rapids: Eerdmans, 2003), 31–35, 69; Seth Turner, "The Interim, Earthly Messianic Kingdom in Paul", *Journal for the Study of the New Testament* 25:3 (2003): 323–42; L. Joseph Kreitzer, *Jesus and God in Paul's Eschatology* (Sheffield: JSOT, 1987), 131–70; George Wesley Buchanan, *New Testament Eschatology: Historical and Cultural Background* (Lewiston: Edwin Mellen, 1993), 90–120; George Howard, *Paul: Crisis in Galatia: A Study in Early Christian Theology* (Cambridge: Cambridge University Press, 1979), 66, 79–81; Brad R. Braxton, *No Longer Slaves: Galatians and African-American Experience* (Collegeville: Liturgical, 2002), 69, 72.

[238] Colin G. Kruse, *Paul, the Law and Justification* (Leicester: Apollos, 1996), 124. Cf. John C. Poirier and Joseph Frankovic, "Celibacy and Charism in 1 Cor 7:5–7", *Harvard Theological Review* 89:1 (1996): 1–18.

son's attention is not divided. He/she does not have to think about pleasing their spouse. They can devote themselves fully to the Lord in body and spirit (1 Cor 7:32–35).

To ensure that the Corinthians do not lose sight of the advantages of celibacy as he extols the goodness of marriage, Paul uses a second illustration – the slave who can gain his freedom should take advantage of the opportunity (1 Cor 7:21b). The correlation of this illustration to celibacy is supported by Paul's use of "bound" (δέδεσαι)/ "free" (λέλυσαι) language to describe celibacy in 1 Cor 7:27. Paul's point by analogy is that "the person who is already celibate or who has been married and is now once again single is urged to take advantage of this opportunity to remain single-mindedly devoted to the Lord (cf. v 35)".[239]

When 1 Cor 7:17–24 is interpreted in this way, the pericope is not a digression from Paul's discussion of marriage and celibacy in 1 Cor 7 but is integral to it. Dawes's proposal allows for the possibility that circumcision and slavery are not illustrations that mean the same thing. Rather, they are complementary.[240] This means that Paul's identification of circumcision and foreskin with the language of calling does not necessarily imply that a slave has a lifelong situation-calling to be a slave.

How does 1 Cor 7:17–24 inform one's understanding of 1 Cor 9:19–23? Since Paul was circumcised (Phil 3:5), and his rule in all the churches was for Jews to remain Jews and not Gentilise themselves (1 Cor 7:17), one would reasonably assume that Paul observed his own rule and consistently lived as a Jew. This has implications for interpreting 1 Cor 9:19–23, which will be discussed in chapters 4–5.

2.3 Summary and Conclusion

This chapter addressed the intertextual argument given by scholars for why 1 Cor 9:19–23 precludes a Torah-observant Paul. It was shown that key texts for the "occasional conformity" reading of 1 Cor 9:19–23 can be interpreted in a way consistent with a Torah-observant Paul. The expression διὰ τοὺς Ἰουδαίους (Acts 16:3) in the Lukan narrative context in all likelihood refers to the timing of Timothy's circumcision and not the circumcision itself. Statements such as "circumcision is nothing" (1 Cor 7:19; cf. Gal 5:6 and 6:15) are rhetorical devices aimed at underscoring that Jewishness, like everything else, is relativised in Christ. With respect to Gal 3:28, the soteriological

---

[239] Dawes, "'But if you can gain your freedom' (1 Corinthians 7:17–24)", 696.

[240] A similar use of complementary illustrations occurs in 1 Cor 3:5–7 and 1 Cor 15:35–44. See Dawes, "'But if you can gain your freedom' (1 Corinthians 7:17–24)", 686–89; Ciampa and Rosner, *The First Letter to the Corinthians*, 308, 321–22.

context, the correspondence between the first and third pair, the semantic range of εἷς, and Paul's reference to "Jews" and "Gentiles" in his letters (Gal 2:3, 12, 14; Rom 11:13; cf. Eph 2:11; Col 4:10–11; Acts 21:39; 22:3), are all nodal points that, when pressed, reveal the weakness of the erasure reading of the passage. Paul's "former way of life in Judaism" (Gal 1:13–14; cf. Phil 3:8) does not have to refer to common Judaism but can refer to a right wing form of Pharisaic Judaism. In Rom 14, Paul is not indifferent to unclean food (by Torah standards) but clean food that the weak considered defiled by association (κοινός). The weak were concerned about accidental mixtures. Paul's statement to Peter in Gal 2:14 is intra-Jewish polemic. Paul may have been echoing the language of the individuals from James who accused Peter of "living like a Gentile" because he ate *with Gentiles*. Alternatively, Gal 2:14 can be understood as polemical hyperbole. Paul may have been reminding Cephas that his Jewish upbringing, education and standard of Jewish living were all *Gentile-like* by Pharisaic standards. Contrary to the view of Richardson and Gooch, Sanders, Carson, Barclay, Dunn, Horrell, Martyn, Sechrest and others, there is little evidence that Paul no longer considered himself a Jew. Moreover, passages such as Acts 21:17–26, Gal 5:3, Rom 2:25, 4:11–12, 16, 11:29, and 1 Cor 7:17–24, lend support to an intertextual case that Paul remained a Torah-observant Jew.

Chapter 3

Contextual Issues: Paul's Stance on Food Offered to Idols (1 Cor 8:1–11:1)

This chapter addresses the second rationale given for why 1 Cor 9:19–23 precludes a Torah-observant Paul: 1 Cor 9:19–23 is consonant with Paul's permissive stance on idol-food in 1 Cor 8 and 10, which was a radical break from Judaism. After an overview of the exegetical problem, which centres on the question of whether Paul sanctioned the eating of idol-food on some occasions, the Jewishness of Paul's view and the role of 1 Cor 9 in the pericope will be considered.

3.1 Overview of the Exegetical Problem

Contemporary scholarship has tended to focus on four main issues surrounding 1 Cor 8:1–11:1: (1) Is 1 Cor 8:1–11:1 a compositional unity? (2) Did Paul address two factions that diverged over the issue of idol-food? (3) Did Paul forbid eating idol-food on some occasions but not others? And (4) What is the relationship between Paul's stance on idol-food and the apostolic decree (Acts 15:1–16:5; 21:25)? Each of these issues will be discussed below.

3.1.1 Is 1 Cor 8:1–11:1 a Compositional Unity?

Johannes Weiss contended that 1 Cor 10:1–22 should be partitioned from 1 Cor 8:1–11:1 to resolve inconsistencies in Paul's instructions about idol-food.[1] He proposed that 1 Cor 10:1–22 was part of an earlier letter mentioned in 1 Cor 5:9. Héring, Schmithals and Yeo have built on Weiss's theory and maintain that 1 Cor 9 is also an example of editorial misplacement.[2] Efforts to

---

[1] Johannes Weiss, *Der erste Korintherbrief* (Göttingen: Vandenhoeck & Ruprecht, 1910), 212–13.

[2] Weiss, *Der erste Korintherbrief*, xl–xliii, 212–13; Héring, *The First Epistle of Saint Paul to the Corinthians*, xii–xiv; Walter Schmithals, *Gnosticism in Corinth: An Investigation of the Letters to the Corinthians* (trans. J. E. Steely; Nashville: Abringdon, 1971), 92–92, 334; Khiok-Khng Yeo, *Rhetorical Interaction in 1 Corinthians 8 and 10: A Formal Analysis with Preliminary Suggestions for a Chinese, Cross-Cultural Hermeneutic* (Leiden: Brill, 1995), 76–83; Robert Jewett, "The Redaction of 1 Corinthians and the Trajectory of the Pauline School", *Journal of the American Academy of Religion* 44:4 (1978): 396–404; Gerhard Sellin,

break up 1 Cor 8:1–11:1 have received minimal support from scholars for two reasons. First, there is little textual evidence to support the suggested partitions and reconstructions.[3] Second, possible inconsistencies in Paul's stance on idol-food can be explained in alternative ways that have proven more plausible. Regarding 1 Cor 9 in particular, "Vocabulary links reveal its direct relationship to chapters 8 and 10. References to Paul's personal practice appear also in 8:13 and 11:1".[4] The chapter also shows "rhetorical skill in its organization and its placement".[5] Sibinga's analysis of paragraph substructure confirms that 1 Cor 8:1–11:1 is a compositional unity and that chapter 9 is not a *corpus alienum*.[6] For the purpose of this study, the literary integrity of 1 Cor 8:1–11:1 is assumed.[7]

3.1.2 Did Paul Address Two Factions That Diverged Over the Issue of Idol-food?

Some scholars argue that Paul was writing to two factions: the "strong" who claimed the right to eat idol-food and the "weak" who maintained that such food was dangerous.[8] Proponents of the "two factions" view include Weiss,

---

"Hauptprobleme des Ersten Korintherbriefes", *Aufstieg und Niedergang der Römischen Welt* 2.25.4 (1987): 2964–82.

[3] Horrell, *Solidarity and Difference*, 170; Robinson Butarbutar, "Resolving a Dispute, Past and Present: An Exegetical Study of Paul's Apostolic Paradigm in 1 Corinthians 9" (Th.D diss., Trinity Theological College, 1999), 95–96.

[4] Garland, *1 Corinthians*, 396. See Wendell Willis, "An Apostolic Apologia: The Form and Function of 1 Corinthians 9", *Journal for the Study of the New Testament* 24 (1985): 39, for lexical and thematic connections.

[5] Willis, "An Apostolic Apologia", 39. "Most recent work, however, has affirmed the unity of the passage, and indeed of 1 Corinthians as a whole, a conclusion with which I fully concur. There are no compelling textual or literary grounds for the hypothesis of literary partition, and both the form of the argument – a broadly chiastic ABA' pattern with an apparent digression at its heart – and the tensions between its various parts are features encountered elsewhere in Paul, indeed in passages that seem to be classic examples of Pauline argumentation (e.g., 1 Corinthians 12–14; Rom. 1.18–3.20; 9–11). Though complex, the passage is best understood as a coherent and integrated unit" (Horrell, *Solidarity and Difference*, 170). Cf. David G. Horrell, "Theological Principle or Christological Praxis? Pauline Ethics in 1 Corinthians 8.1–11.1", *Journal for the Study of the New Testament* 67 (1997): 84.

[6] Joost Smit Sibinga, "The Composition of 1 Cor. 9 and Its Context", *Novum Testamentum* 40 (1998): 138, 143.

[7] Margaret M. Mitchell, *Paul and the Rhetoric of Reconciliation: An Exegetical Investigation of the Language and Composition of 1 Corinthians* (Tübingen: Mohr Siebeck, 1991), 126–49, 237–58, uses literary rhetorical analysis to establish the compositional unity of 1 Cor 8:1–11:1. For a response to Mitchell, see Yeo, *Rhetorical Interaction in 1 Corinthians 8 and 10*, 76–77.

[8] John Fotopoulos, *Food Offered to Idols in Roman Corinth: A Social-Rhetorical Reconsideration of 1 Corinthians 8–10* (Tübingen: Mohr Siebeck, 2003), 189 n. 34, notes that "although many scholars refer to those who advocate eating idol-food as the Strong, this term is not used by Paul in 1 Cor 8:1–11:1 as a title given specifically to the group advocating idol-

Barrett, Theissen, Murphy-O'Connor, Mitchell, Witherington, Schrage, Merklein, Fotopoulos and Horrell.[9] Following Mitchell, rhetorical theory is often employed to support the two factions view. Other scholars assert that Paul's reference to strong and weak was hypothetical (there was no division in reality) and that the Corinthian community as a whole upheld the right to eat idol-food. This group of scholars includes Conzelmann, Hurd, Fee, Gooch, Yeo, Cheung and Smit.[10]

The position taken in this study is that the strong and weak were not hypothetical categories. This stated, I do not find the view that 1 Corinthians is a work of anti-factionalism or deliberative rhetoric (Mitchell) based on ancient rhetorical categories convincing. More evidence is needed to demonstrate that Paul used standard Greco-Roman rhetorical techniques when he wrote 1 Corinthians and that factionalism is a central theme in 1 Cor 8:1–11:1. Cheung is correct that "In view of the multifarious nature of the problems and conflicts revealed in 1 Corinthians, to see the thematic and rhetorical unity of the letter under the categories of factionalism and reconciliation seems reductionistic". He rightly adds that "rhetorical analyses can be most helpful in discerning and explaining the logic and structure of Paul's argument. But they can be very misleading when the actual historical situation is unclear or misconstrued".[11]

---

food consumption. Paul refers to those who advocate eating idol-food as those who possess 'knowledge' (8:10). The term 'Strong', however, is the logical opposite of 'Weak', a term that Paul uses in reference to those opposed to idol-food consumption (8:9). Paul does, though, tell those in favor of eating idol-food that God will not let them be tested beyond their 'strength' (10:13), and he asks them if they are 'stronger' than the Lord (10:22)".

[9] Weiss, *Der erste Korintherbrief*, 211–12; Barrett, "Things Sacrificed to Idols", 138–53; Gerd Theissen, "The Strong and the Weak in Corinth: A Sociological Analysis of a Theological Quarrel", in *The Social Setting of Pauline Christianity: Essays on Corinth* (Philadelphia: Fortress, 1982), 121–44; Jerome Murphy-O'Connor, "Freedom or the Ghetto", *Revue biblique* 85 (1978): 544; Mitchell, *Paul and the Rhetoric of Reconciliation*, 126–49; Ben Witherington III, *Conflict and Community in Corinth: A Socio-Rhetorical Commentary on 1 and 2 Corinthians* (Grand Rapids: Eerdmans, 1995), 186–230; Schrage, *Der erste Brief an die Korinther*, 2:220; Helmut Merklein, *Der erste Brief an die Korinther* (Gütersloh: Gütersloher Verlagshaus, 2000), 2:169–71; Fotopoulos, *Food Offered to Idols in Roman Corinth*, 188–91; Horrell, *Solidarity and Difference*, 170–71.

[10] Conzelmann, *A Commentary on the First Epistle to the Corinthians*, 147; John C. Hurd, *The Origin of 1 Corinthians* (London: SPCK, 1965), 148; Gordon D. Fee, "Εἰδωλόθυτα Once Again: An Interpretation of 1 Corinthians 8–10", *Biblica* 61 (1980): 176–79; Fee, *The First Epistle to the Corinthians*, 359; Peter D. Gooch, *Dangerous Food: 1 Corinthians 8–10 in Its Context* (Ontario: Wilfrid Laurier University Press, 1993), 62–68; Yeo, *Rhetorical Interaction in 1 Corinthians 8 and 10*, 194; Alex T. Cheung, *Idol Food in Corinth: Jewish Background and Pauline Legacy* (Sheffield: Sheffield Academic Press, 1999), 87–88; Joop Smit, *"About the Idol Offerings": Rhetoric, Social Context, and Theology of Paul's Discourse in First Corinthians 8:1–11:1* (Leuven: Peeters, 2000), 10.

[11] Cheung, *Idol Food in Corinth*, 316, 318–19. See Cheung, 314–19, for his complete response to Mitchell.

3.1.3 Did Paul Forbid Eating Idol-Food on Some Occasions but Not Others?

Paul refers to four venues in which the Corinthians would have encountered food offered to idols: (1) in the "temple of an idol" (1 Cor 8:10); (2) at the "table of demons", possibly a literal table on which sacrificial food was placed in temple precincts (1 Cor 10:21);[12] (3) at the "meat market" (1 Cor 10:25); and (4) when invited to a meal by an "unbeliever", presumably at a private residence (1 Cor 10:27). There is widespread agreement that Paul prohibited the eating of idol-food from venues 1 and 2 (the temple and table of demons). There is also general acknowledgement that venues 3 and 4 (1 Cor 10:23–11:1) are related; the food for the meal at the private residence was likely purchased at the *macellum* (meat market).

This notwithstanding, there is little agreement over *why* Paul forbids the consumption of food from the temple and table of demons but not from the marketplace and table of non-Jesus-believers. This study concurs with Fotopoulos that Paul likely prohibits the eating of idol-food from venues 1 and 2 (1 Cor 8:1–10:22) because of the idolatrous context, "Paul not only rejected the consumption of idol-food in temples because of the relationship that was actualized with pagan deities, but also because of the sexual encounters which oftentimes accompanied such meals and were considered by Paul to be immoral Christian behaviour".[13]

The commonly held view among scholars that Paul was indifferent to idol-food, and that his concern for the weak not to stumble accounts for his proscriptive comments in 1 Cor 8:1–10:22, does not reflect all of the data. It seems more likely that concerns about the weak *and* concerns about idolatry are in view, "Abstention for the sake of the weak and abstention in order to avoid idolatry are not mutually exclusive arguments. On the contrary, they are mutually reinforcing in their prohibition of the consumption of idol-food. This is clearly how native Greek speakers and rhetoricians such as Origen and Chrysostom understood Paul's argument".[14]

But if Paul is concerned about idolatry, how can he permit the eating of food from the *macellum* (venues 3–4) given that much of the food sold was offered to idols at local temples, including the imperial cult?[15] Various rationales for Paul's approach have been proposed. The most plausible explanation, however, may be that there was sufficient ambiguity about the origin of *ma-*

---

[12] Fotopoulos, *Food Offered to Idols in Roman Corinth*, 175.

[13] Fotopoulos, *Food Offered to Idols in Roman Corinth*, 39. Cf. Karl-Gustav Sandelin, "Drawing the Line: Paul on Idol Food and Idolatry in 1 Cor 8:1–11:1", in *Neotestamentica et Philonica: Studies in Honor of Peder Borgen* (ed. David E. Aune et al.; Leiden: Brill, 2003), 125; Cheung, *Idol Food in Corinth*, 296.

[14] Cheung, *Idol Food in Corinth*, 96.

[15] Fotopoulos, *Food Offered to Idols in Roman Corinth*, 156.

cellum food to make the status of the food indeterminate.[16] Thus questions of conscience did not need to be raised (1 Cor 10:25); one could thank the Lord for his abundant provision (1 Cor 10:26, 30).

For an exegetical study of 1 Cor 8:1–11:1 that arrives at the above position, see Alex Cheung's *Idol Food in Corinth: Jewish Background and Pauline Legacy*. A rehearsal of his arguments in chapter 3 need not detain us here. Cheung makes a compelling case that "Paul urges abstention from idol food if it is known to be such, but one is not guilty if one eats idol food unknowingly".[17] He adds, "This somewhat casuistic approach to marketplace food and dinner invitations by unbelievers finds strong parallels in biblical case laws". Cheung cites Exod 21:28–29 and 22:2–3 among other passages where a biblical law is introduced and a clarification of the law is appended. In each case, the clarification does not overturn the law but serves to define the contours of the law's application. Cheung concludes, "In the same way, Paul affirms the general prohibition against eating idol food, but attaches an explanation that eating food of unknown origins does not constitute eating idol food. But once the idolatrous status of the food is known, the status of such eating changes accordingly and is then subject to the original general prohibition".[18]

Notably, an underlying implication of the above position is that Paul did not consider idol-food to be intrinsically dangerous. It was not the essence of the food that was the problem. Rather, it was knowingly eating food offered to a false god that was the problem (1 Cor 10:19–20). That idol-food in itself was not harmful is implied by Paul's permission to eat indeterminate food sold at the *macellum*. The allowance leads to the possibility that idol-food could unknowingly be consumed. Paul evidently did not believe that accidental consumption of idol-food would be harmful or he would not have had such a policy. In this sense, there is a parallel between Paul's view of unclean food and food offered to idols.[19] In both cases, Paul did not consider food *in itself* to be a source of spiritual contamination. Paul was not concerned about accidental mixture or consumption. Contrary to the traditional view in Pauline studies, there is no direct evidence that Paul was indifferent to unclean food or idol-food. Jews were called to abstain from both kinds of forbidden food. According to Luke, Gentiles were exempt from the Lev 11 dietary laws but apparently not from the Exod 34:15 warning to avoid idol-food (Acts 15:19–20, 28–29; 21:25).

---

[16] M. Isenberg, "The Sale of Sacrificial Meat", *Classical Philology* 70 (1975): 272; Fotopoulos, *Food Offered to Idols in Roman Corinth*, 188.

[17] Cheung, *Idol Food in Corinth*, 300–301; cf. 152–64.

[18] Cheung, *Idol Food in Corinth*, 301. Tomson, *Paul and the Jewish Law*, 203–20, argues that Paul's approach in principle is consistent with later halakhah. For a response to Tomson, see Cheung, *Idol Food in Corinth*, 306–308.

[19] See the discussion on Rom 14:14 ("nothing is unclean *in itself*") in 2.1.4 above.

The *residential* context appears to be another factor in Paul's decision-making. Paul writes, "If an unbeliever invites you to a meal and you are disposed to go, eat whatever is set before you without raising any question on the ground of conscience" (1 Cor 10:27). A private residence differed from a temple. The former was a house of the gods while the latter was a house of worshipers. Though worship occurred in the home, it was not a place that people visited in order to worship. Paul had to draw the line somewhere to distinguish between idolatrous and non-idolatrous behaviour. It would seem that one factor in the formulation of his stance on idol-food was the distinction between temple and home.

Having said this, even in the residential context, if someone identified the food being served as "offered in sacrifice" (ἱερόθυτόν), Paul instructed the Corinthians not to eat it (1 Cor 10:28);[20] the status of the food was no longer indeterminate.[21] Moreover, Paul seems to indicate in 1 Cor 10:28 that if a person has a sensitive (or malicious) enough conscience (or consciousness) to inform the Jesus-believer about the presence of idol-food on the table, the Jesus-believer should have the consideration not to eat idol-food. As Garland persuasively argues, to eat the food after being told it had been offered to idols would have implied that one could worship the Lord and consciously participate in idolatry:[22]

1. It would compromise their confession of the one true God with a tacit recognition of the sanctity of pagan gods.
2. It would confirm rather than challenge the unbeliever's idolatrous convictions and would not lead the unbeliever away from the worship of false gods.[23] If a Christian eats what a pagan acquaintance regards as an offering to a deity, it would signal the Christian's endorsement of idolatry.
3. It would disable the basic Christian censure of pagan gods as false gods that embody something demonic and make that censure seem hypocritical.[24]

---

[20] Witherington, *Conflict and Community in Corinth*, 238–42, 247–48, argues for a distinction in meaning between ἱερόθυτόν and εἰδωλόθυτα. Contra Fotopoulos, *Food Offered to Idols in Roman Corinth*, 24; Cheung, *Idol Food in Corinth*, 320.

[21] Zetterholm, *The Formation of Christianity in Antioch*, 148.

[22] Paul's scenario in 1 Cor 10:27-28 involves "an unbeliever" serving idol-food to his guests. The implication may be that Jesus-believers would not knowingly do this.

[23] Conzelmann, *A Commentary on the First Epistle to the Corinthians*, 178; John Ruef, *Paul's First Letter to Corinth* (Philadelphia: Westminster, 1977), 102.

[24] Garland, *1 Corinthians*, 497. Cf. David E. Garland, "The Dispute Over Food Sacrificed to Idols (1 Cor 8:1–11:1)", *Perspectives in Religious Studies* 30:2 (2003): 195–96; Cheung, *Idol Food in Corinth*, 159. "His [Paul's] approach to this issue is very close to that of the rabbis. Tomson (1990:214) concludes (from *t. Ḥul.* 2:18; *m. Ḥul. 2:8*; *m. Zebaḥ.* 1:1), 'The Rabbinic view of idolatry is not so much concerned with material objects or actions as with the spiritual attitude with which these are approached by the gentiles' . . . The rabbis absolutely prohibited direct or indirect contact with pagan rites, but they ruled that Jews could intermingle with Gentiles unless it became clear that the latter were engaged in some religious activity

The two questions in 1 Cor 10:29b–30, which Barrett regards as "notoriously difficult" whatever position one takes,[25] would seem to be "responses to 10:27 after a parenthetic interruption in 10:28–29a":[26]

Paul gives the Corinthians the latitude to attend a banquet thrown by an unbeliever without raising any question on the ground of conscience. He then interrupts this thought with a parenthetical observation. If someone announces that the food has been offered in sacrifice, they are to abstain. The conscience *does* come into play in this situation – that is, the conscience of the other. Paul then returns to the thought in 10:27 to explain why it is permissible to eat whatever is served at an unbeliever's house. If one can partake with thankfulness to the one true God, how can one be denounced for eating that over which one has said a prayer of thanksgiving? When someone specifies the food is sacrificial food, the situation is different; the Christian must not eat. In all other cases, the Christian may eat even if the food may have been sacrificed to an idol without the Christian knowing it. The freedom in 10:29b refers to freedom "from the power of idolatry".[27]

A corroborating argument in support of the view that Paul did not permit the intentional consumption of idol-food is that the early church fathers from the second century onward uniformly opposed the conscious eating of food offered to idols. Cheung's extensive investigation of these sources leads him to conclude that the modern interpretation of 1 Cor 8:1–11:1 (idol-food was a matter of indifference for Paul) is unattested in early Christian thought:

> A virtually exhaustive survey of early Christian writings turns up no evidence that any early Christian writer had any inkling of what would become the traditional understanding of Paul's approach. Significantly, what is usually considered the heart of Paul's argument – that idol food is something indifferent and should be avoided only for the sake of the weak – did not once surface in a plethora of writings about this extremely important issue in early Christianity . . . The Pauline argument that to eat idol food was to have fellowship with demons was so persuasive and definitive that it became *the* Christian argument against eating idol food . . . When there is absolutely no evidence for any competing interpretations, such an early, widespread, and uniform understanding of Paul's approach cannot be dismissed except by internal evidence of the most persuasive sort. But, as argued earlier, the internal evidence of 1 Corinthians provides no clear support for the traditional view but is consistent with the view that Paul at root urged the avoidance of idol food.[28]

. . . They assumed that individuals could discern when the Gentile was engaged in idolatrous practices" (Garland, *1 Corinthians*, 496).

[25] Barrett, *A Commentary on The First Epistle to the Corinthians*, 242.

[26] Garland, *1 Corinthians*, 499. Cf. C. T. Craig, "The First Epistle to the Corinthians (Exegesis)", in *The Interpreter's Bible* (ed. G. Buttrick; Nashville: Abingdon, 1953), 10:120; F. F. Bruce, *I and II Corinthians* (Grand Rapids: Eerdmans, 1971), 100–101; Blomberg, *1 Corinthians*, 203; Hays, *First Corinthians*, 177–78; Derek Newton, *Deity and Diet: The Dilemma of Sacrificial Food at Corinth* (Sheffield: Sheffield Academic Press, 1998), 377.

[27] Garland, *1 Corinthians*, 499. See F. S. Jones, *"Freiheit" in den Briefen des Apostels Paulus: Eine historische, exegetische und religionsgeschichtliche Studie* (Göttingen: Vandenhoeck & Ruprecht, 1987), 194; Tomson, *Paul and the Jewish Law*, 216.

[28] Cheung, *Idol Food in Corinth*, 298–99. Dunn, *The Theology of Paul the Apostle*, 704, concurs.

According to the early church fathers, the only Christian groups that considered idol-food a matter of indifference were the heretics mentioned in John's Apocalypse (Rev 2:14–15, 19–20) and the Gnostic sects – the Valentinians, Basilidians and Saturnilians.[29] Irenaeus writes of these groups, "Others, again, following upon Basilides and Carpocrates, have introduced promiscuous intercourse and a plurality of wives, and are indifferent about eating meats sacrificed to idols, maintaining that God does not greatly regard such matters".[30]

To sum up, Paul's stance on idol-food appears to be twofold: (1) Jesus-believers should not eat food in a pagan cultic context; (2) Outside of a pagan cultic context, "the rule applies: what is not specified with regard to pagan cult is permitted, but what is specified is forbidden".[31]

3.1.4 What Is the Relationship Between Paul's Stance on Idol-Food and the Apostolic Decree (Acts 15:1–16:5; 21:25)?

Hurd has argued that a fundamental reason for the seeming inconsistency in Paul's stance on idol-food is that Paul originally permitted the Corinthian Jesus-believers to eat idol-food, but later the Jerusalem leaders pressured Paul to implement the apostolic decree, which prohibited idol-food.[32] Barrett maintains a similar view. He asserts, however, that a "counter-mission" at Corinth sought to enforce the apostolic decree under the "aegis of Peter".[33] Hurd (contra Barrett) is correct that the apostolic decree was widely observed in the early church.[34] If Luke (the earliest source for the apostolic decree) is accurate, Paul likely implemented the apostolic decree at Corinth as he did at other congregations (cf. Acts 15:22–16:5). There is no evidence, however, that Paul's views conflicted with the decree or that Paul's directions concerning idol-food are internally inconsistent (3.1.1 and 3.1.3).[35]

---

[29] John C. Brunt, "Rejected, Ignored, or Misunderstood? The Fate of Paul's Approach to the Problem of Food Offered to Idols in Early Christianity", *New Testament Studies* 31 (1985): 118–19. See Cheung, *Idol Food in Corinth*, 253–56. The point here is that the early church fathers so opposed the view that idol-food was a matter of indifference that they labelled it a heresy.

[30] Irenaeus, *Haer.* 1.28.2 (*ANF* 1.353); cf. 1.24.5 (*ANF* 1.324); 1.6.3 (*ANF* 1.212).

[31] Smit, *"About the Idol Offerings"*, 65. Cf. Garland, "The Dispute Over Food Sacrificed to Idols (1 Cor 8:1–11:1)", 193–94; Cheung, *Idol Food in Corinth*, 296.

[32] Hurd, *The Origin of 1 Corinthians*, 147–49, 240–64, 273–96.

[33] Barrett, "Things Sacrificed to Idols", 150.

[34] Richard Bauckham, "James and the Jerusalem Community", in *Jewish Believers in Jesus: The Early Centuries* (ed. Oskar Skarsaune and Reidar Hvalvik; Peabody: Hendrickson, 2007), 74–75; Bauckham, "James and the Jerusalem Church", 464; Tomson, *Paul and the Jewish Law*, 178.

[35] David R. Catchpole, "Paul, James, and the Apostolic Decree", *New Testament Studies* 23 (1977): 428–44, argues that Paul opposed the decree. Conzelmann, *A Commentary on the First Epistle to the Corinthians*, 138, contends that Paul was not aware of it.

Despite the absence of an explicit reference to the apostolic decree in 1 Corinthians, Paul's "rule in all the churches" (1 Cor 7:17–20) is equivalent to the underlying principle of the decree.[36] Both the Jerusalem Council decision in Acts 15 and Paul's rule in all the churches indicate that Jews should remain Jews and Gentiles should remain Gentiles. What of specific commandments? Paul emphasizes in 1 Cor 7:19 that Jews and Gentiles are to keep the "commandments of God" (1 Cor 7:19). The expression "keeping the commandments of God" (τήρησις ἐντολῶν θεοῦ) follows Paul's exhortation for Jews and Gentiles "to lead the life that the Lord has assigned, to which God called you" (1 Cor 7:17).[37] Since the κλήσει ("calling") differed between Jew and Gentile (1 Cor 7:18, 20), it is reasonable to assume that in Paul's thought the "commandments of God" differed as well.[38]

What were the "commandments of God" for Gentile believers? Given that Luke portrays Paul as delivering the apostolic decree to Gentile believers, it is reasonable to assume (based on Luke) that "keeping the commandments of God" for Gentiles included responsibility to "obey the regulations" (φυλάσσειν τὰ δόγματα [Acts 16:4]),[39] the "requirements" (ἐπάναγκες), listed in the apostolic decree (Acts 15:28; 21:25). One of these "regulations/requirements" was to "abstain from what has been sacrificed to idols" (εἰδωλοθύτων). It has been shown above (3.1.3) how Paul's instructions in 1 Cor 8:1–11:1 can be interpreted to mean that Gentile believers in Corinth were to abstain from what they knew to be idol-food. Marcel Simon considers 1 Cor 8:1–11:1 to "represent a sort of commentary on the Decree".[40] Notably, this is not a recent view. The early church fathers read Paul "in light of the Decree, which was assumed to have the full authority of the apostles".[41]

But if Paul implemented the contents of the apostolic decree, why did he not mention the decree in his letter to the Corinthians? One possible explanation is that Paul had already opposed the eating of idol-food prior to the formulation of the decree.[42] In other words, the decree added nothing to his "rule

---

[36] Conzelmann, *A Commentary on the First Epistle to the Corinthians*, 126 n. 12.

[37] Collins, *First Corinthians*, 284. Circumcision is "nothing" with respect to eschatological blessing (2.1.2.1 and 2.2.3 above). By contrast, "keeping the commandments of God" refers to the living out of different callings in concrete terms.

[38] Tomson, "Paul's Jewish Background in View of His Law Teaching in 1 Cor 7", 267–68. See 2.2.3 above.

[39] Cf. δόγμα in Eph 2:15; Col 2:14.

[40] Marcel Simon, "The Apostolic Decree and its Setting in the Ancient Church", in *Le Christianisme Antique et son contexte religieux: Scripta Varia* (Tübingen: Mohr Siebeck, 1981), 2:429–30. "The whole thrust of the section is to confirm the ruling of the apostolic decision at Jerusalem in Acts 15" (R. B. Terry, *A Discourse Analysis of First Corinthians* [Dallas: Summer Institute of Linguistics, 1995], 44).

[41] Brunt, "Rejected, Ignored, or Misunderstood?" 121.

[42] See Günther Bornkamm, *Paul* (ed. D. Stalker; New York: Harper & Row, 1971), 42.

in all the churches" (1 Cor 7:17). The same point may be made with respect to Gal 2, as Bockmuehl has suggested, "Paul may well fail to mention the Decree in Gal 2 because its meaning indeed 'contributed nothing' (Gal 2.6) to the Gentile mission: nothing, that is, beyond the moral demands that pertain to it in any case, and which Paul takes for granted and consistently upholds, even in Galatians (5.19–21, 23b). In 1 Corinthians 5–10 in particular, Paul's practical exhortation clearly parallels the halakhic concerns of Acts 15".[43]

Two observations may be made in support of this argument. First, since the available evidence outside of 1 Corinthians indicates that first-century Judaism and the early church prohibited idol-food, there is good reason to believe that this sentiment was pervasive in the early stages of the Gentile mission.[44] After all, the apostles were all Jews. If Paul is viewed in his historical context as a Pharisee who became a follower of the Messiah Jesus, it is only reasonable to assume that Paul also expected Gentile believers to avoid idol-food as an expression of their renunciation of idolatry.

Second, in one of Paul's earliest letters, he mentions the Thessalonians who turned from idols to serve the living God (1 Thess 1:9). Cheung asks, "Now, how did the Thessalonian Christians turn from idols? In a culture where sharing meals was the mode and norm for social intercourse, arguably one of the first and most visible ways of turning from idols was to reject idol food".[45] If Paul held this outlook when he established the congregation in Corinth, which is reasonable (1 Cor 6:9–11),[46] and the Corinthians over time drifted away from his position on idol-food thus prompting a first and second letter (1 Corinthians) to be written, then Paul may have seen it as counterproductive to refer to a later ruling to validate his earlier teaching.[47] Pointing the Corinthians back to his original instructions, his "rule in all the churches" and the "commandments of God" (which, for Gentiles may have included a kind of proto-Rabbinic form of the Noachide Commandments among other directives)[48] was a more effective way of steering the Corinthians back to first principles.

If idol-food was not a matter of indifference for Paul, if it was problematic, why did he not require the Corinthian Jesus-believers to live by a higher standard and confirm that all food purchased at the *macellum* was free of contact with idols? Or why did he not instruct Gentile believers to purchase food that

---

[43] Bockmuehl, *Jewish Law in Gentile Churches*, 168. Also Cheung, *Idol Food in Corinth*, 190–91.

[44] Fotopoulos, *Food Offered to Idols in Roman Corinth*, 183–84.

[45] Cheung, *Idol Food in Corinth*, 110.

[46] Fotopoulos, *Food Offered to Idols in Roman Corinth*, 186–87.

[47] Cheung, *Idol Food in Corinth*, 194, arrives at the same conclusion.

[48] Note *Jub.* 7.20. See Bockmuehl, *Jewish Law in Gentile Churches*, 145–73; Taylor, "The Jerusalem Decrees (Acts 15.20, 29 and 21.25) and the Incident at Antioch (Gal 2.11–14)", 373–77.

had been properly slaughtered and supervised by Jews, thereby avoiding the possibility of eating idol-food altogether? Bruce Winter conjectures that Paul originally directed the Gentile believers to purchase food suitable for Jews at the meat market. After Paul left Corinth, however, Winter speculates that the city terminated the right of Jews to have their own food brought in (the city of Sardis censured Jews in this way),[49] thus depriving the Corinthian Jewish community and Gentile believers of access to properly slaughtered and supervised food. Faced with this new situation, Paul permitted the Corinthians to adopt a more relaxed policy on food sold at the meat market.[50]

Though plausible, Winter's historical reconstruction lacks evidence that the Corinthian magistrates barred Jewish food from the city's *macellum*. A more likely explanation for why Paul did not expect the Gentile believers to live by a higher standard with respect to *macellum* food is that Paul wanted them to remain integrated in Corinthian Gentile society. They were to continue eating with non-Jesus-believers and not "go out of the world" (1 Cor 5:9–11). They were not to separate from unbelieving spouses (1 Cor 7:12–13). They were not to become Jews (1 Cor 7:18). This outlook sets the course for Paul's decision-making with respect to meat sold in the *macellum*.[51] Paul lived in Corinth and knew that if the Gentile believers were to remain ensconced in Corinthian society, they would have to accommodate on the issue of meat market food.[52] It would have been extremely difficult (and impossible in some cases) to continue eating with their unbelieving Gentile spouses, friends and business associates if Gentile believers were limited to Jewish supervised food or *macellum* food confirmed to be free of contact with idols.[53]

Paul's instructions in 1 Corinthians should not be seen as inconsistent with the apostolic decree.[54] Like the Decalogue, which was fleshed out in hundreds of applications (Philo, *On the Special Laws* I–IV), the decree was issued in general terms and required interpretation. James and those zealous for the

---

[49] Josephus, *Ant*. 14.261.

[50] Bruce W. Winter, *After Paul Left Corinth: The Influence of Secular Ethics and Social Change* (Grand Rapids: Eerdmans, 2001), 287–301.

[51] John P. Dickson, *Mission-Commitment in Ancient Judaism and in the Pauline Communities: The Shape, Extent and Background of Early Christian Mission* (Tübingen: Mohr Siebeck, 2003), 228–31, 261; Garland, *1 Corinthians*, 493; Garland, "The Dispute Over Food Sacrificed to Idols (1 Cor 8:1–11:1)", 185.

[52] Zetterholm, "Purity and Anger", 12; Fotopoulos, *Food Offered to Idols in Roman Corinth*, 177, 187–88, 258; Cheung, *Idol Food in Corinth*, 38.

[53] Gooch, *Dangerous Food*, 106; Justin J. Meggitt, "Meat Consumption and Social Conflict in Corinth", *Journal of Theological Studies* (1994): 137–41.

[54] Zetterholm, *The Formation of Christianity in Antioch*, 143–49; Peter S. Zaas, "Paul and the Halakhah: Dietary Laws for Gentiles in 1 Corinthians 8–10", in *Jewish Law Association Studies VII: The Paris Conference Volume* (ed. S. M. Passamaneck and M. Finley; Atlanta: Scholars, 1994), 234; cf. Nanos, *The Mystery of Romans*, 166–238.

Torah in Jerusalem were legally minded and understood that in order to apply the decree to real life, their words would need to be defined; different standards of observance would emerge, some stricter than others. According to Luke, the Jerusalem leaders gave Paul and Barnabas the task of delivering the decree to the Gentile believers (Acts 15:22–16:4). There is no direct evidence in Acts or the Pauline corpus that Paul ever rejected the decree. It is reasonable to assume, therefore, that Paul's directives on idol-food in 1 Cor 8:1– 11:1 are not inconsistent with the decree but are an application of his principle not to eat food offered to idols (instructions which it has been argued preceded the decree). Paul understood the situation on the ground and applied this principle in such a way that Gentile believers remained integrated in Corinthian Gentile society, a view consistent with the Jerusalem Council's decision that Gentiles were to remain Gentiles.

3.2 The Jewishness of Paul's View

Scholars often refer to Paul's stance on idol-food as un-Jewish. C. K. Barrett is commonly quoted as stating that "Paul is nowhere more un-Jewish than in this μηδὲν ἀνακρίνοντες ['without raising questions', 1 Cor 10:27]".[55] Gordon Fee describes Paul as an "absolutely liberal" Jew who goes "quite over against his own Jewish tradition".[56] But how is it known that mainstream Jews never ate indeterminate food from the *macellum*? What if the Jewish supervised food was too expensive for them? What then did they eat? It is likely that some Jews ate indeterminate food from the *macellum* regularly or on occasion. E. P. Sanders concurs, "One of Paul's responses as he wrestled with the problem of meat offered to idols was, When a guest, do not raise the question, but do not eat the meat if its origin is pointed out (1 Cor 10:27–29). This may well have been a common Jewish attitude when dining with pagan friends. Barrett thinks that this is Paul's most *un*Jewish attitude. My own guess is that it too has a home somewhere in Judaism".[57] From Sanders's perspective,

it should be borne in mind that many Jews wanted to fit into the common culture, as long as doing so did not involve blatant idolatry. Some Jews participated in the main socializing aspects of Gentile city life – theatres, gymnasia and civil government. "These activities included at least passive contact with idolatry, and they show willingness to overlook formal, civic idolatry in order to participate in the broader civilization". Such Jews may have taken the very attitude towards food which Paul recommended in 1 Cor 10.27–29, and for very

---

[55] Barrett, "Things Sacrificed to Idols", 49.
[56] Fee, *The First Epistle to the Corinthians*, 360 n. 10(3).
[57] Sanders, *Jewish Law from Jesus to the Mishnah*, 281.

similar reasons ... We cannot quantify, but we may suppose that Jewish attitudes towards pagan meat varied.[58]

What did Jews in Sardis do when properly slaughtered and supervised food was banned from the *macellum* in their city? It is not inconceivable, given these kinds of circumstances, that Jews adapted by lowering the bar a notch, permitting indeterminate food but drawing the line at food known to be offered to idols. Gentile believers in Corinth were similarly constrained by their circumstances because they were Gentiles. For example, what did the wives of unbelieving Gentile husbands do if their husbands required them to purchase food from a specific butcher at the *macellum*? Paul was aware of these realities on the ground.

The principle of lowering the bar somewhat concerning indeterminate or forbidden foods (but not doing away with the bar altogether) due to overriding circumstances is well attested in Rabbinic literature. For example, the *Mishnah* lists situations when one may legitimately eat on Yom Kippur (the Day of Atonement), a fast day, "A pregnant woman who smelled food [and grew faint] – they feed her until her spirits are restored ... He who is seized by ravenous hunger – they feed him, *even unclean things*, until his eyes are enlightened" (*m. Yoma* 8.5–6).[59] Notably, even unclean food (e.g. pork and shellfish) may be given to a person with a "ravenous hunger" on Yom Kippur, which is only 24 hours long! As for the pregnant woman, the Talmud comments that she "smelled the [forbidden] flesh of a sacrifice, or of pork [for which she has a morbid craving]". What is the ruling? The rabbis decide that the forbidden meat should not be withheld from her. It should be given to her, however, in increasing increments (from smaller to greater measures, gravy to meat) until her craving is satisfied. Little by little, the bar is lowered until she is satisfied:

If a pregnant woman smelled the [forbidden] flesh of a sacrifice, or of pork [for which she has a morbid craving], we put a reed into the gravy and place it in her mouth. If she then feels that her craving has been satisfied, it is well; if not, she is fed the fat meat itself (*b. Yoma* 82a).[60]

While this is explained as a case of *pikkuaḥ nefesh* (saving a human life), there is some question as to whether the mother or fetus is really in mortal danger because of the craving. The situation is akin to the man with the rav-

---

[58] Sanders, *Jewish Law from Jesus to the Mishnah*, 281; quotation from E. P. Sanders, "Jewish Association With Gentiles and Galatians 2:11–14", in *The Conversation Continues: Studies in Paul and John in Honor of J. Louis Martyn* (ed. Robert T. Fortna and Beverly R. Gaventa; Nashville: Abingdon, 1990), 180. Cf. Peder Borgen, "The Early Church and the Hellenistic Synagogue", in *Paul Preaches Circumcision and Pleases Men: And Other Essays on Christian Origins* (Trykk: Tapir, 1983), 93–94.

[59] Trans. Neusner; italics mine.

[60] Moshe Zemer, *Evolving Halakhah: A Progressive Approach to Traditional Jewish Law* (Woodstock: Jewish Lights, 1999), 26–27.

enous hunger on the Day of Atonement. There is distress but no real danger to life itself. The point is that later Jewish tradition identified overriding circumstances in which Jews could eat forbidden food. These rulings should not be thought of as indifference to Jewish dietary laws and food prohibitions. Similarly, the fact that Paul permitted Gentile believers to purchase indeterminate food from the meat market does not mean that his decision is un-Jewish. He may have viewed it as a necessary accommodation given the unique circumstances of the Gentile believers.

Following Sanders, Magnus Zetterholm conjectures that Paul's approach was consistent with how some mainstream Jews approached the matter of pagan meat. Zetterholm speculates that Paul may have relied on a proto-Rabbinic halakhah that considered sold objects to be generally "non-sacral" in status:

The reason Paul finds food bought at the market least problematic is presumably also the lack of an immediate cultic context, and it is not inconceivable that here Paul draws from a local Jewish halakhah concerning food bought at the market in Corinth when creating a set of rules for Gentile Jesus-believers. Rabbinic literature shows that the rabbis discussed the extent to which the act of selling disconnects objects from a ceremonial context. In the Tosefta, R. Jehuda ha-Nasi is said to have advocated the view that selling in general signified a nonsacral status for an object (see *m. Avodah Zarah* 4:4–5; cf. *t. Avodah Zarah* 5:5; see also Tomson 1990:217–18). The other rabbis disagreed, but the discussion shows that some Jews could argue in this direction. Therefore, it is not impossible that Corinthian Jews argued that food bought at the market no longer had a ceremonial significance attached to it owing to the act of selling. In fact, Paul's view on this matter might indicate that this was the case.[61]

Zetterholm's hypothesis is plausible and represents one more reason to question Barrett's assertion that Paul was indifferent to idol-food. To the above, additional evidence may be adduced that Paul's stance on idol-food was based on Jewish principles of exegesis: (1) Paul alludes to the *Shema* (Deut 6:4), the central tenet of the Jewish faith, at the beginning of his discourse (1 Cor 8:4, 6);[62] (2) Israel's Scriptures are employed to condemn idolatry: Exod 32:6 (1 Cor 10:7), Num 25:1, 9 (1 Cor 10:8) and Deut 32:17 (1 Cor 10:20); (3) Paul commands the Corinthians to avoid the sin of idolatry, "Do not become idolaters (μηδὲ εἰδωλολάτραι γίνεσθε) as some of them did" (1 Cor 10:7); (4) Paul quotes Psalm 24:1 as a basis for his lenient ruling on food sold at the *macellum* (1 Cor 10:26). In the *Tosefta* (*Ber.* 4.1), the rabbis teach, "A man must not taste anything until he has blessed it. As it is said: (Ps. 24.1) 'The

---

[61] Zetterholm, "Purity and Anger", 15. Also notes 18 and 24 above.

[62] See N. T. Wright, *The Climax of the Covenant: Christ and the Law in Pauline Theology* (London: T & T Clark, 1991), 120–36; Smit, *"About the Idol Offerings"*, 24, 75; Leslie Hoppe, *There Shall Be No Poor Among You: Poverty in the Bible* (Nashville: Abingdon, 2004), 33.

earth is the LORD's, and all its fullness'";⁶³ (5) Paul formulates his position on idol-food in a way that is similar to biblical case law.⁶⁴

A final argument that Paul's stance on idol-food has a Jewish basis is the apostle's use of the term σκανδαλίζω (to stumble) twice in 1 Cor 8:1–13. Paul writes, "Therefore, if food causes my brother to stumble (σκανδαλίζει), I will never eat meat again, that I might not cause my brother to stumble (σκανδαλίσω)".⁶⁵ Notably, the verb σκανδαλίζω is not attested outside of Jewish literature and the metaphorical use of the noun σκάνδαλον is limited to the Septuagint and New Testament.⁶⁶ In the Pauline corpus, these terms function as Jewish Greek:

> Both formally and materially the NT use of σκάνδαλον and σκανδαλίζω is exclusively controlled by the thought and speech of the OT and Judaism. How far the words are from Greek thought may be seen not only from their absence from Greek literature but also from the need which the fathers repeatedly felt to explain the meaning of the NT σκάνδαλον.⁶⁷

Given the distinctively Jewish use of σκάνδαλον and σκανδαλίζω in the New Testament, which is informed by the Septuagint, it may be reasonably assumed that Paul's use of σκανδαλίζω in 1 Cor 8:13 is ultimately rooted in Israel's Scriptures. The Torah commands Israel not to *"put a stumbling block* (LXX: σκάνδαλον; MT: מכשל) *before the blind"* (Lev 19:14).⁶⁸ If it can be demonstrated that Lev 19:14 was interpreted metaphorically in first-century non-Christian Judaism, a compelling argument could be made that Paul's 1 Cor 8:13 ethic (do not metaphorically cause to "stumble" the weaker brother) derived from Jewish ethical categories of thought and legal tradition surrounding Lev 19,⁶⁹ especially since Lev 19 was a primary source of ethical teaching in the Second Temple period.⁷⁰ Is there any evidence that Lev 19:14 was interpreted metaphorically in Second Temple Judaism?

---

⁶³ See David Instone-Brewer, *Traditions of the Rabbis From the Era of the New Testament* (Grand Rapids: Eerdmans, 2004), 1:72–74.

⁶⁴ Cheung, *Idol Food in Corinth*, 300–302; cf. Exod 21:28–29; 22:2.

⁶⁵ Paul also uses the terms πρόσκομμα (stumbling block) and ἀπρόσκοπος (not stumbling) in 1 Cor 8:9 and 10:32 respectively. The LXX translates מכשול (Lev 19:14) and מוקש as σκάνδαλον or πρόσκομμα. They are used synonymously in the New Testament (Guhrt, *NIDNT* 2:705, 707–708; Stählin, *TDNT* 7:341).

⁶⁶ Stählin, *TDNT* 7:340. "The noun *skandalon*, from a root meaning jump up, snap shut, was originally the piece of wood that kept open a trap for animals. Outside the Bible it is not used metaphorically, though its derivative *skandalēthron* (e.g. a trap set through questions) is so used. No non-biblical example of *skandalizō* has been found" (Guhrt, *NIDNT* 2:707).

⁶⁷ Stählin, *TDNT* 7:344.

⁶⁸ The *skandalon* command is attested in 4Q367 2a–b, 13 without expansion or commentary. It occurs in a quotation of Lev 19:1–4, 9–15 that is confirmatory of the MT orthography.

⁶⁹ Rosner, *Paul, Scripture and Ethics*, 50–51; Tomson, *Paul and the Jewish Law*, 252–53.

⁷⁰ Gregory E. Sterling, "Was There a Common Ethic in Second Temple Judaism?" in *Sapiential Perspectives: Wisdom Literature in Light of the Dead Sea Scrolls* (ed. John J. Collins et al.; Leiden: Brill, 2004), 193. "It appears that Leviticus 19 and Deuteronomy 22

Qumran literature frequently uses the term "stumbling block" (מכשול) metaphorically[71] and refers to the blessing of having "no stumbling block (מכשול) in your congregation (עדת)".[72] Moreover, the Damascus Document from the late Hasmonean or early Herodian period interprets the "blind person" in Deut 27:18 (the counterpart text to Lev 19:14) as an individual who lacks knowledge:

ואם [את בתו יתן איש לאי]ש את כול מומיה יספר לו למה יביא עליו את משפט
[הארור אשר אמ]ר משגה עור בדרך. וגם אל יתנהת לאשר לוא הוכן לה כי
[הוא כלאים ש]ור וחמור ולבוש צמר{ו}ופשתים יחדיו.

And if [a man gives his daughter to betro]th, he shall tell him about all her defects, lest he bring upon himself the judgment of [the curse, which says,] he who leads the blind astray on the road (Deut 27:18) (4Q271 3, 7–10 = 4Q270 5, 14–17; 4Q269 9, 1–3).[73]

The above passage underscores the responsibility of a father to inform a prospective son-in-law about his daughter's defects (כול מומיה יספר לו), a reference to sexual history or appearance.[74] To not provide this information would make the father guilty of leading "the blind astray" and incur the curse of Deut 27:18, "Cursed be anyone who misleads a blind person on the road".

4Q Instruction^a (4Q415 11, 6–7), which is likely from the Herodian period, similarly states that it is a "stumbling block" (כמכשול) for the father not to inform the groom of the daughter's defects (כ]ול מומיה ספר לו):

[כ]ול מומיה ספר לו ובגויתיה הבינת]ו -- . כיא נגף] באו[פ]ל] [תהיה לו כמכשול לפניו ׃

Describe [a]ll her blemishes to him ... and make known [to him] (about) her bodily parts ... for when in the dark his foot stumbles, it will be a stumbling block before him (4Q415 11, 6–7 = 4Q418 167a+b 6–7).[75]

---

were the most significant biblical law codes. Leviticus 19 was of fundamental importance for these authors as a counterpart to the Decalogue. Writing about its importance for Pseudo-Phocylides, Pieter van der Horst [1978:67] said: 'One might tentatively conclude that in Judaism at the beginning of our era Lev. XIX was regarded as a central chapter in the Torah'. Leviticus 20 is also significant. It is part of the sexual code in Leviticus 18 and 20 . . . These chapters appear to have formed the basis for ethical instruction in the Diaspora" (Sterling, "Was There a Common Ethic in Second Temple Judaism?" 186): See Richard D. Hecht, "Scripture and Commentary in Philo [Appendix: Leviticus 19 in the Philonic Corpus]", in *Society of Biblical Literature Seminar Papers 1981* (ed. Kent H. Richards; Atlanta: Society of Biblical Literature, 1981), 138–58, for a discussion of Lev 19 in Philo. Paul quotes from Lev 19 in Gal 5:14 and Rom 13:9.

[71] See 1QS II, 12–17; 4Q372 8, 7; 4Q415 11, 7; 4Q430 1, 3; 1QH^a XII, 15; cf. 4Q430 1, 3.

[72] 4Q285 8, 9; 11Q14 2, 13.

[73] See Joseph M. Baumgarten, *Qumran Cave 4. XIII: The Damascus Document* (Oxford: Clarendon, 1996), 18:123–83.

[74] Cf. 4Q271 3, 10–15; 4Q270 5, 17–21; 4Q269 9, 4–8.

[75] Lawrence H. Schiffman, trans., "Halakhic Elements in the Sapiential Texts from Qumran", in *Sapiential Perspectives: Wisdom Literature in Light of the Dead Sea Scrolls* (ed. John J. Collins et al.; Leiden: Brill, 2004), 97.

When 4Q271 3, 7–10 and 4Q415 11, 6–7 are read together, it is evident that Qumran law could relate Deut 27:18 and Lev 19:14 and interpret them metaphorically.

Josephus also interpreted Deut 27:18 metaphorically and links the passage to the first part of Lev 19:14:

> One must point out the road to those who are ignorant of it, and not, for the pleasure of laughing oneself, impede another's business by misleading him. Similarly, let none revile the sightless or the dumb.[76]

The blind here are those who lack knowledge and are easily led astray. In his commentary on *Judean Antiquities 1–4*, Feldman notes that Josephus "appears to extend the injunction against putting a stumbling block in front of the blind (Lev. 19:14, Deut. 27:18) into a law that one must point out the road to those who are ignorant of it".[77] Josephus' interpretation matches the *Fragmentary Targum* (MS Paris) on Lev 19:14 and *Targum Pseudo-Jonathan* on Deut 27:18.

In Rabbinic literature, "the blind" in Lev 19:14 is "interpreted metaphorically to represent any person or group that is unaware, unsuspecting, ignorant, or morally blind, and individuals are prohibited from taking advantage of them or tempting them to do wrong . . . It is also a call to action demanding that society and people do everything possible to help the weak".[78] The application of the Lev 19:14 *skandalon* command extends to situations in which one individual tempts another (whether Jew or Gentile) to eat forbidden food:

> R. Nathan [mid 2nd century] said: How do we know that a man must not hold out a cup of wine to a Nazirite or the limb of a living animal to the children of Noah? Because it is stated, *thou shalt not put a stumbling-block before the blind* (Lev. 19:14) (*b. Pesaḥ.* 22b).[79]

The rabbis also applied the *skandalon* command to situations where a stumbling block led Gentiles to commit idolatry (*b. Ned.* 62b). In making this application, the rabbis were well aware that the Scriptures use "stumbling block" language to refer to Israel's fall into idolatry. For example, in his farewell speech, Joshua cautions Israel not to associate with the surviving peoples in the land lest their gods become stumbling blocks (σκάνδαλα) (Josh 23:13; cf. vv. 7, 16). After Joshua's death, the angel of the Lord accuses Israel of not driving out the former inhabitants of the land and destroying their

---

[76] Josephus, *Ant.* 4.276 (Thackeray, LCL).

[77] Louis H. Feldman, *Flavius Josephus, Translation and Commentary: Judean Antiquities Books 1–4* (ed. Steve Mason; Leiden: Brill, 2000), 3:445. Also Jeffrey H. Tigay, *Deuteronomy* (Philadelphia: The Jewish Publication Society, 1996), 255.

[78] Hershey H. Friedman, "Placing a Stumbling Block Before the Blind Person: An In-Depth Analysis", n.p. [cited 19 December 2010]. Online: http://www.jlaw.com/Articles/placingstumbling.html.

[79] See Num 6:3 and Gen 9:4. Cf. *b. Ned.* 81b; *b. Pesaḥ.* 50b–51a; *y. Ber.* 8, 12a.

altars. As a consequence, the angel declares "their gods shall be to you for a stumbling block (σκάνδαλον)" (Judg 2:3). The prophet Hosea proclaimed, "Ephraim, joined with idols (εἰδώλων), has laid stumbling-blocks (σκάνδαλα) in his own way" (Hos 4:17).[80] Looking back over Israel's unfaithfulness, the Psalmist cries out, "They destroyed not the nations which the Lord told them to destroy . . . And they served their graven images; and it became a stumbling block to them (ἐγενήθη αὐτοῖς εἰς σκάνδαλον)" (Ps 105[106]:34–36). In all likelihood, it is not a coincidence that Paul uses σκανδαλίζω language in the same pericope that he focuses on the danger of eating food offered to idols. Pointing to the LXX usage of σκάνδαλον in reference to the trap of idolatry, Cheung contends, "This is probably the source of Paul's usage".[81]

In light of the above, it is reasonable to assume that underlying Paul's 1 Cor 8:13 concern for the weak stumbling are Jewish ethical categories of thought. The following arguments form a cumulative case: (1) The verb σκανδαλίζω is unattested outside of Jewish literature; (2) Some first-century Jews interpreted the σκάνδαλον commandment (Lev 19:14) metaphorically; (3) In 1 Cor 8:13, Paul uses σκανδαλίζω metaphorically to caution those who claimed to have knowledge against causing to stumble the weak (who lacked knowledge). In Rom 14:13, Paul again uses σκάνδαλον metaphorically to caution Jesus-believers in Rome about causing to stumble each other; (4) The LXX uses σκάνδαλον language to describe Israel's fall into idolatry. Thus, it is probably not coincidental that Paul uses σκανδαλίζω language twice in the context of warning the Corinthians about eating idol-food; and (5) Lev 19 was a primary source of ethical instruction in the Diaspora.

3.3 The Function of 1 Cor 9

It was asserted in 3.1.1 that 1 Cor 8:1–11:1 is a compositional unity and that chapter 9 is not a corpus alienum. Here a brief comment will be made on the function of 1 Cor 9 in the pericope. It does not appear that 1 Cor 9 is a defence (ἀπολογία, v. 3) of Paul's apostolic office or of his right to financial support, or even of his right to forego financial support. Rather, the central point of 1 Cor 9 is Paul's renunciation of all rights (even those rights provided

---

[80] Wis 14.11 describes "idols" (εἰδώλοις) as "stumbling blocks for human souls (εἰς σκάνδαλα ψυχαῖς ἀνθρώπων)". Qumran literature identifies idolatry as a stumbling block in 1QH^a XII, 15, "With a willful heart they look about and seek You in idols (גלולים). They have set the stumbling block (מכשול) of their iniquity before themselves, and they come" (cf. 4Q430 1, 3).

[81] Cheung, *Idol Food in Corinth*, 129.

by Mosaic law and the Lord Jesus' command) for the sake of the gospel.[82] Though free, Paul has made himself a slave to all (1 Cor 9:1, 19).[83] Like an athlete, he practises voluntary restraint in the service of Christ (1 Cor 9:24–27).[84] As Wendell Willis puts it, Paul wants to show that he has given up everything "in order not to be an 'obstacle' (ἐγκοπή) in the way of the gospel [1 Cor 9:12]. This is a major theme in chs. 8 and 10: that Christians should not put a 'stumbling block' (πρόσκομμα, 8.9) before other Christians, nor do anything that would 'scandalize' (σκανδαλίζειν, 8.13) them.[85] Rather, Christians are to do every thing possible to be 'inoffensive' (ἀπρόσκοπος, 10.32) to all men".[86] Thus, 1 Cor 9 is not a "digression"[87] or "interruption"[88] or "Excurs"[89] from 1 Cor 8:1–13 and 10:1–11:1, but an integral part of Paul's argument in 1 Cor 8:1–11:1.[90]

3.4 Summary and Conclusion

This chapter addressed the contextual argument given by scholars for why 1 Cor 9:19–23 precludes a Torah-observant Paul. It was shown that it is an overstatement to say that Paul held a permissive stance on idol-food that burst the bounds of Second Temple Judaism. Paul's position on idol-food was twofold: (1) Jesus-believers were not to eat food in a pagan cultic context; and (2) Outside of a pagan cultic context, indeterminate food was permitted, while known idol-food was forbidden. Paul's approach to idol-food was consistent with the apostolic decree, but it was a more contextualized application of the principle. When the 1 Cor 8:1–11:1 pericope and its background are examined for evidence of Jewish influence, it becomes apparent that Paul's perspective on idol-food is informed by Jewish thought. First, Paul refers to passages in Israel's Scriptures that condemn idolatry. Second, the formulation of Paul's

---

[82] Garland, "The Dispute Over Food Sacrificed to Idols (1 Cor 8:1–11:1)", 190.

[83] "Paul had shown the Corinthians that rights were not for self, but for service" (Michael Li-Tak Shen, "Paul's Doctrine of God and the Issue of Food Offered to Idols in 1 Corinthians 8:1–11:1" [Ph.D. diss., Dallas Theological Seminary, 2003], 200; cf. 198).

[84] See Robert S. Dutch, *The Educated Elite in 1 Corinthians: Education and Community Conflict in Graeco-Roman Context* (London: T & T Clark, 2005), 219–48, for a study of the athlete imagery in 1 Cor 9:24–27.

[85] Hays, *First Corinthians*, 149, calls this Paul's "principle of self-limitation".

[86] Willis, "An Apostolic Apologia", 36.

[87] Witherington, *Conflict and Community in Corinth*, 191; Barrett, *A Commentary on The First Epistle to the Corinthians*, 200.

[88] Conzelmann, *A Commentary on the First Epistle to the Corinthians*, 151.

[89] H. Lietzmann, *Die Briefe des Apostels Paulus: An die Korinther I, II* (ed. W. G. Kümmel; Tübingen: Mohr Siebeck, 1949), 43.

[90] Cheung, *Idol Food in Corinth*, 138–39.

stance on idol-food resembles biblical case law. Third, Paul's approach is not as original or un-Jewish as scholars typically assume. Contrary to Barrett and Fee, there is no evidence that all Jews avoided *macellum* food. Fourth, the principle of lowering the bar with respect to indeterminate (or even forbidden foods) due to overriding circumstances is attested in later Jewish literature. Paul may have considered his stance on indeterminate food a necessary adaptation given the unique circumstances of the Gentile believers. Fifth, some Jews in Corinth may have regarded sold objects to be "non-sacral" in status. This would have mitigated the problem of eating indeterminate food from the *macellum*. The early rabbis adopted a similar approach by focusing on the question of idolatrous or non-idolatrous intention. Sixth, Paul's ethic of not causing the weaker brother to stumble (σκανδαλίζω) is probably rooted in Jewish ethical categories of thought and legal tradition surrounding Lev 19. All of these points problematise the contextual argument behind the traditional view that 1 Cor 9:19–23 precludes a Torah-observant Paul. A compelling case can be made that Paul worked within Jewish contours of flexibility to respond to the issue of idol-food in Corinth.

Chapter 4

Textual Issues: Variations on the Setting and Language of 1 Cor 9:19–23

This chapter addresses the third rationale given for why 1 Cor 9:19–23 precludes a Torah-observant Paul: The nomistic language in 1 Cor 9:19–23 demonstrates that Paul did not consider himself to be under the jurisdiction of Mosaic law. Before this argument can be engaged, however, it is necessary to consider the possible background of Paul's accommodation language. Attention needs to be given to the query, "What first-century setting(s) may inform the meaning of Paul's 'all things to all people' discourse?" Analogues of accommodation in Greco-Roman *topoi* as well as in Jewish literature will be surveyed below. Integral to the Jewish background, gospel traditions will also be considered. In the final section, the focus will shift from setting to language. Eight key words and phrases will be discussed. It will be shown that neither the setting nor the language of 1 Cor 9:19–23 necessitates the view that 1 Cor 9:19–23 is incompatible with a Torah-observant Paul.

4.1 Greco-Roman Thought

While there is no evidence that Paul formally studied Greek literature, it is reasonable to assume that Paul had some exposure to Greco-Roman philosophical traditions and rhetoric because it was part of the intellectual culture of his day. A number of scholars conjecture that Paul's language in 1 Cor 9:19–23 can be understood against this Hellenistic background.[1]

4.1.1 Servile Flatterer

Peter Marshall (1987) contends that Paul's opponents accused him of being a "servile flatterer", that is, "one who deliberately adapts his conduct to that of others for his own ends".[2] His adversaries labelled him a sycophant who be-

---

[1] Clarence E. Glad, "Paul and Adaptability", in *Paul in the Greco-Roman World: A Handbook* (ed. J. Paul Sampley; Harrisburg: Trinity Press International, 2003), 26. Cf. Huttunen, *Paul and Epictetus on Law*, 32–36.

[2] Peter Marshall, *Enmity in Corinth: Social Conventions in Paul's Relations with the Corinthians* (Tübingen: Mohr Siebeck, 1987), 309.

came all things to all people. The 1 Cor 9:19–23 pericope is thus Paul's response to this reproach, "Rather than respond in kind or deny the accusations, he takes up the language of the invective . . . to describe his work as an apostle".[3] Paul speaks "tongue in cheek".[4] His ironic use of the servant metaphor, the ethic of "pleasing all" and the notion of "gain" are all intended to communicate in a subtle and subversive way that Paul's slavery is self-imposed and for the purpose of saving others. A shortcoming of Marshall's discussion is that he does not address the Jewish/nomistic language in the 1 Cor 9:19–23 pericope (Jews, under the law, without the law, not without the law of God, in Christ's law). As it will become apparent below, non-Jewish Hellenistic background interpretations of 1 Cor 9:19–23 tend to avoid engagement with the 1 Cor 8:1–11:1 literary context and Paul's Jewish/nomistic language in particular.

4.1.2 Antisthenes' Odysseus

Abraham Malherbe (1989) conjectures that Paul "describes himself in a manner that echoes Antisthenes' Odysseus" in 1 Cor 9:19–23.[5] The comparison is based on the first line of Homer's *Odyssey*, "Tell me, Muse, of the *polytropic* man" – literally, a man of many turns.[6] Malherbe conjectures that Paul became "all things to all people" in the same way that Antisthenes' Odysseus adapted his speech ("tropes") to others in order to save them.[7] Antisthenes notes that even Pythagoras instructed his followers to speak to children in childlike expressions, to women in womanlike expressions, to governors in governmental expressions, and to young men in youthful expressions.[8] In this sense, Malherbe portrays Paul as a polytropic man in the Antisthenic tradition. Like Marshall, Malherbe does not grapple with Jewish/nomistic language in 1 Cor 9:20–21 or the literary context of the passage.

---

[3] Marshall, *Enmity in Corinth*, 315–16. Also Chadwick, "'All Things to All Men' (I Cor IX.22)", 263; F. F. Bruce, "'All Things to All Men': Diversity in Unity and Other Pauline Tensions", in *Unity and Diversity in New Testament Theology: Essays in Honor of George E. Ladd* (ed. Robert A. Guelich; Grand Rapids: Eerdmans, 1978), 92. Contra Brian J. Dodd, *Paul's Paradigmatic "I": Personal Example as Literary Strategy* (Sheffield: Sheffield Academic Press, 1999), 108.

[4] Marshall, *Enmity in Corinth*, 316.

[5] Abraham J. Malherbe, "Antisthenes and Odysseus, and Paul at War", in *Paul and the Popular Philosophers* (Minneapolis: Fortress, 1989), 119.

[6] Antisthenes, Scholium on *Od.* 1.1.

[7] Malherbe, "Antisthenes and Odysseus, and Paul at War", 99–101.

[8] Malherbe, "Antisthenes and Odysseus, and Paul at War", 100–101; W. B. Stanford, *The Ulysses Theme: A Study in the Adaptability of a Traditional Hero* (New York: Basil Blackwell & Mott, 1968), 99.

4.1.3 *Enslaved Leader* Topos

Dale Martin (1990) maintains that 1 Cor 9:19–23 reflects Paul's view of himself as an "enslaved leader".[9] Paul lowers his social status (in the eyes of others) and takes on work considered by some to be demeaning in order to win those of a lower position in society (the weak). Paul's actions echo the Hellenistic demagogues who align themselves with the lower class and adopt their lifestyle rather than follow the benevolent patriarchal model.[10] In this way, the enslaved leader does not relinquish authority but confirms it, "He becomes the patron of all the people".[11]

Martin understands Paul's self-enslavement as a missionary strategy to the weak and a rhetorical strategy for communicating his leadership model to the strong. It also communicates the theological principle that self-humbling precedes salvation. In 1 Cor 9:19–23, Paul "plays on the soteriological meanings of metaphorical slavery by showing that his own self-lowering will bring not only the salvation of his converts but his own eschatological salvation as well (9:23, 27)".[12] Consistent with the above studies by Marshall and Malherbe, Martin avoids engaging Jewish/nomistic language in 1 Cor 9:20–21.

4.1.4 *Political Commonplaces About the Factionalist and the Non-Partisan*

Margaret Mitchell (1991) submits that 1 Cor 9:19–23 reflects Paul's view of himself as a "non-factionalist – he is a member of no party, because he shares equally with all and is a partner (συγκοινωνός), not of men or factions, but of the gospel". Mitchell adds that Paul's "all things to all people" language reflects his rhetorical strategy and mediator role as a "conciliator of the factions".[13] Paul is a political chameleon but not for self gain.[14] He adapts to all in order to save others.[15] Like Marshall, Malherbe and Martin, Mitchell does not address the meaning of Paul's Jewish/nomistic language in 1 Cor 9:20–21.

---

[9] Dale B. Martin, *Slavery as Salvation: The Metaphor of Slavery in Pauline Christianity* (New Haven: Yale University Press, 1990), 117–35.

[10] Martin, *Slavery as Salvation*, 125–26.

[11] Martin, *Slavery as Salvation*, 134.

[12] Martin, *Slavery as Salvation*, 132.

[13] Mitchell, *Paul and the Rhetoric of Reconciliation*, 133–34, 248 n. 344.

[14] Cf. Stephen Barton, "'All Things to All People': Paul and the Law in the Light of 1 Corinthians 9.19–23", in *Paul and the Mosaic Law* (ed. James D. G. Dunn; Tübingen: Mohr Siebeck, 1996), 277.

[15] Mitchell, *Paul and the Rhetoric of Reconciliation*, 134. Mitchell highlights the importance of the Proteus tradition for understanding the political commonplace behind 1 Cor 9:19–23. See Plutarch, *Mor.* 96F–97; cf. *Alc.* 23.4–6; Virgil, *Georg.* 4.407–13; Philo, *Ios.* 34. Also Samuel Vollenweider, *Freiheit als neue Schöpfung: Eine Untersuchung zur Eleutheria bei Paulus und in seiner Umwelt* (Göttingen: Vandenhoeck & Ruprecht, 1989), 216–17 n. 86–87; Marshall, *Enmity in Corinth*, 70–90, 309–17; Meeks, "The Christian Proteus", 435–44.

4.1.5 Epicurean Psychagogic Technique

Clarence Glad (1995) argues that 1 Cor 9:19–23 reflects the psychagogic method of Late Republic Epicureans in Athens, Naples and Herculaneum as described in Philodemus' *On Frank Criticism*. Glad uses the term "psychagogy" or "guidance of the soul" to "describe a mature person's leading of neophytes in an attempt to bring about moral reformation by shaping the neophyte's view of himself and of the world".[16] Paul was a flexible guide who adapted to the status of his clients, the weak. He also "gives the wise of Corinth an example of how to treat the weak and suggests that they implement a proper form of psychagogic guidance".[17] The Corinthians were to participate in a communal participatory psychagogy (contra Malherbe's Cynic image of Paul)[18] that was analogous to the ethos of Epicurean communities.[19]

Glad rejects Marshall's thesis that Paul's "all things to all people" language is an ironic echo of his opponents' accusations and instead views it as an expression of Paul's versatile method of recruitment and psychagogy.[20] Paul's "unrestricted openness in associating with all types of people",[21] and his concern for weak neophytes, reflects a psychagogic orientation to "save" all, a term commonly used by moralists.[22]

A weakness of Glad's study is that he fails to present direct evidence that Paul draws from this strand of Epicurean thought. Glad "appears to read one particular background, of philosophical psychagogy, onto Paul's actual argument in 1 Corinthians 9 more heavily than that text can bear . . . Hence in his interpretation (and that of Martin, which applies the demagoguery *topos* to Paul) it is perhaps the case that what is gained from the wider historical context is at the cost of a loss in engagement with the immediate literary and rhetorical context of the argument".[23] Glad's interpretation of Paul's Jewish/nomistic language in 1 Cor 9:20–21 will be discussed in section 4 below.

---

[16] Clarence E. Glad, *Paul and Philodemus: Adaptability in Epicurean and Early Christian Psychagogy* (Leiden: Brill, 1995), 2.

[17] Glad, *Paul and Philodemus*, 3.

[18] "The Cynics' preoccupation with the individual contrasts with Paul's communal concern; Paul is a founder of communities, 'of which the Cynics had none'" (Glad, *Paul and Philodemus*, 6).

[19] Glad, *Paul and Philodemus*, 7–12.

[20] Glad, *Paul and Philodemus*, 16–17.

[21] Glad, "Paul and Adaptability", 28.

[22] Glad, *Paul and Philodemus*, 251, 253–54. Cf. Hodge, *If Sons, Then Heirs*, 124.

[23] Margaret M. Mitchell, "Pauline Accommodation and 'Condescension' (συγκατάβασις): 1 Cor 9:19–23 and the History of Influence", in *Paul Beyond the Judaism/Hellenism Divide* (ed. Troels Engberg-Pedersen; Louisville: Westminster John Knox, 2001), 200.

4.1.6 Sophistic Deception to Deceive the Deceived

Mark Given (2001) posits that 1 Cor 9:19–23 reflects Paul's apocalyptic epistemology and sophistic rhetorical strategy. Like Socrates, Paul deceived the deceived of the world for their own good through intentional ambiguity, cunning and deception, what Given calls "true rhetoric".[24] He was indeed a chameleon for the sake of Christ.[25] Given concurs with Barrett that Paul's Jewish practices were a "guise he could adopt or discard at will".[26] The apostle deceived his Jewish audience by masquerading as an observant Jew in order to save them, "This is why Paul speaks of becoming 'like' a Jew. He can temporarily and cunningly 'become like' a practicing Jew, but he cannot actually 'become' a practitioner of Judaism again (Gal 1:13; 2:18)".[27] Paul can do this because he is indifferent to the dietary laws and other Torah commandments.[28]

A weakness in Given's case is that Paul explicitly states in 2 Cor 4 that he does not minister in a deceptive way – "we refuse to practise cunning or to falsify God's word; but by the open statement of the truth we commend ourselves to the conscience of everyone in the sight of God" (2 Cor 4:2; cf. 12:16). Given responds to 2 Cor 4:2 by pointing out that Paul describes his gospel as veiled in the subsequent verse (2 Cor 4:3). But is Paul's "true rhetoric" responsible for the veil? On the contrary, Paul blames the veil on the "god of this world" who has "blinded the minds of the unbelievers, to keep them from seeing the light of the gospel" (2 Cor 4:4). Given presents no counter evidence that Paul's gospel deceives.[29] Another shortcoming in Given's case is the assertion that Paul follows an "ends justifies the means" ethic.[30] Paul rejects this charge in Rom 3:7–8, a passage that Given does not address.

4.1.7 A Synthetic View

In her study on the history of influence of 1 Cor 9:19–23, Margaret Mitchell (2001) refers to the various Greco-Roman *topoi* surveyed above (with the exception of Given's sophistic rhetorical strategy) and concedes that it is not possible to identify the specific strand(s) of Hellenistic thought that influenced Paul's language of adaptability in 1 Cor 9:19–23. The proposals are

---

[24] Mark D. Given, "True Rhetoric: Ambiguity, Cunning, and Deception in Pauline Discourse", in *Society of Biblical Literature 1997 Seminar Papers* (Atlanta: Scholars, 1997), 531; Given, *Paul's True Rhetoric*, 3, 23–24, 37, 117.
[25] Given, *Paul's True Rhetoric*, 105.
[26] Barrett, *A Commentary on The First Epistle to the Corinthians*, 211.
[27] Given, *Paul's True Rhetoric*, 106–107; cf. 36.
[28] Given, *Paul's True Rhetoric*, 112–13.
[29] Given, "True Rhetoric", 535–36; Given, *Paul's True Rhetoric*, 23.
[30] Given, *Paul's True Rhetoric*, 117.

"equally feasible" because of the limited data.[31] Moreover, Mitchell raises the possibility that Paul was influenced by a synthesis of Greco-Roman traditions, "One may legitimately question whether each of these options represents an individual and independent 'tradition' separable from the others, which Paul would have singularly encountered and adapted in 1 Corinthians 9 in some direct way".[32] Paul may have simply "caught" what was "in the air" and naturally fused this with Hellenistic Jewish conceptions of accommodation.[33]

While this last analysis is the most nuanced of the above assessments, Mitchell appears to overstate the evidence that Paul's language in 1 Cor 9:19–23 must reflect non-Jewish Hellenistic thought in some way. Mitchell's assumption lacks support. As John Barclay has noted, "Paul makes little attempt to express his new commitment in the terms or categories of Hellenistic culture. Despite years of association with Gentiles, Paul's letters show little acculturation in the core of his theology and he rarely attempts to effect any cultural synthesis with the Greco-Roman world he sought to evangelize".[34] With no explicit attributions or quotations in the literary context to give weight to the argument that Paul draws on Greco-Roman *topoi* in 1 Cor 9:19–23, all of the above proposals must be considered mere conjecture. Moreover, each of the studies surveyed (with the exception of Glad and Given) avoid commenting on Paul's Jewish/nomistic language in 1 Cor 9:19–23, a reflection of their inability to explain the meaning of the text in detail.

4.2 Jewish Thought

The case for a Jewish accommodation setting of 1 Cor 9:19–23 has significantly more text-based support than the arguments surveyed in the previous section. As noted in section 3.2, Paul employs Jewish sources to formulate his stance on food offered to idols in 1 Cor 8 and 10. In the relinquishment of rights/accommodation chapter (1 Cor 9), Paul quotes from Israel's law with the lead-in, "Do I say this on human authority? Does not the law also say the same? For it is written in the law of Moses" (1 Cor 9:8–9). The dominical command in 1 Cor 9:14 refers to a Jewish teacher. The two other contemporary individuals mentioned in the chapter (Cephas and Barnabas) are both Jews. 1 Cor 9:19–23 uses νόμος and compounds of νόμος nine times. Paul refers to being "under the law", "as one without the law", "not without the

---

[31] Mitchell, "Pauline Accommodation and 'Condescension' (συγκατάβασις)", 198–99.

[32] Mitchell, "Pauline Accommodation and 'Condescension' (συγκατάβασις)", 199.

[33] Mitchell, "Pauline Accommodation and 'Condescension' (συγκατάβασις)", 201, 214, 301–302 n. 16.

[34] Barclay, *Jews in the Mediterranean Diaspora*, 387. See Mitchell, "Pauline Accommodation and 'Condescension' (συγκατάβασις)", 300 n. 12, for a response to Barclay.

law of God" and "in Christ's law" – terminology that draws attention to Jewish law as a point of reference. These Jewish touchstones in 1 Cor 9:19–23 and 8:1–11:1 give weight to the argument that Paul's "all things to all people" language is informed by a Jewish accommodation setting. But what specific Jewish accommodation setting could Paul be drawing from? In this section, I will examine adaptation exhibited in Jews associating with fellow Jews, Jews associating with Gentiles, Jewish outreach and the ideal Jewish guest and host.

4.2.1 Jews Associating With Jews

During the last third of the twentieth century, a sea change occurred in the way New Testament scholars viewed first-century Judaism. It is now widely accepted that Second Temple Judaism was far more diverse than theologians and exegetes had previously recognized. Torah-observant Jews in this period varied greatly in thought and practice. Judaism was pluriform and sectarian. The implication of such diversity is that accommodation was necessary for Jews to associate closely with one another. Discussed below will be Pharisees living as priests, Pharisaic accommodation to mainstream Jews, the limits of Pharisaic accommodation, and the standards of table-fellowship at Qumran and in Pharisee homes. Commensality issues are primarily focused on in this section because the background is necessary to establish my case.

4.2.1.1 Pharisees Living as Priests

Few have disputed that Pharisees were scrupulous about what they ate and with whom they ate. There is less agreement over why they were so exacting. Gedalyahu Alon and Jacob Neusner have argued that Pharisees pursued holiness above and beyond the requirements of the law.[35] Toward this end, Pharisees ate their food in a state of ritual purity *as though they were priests*. Jacob Neusner writes:

> But the Pharisees held that even outside of the Temple, in one's own home, the laws of ritual purity were to be followed in the only circumstance in which they might apply, namely, at the table. Therefore, one must eat secular food (ordinary, everyday meals) in a state of ritual purity *as if one were a Temple priest*. The Pharisees thus arrogated to themselves – and to all Jews equally – the status of the Temple priests, and performed actions restricted to priests on account of that status. The table of every Jew in his home was seen as being like the table of

---

[35] Gedalyahu Alon, *Jews, Judaism and the Classical World: Studies in Jewish History in the Times of the Second Temple and Talmud* (Jerusalem: The Magnes Press, 1977), 219; Jacob Neusner, *From Politics to Piety: The Emergence of Pharisaic Judaism* (New York: Ktav, 1979), 83; Jacob Neusner, "The Fellowship (חבורה) in the Second Jewish Commonwealth", *Harvard Theological Review* 53 (1960): 126–27.

the Lord in the Jerusalem Temple. The commandment, "You shall be a kingdom of priests and a holy people", was taken literally.[36]

E. P. Sanders has countered that Pharisees were concerned only that food reserved for the priests (second tithe, sacrifices and heave offerings) was kept pure.[37] Bruce Chilton dismantles Sanders's case piece by piece and notes that "there is now broad agreement that Neusner is correct, and that the issue of purity marked out Pharisaic practice from the practice of priests and Jews generally".[38] In more recent discussion, Hannah Harrington has sided with Alon and Neusner (*pace* Sanders), concluding that the evidence overwhelmingly favours the view that the Pharisees approached meals and dining contexts *as though* they were priests:

> In summary, it is clear that although the Pharisees did not adopt the total regimen required for a priestly way of living, *they did think it important to eat like priests* and to consider their own ordinary food as holy in some degree . . . What is evident is a conscious effort to make an extension of the laws for priestly food to the private home. This necessitated the separation of menstruating women whenever possible from preparing food. It also meant the refusal to eat food which may have contracted corpse impurity or any other biblical type of impurity. *In no way do the Pharisees think of themselves as priests*, but they do strive for a holiness above and beyond what the Torah prescribed for the lay Israelite.[39]

Joachim Schaper has corroborated Harrington's assessment,[40] and more recently Crossley has argued that the Pharisees sought to "imitate the priesthood" at the table, even as they fully recognized that they were not priests.[41]

Compelling evidence for the "became as priests at the table" position is that the synoptic gospels depict Pharisees as concerned about ritual handwashing,[42] something expected of priests but not ordinary Jews (Exod 30:17–

---

[36] Neusner, *From Politics to Piety*, 83; cf. Jacob Neusner, *The Idea of Purity in Ancient Judaism: The Haskell Lectures, 1972–1973* (Leiden: Brill, 1973), 65.

[37] Sanders, *Jewish Law from Jesus to the Mishnah*, 197, 209.

[38] Chilton, "The Purity of the Kingdom as Conveyed in Jesus' Meals", 479.

[39] Hannah K. Harrington, "Did the Pharisees Eat Ordinary Food in a State of Ritual Purity?" *Journal for the Study of Judaism in the Persian, Hellenistic and Roman Period* 1995 (26): 53–54, emphasis mine.

[40] Joachim L. W. Schaper, "The Pharisees", in *The Cambridge History of Judaism* (ed. William Horbury et al.; Cambridge: Cambridge University Press, 1999), 3:420. Also Joel B. Green, *The Gospel of Luke* (Grand Rapids: Eerdmans, 1997), 247; Roland Deines, *Jüdische Steingefäße und pharisäische Frömmigkeit: Ein archäologisch-historischer Beitrag zum Verständnis von Johannes 2,6 und der jüdischen Reinheitshalacha zur Zeit Jesu* (Tübingen: Mohr Siebeck, 1993), 243–46.

[41] Crossley, *The Date of Mark's Gospel*, 94.

[42] Harrington, "Did the Pharisees Eat Ordinary Food in a State of Ritual Purity?" 53, replies to Sanders's assessment of Mark 7. *Pace* Hyam Maccoby, *Ritual and Morality: The Ritual Purity System and its Place in Judaism* (Cambridge: Cambridge University Press, 1999), 157f, who interprets Pharisaic handwashing as hygienic, and Chaim Milikowsky, "Reflections on Hand-Washing, Hand-Purity and Holy Scripture in Rabbinic Literature", in

21; 40:31, though note Lev 15:11). While "non-priestly" motivations for Pharisaic ritual handwashing are plausible,[43] Pharisaic preoccupation with preserving the purity of *priestly food* (the second tithe, sacrifices and heave offerings) lends support to the argument that Pharisees focused on how the priests ate. Evidence of first-century Jews observing supererogatory commandments that emulated the priesthood, such as the Nazirite vow with its temporary lay-priest requirements (Philo, *Spec.* 1.247–54),[44] adds to the cumulative case that Pharisaic ritual handwashing was modelled after priestly practice.

If Alon, Neusner, Harrington, Deines, Schaper and Crossley are correct, then fundamental to Pharisaic identity was the non-priestly imitation of the priest who followed a narrower definition of Torah observance than ordinary Jews. Pharisees were "priests *manqués*".[45] Paul would have grown up living as a priest with respect to his ritual purity standards at the table, though he was not a priest. Without stretching this too far, one could say that Paul became as a priest when it came to ritual purity practices surrounding food and table-fellowship. Could this be a Jewish analogue to Paul's γίνομαι . . . ὡς . . . μὴ ὢν αὐτός ("I became as . . . though I myself am not") conduct described in 1 Cor 9:19–23? Living as a priest at the table (though not being a priest) would have been a formative experience for Paul, and may have ingrained in him the normativeness and value that can result from living as another at the table. It may be speculated that Paul's imitation of priestly conduct at meals would have set a precedent for his later "I became as . . . though I myself am not" behaviour. Possible evidence that the two are related is that Paul explic-

---

Purity and Holiness: The Heritage of Leviticus (ed. M. J. H. M. Poorthuis and J. Schwartz; Leiden: Brill, 2000), 149–62, who distinguishes "impurity of the hands" from "washing the hands". For a response to both arguments, see John C. Poirier, "Purity Beyond the Temple in the Second Temple Era", *Journal of Biblical Literature* 122:2 (2003): 248–56; John C. Poirier, "Why Did the Pharisees Wash Their Hands?" *Journal of Jewish Studies* 47 (1996): 217–33.

[43] Eyal Regev, "Non-Priestly Purity and Its Religious Aspects According to Historical Sources and Archaeological Findings", in *Purity and Holiness: The Heritage of Leviticus* (ed. M. J. H. M. Poorthuis and J. Schwartz (Leiden: Brill, 2000), 237–44; Eyal Regev, "Pure Individualism: The Idea of Non-Priestly Purity in Ancient Judaism", *Journal for the Study of Judaism in the Persian, Hellenistic, and Roman Periods* 31 (2000): 176–202.

[44] "Because of the similarities to the injunctions placed on priests to avoid wine whilst in sacred service, the Nazirite's time under the vow was considered to be priest-like" (Chepey, *Nazirites in Late Second Temple Judaism*, 51). Markus Bockmuehl contends that Nazirites would have been regarded as temporarily comparable in status to priests, offering to "layfolk of both sexes and all walks of life a temporary share in quasi-priestly status" (Bockmuehl, *Jewish Law in Gentile Churches*, 39). Also Koet, "Why did Paul shave his hair (Acts 18, 18)?" 134.

[45] Albert I. Baumgarten, *The Flourishing of Jewish Sects in the Maccabean Era: An Interpretation* (Leiden: Brill, 1997), 99 n. 54.

itly mentions the priesthood and their food before and after 1 Cor 9:19–23 (9:13 and 10:18).[46]

4.2.1.2 Pharisaic Accommodation to Mainstream Jews

Under the reign of John Hyrcanus I (135–104 BCE) and Salome Alexandra (78–69 BCE), the Pharisees exerted some measure of halakhic influence over Jews in the land of Israel.[47] A number of scholars maintain that the Pharisees at this time instituted their halakhah in society in an accommodating way, and that this accounts for Josephus' multiple references to popular support for the Pharisees. Relative to the Sadducees and Essenes,[48] who were stringent in their implementation (or hoped for enactment) of sectarian purity law in Israel, the Pharisees were lenient and flexible:

> Why did Pharisaic, as opposed to Sadducaic/Essenic, halakha appeal to so many Palestinian Jews in the Hasmonaean era? . . . One particularly interesting aspect of Pharisaic halakha is its leniency in matters of ritual purity . . . The Essenic concept was much stricter, probably caused by the wish to err on the side of caution rather than run the risk of violating divine prescripts. The Pharisees took a different stance. They were open to the insight that the Law had to be adjusted to the living-conditions of the people.[49]

Joseph Baumgarten confirms in his study of Pharisaic/Sadducean halakhah on the *Ṭebul Yom* (one who is immersed but awaits sunset to be declared pure), bones of animals, and *niṣṣoq* (an unbroken stream of liquid) that Pharisaic halakhah was less strict than Saducean/Qumran halakhah, "We have so far found indications that in three of the four disputes between Pharisees and Sadducees concerning ritual purity, the Qumran view was likely to have been in harmony with that of the Sadducees. It should also be noted in all three of the foregoing cases the Sadducees held the position of greater stringency . . . Returning to the *Ṣaddûqîm* in tannaitic texts [e.g. *m. Yad.* 4.6–7], we have found their complaints about Pharisaic laxities in the sphere of purity to be consistent with the laws found in the *Temple Scroll* and other Qumran writings".[50]

Alon describes Pharisaic halakhah as a middle approach between two extremes (Essene and Sadducean halakhah).[51] The Pharisees attempted to balance the principle of accommodation with the principle that priestly sanctity extended to all Jews. Neusner concurs that the Pharisaic approach to purity laws was "on the whole, moderate, given the range of possibilities that pre-

---

[46] See Newton, *Deity and Diet*, 60–70.
[47] Schaper, "The Pharisees", 411–15; Josephus, *Ant.* 13.288–99, 400–15.
[48] Josephus, *Ant.* 13.298.
[49] Schaper, "The Pharisees", 407–408.
[50] Joseph M. Baumgarten, "The Pharisaic-Sadducean Controversies about Purity and the Qumran Texts", *Journal of Jewish Studies* 31 (1980): 165, 168–69.
[51] Alon, *Jews, Judaism and the Classical World*, 233–34.

sented themselves to the sages".⁵² While Qumran sectaries implemented a stringent purity halakhah, the Pharisees by contrast took "advantage of Scripture's ambivalence to ease the life of the community rather than to lay unnecessary burdens upon it".⁵³

Of course, this liberal evaluation of the Pharisees is not absolute. Depending on the time and place, the Pharisees could be assessed differently, especially if the comparison were not with the very strict sects but with the less strict Jews or sinners. For instance, the gospel writers describe the Pharisees as religious leaders who imposed burdens on the people and who did not help to alleviate these burdens (these passages will be surveyed in chapter 5).

To sum up, when the Pharisees are viewed against the backdrop of pluriform Second Temple Judaism, Pharisaic halakhah appears accommodation-oriented (relative to the Sadducees and Essenes). From another perspective, that of the gospel writers who closely associated with Jewish sinners and Gentiles, the Pharisees appeared rigid and burden imposing. The two assessments are not mutually exclusive but reflect different contexts and points of view. Given that Pharisees likely viewed themselves as proponents of accommodation, it is easy to see how Paul's Pharisaic background could have influenced the development of a lenient halakhah in 1 Cor 8:1–11:1. Pamela Eisenbaum suggests in her book *Paul Was Not a Christian*, "Perhaps Paul had a more flexible view of Torah to start with, and thus perhaps his seemingly 'looser' interpretations of various commandments derive from his training as a Pharisee".⁵⁴ Along the same lines, Pharisaic concern not to cause the public to stumble but to alleviate difficulty could have been a factor that contributed to Paul's 1 Cor 9:19–23 (cf. 10:32–33) accommodation-oriented approach to Jews, Gentiles and the weak.⁵⁵

4.2.1.3 The Limits of Pharisaic Accommodation and Jesus' Association With Sinners

The quest for holiness in Pharisaic life, as reflected in priestly conduct, meant that Pharisees avoided contact with people, even whole groups, who were assumed to be morally and ritually impure. There is no evidence of variegation between the school of Hillel and Shammai in this respect. Though Pharisees were accommodation-oriented relative to Sadducees and Essenes, the data

---

⁵² Neusner, "The Fellowship (חבורה) in the Second Jewish Commonwealth", 137.

⁵³ Hannah K. Harrington, *The Impurity Systems of Qumran and the Rabbis: Biblical Foundations* (Atlanta: Scholars, 1993), 264. Cf. Ottenheijm, "Impurity Between Intention and Deed", 142; Roland Deines, "The Pharisees Between 'Judaisms' and 'Common Judaism'", in *Justification and Variegated Nomism: The Complexities of Second Temple Judaism* (ed. D. A. Carson et al.; Tübingen: Mohr Siebeck, 2001), 1:497.

⁵⁴ Pamela Eisenbaum, *Paul Was Not a Christian: The Original Message of a Misunderstood Apostle* (New York: HarperOne, 2009), 131.

⁵⁵ Richardson and Gooch, "Accommodation Ethics", 124 n. 17.

suggest that they reached their limits of accommodation when it came to association with tax collectors and sinners.

The consistent witness of the synoptic gospels is that the Pharisees were critical of Jesus because he ate with tax collectors and sinners (Matt 9:10; 11:19; Mark 2:16; Luke 5:30; 7:34; 15:1). While a few have called into question the historicity of these accounts (despite their multiple attestation),[56] it is notable that "a wide variety of scholars who disagree on virtually everything else include this motif in their respective pictures of the historical Jesus".[57]

Who were the "tax collectors and sinners" in the gospels? Sanders argues that in first-century Judaism, sinners were "the wicked . . . those who sinned wilfully and heinously and who did not repent".[58] They were individuals who "*by the normal standards of Judaism* were *wicked*. They were doubtless also [ritually] impure".[59] In Greco-Roman literature tax collectors were those who "trafficked in prostitution and slavery, particularly to brothel keepers and pimps".[60] In this sense, they were the archetype sinners.

Dunn adds a crucial nuance to Sanders's argument. Jewish "sinners" were *like Gentiles*, people outside the boundaries of the law and thus law-less in their actions (ἄνομος).[61] According to Dunn,

> "sinner" is used more or less as a synonym for "Gentile" (Ps. 9.17; Tobit 13.8[6]; *Jub.* 23.23–4; *Pss. Sol.* 1.1; 2.1–2; Luke 6.33=Matt. 5.47; Mark 14.41 pars.; Gal. 2.15) . . . their conduct lay outside the boundary of the law. They were literally lawless.[62]

---

[56] E.g. Dennis E. Smith, "The Historical Jesus at Table", in *Society of Biblical Literature 1989 Seminar Papers* (ed. David J. Lull; Atlanta: Scholars, 1989), 482, 486. Dunn, *Jesus, Paul and the Law*, 69–71, responds to Sanders's assertion in *Jesus and Judaism*, 265, that the gospel accounts are "unrealistic" and that there was "no substantial conflict between Jesus and the Pharisees with regard to Sabbath, food and purity laws". Dunn concludes that Sanders's case is a "policy of desperation".

[57] Smith, "The Historical Jesus at Table", 466. See Dwayne H. Adams, *The Sinner in Luke* (Eugene: Pickwick, 2008), 69–73; Dietmar Neufeld, "Jesus' Eating Transgressions and Social Impropriety in the Gospel of Mark: A Social Scientific Approach", *Biblical Theology Bulletin* 30:1 (2000): 15; Kathleen E. Corley, "Jesus' Table Practice: Dining with 'Tax Collectors and Sinners', including Women", in *Society of Biblical Literature 1993 Seminar Papers* (ed. Eugene H. Lovering; Atlanta: Scholars, 1993), 444; Kathleen E. Corley, *Private Women, Public Meals: Social Conflict in the Synoptic Tradition* (Peabody: Hendrickson, 1993), 91; S. Scott Bartchy, "Table Fellowship", in *Dictionary of Jesus and the Gospels* (ed. Joel B. Green and Scot McKnight; Downers Grove: InterVarsity, 1992), 797.

[58] Sanders, *Jesus and Judaism*, 177.

[59] Sanders, *Jesus and Judaism*, 187.

[60] Corley, "Jesus' Table Practice", 447. Cf. Matt 21:32; 18:11; Dio Chrysostom, *Or.* 4.98; 14.14; Lucian, *Men.* 11; Theophrastus, *Char.* 6; Plutarch, *Mor.* 236C; Cicero, *Verr.* II.1.39.101.

[61] "The 'sinner' for the Jew was primarily a person who was the antithesis of the 'righteous'. The 'sinner' violated the Law of God and was unwilling to repent" (Adams, *The Sinner in Luke*, 67).

[62] Dunn, *Jesus, Paul and the Law*, 73–74.

Norman Perrin and Dennis Smith refer to these sinners as "Jews who had made themselves as Gentiles".[63]

The Pharisaic use of the term "sinner" was probably laden with sectarian overtones.[64] The sinners Jesus consorted with were thus not only wicked based on the standards of common Judaism but particularly wicked from the perspective of the Pharisee sect. It is likely that the Pharisees did not use the epithet "sinner" as a synonym for all non-Pharisees. Rather, the term was probably reserved for Jews who publicly contravened important aspects of Pharisaic halakhah thereby implicitly calling into question the role of the Pharisees as Jewish legal decisors:[65]

> It is precisely those who were "scrupulous" in their adherence to the law and the ancestral customs who would be most liable to criticize others whose observance was, in their eyes, significantly less scrupulous (= *un*scrupulous) . . . the sin of the "sinners" is that they stand outside the boundaries of righteousness as defined by the "righteous". We need not assume that the Pharisees were as rigid as the Essenes: they did not necessarily regard all non-Pharisees as sinners – perhaps only those who made light of Pharisaic concerns.[66]

It seems that the Pharisees regarded sinners as contaminated people by the standards of Pharisaic halakhah. To associate with sinners was to share in their wickedness. To eat with sinners was to cross the limits of Pharisaic halakhah, which defined the contours of a life of holiness and purity. What were the Pharisees particularly concerned about? Notably, a significant portion of Pharisaic halakhah focused on the production, tithing and cooking of food in a way that ensured its ritual purity status:

> The Houses' rulings [of Hillel and Shammai] pertaining either immediately or ultimately to table-fellowship involve preparation of food, ritual purity relating directly to food or indirectly to the need to keep food ritually clean, and agricultural rules concerning the proper

---

[63] Norman Perrin, *Rediscovering the Teaching of Jesus* (New York: Harper and Row, 1967), 93–94; Smith, "The Historical Jesus at Table", 481; cf. Bird, *Jesus and the Origins of the Gentile Mission*, 106–107; Adams, *The Sinner in Luke*, 65–66.

[64] Some scholars describe this sectarian conflict as one between the *ḥaberim* and the *'ammei ha-aretz*. Oppenheimer (1977) argues that the *ḥaber* and *'am ha-aretz* existed in the first century (*pace* Shaye J. D. Cohen, review of Aharon Oppenheimer, *The 'Am Ha-Aretz: A Study in the Social History of the Jewish People in the Hellenistic-Roman Period*, *Journal of Biblical Literature* 97 [1978]: 596–97). Others view the *ḥaber* and *'am ha-aretz* as a literary creation of the early rabbis. Cf. Peter Haas, "The Am Ha'Arets as Literary Character", in *From Ancient Israel to Modern Judaism: Intellect in Quest of Understanding* (ed. Jacob Neusner et al.; Atlanta: Scholars, 1989), 2:139–53. What is clear is that these constructs cannot be superimposed on the gospel accounts so as to identify the *ḥaberim* with "Pharisees" and the *'ammei ha-aretz* with "sinners" (= the masses). See David A. Neale, *None But the Sinners: Religious Categories in the Gospel of Luke* (Sheffield: Sheffield Academic Press, 1991), 40–67, for a review of the problem.

[65] See Matt 23:2–3.

[66] Dunn, *Jesus, Paul and the Law*, 76–77; cf. Morna D. Hooker, *A Commentary on the Gospel According to St. Mark* (London: A & C Black, 1991), 96.

growing, tithing, and preparation of agricultural produce for table use. The agricultural laws relate to producing or preparing food for consumption, assuring either that tithes and offerings have been set aside as the law requires, or that conditions for the nurture of crops have conformed to biblical taboos. Of the 341 individual Houses' legal pericopae, no fewer than 229, approximately 67 per cent of the whole, directly or indirectly concern table-fellowship.[67]

When the Pharisaic preoccupation with eating food in a state of ritual purity is understood, it becomes apparent that the maintenance of purity "extends as well to those with whom one eats . . . The body, then, must be carefully guarded: the mouth must be regulated so that only clean food, tithed, properly prepared, served in appropriate vessels, *and eaten in clean company* enter the physical body by means of hands ritually washed".[68] Sinners were unfit for table-fellowship because of their moral impurity and lack of responsiveness to Pharisaic halakhah, particularly with respect to ritual purity issues.

An important implication of this portrait of Pharisees and sinners is that the two groups represented two poles of the religious spectrum in mainstream society in first-century Israel, with the common people comprising the middle. The gospels focus on three main groups of people Jesus ate with: the common people, the Pharisees (in Luke) and the sinners. An intriguing possibility arises from the recognition of this variegated social landscape: If Paul was aware of Jesus' open table-fellowship, and this gospel tradition informed his approach to commensality issues (as will be suggested in chapter 5), could Paul have ordinary Jews, Pharisees and sinners in mind when he refers to his efforts to win "Jews", "those under the law" and "those without the law" in 1 Cor 9:19–23? This question will be revisited later.

4.2.1.4 Standards of Table-Fellowship at Qumran and in Pharisee Homes

To round off the discussion of different standards of commensality in the Second Temple period, the issue of how Qumran Jews differed from Pharisees with respect to table-fellowship will be briefly commented on. The query addressed here is: "What did one have to do to eat with a Qumran Jew?"

In *The Purity Texts* (2004), Harrington surveys food and commensality-related halakhah at Qumran. Four of her observations are notable:

Candidates for membership in the community were put on probation and examined for a whole year before they were allowed to eat the communal food; at least two years of proba-

---

[67] Neusner, *From Politics to Piety*, 86. Sanders, "Jewish Association With Gentiles and Galatians 2:11–14", 177–79, disputes the accuracy of Neusner's figure but concedes that food and table-fellowship were central concerns of Pharisaic halakhah.

[68] Jerome H. Neyrey, "Ceremonies in Luke-Acts: The Case of Meals and Table Fellowship", in *The Social World of Luke-Acts: Models for Interpretation* (ed. Jerome H. Neyrey; Peabody: Hendrickson, 1991), 383, italics mine.

tion were necessary in order to drink communal liquids (1QS 6.17–21; *War* 2.138; cf. CD 15.14–15).[69]

[Ordinary food was] harvested, stored and eaten in a state of ritual purity; all members had to bathe before eating it (1QS 5.13; cf. *War* 2.129).[70]

[The] members wore white before eating the meal and no physically impaired person could partake of it (*War* 2.129–131; *Ant.* 18.21; 1Q28a 2.3–10; cf. 1Q33 7.4–6).[71]

Food could also be contaminated if a transgressor ate of it . . . Members who violated community rules were excluded from the table (1QS 7.2–21; 8.22–24; *War* 2.143).[72]

What did one have to do to eat with a Qumran Jew? He had to wait at least a year before he could share table-fellowship with the community (referred to as "the Many") and at least two years before he could participate in communal drink. This was to ascertain that the individual was trustworthy with respect to ritual purity.[73] Before every meal, he had to ritually bathe and put on white clothes. Any transgression of the community's rule would result in either a reduction of the member's food allowance or exclusion from the table altogether (1QS).[74] At such times, the member was not permitted to eat food that was grown or prepared outside of the community.

The Qumran community represents one end of the Jewish religious spectrum with respect to commensality. The only way to eat with a Qumran Jew was to become a full member of the community. Even an observant outsider could not share table-fellowship with a Qumran Jew for an evening. By contrast, the Pharisees were more open to sharing meals with people who were from outside their sect. Jesus could be invited to Pharisaic homes as long as he adapted to Pharisaic standards of ritual purity. A. Baumgarten notes, "Whether Jesus was a Pharisee or not, he could meet their standards and join a Pharisee at dinner by immersion, unlike the requirements at Qumran or the Essenes, where a long period of preparation was required before a potential member was eligible to share in the food of the order".[75]

In this respect, the Pharisees can be characterized as a more flexible and accommodation-oriented sect. Their standard of commensality appears strict in the gospels because they are being compared with Jesus' open table-fellowship. When Pharisees are placed side by side with Qumran Jews, however, they are remarkably liberal:

---

[69] Harrington, *The Purity Texts*, 24.
[70] Harrington, *The Purity Texts*, 23.
[71] Harrington, *The Purity Texts*, 23.
[72] Harrington, *The Purity Texts*, 24.
[73] James D. G. Dunn, "Jesus, Table-Fellowship, and Qumran", in *Jesus and the Dead Sea Scrolls* (ed. James H. Charlesworth; New York: Doubleday, 1992), 261–62.
[74] Baumgarten, *The Flourishing of Jewish Sects in the Maccabean Era*, 95–96.
[75] Baumgarten, *The Flourishing of Jewish Sects in the Maccabean Era*, 99–100.

The moderate nature of Pharisaic food regulations would help explain how they could participate in the life of the court over many years of the Second Temple period, at times even banqueting with the King, as in the story in Josephus, *Ant.* 13.289 and *bQidd.* 66a . . . Nevertheless, Pharisees demanded a degree of stringency concerning those with whom they ate, as a matter of purity. If the conjectures above are correct, Pharisees could only eat with other Pharisees, or with those who maintained their standards (perhaps only temporarily). The Pharisees thus supply an example of a sect erecting purity barriers concerning food, albeit more modest ones, as appropriate for a reformist group, differentiating between its members and other Jews.[76]

4.2.2 Jews Associating With Gentiles

Jewish analogues of accommodation may also be detected in Jewish association with Gentiles. In the Second Temple period, outside of Jesus-believing circles, some Jews ate with Gentiles and other Jews did not. The evidence for this will be discussed below, as well as the secondary question of what was normative and the conditions under which table-fellowship could occur.

4.2.2.1 Evidence That Some Jews Did Not Eat With Gentiles

Though "Gentiles are not a category of impurity anywhere in the Torah",[77] Qumran Jews considered non-Jews intrinsically impure (morally and ritually) due to their exposure to and participation in idolatry.[78] To eat with a Gentile was to become defiled (*Jub.* 22.16). It may be argued *mutatis mutandis* that if Pharisees viewed Jewish sinners as impure and unfit to eat with, how much more would they have considered Gentile sinners off limits. Since Qumran Jews and Pharisees represented one end of the Jewish religious spectrum relative to the mainstream, it is not possible to extrapolate from this data that all Jews were like Qumran Jews and Pharisees in their view of Gentiles.

The Apocrypha and Pseudepigrapha make mention of Jews who refrain from table-fellowship with Gentiles, but in each instance there is no direct evidence of a Jewish ban on eating with Gentiles.[79] Rather, the data invite speculation that idolatry-related circumstances surrounding the meal prompted the avoidance of table-fellowship (e.g. the meal consisted of food offered to idols or took place in a pagan cultic setting). As Sanders points out, the texts "show that the problem was the food, in particular Gentile meat and wine . . . All these passages have at least the implied paraenetic purpose of advising Jews

---

[76] Baumgarten, *The Flourishing of Jewish Sects in the Maccabean Era*, 100.

[77] Harrington, *The Purity Texts*, 112–27.

[78] *Pace* Hayes, *Gentile Impurities and Jewish Identities*, 45–67, who introduces the category of genealogical impurity (esp. 19–34) and rejects the notion of intrinsic moral or ritual impurity. See Klawans, *Impurity and Sin in Ancient Judaism*, 79–82; Bauckham, "James and the Jerusalem Church", 91–142.

[79] *Pace* Esler, *Community and Gospel in Luke-Acts*, 76–83.

of what to do in Gentile lands or at Gentile tables: Avoid the meat and wine, and preferably bring your own food".[80]

In *Joseph and Aseneth* 7.6–7, Joseph declines to eat with Egyptians but there is no explanation why. If the refusal was due solely to his avoidance of idolatry and idol-food, as hinted later in the text (*Jos. Asen.* 8.5), it stands to reason that the removal of the stumbling block would result in the possibility of non-idolatrous table-fellowship with Gentiles.

In Add Esth 14.17 C, Esther states that she has not eaten from Haman's table or "honored the king's feast or drunk the wine of libations". In the first case, she did not eat with a wicked man who attempted to exterminate her people. In the third instance, she abstained from wine offered to idols. It is plausible that the second reference (not "honored the king's feast") implies that she did not eat idol-food or participate in idolatry when dining with the king. Alternatively, not honouring the king's feast could point to the avoidance of wickedness and idolatry. There is no direct statement that Esther avoided *all* meals with her husband, the king, or with all Gentiles. In fact, she prepares two dinners for the king and Haman (Esth 5:5–8; 6:14–7:1).

In Dan 1:8, the reader is told that Daniel "resolved that he would not *defile* (ἀλισγηθῇ) himself with the *royal rations of food and wine*". Subsequently, in verse 12, the text indicates that Daniel was willing to eat *vegetables* or *seeds* (זֵרְעִים). Daniel's concern to avoid wine suggests that the issue was not unclean food (there is no wine prohibition in the Torah) but food offered to idols.[81] He seems to have reasoned that vegetables (or seeds) were less likely to be offerings. Significantly, this text does not indicate that Daniel sought to avoid Gentiles or table-fellowship with Gentiles, but only that he sought to avoid defiling food. Daniel may have been willing to eat the same food at a Gentile's table so long as the setting was not idolatrous.

A similar story is found in Tobit 1.11. Tobit relates, "After I was carried away captive to Assyria and came as a captive to Nineveh, everyone of my kindred and my people ate the food of the Gentiles, but I kept myself from eating the food of the Gentiles". What does the author mean when he says that Tobit kept himself "from eating the food of the Gentiles"? Read straight up, it may simply mean that Tobit refrained from eating forbidden food; he observed the biblical dietary laws and did not eat idol-food. This does not necessarily exclude the possibility of table-fellowship with Gentiles if forbidden food is not being served. Once again, the issue of circumstance must be addressed in order to make an accurate determination about the writer's perspective on table-fellowship with Gentiles.

---

[80] Sanders, "Jewish Association With Gentiles and Galatians 2:11–14", 177.

[81] The "royal rations of food and wine" were from the table of a pagan king.

In Greco-Roman literature, Diodorus, Tacitus and Philostratus describe Jews as a people that avoided table-fellowship with outsiders.[82] Crossley, however, points out that these writers "never discuss the question of table-fellowship between Jews and Gentiles *on Jewish terms*".[83] In other words, none of the authors address the question of whether Jews could eat with Gentiles in contexts that were non-idolatrous and where idol-food was not being served.[84]

4.2.2.2 Evidence That Some Jews Ate With Gentiles

Two Second Temple Jewish texts that describe Jews and Gentiles eating together will now be examined. In Judith 12.17–19, the reader is informed that Judith "ate and drank" with Holofernes, an Assyrian general. Notably, Judith ate "what her maid had prepared". The implication is that her food was not the same as Holofernes' food. Is Judith depicted as a law-breaker or a renegade Jew? On the contrary, she is portrayed as a pious Jew. Every night that she was in Holofernes' camp, she ritually purified herself through immersion at a nearby spring (Jdt 12.7–9), an indication of her commitment to ritual purity. The story suggests that under certain conditions it was possible for a Torah-observant Jew to eat with a Gentile. These conditions included ritual immersion and eating food prepared by Jews (or in accordance with Jewish custom).

The *Letter of Aristeas* provides another example of Jews and Gentiles eating together. In this detailed text, the high priest Eleazar receives a request from king Ptolemy to send a contingent of seventy-two Jews, six from each of the tribes of Israel, to Alexandria to translate the law of God from Hebrew to Greek (*Let. Aris.* 38). Eleazar writes to the king that he will send seventy-two elders, all humble men of noble character, experts in Jewish law and literature (*Let. Aris.* 39, 121–122). After an extended apologetic on the biblical dietary laws and the role of Mosaic law in keeping Israel distinct from the nations (*Let. Aris.* 128–169, esp. 139–142),[85] Eleazar sends off the envoys. Upon their arrival, the Egyptian king honours them with a banquet. Significantly, the king has prepared food for the seventy-two elders that meets Jewish stand-

---

[82] Diodorus Siculus, *Bibliotheca Historica* 34.1.2; Tacitus, *Historiae* 5.5.2; Philostratus, *Life of Apollonius of Tyana* 5.33. See Menachem Stern, *Greek and Latin Authors on Jews and Judaism* (Jerusalem: Israel Academy of Sciences and Humanities, 1974), 1:182–83; 2:219, 341.

[83] Crossley, *The Date of Mark's Gospel*, 145. See Stern, *Greek and Latin Authors on Jews and Judaism*, 1:182–83.

[84] Philostratus, *Life of Apollonius* 5.33, seems to suggest that Jews do not eat with Gentiles because they avoid idol-food.

[85] See John J. Collins, *Jewish Cult and Hellenistic Culture: Essays on the Jewish Encounter with Hellenism and Roman Rule* (Leiden: Brill, 2005), 14.

ards. It is clear from the text that the king and the seventy-two elders eat and drink the same food together:[86]

> "Everything of which you partake", he said, "will be served in compliance with your habits; it will be served to me as well as to you". They expressed their pleasure and the king ordered the finest apartments to be given to them near the citadel, and the preparations for the banquet to be made (*Let. Aris.* 181).[87]

The text goes on to explain that the king's servant, Dorotheus, was conscientious to make certain that the preparations were in keeping with Jewish law and custom (*Let. Aris.* 182–83). Preparations included the elimination of priests and other functionaries who performed idolatrous rites at the king's banquets (*Let. Aris.* 184). In their place, Dorotheus asked Eleazar, the senior Jewish priest in the delegation, to say a prayer to the God of Israel before the meal (*Let. Aris.* 184–85). On the seventh day of the banquet, the number of Gentile guests increased so as to include a large number of ambassadors from various cities (*Let. Aris.* 275).

The *Letter of Aristeas* suggests that some Jews ate with Gentiles in the Second Temple period. Several aspects of the story are notable: (1) Eleazar the high priest is invoked as an authority that permitted the Jew-Gentile table-fellowship; (2) The Torah's dietary laws are upheld; (3) The participants in the meal include Torah-observant Jews who are trained in Mosaic law. They are not renegade Jews but elders of the twelve tribes known for their noble character and wisdom; and (4) Table-fellowship was possible because the king adapted to Jewish sensibilities. The food served was in accordance with Jewish law and custom. Also, all elements of idolatry were removed.

The *Letter of Aristeas* implies that under certain conditions even pious Jews could eat with Gentiles. The letter explicitly acknowledges that Israel is to remain distinct from the nations (*Let. Aris.* 139, 142). How is this consistent with the Jew-Gentile banquet? Sanders explains, "Here separatism is accepted, in no contradiction to the story of banqueting with the king. The latter had shown respect for God's law, including the restrictions on food, and so dining with him was compatible with Jewish separatism".[88]

Esler objects on philological grounds to calling king Ptolemy's banquet "table-fellowship". His underlying assumption is that a ban existed in the Jewish world on table-fellowship with Gentiles. But what is the textual basis for this? After a point-by-point response to Esler's hypothesis, Zetterholm concludes that the evidence for a ban is wanting:

---

[86] *Pace* Esler, *Community and Gospel in Luke-Acts*, 82.

[87] R. J. H. Shutt, trans., "Letter of Aristeas: A New Translation and Introduction", in *The Old Testament Pseudepigrapha* (ed. James H. Charlesworth; London: Darton, Longman & Todd, 1985), 2:7–34.

[88] Sanders, "Jewish Association With Gentiles and Galatians 2:11–14", 182.

[Esler] presumes a rather stereotyped picture of Judaism and Jews . . . Judaism was diversified not only with regard to different factions: the Jews of the first century CE also had different ideas of how to carry out the commandments in the torah . . . We must conclude that there unquestionably existed a certain reluctance among Jews to associate with Gentiles. As Sanders states, "Jews were in general less willing to mix than were the other peoples of the empire". In spite of this, social intercourse existed in almost every area of life with one general exception – marriage. *As for table-fellowship between Jews and Gentiles, we have seen that it did exist and was perfectly possible, given the right circumstances, which must have depended on the specific individual's degree of halakhic observance. This may have varied for different groups and probably even geographically.* We have noted that some groups may have considered all table-fellowship with Gentiles abominable while other groups had a more open attitude . . . *table-fellowship was possible even in the home of a Gentile, although the reluctance to eat with a Gentile would generally have been much less if the meal were to be taken in the home of the Jew, where the Jew was in control of what was served and knew where the ingredients came from.*[89]

Dunn similarly critiques Esler in his rejoinder. First-century Jews and Gentiles were not two undifferentiated groups:

Regrettably Esler's discussion is vitiated by the fact that he views the whole discussion in terms of two monolithic and undifferentiated blocks – Jews and Gentiles . . . "Gentiles" were not an undifferentiated mass . . . Nor has Esler really taken on board the significance of my talk of "*less scrupulous* Jews". The "Jews" too were not an undifferentiated mass living in uniform life-patterns. The evidence collected above (ch. 3) confirms that there was a spectrum of law observance regarding table-fellowship *within* Judaism.[90]

To sum up, amid the diversity of late Second Temple Judaism, some Jews ate with Gentiles and other Jews did not.[91] There is evidence of Jews refraining from table-fellowship with Gentiles as a rule at Qumran, and it may be reasonably assumed that the Pharisees did the same. Further data, however, suggest that differentiation existed in the Jewish mainstream and that commensality traditions were not uniform (cf. Acts 10:28).[92] Most texts that directly

---

[89] Zetterholm, *The Formation of Christianity in Antioch*, 150, 155; cf. Magnus Zetterholm, "A Covenant for Gentiles? Covenantal Nomism and the Incident at Antioch", in *The Ancient Synagogue from Its Origins Until 200 C.E.: Papers Presented at an International Conference at Lund University, October 14–17, 2001* (ed. Birger Olsson and Magnus Zetterholm; Stockholm: Almqvist & Wiksell International, 2003), 176, italics mine. Philo appears to have attended Gentile banquets (*Ebr.* 217–19, 177; *Prob.* 26, 141; *Prov.* 2.58).

[90] Dunn, *Jesus, Paul and the Law*, 181.

[91] Andrew E. Arterbury, *Entertaining Angels: Early Christian Hospitality in its Mediterranean Setting* (Sheffield: Phoenix, 2005), 162–63; Nanos, *The Galatians Debate*, 296–97; Bockmuehl, *Jewish Law in Gentile Churches*, 57–61; Barclay, *Jews in the Mediterranean Diaspora*, 147, 435–36; Tomson, *Paul and the Jewish Law*, 231; Sanders, "Jewish Association With Gentiles and Galatians 2:11–14", 180; James D. G. Dunn, "The Incident at Antioch (Gal. 2:11–18)", *Journal for the Study of the New Testament* 18 (1983): 23.

[92] From Peter's perspective, it was "taboo" (ἀθέμιτόν) for Jews to associate with foreigners (ἀλλοφύλῳ) (Acts 10:28). Polytheistic Gentiles may be in view. Zetterholm, "Purity and Anger", 8, argues that "the fears concerning Cornelius' impurity originated from his in-

address Jew-Gentile table-fellowship do not exclude the possibility that under certain circumstances Jews could eat with Gentiles.[93]

What were these circumstances? Piecing together the evidence, it would seem that a Jew would not typically eat in an idolatrous context. As well, Jews observed the Torah's dietary laws when they ate with Gentiles. This would require the Jew to host the Gentile, or the Gentile to host the Jew but adjust the menu to the Jew's satisfaction, or for the Jew to bring his own food when eating in a Gentile's home.[94]

The above findings are consistent with the conclusion in chapter 3 that Paul did not burst the bounds of Judaism when he shared table-fellowship with Gentiles. Like Judith and the seventy-two elders who ate with King Ptolemy of Egypt, Paul found a way to remain within the contours of Jewish law. Dunn envisions "strict Jews avoiding table-fellowship as far as possible, and those less scrupulous in matters of tithing and purity willingly extending and accepting invitations to meals where such Gentiles would be present".[95] In the same way, Paul's "less scrupulous" *modus operandi* may be viewed as an halakhic accommodation relative to the strict Pharisaic background from which he came and continued to identify with (Phil 3:5; Acts 23:6; 26:5).

4.2.3 Jewish Outreach

In the mid-twentieth century, Henry Chadwick and David Daube argued for a Jewish missionary-apologetic[96] setting of 1 Cor 9:19–23. They proposed that

---

volvement in Roman religion . . . the information in Acts 10:1 that he was a Roman officer makes it impossible to imagine that he was not involved in any way in cultic activities that, from a Jewish perspective, must have been defined as idolatry".

[93] Crossley, *The Date of Mark's Gospel*, 147. Even if Esler, *Community and Gospel in Luke-Acts*, 77, were correct that "as a general rule Jews did refrain from eating with Gentiles", it is only necessary to make a reasonable case that some Jews outside of Jesus-believing circles ate with Gentiles and that they were not regarded as bursting the bounds of Judaism. Jdt 12.17–19 and *Let. Aris.* 181 would seem to be sufficient evidence.

[94] Bockmuehl, *Jewish Law in Gentile Churches*, 58; Barclay, *Jews in the Mediterranean Diaspora*, 435. Contemporary Orthodox Jews adopt the same approaches when they want to eat with Gentiles. See Shimon Apisdorf, *Kosher for the Clueless But Curious* (Baltimore: Leviathan, 2005), 68–81; Blu Greenberg, *How to Run a Traditional Jewish Household* (London: Jason Aronson, 1989), 113–19. "An infinite number of permutations is available to the Jew who might want to, more or less, eat like a Jew while joining his or her gentile neighbor in food or drink. She might, for example, compromise the restriction on gentile bread – the substance of which is kosher – while observing restrictions on prohibited substances and mixtures. He might use the law to negotiate more lenient boundaries between 'permitted' and 'prohibited', eating cold vegetables with his gentile business partner while failing to symbolize his extreme piety" (David C. Kraemer, *Jewish Eating and Identity Through the Ages* [London: Routledge, 2007], 124).

[95] Dunn, "The Incident at Antioch (Gal. 2:11–18)", 23.

[96] The term "missionary-apologist" or "missionary-apologetic" is used to emphasize a wider definition of outreach.

Paul's principle of flexibility was not a radical break from Judaism but rather the *modus operandi* of Second Temple Jewish missionary-apologists who attempted to "win" Gentiles to the God of Israel. In this section, the principal arguments put forward by Chadwick and Daube will be examined and their viability considered. Matthew 23:15 will then be taken up and the possibility that Paul emulated Pharisaic methods of outreach.

4.2.3.1 Henry Chadwick and Philo's QG 4.69

Henry Chadwick presented a paper on 1 Cor 9:19–23 at the ninth General Meeting of the *Studiorum Novi Testamenti Societas* in Marburg, Germany, September 10, 1954; Rudolf Bultmann chaired the event. The paper was published a year later in volume one of *New Testament Studies*.[97] The eloquence of the article, the esteemed reputation of Henry Chadwick and the success of *New Testament Studies* made Chadwick's statement on 1 Cor 9:19–23 a seminal contribution to the field of Pauline studies. "All Things to All Men (I Cor. IX.22)" continues to be referenced in all major treatments of 1 Corinthians 9:19–23 to this day.

Though Chadwick did not write a follow-up article on 1 Cor 9:19–23, he briefly commented on the passage in two subsequent lectures in the 1960's.[98] In both, he tantalizingly refers to an obscure passage in Philo (not referred to in his 1955 article)[99] that elucidates Paul's words in 1 Cor 9:19–23. In the first of these addresses, The Manson Memorial Lecture delivered at the University of Manchester on November 8, 1965, Chadwick holds up *Quaestiones et solutiones in Genesin* 4.69 (hereafter referred to as *QG* 4.69) as an illustration of how Philo could be used as a source for better understanding Paul:

> More important is a very interesting passage of Philo's *Questions on Genesis* (iv. 69) where he discusses how far one is under an obligation to tell the whole truth about everything. Must one always say all that is in one's heart? Or may some reserve be practiced without loss of integrity? Because of the evil in the world, Philo says, the wise man needs much versatility. He must "imitate those hypocrites who say one thing and do another to save whom they can", though "it is not right for this to occur in all cases". Unhappily Philo does not satisfy our curiosity by telling us what cases he disapproves. *But comparison with 1 Corinthians ix shows that both St. Paul and Philo reflect a continuing discussion in the hellenistic synagogue concerning the serious obligations of a missionary and apologist to be entirely frank and the extent to which he may be allowed to use tact in presenting his case.*[100]

---

[97] Chadwick, "'All Things to All Men' (I Cor IX.22)", 261–75.

[98] In each lecture, Chadwick devotes a paragraph to 1 Cor 9:19–23.

[99] Chadwick was unaware of *QG* 4.69 at the time. From personal correspondence with Henry Chadwick, 15 November 2003.

[100] Henry Chadwick, "St. Paul and Philo of Alexandria", *Bulletin of the John Rylands Library* 48 (1965): 297–98, emphasis mine.

Some two years later, on February 27, 1968, Chadwick presented The Ethel M. Wood Lecture at the University of London where he once again cited *QG* 4.69 as crucial for understanding 1 Cor 9:19–23.[101]

When I came across Chadwick's 1965/68 comments,[102] I expected to find at least some response in the secondary literature. After much searching, however, it appears that Chadwick's two paragraphs went largely unnoticed and were eclipsed by his popular 1955 article, assumed to be his final word on 1 Cor 9:19–23. Among the hundreds of works written over the past forty years on Pauline accommodation, Jewish proselytizing and Philo's view of Judaism, none to my knowledge discuss *QG* 4.69. To check my findings, I asked Henry Chadwick if he knew of anyone who had interacted with his 1965/68 comments on 1 Cor 9:19–23. He replied that he has received no response to date and remains "convinced" that "*Questions on Genesis* 4.69 is crucial for 1 Cor 9".[103] If Chadwick is correct, a weighty piece of first-century evidence may be brought to bear on the study of 1 Cor 9:19–23. But is he right?

The Text of QG *4.69*

QG 4 is one of the few works of Philo that survives mainly in Armenian and Latin with only fragmentary attestation in Greek.[104] When translating *QG* 4.69 for *LCL*, Ralph Marcus was fortunate to have both the Armenian translation *and an extant Greek fragment of the text*, which he cites in the critical apparatus and is reproduced in Appendix A of Supplement II of the Loeb edition.[105] Below is Marcus's English translation of *QG* 4.69 with the Greek fragment from the Norwegian Philo Concordance Project:[106]

From the Armenian: (Gen. xx. 16) Why does Abimelech say to Sarah, "Behold, I have given a thousand (pieces of) silver to thy brother. Let this be for the honour of thy face and of all women who are with thee, and speak the truth about everything"? He is deserving of approval

---

[101] Henry Chadwick, *The Enigma of St Paul* (London: Athlone, 1969), 13–14. Chadwick refers to "two passages" in his 1968 lecture. The second (Philo, *Cher.* 15) is identified in his 1965 lecture at the end of his comment on *QG* 4.69 and is given for comparison sake.

[102] I am grateful to Prof. William Horbury for suggesting that I read Chadwick's 1965 Manson Memorial Lecture.

[103] From personal correspondence with Henry Chadwick, 15 November 2003.

[104] Earle Hilgert, "The *Quaestiones*: Texts and Translations", in *Both Literal and Allegorical: Studies in Philo of Alexandria's* Questions and Answers on Genesis and Exodus (ed. David M. Hay; Atlanta: Scholars, 1991), 8; Ralph Marcus, *Questions and Answers on Genesis* (Cambridge: Harvard University Press, 1953), vii–viii.

[105] Ralph Marcus, *Questions and Answers on Exodus* (Cambridge: Harvard University Press, 1953), 219–20. See J. Rendel Harris, *Fragments of Philo Judaeus* (Cambridge: Cambridge University Press, 1886), 35; Françoise Petit, *Philo, Quaestiones in Genesim et in Exodum: fragmenta graeca* (Paris: Éditions du Cerf, 1978), 165–66.

[106] Peder Borgen, Kare Fuglseth and Roald Skarsten, *The Norwegian Philo Concordance Project* (database v. 1.0, Accordance edition, 2005).

who has imposed also upon himself a penalty for an involuntary sin for the consolation and assuagement and the honour of the face (of Sarah). *From the Greek*: But the expression "speak the truth about everything" is the injunction of an unphilosophical and unlearned man. For if human life were properly directed and admitted nothing false, it would be proper to speak the truth to everyone about everything. But since hypocrisy of an evil kind acts with authority as if in a theatre, and arrogance [falsehood] is concealed with [covers over] the truth, the wise man requires a versatile art from which he may profit in imitating those mockers [hypocrites] who say one thing and do another in order to save whom they can. τὸ δὲ "πάντα ἀλήθευσον" ἀφιλοσόφου καὶ ἰδιώτου παράγγελμα. εἰ μὲν γὰρ ὁ τῶν[107] ἀνθρώπων βίος εὐώδει μηδὲν παραδεχόμενος ψεῦδος, εἰκὸς ἦν ἐπὶ παντὶ πρὸς πάντας ἀληθεύειν. ἐπειδὴ δὲ ὑπόκρισις ὡς ἐν θεάτρῳ δυναστεύει καὶ τὸ ψεῦδος παραπέτασμα τῆς ἀληθείας ἐστί, τέχνης δεῖ τῷ σοφῷ πολυτρόπου, καθ' ἣν ὠφελήσει, μιμούμενος τοὺς ὑποκριτὰς οἳ ἄλλα λέγοντες ἕτερα δρῶσι[108] ὅπως διασώσωσιν οὓς δύνανται. *From the Armenian*: Now it is not right for this to happen in all cases. For it is profitable for a counselor of evil to speak falsely about everything to his hearers, while a salutary nature is peculiar to virtue.[109]

Based on the above text, Chadwick contends that there was "lively discussion in the Greek synagogues about the intellectual integrity of the missionary-apologist, seeking to interpret his faith to people with strong prejudices".[110] Chadwick suggests that Philo participates in this conversation and affirms the importance of flexibility and adaptability:

How far might he [the missionary-apologist] go in accepting their language and principles in making his faith intelligible and acceptable to them? His purpose, says Philo, is to save whom he can; yet there are limits imposed by personal integrity and by loyalty to the truth. What are these limits, we at once ask. But at this critical moment Philo's discussion tantalizingly breaks off. At least it is evident that he regarded a certain flexibility and adaptability as both necessary and right. He felt it a merit to use tact in presenting a case, and no doubt wisely declined to lay down a general rule.[111]

If Chadwick is correct, the issue in *QG* 4.69 is whether one must speak the truth to everyone about everything (παντὶ πρὸς πάντας) and the extent to which a Jewish missionary-apologist may adapt his language and lifestyle in order to make his faith intelligible to his audience so as to save them. Significantly, the last words in the Greek fragment of *QG* 4.69 ("in order to save whom they can") are evocative of 1 Cor 9:22, "I have become all things to all people, that I might by all means save some". Can Chadwick's missionary-apologetic reading of *QG* 4.69 be sustained?

---

[107] The fragment from Harris and Marcus has μέν instead of τῶν. Petit, *Philo, Quaestiones in Genesim et in Exodum*, 165, has τῶν.

[108] The fragment from Harris and Marcus has μέν instead of δρῶσιν. Petit, *Philo, Quaestiones in Genesim et in Exodum*, 166, has δρῶσι.

[109] Philo, *QG* 4.69 (Marcus, LCL).

[110] Chadwick, *The Enigma of St Paul*, 13–14.

[111] Chadwick, *The Enigma of St Paul*, 14.

Jewish Missionary-Apologetic Activity in QG *4.69?*

Who are the ones who seek to "save whom they can" (διασώσωσιν οὓς δύνανται) in *QG* 4.69? In order to answer this question, it is helpful to consider Philo's audience. Two observations are noteworthy: First, *QG* 4 is a commentary on the Torah. The questions asked, and the answers given, were of direct relevance to Jews. Second, the book divisions of *QG* 4 roughly correspond to the divisions of the one-year (Babylonian) Torah reading cycle for the book of Genesis.[112] It may be reasonably inferred that Philo's commentary was written for Jews who followed the weekly Torah readings in the synagogues. These individuals wanted to better understand the meaning of the text and its contemporary application.

Given the likelihood of a Hellenistic synagogue setting, the expression "in order to save whom they can" could very well refer to Jewish missionary-apologists who sought to draw Gentiles to the God of Israel, as Chadwick contends. Philo speaks of Jews using their freedom of speech in the marketplace to share with all men the Torah's benefits, which he regards as profitable and necessary (*Spec.* 1.319–23). Philo informs his reader that Moses "invites" all Gentiles to become members of Israel (*Virt.* 175, 178). The Torah was translated into Greek in order to communicate the benefits of Judaism to the Gentile world (*Mos.* 2.27). The translators commenced their work by praying that the "greater part, or even the whole, of the human race might be profited and led to a better life by continuing to observe such wise and truly admirable ordinances" (*Mos.* 2.36). Gentiles who attended the annual Septuagint festival in Pharos stirred Philo's longing for the day when all Gentiles would leave their vain religious traditions and embrace the one true God and his laws (*Mos.* 2.43–44).

Philo uses salvation imagery to describe the experience of proselytes. They are like blind men who can now see; conversion is a crossing over from "deepest darkness" to the "most radiant light" (*Virt.* 179). Proselytes to Judaism see through the "great delusion [that] has taken hold of the larger part of mankind" (*Dec.* 52). They turn from the "ridiculous" religion of Egypt to the "road from which none can stray" (*Dec.* 76–79, 81). They arrive at a "higher state" and obtain the "approval" of God (*Spec.* 1.51; cf. 1.309; *Virt.* 102). Conversion produces an immediate and supernatural transformation of the soul. All of the virtues are manifest (*Virt.* 181–82). The convert is awarded "a place in heaven firmly fixed" in contrast to those who are "dragged right down and carried into Tartarus itself and profound darkness" (*Praem.* 152). Given Philo's outspoken interest in bringing Gentiles to the knowledge of

---

[112] James R. Royse, "The Original Structure of Philo's *Quaestiones*", *Studia philonica* 4 (1976–77): 62; Marcus, *Questions and Answers on Genesis*, xv.

God and his laws, it is within the realm of plausibility that *QG* 4.69 refers to Jewish missionary-apologists among Gentiles.

What other interpretations are possible? Petit suggests that *QG* 4.69 may refer to physicians who seek to save their patients by concealing the truth.[113] The text could also refer to a civilian who gives false information to the enemy in order to save his people from being conquered. Philo mentions both of these scenarios in *De cherubim* 15:

> On the other hand, if the physician who purposes to use purge or knife or hot iron to benefit his patient, conceals the truth from him, that he may not shirk the treatment through anticipation of its terror, or collapse and faint when exposed to it, we have an action contrary to duty in itself yet in its actual execution right. So too with the wise man who, fearing that the truth may strengthen the enemy's position, gives them false information to save his country.[114]

The physician who saves his patient is mentioned again in *QG* 4.45 (cf. *QG* 4.204). Another possibility is that *QG* 4.69 refers to Jews engaged in missionary-apologetic work among Jews rather than Gentiles. Perhaps it refers to zealous Pharisees who "cross sea and land" to make Jewish disciples of the Pharisee sect (Matt 23:15).

More study is needed to determine if the Gen 20 context sheds light on the identity of those who seek to "save whom they can". In Gen 20, Abraham is described as concealing vital information about himself from Abimelech, the king of Gerar; Abraham identifies himself as Sarah's brother, but not husband, in order to save his life (Gen 20:11). One potential area of exploration would be to consider whether Philo's reading of Gen 20 is informed by traditions surrounding Abraham the proselytizer-apologist *par excellence* in Gen 12 (*Jub.* 12.1–8; Josephus, *Ant.* 1.161–68; *Tg. Onq.* 12:5; *SifreDeut* 32.2).[115]

QG 4.69 is an intriguing text and one that warrants further study. In light of the various possible explanations of those who "seek to save whom they can", and the lack of any data in the immediate literary context that clarify who Philo is describing, it must be acknowledged that an impasse has been reached. The ambiguity is significant enough that a definitive statement cannot be made about the meaning of this text.

4.2.3.2 David Daube and Jewish Missionary-Apologetic Background

In 1947, David Daube published two articles that explored the possible influence of Jewish missionary-apologetic practice in 1 Cor 9:19–23: "Jewish Mis-

---

[113] Petit, *Philo, Quaestiones in Genesim et in Exodum*, 166.

[114] Philo, *Cher.* 15 (Colson and Whitaker, LCL). Cf. Cicero, *De Officiis* 3.50–53.

[115] One cannot read Gen 20 without recalling Gen 12, the first time that Abraham conceals information to save his life. There are numerous parallels between the two texts in addition to the fact that the later incident alludes to the earlier incident (Gen 20:13).

sionary Maxims in Paul" and "Κερδαίνω as a Missionary Term".[116] In both articles, Daube argued that Paul was drawing on a "living element" in Second Temple Judaism when he spoke of becoming all things to all people.

This section builds on Daube's case that Paul's accommodation-oriented approach to outreach was influenced by Pharisaic proselytizing methods. In order to evaluate the likelihood of this possibility, however, the prior question needs to be asked, "Did proselytizing Pharisees exist in the first century?" After a brief overview of contemporary scholarship on Jewish missionary-apologetic activity in the Greco-Roman period, the importance of Matt 23:15 will be addressed.

Recent Scholarship on Jewish Missionary-Apologetic Activity in the First Century

Martin Goodman (1994), Scot McKnight (1991) and Rainer Riesner (2000) maintain that there is little to no evidence for active Jewish proselytizing among Gentiles in the first century. By contrast, John Dickson, James Carleton Paget, Peder Borgen and Louis Feldman contend that the evidence for such proselytizing exists, but the minimalist position levels down a diverse Second Temple Judaism and employs a definition of "missionary" that is overly narrow.[117]

Goodman, McKnight and Riesner offer an important corrective to the maximalist view taken up for example by Dieter Georgi that Second Temple Judaism as a whole was a missionary-apologetic religion.[118] In my view, however, the medial stance as represented by Dickson, Carleton Paget, Borgen and Feldman best accounts for the evidence.[119] It makes the most sense of the broad spectrum of historical data, which, when cumulatively read, suggests that some Jews in some geographic locations were proselytizing Gen-

---

[116] David Daube, "κερδαίνω as a Missionary Term", *Harvard Theological Review* 40 (1947): 109–20; David Daube, "Jewish Missionary Maxims in Paul", *Studia Theologica* 1 (1947): 158–69; David Daube, *The New Testament and Rabbinic Judaism* (London: Athlone, 1956), 336–61; David Daube, *New Testament Judaism: Collected Works of David Daube* (ed. Calum Carmichael; Berkeley: The Robbins Collection, 2000), 2:561–82.

[117] Dickson, *Mission-Commitment in Ancient Judaism and in the Pauline Communities*, 1–85; James Carleton Paget, "Jewish Proselytism at the Time of Christian Origins: Chimera or Reality?" *Journal for the Study of the New Testament* 62 (1996): 65–103; Peder Borgen, "Proselytes, Conquest, and Mission", in *Recruitment, Conquest and Conflict: Strategies in Judaism, Early Christianity, and the Greco-Roman World* (ed. P. Borgen et al.; Atlanta: Scholars, 1998), 57–77; Louis H. Feldman, *Jew and Gentile in the Ancient World: Attitudes and Interactions from Alexander to Justinian* (Princeton: Princeton University Press, 1993).

[118] Dieter Georgi, *The Opponents of Paul in Second Corinthians* (Edinburgh: T & T Clark, 1987), 83–228.

[119] Also Michael F. Bird, *Crossing Over Sea and Land: Jewish Missionary Activity in the Second Temple Period* (Peabody: Hendrickson, 2010), 149–56.

tiles (e.g. Josephus, *Ant.* 20.17–96; Dio, *Hist.* 57.18.5a; Matt 23:15), as Shaye Cohen concedes:

> Was Judaism in antiquity a missionary religion? We must be wary of simplistic generalizations. There were many varieties of Judaism in antiquity and no single one of them was "normative" or "orthodox". Judaism changed radically during the centuries under review (from the Maccabees, mid-second-century B.C.E., to the fifth century C.E.), and there is no reason to assume that its attitude toward conversion and converts (or anything else, for that matter) was uniform or remained unchanged during that entire period. The evidence surveyed here indicates that there may have been missionary trends among some segments of diaspora and Palestinian Jewry in the first century C.E.[120]

Dickson's 2003 monograph on *Mission-Commitment in Ancient Judaism and in the Pauline Communities* reinforces this argument by demonstrating that, independent of the texts most debated, a number of other texts point to a general "missions-commitment" in ancient Judaism, which served as a seedbed for overt missionary-apologetic activity (e.g. Philo, *Mos.* 1.149; *Ios* 85–87; Josephus, *J. W.* 7.45; *Ant.* 8.115–17; 2 Macc 9.13–17; Tob 13.3–6). This would suggest that Daube's proposal that 1 Cor 9:19–23 reflects the influence of Pharisaic missionary-apologetic practice does not appear to be precluded by a lack of evidence for Jewish proselytizing activity in the Second Temple period.

Matt 23:15 and Proselytizing Pharisees

Since Paul lived as a Pharisee and came from a family of Pharisees (Phil 3:5; Gal 1:14; Acts 23:6; 26:5), it is within the bounds of possibility that his 1 Cor 9:19–23 approach to mission was in some way influenced by Pharisaism. In order to determine the plausibility of this, three questions need to be asked: Did the Pharisees proselytize? If they did, whom did they proselytize and how did they proselytize?

Is there any direct evidence that the Pharisees engaged in active missionary-apologetic activity? Notably, explicit evidence is provided in Matt 23:15:[121]

---

[120] Shaye J. D. Cohen, "Was Judaism in Antiquity a Missionary Religion?" in *Jewish Assimilation, Acculturation and Accommodation: Past Traditions, Current Issues and Future Prospects* (ed. Menachem Mor; New York: University Press of America, 1992), 20.

[121] The case for the authenticity of the logion is presented in Michael F. Bird, "The Case of the Proselytizing Pharisees? – Matthew 23.15", *Journal for the Study of the Historical Jesus* 2:2 (2004): 120–22; Bird, *Crossing Over Sea and Land*, 66–70; W. D. Davies and Dale C. Allison, *The Gospel According to Saint Matthew* (Edinburgh: T & T Clark, 1997), 3:287–88; Scot McKnight, *A Light among the Gentiles: Jewish Missionary Activity in the Second Temple Period* (Minneapolis: Fortress, 1991), 106–107; Martin Goodman, *Mission and Conversion: Proselytizing in the Religious History of the Roman Empire* (Oxford: Clarendon, 1994), 69.

> Woe to you, scribes and Pharisees, hypocrites! For you cross sea and land to make a single convert (προσήλυτον), and you make (ποιεῖτε) the new convert twice as much a child of hell as yourselves (Matt 23:15).

Matthew depicts the Pharisees as a group that engaged in *proselytizing* activities. Shaye Cohen, a minimalist, concedes that Matt 23:15 is an "ancient source that explicitly ascribes a missionary policy to a Jewish group".[122] Matt 23:15 does not indicate the extent of their conversionary efforts. The text, however, implies that Pharisaic outreach was widespread enough that it caught Jesus' attention and he considered it worthy of comment. If proselytizing had been an insignificant aspect of the group's activities, there would have been no force to Jesus' words. As for geographic extent, while no locations are given, the text seems to hint that the Pharisees were involved in missionary-apologetic work outside of the land of Israel ("you cross sea and land").

Whom did the Pharisees proselytize? The response to this question in contemporary scholarship often depends on whether the interpreter is a minimalist or maximalist on the issue of Jewish missionary-apologetic activity in the Second Temple period.[123] Maximalists typically interpret the passage as a reference to Pharisaic proselytism of Gentiles. By contrast, Martin Goodman, a minimalist, maintains that Matt 23:15 refers to Pharisaic proselytism of ordinary Jews. They sought to win them to Pharisaic halakhah:

> Is the conversion of Jews to Pharisaism something that Pharisees would have found desirable in the first century? There is little explicit evidence, but it seems at least possible. Pharisees believed that they alone could interpret the Torah correctly and it would seem obvious that, like the prophets of old calling the people to repent, they should feel a duty to teach the rest of the Jews how to live righteously and bring divine blessings on the community . . . It is reasonable to suppose that they might wish as many Jews as possible to "become Pharisees", although precisely how such a conversion would be marked (other than by the self-description of the convert) is unclear.[124]

Irina Levinskaya adds to the cogency of Goodman's argument by pointing out that Jesus' woe in verse 15 is linked to the woe before it which concerns Jews, not Gentiles, "Both woes are connected and develop the same idea with rhetorical intensification. Apparent reference to Gentile proselytes in this Jewish context [v. 15] would weaken the strength of accusation and the connection between the two parts. Besides, it is difficult to explain why Gentiles who

---

[122] Cohen, "Was Judaism in Antiquity a Missionary Religion?" 18; cf. Shaye J. D. Cohen, "Adolph Harnack's 'The Mission and Expansion of Judaism': Christianity Succeeds Where Judaism Fails", in *The Future of Early Christianity: Essays in Honor of Helmut Koester* (ed. Birger A. Pearson; Minneapolis: Fortress, 1991), 167.

[123] Levinskaya, *The Book of Acts in Its Diaspora Setting*, 36.

[124] Martin Goodman, "Jewish proselytizing in the first century", in *The Jews Among Pagans and Christians in the Roman Empire* (ed. Judith Lieu et al.; London: Routledge, 1994), 61–62.

converted to Judaism would be worse than their Pharisaic teachers".[125] Bird helpfully notes that "in 4Q266frag. 5, 1.15 initiates are called the 'converts of Israel'".[126]

In addition to Goodman's intra-Jewish reading of Matt 23:15, a number of other minimalist interpretations of Matt 23:15 have been put forward:[127] Graetz interprets Matt 23:15 to mean "You compass sea and land to make one particular proselyte [Flavius Clemens]". Friedlaender asserts that Matt 23:15 refers to Eleazar's conversion of Izates described by Josephus. Jellinek argues that the Pharisees made one proselyte from among the Gentiles each year as a reminder that the nations would one day be fully converted. Finally, Munck maintains that Matt 23:15 has the matrimonial alliances of the Herod family in view.[128] The trouble with each of these interpretations (except Goodman's) is that the amount of proselytism is so negligible as to render Jesus' words inapposite.

A more recent explanation proposed by Bird is that Matt 23:15 does not refer to Pharisaic proselytism of Gentiles but rather an attempt on the part of the zealous wing of the Pharisees to enlist Gentile sympathizers (God-fearers) in support of their "religious-political ideology".[129] While this is certainly plausible, Bird's argument does not convincingly explain Jesus' remark: "you make the new convert twice as much a child of hell as yourselves". Bird contends this means "the proselyte will share the fate of his mentor and burn like Jerusalem in the ashes of *gehenna* in the aftermath of the terror wrought by the Roman legions". This reading, however, seems forced; I find Goodman's view more persuasive.

Carleton Paget, who takes a medial position on first-century proselytism, considers Goodman's interpretation of Matt 23:15 wide of the mark since there is no attestation in Second Temple Jewish literature of προσήλυτος being used to describe a Jew who became a member of a Jewish sect:

First, we have no evidence of the use of προσήλυτος to refer to a Jewish convert to a Jewish sect . . . Secondly, while it is certainly true that the term προσήλυτος is not found very often in first-century Jewish literature, in the places where it does occur, it overwhelmingly has the sense of a Gentile convert to Judaism. This is the case both with the usage of the term in the LXX, Acts, and Philo . . . In the end the argument of Goodman, and more explicitly

---

[125] Levinskaya, *The Book of Acts in Its Diaspora Setting*, 39. The Goodman-Levinskaya case is strengthened by the fact that there is arguably (though controversially) no explicit interest in a Gentile mission in the bulk of Matthew until ch. 28.

[126] Bird, "The Case of the Proselytizing Pharisees? – Matthew 23.15", 126. Cf. Josephus, *War* 2.142; Justin Martyr, *Dial*. 122.5 ("Christ and his proselytes").

[127] Graetz, Friedlaender and Jellinek are cited in Bernard Bamberger, *Proselytism in the Talmudic Period* (Cincinnati: Hebrew Union College Press, 1939), 267–73.

[128] Munck, *Paul and the Salvation of Mankind*, 266.

[129] Bird, "The Case of the Proselytizing Pharisees? – Matthew 23.15", 127–37.

McKnight, has a circular feel to it. Mt. 23.15 cannot refer to Jewish proselytic activity because evidence for such activity has not been found elsewhere.[130]

Carleton Paget may be correct that προσήλυτος in Matt 23:15 should be rendered "convert [to Judaism]" on the basis of the extant sources. At the same time, it is possible that a specific term for "a Jew won to a Jewish sect through proselytizing-like activity" did not exist and that the word προσήλυτος was borrowed to describe this type of experience. Moreover, Goodman presents first-century evidence that the term προσήλυτος was used at times in a non-technical sense:

> First, it should be noted that the term is very rare in the first century except in quotations from the Septuagint. It was hardly used by Philo and never used by Josephus. Apart from the passage in Matthew, the only book of the whole new Testament where it is found is Acts, where it occurs three times (Acts 2:11; 6:5; 13:43). It was clearly *becoming* a technical term among Jews for a converted Gentile, and had been doing so since the time of the Septuagint translation of the third and second centuries BC (see Allen 1894), but its meaning was not yet confined to this sense alone. An examination of Philo's use of the term may illustrate this continuing flexibility. In referring to Gentile converts to Judaism Philo preferred to use the word *epēlus*. *Prosēlytos* appears only when it is already found in the Septuagint which Philo was quoting ... What I suggest, therefore, is that *prosēlytos* in the first century had both a technical and a non-technical sense, and that in that latter sense it could quite easily be applied to Jews.[131]

Carleton Paget's interpretation has weight given its philological support and congruence with the medial position on Jewish proselytism in the first century. This notwithstanding, the combined data corroborates Goodman's position in my view. It is unlikely that the Pharisees were critical of Jesus eating with Jewish sinners when they were at the same time planning missions to Gentile sinners.[132] The concern for one but not the other strikes me as un-

---

[130] Paget, "Jewish Proselytism at the Time of Christian Origins: Chimera or Reality?" 96–97. Cf. Dickson, *Mission-Commitment in Ancient Judaism and in the Pauline Communities*, 39–46; Louis H. Feldman, "Was Judaism a Missionary Religion in Ancient Times?" in *Jewish Assimilation, Acculturation and Accommodation: Past Traditions, Current Issues and Future Prospects* (ed. Menachem Mor; New York: University Press of America, 1992), 29–30.

[131] Goodman, *Mission and Conversion*, 62–63. "In regard to the Pharisees, someone who previously did not tithe, separate *terumah*, and observe certain purity rules, as a result of contact with Pharisees, has undergone 'radical re-socialization'; such an individual has been 'converted' to be a Pharisee. The Pharisaic observances and rules governing the admission of participants to table fellowship with them are the 'basic tool' for re-socializing non-Pharisees to their new, distinctive social identity. Hence, people who chose to follow Pharisaic rules, to 'be as to the law a Pharisee', could plausibly be viewed as converts to Pharisaism" (Jonathan D. Brumberg-Kraus, "Were the Pharisees a Conversionist Sect? Table Fellowship as a Strategy of Conversion (2002)", n.p. [cited 19 December 2010]. Online: http://acunix.wheatonma.edu/jkraus/articles/Pharisees.htm). Cf. Alan F. Segal, *Paul the Convert: The Apostolate and Apostasy of Saul the Pharisee* (New Haven: Yale University Press, 1990), 74, 104.

[132] "In addition, it is more plausible to understand the Pharisaic activity as having to do with Gentiles who were already associated with the synagogue than with any sort of direct

realistic. More true to life and consistent with what is known of Pharisaic Judaism is Goodman's explanation that the Pharisees sought to win "converts" from among the masses of ordinary Jews.

How would they have proselytized? In his essay, "Were the Pharisees a Conversionist Sect? Table Fellowship as a Strategy of Conversion" (2002), Jonathan Brumberg-Kraus takes up the evidence of Matt 23:15 and argues that Pharisees situated themselves in the day-to-day lives of ordinary Jews in Israel and the Diaspora in order to proselytize among the masses. Their method of outreach was not primarily teaching in the marketplace, as Philo envisioned some Jews doing (*Spec.* 1.319–23), but rather table-centred hospitality. They invited Jews into their homes and ate with them:

Table fellowship was the principal practice used by the Pharisees to win adherents to their religious movement in the first century C.E. The Pharisees' gathering together to eat properly tithed food in a state of ritual purity, and the procedures for acquiring food and maintaining households or other spaces fit for such gatherings, were strategies to influence non-Pharisees to conform to a Pharisaic way of life . . . the particular *behaviors* of tithing, observance of purity laws, and table fellowship themselves functioned as *means of proselytizing* . . . Tithing and observance of purity rules . . . were a means of "outreach" . . . the Pharisees' engagement with non-Pharisees was an implicit invitation to non-Pharisees to accept their categories, to make distinctions like a Pharisee – in effect, to act like a Pharisee.[133]

The thesis that table-fellowship was a "principal" means the Pharisees used to bring new members into their sect is an explanation that fits the historical data. The Pharisees focused on food and the table. To eat in the home of a Pharisee must have been a special experience for an ordinary Jew. It stands to reason that Pharisaic hospitality would have been a natural means of outreach.[134]

---

proselytizing activity to the wider Gentile world. We have plenteous evidence for the former but very little for the latter" (Terence L. Donaldson, *Judaism and the Gentiles: Jewish Patterns of Universalism [to 135 CE]* [Waco: Baylor University Press, 2007], 415).

[133] Brumberg-Kraus, "Were the Pharisees a Conversionist Sect?" n.p.

[134] Consider a contemporary analogy: the Chabad (Lubavitch) sect of Hasidic Judaism. Chabad is the most prominent group of ultra-Orthodox Jews in the world and the fastest growing due to their active missionary efforts among Jews. Chabad sends out *shlichim* (the Hebrew equivalent of "apostles") to Jewish communities around the globe. There are now over four thousand *shlichim* in 62 countries. See Sue Fishkoff, *The Rebbe's Army: Inside the World of Chabad-Lubavitch* (New York: Schocken, 2003), 10. Far from being insular, Chabad missionaries have woven themselves into the fabric of the Jewish mainstream and they receive the popular support of the Jewish world, "Here are Jews who live according to the strictest interpretation of Jewish law, who adhere to rigid lifestyle constraints . . . but who – alone among Hasidim – nevertheless have made it their mission to engage the modern world . . . They are zealous about their own kashrut (observance of kosher laws), but they open their arms to Jews who eat pork and drive on Shabbat. The Chabad shliach is nonjudgmental and welcoming toward other Jews, while maintaining his own 'authentic' credentials through strict adherence to Jewish law. This combination of operational flexibility and personal scru-

Returning to Paul, is there any indication in 1 Cor 9:19–23 that his missionary-apologetic approach was influenced by Pharisaic proselytizing methods? Though there is no explicit statement along these lines, it is notable that Paul instructs the Corinthians to remain integrated in society (as the Pharisees were) thus facilitating outreach (1 Cor 5:9–10; 7:16; 10:31–11:1).[135] Moreover, five times in 1 Cor 9:19–22 Paul uses the word κερδαίνω (which Daube and most commentators [4.4.7] consider a technical term for winning Jewish proselytes). Finally, the literary context of 1 Cor 9:19–23 (8:1–11:34) is focused on food, table-fellowship and hospitality. Was it a coincidence that Paul describes his missionary-apologetic method in a commensality context? This question will be revisited in chapter 5.

4.2.4 The Ideal Guest and Host

Hospitality was a context in which accommodation frequently took place in first-century Jewish life. Welcoming and visiting were ethics informed by the biblical narrative and the lives of Israel's patriarchs in particular. Abraham was seen as the ideal host,[136] and the angels who visited Abraham were viewed as exemplary guests.[137] The aim of this section is not to argue that

---

pulousness can be disarmingly compelling" (Fishkoff, *The Rebbe's Army*, 22–23, 26–27). Chabad Jews view outreach as an expression of Torah piety. Open table-fellowship and accommodation within limits (*hislabshus* – a Kabbalistic term for divine accommodation) is necessary to win fellow Jews to a Torah-true life. The primary way that Chabad Jews reach out to ordinary Jews and make new members of their sect is through hospitality and table-fellowship as Fishkoff describes in her chapter "Torah and Chicken Soup". Chabad houses can be found in almost every major city in the world and in many suburban communities. They are often private residences purchased to serve as outreach centers. Outreach mainly occurs by inviting people to strictly kosher meals where all aspects of life and Judaism are discussed in a welcoming environment. The second volume of the Chabad missionary training manual (*Shlichus: Outreach Insights*) has the following entry on Shabbos (Sabbath) meals at the Chabad House, "*Shabbos Table* – As mentioned earlier, this is really where so much *kiruv livovos* [outreach through hospitality] actually happens. At the end of the day, it's not the lecture but the cholent [a slow-cooked stew traditionally served on Shabbos afternoons] that turns people on to Yiddishkeit [Jewishness]. In large measure, it is experiencing a real Shabbos with a real Yiddishe [Jewish] family for the first time that so impresses people. The Shabbos atmosphere, the children, the togetherness, all go a long way to make people want this kind of life for themselves" (Chana Piekarski, ed., *Shlichus: Outreach Insights: A Panorama of Programs and Projects* [Brooklyn: Nshei Chabad, 1996], 249). Cf. Chana Piekarski, ed., *Shlichus: Meeting the Outreach Challenge: A Resource Handbook for Shluchim* (Brooklyn: Nshei Chabad, 1991), 118–20.

[135] See Dickson, *Mission-Commitment in Ancient Judaism and in the Pauline Communities*, 228–31.

[136] Josephus, *Ant.* 1.196–200; Philo, *Abr.* 107–115; *QG* 4.8–10. *T. Ab.* RecLng. 20.15 closes with the exhortation, "Let us too, my beloved brothers, imitate the hospitality of the patriarch Abraham" (cf. 1.1–7).

[137] Philo, *Abr.* 107–8, 115, 118; *T. Ab.* RecLng 4.7–10; RecShrt. 4.15.

4.2 Jewish Thought

Paul was directly influenced by these stories. Rather, I propose that these stories fostered an ideal of hospitality that was in the air in Second Temple Judaism – the ideal guest adapted to his host and the ideal host served his guest. Paul would have been familiar with this Jewish hospitality ethic given his traditional upbringing and the Pharisaic-Hillelite teaching that a person should conform to the customs of those around him, "Hillel the Elder says, 'Do not appear naked [where others go clothed], and do not appear clothed [where others go naked], and do not appear standing [where others sit], and do not appear sitting [where others stand]'" (*t. Ber.* 2.21).[138] In considering Jewish analogues to 1 Cor 9:19–23, attention should be given to the possibility that Paul's principle of accommodation reflects the Jewish ethic of a guest seeking to please his host by following the way of his host.

The paradigmatic example of accommodation-oriented hospitality in Israel's Scriptures is when the Lord and two angels appear as humans and eat with Abraham, the exemplary host (Gen 18). First-century writers give special attention to the hospitality and adaptability described in this text. In Gen 18, the Lord (MT: יהוה; LXX: θεός) is described as a man who visited Abraham. Accompanying the Lord were two angels who also seemed to be men:[139]

The LORD appeared to Abraham by the oaks of Mamre (ממרא), as he sat at the entrance of his tent in the heat of the day. He looked up and saw *three men* (MT: שלשה אנשים; LXX: τρεῖς ἄνδρες) standing near him (Gen 18:1–2).

The Lord is depicted in the text as standing, sitting, having his feet washed, eating, and talking with Abraham and the other two "men" (Gen 18:2–5, 8, 16–17). He receives Abraham's hospitality.

While the Hebrew and Greek Genesis describe the men who appeared to Abraham in Gen 18–19 as the Lord and two angels, Josephus and Philo substitute a third angel for the Lord. Josephus comments that Abraham "saw three angels" (*Ant.* 1.196) who were "young men of remarkably fair appearance" (*Ant.* 1.200). Philo describes the men in Gen 18 as "angels" who were "transformed from their spiritual and soul-like nature into human shape" (*Abr.* 113). He writes:

---

[138] Jacob Neusner, *The Tosefta: Translated from the Hebrew With a New Introduction* (Peabody: Hendrickson, 2002), 13, includes brackets. Cf *Let. Aris.* 257; Sir 32.1–2; *Gen. Rab.* 48.14; *Exod. Rab.* 42.5; *Der. Er. Rab.* 7.7: "This is the general rule: A man should not deviate from the custom of his companions or from society". The argument for Paul's knowledge of Hillelite teaching is strengthened by Luke's account that Paul was educated "at the feet of Gamaliel" (Acts 22:3; cf 5:34), possibly the son or grandson of Hillel. See Peter J. Tomson, "Gamaliel's Counsel and the Apologetic Strategy of Luke-Acts", in *The Unity of Luke-Acts* (ed. J. Verheyden; Leuven: Leuven University Press, 1999), 585–604; Günter Stemberger and Markus Bockmuehl, *Introduction to the Talmud and Midrash* (Edinburgh: T & T Clark, 1996), 67.

[139] That two of the three men were angels is evident from Gen 19:1 (MT: שני המלאכים; LXX: οἱ δύο ἄγγελοι) and 19:15 (MT: המלאכים; LXX: οἱ ἄγγελοι).

When at noon he saw three travelers in the form of men (ὡς ἄνδρας), for their diviner nature was not apparent to him, he ran to them and earnestly begged of them not to pass his tent but to enter as was fitting and partake of hospitality. But they, knowing, not so much by his words as by the feeling he showed that he spoke the truth, assented without hesitation. And he, his soul full of joy, was eager to carry out the reception without delay . . . I do not know how to express the vast happiness and blessedness of that house where angels did not shrink from halting and receiving hospitality from men – angels, those holy and divine beings, the servitors and lieutenants of the primal God whom He employs as ambassadors . . . It is a marvel indeed that though they neither ate nor drank they gave the appearance of both eating and drinking. But that is a secondary matter; the first and greatest wonder is that, though incorporeal, they assumed human form to do kindness to the man of worth (*Abr.* 107–108, 115, 118).

Philo notes that the angels were "as men" and that Abraham was unaware of their true identity. The "first and greatest wonder" for Philo is their adaptability: Those who are not humans became as humans. A "secondary matter", but obviously of some importance to Philo is that the angels gave the *appearance* of eating and drinking, though in actuality they did not eat or drink.

Why did the angels pretend to eat rather than simply say they did not eat because they were angels? It appears that they wanted to be proper guests. Philo states that "they assumed human form to do kindness to the man of worth". It may be speculated that the adaptation was an expression of kindness because it enabled them to receive Abraham's hospitality, which they knew Abraham would offer them.[140] Abraham was known in the ancient world for his magnanimous hospitality. Philo indicates that the angels sought to please Abraham as guests by going to extreme lengths in their adaptation.

As Abraham sought to please the angels – represented by his running to meet them, bowing before them, referring to himself twice as their "servant" (v. 3 MT: עבדך; LXX: παῖδά σου; v. 5 MT עבדכם; LXX παῖδα ὑμῶν), bringing water for their feet,[141] joyfully offering them hospitality – the angels in turn sought to please Abraham by accepting his offer of hospitality and appearing to eat what was set before them.[142] The angels went as far as they could go in their adaptation for the sake of being good guests. Philo, however, implies that they had their limits as a result of being angels by nature.

Having commented on the Genesis 18 story as told by the Hebrew and Greek Genesis, Josephus and Philo, a related account in the *Testament of Abraham* will now be examined. The *Testament of Abraham* (written around 100 CE)[143] maintains that Michael was one of the angels who visited Abra-

---

[140] David Goodman, "Do Angels Eat?" *Journal of Jewish Studies* 37 (1986): 174.

[141] See Andrew E. Arterbury, "Abraham's Hospitality among Jewish and Early Christian Writers: A Tradition History of Gen 18:1–16 and Its Relevance for the Study of the New Testament", *Perspectives in Religious Studies* 30:3 (2003): 361, 368.

[142] Cf. *Num. Rab.* 10.5: "When he brought them into his house . . . they did not like to deprive him of the exercise of hospitality and so they ate with him".

[143] "It seems best to assume a date for the original of c. A.D. 100, plus or minus twenty-five years" (E. P. Sanders, "Testament of Abraham: A New Translation and Introduction", in

ham in Genesis 18 (*T. Ab.* RecLng. 6.4).¹⁴⁴ A number of years after the birth of Isaac, Michael reappears to Abraham to announce the patriarch's imminent death. Michael, however, is overcome by Abraham's godly character, which includes his generous hospitality. He is awestruck by him and cannot bring himself to fulfil the mission.

Michael returns to heaven and reports to the Lord, "For I have not seen a man like him on the earth – merciful and *hospitable*, just, truthful, God-fearing, abstaining from every evil deed" (*T. Ab.* RecLng. 4.6). The Lord replies to Michael that he should return and follow Abraham's custom in all things, particularly with regard to what he eats, "Go, Michael Commander-in-chief, to my friend Abraham, and *whatever he says to you, this indeed do, and whatever he eats, you indeed eat along with him*" (*T. Ab.* RecLng. 4.7). The Lord calls Michael to adapt as a gracious guest and eat what is set before him. But Michael is hesitant to eat what is "earthly and corruptible". He is unsure how to accommodate to his host:

Lord, all the heavenly spirits are incorporeal, and they neither eat nor drink; and he has set a table with an abundance of good things that are earthly and corruptible. And now, Lord, what shall I do? How shall I remain undiscovered while sitting with him at one table with these things? (*T. Ab.* RecLng. 4.9).

The Lord replies to Michael:

Go down to him, and do not worry about this; for while you are sitting with him I shall send upon you an all-devouring spirit, and it will consume from your hands and through your mouth all that is on the table, and you may freely rejoice together with him (*T. Ab.* RecLng. 4.10).¹⁴⁵

This late first-century/early second-century CE dialogue between the Lord and Michael gets to the heart of what it meant to be an ideal guest. First, the Lord commands Michael to go to Abraham. Second, Michael is to adapt to Abraham's customs. Third, Michael is to eat what Abraham eats. Michael

---

The Old Testament Pseudepigrapha [ed. James H. Charlesworth; New York: Doubleday, 1983], 1:875); "There is widespread agreement that *T. Abr* is a Jewish work, written in Greek ... The date is usually put in the first century CE, on the basis of parallels to other Hellenistic Jewish writings" (John J. Collins, "The Genre Apocalypse in Hellenistic Judaism", in *Apocalypticism in the Mediterranean World and the Near East. Proceedings of the International Colloquium on Apocalypticism* [ed. David Hellholm; Tübingen: Mohr Siebeck, 1983], 541). Cf. Dale C. Allison, *Testament of Abraham* (Berlin: Walter de Gruyter, 2003), 39. James R. Davila, *The Provenance of the Pseudepigrapha: Jewish, Christian, or Other?* (Leiden: Brill, 2005), 205, suggests the possibility that "the *Urtext* of the *Testament of Abraham* was compiled by a Gentile Christian who was less concerned with boundary maintenance than most of the other surviving Christian literature".

¹⁴⁴ See Allison, *Testament of Abraham*, 162. Unless otherwise noted, I follow Allison's translation of the Greek text from Schmidt's 1986 critical edition.

¹⁴⁵ Stone includes the variant ἐν πᾶσιν (IG BJQ) and translates the last line of the text "Rejoice together with him *in everything*". See Michael E. Stone, *The Testament of Abraham: The Greek Recensions* (Missoula: Society of Biblical Literature, 1972), 11.

does not have a problem with the first and second orders. However, the third order conflicts with his nature. He was not created to eat things that are earthly and corruptible. At this point, the Lord presents a clever solution that enables Michael to have table-fellowship with Abraham without violating his nature. All of this is done because Michael is concerned "not to offend Abraham's hospitality".[146]

In the shorter recension of the *Testament of Abraham*, the Lord instructs Michael in greater detail how to adapt to his host and identify with him, "My dear Michael, rise and go to Abraham. *And if you see him eat anything, you also eat some of it.* And wherever he sleeps, you also sleep with him" (*T. Ab.* RecShrt. 4.15):

Testament of Abraham (RecLng. 4.7)	*Testament of Abraham* (RecShrt. 4.15)
Go, Michael Commander-in-chief, to my friend Abraham, and whatever he says to you, this indeed do, *and whatever he eats, you indeed eat along with him* (καὶ ὅτι ἂν ἐσθίῃ συνέσθιε καὶ σὺ μετ' αὐτοῦ)	My dear Michael, rise and go to Abraham. *And if you see him eat anything, you also eat some of it* (καὶ εἴ τι ἂν ἴδῃς αὐτὸν ἐσθίοντα, φάγῃ καὶ σὺ ἐξ αὐτῶν). And wherever he sleeps, you also sleep with him.

The shorter recension portrays the Lord as responsive to Michael's concern not to offend Abraham's hospitality, even to the point of sleeping with Abraham. Once again, the extent of the angel's adaptation to Abraham's hospitality may be seen. Since Michael is incorporeal by nature, there is no need for him to sleep. Yet he will become like Abraham and pretend to sleep out of a desire to please Abraham.

The imagery of angels as guests was in the air in the first century (Heb 13:2).[147] Even Paul refers to angels as guests in Gal 4:14 ("[you] welcomed me as an angel of God") in a possible allusion to Abraham as the exemplary host in Gen 18.[148] In his 2005 monograph *Entertaining Angels: Early Christian Hospitality in its Mediterranean Setting*, Andrew Arterbury identifies the angelic response to hospitality in *T. Ab.* 4.7, 10 as "standard etiquette for a guest" in the first-century Mediterranean world. He also compares the Lord's

---

[146] Kevin P. Sullivan, *Wrestling With Angels: A Study of the Relationship between Angels and Humans in Ancient Jewish Literature and the New Testament* (Leiden: Brill, 2004), 191. Cf. *Num. Rab.* 10.5.

[147] Arterbury, "Abraham's Hospitality among Jewish and Early Christian Writers", 375, argues for a possible allusion to Gen 18 in Heb 13:2 (cf. Philo, *Abr.* 107–110; *QG* 4.10; Josephus, *Ant.* 1.196, 200; *T. Ab.* RecLng. 1). There is likely a connection between the encouragement to show hospitality in Heb 13:2 and the identification language ("as though you were" [ὡς]) in Heb 13:3. Jewish hospitality involved putting oneself in the shoes of a stranger (Deut 10:17–19).

[148] See Sullivan, *Wrestling With Angels*, 124; Nancy L. Calvert, "Abraham Traditions in Middle Jewish Literature: Implications for the Interpretation of Galatians and Romans" (Ph.D. diss., University of Sheffield, 1993), 236; Betz, *Galatians*, 226.

instruction in *T. Ab.* 4.7 ("whatever he eats, you indeed eat along with him") to Jesus' rule of adaptation in Luke 10:8 ("eat what is set before you").[149] *T. Ab.* indicates that a guest is to become like his host. The guest is to do what the host does, follow the instructions of the host, eat what the host eats and, if invited, even sleep where the host sleeps. The guest leaves his own preferences at the door and adopts an attitude of seeking to please his host *in everything* once he enters the host's home. He is to accommodate as much as possible within the limitations of his being and conscience.

How do these Second Temple Jewish stories of angelic adaptation inform one's understanding of Paul's principle of adaptation in 1 Cor 9:19–23? It has been noted previously that 1 Cor 9:19–23 is set in a literary context that focuses on food, table-fellowship and being a guest. The significance of this will be unpacked in chapter 5. For now, it is enough to note that Paul's way of thinking expressed in 1 Cor 9:19–23 and 10:31–33 is comparable to the mindset of a first-century Jewish guest who seeks to please his host in everything.

4.3 Gospel Traditions

Many exegetes have argued that Paul's 1 Cor 9:19–23 principle of adaptation is rooted in gospel traditions.[150] Seyoon Kim (2003) contends that the passage reflects Paul's ethic of imitating the teaching and example of Christ, including his self-giving death on the cross. This is supported by Paul's reference to being "in Christ's law" in 1 Cor 9:21 and his recapitulation, "Be imitators of me, as I am of Christ" (1 Cor 11:1). What did this mean practically?

Kim identifies six areas of imitation that are reflected in 1 Cor 8:1–11:1. These include: Jesus' double command of love (Mark 12:28–34), not causing to stumble the little ones (Mark 9:42–50), being a servant of all (10:44–45), Jesus' teaching about food and purity (Mark 7:15), Jesus' self-giving death on the cross and his open table-fellowship with sinners.[151] Paul sought to follow Jesus' conduct in all of these areas. Kim concludes, "Since Paul echoes such sayings of Jesus and such conduct of his especially clearly in the crucial passages, 1 Cor 8:13; 9:19–22; and 10:23–33, where he gives himself as an example for the Corinthians' imitation, saying that he himself is an imitator of Christ (11:1), it is clear that in seeking to imitate Christ Paul has in view these teachings and the conduct of Jesus".[152]

Kim's overall case for an *imitatio Christi* ethic reflected in 1 Cor 9:19–23 is exegetically sustainable as will be seen in chapter 5. Two of Kim's sub-

---

[149] Arterbury, *Entertaining Angels*, 143.
[150] Proponents of this view are noted in 5.3 and 5.4 below.
[151] Kim, "Imitatio Christi (1 Corinthians 11:1)", 224.
[152] Kim, "Imitatio Christi (1 Corinthians 11:1)", 224.

points, however, are less defensible. First, Kim leaps to the assumption that ὑπὸ νόμον ("under the law") refers to being under the authority of Mosaic law.[153] He provides no evidence for this, nor does he engage alternative interpretations of the text.

Second, Kim contends that Paul followed Jesus' teaching and conduct with respect to Jewish food and purity laws, and presumes on the basis of Mark 7:15, 19b that Jesus nullified these laws. But is this the only way to read Mark 7? A case can be made that Jesus' *mashal* in Mark 7:15 concerns the *Pharisaic tradition* of eating ordinary food in a state of ritual purity (Mark 7:1–5; Matt 15:1–2, 20) rather than the biblical food/purity laws. That Mosaic law is not at issue is implied by Jesus' criticism of the Pharisees, "You have a fine way of rejecting the commandment of God in order to keep your tradition! For Moses said . . ." (Mark 7:9–10; Matt 15:3–4). Moreover, Mark 7:15 is consistent with the Jewish idiom of dialectic negation:

> Grammatically speaking, Mark 7.15 – as well as the Old Testament passages [Jer 7:22–23; Hos 6:6] – may be understood as a "dialectic negation". As a Semitic idiom, the formula "not A, but B" (οὐ . . . ἀλλά) can be rendered "not so much A, but rather B". Though one aspect is categorically rejected by the emphasis of the opposite, the purport of Mark 7:15 would in effect be: "A man is not so much defiled by that which enters him from outside as he is by that which comes from within". Thus it seems clear that no more than the quoted Old Testament passages aim at abolishing the sacrifice cult does Mark 7:15 intend to abrogate the food laws or the cultic laws on purity in general. It only relativizes them in stressing the importance of morality.[154]

Mark 7:19b can be read in a way that does not imply nullification of the Jewish food/purity laws. As I have argued elsewhere,[155] Mark's editorial comment may reflect his Gentile audience (alluded to in Mark 7:3)[156] and the apostolic decree that *exempted only Gentiles* from the biblical dietary laws (Acts 15:19–29). This exemption "was not because these portions of the Torah had been abolished but because their applicability was limited to Jews . . . In this light, Mark 7:19b is most accurately understood as a halakhic comment by Mark and not an 'apocalyptic pronouncement that all foods are (now) clean'. What was effectually abolition from the Gentile Christian perspective was halakhic application from the Jewish Christian perspective. Given this wider picture of the early Church's ecclesiology, the use of abolition vocabulary (e.g. 'revoked', 'abrogated', 'invalidated') by modern commentators to explain the Markan parenthesis is certainly anachronistic, for it disregards the validity of these laws for Jewish Christians".[157]

---

[153] Kim, "Imitatio Christi (1 Corinthians 11:1)", 202.

[154] Tom Holmén, *Jesus and Jewish Covenant Thinking* (Leiden: Brill, 2001), 240–41.

[155] Rudolph, "Jesus and the Food Laws", 291–311.

[156] The gospel includes seven Aramaic names/expressions written in Greek that Mark translates for his non-Jewish audience (3:17; 5:41; 7:11, 34; 14:36; 15:22, 34).

[157] Rudolph, "Jesus and the Food Laws", 306.

Building on his unsupported reading of Mark 7:15, 19b, Kim argues that Paul was able to associate with Gentiles (1 Cor 9:21) because Jesus nullified the Jewish food/purity laws. Here Kim wrongly assumes that Paul could not have associated with Gentiles unless he violated the Jewish food/purity laws:

> This line of reasoning suggests that Paul not only sees "the law of Christ" as emphasizing the love command but also dispensing with the food/purity rules of the law of Moses. With the "law of Christ" Paul refers to Jesus setting aside the food/purity rules as well as his stressing the love command. Only so could Paul, guided by "the law of Christ", accommodate himself to the Gentiles "as one outside the law", that is, ignoring the food/purity regulations of the law of Moses. This conclusion points to Jesus' ruling about food/purity in Mark 7:15/Matt 15:11, the *mashal* saying of Jesus whose intent Mark correctly interprets: "Thus he declared all foods clean" (Mark 7:19).[158]

As shown in chapter 3, some Diaspora Jews associated with Gentiles without violating Mosaic law. Kim seems unaware of this Jewish background. Instead of recognizing the diversity of Second Temple Judaism, he unwarrantably portrays Jews and Gentiles as two monolithic and undifferentiated groups.

Kim goes on to discuss Rom 14:14, 20 and assumes the traditional discontinuity reading without any exegetical treatment of the text or discussion of alternative readings.[159] As it has already been shown in 2.1.4, however, a case can be made that Rom 14 does not indicate Paul was indifferent to the biblical food laws but to clean food that the weak incorrectly considered defiled by association. In Rom 14, Paul argues that no food is unclean *in itself*, a perspective consistent with Mosaic law and Pharisaic-Hillelite teaching.[160]

4.4 Variations on the Language of 1 Cor 9:19–23

Having surveyed various settings that may inform the meaning of Paul's principle of adaptation and flexibility, the semantic elements in 1 Cor 9:19–23 will now be examined. Eight key words and phrases may be identified in the pericope: "free" (ἐλεύθερος), "I became as" (ἐγενόμην . . . ὡς), "under the law" (ὑπὸ νόμον), "without the law" (ἄνομος), "though I am not without the law of God" (μὴ ὢν ἄνομος θεοῦ), "in Christ's law" (ἔννομος Χριστοῦ), "win" (κερδήσω) and "weak" (ἀσθενεῖς). My aim below is to review how these terms have been understood in Pauline scholarship, to draw some preliminary conclusions about their likely meaning and to consider the implications of this language for whether Paul remained (or did not remain) a Torah-observant Jew.

---

[158] Kim, "Imitatio Christi (1 Corinthians 11:1)", 203.
[159] Kim, "Imitatio Christi (1 Corinthians 11:1)", 204–206.
[160] Ottenheijm, "Impurity Between Intention and Deed", 146.

4.4.1 "Free" (ἐλεύθερος)

A recent in-depth treatment of the term ἐλεύθερος in 1 Cor 9 is Lincoln Galloway's 2004 monograph *Freedom in the Gospel: Paul's Exemplum in 1 Cor 9 in Conversation with the Discourses of Epictetus and Philo*. Galloway concludes that "Paul's freedom (9:1, 19) links his call (οὐκ εἰμὶ ἀπόστολος 9:1) with his mission to all (9:19, 22) . . . Over the din of competing interests – Jews, those under the law, those outside the law, the weak – Paul emphasizes a mission to all".[161] For Paul, being ἐλεύθερος meant that he was "free from all" (ἐκ πάντων; ESV, NET); he did not "belong" to any man (NIV); he was "not a slave to any human being" (NJB). Paul counts himself free from all people; he can thus voluntarily relinquish his rights (described in 1 Cor 9:1–18) and become a slave to all (πᾶσιν ἐμαυτὸν ἐδούλωσα) in accordance with his call to all.[162] There is no indication in the text that Paul's freedom precluded Torah observance.

By contrast, Peter O' Brien asserts that ἐλεύθερος (1 Cor 9:19) means that Paul is *free* from the requirements of Mosaic law:

> He speaks of himself "as being free" (v. 19), "as not under the law" (v. 20), "as not without law toward God", "but under the law of Christ" (v. 21). Most interpreters agree that these four clauses are concessive ("Though I am free", etc.; cf. NIV, RSV, JB) with the expressions indicating Paul's freedom from the law, especially in matters of Jewish (religious) legal requirements.[163]

There are several weaknesses with O'Brien's interpretation. First, there is no indication in 1 Cor 9:1, 19 that ἐλεύθερος refers to freedom from Mosaic law.[164] Second, the language "free from all . . . slave to all" (v. 19) indicates that people are the referent. Third, since Paul contrasts ἐλεύθερος with ἐδούλωσα (to enslave) in 1 Cor 9:19, it seems reasonable to interpret "freedom" in light of Paul's discussion on *freedom from human masters* in 1 Cor 7:21–23.[165] This is the probable antecedent of the 1 Cor 9:1, 19 usage.[166] The

---

[161] Lincoln E. Galloway, *Freedom in the Gospel: Paul's Exemplum in 1 Cor 9 in Conversation with the Discourses of Epictetus and Philo* (Leuven: Peeters, 2004), 188.

[162] Schrage, *Der erste Brief an die Korinther*, 2:338; Thiselton, *The First Epistle to the Corinthians*, 700–701.

[163] Peter T. O'Brien, *Gospel and Mission in the Writings of Paul: An Exegetical and Theological Analysis* (Grand Rapids: Baker, 1995), 93–94; cf. Gooch, *Partial Knowledge*, 136. Contra Fee, *The First Epistle to the Corinthians*, 426.

[164] Jones, *"Freiheit" in den Briefen des Apostels Paulus: Eine historische, exegetische und religionsgeschichtliche Studie*, 52–53; Rietveld, "A Critical Examination of 1 Corinthians 9:19–23 as it Pertains to Paul's Missionary and Apologetic Strategy", 55; August Ludwig Christian Heydenreich, *Commentarius in priorem divi Pauli ad Corinthios epistolam* (Marburgi: J. C. Krieger, 1825–1828), 2:39.

[165] Wayne Coppins, *The Interpretation of Freedom in the Letters of Paul: With Special Reference to the 'German' Tradition* (Tübingen: Mohr Siebeck, 2009), 55–77.

concept of not having a human master may also be related in Paul's mind to not being a man pleaser (Gal 1:10; 1 Cor 10:32–33). To sum up, when Paul says in 1 Cor 9:19 that he is "free", he does not mean free from Mosaic law but free from human masters and free from the need to please men for his own advantage. Paul's freedom from having human masters meant that his self-enslavement to serve all (as an apostle) was a voluntary act of relinquishing his rights. As Bornkamm puts it, "Freedom is here thought of not as a right, but as renunciation of one's right for the sake of another".[167] This is the underlying significance of 1 Cor 9:19 in my view.

4.4.2 "I Became as" (ἐγενόμην . . . ὡς)[168]

Glad contends that Paul's expression ἐγενόμην . . . ὡς (1 Cor 9:20–21) refers to "Paul's willingness to *associate* with all" (italics mine).[169] To become "as a Jew . . . as one under the law . . . as one without the law" meant to *associate* with different groups of people. Conversely, Given maintains that ἐγενόμην . . . ὡς refers to "temporarily assuming a different identity".[170] Imitation is involved. Paul temporarily and cunningly became like the people he sought to win.

Given presents two reasons why Glad's interpretation of ἐγενόμην . . . ὡς is flawed. First, Paul would have used a different word or expression if he meant *association*. The apostle employs συναναμίγνυσθαι in 1 Cor 5:9, 11 and συναπαγόμενοι in Rom 12:16. Why did he not use these terms? Second, there is no attestation of ἐγενόμην . . . ὡς that conveys the meaning "association": "There is, in fact, no example in the NT or LXX where this construction is used simply to express a willingness to associate with someone. Whether it is used in a literal or figurative mode, it refers to concrete, observable changes".[171]

Given's critique of Glad is uneven. On the first point, Given concedes that the NT and LXX use various words to express the idea of association (Acts

---

[166] P. D. Gardner, *The Gifts of God and the Authentication of a Christian: An Exegetical Study of 1 Corinthians 8:1–11:1* (Lanham: University Press of America, 1994), 96–98; Barrett, *A Commentary on The First Epistle to the Corinthians*, 210.

[167] Bornkamm, *Paul*, 174. Also Kenneth V. Neller, "1 Corinthians 9:19–22, A Model for Those Who Seek to Win Souls", *Restoration Quarterly* 29 (1987): 132; Back, *All Things to All Men*, 10.

[168] Tomson, *Paul and the Jewish Law*, 276–77, argues in support of the late variant (G) that omits ὡς. I am not convinced by Tomson's argument since, as Mitchell ("Pauline Accommodation and 'Condescension' [συγκατάβασις]", 299 n. 2) has pointed out, "there are no grounds for such a significant shift in semantic meaning of the elided verb (in this particular case or in Greek generally)".

[169] Glad, *Paul and Philodemus*, 259–60.

[170] Given, *Paul's True Rhetoric*, 106–107.

[171] Given, *Paul's True Rhetoric*, 109.

10:28; Wis 6.23; 8.4; Sir 9.4; 13.2, 16). There is no reason that Paul had to use the same word in 1 Cor 9:20–21 that he used in 1 Cor 5:9, 11. Paul uses synonyms as all good writers do. Moreover, if Paul intended to emphasize *identification* through association, the expression ἐγενόμην . . . ὡς would have been a fitting way to communicate this nuance.

Given's philological argument that ἐγενόμην . . . ὡς includes the connotation "concrete, observable changes" should be accepted. This does not necessarily mean, however, that Glad is incorrect that ἐγενόμην . . . ὡς refers to association. Glad's argument may simply be insufficient. It has been shown above that, in the first-century, table-fellowship involved guests adapting to the customs and way of life of their host. If 1 Cor 9:19–23 refers to accommodation-oriented table-fellowship with all, the expression ἐγενόμην . . . ὡς could refer to both association and adaptation that is concrete and observable.

There are two problems with Given's hyper-literal interpretation of ἐγενόμην . . . ὡς. The ethical problem of a sophistic deception to deceive the deceived has already been addressed in 4.1.6. The second weakness has been raised by Sanders, "The problem is the practical one . . . how could he [Paul] have been a Jew to the Jews and a Gentile to the Gentiles *in the same church*?"[172] Paul's statement "I have become all things to all people" could not have been intended hyper-literally.

At the same time, going to the other extreme and arguing, as Sanders does, that ἐγενόμην . . . ὡς is hyperbole is no more of a solution. Given's philological argument and Paul's nomistic language in 1 Cor 9:19–23 prevents us from taking this step. It may be concluded that the medial position that combines the nuance of "association" and "concrete, observable changes" is the most plausible explanation of ἐγενόμην . . . ὡς. Moreover, 1 Cor 9:19–23 seems to assume a homogenous context. If Paul became a Jew to the Jews, it may be presumed that Gentiles were not around and vice versa.

In what type of situation would all of these factors have converged? As already noted, receiving hospitality in a household context would have naturally involved association and "concrete, observable changes" (with respect to adaptation). A household setting would have also been an environment where Paul would have encountered a homogeneous grouping (in contrast to the church in Corinth). Also, a household represents a common way of life, uniformity of custom, and in the case of Jewish households, a single standard of *halakhah*. Guests are expected to conform to the standard of the household they enter even if their standard is different. Thus, Paul's ἐγενόμην . . . ὡς ethic in a household setting would not have been a deception but a common and reasonable expectation. Receiving hospitality in a household context would have also naturally led to conversation and an opportunity for Paul to "win" (κερδαίνω) the household to the truth of the gospel.

---

[172] Sanders, *Paul, the Law, and the Jewish People*, 185–86.

4.4.3 "Under the Law" (ὑπὸ νόμον)[173]

Most contemporary studies of 1 Cor 9:20 interpret the expression ὑπὸ νόμον as a reference to "Jews living under the authority of Mosaic law"[174] or "proselytes living under the authority of Mosaic law".[175] The second interpretation ("proselytes" as a subset of "Jews") has the benefit of avoiding repetition in Paul's list. In both readings, however, ὑπὸ νόμον is assumed to be a reference to the Torah-observant life. Thus, when Paul says that he is not ὑπὸ νόμον, he means that he does not consistently observe the Torah as other Jews do. He does not consider the laws of the Torah obligatory.

Few have challenged this consensus interpretation of ὑπὸ νόμον,[176] a surprising find since the meaning of ὑπὸ νόμον elsewhere in the Pauline corpus

---

[173] Tomson, *Paul and the Jewish Law*, 277–79, follows a textual tradition that omits the clause μὴ ὢν αὐτὸς ὑπὸ νόμον ("though I myself am not under the law"). See D^grc C K Ψ 81 88 256 326 330 451 460 614 629^c 1175 1241 1518 1881 1984 1985 2138 2492 Byz Lect syr^p eth. Origen Chrysostom. I am not convinced by Tomson's case since the variant is not well attested and is likely due to deletion by homoioteleuton (Mitchell, "Pauline Accommodation and 'Condescension' [συγκατάβασις]", 299 n. 2). Bruce M. Metzger, *A Textual Commentary on the Greek New Testament* (Stuttgart: Deutsche Bibelgesellschaft, 1998), 493, comments, "The words, which are decisively supported by (𝔓^46) ℵ A B C D* F G P it vg syr^h cop^sa goth arm, probably fell out by accident in transcription, the eye of the copyist passing from ὑπὸ νόμον to ὑπὸ νόμον". Inclusion is also supported by 33 104 181 436 630 1739 1877 2127 2495 it^ar, d, dem, e, f, g, x, z vg syr^h cop^sa, bo goth arm.

[174] Schrage, *Der erste Brief an die Korinther*, 2:341–43; Thiselton, *The First Epistle to the Corinthians*, 702–704; Morna D. Hooker, "A Partner in the Gospel: Paul's Understanding of His Ministry", in *Theology and Ethics in Paul and His Interpreters: Essays in Honor of Victor Paul Furnish* (ed. Eugene H. Lovering and Jerry L. Sumney; Nashville: Abingdon, 1996), 84–85; Gardner, *The Gifts of God and the Authentication of a Christian*, 100. Also Fee, *The First Epistle to the Corinthians*, 428–29; Meyer, *Paul's First Epistle to the Corinthians*, 1:271; Ellicott, *St. Paul's First Epistle to the Corinthians*, 167.

[175] Edwin D. Freed, *The Morality of Paul's Converts* (London: Equinox, 2005), 136. Also Ciampa and Rosner, *The First Letter to the Corinthians*, 423, 426; Blomberg, *1 Corinthians*, 184; G. G. Findlay, "St. Paul's First Epistle to the Corinthians", in *The Expositor's Greek Testament* (ed. W. R. Nicoll; Grand Rapids: Eerdmans, 1961), 2:854; Robertson and Plummer, *A Critical and Exegetical Commentary on the First Epistle of St. Paul to the Corinthians*, 191; Godet, *Commentary on the First Epistle of St. Paul to the Corinthians*, 37; C. F. G. Heinrici, *Das erste Sendschreiben des Apostel Paulus an die Korinther* (Berlin: Hertz, 1880), 250 n. 4. Note Josephus' reference to proselytes in *Ag. Ap.* 2.210: ὑπὸ τοὺς αὐτοὺς ἡμῖν νόμους ("under . . . the laws"). Conzelmann, *A Commentary on the First Epistle to the Corinthians*, 160 n. 23, sees no evidence that proselytes are in view. Blomberg (cited above) and Neller ("1 Corinthians 9:19–22", 134) include God-fearers within the category of ὑπὸ νόμον.

[176] The exceptions: Origen (*Fr. 1 Cor.* XLIII.513.14) understood ὑπὸ νόμον as a reference to Samaritans. See Darrell D. Hannah, *The Text of 1 Corinthians in the Writings of Origen* (Atlanta: Scholars, 1997), 238; Claude Jenkins, "Origen on 1 Corinthians", *Journal of Theological Studies* 9 (1908): 513. Richard A. Horsley, *1 Corinthians* (Nashville: Abingdon, 1998), 131, maintains that "Jews" = Judeans and "under the law" = Diaspora Jews. The

is a source of longstanding controversy in Pauline studies. Outside of 1 Cor 9:20, various meanings of ὑπὸ νόμον have been proposed. For example, ὑπὸ νόμον appears twice in Rom 6:14–15. Here ὑπὸ νόμον is juxtaposed with ὑπὸ χάριν ("under grace"). According to Moo, in the Romans context, to be "'under law' is to be subject to the constraining and sin-strengthening regime of the old age".[177] Others have interpreted ὑπὸ νόμον in Rom 6:14–15 to mean under the condemnation of the law or under a works-righteousness approach to the law.[178]

---

weakness of this proposal is that "Jews" (not "Judeans") are juxtaposed with "Greeks" (i.e. Gentiles) in every other occurrence of Ἰουδαῖος in the letter (1 Cor 1:22; 10:32; 12:13). Nanos ("A Torah-Observant Paul?" 37) argues that "Jews" = "Judeans" and "under the law" = "proselytes". The problem with the rendering "Judeans" has been noted. How did Paul become as a proselyte? If this is no different from becoming "as a Jew", there is redundancy. Also, why would Paul add the restrictive clause ("though I myself am not a proselyte" [v. 20b])? Was Paul concerned that people would think he was a proselyte? This is unlikely. Caroline Johnson Hodge, "Apostle to the Gentiles: Construction of Paul's Identity", *Biblical Interpretation* 13:3 (2005): 284–85, identifies ὑπὸ νόμον with Gentiles who are "enslaved" to the law. But she offers no evidence from the Corinthian correspondence to support this position and appears to superimpose her view of the Galatians setting onto 1 Cor 9. Cf. Lloyd Gaston, *Paul and the Torah* (Vancouver: University of British Columbia Press, 1987), 30. Collins, *First Corinthians*, 354, contends that "under the law" (1 Cor 9:20) refers to being under law of any kind. Paul's reference to "Jews" in 1 Cor 9:20a would seem to warrant against this. Alternatively, Thielman, "The Coherence of Paul's View of the Law", 243–46, asserts that ὑπὸ νόμον in 1 Cor 9:20 refers to "being under those aspects of the law which are distinctively Jewish . . . in particular the food laws". Also Stephen Westerholm, *Perspectives Old and New in Paul: The "Lutheran" Paul and His Critics* (Grand Rapids: Eerdmans, 2004), 172, 203, 432; Stephen Westerholm, *Israel's Law and the Church's Faith: Paul and His Recent Interpreters* (Grand Rapids: Eerdmans, 1988), 200–203; Kistemaker, *1 Corinthians*, 306; Grosheide, *Commentary on the First Epistle to the Corinthians*, 212; Hodge, *An Exposition of the First Epistle to the Corinthians*, 165; Godet, *Commentary on the First Epistle of St. Paul to the Corinthians*, 38; John Calvin, *The First Epistle of Paul the Apostle to the Corinthians* (trans. John W. Fraser; London: Oliver and Boyd, 1960), 195. There is no direct evidence, however, that Paul compartmentalized the law into "moral" and distinctively Jewish/ceremonial sections. Rather, Paul writes in Gal 5:3, "I testify to every man who lets himself be circumcised that he is obliged to obey the entire law". If Paul observed part of the law *ad hoc.*, his oath would have had no force. Cf. Jas 2:10; Räisänen, *Paul and the Law*, 71–72; Watson, *Paul, Judaism and the Gentiles*, 29. Thielman's argument has three additional problems: (1) Unnecessary repetition in 1 Cor 9:20a–b; (2) In v. 20, Paul would be claiming to be under a section of the law, and then in v. 21 he would be claiming to embrace "God's law" as a whole (the implication also of 1 Cor 9:8–9); and (3) The argument assumes that Jews are simpletons (see 1.3 above).

[177] Douglas J. Moo, *The Epistle to the Romans* (Grand Rapids: Eerdmans, 1996), 389.

[178] C. E. B. Cranfield, *A Critical and Exegetical Commentary on The Epistle to the Romans* (Edinburgh: T & T Clark, 1975), 1:320; Hans Hübner, *Law in Paul's Thought* (Edinburgh: T & T Clark, 1984), 134–35; C. F. D. Moule, "Obligation in the Ethic of Paul", in *Christian History and Interpretation: Studies Presented to John Knox* (ed. W. R. Farmer et al.; Cambridge: Cambridge University Press, 1967), 394–95.

The meaning of ὑπὸ νόμον in Galatians 3:23, 4:4, 5, 21 and 5:18 has also been the subject of vigorous debate.[179] Proposed meanings of the expression may be grouped into three categories: (1) Under a legal or legalistic system of the law;[180] (2) Under the condemnation or curse of the law;[181] and (3) Under the guiding, restraining influence of the law.[182] It is uncertain if Paul uses ὑπὸ νόμον in a consistent way throughout Galatians. Moreover, many scholars maintain that Paul does not use ὑπὸ νόμον in Galatians in the same way that he uses it in Rom 6:14–15 and 1 Cor 9:20. In his 2007 monograph on Paul's use of νόμος in Gal 5:13–6:10, Todd Wilson argues that Paul employs ὑπὸ νόμον in this context as a shorthand for being "under the curse of the law" (Gal 3:10, 13). Wilson, however, is less confident about what Paul means by the expression ὑπὸ νόμον in Romans and 1 Corinthians:

> While we have seen strong evidence to suggest that "under Law" serves as shorthand for "under the curse of the Law" in Galatians, it has not been my intention to argue that this phrase functions as a technical term for Paul with a uniform meaning everywhere else it occurs. Paul's use of "under Law" as shorthand for "under the curse of the Law" may very well have been an *ad hoc* device used only in Galatians to address the particular situation in Galatia. *There is no reason why this could not have been the case, nor why Paul might not have used the expression "under Law" (or any other phrase) one way in Galatians and another way in some other letter.* This is not intended to sidestep the issue of Paul's other uses of "under Law" in Rom 6.14–15 or 1 Cor 9.20–21. I am less confident, however, about how to understand Paul's use of the expression in those contexts, even though a reference to the curse of the Law is not impossible in either one, particularly not in Romans.[183]

---

[179] William N. Wilder, *Echoes of the Exodus Narrative in the Context and Background of Galatians 5:18* (New York: Peter Lang, 2001), 5–119, 251–65.

[180] E. de W. Burton, *A Critical and Exegetical Commentary on the Epistle to the Galatians* (Edinburgh: T & T Clark, 1921), 176; A. Oepke, *Der Brief des Paulus an die Galater* (Berlin: Evangelische Verlagsanstalt, 1984), 176; H. Schlier, *Der Brief an die Galater* (Göttingen: Vandenhoeck & Ruprecht, 1962), 250; R. A. Cole, *The Letter of Paul to the Galatians* (Grand Rapids: Eerdmans, 1989), 209.

[181] U. Borse, *Der Standort des Galaterbriefes* (Köln: PeterHansten, 1972), 60–61; H. N. Ridderbos, *The Epistle of Paul to the Churches of Galatia* (Grand Rapids: Eerdmans, 1953), 204–205; I.-G. Hong, *The Law in Galatians* (Sheffield: JSOT, 1993), 175.

[182] Betz, *Galatians*, 281; John M. G. Barclay, *Obeying the Truth: A Study of Paul's Ethics in Galatians* (Edinburgh: T & T Clark, 1988), 116; Martyn, *Galatians*, 496; Richard N. Longenecker, *Galatians* (Waco: Word, 1990), 246; Dunn, *The Epistle to the Galatians*, 301. See Todd A. Wilson, "'Under Law' in Galatians: A Pauline Theological Abbreviation", *Journal of Theological Studies* 56:2 (2005): 383, for a discussion of these three options.

[183] Todd A. Wilson, *The Curse of the Law and the Crisis in Galatia: Reassessing the Purpose of Galatians* (Tübingen: Mohr Siebeck, 2007), 44, italics mine; cf. Wilson, "'Under Law' in Galatians", 390–91. Garland, *1 Corinthians*, 430, adopts this reading of ὑπὸ νόμον in 1 Cor 9:20, "'To be under the law' means to be judged by the law (Rom. 2:12), to be under divine wrath as a violator of the law (Rom. 4:15), and under a curse (Gal. 3:10). Paul was willing to endure that judgment and punishment to win Jews". Garland adds that Paul submitted to the forty lashes minus one five times (2 Cor 11:24; cf. Deut 25:3), "He bowed to syna-

My point in rehearsing the various interpretations of ὑπὸ νόμον outside of 1 Corinthians is to show that Paul used the phrase with different nuances in different contexts and that contemporary scholars are divided over what Paul meant by ὑπὸ νόμον in each circumstance.[184] If this is the case with respect to Romans and Galatians, why should it be assumed that the meaning of ὑπὸ νόμον is straightforward and self-evident in 1 Cor 9:20? The context of 1 Cor 8:1–11:1 does not require the standard interpretation ("under [the authority of] the law") and the second restrictive clause in 1 Cor 9:21 ("though I am not without the law of God [μὴ ὢν ἄνομος θεοῦ]") would seem to call this reading into question. For these reasons, one should be particularly careful when elucidating this phrase. Having established that ambiguity surrounds Paul's use of ὑπὸ νόμον throughout the Pauline corpus, and that ὑπὸ νόμον may be used in different ways by Paul, consideration should be given to the possibility of a non-standard reading of ὑπὸ νόμον in 1 Cor 9:20.

It is notable that within the Corinthian correspondence, Paul uses νόμος in a way that is atypical at least once. Paul writes in 1 Cor 15:56a, "The sting of death is sin, and the power of sin is the law". What does this mean? Chris Vlachos argues compellingly in his 2009 monograph on the law-critical epigram in 1 Cor 15:56 that νόμος is here a referent to *"divine law in general"*.[185] Moreover, Vlachos asserts that the meaning of νόμος in 1 Cor 15:56a is being refracted through the story of Adam's response to God's commandment in Gen 3, "Paul's understanding of the law-sin nexus may be best explicated ... by reference to the Fall account itself, which, it would appear, contains the story behind the moral of 1 Cor 15:56".[186] As divine law, νόμος includes Mo-

---

gogue discipline to maintain his Jewish connections (Harvey 1985:93)". This novel reading of 1 Cor 9:20 deserves consideration. However, three weaknesses should be pointed out: (1) There is unnecessary repetition since "Jews" are "those under the law" (1 Cor 9:20); (2) A lack of contextual support; and (3) The connection between being "under [the curse of] the law" and submitting to synagogue discipline is a stretch.

[184] Stephen Westerholm, "Sinai as Viewed from Damascus: Paul's Reevaluation of the Mosaic Law", in *The Road from Damascus: The Impact of Paul's Conversion on His Life, Thought, and Ministry* (ed. Richard N. Longenecker; Grand Rapids: Eerdmans, 1997), 162.

[185] Chris A. Vlachos, *The Law and the Knowledge of Good and Evil: The Edenic Background of the Catalytic Operation of the Law in Paul* (Eugene: Pickwick, 2009), 76. Cf. Rom 7:9, 11. Also Harm W. Hollander, "The Meaning of the Term 'Law' (NOMOS) in 1 Corinthians", *Novum Testamentum* 40 (1998): 132; Sebastian Schneider, *Vollendung des Auferstehens. Eine exegetische Untersuchung zu 1 Kor 15,51–52* (Frankfurt: Phil.-Theol. Hochschule St. Georgen, 1994), 53; Harm W. Hollander, and J. Holleman, "The Relationship of Death, Sin and Law in 1 Cor 15:56", *Novum Testamentum* 35:3 (1993): 279; Collins, *First Corinthians*, 582–83.

[186] Vlachos, *The Law and the Knowledge of Good and Evil*, 86; cf. 1 Cor 15:21–22, 44–49.

saic law but is not limited to it. In other words, Mosaic law is not Paul's central focus in 1 Cor 15:56a.[187]

A similar atypical use of νόμος may occur in 1 Cor 9:20. Here Paul indicates that he is not "under the law". But what is the "law" he is not under? Most commentators assume that it is Mosaic law or its distinctively Jewish commandments. There is another possibility, however, not often considered. Since Paul could "both narrow and broaden" the inflection of νόμος,[188] Paul's focus in 1 Cor 9:20 could be on sectarian interpretation and expansion of Mosaic law.[189] As shown throughout this chapter, Second Temple Judaism was diverse and this diversity was reflected in variegated approaches to the law. The term ὑπὸ νόμον in 1 Cor 9:20 may refer to those who were under a Pharisaic interpretation of the law as Bishop John Lightfoot proposed at Cambridge in 1664:

> He distinguished, as it seems by the verse before, between the "Jews", and those that are "under the law": which may be understood of the Jews in general, and of the Pharisees in particular; because the Pharisees seemed more to subject themselves to the law than the rest of the nation.[190]

Notably, Paul uses νόμος in reference to Pharisaic interpretation of Mosaic law in Phil 3:5. He was no longer κατὰ νόμον Φαρισαῖος – "according to [sectarian standards of the] law, a Pharisee" (Phil 3:5). Eating ordinary food in a state of ritual purity was no longer Paul's consistent lifestyle. When associating with Pharisees in a table-fellowship context, however, he could adapt to Pharisaic standards of ritual purity in order to please his host. 1 Cor 9:20 may thus be elucidated as follows, "To those under [a Pharisaic interpretation of] the law I became as one under [a Pharisaic interpretation of] the law (though

---

[187] "Hong is surely correct to note that Paul 'cannot think of it [divine law] without an awareness of the Mosaic law as its supreme example'. Yet this being so, Paul does not appear to be pondering Mosaic law in his Corinthian epigram but divine law in general and its relation to sin" (Vlachos, *The Law and the Knowledge of Good and Evil*, 80).

[188] James D. G. Dunn, "Paul and the Torah: The Role and Function of the Law in the Theology of Paul the Apostle", in *The New Perspective on Paul: Collected Essays* (Tübingen: Mohr Siebeck, 2005), 447.

[189] Congruent with this view, Bruce, *I and II Corinthians*, 87, understands νόμος in 1 Cor 9:20 to be "the Jewish law, consisting of the 613 written precepts of the Pentateuch together, probably, with their oral amplification ('the tradition of the elders') accepted as the divinely appointed way of life".

[190] John Lightfoot, *A Commentary on the New Testament from the Talmud and Hebraica: Matthew – 1 Corinthians* (Peabody: Hendrickson, 1979), 4:222. Gerard Sloyan, "Did Paul Think That Jews and Jewish Christians Must Follow Torah?" in *Bursting the Bonds? A Jewish-Christian Dialogue on Jesus and Paul* (Maryknoll: Orbis, 1990), 172, also identifies the term ὑπὸ νόμον with Pharisees, "This seems to hint at a distinction between ordinary Jews and a new class of Law observants ('those under the Law') who were perhaps the 'separated' or *perushim* to which he gave his allegiance as a young man".

I myself am not under [a Pharisaic interpretation of] the law) so that I might win those under [a Pharisaic interpretation of] the law".

In the same way that νόμος in 1 Cor 15:56a may be refracted through the "edenically informed" tradition of the Fall in Gen 3, which serves as its "theological substructure",[191] Paul's use of νόμος in 1 Cor 9:20 may be refracted through the "halakhically informed" *tradition of the elders* (παράδοσιν τῶν πρεσβυτέρων) which interprets Mosaic law (Mark 7:3–5; Josephus, *Ant.* 13.297; Gal 1:14). The expression τοῖς ὑπὸ νόμον ("those under the law") would thus refer to "Pharisees". Alternatively, τοῖς ὑπὸ νόμον may refer more broadly to Jews who were like Pharisees, viz. those who scrupulously observed the law. August L. C. Heydenreich notes in his commentary on 1 Corinthians that this interpretation avoids the problem of repetition in 1 Cor 9:20 (Jews = those under the law):

> Οἱ Ἰουδαῖοι are Jews in general, people devoted to mosaic religion. To be distinguished from them are οἱ ὑπὸ νόμον, either: *the more zealous* (*acriores*) patrons and defenders of Mosaic law, such as *v.c.* the Pharisees were, very tenacious of those laws, binding themselves and others to them very tightly (*strictissime*), Gal. 4.21 . . . Against those who take τοῖς ὑπὸ νόμον *to be exactly the same people as* τοῖς Ἰουδαίοις, there stands this very weighty objection, namely that there are no reasons why we should think that the Apostle repeated the same thing in other words . . . Others agree with us in this, indeed, that τοὺς Ἰουδ. *are professors of Jewish religion in general*, and τοὺς ὑπὸ νόμον *rigorous Jews*, observing the Mosaic law as strictly as possible.[192]

Peter Richardson concurs that τοῖς ὑπὸ νόμον in 1 Cor 9:20 refers to Jews who are particularly strict in their observance of Torah:

> In 1 Corinthians 9:19ff. the meaning of *Ioudaios* is not necessarily equivalent to "being under law". It seems to mean instead a Jew who is not particularly scrupulous about his observance, whereas the next phrase represents the one who is scrupulous.[193]

Markus Bockmuehl arrives at the same position:

> When he eats with conservative Jews, on the other hand, he is prepared to accommodate himself to their stricter parameters of observance. Thus, "not being under the law" means that while Paul himself does not affirm the narrowly ethnic type of halakhah, he can happily adapt to it and operate within it, if thereby he can win some of his stricter compatriots.[194]

More recently, Richard Phua, in his 2005 monograph *Idolatry and Authority: A Study of 1 Corinthians 8.1–11.1 in the Light of the Jewish Diaspora*, raises the possibility that ὑπὸ νόμον in 1 Cor 9:20 may refer to "strict Jews":

---

[191] Vlachos, *The Law and the Knowledge of Good and Evil*, 8, 10.
[192] Heydenreich, *Commentarius in priorem divi Pauli ad Corinthios epistolam*, 2:41–42; trans. J. M. F. Heath.
[193] Richardson, *Israel in the Apostolic Church*, 122.
[194] Bockmuehl, *Jewish Law in Gentile Churches*, 171.

To the Jews, Paul says he becomes "like" (ὡς) a Jew. However, he does not say anything about the Law, which may suggest that there are Jews who, though they may be Jews, do not adhere strictly to the Law (see chapter 4 above). The second group, those under the Law, could refer to the Jews who may be described as strict Jews with regard to their strict adherence to the Law of Moses.[195]

If Heydenreich, Richardson, Bockmuehl and Phua are correct, "those under the law" might be interpreted to mean more broadly "those under [strict interpretation of] the law".[196] It follows that Paul's statement "I myself am not under the law" need not imply that Paul ceased to be a Torah-observant Jew. It would only mean that he stopped living according to Pharisaic or particularly strict standards of Torah observance as a consistent lifestyle. This argument will be unpacked in chapter 5.

4.4.4 "Without the Law" (ἄνομος)

Paul writes in 1 Cor 9:21, "To those without the law (ἀνόμοις) I became as one without the law (ὡς ἄνομος) . . . so that I might win those without the law (ἀνόμους)". Who are the ἀνόμους? Most commentators identify the ἀνόμους as Gentiles. This is almost certain given the 1 Cor 8:1–11:1 context and the recapitulation of 1 Cor 9:19–23 in 1 Cor 10:32–33 which refers to Jews and Greeks (Gentiles). But the question still remains, "Why did Paul use the term ἀνόμοις ('those without the law') instead of ἔθνεσιν ('Gentiles'; 1 Cor 1:23) or Ἕλλησιν ('Greeks'; 1 Cor 10:32)?" In answer to this question, Stowers proposes that Paul wanted to emphasize that these people were sinners. Stowers notes that the primary meaning of ἄνομος is not "without law" but "*lawless*" in the sense of being "*against the law*":

In sum, *anomos* and its cognates almost always mean evil, wicked, or sinful in Jewish literature before 70 C.E., and the vast majority of examples refer to Jews or to the wicked in general and not to gentiles. It comes as no surprise, then, that the *RSV* employs transgressor, lawless men, lawlessness, evildoer, iniquity, and wickedness to translate *anomos* and *anomia*. The exceptions, of course, remain "outside the law" for *anomos* in 1 Cor 9:21 and "without the law" for *anomōs* in Rom 2:12. Judging from pagan, Jewish, and Christian usage, either Paul forged a nearly unique usage in these two texts that is at odds with other Jewish writers or the traditional reading is highly questionable. The accepted reading seems even more problematic on the realization that Paul himself uses these terms in the normal way elsewhere. In Rom 4:7 he quotes Ps 31:1. There the *RSV* translates *hoi anomiai* as "iniquities". In 6:9 the *RSV* renders *anomia* as "iniquity". Both texts parallel the terms with "sin" (*hamartia*).[197]

---

[195] Richard Liong-Seng Phua, *Idolatry and Authority: A Study of 1 Corinthians 8.1–11.1 in the Light of the Jewish Diaspora* (London: T & T Clark, 2005), 193.

[196] Cf. Brad H. Young, *Paul the Jewish Theologian: A Pharisee among Christians, Jews, and Gentiles* (Peabody: Hendrickson, 1997), 20.

[197] Stanley K. Stowers, *A Rereading of Romans: Justice, Jews, and Gentiles* (New Haven: Yale University Press, 1994), 137; cf. Thomas C. Edwards, *A Commentary on the First Epistle to the Corinthians* (London: Hodder and Stoughton, 1903), 238.

Based on this evidence, Glad concurs that Paul associated closely with *sinners* (ἀνόμους) in an attempt to win them, "In his effort to benefit others, Paul was then willing to associate with people of different moral standing . . . Reverberations of the issues hinted at in 1 Cor 9:19–23 are found in its wider context in Paul's concern with a right and wrong form of association between different types of people both within and outside the community . . . Discussions on matters relating to the association with outsiders and the immoral occur in chapters 5–7, 9–10, and 14".[198]

The Stowers-Glad thesis makes an important contribution to understanding the meaning of ἄνομοι in 1 Cor 9:21. This not withstanding, Given is correct that some texts identify ἄνομοι with Gentiles (Wis 17; Acts 2:23) and context is the final decisor.[199] How then should ἀνόμοις be rendered in 1 Cor 9:19–23? I conclude with Richard Hays that ἀνόμοις (1 Cor 9:21) probably means "lawless" or "sinners".[200] However, the idol-food context of 1 Cor 8:1–11:1, and the recapitulation of 1 Cor 9:19–23 in 10:32–33 (which includes "Greeks"), would suggest that ἀνόμοις in 1 Cor 9:21 more accurately refers to "lawless Gentiles" or "Gentile sinners",[201] comparable to ἐθνῶν ἁμαρτωλοί ("Gentile sinners") in Gal 2:15. As Augustine put it, *"Now, whom does he wish to designate here except the Gentiles whom we call pagans"* (*Op. mon.* 11 [12]).[202]

4.4.5 "Though I Am Not Without the Law of God" (μὴ ὢν ἄνομος θεοῦ)

Paul writes in 1 Cor 9:21, "To those without the law/the lawless I became as one without the law/the lawless (though I am not without the law of God [μὴ ὢν ἄνομος θεοῦ]) . . ." Here Paul seems to clarify that his close association with Gentile sinners (for outreach purposes) should not be interpreted as a neglect or abandonment of "God's law" (νόμος θεοῦ).[203] But what exactly does Paul mean by νόμος θεοῦ ("God's law")? Notably, most commentators do not attempt to explicate this expression. It should be pointed out that if νόμος θεοῦ is a synonym for the "law of Moses", then the restrictive clause may be Paul's way of saying, "Do not misunderstand the nature of my association with Gentile sinners. I remain fully Torah observant". Such a declaration would be similar to the one Luke relates in Acts 21:24: "Thus all will

---

[198] Glad, *Paul and Philodemus*, 258.

[199] Given, *Paul's True Rhetoric*, 107.

[200] Hays, *First Corinthians*, 154. *Pace* Michael Winger, "The Law of Christ", *New Testament Studies* 46 (2000): 545–46; Thiselton, *The First Epistle to the Corinthians*, 703–704; Witherington, *Conflict and Community in Corinth*, 212.

[201] Schrage, *Der erste Brief an die Korinther*, 2:343 n. 377.

[202] Trans. Muldowney (FC). Cf. Gardner, *The Gifts of God and the Authentication of a Christian*, 102.

[203] Thiselton, *The First Epistle to the Corinthians*, 704.

know that there is nothing in what they have been told about you, but that you yourself also live in observance of the law (φυλάσσων τὸν νόμον)" (ESV).

Is there any basis for identifying "God's law" in 1 Cor 9:20 with "Mosaic law"? In point of fact, there is broad support given the common use of the locution in Second Temple Jewish literature. Throughout Israel's Scriptures and the apocryphal writings, Mosaic law is referred to as "the law of God" or "God's law" (νόμου τοῦ θεοῦ/νόμου θεοῦ).[204] Josephus likewise refers to the law of Moses as the law of God (νόμῳ τοῦ θεοῦ) in *Ant.* 11.121, 124, 130. Paul uses the same expression (νόμῳ τοῦ θεοῦ) in Rom 7:22 and 8:7 (cf. 7:25).

While Paul's use of νόμῳ τοῦ θεοῦ in Romans is sometimes interpreted to mean "will of God",[205] most exegetes maintain that νόμῳ τοῦ θεοῦ in Rom 7:22 is a direct reference to the law of Moses. Schreiner writes, "Obviously, νόμος refers to the Mosaic law in verse 22 . . . and in verse 25".[206] Dunn concurs, "Here beyond question, as most agree, νόμος is the Torah ('the law of God'), not just 'God's will in a general sense' (Käsemann)".[207] Moo similarly asserts, "'The law of God' is again the Mosaic law, the torah, to which Paul as a Jew was devoted".[208] J. Louis Martyn considers Paul's reference to "God's law" in Rom 7:22 "a literal and specific reference to 'the Law of Moses'".[209] Michael Winger concedes that "νόμος θεοῦ, invoked without any further explanation, is likely to be understood as Jewish law".[210]

The meaning of "God's law" in 1 Cor 9:21 is informed by Paul's explicit reference to Mosaic law earlier in chapter 9. Paul writes, "*Do I say this on human authority?* Does not *the law* (ὁ νόμος) also say the same? For it is written in *the law of Moses* (τῷ Μωϋσέως νόμῳ), 'You shall not muzzle an ox while it is treading out the grain'" (1 Cor 9:8–9). Here Paul emphatically cites the law of Moses as a divine authority,[211] "This authoritative law is not

---

[204] See LXX Josh 24:26; Ezra 7:12, 14, 21, 25 (2x); Neh 8:8, 18; 10:29(28), 30(29); Ps 36(37):31; Isa 30:9; Hos 4:6; Sir 41.8; Bar 4.12; 1 Esd 8.19, 21, 23–24; 3 Macc 7.10, 12; 2 Esd 7.20; 4 Macc 13.22.

[205] T. J. Deidun, *New Covenant Morality* (Rome: Biblical Institute, 1981), 199, 203.

[206] Thomas R. Schreiner, *Romans* (Grand Rapids: Baker, 1998), 375–76.

[207] James D. G. Dunn, *Romans 1–8* (Dallas: Word, 1988), 393.

[208] Moo, *The Epistle to the Romans*, 461.

[209] J. Louis Martyn, "*Nomos* Plus Genitive Noun in Paul: The History of God's Law", in *Early Christianity and Classical Culture: Comparative Studies in Honor of Abraham J. Malherbe* (ed. John T. Fitzgerald et al.; Leiden: Brill, 2003), 575.

[210] Winger, "The Law of Christ", 545.

[211] Thomas L. Brodie, "The Systematic Use of the Pentateuch in 1 Corinthians", in *The Corinthian Correspondence* (ed. R. Bieringer; Leuven: Leuven University Press, 1996), 445, notes that the "acknowledgement is lavish"; cf. Thielman, "The Coherence of Paul's View of the Law", 244. The fact that Paul does not make use of his right granted by Mosaic law does not mean that he rejected the authority of the law any more than his non-use of the right granted by Christ (1 Cor 9:14–15) means that he rejected the authority of Christ. Paul em-

some new Torah of Christ or ethic of guidance by the Holy Spirit, but, specifically, the law of Moses – the Jewish Torah".[212] Thus, "law of Moses" in 1 Cor 9:8–9 sets the default and prepares the reader to know how to interpret "God's law" in 1 Cor 9:20.

A final argument for a "law of Moses" reading of "God's law" in 1 Cor 9:21 is that Paul's rule in all the churches (1 Cor 7:17–20) stipulated that Jews were to remain practising Jews (the equivalent of "obeying the commandments of God for Jews") and not live as Gentiles:

> This is my rule in all the churches. Was anyone at the time of his call already circumcised? Let him not seek to remove the marks of circumcision [περιτετμημένος τις ἐκλήθη, μὴ ἐπισπάσθω]. Was anyone at the time of his call uncircumcised? Let him not seek circumcision. Circumcision is nothing, and uncircumcision is nothing; but *obeying the commandments of God* (τήρησις ἐντολῶν θεοῦ) is everything. Let each of you remain in the condition in which you were called [ἕκαστος ἐν τῇ κλήσει ᾗ ἐκλήθη, ἐν ταύτῃ μενέτω] (1 Cor 7:17–20).

I contend that the second restrictive clause in 1 Cor 9:19–23 ("though I am not without the law of God") points back to 1 Cor 7:17–20.[213] Frank Thielman concurs, "'The law of God' here, moreover, is probably identical with 'the commandments of God' in 7:19".[214] The two passages (1 Cor 7:17–20; 9:21) side by side suggest that Paul continued to live according to "God's law" (i.e. "the law of Moses" of 1 Cor 9:8–9). Paul was circumcised and thus called to live the circumcised life as defined by the commandments of God in the Torah incumbent upon Jews. It is reasonable to assume that Paul kept his own rule (2.2.3).

My proposal to read the second restrictive clause ("though I am not without the law of God") in light of *Paul's calling to live as a Jew and not as a Gentile* (1 Cor 7:17–20) is not new. Augustine posited the same interpretation in *c*. 400 C.E. After quoting 1 Cor 9:19–22, Augustine comments:

> His actions were the manifestation of a free and openly acknowledged conviction which prompted him to say: "Was one called having been circumcised? Let him not become uncircumcised [1 Cor 7:18]", *that is, let him not live as if he had not been circumcised*... Because of the view which he expressed in the words: "Was one called having been circumcised? Let him not become uncircumcised. Was one called being uncircumcised? Let him not be circumcised [1 Cor 7:18]", *he actually conformed to obligations* which he was considered to have simulated by those who did not understand or who paid scant attention. For, he was a Jew and he was called after having been circumcised; he did not wish to return to his former

---

phasizes his regard for the "law of Moses" as "*law*" and directly refers to it as a divine authority.

[212] Thielman, "The Coherence of Paul's View of the Law", 241.

[213] See Conzelmann, *A Commentary on the First Epistle to the Corinthians*, 160; Edgar Krentz, "Paul: All Things to All People – Flexible and Welcoming", *Currents in Theology and Mission* 24:3 (1997): 240; Coppins, *The Interpretation of Freedom in the Letters of Paul*, 55–77.

[214] Thielman, *Paul and the Law*, 104; cf. 101; Thielman, "The Coherence of Paul's View of the Law", 239; Garland, *1 Corinthians*, 432.

state, that is, he was unwilling to live as if he had not been circumcised. For, this was within his power. He was not under the Law as were those who observed it slavishly; nevertheless, he was in the law of God and of Christ. For the Law of the Jews was not one law and that of God another.[215]

Augustine interpreted 1 Cor 7:17–24 to mean that Jews were *called* to live as Jews and not to Gentilise themselves. Moreover, he saw that the literary context connected 1 Cor 7:17–24 to 9:19–23 and he interpreted the latter in light of the former.[216] Paul remained a Jew because he was called by God to be a Jew. In chapter 5, the meaning of the second restrictive clause ("though I am not without the law of God") will be further unpacked.

4.4.6 "In Christ's Law" (ἔννομος Χριστοῦ)

The term ἔννομος Χριστοῦ (1 Cor 9:21) is an enigma in New Testament studies. Below I will briefly survey how contemporary scholars have interpreted the expression and offer some preliminary conclusions.

Graham Stanton posits that "'I am under Christ's jurisdiction' catches the sense".[217] For Stanton, ἔννομος Χριστοῦ (1 Cor 9:21) = τὸν νόμον τοῦ Χριστοῦ (Gal 6:2),[218] with νόμος referring to the law of Moses in both texts.[219] The "subtle play on words" in 1 Cor 9:20–21 prevented Paul from using the exact term again. Wilson similarly interprets "each of the four uses of νόμος in 5.13–6.10 as a reference to the Law of Moses (including the Law

---

[215] Augustine, *Op. mon.* 11 [12]; trans. Muldowney [FC], italics mine. Cf. Schrage, *Der erste Brief an die Korinther*, 2:351.

[216] "In 1 Corinthians 7, Paul responded to the first of a series of questions or issues the Corinthian Christians had raised with him by letter. 1 Corinthians 8–10 takes up a second issue. 1 Corinthians 7 is, therefore, an important part in the literary context of 1 Cor 9:19–23" (Hall, "All Things to All People", 145). Both sections (1 Cor 7:17–24 and 1 Cor 9:19–23) refer to (1) Jews and Gentiles; (2) God's law/commandments; and (3) Being free/slave. The term Paul uses in 1 Cor 7:17 to refer to his *rule* in all the churches (διατάσσω) is the same word he uses in 1 Cor 9:14 to refer to the Lord's *command* (διατάσσω). 1 Cor 7:16 and 9:22 are the only two places in the letter where Paul refers to one person saving another. See Peter Richardson, "'I Say, Not the Lord': Personal Opinion, Apostolic Authority and the Development of Early Christian Halakhah", *Tyndale Bulletin* 31 (1980): 65–86.

[217] Graham Stanton, "The Law of Christ: A Neglected Theological Gem?" in *Reading Texts, Seeking Wisdom: Scripture and Theology* (ed. David F. Ford and Graham Stanton; London: SCM, 2003), 174.

[218] Also Bouwman, *Berufen zur Freiheit*, 92.

[219] "Gal. 6.2 is the thirty-first of Paul's references in Galatians to νόμος, law. In nearly all the preceding instances the reference is to '*the* Law', that is, the law of Moses. So it is most unlikely that without alerting his listeners Paul changes tack and refers to the teaching of Jesus as 'law', or to 'showing love for others' (i.e. bearing the burdens of others) as 'law'" (Stanton, "The Law of Christ", 172). See also Martyn, *Galatians,* 555. Contra Donald B. Garlington, "Burden Bearing and the Recovery of Offending Christians (Galatians 6:1–5)", *Trinity Journal* 12 (1991): 166–67, who argues that "'the law of Christ', as in 1 Cor 9:21, is purposely set in contrast to the law of Moses".

of Christ in 6.2)".²²⁰ J. Louis Martyn concurs, "The expression ἔννομος Χριστοῦ in 1 Cor 9:21b is surely to be taken together with ὁ νόμος τοῦ Χριστοῦ of Gal 6:2, *the Law [of Moses/God's Law] as it has been taken in hand by Christ*".²²¹ By contrast, Winger doubts that there is a correspondence between ἔννομος Χριστοῦ (1 Cor 9:21) and τὸν νόμον τοῦ Χριστοῦ (Gal 6:2) but offers no reason.²²²

Dodd considers dominical commands (1 Cor 7:10; 9:14) to be "constituent elements in the 'law of Christ'".²²³ Furnish, however, rejects this argument given that ἔννομος Χριστοῦ (1 Cor 9:21) is "not the principal matter in the context, but is inserted to guard against a possible misunderstanding of the preceding remark".²²⁴ Also, dominical commands do not appear in the context of τὸν νόμον τοῦ Χριστοῦ in Gal 6:2.²²⁵ A more nuanced argument to deflect Furnish's criticism is put forward by Dunn who equates ἔννομος Χριστοῦ with Christ's ethic of loving one's neighbour, "As one could fulfill the law by loving one's neighbor, so one could love the neighbor by keeping the law".²²⁶

Hays argues that "By using the expression 'under Christ's law' . . . [Paul] is asserting that the pattern of Christ's self-sacrificial death on the cross has now become the normative pattern for his own existence".²²⁷ Horrell concurs, "The wider context of 1 Cor 9.21 thus adds further plausibility to the idea that the νόμος of Christ to which Paul conforms is exactly what Hays has seen as the law of Christ in Gal. 6.2: a normative pattern determined by 'the paradigmatic self-giving of Jesus Christ' (Hays 1987:275)'".²²⁸ Carson and Thiselton adopt a view equivalent to Dodd and Hayes/Horrell combined.²²⁹

Glad contends that ἔννομος Χριστοῦ (1 Cor 9:21) points to Paul's imitation of Christ's table-fellowship with sinners (1 Cor 11:1).²³⁰ Paul employed

---

[220] Todd A. Wilson, "The Law of Christ and the Law of Moses: Reflections on a Recent Trend in Interpretation", *Currents in Biblical Research* 5:1 (2006): 129–50; cf. Wilson, *The Curse of the Law and the Crisis in Galatia*, 141.

[221] Martyn, "*Nomos* Plus Genitive Noun in Paul", 584 n. 23, emphasis mine; also Schrage, *Der erste Brief an die Korinther*, 2:345.

[222] Winger, "The Law of Christ", 545.

[223] C. H. Dodd, "ENNOMOS KRISTOU", in *Studia Paulina in honorem J. de Zwaan* (Haarlem: Bohn, 1953), 108. Similarly, Conzelmann, *A Commentary on the First Epistle to the Corinthians*, 161; Witherington, *Conflict and Community in Corinth*, 213.

[224] Victor P. Furnish, *Theology and Ethics in Paul* (New York: Abingdon, 1968), 61.

[225] Cf. Ernst Bammel, *Judaica et Paulina: Kleine Schriften* (Tübingen: Mohr Siebeck, 1997), 2:324.

[226] James D. G. Dunn, "'The Law of Faith', 'the Law of the Spirit' and 'the Law of Christ'", in *Theology and Ethics in Paul and His Interpreters: Essays in Honor of Victor Paul Furnish* (ed. Eugene H. Lovering and Jerry L. Sumney; Nashville: Abingdon, 1996), 78.

[227] Hays, *First Corinthians*, 154.

[228] Horrell, *Solidarity and Difference*, 231.

[229] Carson, "Pauline Inconsistency", 12; Thiselton, *The First Epistle to the Corinthians*, 704.

[230] Glad, *Paul and Philodemus*, 257–60.

the term ἔννομος Χριστοῦ ("in Christ's law") to defend his accommodation-oriented association with immoral persons for the purpose of outreach (τοῖς ἀνόμοις ὡς ἄνομος . . . ἵνα κερδάνω τοὺς ἀνόμους [1 Cor 9:21]). The apostle anticipated that some might interpret his association with the Gentile lawless to mean that Paul himself was lawless.

This study is largely in agreement with scholars who identify ἔννομος Χριστοῦ (1 Cor 9:21) with τὸν νόμον τοῦ Χριστοῦ (Gal 6:2). One would reasonably expect, however, some modulation in the way the expressions are used given the different audiences and settings. Given that νόμος θεοῦ in 1 Cor 9:20 almost certainly means "law of Moses", and given the consistent meaning of νόμος as "law of Moses" leading up to Gal 6:2, it is likely that ἔννομος Χριστοῦ refers to the "law of Moses" (*pace* Hays and Horrell). Lastly, ἔννομος Χριστοῦ does seem related to Paul's *imitatio Christi* ethic in 1 Cor 11:1 (as Kim argues), "Be imitators of me, as I am of Christ" (μιμηταί μου γίνεσθε καθὼς κἀγὼ Χριστοῦ). A reading that brings together the interpretations of Stanton, Wilson, Martyn and Glad may thus be proposed: ἔννομος Χριστοῦ *refers to God's law (the law of Moses) in the hand of Christ as reflected in Christ's association with sinners.* This will be discussed further in chapter 5.

4.4.7 "Win" (κερδήσω)

David Daube's 1947 essay "Κερδαίνω as a Missionary Term"[231] is the seminal statement on the term κερδαίνω, which is used five times in 1 Cor 9:19–22. Daube argues that the meaning of κερδαίνω, in the sense of "to win over an unbeliever to your faith" (e.g. 1 Cor 9:19–22; 1 Pet 3:1) or "to win back a sinner to the way of life required by his and your faith" (e.g. Matt 18:15), is rooted in pre-Christian Judaism. Stated differently, Paul's use of κερδαίνω was thoroughly Jewish. A full discussion of Daube's philological argument need not detain us here. What is important to note is that Daube concedes that the evidence is wanting for the use of κερδαίνω in reference to Jewish proselytism of Gentiles. Daube maintains, however, that sufficient evidence exists to demonstrate that Jews employed κερδαίνω in the sense of "to win back a [Jewish] sinner" and he infers that the connotation "to win over Gentile proselytes" would have been a natural extension of this usage.

Significantly, most contemporary studies of 1 Cor 9:19–23 that cite Daube agree with his conclusion on κερδαίνω.[232] Craig Keener notes that "commen-

---

[231] Daube, "κερδαίνω as a Missionary Term", 109–20; Daube, *The New Testament and Rabbinic Judaism*, 352–61; Daube, *New Testament Judaism*, 575–82.

[232] Notable exceptions include Schnabel, *Early Christian Mission*, 2:959; Garland, *1 Corinthians*, 429 n. 12; Vollenweider, *Freiheit als neue Schöpfung*, 208; Carson, "Pauline Inconsistency", 9–10.

tators follow D. Daube".²³³ Thiselton writes, "Daube shows that it [κερδαίνω] was probably a technical term for 'winning a proselyte' in Judaism, reflecting the Hebrew נשכר (*niskar*, the Niphal of *sakar, to hire, to gain*)".²³⁴ Schrage concurs that κερδαίνω "is probably taken from Judaism. According to Daube, we have here in κερδαίνειν a technical term for the Hebrew נשכר and השתכר in the meaning to win proselytes or to win back sinners".²³⁵ Fee remarks, "Daube has demonstrated that its Hebraic counterpart had already been taken over into Judaism as missionary language".²³⁶

How does this study evaluate Daube's case and the half-century of scholarly consensus behind it? Despite Daube's uncritical use of rabbinic sources, it appears that his instincts were likely correct, even if the first-century evidence is largely circumstantial. Paul employs κερδαίνω five times in 1 Cor 9:19–22. The emphatic use of the term would seem to suggest that Paul is drawing on a pre-existing meaning of the term which Daube convincingly argues is Jewish in origin. Exegetes are at a loss to explain Paul's locution (which does not appear in Greco-Roman sources) in any other way. In short, Daube provides a reasonable and convincing case.

Two additional observations are noteworthy. First, Daube does not anticipate Goodman's interpretation of Matt 23:15 that Pharisees actively sought Jewish converts to Pharisaic Judaism. Nevertheless, Daube's conclusions fit Goodman's argument for intra-Jewish proselytizing. The two proposals are mutually supportive and add to the case that Paul was drawing from a living element in first-century Judaism when he said that he became as a Jew to the Jews in order to win Jews.

Second, if the term κερδαίνω was used by Pharisees (which is plausible given Paul's Pharisaic background and the evidence for Pharisaic proselytizing [Matt 23:15]), then it may be reasonably conjectured that Paul not only borrowed the word, but that he used it in a way consonant with its Pharisaic usage, viz. recruiting new members through table-fellowship and living among the masses.

---

²³³ Craig S. Keener, *1–2 Corinthians* (Cambridge: Cambridge University Press, 2005), 80.
²³⁴ Thiselton, *The First Epistle to the Corinthians*, 701. Cf. *BAGD* 429; *EDNT* 2:283–84.
²³⁵ Schrage, *Der erste Brief an die Korinther*, 2:339.
²³⁶ Fee, *The First Epistle to the Corinthians*, 427 n. 24. Also Rode, "El Modelo de Adaptación de Pablo Según 1 Corintios 9:19–23", 336; Butarbutar, "Resolving a Dispute, Past and Present", 222; O'Brien, *Gospel and Mission in the Writings of Paul*, 95; Gardner, *The Gifts of God and the Authentication of a Christian*, 98–99; Neller, "1 Corinthians 9:19–22", 139; Richardson and Gooch, "Accommodation Ethics", 95, 120–21; M. J. Joseph, "A Leap into the 'Slavery of Paul' from an Indian Angle", *The Indian Journal of Theology* 26:2 (1977): 74; Conzelmann, *A Commentary on the First Epistle to the Corinthians*, 160; Barrett, *A Commentary on The First Epistle to the Corinthians*, 211; H. J. Schoeps, *Paul: The Theology of the Apostle in the Light of Jewish Religious History* (trans. Harold Knight; Philadelphia: Westminster, 1961), 231.

4.4.8 "Weak" (ἀσθενεῖς)[237]

There are various positions on "the weak" (1 Cor 9:22) in contemporary scholarship. Some argue that Paul's "win" and "save" language in 1 Cor 9:19–23 indicates that the weak are non-Jesus-believers.[238] This view is supported by Paul's closing statement, "I do it all for the sake of the gospel" (1 Cor 9:23). Witherington thus infers that winning the weak refers to Paul's "way of evangelizing and presenting the gospel to the lost".[239]

On the other hand, a large number of scholars maintain that Paul's view of salvation is more complex.[240] He wrote to the Philippians: "*work out your own salvation* with fear and trembling" (Phil 2:12). Paul comments at the beginning of the Corinthian letter, "For the message about the cross is foolishness to those who are perishing, but to us who are *being saved* it is the power of God" (1 Cor 1:18). Moreover, Paul refers to "weak" Jesus-believers who stumble and fall, even to the point of destruction, over the issue of idol-food (1 Cor 8:7–11). As Richard Hays points out, these texts suggest that the weak in view are Jesus-believers, or include Jesus-believers, whom Paul is leading along the path of salvation:

The weak Christians, as we have already seen in chapter 8, are in danger – in Paul's view – of falling away from Christ and therefore not being saved (see also the illustration in 10:1–13). Thus, his continuing identification with the weak aims not only to gain converts but also to strengthen their adherence to the community and to help them along the path to salvation.[241]

A further argument in support of Hays's position is that the semantic range of κερδαίνω ("to win") includes the sense of "*to win back* a sinner to the way of life required by his faith" (as Daube contends; cf. κερδαίνω in Matt 18:15).

---

[237] The word ὡς is added before ἀσθενεῖς in ℵ² C D F Maj. Omission receives strong support from P⁴⁶ ℵ* A B 1739.

[238] Garland, *1 Corinthians*, 434; David A. Black, "A Note on 'the Weak' in 1 Corinthians 9:22", *Biblica* 64 (1983): 240–42; cf. Nanos, "The *Polytheist* Identity of the 'Weak', and Paul's Strategy to 'Gain' Them", 179–210.

[239] Witherington, *Conflict and Community in Corinth*, 213.

[240] Horrell, *Solidarity and Difference*, 260; O'Brien, *Gospel and Mission in the Writings of Paul*, 95; Schrage, *Der erste Brief an die Korinther*, 2:346–47. Also Barton, "All Things to All People", 279; Glad, *Paul and Philodemus*, 274–76; Back, *All Things to All Men*, 13; Gardner, *The Gifts of God and the Authentication of a Christian*, 99; Blomberg, *1 Corinthians*, 184; Kistemaker, *1 Corinthians*, 309; Thielman, "The Coherence of Paul's View of the Law", 244; Neller, "1 Corinthians 9:19–22", 136–38; Fee, *The First Epistle to the Corinthians*, 431; Carson, "Pauline Inconsistency", 14; Morris, *The First Epistle of Paul to the Corinthians*, 136; Ebeling, *The Truth of the Gospel*, 115; Meeks, "The Christian Proteus", 438; Barrett, *A Commentary on The First Epistle to the Corinthians*, 215; Lietzmann, *Die Briefe des Apostels Paulus*, 43; Moffatt, *The First Epistle of Paul to the Corinthians*, 123; Robertson and Plummer, *A Critical and Exegetical Commentary on the First Epistle of St. Paul to the Corinthians*, 192; Meyer, *Paul's First Epistle to the Corinthians*, 1:273; Godet, *Commentary on the First Epistle of St. Paul to the Corinthians*, 39.

[241] Hays, *First Corinthians*, 155.

Finally, some scholars regard the weak as weaker members of society. Paul refers to the weak in this way in 1 Cor 1:26–29, "Consider your own call, brothers and sisters: not many of you were wise by human standards, not many were powerful, not many were of noble birth. But God chose what is foolish in the world to shame the wise; God chose what is weak (ἀσθενῆ) in the world to shame the strong; God chose what is low and despised in the world, things that are not, to reduce to nothing things that are, so that no one might boast in the presence of God". Thiselton concludes that the "weak" were the economically vulnerable and dependent:

> Hence these are people who are most probably the vulnerable in sociopolitical terms, forced into dependency on patrons, owners, or employers . . . The weak stand in contrast to those with "social power, influence, political status . . . ability or competence in a variety of areas" and by contrast have "low social standing" and crave for identity, recognition, and acceptance.[242]

Paul thus became weak to the weak in the sense that he "voluntarily enslaved himself".[243] He "took on the lifestyle and condition of the weak . . . he lowered himself to the social status of the weak by refusing the patronage of the rich and becoming a manual labourer [1 Cor 4:10b, 12a]".[244] Paul may have also viewed his ethic of becoming weak to the weak as an imitation of Christ who became weak to the weak:

> "For while we were still weak, at the right time Christ died for the ungodly" (Rom 5:6). The gospel is the story of the Son of God taking on weakness for the sake of humankind, and Paul asserts that he follows this same divine paradigm (2 Cor 13:4; cf. 2 Cor 8:9; 6:10). This is why he boasts in his weakness (2 Cor 11:30; 12:5, 9–10; 13:9), because God's power is made perfect in weakness and is more effective in winning others to the gospel of Christ's cross.[245]

How should the data be evaluated? It seems plausible that each of these perspectives adds to the overall picture. They are not mutually exclusive. 1 Cor 9:19–23 focuses on non-Jesus-believers. This does not necessarily mean, however, that Jesus-believers are excluded from the purview of 1 Cor 9:22. In all likelihood, Paul has non-Jesus-believers *and* Jesus-believers in mind in 1 Cor 9:22, the latter indicated by Paul's reference to the "weak" in the Corinthian congregation for whom idol-food is a stumbling block (1 Cor 8:7, 9–10). Perhaps some of these Jesus-believers were also economically vulnerable and dependent (1 Cor 1:26–29). Paul became weak to the weak by voluntarily becoming economically vulnerable and closely associating with these people. He toiled to earn a living as a tentmaker among them (Acts 18:3). The lack of

---

[242] Thiselton, *The First Epistle to the Corinthians*, 705–706. Cf. Theissen, "The Strong and the Weak in Corinth", 121–43.

[243] Neller, "1 Corinthians 9:19–22", 138.

[244] Hays, *First Corinthians*, 154–55; cf. Barton, "All Things to All People", 285; Martin, *Slavery as Salvation*, 123–24.

[245] Garland, *1 Corinthians*, 434.

the ὡς in 1 Cor 9:22 may indicate that his adaptation was not temporary but a consistent lifestyle (Acts 18:11, 18). In becoming weak to the weak, Paul imitated Christ (the Jewish Messiah)[246] who lowered himself so that the poor could be lifted up.[247]

4.5 Summary and Conclusion

This chapter responded to the textual arguments given by scholars for why 1 Cor 9:19–23 precludes a Torah-observant Paul. It was found that the case for a Jewish accommodation setting of 1 Cor 9:19–23 is strong given Paul's use of Jewish sources and nomistic language in 1 Cor 8:1–11:1. By contrast, there are no explicit attributions or quotations in the literary context of 1 Cor 9:19–23 to give weight to the argument that Paul draws on Greco-Roman *topoi*.

---

[246] Paul viewed Christ as the Jewish Messiah. This is apparent from the apostle's use of Χριστός with the titular article in Rom 9:5 and 15:3, 7 and his identification of Christ with the Jewish people in both texts (Rom 9:3–5; 15:8). See Wright, *The Climax of the Covenant*, 41–55; Hafemann, "Eschatology and Ethics", 172; James D. G. Dunn, *Romans 9–16* (Dallas: Word, 1988), 838; Davies, *Jewish and Pauline Studies*, 123–24; *pace* I. Howard Marshall, "A New Understanding of the Present and the Future: Paul and Eschatology", in *The Road from Damascus: The Impact of Paul's Conversion on His Life, Thought, and Ministry* (ed. Richard N. Longenecker; Grand Rapids: Eerdmans, 1997), 53. In Pauline Messianism, Christ is "a servant (διάκονον) of the circumcised" (Rom 15:8). He is the Isaiah 11 "Root of Jesse" (Rom 15:12; LXX Isa 11:1, 10). It is notable that the Root of Jesse is concerned about the poor and the meek (Isa 11:4; cf. 42:3). See Seyoon Kim, *Paul and the New Perspective: Second Thoughts on the Origin of Paul's Gospel* (Grand Rapids: Eerdmans, 2002), 126–27. Empowered by the Spirit of God – with wisdom, understanding and *strength* (ἰσχύος; Isa 11:2) – the Jewish Messiah, upheld the weak.

[247] Paul writes of Christ's accommodation, "For you know the generous act of our Lord Jesus Christ, that though he was rich, yet for your sakes he became poor, so that by his poverty you might become rich" (2 Cor 8:9). Paul's use of the same language ("as poor, yet making many rich" [2 Cor 6:10]) to describe his own life suggests that Paul sought to imitate Christ's self-emptying generosity. Cf. 1 Cor 9:19; 11:1; 2 Cor 11:7; Rom 12:16; 15:1–3 and the Jewish view of divine hospitality and accommodation (Lev 19:9–10; Deut 10:16–19; Ps 113:4–8; Isa 42:1–4; 52:13–53:12; 61:1–2; Josephus, *Ant*. 4.231–237; Philo, *Virt*. 90–91; *Spec*. 1.307–308; 4.73–74). "In the context of a banquet given by a Pharisee, Jesus [in Luke's account] instructs the guests regarding whom to 'invite' (14:13, 21). They are to 'invite' those who cannot repay (14:14). In specific terms they are told to 'invite' the 'poor', the 'crippled', the 'lame', and the 'blind' (14:13, 21). Luke links the theme of 'inviting' (καλέω) to Jesus' table fellowship with 'toll-collectors and sinners' and his mission of 'calling' (καλέσαι) them to repentance in 5:32. The 'invitation' to the 'poor', 'crippled', 'lame', and 'blind' links the narrative to 7:21–22 and the blending of Isa 35:5 with Isa 61:1; and to the Nazareth proclamation of 4:18 . . . All of the key terms – 'seek', 'lost', and 'save' – which have been identified in Ezekiel 34 as referring to the role of the future Davidic shepherd-prince, are included as part of the defining elements of the mission of Jesus in Luke" (Adams, *The Sinner in Luke*, 154, 160; cf. 69–104, 186–87).

Possible Jewish analogues to Pauline accommodation were identified in Jews associating with Jews, Jews associating with Gentiles, Jewish outreach and the ideal Jewish guest. Kim argues convincingly that Paul's principle of adaptation stems from Paul's *imitatio Christi* ethic. However, Kim's assertion that Paul was able to associate with Gentiles only because of Jesus' nullification of the Jewish food/purity regulations (Mark 7:15, 19b) lacks historical and biblical support. Concerning Paul's specific language in 1 Cor 9:19–23: the term ἐλεύθερος ("free") in 1 Cor 9:19 probably does not mean free from Mosaic law but free from human masters. The expression ὑπὸ νόμον ("under the law") in 1 Cor 9:20 does not necessarily mean "under [the authority of] the law"; it can denote Jews who observed Pharisaic halakhah (κατὰ νόμον Φαρισαῖος [Phil 3:5]) or Jews who strictly observed the law. In these readings, "under the law" is a subset of "Jews". By contrast, the traditional interpretation of ὑπὸ νόμον introduces an unnecessary repetition into the 1 Cor 9:19–23 pericope. The term ἄνομος (1 Cor 9:21) probably refers to "lawless Gentiles". The phrase νόμος θεοῦ ("law of God") in 1 Cor 9:21b in all likelihood is coterminous with law of Moses and equivalent to the ἐντολῶν θεοῦ ("commandments of God") in 1 Cor 7:19. Contextually, Paul's use of ἔννομος Χριστοῦ ("in the law of Christ") in 1 Cor 9:21b would seem to represent the law of Moses in the hand of Christ as iterated in Christ's association with sinners. This chapter has shown that neither the setting nor the language of 1 Cor 9:19–23 necessitates the consensus view that 1 Cor 9:19–23 precludes a Torah-observant Paul.

Part I (chapters 2–4) of this monograph has focused on destabilising the traditional view of 1 Cor 9:19–23. In keeping with the primary thrust of the monograph, I have pointed out holes in the intertextual, contextual and textual arguments behind the consensus reading and have demonstrated that scholars overstate their case when they use 1 Cor 9:19–23 as incontrovertible evidence that Paul was not Torah observant. In Part II (chapter 5), I will focus on the secondary aim of the monograph – to offer an interpretation of 1 Cor 9:19–23 that is compatible with a Torah-observant Paul.

Part II

A Proposed Interpretation of 1 Cor 9:19–23

Chapter 5

Imitating Christ's Accommodation and Open Table-Fellowship

Chapters 2–4 addressed the three rationales given by scholars for why 1 Cor 9:19–23 precludes a Torah-observant Paul. In this chapter, the data will be brought together and a proposal made for how 1 Cor 9:19–23 can be understood as the discourse of a Jew who remained within the bounds of pluriform Second Temple Judaism. I will present an exegetical case that 1 Cor 9:19–23 reflects Paul's ethic of imitating Christ's accommodation and open table-fellowship.

5.1 The Exegetical Context of 1 Cor 9:19–23

The thesis that Paul followed Christ's example of accommodation finds support in the correlation between 1 Cor 9:19–23 and 10:32–11:1. Almost all recent studies of 1 Cor 8:1–11:1 note that Paul echoes 1 Cor 9:19–23 in 10:32–33, providing a kind of recapitulation of his earlier comments.[1] Five reasons

---

[1] Horrell, *Solidarity and Difference*, 177; Thiselton, *The First Epistle to the Corinthians*, 794; Collins, *First Corinthians*, 390. Also Garland, *1 Corinthians*, 501–502; Fotopoulos, *Food Offered to Idols in Roman Corinth*, 247–49; Kim, "Imitatio Christi (1 Corinthians 11:1)", 199; Dickson, *Mission-Commitment in Ancient Judaism and in the Pauline Communities*, 253; Shen, "Paul's Doctrine of God and the Issue of Food Offered to Idols in 1 Corinthians 8:1–11:1", 234; Rode, "El Modelo de Adaptación de Pablo Según 1 Corintios 9:19–23", 341–42; Robert L. Plummer, "Imitation of Paul and the Church's Missionary Role in 1 Corinthians", *Journal of the Evangelical Theological Society* 44:2 (2001): 222, 225–26; Horsley, *1 Corinthians*, 142; Newton, *Deity and Diet*, 380; Hays, *First Corinthians*, 179; Horrell, "Theological Principle or Christological Praxis?" 106; Barton, "All Things to All People", 273; Schrage, *Der erste Brief an die Korinther*, 2:475–76; O'Brien, *Gospel and Mission in the Writings of Paul*, 91–92; Hall, "All Things to All People", 142; Fee, *The First Epistle to the Corinthians*, 489–90; Neller, "1 Corinthians 9:19–22", 137; William S. Kurz, "Kenotic Imitation of Paul and of Christ in Philippians 2 and 3", in *Discipleship in the New Testament* (ed. Fernando F. Segovia; Philadelphia: Fortress, 1985), 108; Christian Wolff, *Der erste Brief des Paulus an die Korinther* (Berlin: Evangelische Verlagsanstalt, 1982), 2:63; Orr and Walther, *1 Corinthians*, 256; Barrett, *A Commentary on The First Epistle to the Corinthians*, 245; Hurd, *The Origin of 1 Corinthians*, 128–30; Willis Peter De Boer, *The Imitation of Paul: An Exegetical Study* (Kampen: J. H. Kok, 1962), 158.

may be given in support of this assertion: First, the people groups mentioned in the two texts appear to correspond:[2]

1 Cor 9:20–22	1 Cor 10:32
Jews/those under the law	Jews
Those outside the law	Greeks

Second, σῴζω ("save") language occurs in both passages (1 Cor 9:22; 10:33). Third, the slave metaphor is employed in both sections (1 Cor 9:19, 22; 10:33). Fourth, the only examples of two πᾶς words side-by-side in the Pauline corpus are in 1 Cor 9:19 and 10:33:

1 Cor 9:19	1 Cor 10:33
πάντων πᾶσιν	πάντα πᾶσιν
πλείονας	πολλῶν

Fifth, 1 Cor 10:32–33 is located at the conclusion of the 1 Cor 8–10 pericope where Paul restates his main points.[3] For these five reasons, it is reasonable to view 1 Cor 10:32–33 as a recapitulation of 1 Cor 9:19–23.

Is 1 Cor 11:1 ("Be imitators of me . . .") a continuation of the recapitulation in chapter 10? Gordon Fee calls the split between 10:33 and 11:1 "one of the most unfortunate chapter divisions in the NT".[4] The NA[27] places 11:1 in the paragraph that begins with 10:31, making 11:2 the de facto beginning of the next chapter. What is the exegetical basis for this linking of 11:1 with 10:32–33 over 11:2–3? To begin with, there is a flow of thought suggested by the repetition of καθὼς κἀγώ in 10:33–11:1. In addition, throughout 1 Cor 8–10 but especially in 1 Cor 9, Paul describes the way he serves different people in different ways (stressing the first person singular in 1 Cor 9:19–23), and in so doing puts himself forward as a model. In this regard, 1 Cor 11:1 naturally points back to Paul's example in 1 Cor 8–10 and 9:19–23 in particular. Note

---

[2] Horrell, *Solidarity and Difference*, 260; Barton, "All Things to All People", 279, 284; Kim, "Imitatio Christi (1 Corinthians 11:1)", 200; Plummer, "Imitation of Paul and the Church's Missionary Role in 1 Corinthians", 225–26; Back, *All Things to All Men*, 10, 12–13; Gardner, *The Gifts of God and the Authentication of a Christian*, 99; Hall, "All Things to All People", 142; Neller, "1 Corinthians 9:19–22", 137; Willis, "An Apostolic Apologia", 38. Given Paul's "win" and "save" language in 1 Cor 9:19–23, some commentators call into question a correspondence between "the weak" (1 Cor 9:22) and members of "the *ekklesia* of God" (1 Cor 10:32). See Garland, *1 Corinthians*, 433; Schrage, *Der erste Brief an die Korinther*, 2:345–46. However, Paul's reference in 1 Cor 8:9–13 to "weak believers" who are "members of your family" would suggest that Jesus-believers are at least partly in view. Cf. 4.4.8 above. The term ἀσθενής appears three times in 1 Cor 8:7–10 in reference to members of the *ekklesia* (cf. Rom 14:1–15:1). Moreover, 1 Cor 8:13 is a possible example of Paul becoming weak to the weak.

[3] Jerry L. Sumney, "The Place of 1 Corinthians 9:24–27 in Paul's Argument", *Journal of Biblical Literature* 119:2 (2000): 333; Hays, *First Corinthians*, 179; Kim, "Imitatio Christi (1 Corinthians 11:1)", 201.

[4] Fee, *The First Epistle to the Corinthians*, 490.

also 1 Cor 8:12–13 where the thought moves immediately from Christ's identification with the weak to Paul's identification with the weak. I am not aware of any commentator or translator who questions the NA^{27} decision to make 1 Cor 11:1 the conclusion of 10:31–33.

What has been questioned by at least one scholar is whether "of Christ" in 1 Cor 11:1 (μιμηταί μου γίνεσθε καθὼς κἀγὼ Χριστοῦ ["Be imitators of me, as I am *of Christ*"]) necessarily implies that Paul imitated Christ. Brian Dodd argues that the genitive is shorthand for "belonging to Christ" and "takes on the weight of a technical term" in the letter (1 Cor 1:12; 2:16; 3:23; 6:15; 7:22; 12:27; 15:23).[5] Paul's exhortation to the Corinthians in 1 Cor 11:1 should therefore not be interpreted as "Follow my example, as I follow the example of Christ", but "Imitate my example that I have portrayed in 1 Corinthians, because I am possessed by my master, Christ".[6]

While Dodd's interpretation is possible, he overstates the case for a technical use of Χριστοῦ in the letter.[7] Moreover, καθὼς κἀγὼ Χριστοῦ serves as the reason *why* the Corinthians should be imitators of Paul (μιμηταί μου γίνεσθε). Would the fact that Paul *belonged* to Christ be sufficient justification to imitate him? Did not all the Corinthian Jesus-believers belong to Christ, even those whom Paul corrected? A more compelling reason why the Corinthians should imitate Paul is that he *imitated* Christ. He conformed his life to the Lord Jesus, a standard he appeals to elsewhere in his letters (e.g. Phil 2:5–8; Rom 15:1–3, 7; 2 Cor 8:9; cf. Eph 4:32–5:1). Finally, as Horrell notes, the repeated use of καθὼς κἀγώ in 1 Cor 10:33 and 11:1 indicates a deliberate analogy between Paul's *imitatio Christi* way of relating to Christ and the Corinthians imitating Paul:

> However, *pace* Dodd (p. 158), in only two of the above list of occurrences (given by Dodd) of Χριστου in 1 and 2 Corinthians is there any sense of the phrase being a "technical term", a "cipher" (1 Cor. 15.23; 2 Cor. 10.7) and the parallelism conveyed by καθὼς κἀγώ in 11.1 (cf. 10.33) speaks more strongly for the usual interpretation, which takes imitation to be implied in the second clause as stated in the first. If Dodd's reading were correct, we would have expected ἐγὼ γάρ rather than καθὼς κἀγώ.[8]

It may be concluded that 1 Cor 11:1 is properly interpreted, "Be imitators of me, as I am [an imitator] of Christ".

---

[5] Brian J. Dodd, "The Story of Christ and the Imitation of Paul in Philippians 2–3", in *Where Christology Began: Essays on Philippians 2* (ed. Ralph P. Martin and Brian J. Dodd; Louisville: Westminster/John Knox, 1998), 158.

[6] Dodd, "The Story of Christ and the Imitation of Paul in Philippians 2–3", 157. Also Dodd, *Paul's Paradigmatic "I"*, 19, 28–29, 113, 187.

[7] Cf. 1 Cor 1:12. See Horrell, *Solidarity and Difference*, 179 n. 50; Garland, *1 Corinthians*, 502–503.

[8] Horrell, *Solidarity and Difference*, 179 n. 50; cf. De Boer, *The Imitation of Paul*, 162–63.

What are the implications of viewing 1 Cor 10:32–11:1 as a recapitulation of 1 Cor 9:19–23? The correlation suggests that Paul's accommodation described in 1 Cor 9:19–23 was modelled after Christ's example. The logic of this argument may be summed up as follows:

Premise A	1 Cor 11:1 ("Be imitators of me, as I am of Christ") continues the thought of 1 Cor 10:32–33
Premise B	1 Cor 10:32–33 is a recapitulation of 1 Cor 9:19–23
Conclusion C	1 Cor 9:19–23 reflects Paul's *imitatio Christi* ethic

One of the strengths of the above argument is that it is backed up by widespread agreement on propositions A and B. While the conclusion (C) is less recognized, an increasing number of scholars have adopted this interpretation of the text.[9]

5.2 "Interchange" in Paul's Letters

It has been argued that Paul's accommodation was based on Christ's example, but what was this example? Does Paul refer in his letters to Christ's accommodation? In what way did Christ become "all things to all people"? Morna Hooker finds a reasonable answer to this query in Pauline texts where Christ is described as entering into the life experience of others – what Hooker calls "interchange".[10] *Interchange* describes "the self-identification of Christ with men and women which, in turn, results in their sharing in what he is".[11] Examples of "interchange" may be found, according to Hooker, throughout Paul's letters (2 Cor 5:21; 8:9; Gal 3:13–14; 4:4–5; Rom 8:3–4; Phil 2:5–8).

The last passage mentioned, Phil 2:5–8, bears particular resemblance to 1 Cor 9:19–23/10:32–11:1 with respect to *renunciation of rights*:

Let the same mind be in you that was in Christ Jesus, who, though he was in the form of God, did not regard equality with God as something to be exploited, but emptied himself, taking the form of a slave, being born in human likeness. And being found in human form, he humbled himself and became obedient to the point of death – even death on a cross (Phil 2:7).

Both texts (Phil 2:7 and 1 Cor 9:19–23/10:32–11:1) include a call to imitate Christ through self-giving. There is the noun and verbal use of the term "slave" (δούλου/ἐδούλωσα). There is also a similar use of the verb γίνομαι to describe accommodation.

---

[9] E.g. Horrell, *Solidarity and Difference*, 179; Garland, *1 Corinthians*, 435–36; Kim, "Imitatio Christi (1 Corinthians 11:1)", 221; Hooker, "A Partner in the Gospel", 96; Richardson and Gooch, "Accommodation Ethics", 124–25.

[10] Morna D. Hooker, "Interchange in Christ", *Journal of Theological Studies* 22 (1971): 349–61.

[11] Hooker, "A Partner in the Gospel", 90; cf. Irenaeus, *Adv Haer.* V praef.

In the six "interchange" passages mentioned above, the Son of God is described as having accommodated himself to human experience. Through self-humbling, he became sin, poor, cursed, under the law, a servant. He entered the world and took on human flesh so that human flesh could become like him. Paul also reminds his readers that Christ's accommodation to humanity did not displace his identity as the Son of God. The Son was in the "likeness" (ὁμοιώματι) of sinful flesh and in the "form" (μορφῇ) of a slave (Phil 2:7). Despite becoming poor and sin, he remained rich and without sin. There is an element of paradox.[12]

Finally, in one of these "interchange" texts, Gal 4:4–5, Paul describes the Son of God as taking on Jewish identity: He was "born of a woman, born under the law, in order to redeem those who were under the law". In short, *Christ became a Jew to the Jews to redeem Jews.* "Interchange" then is one way to describe Paul's understanding of Christ's accommodation. Christ entered the life experience of human beings and identified with them, as the second Adam (1 Cor 15:22, 45), so that human beings could enter into his life. He entered into the life experience of Jews as a Jew so that Jews could enter into his life.[13]

---

[12] Hooker, "A Partner in the Gospel", 92; Morna D. Hooker, *From Adam to Christ: Essays on Paul* (Cambridge: Cambridge University Press, 1990), 8. A similar paradox is implied in 1 Cor 9:21–22. Paul became as a Gentile to Gentiles without displacing his Jewish identity (2 Cor 11:22; Rom 11:1). He became weak to the weak without compromising his strength (Rom 15:1).

[13] Christ's identity as a Jew, the "son of David", is central to Paul's gospel – "the gospel concerning his Son, who was descended from David according to the flesh" (Rom 1:3; cf. 9:5; 15:12). See also 2 Tim 2:8, "Remember Jesus Christ, raised from the dead, a descendant of David – that is my gospel" (2 Tim 2:8). The order is notable – "raised from the dead, descended from David" (cf. Rev 22:16). "The New Testament documents, both early and late, recall that the Word became *Jewish* flesh and lived, died, and rose among us . . . But it remains significant that scholars who otherwise affirm the Jewish identity of Jesus are often content to sideline his resurrection as irrelevant. Even those who do take it seriously do not always make enough of one crucial fact: the one who is raised is none other than the crucified Messiah of Israel and 'King of the Jews'. For the early Christians, it was the resurrection that confirmed this identity; indeed, it is theologically vital for the New Testament witnesses that Jesus' identity did not change on Easter Sunday (Acts 2:36; 17:3; 26:23; cf. Luke 24:26; Rom 1:3–4; Phil 2:9–11; John 20:28–31). In the resurrection God made Jesus visibly 'both Lord and Messiah' of Israel, the Son of David who is 'Son of God with power' (Acts 2:36; Rom 1:3–4) – and, in one of the most radically Jewish and radically Nicene of all early christological affirmations, God bestowed on him 'the name that is above every name' – the very name of YHWH (Phil 2:9; cf. Eph 1:20–21; Heb 1:3b–4; also John 17:11–12; Rev 1:4–8). For the first Christians, in other words, it was 'seeing the Word' in the resurrection that crucially corroborated the identity of Jesus the Jew as Messiah and Lord God of Israel. In the witness of the apostles – including the apostle to the Gentiles – the New Testament's implied readers firmly appropriated this truth" (Markus Bockmuehl, "God's Life as a Jew: Remembering the Son of God as Son of David", in *Seeking the Identity of Jesus: A Pilgrimage* [ed. Beverly

Returning to 1 Cor 9:19–23, Hooker and Garland make a convincing case that Paul, in imitation of Christ, sought to enter into the life experience of Jews, Gentiles and the weak so that they could enter into his life experience of being in Christ.[14] It is important to point out that this argument does not require that Paul knew particular Jesus traditions. Paul understood the pattern of Christ's life – that Christ accommodated to the situation of others for the sake of others – and this served as Paul's model of accommodation-oriented ministry (2 Cor 8:9 with 6:10).[15] In sections 5.3 and 5.4, it will be argued, independent of Hooker's "interchange" case, that Paul was aware of specific Jesus traditions that may be described as "Jesus' example and rule of adaptation".

Roberts Gaventa and Richard B. Hays; Grand Rapids: Eerdmans, 2008], 75–78). Cf. Markus Bockmuehl, *Seeing the Word: Refocusing New Testament Study* (Grand Rapids: Baker Academic, 2006), 220–28; Bruce D. Marshall, *Trinity and Truth* (Cambridge: Cambridge University Press, 2000), 178. The monophysite debate in the fifth through seventh centuries required a vocabulary rich in nuance to describe how Christ's humanity coexisted with his divinity without diminishment of either nature. Pseudo-Cyril described the relationship between Christ's divinity and humanity as two natures "enveloping one another" and "penetrating each another" in asymmetrical fashion "without forming a hybrid" or *tertium quid*. Asymmetrical "mutual containment" of the two natures did not level down Christ's humanity (Eutychianism) but rather had the effect of drawing out its fullness. John of Damascus referred to this relationship as perichoresis (*De Fide* 3.17) and described it as the glowing of iron penetrated by fire. This asymmetrical relationship is reflected in the fact that "iron becomes fiery, yet fire does not become iron" (John of Damascus, *Contra Jacobitas* 52.41–43). Significantly, perichoresis vocabulary can be heuristically used to describe the relationship between Christ's divinity and the particularity of his humanity as the son of David. It can also be used to describe how Paul may have viewed himself as a Jew "in Christ" even as this monograph has sought to make room for the possibility that Paul understood new creation identity and Jewish identity (or "nature" [Gal 2:15: φύσει Ἰουδαῖοι]) as coexisting in union, without one diminishing the other. Borrowing John of Damascus's illustration, perhaps Paul saw his new creation identity in Christ as a fire that caused his Jewishness to glow all the brighter. Judith Gundry-Volf, "Beyond difference?" 27–30, comes close to this idea when she writes, "'Paul can speak of being a 'new creation' (καινὴ κτίσις) without implying the erasure of differences, only their revalorization . . . 'put on Christ' (in baptism) connotes a kind of eschatological transformation that takes up rather than leaves out the differences in the body . . . Though believers 'put on' the *one* Christ, he 'puts on' their *differentiated* 'flesh' – to reappropriate Paul's metaphor – and 'lives in me' [Gal 2:20], that is, in each individually differentiated 'me'". *Pace* Gundry-Volf, 29, revalorization in Paul's thought can be described as an eschatological celebration of distinct callings *in Christ* that reflect the beauty and diversity of creation, including an economy of mutual blessing between Israel and the nations. See Tucker, *You Belong to Christ*, 232; Campbell, *Paul and the Creation of Christian Identity*, 87–96; Soulen, *The God of Israel and Christian Theology*, 114–77.

[14] Hooker, "A Partner in the Gospel", 83–100; Garland, *1 Corinthians*, 435–36. Note the "interchange" language in Gal 4:12.

[15] See 4.4.8 above.

5.3 Paul's Knowledge of Jesus Tradition

Some would object to the above *imitatio Christi*/"interchange" understanding of Christ's accommodation in Paul's thought on the grounds that Paul did not seek to imitate the earthly Jesus but rather the pre-existent Jesus, the Christ of faith revealed in the saving events of the *kerygma*. Rudolf Bultmann wrote, "When [Paul] refers to Christ as an example he is thinking not of the historical Jesus but of the pre-existent Jesus".[16] Bultmann's position has been followed by Käsemann, Beare, Dahl, Martin, Betz, Furnish, Collange, Schulz, Merk, and B. Dodd, among others. Regarding 1 Cor 11:1, Wolfgang Schrage is certain. Paul "speaks not of imitating Jesus but of imitating Christ . . . an exemplary element is indeed present, but the example is not the earthly Jesus . . . Certainly any attempt to copy or imitate the life of Jesus that views Jesus as a model is not Pauline".[17]

But is Bultmann's dichotomy between the Jesus of history and the Christ of faith tenable? There does not appear to be any evidence for this distinction in Paul's exhortations to imitate Christ (1 Cor 11:1; Phil 2:5–11; Rom 15:1–3, 7; 2 Cor 8:9; 10:1; cf. Eph 5:1–2, 25). What drives the view that Paul did *not* imitate the earthly Jesus? One explanation, according to Hooker, is that many of these scholars hold to a "Lutheran" reading of Paul that identifies imitation of the earthly Jesus as works.[18]

A second and more widespread objection to the view that Paul imitated the earthly Jesus is that Paul knew very little about Jesus' life and teachings. Bultmann claimed that "the teaching of the historical Jesus plays no role, or practically none, in Paul".[19] This was famously argued on the basis of 2 Cor 5:16, Gal 1:11–12 and an argument from silence. Recent scholarship, however, has largely dismissed this interpretation of 2 Cor 5:16 and Gal 1:11–12, thus reopening the question of whether Paul knew more about the earthly Jesus than his letters explicitly indicate. The Jesus-Paul debate has engaged many scholars and a rehearsal of the main arguments by minimalists and maximalists has been skilfully accomplished by David Wenham (1995) and Michael Thompson (1991), who conclude that Paul was aware of a number of Jesus traditions. A more thorough discussion of the plausibility of their findings need not detain us here. In the remainder of this section, attention will be focused on references to the life and teachings of Jesus within 1 Corinthians.

---

[16] Rudolf Bultmann, *Theology of the New Testament* (New York: Scribner, 1951), 1:188; cf. Rudolf Bultmann, "Die Bedeutung des geschichtlichen Jesus für die Theologie des Paulus", in *Glauben und Verstehen* (Tübingen: Mohr Siebeck, 1933), 1:206.

[17] Wolfgang Schrage, *The Ethics of the New Testament* (Edinburgh: T & T, 1988), 208.

[18] Hooker, *From Adam to Christ*, 7.

[19] Bultmann, *Theology of the New Testament*, 1:35.

Scholars largely agree that Paul refers to dominical sayings in 1 Cor 9:14 and 7:10–11.[20] In 1 Cor 9:14, only five verses away from the accommodation passage, Paul writes, "In the same way, the Lord commanded that those who proclaim the gospel should get their living by the gospel". This appears to allude to Jesus' teaching in Luke 10:7 and Matthew 10:10. Two chapters earlier, Paul lays down Jesus' command that the wife should not separate from her husband (1 Cor 7:10–11; cf. Mark 10:9, 11–12; Matt 19:6, 9; Luke 16:18).[21] Two chapters after the accommodation passage, Paul refers to what Jesus did and said on the night he was betrayed (1 Cor 11:23–25; cf. Mark 14:12–25; Matt 26:20–29; Luke 22:14–23).

Richard Horsley notes that the terms "received" and "handed on" in 1 Cor 11:23 (here applied to Jesus tradition) were "virtually technical terms in Jewish culture for the transmission of important traditions such as customs, rituals, and ethical teachings".[22] Paul uses the terms a second time with reference to Jesus tradition in 1 Cor 15:3, "For I *handed on* to you as of first importance what I in turn had *received* . . ." (παρέδωκα γὰρ ὑμῖν ἐν πρώτοις, ὃ καὶ παρέλαβον). These texts (1 Cor 7:10–11; 9:14; 11:23–25; 15:3) demonstrate that Paul was familiar with Jesus traditions and had them in mind when he wrote 1 Corinthians 9 and 11.[23] This adds to the cumulative case that Paul's interest in the imitation of Jesus was rooted in gospel traditions.

5.4 Jesus as "All Things to All People" in the Gospels

Paul depicts Christ's incarnation as a form of divine accommodation (Gal 4:4–5) and Jesus' self-giving death on the cross as the climactic expression of this accommodation (Phil 2:5–8). In this section, I will examine the period between Jesus' birth and death and ask whether the gospels include additional examples of Jesus' accommodation (or teachings by Jesus on the subject of accommodation). In each case, consideration will be given to evidence that Paul was familiar with these traditions.

---

[20] James D. G. Dunn, "Jesus Tradition in Paul", in *Studying the Historical Jesus: Evaluations of the State of Current Research* (ed. Bruce Chilton and Craig Evans; Leiden: Brill, 1994), 160–61.

[21] See David Wenham, "Paul's Use of the Jesus Tradition: Three Samples", in *Gospel Perspectives: The Jesus Tradition Outside the Gospels* (ed. David Wenham; Eugene: Wipf and Stock, 1984), 5:7–15.

[22] Horsley, *1 Corinthians*, 160.

[23] Kim, *Paul and the New Perspective*, 219; Traugott Holtz, "Paul and the Oral Gospel Tradition", in *Jesus and the Oral Gospel Tradition* (ed. Henry Wansbrough; Sheffield: Sheffield Academic Press, 1991), 382–85.

5.4.1 A Slave of All

Johannes Weiss, F. F. Bruce, and Rainer Riesner, among others, have noticed a possible echo of Mark 10:44–45 in 1 Cor 9:19.[24] Paul describes himself in 1 Cor 9:19 as a "slave to all" (πᾶσιν . . . ἐδούλωσα) even as in Mark 10:44–45 Jesus called the one who followed him to be a "slave of all" (πάντων δοῦλος). Since Paul calls the Corinthians to be imitators of him as he is of Christ, and the above A–C reasoning (5.1) links 1 Cor 9:19 to 1 Cor 11:1, it may be reasonably inferred that Paul consciously imitated Jesus, the "slave of all". Like Jesus, Paul renounced all rights for the sake of the gospel. Though free, Paul made himself a slave to all (1 Cor 9:1, 19).

5.4.2 Eating With Sinners, Pharisees and Ordinary Jews[25]

Is there any example in the gospels of Jesus accommodating himself to another's customs or way of life for the sake of ministry? Significantly, all three synoptic gospels record that Jesus ate with "tax collectors and sinners" (to the consternation of the Pharisees) in order to "save" the lost (Luke 19:7–10) and "call" disciples (Mark 2:14, 17; Matt 9:9, 13; Luke 5:27, 32).

Jesus' willingness to receive hospitality from unrepentant sinners was a form of accommodation (cf. 2 John 10–11).[26] Josephus describes first-century Jews as Torah observant but notes that Torah observance took on different forms: some Jews were not strict, others "strict" and others "extremely strict".[27] With respect to Jesus' Torah observance, it would appear that his level of strictness was somewhere in the middle of the spectrum between sinners and Pharisees. This is implied by Luke's account that Pharisees were willing to eat with Jesus but not with tax collectors and sinners (Luke 5:27–32; 7:34–36; 11:37; 14:1; 15:1–3).[28] Jesus was a mainstream Jew, like the crowds with whom he ministered and with whom he ate (Matt 14:16–21; 15:32–38; Mark 6:37–44; 8:2–9; Luke 9:12–17; John 6:5–13).

Jesus' statement "I have come to call not the righteous but sinners" (attested in all three synoptic gospels), and his parable of the lost sheep (Luke 15:7), suggest that his ministry to sinners was not an ancillary aspect of his

---

[24] Weiss, *Der erste Korintherbrief*, 243; Bruce, *I and II Corinthians*, 86; Rainer Riesner, "Paulus und die Jesus-Überlieferung", in *Evangelium, Schriftauslegung, Kirche* (ed. J. Adna et al.; Göttingen: Vandenhoeck & Ruprecht, 1997), 364.

[25] The three groups are depicted in Luke 7:29–30.

[26] Klawans, *Impurity and Sin in Ancient Judaism*, 143–57, argues persuasively that Jesus was concerned about moral and ritual impurity, and that he prioritized the former over the latter.

[27] Josephus, *Ant.* 1.14; 20.38–46, 201; *C. Ap.* 2.144, 175, 187; *J.W.* 1.110; 2.119; cf. Philo, *Spec.* 1.186; Michael Winger, "Act One: Paul Arrives in Galatia", *New Testament Studies* 48 (2002): 559 n. 28; Gregory E. Sterling, "'Thus are Israel': Jewish Self-Definition in Alexandria", *The Studia Philonica Annual* 7 (1995): 15. See sections 4.2.1, 4.2.2 and 4.4.3 above.

[28] See Green, *The Gospel of Luke*, 247; Bockmuehl, *Jewish Law in Gentile Churches*, 10–12.

ministry; it was central. In fulfilling his mission, accommodation was essential. Accommodation enabled intimate communication to take place and this led to Jesus becoming a "friend of tax collectors and sinners", many of whom became his followers (Luke 7:34; Matt 11:19; Mark 2:15).

By viewing Jesus' table-fellowship with sinners as an accommodation, I do not mean to suggest that he violated the biblical dietary laws. There is no evidence that Jesus ate unclean food, and Peter's negative response to the Lord's command to eat unclean food in Acts 10:14 ("By no means, Lord; for I have never eaten anything that is profane or unclean") implies that neither Jesus nor Peter ate forbidden food in the homes of sinners.

It may be assumed that Jesus accommodated to stricter levels of ritual purity when he ate with Pharisees unless he had a specific reason not to.[29] As William Loader observes, Jesus' table-fellowship with Pharisees "implies sufficient acceptance of Pharisee norms on the part of Jesus as to make such fellowship possible".[30] In all likelihood, Jesus' accommodation typically included ritual immersion at one of the local *miqva'ot*, handwashing and associated blessings (Mark 7:1–5).[31]

By associating with all through open table-fellowship, one could say that Jesus became all things to all people (sinners, Pharisees and ordinary Jews). One might even call this a form of "interchange", for "shared meals symbolized shared lives – intimacy, kinship, unity".[32] Jesus entered the lives of all, through table-centred fellowship, so that all could enter his life. In their article on 1 Cor 9:19–23, Richardson and Gooch conclude that "Jesus accommodated himself in his eating customs to the situation of others and with the object of influencing their relationship with God".[33]

5.4.3 Paul's Awareness of Jesus' Example of Adaptation

Was Paul familiar with the tradition that Jesus ate with sinners and Pharisees? Paul was a Pharisee and, as it was noted, the Pharisees found fault with Jesus for eating with sinners. If the Pharisees retained a living memory of Jesus eating with sinners, it is probable that Paul would have been aware of the tradition.[34] Moreover, as shown above, the gospels indicate that the early church regarded Jesus' ministry to tax collectors and sinners as a principal focus of

---

[29] In Luke 11:37–41, Jesus teaches a lesson related to the fact that he did not ritually wash before dinner.

[30] William R. G. Loader, *Jesus' Attitude Towards the Law: A Study of the Gospels* (Tübingen: Mohr Siebeck, 1997), 318; cf. Kalervo Salo, *Luke's Treatment of the Law: A Redaction-Critical Investigation* (Helsinki: Suomalainen Tiedeakatemia, 1991), 94–95.

[31] See Poirier, "Purity Beyond the Temple in the Second Temple Era", 247–65.

[32] Green, *The Gospel of Luke*, 246. Cf. Bartchy, "Table Fellowship", 796; Robert A. Guelich, *Mark 1–8:26* (Dallas: Word, 1989), 103.

[33] Richardson and Gooch, "Accommodation Ethics", 132–33.

[34] Cf. Gal 1:13, 23; Acts 8:3.

his ministry. This raises the likelihood that Paul knew of the tradition after joining the sect he formerly persecuted. He may likewise have known that Jesus ate with Pharisees.

Alexander Wedderburn contends that the early church was more open to the inclusion of Gentiles as a result of this tradition: "In other words, they would have argued that if Jesus was a friend ... of 'sinners' (Matt 11.19/Luke 7.34) then he was also a friend of Gentiles who were also classed among 'sinners'".[35] Dunn agrees with this assessment in his discussion of Mark 2:15–17:

> It is hard then to believe that the memory of such an episode and its accompanying Jesus-saying played no part in the earliest communities' wrestling with the equivalent questions of their own day. Particularly in a situation where "sinners" was more or less synonymous with "Gentiles" (Gal 2.15; cf. Mark 10.33 with 14.41, and Matt. 5.47 with Luke 6.33), the pericope's applicability when the issue of table-fellowship between Jewish and Gentile believers began to emerge as an issue must have been obvious.[36]

It may be concluded that Paul probably knew that Jesus ate with sinners and Pharisees. Paul likely saw these sinners, whom Jesus welcomed, as paradigmatic of Gentile sinners.[37]

5.4.4 Jesus' Rule of Adaptation

In this section, it will be proposed that Paul not only knew of Jesus' example of adaptation but that he also knew of Jesus' rule of adaptation given to the 70/72,[38] namely: "eat what is set before you" (Luke 10:8). While it is not necessary to win this argument to make the case that Paul imitated Jesus' example of adaptation, it adds to the cumulative evidence.

Christopher Tuckett considers the words "eat what is set before you" in Luke 10:8 a "secondary insertion into the tradition, possibly via dependence on the Pauline tradition (cf. 1 Cor 10,27)".[39] Viewed in this way, Luke 10:8 reflects the later Gentile mission, a mission in which some Jesus-believing

---

[35] Alexander J. M. Wedderburn, "Paul and Jesus: Similarity and Continuity", in *Paul and Jesus: Collected Essays* (ed. A. J. M. Wedderburn; Sheffield: Sheffield Academic Press, 1989), 136. Also Richard A. Burridge, *Imitating Jesus: An Inclusive Approach to New Testament Ethics* (Grand Rapids: Eerdmans, 2007), 149.

[36] Dunn, *Jesus, Paul and the Law*, 19; James D. G. Dunn, "Mark 2.1 – 3.6: A Bridge between Jesus and Paul on the Question of the Law", *New Testament Studies* 30 (1984): 404. Cf. Matt 18:17; Dunn, "Jesus Tradition in Paul", 172; Crossley, *The Date of Mark's Gospel*, 143; Bockmuehl, *Jewish Law in Gentile Churches*, 81; Larry W. Hurtado, *Mark* (Peabody: Hendrickson, 1989), 40; C. F. Evans, *Saint Luke* (London: SCM, 1990), 307; Richardson and Gooch, "Accommodation Ethics", 134; *pace* Guelich, *Mark 1–8:26*, 103.

[37] Dickson, *Mission-Commitment in Ancient Judaism and in the Pauline Communities*, 254.

[38] 70 (p^{45}, ℵ, A, C); 72 (p^{75}, B, D).

[39] Christopher M. Tuckett, "Paul and the Synoptic Mission Discourse?" *Ephemerides Theologicae Lovanienses* 60 (1984): 378.

Jews supposedly abandoned the Jewish dietary laws in order to eat with Gentiles.[40]

A considerable weakness in the above argument, however, is that there is no consensus of opinion on the origin of Luke 10:8,[41] a fact that Tuckett concedes in his most recent comments on the text ("the evidence is ambiguous").[42] Some consider Luke 10:8 to be a Lukan creation[43] or redaction[44] or insertion into Q,[45] while others view it as possible Q material from an earlier or later period[46] or even pre-Q.[47]

Tuckett offers no evidence that Luke 10:8 is a "secondary insertion into the tradition". Moreover, that the words of Luke 10:8 ("eat what is set before you") appear in 1 Cor 10:27 does not prove Lukan dependence on Paul. It may be the other way around (e.g. 1 Cor 9:14 is probably dependent on the Jesus tradition behind Luke 10:7). In support of the view that Paul was dependent on a tradition similar to Luke 10:8 ("eat what is set before you") in 1 Cor 10:27, it is not necessary to prove that Luke 10:8 is an authentic Jesus tradition. I only need to make a reasonable case that a similar tradition could have circulated prior to the writing of 1 Corinthians.

A good case for this can be made.[48] First, the *Gospel of Thomas* includes the dominical command found in Luke 10:8:

---

[40] David R. Catchpole, *The Quest for Q* (Edinburgh: T & T Clark, 1993), 176; Evans, *Saint Luke*, 448–49.

[41] Risto Uro, *Sheep among the Wolves: A Study on the Mission Instructions of Q* (Helsinki: Suomalainen Tiedeakatemia, 1987), 27–28.

[42] Christopher M. Tuckett, *Q and the History of Early Christianity* (Peabody: Hendrickson, 1996), 399.

[43] Paul Hoffmann, *Studien zur Theologie der Logienquelle* (Münster: Aschendorff, 1972), 276–83.

[44] Siegfried Schulz, *Q – die Spruchquelle der Evangelisten* (Zürich: Theologischer Verlag, 1972), 407.

[45] Catchpole, *The Quest for Q*, 151–88.

[46] Uro, *Sheep among the Wolves*, 222; I. Howard Marshall, *The Gospel of Luke: A Commentary on the Greek Text* (Exeter: Paternoster, 1978), 421; Rudolf Laufen, *Die Doppelüberlieferung der Logienquelle und des Markusevangeliums* (Bonn: Peter Hanstein, 1980), 218–20; Richardson and Gooch, "Accommodation Ethics", 135–36.

[47] P. Sellow, "Early Collections of Jesus' Words" (Ph.D. diss., Harvard Divinity School, 1985), 131–33.

[48] James M. Robinson, Paul Hoffmann and John S. Kloppenborg, eds., *The Critical Edition of Q* (Leuven: Peeters, 2000), lxxxii, 170–71, accept Luke 10:8 (ἐσθίετε τὰ παρατιθέμενα ὑμῖν) as one of the "reconstructions that are probable but uncertain". Other Q editions arrive at the same position: Burton L. Mack, *The Lost Gospel: The Book of Q and Christian Origins* (San Francisco: HarperCollins, 1993), 260–61; Robert J. Miller, ed., *The Complete Gospels: Annotated Scholars Version* (Sonoma: Polebridge, 1992), 249–300. Without endorsing these constructions, they are noted to show that divergent source-critical methodologies arrive at a common view that the tradition behind Luke 10:8 is early.

When you go into any land and walk about in the districts, if they receive you, *eat what they will set before you*, and heal the sick among them. For what goes into your mouth will not defile you, but that which issues from your mouth – it is that which will defile you (*Gos. Thom.* 14).[49]

As F. F. Bruce notes, the *Gospel of Thomas* links the tradition of Luke 10:8 to Matt 15:11.[50] Notably, Jesus does not comment here on the biblical dietary laws but on the Pharisaic view that eating clean food with ritually unwashed hands "defiles" (κοινόω). While it is unclear whether the *Gospel of Thomas* contributes an independent witness to the authenticity of the Luke 10:8 saying, the connection it makes between Jesus' rule of adaptation and Matt 15:11 lends support to an intra-Jewish reading of the tradition since the redactor likely knew that Matt 15:1–20 focused on Jesus' criticism of Pharisaic halakhah and not the biblical food laws.[51]

Second, while Luke is the only canonical gospel that includes the saying "eat what is set before you", Matthew's gospel may imply the same through a conflated version of the Luke 10:5–8 pericope. Matthew 10:10–11 states that "laborers deserve their food (τροφῆς). Whatever town or village you enter, find out who in it is worthy, and stay there until you leave".[52]

Third, Jesus' rule of adaptation reflects Jesus' example of adaptation at the table, which the disciples were called to imitate. Rather than a secondary insertion into the tradition, it is more likely a development of Luke's theme of how Jesus dealt with differing standards of Torah observance at the table. The placement of the rule of adaptation between Luke 7:34 and 15:1–7/19:1–10 is significant. In all of these passages, Jesus is described as eating in the homes of tax collectors and sinners, where the standard of Torah observance was presumably less strict relative to Pharisees and ordinary Jews. In this sense, Jesus' instruction to the 70/72 about adaptation ("eat what is set before you") would seem to be a call to imitate Jesus' accommodation-oriented table-fellowship in the same way that Jesus' call to heal the sick and proclaim the kingdom in the adjacent verse (Luke 10:9) is a call to imitate the way Jesus ministered in word and deed (see esp. v. 16).[53]

---

[49] T. O. Lambdin, *Nag Hammadi Codex 2,2–7* (ed. Bentley Layton; Leiden: Brill, 1989), 1:60–61.

[50] F. F. Bruce, *Jesus and Christian Origins Outside the New Testament* (Grand Rapids: Eerdmans, 1974), 119.

[51] In Matt 15, Jesus is engaged in an intra-Jewish debate over Pharisaic standards of ritual purity (Matt 15:1–2, 20). The biblical dietary laws are not in view.

[52] The *Didache* 13:1–2 preserves a similar tradition, "But every genuine prophet who wishes to settle among you 'is worthy of his food (τροφῆς)'. Likewise, every genuine teacher is, like 'the worker, worthy of his food (τροφῆς)'".

[53] Geoffrey Burn, "Hospitality and Incarnational Vulnerability in Luke 10.1–12", *Theology* 103:816 (2000): 446; Judith Lieu, *The Gospel of Luke* (London: Epworth, 1997), 83.

In light of Jesus' almost exclusive ministry to Jews,[54] and his instructions to the twelve not to go among the Gentiles[55] (Luke introduces the Gentile mission in Acts 10), commentators should not be quick to assume that Gentiles and unclean food are in view in Luke 10:7–8.[56] As John Nolland observes, "There is no interest here in issues of kosher food".[57] Chilton agrees that Jesus' rule "presupposes that what the disciples eat, within any house which might receive them, is clean".[58] Nor should it be presumed without evidence that the issue is unappetizing food. Given the intra-Jewish context, the issue was probably accidental mixtures or food considered to be κοινός (2.1.4).

The Lukan focus on halakhic diversity with respect to table-fellowship suggests, from a narrative perspective, that Jesus anticipated his followers would receive hospitality from Jews whose strictness of Torah observance at the table was less than their own.[59] A stricter level of observance by their host would not have caused them to refrain from eating.

Contrary to the view of some scholars, there is no evidence that Galilean Jews were less strict in their Torah observance than other Jews. Lawrence Schiffman concludes in his study of Galilean halakhah that the Galileans were particularly stringent, "Our examination of the specific references in tannaitic sources to differences between the Galileans and Judeans has revealed that, in most cases, the Galileans were more stringent in regard to the law than their Judean coreligionists . . . In no case did the sources portray the Galileans as lenient or less observant".[60] Dunn has argued for a Pharisaic presence in Galilee and notes that the first-century sages Yochanan ben Zakkai and Hanina ben Dosa were from the village of Arav in Galilee.[61] Josephus (*Ant.* 20.23) refers to a "very strict" (πάνυ ἀκριβής) Jew named Eleazar from Galilee who convinced the king of Adiabene to be circumcised. *Mikvaot* (Jewish ritual baths) have been found in early Roman Sepphoris, an indication that ritual purity was a concern among the Galileans.[62] All of this adds to the cumulative case that when Jesus commanded his disciples to eat what was set before them, he likely meant that they were not to maintain a narrow definition of Torah observance at the table, thus preventing them from receiving hospi-

---

[54] Matt 15:21–28; Mark 7:24–30.

[55] Matt 10:5.

[56] Schnabel, *Early Christian Mission*, 1:325.

[57] John L. Nolland, *Luke 9:21–18:34* (Dallas: Word, 1993), 553.

[58] Chilton, "The Purity of the Kingdom as Conveyed in Jesus' Meals", 486.

[59] Richardson and Gooch, "Accommodation Ethics", 135.

[60] Lawrence H. Schiffman, "Was There a Galilean Halakhah?" in *The Galilee in Late Antiquity* (ed. L. Levine; New York: The Jewish Theological Seminary of America, 1992), 156.

[61] Dunn, *Jesus, Paul and the Law*, 77–79.

[62] Mark A. Chancey, *The Myth of a Gentile Galilee* (Cambridge: Cambridge University Press, 2003), 71, 79.

tality. There is no evidence that Jesus called his disciples to be willing to violate the biblical food laws.[63] Rather, the intra-Jewish context suggests that Jesus called his disciples to a lifestyle of flexibility within the contours of Jewish law. They were to eat with the less strict, the strict and the very strict, adapting to the custom of their Jewish host without reservation.

5.4.5 Paul's Awareness of Jesus' Rule of Adaptation

Was Paul familiar with Jesus' rule of adaptation ("eat what is set before you")? A case has been presented that the rule was early and that it reflected Jesus' own practice of adapting to different standards of Torah observance at the table (Mark 2:15; Matt 11:19; Luke 7:34). Paul was probably aware of the tradition that Jesus ate with sinners, Pharisees and ordinary Jews. This raises the likelihood that he also knew of Jesus' rule of adaptation concerning commensality.

Paul's 1 Cor 9:14 reference to a dominical saying ("the Lord commanded that those who proclaim the gospel should get their living by the gospel"), a probable allusion to the tradition in Luke 10:7 ("for the labourer deserves to be paid"), adds to the likelihood that Paul was aware of Jesus' rule of adaptation redacted in Luke 10:8. Significantly, the Luke 10:7 command occurs between two versions of Jesus' rule of adaptation:

Remain in the same house, eating and drinking whatever they provide, for the labourer deserves to be paid. Do not move about from house to house. Whenever you enter a town and its people welcome you, eat what is set before you (Luke 10:7–8).

It should be pointed out that the issue of how to deal with different standards of Torah observance in Diaspora Jewish households was personally relevant to Paul. Jews varied widely in their perspectives on ritual purity and defilement by association,[64] and Paul would have had to decide ahead of time how to approach this diversity, especially as one who was accustomed to a Pharisaic lifestyle.

Luke describes Paul as visiting the local synagogue "first" when he entered a Gentile city (Acts 13:46). If Luke's account is accurate on this point, and there is reason to think it is (2 Cor 11:24; Rom 1:16; 1 Cor 9:20), Paul was likely offered hospitality by Jews and monotheistic Gentiles who attended these synagogues (Acts 16:15; 17:7; 18:7–8; 20:20–21; 21:8, 16). His hosts would have spanned the spectrum from less strict to very strict.

Through preaching in public places where non-Jews gathered, Paul was probably also offered hospitality by polytheistic Gentiles who wanted to learn

---

[63] Crossley, *The Date of Mark's Gospel*, 114.
[64] Dunn, *Jesus, Paul and the Law*, 139–40; Dunn, "The Incident at Antioch (Gal. 2:11–18)", 15; Regev, "Non-Priestly Purity and Its Religious Aspects According to Historical Sources and Archaeological Findings", 223–44; Sanders, "Jewish Association With Gentiles and Galatians 2:11–14", 172. See Tob 1.6–8; Josephus, *Ant.* 14.245; Philo, *Legat.* 156; *Spec.* 1.153.

more about his message (cf. Acts 16:34; 17:16–34).⁶⁵ Paul indicates in 1 Cor 10:27–30 that he was not opposed to eating with such Gentiles. At the end of Acts, Luke portrays Paul as a man who, like Jesus, "welcomed all (πάντας) who came to him":⁶⁶

> Our proposal is that Jesus' mission to "sinners" and his comments about Gentiles in Luke prepare the reader for the mission to Gentiles in Acts. J. T. Sanders draws a similar conclusion by noting that the place of the toll-collectors and "sinners" in the Gospel (Luke) is taken by the Gentiles in Acts . . . Luke uses a term that, according to our research, referred to Jewish "sinners" and to Gentiles in general . . . Acts ends with Paul following the pattern that Jesus established in the Gospel. Jesus "welcomed" "sinners" as a means of inviting them into the kingdom. Luke used this as his closing image in Acts. Paul "welcomed" all who came to see him and he preached to them about the Lord Jesus Christ (Acts 28:30–31).⁶⁷

It is likely that the knowledge of Jesus' example and rule of adaptation provided Paul with an authoritative criterion to follow as he encountered a variety of foods and food-related customs in Jewish and Gentile homes. Commentators often overlook that Paul restates Jesus' rule of adaptation in 1 Cor 10:27 (A 2005 *TLG* search found that a comparable use of ἐσθίετε with παρατίθημι is unattested in pre-Christian Greek literature):

Luke 10:8	1 Cor 10:27
Eat what is set before you	Eat whatever is set before you
ἐσθίετε τὰ παρατιθέμενα ὑμῖν	πᾶν τὸ παρατιθέμενον ὑμῖν ἐσθίετε

Adding weight to the argument for literary dependence, Biörn Fjärstedt notes in his dissertation on synoptic traditions in 1 Corinthians that a number of lexical correspondences exist between 1 Cor 9 and Luke 10:7–8, beginning with Paul's 1 Cor 9:14 reference to the dominical saying preserved in Luke 10:7.⁶⁸ Fjärstedt lists the following lexical correspondences between the blocks of material:⁶⁹

---

⁶⁵ "Paul Minear has proposed that for Luke 'table fellowship as interpreted by table talk *constituted the gospel*' . . . the Acts of the Apostles may be read, structurally, as a collection of guest and host stories about the missionary ventures generated in the Spirit-led communities of Jerusalem and Antioch. Often the names of individuals are reported for no other reasons, it seems, than to point up their exemplary hospitality to such notable figures as Peter, Paul, Barnabas, and so on" (John Koenig, *New Testament Hospitality: Partnership with Strangers as Promise and Mission* [Eugene: Wipf and Stock, 2001], 86–87); Paul Minear, *Commands of Christ: Authority and Implications* (Nashville: Abingdon, 1972), 180.

⁶⁶ The Western text adds "(both) Jews and Greeks".

⁶⁷ Adams, *The Sinner in Luke*, 192–93. Cf. Luke 9:11 ("and he welcomed them, and spoke to them about the kingdom of God") with Acts 28:30–31 ("and welcomed all who came to him, proclaiming the kingdom of God").

⁶⁸ Biörn Fjärstedt, *Synoptic Traditions in 1 Corinthians: Themes and Clusters of Theme Words in 1 Corinthians 1–4 and 9* (Uppsala: Theologiska Institutionen, 1974), 74–76.

⁶⁹ Dale Allison believes that Fjärstedt's observations on 1 Cor 9 and Luke 10 have advanced the argument for Pauline dependence on the mission discourse, "Fjärstedt has prob-

5.4 Jesus as "All Things to All People" in the Gospels 189

1 Cor 9	Verse	Luke 10	Verse
ἀπόστολος	1	ἀπέστειλεν	1
ἀπόστολος	2	ἀποστέλλω	3
ἀποστολῆς	2	ἀποστείλαντά	16
ἀπόστολοι	5	ἀπέστειλεν	(9:2)
ἐξουσίαν	4	ἐξουσίαν	19
ἐξουσίαν	5		
ἐξουσίαν	6	ἐξουσίαν	(9:1)
ἐξουσίας	12		
ἐξουσίᾳ	12		
ἐξουσίᾳ	18		
ἔργον	1	ἐργάται	2
ἐργάζεσθαι	6	ἐργάτας	2
ἐργαζόμενοι	13	ἐργάτης	7
φαγεῖν	4	ἐσθίοντες	7
ἐσθίει	7	ἐσθίετε	8
ἐσθίει	7		
ἐσθίουσιν	13		
πεῖν	4	πίνοντες	7
μισθόν	17	μισθοῦ	7
μισθός	18		
θερίσομεν	11	θερισμός	2
		θερισμοῦ	2
		θερισμόν	2
εὐαγγελίζωμαι	16	λέγετε...ἤγγικεν... ἡ βασιλεία	9
εὐαγγελίσωμαι	16	εἴπατε...ἤγγικεν ἡ βασιλεία	10–11
εὐαγγελιζόμενος	18	εὐαγγελιζόμενοι	(9:6)
εὐαγγελίῳ	12		
εὐαγγέλιον	14		
εὐαγγελίου	14		
εὐαγγέλιον	18		

---

ably made his case for at least one text. The parallels between 1 Cor 9 and Luke 10 are extensive and the thoughts are similar . . . That most of these parallels mark a real connection is strongly re-enforced by the explicit citation of the Lord's command in 1 Cor. 9.14 (see above). Thus, despite its flaws, Fjärstedt's dissertation establishes at least one important link between the apostle Paul and the Jesus tradition; and of special consequence is the conclusion that Paul knows more than isolated sayings. He seems to know a block of material, a missionary speech" (Dale C. Allison, "The Pauline Epistles and the Synoptic Gospels: The Pattern of the Parallels", *New Testament Studies* 28 [1982]: 9–10); cf. Dale C. Allison, "Paul and the Missionary Discourse", *Ephemerides Theologicae Lovanienses* 61 (1985): 369–75. Tuckett, "Paul and the Synoptic Mission Discourse?" 381, adopts a minimalist position on the Fjärstedt-Allison hypothesis, conceding only that "Paul knew and used one saying, the workman saying, from this discourse". See F. Neirynck, "Paul and the Sayings of Jesus", in *L'Apôtre Paul: Personnalité, Style et Conception du Ministère* (ed. A. Vanhoye; Leuven: Leuven University, 1986), 277. Without adopting Fjärstedt's maximalist view, I would suggest that even if only a few of Fjärstedt's lexical parallels are valid in addition to the workman saying, they would be confirmatory of the case that Paul appropriated Jesus' rule of adaptation in 1 Cor 10:27.

1 Cor 9	Verse	Luke 10	Verse
εὐαγγελίῳ	18		
κηρύξας	27	κηρύσσειν	(9:2)

In considering these lexical parallels, it is important to remember that Paul addresses in 1 Cor 9 the very issue that Jesus addresses in Luke 10 – provision for the lodging and sustenance of those sent out for ministry.[70]

Bearing in mind other echoes of Jesus tradition in 1 Cor 7–11, it is highly plausible that Paul applied Jesus' rule of adaptation (which probably concerned clean food of doubtful or defiled status) to the Corinthian Gentile context where food sacrificed to idols and indeterminate food was a foremost concern. I. Howard Marshall concludes that there is "an echo of this verse [Luke 10:8] in 1 Cor. 10.27".[71] Eckhard Schnabel concurs, "This evidence makes the assumption plausible that Paul was familiar with Jesus' missionary discourse, at least in the version of Lk 10".[72] Wenham agrees that Paul is "applying the general instruction to apostles about receiving hospitality (which he has been thinking about) to the specific question facing the Corinthians".[73] The restrictive clause in 1 Cor 9:21 ("though I am not without the law of God") and 1 Cor 10:28 ("do not eat [μὴ ἐσθίετε]" if your host tells you the food has been sacrificed) is a reminder that Paul adapted Jesus' halakhic rule to a Gentile setting and that Paul acknowledged exceptions to the rule.

In light of the cumulative evidence, it may be cautiously affirmed that Paul was familiar with Jesus' rule of adaptation. It appears that he was aware of Jesus' words attested in Luke 10:7–8 ("the labourer deserves to be paid . . . eat what is set before you") and that it was integral to the development of his thought on mission-based remuneration and accommodation at the table.

5.5 Paul as "All Things to All People"

In this section, it will be argued that 1 Cor 9:19–23 is informed by Jesus' example and rule of adaptation with respect to commensality. As Jesus became all things to all people through eating with ordinary Jews, Pharisees and sinners, Paul became "all things to all people" through eating with ordinary Jews, strict Jews (those "under the law") and Gentile sinners.

---

[70] David Wenham, *Paul: Follower of Jesus or Founder of Christianity?* (Grand Rapids: Eerdmans, 1995), 190–96; Arterbury, *Entertaining Angels*, 98, 102, 141, 175–79; cf. Victor P. Furnish, *Jesus According to Paul* (Cambridge: Cambridge University Press, 1993), 49.

[71] Marshall, *The Gospel of Luke*, 421.

[72] Schnabel, *Early Christian Mission*, 2:945.

[73] Wenham, *Paul*, 194.

5.5.1 "I Became As" (γίνομαι ... ὡς)

In the ancient world, the circle of people one ate with was an outward expression of the people with whom one identified. This sociological reality is sometimes referred to as "like ate with like"[74] or "like with like".[75] Table-fellowship was the quintessential expression of concord and unity, "In the various cultures underlying the New Testament, dining with someone indicated solidarity with that person. To eat with is to identify with".[76] Against this first-century cultural backdrop, Glad asserts that Paul's γίνομαι ("I became as") language refers to "association",[77] while Given takes it to mean "concrete, observable changes".[78] As argued in 4.4.2, both are probably correct. When Paul wrote that he "became as" others, in all likelihood he did not mean that he imitated them like a chameleon but that he closely associated with them through table-fellowship, and conformed to their customs (within the limits of God's law) in keeping with the Jewish ethic of hospitality:

> ... that relationship, the one between guest and host, is governed by all the most specific rules of etiquette and good conduct – but the most important rule (*always*!) is that the guest show deference to the host by accepting his choices. Of menu. Of wine. Of company. Of table conversation. In other words, the guest in any culture shows subservience and gratitude to his host by *gratefully* accepting what is served for dinner ... Hosts and guests do not have a relationship of equality in any culture; indeed the whole idea of being a guest implies subservience ... The whole point is that the guest is *supposed* to set his own feelings aside out of deference to the host; the relationship rests on the fact that the host calls the shots and the guest gratefully and graciously accepts the inequality of the situation as the price for a free meal.[79]

For Paul, being a guest was a primary way that he came to know people intimately ("extend hospitality to strangers ... Rejoice with those who rejoice, weep with those who weep" [Rom 12:13–14]).[80] Receiving hospitality was more than simply eating together. It was an experience of understanding the host and following the way of the host (e.g. Philo, *Abr.* 107–8, 115, 118; *T.*

---

[74] Neufeld, "Jesus' Eating Transgressions", 20.

[75] Bartchy, "Table Fellowship", 796; cf. Sir 13.16, "All living beings associate with their own kind, and people stick close to those like themselves".

[76] Robert L. Kelley, "Meals with Jesus in Luke's Gospel", *Horizons in Biblical Theology* 17:2 (1995): 123. Cf. Reta Halteman Finger, *Of Widows and Meals: Communal Meals in the Book of Acts* (Grand Rapids: Eerdmans, 2007), 176–77; Rosenblum, *Food and Identity in Early Rabbinic Judaism*, 2–3.

[77] Glad, "Paul and Adaptability", 29.

[78] Given, *Paul's True Rhetoric*, 109.

[79] Martin Samuel Cohen, *Travels on the Private Zodiac: Reflections on Jewish Life, Ritual, and Spirituality* (London Ontario: Moonstone, 1995), 40.

[80] Cf. *Der. Er. Rab.* 7.7: "A man should not rejoice among people who weep or weep when among those who rejoice ... This is the general rule: A man should not deviate from the custom of his companions or from society". See Hilary Le Cornu with Joseph Shulam, *A Commentary on the Jewish Roots of Galatians* (Jerusalem: Academon, 2005), 284, on Gal 4:12–14.

Ab. RecShrt. 4.15; RecLng. 4.7 ["and *whatever he says to you, this indeed do, and whatever he eats, you indeed eat along with him*"]).[81] The *Midrash* similarly describes a universal rule of hospitality that enjoins guests to become like their hosts: "If you go to a town, behave according to its customs". Conzelmann, Bornkamm, Schoeps and Daube maintain that this teaching, which came to be interpreted by Jews as a charge to imitate one's host, goes back to Hillel:[82]

> *There is a saying: "If you go to a town, follow its custom"*. Above, where there is no eating, Moses went up and *made it his business to look and act like them*: "Then I abode in the mount forty days and forty nights. I did not eat bread or drink water" (Deut. 9.9). Below, where there is eating: "And he stood by them under the tree while they ate" (*Gen. Rab.* 48.14).[83]

> *The proverb runs: "If thou goest into a city, thou must act according to its customs"*. When Moses ascended on high, where there is no eating or drinking, *he emulated the heavenly example*, and when the angels descended on earth, where there is eating and drinking, they ate and drank, for it says, And he [Abraham] stood by them under the tree, and they did eat (Gen. 18:18) (*Exod. Rab.* 47.5).[84]

Samuel Vollenweider asserts that the saying is not handed down from Hillel ("Das Dictum stammt nicht von Hillel")[85] but is historically rooted in the first century travel rule echoed by one of the Jewish guests in the *Letter of Aristeas* 257. Vollenweider recognizes the similarity between this travel rule and Pauline accommodation in 1 Cor 9:19–23:

> The *travel rule* in *Let. Aris.* 257 comes in a certain formal nearness to the Pauline accommodation: How can one find a good reception in a foreign land? "If he makes himself similar to all [sich *allen gleichstellt*, Πᾶσιν ἴσος γινόμενος] . . . and presents himself as inferior to his host rather than superior to him. For God is also accustomed in accordance with his nature to accept that which lowers itself". God is here compared with the host, who values modesty and humility. Such a travel rule is also attested in *Gen. Rab.* 48.14 and *Exod. Rab.* 47.5: "From there comes the saying (*Mashal*): 'If you come into a city, then act according to its customs'".[86]

The rule of hospitality, which may indeed go back to Hillel (*t. Ber.* 2.21), combined with the travel rule attested in the *Letter of Aristeas* 257 (Πᾶσιν ἴσος γινόμενος), and the Lord's directive to follow the way of the host in the *Testament of Abraham* RecLng. 4.7 (καὶ ὅτι ἂν ἐσθίῃ συνέσθιε καὶ σὺ μετ᾽

---

[81] See 4.2.4 above.

[82] Conzelmann, *A Commentary on the First Epistle to the Corinthians*, 160 n. 21; Bornkamm, "The Missionary Stance of Paul in 1 Corinthians 9 and in Acts", 195; Schoeps, *Paul*, 231; Daube, *The New Testament and Rabbinic Judaism*, 339; Daube, *New Testament Judaism*, 563; cf. Schrage, *Der erste Brief an die Korinther*, 2:339.

[83] Jacob Neusner, *The Components of the Rabbinic Documents: From the Whole to the Parts IX. Genesis Rabbah Part Five* (Atlanta: Scholars, 1997), 225, emphasis mine. Also *Lev. Rab.* 34.8; *Num. Rab.* 10.6; *Eccl. Rab.* 3.14; *b. B. Meṣiʿa* 86b.

[84] Soncino 1939, emphasis mine.

[85] Vollenweider, *Freiheit als neue Schöpfung*, 218 n. 94.

[86] Vollenweider, *Freiheit als neue Schöpfung*, 218.

αὐτου), provide a reasonable basis to argue that γίνομαι ... ὡς in 1 Cor 9:19–23 describes Paul's adaptation to his host in Jewish and Gentile hospitality settings.[87] *I contend that Paul's "I became as" statements refer to his regular practice of accommodating to his host, especially with respect to eating what was set before him. This made it possible for Paul to share with his host the gospel of God.*[88]

This table-centred interpretation of γίνομαι ... ὡς in 1 Cor 9:19–23 is supported by six observations:

1. "Food and table-fellowship" is a central theme in 1 Cor 8:1–11:1.[89] There are more than twenty-five references to food and commensality in the pericope. Following 1 Cor 11:1, Paul continues his focus on food and table-fellowship by discussing the tradition of the Messiah's last Passover and the covenant meal instituted out of it (1 Cor 11:20–32; cf. 5:6–8).[90]
2. Paul closes chapter 11 with guidelines for proper conduct when the congregation eats together (1 Cor 11:33–34). He reminds them that they are not in their own homes (the implication is that they are guests) and they should think of the others present (1 Cor 11:33).
3. Paul has in mind the scenario of being a guest at an unbeliever's home in 1 Cor 10:27a, "If an unbeliever invites you to a meal ..."
4. In 1 Cor 10:27b, Paul echoes Jesus' rule of adaptation with respect to being a guest in another's home ("eat what is set before you" [cf. Luke 10:8]).
5. In chapter 9 the verses that lead into vv. 19–23 focus on food and receiving hospitality. Paul refers to the "food and drink" (v. 4) he had a right to receive from the Jesus-believers in Corinth, eating from a vineyard and

---

[87] The view that Paul sought to please his host by adapting to his host comes close to Augustine's portrayal of Paul as one who empathized with all, "A person who nurses a sick man becomes, in a sense, sick himself, not by pretending to have a fever but by thinking sympathetically how he would wish to be treated if he were sick himself" (Augustine, *Epist. to Jerome* 40.4; cf. 82; *CSEL* 34:2:379–80; *FC* 12:413–14). See Carolline White, *The Correspondence (394–419) Between Jerome and Augustine of Hippo* (Lampeter: The Edwin Mellen Press, 1990), 168–69. Similarly, Chadwick, "'All Things to All Men' (I Cor IX.22)", 275, suggests that Paul sought to "minimize the gap between himself and his potential converts".

[88] "Thus, from Acts as well as Paul's own letters we begin to get the impression that for the apostle 'meal' and 'gospel' belong together" (Koenig, *New Testament Hospitality*, 55).

[89] "Banquet as Missionary Approach (1 Cor 10:31–11:1). The Corinthians attended meals that both Christ-followers and pagans attended, as seen in 1 Cor 8–10. These meals provided opportunities for mission ... Paul's overarching missionary approach is summarized in 1 Cor 10:31: 'Whether, then, you eat or drink or whatever you do, do all to the glory of God' ... Paul concludes with an imperative 'be an imitator of me'. This imitation relates directly to Paul's missional behaviour" (J. Brian Tucker, "The Role of Civic Identity on the Pauline Mission in Corinth", *Didaskalia* [Winter 2008]: 88–89).

[90] Passover and table-fellowship are also mentioned in 1 Cor 5:6–11. See Jonathan Schwiebert, "Table Fellowship and the Translation of 1 Corinthians 5:11", *Journal of Biblical Literature* 127:1 (2008): 159–64.

drinking milk (v. 7), eating grain (v. 9), sharing in the harvest (v. 10), eating holy food (v. 13).

6. 1 Cor 9:19–23 seems to assume a hospitality context. One of the only occasions when Paul would have been around Jews or Gentiles exclusively was when he ate in a Jewish or Gentile home. Proponents of a hyperliteral interpretation of 1 Cor 9:19–23 are unable to explain how Paul could become a Jew to the Jews and a Gentile to the Gentiles in a larger setting where Jews and Gentiles were present together. I conclude that Paul "became" all things to all people by adapting to his Jewish or Gentile host. By being an accommodating guest at the table, Paul entered into the lives of all so that all could enter into his life in Christ.

5.5.2 "I Became as One Under the Law" (ἐγενόμην . . . ὡς ὑπὸ νόμον)

Though the term Ἰουδαίοις ("Jews") appears before ὑπὸ νόμον ("under the law") in 1 Cor 9:20, I will discuss their meaning in reverse order to make the case that ὑπὸ νόμον is a subset of Ἰουδαίοις. In commenting on 1 Cor 9:20 ("To the Jews I became as a Jew . . . To those under the law I became as one under the law"), Gerard Sloyan writes, "This seems to hint at a distinction between ordinary Jews and a new class of Law observants ('those under the Law') who were perhaps the 'separated' or *perushim* to which he gave his allegiance as a young man".[91] In 4.4.3, it was argued that there is much to commend this interpretation of ὑπὸ νόμον, which goes back to John Lightfoot (1664). One qualification, however, should be added to the Lightfoot-Sloyan reading: "those under the law" may refer more broadly to Jews who scrupulously observed the law. As shown in chapter 4, there was a spectrum of Jewish groups in the Second Temple period that shared similar overlapping commitments to strict Torah observance. "Those under the law" might then be interpreted to mean more broadly "those under [strict interpretation of] the law", as Heydenreich, Richardson, Bockmuehl and Phua have posited.[92]

While this broader interpretation of "under the law" is plausible, the limited textual data seem to support the Lightfoot-Sloyan hypothesis that Paul had Pharisees particularly in mind. For example, Paul uses νόμος in reference to Pharisaic interpretation of the law in Phil 3:5 – "as to the law, a Pharisee" (κατὰ νόμον Φαρισαῖος [Phil 3:5]).[93] Pharisees strictly observed the Torah

---

[91] Sloyan, "Did Paul Think That Jews and Jewish Christians Must Follow Torah?" 172.

[92] Heydenreich, *Commentarius in priorem divi Pauli ad Corinthios epistolam*, 2:41–42; Richardson, *Israel in the Apostolic Church*, 122; Bockmuehl, *Jewish Law in Gentile Churches*, 171; Phua, *Idolatry and Authority*, 193; cf. Young, *Paul the Jewish Theologian*, 20.

[93] "Paul's concise claim, 'in relation to (*kata*) law, a Pharisee', most naturally means living Jewish life according to the Pharisaic interpretation of the law" (Anthony J. Saldarini, *Pharisees, Scribes and Sadducees in Palestinian Society* [Edinburgh: T & T Clark, 1988], 135). Cf. Joseph Sievers, "Who Were the Pharisees?" in *Hillel and Jesus: Comparative Studies of Two Major Religious Leaders* (ed. James H. Charlesworth and Loren L. Johns; Min-

and upheld the "tradition (παράδοσιν) of the elders" (Matt 15:2; Mark 7:3, 5). Josephus describes the Pharisees as keeping "certain regulations handed down (παρέδοσαν) by former generations and not recorded in the Laws of Moses" (Josephus, *Ant.* 13.297; cf. Gal 1:14: παραδόσεων).[94] Despite the ongoing debate over the reliability of Josephus' account, few would disagree with the statement that Pharisaic halakhah was a combination of strict interpretation (relative to the experience of ordinary Jews) and expansion of Mosaic law consistent with the customs of the fathers.

Another factor in support of the Lightfoot-Sloyan hypothesis is that Pharisees lived among the people and were open to table-fellowship if a guest conformed to their halakhic standards (4.2.1.4). This is in contrast to some of the other sectarian groups (e.g. Qumran Jews). Neusner points out:

Both Christians and Pharisees lived among ordinary folk, while the Qumranians did not. In this respect the commonplace character of Pharisaic table-fellowship is all the more striking. The sect ordinarily did not gather *as a group* at all, but in the home. All meals required purity. Pharisaic table-fellowship took place in the same circumstances as did the meals of outsiders. Pharisees were common folk, who ate everyday meals in an everyday way, among ordinary neighbors, not members of the sect.[95]

Paul would have also encountered Jews who were not Pharisees but oriented toward Pharisaic halakhah. Dunn notes that Pharisees in Israel and the Diaspora exerted influence on Jews to be stricter in observance particularly with respect to ritual purity:

We may justifiably infer then that wherever Pharisaic influence was strong during the middle decades of the first century of our era, both within Palestine and among strong concentrations of Jews in the Diaspora, there would be pressure on those who thought of themselves as good

---

neapolis: Fortress, 1997), 145; Bockmuehl, *The Epistle to the Philippians*, 197; L. J. Lietaert Peerbolte, *Paul the Missionary* (Leuven: Peeters, 2003), 140–42.

[94] On παράδοσις, see Günter Stemberger, *Jewish Contemporaries of Jesus: Pharisees, Sadducees, Essenes* (trans. Allan W. Mahnke; Minneapolis: Fortress, 1995), 88–95; Jacob Neusner and C. Thoma, "Die Pharisäer vor und nach der Tempelzerstörung des Jahres 70 n. Chr", in *Tempelkult und Tempelzerstörung (70 n. Chr.)* (ed. S. Lauer; New York: Peter Lang, 1994), 77, 96–98; Martin Hengel and Roland Deines, "E. P. Sanders' 'Common Judaism', Jesus, and the Pharisees: A Review Article", *Journal of Theological Studies* 46 (1995): 17–41; Joseph M. Baumgarten, "The Unwritten Law in the Pre-Rabbinic Period", *Journal for the Study of Judaism in the Persian, Hellenistic, and Roman Periods* 3 (1972): 7–29; Albert I. Baumgarten, "Korban and the Pharisaic Paradosis", *Journal of the Ancient Near Eastern Society of Columbia University* 16–17 (1984/85): 5–17; Albert I. Baumgarten, "The Pharisaic Paradosis", *Harvard Theological Review* 80 (1987): 63–70; D. R. Schwartz, "Hillel and Scripture: From Authority to Exegesis", in *Hillel and Jesus: Comparative Studies of Two Major Religious Leaders* (ed. J. H. Charlesworth and L. L. Johns; Minneapolis: Fortress, 1997), 335–62, esp. 337.

[95] Neusner, *The Idea of Purity in Ancient Judaism*, 67. Also Sanders, *Jewish Law from Jesus to the Mishnah*, 236–42; Saldarini, *Pharisees, Scribes and Sadducees in Palestinian Society*, 286–87, 72. See 5.4.2 above.

Jews to observe the halakhic clarifications of the laws on tithing and purity – that is to say, pressure on devout Jews (including proselytes) to observe strict limits in their practice of table-fellowship.[96]

Eyal Regev confirms that Jewish concern with ritual purity was widespread in Israel and the Diaspora.[97] In addition to eating in the homes of Pharisees and Pharisee-oriented Jews in the cities he visited, it may be reasonably conjectured that when Paul returned to Tarsus or Israel (see Acts 9:11, 28–30; 11:25; 21:39; 22:3; 26:4–5), he received hospitality from Pharisees he knew intimately. After all, he was from a family of Pharisees (Acts 23:6; 26:4–5; cf. Phil 3:5; Gal 1:14).[98] In such situations, it is proposed that Paul became as one under the law to win those under the law.

5.5.2.1 The Reason for Paul's Use of the Term "Under the Law" (ὑπὸ νόμον) in 1 Cor 9:20

Why would Paul use the expression "under the law" (ὑπὸ νόμον) to refer to Pharisees or Jews who strictly adhered to the law? One explanation is that Pharisees and other ardent observers of the law *stood out* among the law-observant populace as particularly zealous for the Torah, "I advanced in Judaism *beyond* many among my people of the same age, for I was *far more zealous* for the traditions of my ancestors" (Gal 1:14). It should be remembered that in a society where it was normative for Jews to be law observant, *if a Jew referred to other Jews as "under the law", it would have likely had the connotation "under the law in a particularly fervent way"*, perhaps comparable in meaning to "zealous for the law" (ζηλωταὶ τοῦ νόμου) in Acts 21:20 (cf. 22:3).[99] In contemporary Israeli parlance, such Jews are referred to as the *haredim* (Hebrew for "ultra-Orthodox") or *frum* (Yiddish for "very religious") in contrast to the *masorti* (Hebrew for "traditional").[100] Each generation of Torah-observant Jews has insider language to describe fellow Jews who are

---

[96] Dunn, *Jesus, Paul and the Law*, 140; Dunn, "The Incident at Antioch (Gal. 2:11–18)", 16. Sanders, "Jewish Association With Gentiles and Galatians 2:11–14", 172, points out that Diaspora Jews did not tithe their food.

[97] Regev, "Non-Priestly Purity and Its Religious Aspects According to Historical Sources and Archaeological Findings", 223–44.

[98] Paul's second and third missionary journeys took him through the region of Tarsus and Jerusalem. Saldarini, *Pharisees, Scribes and Sadducees in Palestinian Society*, 137, 142–43, notes, "It is likely that the Pharisees and their influence extended into Palestine and adjacent areas in Syria and Cilicia . . . The Pharisees had a following in Palestine and probably in the immediately surrounding territories, including Tarsus which was close to Antioch in northern Syria". Consistent with this data, Matt 23:15 indicates that Pharisees crossed "sea and land" for outreach purposes.

[99] According to Luke, Paul used the terms ἀκρίβειαν ("strictly") and ζηλωτής ("zealous") together to describe his Pharisaic upbringing (Acts 22:3).

[100] See Charles S. Liebman, "Introduction", in *Conflict and Accommodation between Jews in Israel: Religious and Secular* (ed. Charles S. Liebman; Jerusalem: Keter, 1990), xiv–xv.

especially scrupulous in their interpretation and application of Jewish law. It is proposed that Paul either coined the term "under the law" or borrowed it from contemporary usage to refer to the *haredim* or *frum* of his day.[101]

A second possibility is that the term ὑπὸ νόμον is ironic and should be in quotes – the Pharisees stood out as "under the law" because they made a show of their strict Torah observance.[102] Matthew writes, "They do all their deeds to be seen by others; for they make their phylacteries [tefillin] broad and their fringes [tsitsit] long" (Matt 23:5; cf. 6:1, 16; Mark 12:40; Luke 20:47).

A *third* possible explanation is that "under the law" is a term that the Pharisees and other strict sects used to describe themselves in contrast to the general populace, "We are the ones who live under the law. We are the true Jews. We are the circumcision". Sometimes very religious Jews today refer to themselves as "Torah-true" Jews[103] or observers of a "Torah-true life".[104]

A *fourth* possible explanation for the term (given Paul's typically negative use of ὑπὸ νόμον in Galatians and Romans) is that the apostle considered narrow interpretation of the law a burden. Very strict Jews were "under [the burden of a stringent interpretation of] the law". Contemporary *frum* Jews understand how a narrowly defined Torah-observant lifestyle can have a negative side due to the loss of personal freedom:

> The narrower our definitions for proper observance, the narrower the path and the harder it is to stay on the derech [way]. The narrower the path, the less room there is for the self. The less room there is to move, make mistakes, or express varying parts of the personality, the more likely a person will fall off the derech . . . narrow definitions of proper observance blur the understanding of proper observance. All things become equated until we lose all sense of priority. *Non-halachic* requirements seem the same as *halachic* ones, for breaches in both areas are met with the same condemnation . . . When communal standards become the measure of *frumkeit* [religiosity] rather than the Torah's, observance starts to become more about what people think, and people then aim to please each other rather than God . . . the more we focus on extra-*halachic* requirements, the greater the possibility that we neglect or forget about the Torah itself.[105]

As one who had lived most of his life as a strict Pharisee and then experienced the relative freedom of common Judaism, Paul intimately understood the restrictive nature of Pharisaic halakhah.

---

[101] Paul noticed the "extremely religious" (δεισιδαιμονεστέρους) among the Gentiles he sought to win (Acts 17:22).

[102] Cf. the *shikmi* Pharisee in *y. Soṭah* 5.5. See Sara Epstein Weinstein, *Piety and Fanaticism: Rabbinic Criticism of Religious Stringency* (London: Jason Aronson, 1997), 149.

[103] Hella Winston, *Unchosen: The Hidden Lives of Hasidic Rebels* (Boston: Beacon, 2005), 184 n. 1.

[104] Fishkoff, *The Rebbe's Army*, 31.

[105] Faranak Margolese, *Off the Derech: Why Observant Jews Leave Judaism* (New York: Devora, 2005), 311–13, 317.

In support of the view that Paul regarded Pharisaic halakhah as a particularly narrow interpretation of the Torah, it is notable that Luke relates Paul's saying that the Pharisees are "the strictest (ἀκριβεστάτην) sect of our religion" (Acts 26:5). That Paul thought of Pharisees as punctilious in their law observance is corroborated by his statement in Phil 3:5–6 that he had been "as to the law, a Pharisee . . . as to righteousness under the law, blameless". The language "as to righteousness under the law, blameless" (κατὰ δικαιοσύνην τὴν ἐν νόμῳ γενόμενος ἄμεμπτος) suggests that Paul perceived Pharisaic halakhah to be especially restrictive. For someone with this perspective, it would have been natural to view Pharisees as "under the law" in the sense of being *under [the burden of a strict interpretation of] the law*. In what ways were the Pharisees demanding as a sect?

Pharisaic halakhah was particularly concerned with eating ordinary food in a state of ritual purity (4.2.1). Neusner comments that in early Rabbinic literature "approximately 67 percent of all legal pericopae [pertaining to Pharisees] deal with dietary laws. These laws concern (1) ritual purity for meals and (2) agricultural rules governing the fitness of food for pharisaic consumption".[106] Sanders disputes the accuracy of Neusner's figure but concedes that food and table-fellowship were central concerns of Pharisaic halakhah.[107] Dunn convincingly demonstrates that Neusner's results are reasonable and that "the purity of the meal table was an important concern among many of the Pharisees of Jesus' time, or at least within a significant faction of the Pharisees".[108] The gospels confirm that Pharisees prioritized the preparation of food, ritual purity, tithing of foods, and table-fellowship (Mark 7:1–5; Matt 15:1–2; 23:23–26; Luke 11:42).

Consistent with the gospels and Acts, Josephus describes the Pharisees as a sect known for their *strict* and *exacting* (ἀκρίβεια) observance of Jewish law.[109] According to Dunn,

when Josephus speaks of the Pharisees he regularly describes them as the party of ἀκρίβεια (*War* 1.110; 2.162; *Ant.* 17.41; *Life* 191; cf. *Ant.* 20.201, and note again the striking correlation in Acts 22.3; 26:5). The word denotes "exactness or precision", and when used in connection with "law" is most naturally taken in a sense like "strictness or severity" (Greek-English Lexicon, ed. H. Liddell and R. Scott). So when we read, for example, in *War* 2.162, that the Pharisees interpreted the laws or customs μετ' ἀκριβείας, the implication is clear that they were well known as those who interpreted the law with scrupulous exactness and strictness in detail. This strongly suggests that the Pharisees also saw themselves in an important sense as guardians of the law and of the ancestral customs (*Ant.* 13.297, 408; 17.41; *Life* 198). Moreover, if Josephus, the self-confessed Pharisee, is any guide, they naturally wished to

---

[106] Jacob Neusner, *Judaic Law From Jesus to the Mishnah: A Systematic Reply to Professor E. P. Sanders* (Atlanta: Scholars, 1993), 253–54.

[107] Sanders, "Jewish Association With Gentiles and Galatians 2:11–14", 177–79.

[108] Dunn, *Jesus, Paul and the Law*, 64–65.

[109] Cf. Stemberger, *Jewish Contemporaries of Jesus*, 90–91.

commend such "strictness" to others (*Ant*. 1.14; 4.309; 5.132; 8.21; 18.345; *Ap.* 2.149, 187, 227–28).[110]

Josephus depicts the Pharisees as intermittently allied with the governing class (*Ant*. 13. 408–409, 423; *J.W.* 1.108–12; 2.262) and concerned with legislating Pharisaic halakhah on the populace – "the regulations (νόμιμα) they had imposed on the people" (*Ant*. 13.296–97).[111]

It is significant that Luke portrays Pharisaic halakhah as a heavy burden. In Acts 15, Luke relates that Jesus-believing Pharisees opposed Paul's stance that Jesus-believing Gentiles were exempt from circumcision. In response to the news of Gentile conversion, "some believers who belonged to the sect of the Pharisees stood up and said, 'It is *necessary* (δεῖ) for them [the Gentile believers] to be circumcised and *ordered* (παραγγέλλειν) to keep the law of Moses'" (Acts 15:5). Luke informs the reader that this view was a source of "no small dissension and debate" between Paul and his opponents in Antioch (Acts 15:2). Immediately after the Pharisees state what they "require" of the Gentile believers, Peter replies that the Pharisee demand is akin to *"placing on the neck of the [Gentile] disciples a yoke that neither our ancestors nor we have been able to bear"* (Acts 15:10).

While most commentators interpret Peter's "under the yoke" language as a reference to being "under the yoke of Mosaic law", the Luke-Acts context gives weight to the argument that Peter was referring to the historic imposition of Pharisaic interpretation of the law (not Mosaic law in general) on the Jewish populace.[112] I contend that he is speaking of being "under the yoke of Pharisaic halakhah".[113]

---

[110] Dunn, *Jesus, Paul and the Law*, 66–67.

[111] Saldarini, *Pharisees, Scribes and Sadducees in Palestinian Society*, 79–106.

[112] According to Josephus, *Ant*. 13.296–299, Pharisaic law was in force during the reigns of Hyrcanus and Salome Alexandra, "Salome gave the Pharisees a free hand in reshaping their role under her reign and ordered the populace to heed their instructions. The 'tradition of the fathers', i.e. Pharisaic halakha, once more became the law of the land" (Schaper, "The Pharisees", 414). Cf. Hillel Newman, *Proximity to Power and Jewish Sectarian Groups of the Ancient Period: A Review of Lifestyle, Values, and Halakhah in the Pharisees, Sadducees, Essenes, and Qumran* (ed. Ruth Ludlam; Leiden: Brill, 2006), 63–73. *Pace* Shaye J. D. Cohen, *Josephus in Galilee and Rome: His Vita and Development as a Historian* (Leiden: Brill, 1979), 223. Weight should be given to the agreement between Josephus and the gospel writers and their proximity to the historical events. A balanced approach would be to "recognize the likelihood that their [the Pharisees'] influence reached well beyond their own ranks" (Dunn, *Jesus, Paul and the Law*, 66).

[113] "As a simple Galilean Jew who observes the Law of cleanliness (Ac 10.14) and can under divine guidance readily fraternize with the Gentiles (Ac 10.28; Ga 2.11–14), Peter and those like him may find the details of the Pharisaic legal tradition too burdensome to observe" (Mbachu Hilary, *Inculturation Theology of the Jerusalem Council in Acts 15: An Inspiration for the Igbo Church Today* [Frankfurt am Main: Peter Lang, 1995], 159).

Three arguments support this interpretation of Acts 15:10. First, the assumption throughout Acts 15 is that Jesus-believing Jews would continue to observe Mosaic law. According to Michael Wyschogrod,

> Acts 15 is decisive in this respect ... After *lengthy* debate (Acts 15:7) the decision is reached, and communicated in a letter, that no further burden beyond the Noachide Laws is to be placed on gentiles. In so doing, Paul's position on the matter is fully vindicated by the authoritative Jerusalem church. Had the thought that with the coming of Christ the Law had been abolished entered anyone's mind in Jerusalem, there could clearly not have ensued a long discussion, settled with some difficulty, as to whether circumcision and the Law ought to be made obligatory for gentiles. If it was no longer obligatory for Jews, how could it possibly become so for others? The only possible explanation dictated by the facts is that the possibility of the Torah not remaining binding for Jews never occurred to anyone in Jerusalem.[114]

Second, Luke disparages narrow interpretation of the law. In Luke 11:37–45, after a negative portrayal of Pharisaic law observance, Jesus is depicted as saying, "Woe also to you lawyers (νομικοῖς)! *For you load people with burdens hard to bear*, and you yourselves do not lift a finger to ease them" (Luke 11:46). Similar language is found in Acts 15:10 in response to Pharisees:

Luke 11:46	Acts 15:10
For you load people with burdens hard to bear (δυσβάστακτα)	by placing on the neck of the disciples a yoke that neither our ancestors nor we have been able to bear (βαστάσαι)

Luke 11:46 and Acts 15:10 were written by the same author and occur in contexts in which Luke focuses on onerous burdens imposed by the Pharisees.[115]

Third, Torah observance is positively portrayed throughout Luke-Acts (e.g. Luke 1:6; 2:21–39;[116] Acts 22:12).[117] These three arguments support the case that Acts 15:10 does not refer to the general application of Mosaic law (the

---

[114] Wyschogrod, *Abraham's Promise*, 194. "If the minimum acceptable is demanded of non-Jews, circumcision and respect for the Torah in its ritual sphere are incumbent on Christians of Jewish origin. Without actually saying so, the Jerusalem Council thus adopts among Christians the principle of a dual relationship with the Law. This duality is made possible by the extent to which the soteriological foundation is, as Peter recalls, the same for both (Acts 15.11)" (Daniel Marguerat, "Paul and the Torah in the Acts of the Apostles", in *Torah in the New Testament: Papers Delivered at the Manchester-Lausanne Seminar of June 2008* [ed. Michael Tait and Peter Oakes; London: T & T Clark International, 2009], 111).

[115] The Nazarene commentary on Isaiah, quoted by Jerome, refers to Pharisees placing a heavy yoke of the *traditions* on the people, "When Christ came and his preaching shone out, the land of Zebulon and the land of Naphtali first of all were freed from the errors of the Scribes and the Pharisees and he shook off their shoulders the very heavy yoke of the Jewish traditions (*traditionum Iudaicarum*)" (Jerome, *Comm. Isa.* 9.1).

[116] "In the course of eighteen verses Luke mentions that they were acting in accordance with the law no fewer than five times (2.22, 23, 24, 27, 39)" (Esler, *Community and Gospel in Luke-Acts*, 112).

[117] See Carras, "Observant Jews in the Story of Luke and Acts", 693–708.

normative way of life of first-century Jews) but to Pharisaic halakhah.[118] Acts 15:10 is thus evidence that Pharisees were viewed by some early Jesus-believers as Jews who were "under the yoke" of a particularly strict interpretation of the law.

Matthew's view of Pharisaic law is similar to Luke's: the Pharisees impose burdens on the people through their narrow interpretations of the Torah. In Matt 11:28–30, Jesus says, "Come to me, all you that are weary and are carrying heavy burdens, and I will give you rest. Take my yoke upon you, and learn from me; for I am gentle and humble in heart, and you will find rest for your souls. *For my yoke is easy, and my burden is light*" (italics mine). This is followed by two stories that portray Pharisaic interpretation of Sabbath law as overly strict and burdensome (Matt 12:1–8, 9–14). In Matt 15:1–20 (cf. Mark 7:1–5), Pharisees rebuke Jesus' disciples for not keeping the "tradition of the elders". Finally, Matthew describes the Pharisees as legislators who "tie up *heavy burdens* (φορτία)*, hard to bear, and lay them on the shoulders of others*" (Matt 23:1–4).[119] Beaton concludes, "The language of heavy burdens seems to relate to Pharisaic halakhah and not to Torah itself".[120]

To sum up the fourth reason that Paul may have used the term ὑπὸ νόμον in 1 Cor 9:20 – the term with its negative valence may have been shorthand for one "under the yoke of Pharisaic halakhah". Pharisees observed narrow interpretations of the Torah that restricted personal freedom and naturally imposed a heavier burden on the individual. The polemical descriptor "under the law" may have subtly expressed the nuance "under heavy burdens [of the law], hard to bear".

5.5.2.2 The Meaning of the Restrictive Clause "Though I Myself Am Not Under the Law" (μὴ ὢν αὐτὸς ὑπὸ νόμον)

What did Paul mean by his qualification in 1 Cor 9:20 – "(though I myself am not under [Pharisaic/strict interpretation of] the law)"? This study submits that Paul remained a Pharisee in kinship, custom and education, but he challenged

---

[118] Given the intra-Jewish/Pharisaic context, Peter's words might be interpreted as follows, "If we mainstream Jews do not want to keep strict Pharisaic interpretations and expansions of the law, why should we impose Pharisaic halakhah on the Gentiles? We are not saved by strict law observance but by grace". When Acts 15:10 is read in this way, Peter is not rejecting Torah observance per se but Torah observance as defined by Pharisaic halakhah for the purpose of eschatological blessing.

[119] Cf. φορτίζω (to burden) in Matt 11:28; Luke 11:46. Note the "shoulder-Pharisee who lays commandments on men's shoulders" (*y. Ber.* 67a) and the *baraita* in *t. Soṭah* 22b.

[120] Richard Beaton, "Messiah and Justice: A Key to Matthew's Use of Isaiah 42.1–4?" *Journal for the Study of the New Testament* 75 (1999): 16 n. 42. See Roger Mohrlang, *Matthew and Paul: A Comparison of Ethical Perspectives* (Cambridge: Cambridge University Press, 1984), 21–23; K. G. C. Newport, *The Sources and Sitz im Leben of Matthew 23* (Sheffield: Sheffield Academic Press, 1995), 124–27.

Pharisaic halakhah by closely associating with Gentile sinners and not consistently eating tithed, ordinary food in a state of ritual purity. It is not known how most Pharisees viewed Paul after he became an apostle to the Gentiles. Pharisaic Judaism was not monolithic; diversity existed in the sect (Acts 15:5) and there was presumably a ladder of halakhic observance that stretched from the novitiate to the extremely strict. Those with a Pharisaic pedigree like Paul may have been given more latitude before being excluded from the group. That Paul was not entirely excluded is suggested by Paul's self-identification as a Pharisee in Acts 23:6 – ἐγὼ Φαρισαῖός εἰμι – and the Pharisee response three verses later, "We find nothing wrong with this man".

5.5.3 "I Became as a Jew" (ἐγενόμην ὡς Ἰουδαῖος)

If ὑπὸ νόμον ("under the law") refers to Pharisees, and perhaps other strict observers of the Torah, it may be inferred that the designation Ἰουδαίοις ("Jews") in 1 Cor 9:20 refers to the larger body of Jews (כל ישראל) in which strict Jews form their subidentity. The name "Pharisees" (פרושים = "the separate ones") appears to imply this meaning.[121] It is notable that separation from the larger group of "Jews" to form a sect did not mean that the Pharisees were exclusivist. On the contrary, as shown in 4.2.1.2, the Pharisees were oriented toward living with the common people and influencing them in the direction of Pharisaic halakhah:

> The exaggerated polarization of the Pharisees' exclusivism and the Christians' inclusivism obscures the phenomenon that exclusivist and inclusivist tendencies often *co-exist* in the same group, particularly in conversionist sects. Thus, despite the separatism implied by their so-called "exclusivist" tithing, purity, and table fellowship practices, and even by their name itself ("Pharisee" comes from the Hebrew word "*perushi*" "one who is set apart"), the Pharisees demonstrated markedly *non-separatist* tendencies. The table fellowship rules distinguished between members and non-members of the Pharisees' "club", but did not discourage non-members from joining the club. On the contrary, the rules were designed to entice non-members to join . . . The Pharisees' apparently conflicting tendencies of separatism and popular appeal could likewise reflect the inherent tension of a conversionist sect both trying to win adherents and to maintain its distinctive boundaries and social identity.[122]

In support of the proposal that, in 1 Cor 9:20, Ἰουδαίοις is Paul's designation for ordinary Jews and ὑπὸ νόμον is Paul's designation for strict Jews, it is significant that in 1 Cor 10:18 Paul moves from the universal to the particular, from the set of all Jews (the people of Israel) to the subset of strict Jews (priests). In Phil 3:5–6 and Acts 22:3, Paul similarly moves from the set of all

---

[121] Emil Schürer, *The History of the Jewish People in the Age of Jesus Christ* (ed. Geza Vermes et al.; Edinburgh: T & T Clark, 1979), 2:396–97.

[122] Brumberg-Kraus, "Were the Pharisees a Conversionist Sect?" n.p.; cf. Wayne A. Meeks, "Since then you would need to go out of the world: 'Group Boundaries in Pauline Christianity'", in *Critical History and Biblical Faith: New Testament Perspectives* (ed. T. J. Ryan; Billanova: College Theology Society, 1979), 7.

Jews (the people of Israel) to the subset of strict Jews (those under Pharisaic halakhah):

Text	Larger Group	Subgroup
1Cor 10:18	the people of Israel	those who eat the sacrifices[123]
Phil 3:5	a member of the people of Israel	as to the law, a Pharisee κατὰ νόμον Φαρισαῖος
Acts 22:3	I am a Jew	educated at the feet of Gamaliel according to the strict manner of the law of our fathers κατὰ ἀκρίβειαν τοῦ πατρῴου νόμου

Josephus likewise describes the Pharisees as a subset of Jews – "a *body of Jews* (Ἰουδαίων) with the reputation of *excelling the rest of their nation* in the observances of religion" (Josephus, *J.W.* 1.110; cf. *Ant.* 17.41; italics mine). Mark refers to "the Pharisees, and all the Jews" (οἱ Φαρισαῖοι καὶ πάντες οἱ Ἰουδαῖοι) (Mark 7:3). Luke distinguishes "all the people" (πᾶς ὁ λαός) from "the Pharisees and the lawyers" (οἱ Φαρισαῖοι καὶ οἱ νομικοί) (Luke 7:29–30). I conclude that in 1 Cor 9:20 Paul moves from the universal to the particular.

It is notable that there is no restrictive clause in 1 Cor 9:20a clarifying "(though I myself am not a Jew)". This is because Paul considered himself to be a Jew. The ὡς in 1 Cor 9:20a does not suggest that Paul regarded himself as a former Jew (as many scholars maintain [1.1.1])[124] but points to the diversity that existed in the worldwide community of "Jews". Far from being monolithic, ordinary Jews were extremely diverse, even as they are today in Israel and the Diaspora.[125] In addition to regional distinctions between Jews (e.g. Judeans, Galileans, etc.), there were "Hellenists" (Ἑλληνιστῶν) and "Hebrews" (Ἑβραίους) (Acts 6:1). Luke refers to Jews who identified culturally as "Parthians, Medes, Elamites, and residents of Mesopotamia, Judea and Cappadocia, Pontus and Asia, Phrygia and Pamphylia, Egypt and the parts of Libya belonging to Cyrene . . . Cretans and Arabs" (Acts 2:9–11). In the course of his travels, Paul encountered the rich cultural tapestry of Jews who lived throughout the Roman Empire. When Paul says "To Jews I became *as a*

---

[123] That Paul refers to priests in 1 Cor 10:18 is corroborated by 1 Cor 9:13, "Do you not know that those who are employed in the temple service get their food from the temple, and those who serve at the altar share in what is sacrificed on the altar?"

[124] E.g. Sechrest, *A Former Jew*, 156, "Thus, when Paul maintains that he can 'become *like* a Jew', he clearly implies that he does not see himself as a Jew in the first place".

[125] Diane K. Tobin, Gary A. Tobin and Scott Rubin, *In Every Tongue: The Racial and Ethnic Diversity of the Jewish People* (San Francisco: Institute for Jewish and Community Research, 2005); James R. Ross, *Fragile Branches: Travels Through the Jewish Diaspora* (New York: Riverhead, 2000); Steven M. Lowenstein, *The Jewish Cultural Tapestry: International Jewish Folk Traditions* (Oxford: Oxford University Press, 2000); Karen Primack, ed., *Jews in Places You Never Thought Of* (Hoboken: Ktav, 1998); Ida Cowen, *Jews in Remote Corners of the World* (Englewood Cliffs: Prentice-Hall, 1971).

Jew", he means that he received hospitality from ordinary Jews in Israel and the Diaspora whose customs and culture were vastly different from his own.

5.5.4 *"I Became as One Without the Law (Though I Am Not Without the Law of God but Am in Christ's Law)"* (ἐγενόμην . . . ὡς ἄνομος, μὴ ὢν ἄνομος θεοῦ ἀλλ' ἔννομος Χριστοῦ)

In response to Sloyan's thesis that Paul adapted to Ἰουδαίοις and ὑπὸ νόμον (1 Cor 9:20) by conforming to different standards of Torah observance (less strict and strict), Lester Dean adds that Paul also adapted to Gentiles without stepping outside of Jewish contours of flexibility.[126] If this was the case, what would 1 Cor 9:21 mean practically? In line with the argument that γίνομαι . . . ὡς refers to close association through table-fellowship and conforming to the ways of one's host, this study contends that Paul, the apostle to the Gentiles, became "as one without the law" (ἄνομος) by visiting Gentile homes, sharing table-fellowship with Gentiles and conforming to the customs of his Gentile host. Through *koinonia* with Gentiles, Paul "became as" a Gentile.

Did becoming "as a Gentile" mean that Paul violated biblical law? There is no evidence that Paul ever knowingly ate idol-food[127] or unclean food.[128] Moreover, on the basis of 1 Corinthians 7, there is good reason to believe that

---

[126] Lester Dean, "A Response to Gerard Sloyan from Lester Dean", in *Bursting the Bonds? A Jewish-Christian Dialogue on Jesus and Paul* (Maryknoll: Orbis, 1990), 174.

[127] Shen, "Paul's Doctrine of God and the Issue of Food Offered to Idols in 1 Corinthians 8:1–11:1", 208–10; Gooch, *Dangerous Food*, 93–95. Contra Hurd, *The Origin of 1 Corinthians*, 128–30, 147–48; Barrett, "Things Sacrificed to Idols", 50.

[128] Kinzer, *Postmissionary Messianic Judaism*, 88. There is no evidence that the "forty lashes minus one" five times (2 Cor 11:24) were due to Paul eating forbidden food. *Pace* C. K. Barrett, *A Commentary on the Second Epistle to the Corinthians* (London: A & C Black, 1973), 296; Anthony E. Harvey, "Forty Strokes Save One: Social Aspects of Judaizing and Apostasy", in *Alternative Approaches to New Testament Study* (ed. Anthony E. Harvey; London: SPCK, 1985), 84. The punishment may have been related to Paul's teaching that Jesus was the "Son of God" (Rom 1:4; 2 Cor 1:19; Gal 2:20; cf. Acts 7:55–58; 9:1–2, 20–21; 18:12–13; 26:11). David E. Garland, *2 Corinthians* (Nashville: Broadman & Holman, 1999), 497, notes, "We cannot know why the synagogue inflicted this punishment on Paul. The best guess is that it was for the serious offense of blasphemy when he proclaimed his faith in Christ, his altered understanding of Judaism with the inclusion of Gentiles in the people of God". See Sanders, *Paul, the Law, and the Jewish People*, 191; E. P. Sanders, "Paul on the Law, His Opponents, and the Jewish People in Philippians 3 and 2 Corinthians 11", in *Anti-Judaism in Early Christianity. Vol. 1. Paul and the Gospels* (ed. Peter Richardson; Ontario: Wilfrid Laurier University Press, 1986), 86–87. Paul may have been perceived as a troublemaker in general (Acts 24:5). Unsubstantiated rumours (according to Luke) that Paul taught Diaspora Jews not to live according to Mosaic law would have compounded the accusations against him (Acts 21:17–26; cf. 6:13–14). Paul Barnett, *The Second Epistle to the Corinthians* (Grand Rapids: Eerdmans, 1997), 542, notes that "we do not know the basis of these punishments that were inflicted on him. Perhaps they arose from false charges and were designed to deter his ongoing presence in a particular town or city".

Paul continued to live as a Torah-observant Jew. First and foremost, as Augustine (*Op. mon.* 11 [12]) maintained, it is reasonable to assume that Paul observed his own "rule in all the churches" that Jews were to remain practising Jews (1 Cor 7:17–20).[129] I contend that this *rule* serves as a principal literary context for interpreting Paul's nomistic language in 1 Cor 9:19–23.[130] The various parallels between 1 Cor 7:17–24 and 9:19–23 add exegetical weight to the assessment that the 1 Cor 7:17–20 rule defined the parameters within which Pauline accommodation took place.[131] By noting the passages before and after 1 Cor 9:19–23 that speak of Jews and Gentiles, one can see the flow of Paul's thought:

1 Cor 7:17–20	⇒	1 Cor 9:19–23	⇒	1 Cor 10:32–11:1
Paul's rule		Paul's principle of adaptation		Paul's model

Conscious that his statement in 1 Cor 9:21 ("I became as one without the law") could be misunderstood to mean that he violated Mosaic law (against his own rule), Paul adds the qualification: "though I am not without the law of God" (μὴ ὢν ἄνομος θεοῦ) (1 Cor 9:21). Paul identifies "the law"/"the law of Moses" as a divine authority in 1 Cor 9:8–9.[132] Finally, I propose that by eating with the law-less, Paul likely imitated the example of Jesus (1 Cor 11:1), who ate with sinners yet remained a fully Torah-observant Jew (Matt 5:17–20).[133]

When Paul was in a Gentile household, how did he observe Jesus' rule of adaptation to "eat what is set before you"? The example given in 1 Cor 10:25–30 suggests that Paul was willing to eat food sold at the meat market

---

[129] See 4.4.5 above.

[130] Tomson, *Paul and the Jewish Law*, 281; Bockmuehl, *Jewish Law in Gentile Churches*, 170–71. Also Bornkamm, "The Missionary Stance of Paul in 1 Corinthians 9 and in Acts", 196.

[131] Hall, "All Things to All People", 145. Also 4.4.5 above.

[132] Cf. Josephus, *Ant.* 4.233; David Instone-Brewer, "1 Corinthians 9.9–11: A Literal Interpretation of 'Do Not Muzzle the Ox'", *New Testament Studies* 38 (1992): 554–65; Jodie Boyer Hatlem and Doug Johnson Hatlem, "Muzzling the Ox: Should Torah Be Normative for Gentile Christians?" *Studies in Christian-Jewish Relations* 5:1 (2010): 1–22; David L. Dungan, *The Sayings of Jesus in the Churches of Paul: The Use of the Synoptic Tradition in the Regulation of Early Church Life* (Oxford: Basil Blackwell, 1971), 10. For Paul to relinquish his right granted by Mosaic law (1 Cor 9:8–9) does not necessarily mean that he views himself free from the constraints of the law. In the same way, Paul relinquishes his right "commanded" by the Lord Jesus (1 Cor 9:14) but this does not necessarily mean that he feels free to depart from the requirements of his Lord. See Fee, *The First Epistle to the Corinthians*, 413 n. 96; *pace* Horrell, *Solidarity and Difference*, 216–22; David G. Horrell, "'The Lord Commanded . . . But I Have Not Used . . .': Exegetical and Hermeneutical Reflections on 1 Cor 9.14–15", *New Testament Studies* 43 (1997): 599. There is a difference between a right and a responsibility. One typically has freedom to relinquish the former but not the latter.

[133] See Crossley's chapter "Jesus' Torah Observance in the Synoptic Gospels", in *The Date of Mark's Gospel*, 82–124; cf. 159–205. Also Bockmuehl, *Seeing the Word*, 189–228; Bockmuehl, *Jewish Law in Gentile Churches*, 3–21; Sanders, *Jesus and Judaism*, 245–69; Anthony E. Harvey, *Jesus and the Constraints of History* (Philadelphia: Westminster, 1982), 36–65.

without raising questions of conscience as long as the origin of the food was indeterminate; he adapted in this manner to Gentiles for the sake of the gospel (1 Cor 10:25–30). It may be speculated that, in Gentile homes, Paul was discriminating in what he ate, abstaining from unclean food like pork but not quibbling over accidental mixtures of clean and unclean food (2.1.4). Consistent with this approach, he probably did not raise questions of conscience concerning how the meat set before him was slaughtered, unless someone indicated that the animal had been strangled (Acts 15:20, 29; 21:25). As it was argued in chapters 3–4, there is no reason to think that Paul's "don't ask" policy with respect to accommodation violated the Torah or that it represented indifference to Jewish food laws. More likely, Paul considered his actions to be within the boundaries of Torah observance. Granted, strict Jews may have rejected Paul's lenient halakhah. But Gentile inclusion in the people of God, the presence of Diaspora Jews who ate with Gentiles within defined contours of Jewish flexibility, and Christ's halakhah of commensality with sinners (which will be discussed below), all would have empowered Paul to regard his dietary adaptation to be within the parameters of Torah observance. Stated differently, far from being indifferent to biblical dietary laws, Paul's ability to adapt to different table-fellowship contexts within biblical limits was an expression of halakhic flexibility consistent with Jesus' example and rule of adaptation.

What did Paul mean by his statement that he was "in Christ's law" (ἔννομος Χριστοῦ [1 Cor 9:21])? Given that Paul uses the term in the context of discussing his ministry to Gentiles ("to those without the law"), I maintain that living "in Christ's law" refers to Paul's Torah-observant accommodation to "Gentile sinners" in the manner of Christ's open table-fellowship with "sinners".[134] When Paul was under Pharisaic halakhah (κατὰ νόμον Φαρισαῖος = ὑπὸ νόμον), in all likelihood he avoided the homes of Jewish sinners; how much more the homes of Gentile sinners. But now Paul was a member of the Nazarene sect and under Christ's halakhah (κατὰ νόμον Χριστός = ἔννομος Χριστοῦ). Christ's halakhah was reflected in Jesus' example of eating with sinners. This Messianic halakhah had the effect of encouraging Paul to associate closely with Gentiles.

It is notable that Paul's use of "law of Christ" (νόμον τοῦ Χριστοῦ) in Gal 6:2 is consistent with my interpretation of ἔννομος Χριστοῦ (1 Cor 9:21). In Gal 6:1, Paul speaks of associating with a brother who has sinned[135] in order

---

[134] The term ἔννομος Χριστοῦ refers to God's law (the law of Moses) in the hand of Christ as reflected in Christ's association with sinners. See 4.4.6 above.

[135] Garlington, "Burden Bearing and the Recovery of Offending Christians (Galatians 6:1–5)", 159; Bruce, *The Epistle to the Galatians*, 260.

to restore him.¹³⁶ That Paul may have in mind Jesus' association with sinners is supported by Paul's instruction in the same verse to come in a spirit of "gentleness" (πραΰτητος). Why gentleness? Paul uses πραΰτητος in 2 Cor 10:1 to describe the Christ/Messiah, a possible allusion to Jesus tradition which describes the Messiah's "yoke" as "gentle" (πραΰς) and his "burden" (φορτίον) as light (Matt 11:29–30).¹³⁷ Donald Garlington concurs, "Ultimately, πραΰτης is conformity to the image of Christ, the meek and gentle (Matt 11:29; 2 Cor 10:1)".¹³⁸

In Gal 6:1–2, Paul may have in mind Jesus' gentleness toward sinners in contrast to the harsh approach of the Pharisees toward the lawless (polemically speaking), which is a natural extension of narrowly defined Torah observance.¹³⁹ Richard Beaton identifies the gentle yoke/light burden language of Matt 11:29–30 as being in direct contradistinction to the Pharisees who "tie up heavy burdens (φορτίον), hard to bear, and lay them on the shoulders of others; but they themselves are unwilling to lift a finger to move them" (Matt 23:4; cf. φορτίον in Luke 11:46).¹⁴⁰

I propose that in keeping with Christ's halakhah (νόμον τοῦ Χριστοῦ) toward the sinner, Paul instructs the Jesus-believer in Gal 6:2 to visit transgressors and serve them as Jesus served sinners so that they can be restored (Gal 6:2; cf. φορτίον in 6:5). In 1 Cor 9:21, Paul speaks of fulfilling Christ's halakhah by visiting the lawless one without participating in their lawlessness. He adapts to them and serves them, thinking of their good above his own, so that they can be saved (1 Cor 10:32–33). Glad arrives at the same conclusion:

Regardless of exactly how one translates the phrase ἔννομος Χριστοῦ, it can, in light of the above contrast and Paul's use of ὁ νόμος τοῦ Χριστοῦ (*hapax*) in Gal 6:2, be construed as Paul's way of emphasizing that although his adaptation towards the immoral could be seen as ungodly it is in complete accord with "Christ's law" and affable behavior. Indeed, it is

---

¹³⁶ Note Matthew's use of κερδαίνω with respect to visiting and restoring a brother who has sinned (Matt 18:15). See Neller, "1 Corinthians 9:19–22", 139.

¹³⁷ Cf. *1 Clem.* 16.17; Wenham, *Paul*, 355; Furnish, *Jesus According to Paul*, 14–17; Michael B. Thompson, *Clothed with Christ: The Example and Teaching of Jesus in Romans 12.1–15.13* (Sheffield: Sheffield Academic Press, 1991), 154–55; Ralph P. Martin, *2 Corinthians* (Waco: Word, 1986), 302; Peter Richardson, "The Thunderbold in Q and the Wise Man in Corinth", in *From Jesus to Paul: Studies in Honour of Francis Wright Beare* (ed. Peter Richardson and John C. Hurd; Waterloo: Wilfrid Laurier University Press, 1984), 91–111; Adolf von Harnack, "'Sanftmut, Huld und Demut' in der alten Kirche", in *Festgabe für Julius Kaftan zu seinem 70. Geburtstag* (ed. A. Titius et al.; Tübingen: Mohr Siebeck, 1920), 113–29. Contra Donald D. Walker, *Paul's Offer of Leniency (2 Cor 10.1): Populist Ideology and Rhetoric in a Pauline Letter Fragment* (Tübingen: Mohr Siebeck, 2002), 10.

¹³⁸ Garlington, "Burden Bearing and the Recovery of Offending Christians (Galatians 6:1–5)", 160.

¹³⁹ Margolese, *Off the Derech*, 318–44.

¹⁴⁰ Richard Beaton, *Isaiah's Christ in Matthew's Gospel* (Cambridge: Cambridge University Press, 2002), 122–73.

Christ's behavior that forms the exemplary pattern of Paul's own affable conduct (1 Cor 11:1) . . . Paul's advice concerning "outsiders" and "insiders" in 1 Cor 5 is congruent with his remarks in 9:19–23 which shows the need for associating with immoral persons – ἄνομοι – *outside* the community in order to recruit or benefit them. That such behavior was seen as "lawless" by some goes without saying. But Paul emphasizes that such a conduct is upright and law-abiding, congruent with the "law of Christ" and explains the need for associating with different types of people in light of recruitment.[141]

This interpretation of "in Christ's law" (ἔννομος Χριστοῦ) adds strength to the central argument of the monograph that 1 Cor 9:19–23 as a whole is informed by Jesus' example and rule of adaptation with respect to commensality. As Jesus became all things to all people through eating with ordinary Jews, Pharisees and sinners, Paul became "all things to all people" through eating with ordinary Jews, strict Jews (those "under the law") and Gentile sinners.

5.5.5 "I Became Weak" (ἐγενόμην . . . ἀσθενής)

Building on the above hermeneutic, it may be conjectured that Paul became weak to the weak by lowering himself as Christ did so that weaker members of society could be lifted up in Christ (1 Cor 1:26–29; 11:1; 2 Cor 6:10; 8:9; 11:7; see 4.4.8).[142] Rather than make use of his rights as an apostle to receive food and drink (1 Cor 9:1–18), Paul "took on the lifestyle and condition of the weak . . . he lowered himself to the social status of the weak by refusing the patronage of the rich and becoming a manual labourer [1 Cor 4:10b, 12a]".[143] Paul toiled to earn a living as a tentmaker in Corinth (Acts 18:3), which resulted in him being invited to the table of the economically vulnerable and dependent. The lack of the ὡς in 1 Cor 9:22 suggests that his adaptation was not temporary but a consistent lifestyle.

Paul also became weak to the weak by adapting to the sensibilities of Jesus-believers for whom certain foods were a stumbling block (1 Cor 8:7–10).[144] Paul describes this scenario in 1 Cor 8:13, "Therefore, if food causes my brother to stumble, I will never eat meat, so that I may not cause my brother to stumble". Paul's concern not to cause the weak to "stumble" (an ethic rooted in the Torah, the Prophets and Jesus tradition)[145] overrode his general policy to eat what was set before him within biblical limits.

---

[141] Glad, *Paul and Philodemus*, 257–58, 260.

[142] Adams, *The Sinner in Luke*, 69–104, 154, 160, 186–87.

[143] Hays, *First Corinthians*, 154–55; cf. Barton, "All Things to All People", 285; Martin, *Slavery as Salvation*, 123–24.

[144] Gooch, *Partial Knowledge*, 114–19.

[145] See 3.2; cf. 1 Cor 8:13 with Mark 9:42; Matt 18:6; Luke 17:2. Also Michael B. Thompson, "The Example and Teaching of Jesus in Romans 12.1–15.13" (Ph.D. diss., University of Cambridge, 1988), 148; Thompson, *Clothed with Christ*, 183–84; Kim, "Imitatio Christi (1 Corinthians 11:1)", 198.

Chapter 6

Conclusion and Implications

Part I (chapters 2–4) of this monograph showed that there are major weaknesses in the intertextual, contextual and textual case for the consensus reading of 1 Cor 9:19–23. Scholars overstate their case when they assert that 1 Cor 9:19–23 is incompatible with a Torah-observant Paul. Part II (chapter 5) demonstrated that 1 Cor 9:19–23 can be read as the discourse of a Jew who lived within the bounds of Mosaic law. It was argued that 1 Cor 9:19–23 is informed by Jesus' example and rule of adaptation with respect to commensality. As Jesus became all things to all people through eating with ordinary Jews, Pharisees and sinners, Paul became "all things to all people" through eating with ordinary Jews, strict Jews (those "under the law") and Gentile sinners. Through accommodation and open table-fellowship, Paul entered into the lives of all so that all could enter into his communion with Christ.

The counter case centred on interpreting 1 Cor 9:19–23 in light of Paul's recapitulation in 1 Cor 10:32–11:1, which concludes with the statement, "Be imitators of me, as I am of Christ". Given the food-related/hospitality context of 1 Cor 8–10, and Paul's reference to dominical sayings that point back to Jesus' example and rule of adaptation (1 Cor 9:14; 10:27/Luke 10:7–8), it was concluded that 1 Cor 9:19–23 reflects Paul's imitation of Jesus' accommodation-oriented table-fellowship with all (Mark 2:15–17; Matt 9:10–13; 11:19; Luke 5:29–32; 7:34–36).

It is important to point out that even if one does not accept my proposed interpretation of 1 Cor 9:19–23 in chapter 5, for it has its strengths and weaknesses, the reassessment of the traditional view in chapters 2–4 still stands as a significant and original contribution to scholarship. The critical reassessment is the larger part of the monograph and the primary thrust; the proposed interpretation is secondary. By demonstrating that the traditional view does not stand up under closer scrutiny, I destabilise the consensus reading and invite scholars to take a fresh look at 1 Cor 9:19–23. This is not a small contribution to New Testament studies because 1 Cor 9:19–23 is used by many scholars as a hermeneutical lens for understanding Paul.

Five implications of the monograph are notable. First, if the initial restrictive clause in 1 Cor 9:20 ("though I myself am not *under the law*") means that Paul no longer viewed Pharisaic (or other strict sectarian) halakhah as a final authority in his life, then Paul was indifferent to certain halakhic interpretations and expansions of Mosaic law but not necessarily to the law itself. The second restrictive clause ("though I am not without the law of God"), and Paul's "rule in all the churches" that Jews are to remain practising Jews and not live as Gentiles (1 Cor 7:17–20), inform the reader that Paul remains within the bounds of Mosaic law, though he challenges Pharisaic interpretation of the law (or narrow definition of Torah observance). In this sense, Paul's lifestyle was fully consistent with the portrait of Jesus in the gospels that a number of contemporary scholars maintain: Jesus lived according to Mosaic law but did not consistently conform his lifestyle to Pharisaic halakhah (Mark 7:1–22; Matt 15:1–20).

Second, Paul's statement – "To those without the law I became as one without the law" (1 Cor 9:21) – cannot be used as incontrovertible evidence that he was indifferent to Jewish law because of the restrictive clause that immediately follows it ("though I am not without the law of God"). In order to establish that Paul was indifferent to the law, one must demonstrate that Paul could not have eaten with Gentiles and stayed within the contours of Jewish flexibility. This study, however, has shown that Second Temple Judaism was diverse and that some first-century Jews did eat with Gentiles without compromising their status as Torah-observant Jews (e.g. the tradition of the seventy-two elders in the *Letter of Aristeas*).

Third, if becoming "all things to all people" refers to Paul's open table-fellowship with Jewish and Gentile families during the course of his missionary journeys, and to the adaptation he exhibited by accommodating to his hosts within the limits of God's law, then it is not judicious for exegetes to use 1 Cor 9:19–23 as a hermeneutical key to explain Paul's ritual purification in the temple described in Acts 21:17–26 (cf. 24:18). The intertextual leap is all the more questionable given Luke's stated reason for Paul's actions. Luke informs his readers that James invited Paul to set the record straight and prove to the zealous Jesus-believing Jews in Jerusalem that *he faithfully observed the Torah as they did* ("Thus all will know that there is nothing in what they have been told about you, but that you yourself also live in observance of the law" [Acts 21:24 ESV]). As Barrett points out, if Paul was not consistently law observant, then his testimony would have been a lie and a deceit, something "not covered by 1 Corinthians 9".[1] The monograph thus encourages a revisiting of the meaning of Acts 21:17–26 and its mirror text (Acts 15).

Even if Acts 21:17–26 is viewed as tendentious evidence, it is nonetheless "the earliest *Wirkungsgeschichte* of Paul's life and teachings with respect to Torah observance. This is how the cultural and practical 'footprint' of Paul's person impressed itself on a Gentile Christian author within living memory of less than a generation of Paul's death"[2] – a compelling reason to re-open criti-

---

[1] Barrett, *The Acts of the Apostles*, 2:1013.
[2] Markus Bockmuehl, personal correspondence, 3 June 2006.

cal dialogue about the meaning of 1 Cor 9:19–23. Since this monograph has a direct bearing on the traditional interpretation of Acts 21:17–26, it is also relevant to the "Paul of Acts and Paul of the Epistles" debate and the larger "historical Paul" discussion

Fourth, the monograph has implications for Jewish-Christian dialogue. On the basis of the traditional interpretation of 1 Cor 9:19–23, Jewish writers have understandably described Paul as a proponent of "trickery", "deceit" and "pious fraud" (1.2). The intertextual case that informs the consensus reading of 1 Cor 9:19–23 portrays Paul's Jewishness as superseded and displaced in Christ. He was a member of the "third entity" church and no longer considered himself to be a Jew (1.1.1). Some scholars refer to Paul as a "former Jew" (2.1.3).[3] All of this reinforces the commonly held view among Jews that "Pauline Christianity" was an anti-Jewish movement. Since this monograph problematises the intertextual reading of 1 Cor 9:19–23, and opens up room for the possibility that Paul remained within the bounds of pluriform Second Temple Judaism, it adds strength to recent studies by Mark Nanos, Anders Runesson, Magnus Zetterholm, Douglas Harink, Markus Bockmuehl, William Campbell, Kathy Ehrensberger, Peter Tomson, Pamela Eisenbaum, Caroline Johnson Hodge, Paula Fredriksen, Joel Willitts, Justin Hardin, Todd Wilson, Brad Braxton, Hilary Le Cornu, Mark Kinzer, J. Brian Tucker, Christopher Zoccali, among others, that conclude Paul has been misunderstood.[4] This in turn has implications for rapprochement between Jews and Christians.

Finally, this study has a bearing on the question, "Did Paul value Jewish continuity?" Daniel Boyarin and John Barclay have debated the degree to which Paul's "indifference" view of Jewish law was intentionally designed to undermine the continued presence of Jews in his churches.[5] Boyarin contends that Paul sought to assimilate Jews and Gentiles into the Hellenistic ideal of "the one"; Paul understood that his theology led directly to Jewish assimilation. Barclay on the other hand sees a measure of cognitive dissonance in Paul's position; perhaps Paul did not realize that indifference to Jewish difference would inevitably lead to the delegitimisation of Jewish existence and to the erasure, or displacement, of Jews from the church. Despite their disagreement over Paul's intentionality, Boyarin and Barclay agree that indifference

---

[3] Sechrest, *A Former Jew*, 156.

[4] See Magnus Zetterholm, *Approaches to Paul: A Student's Guide to Recent Scholarship* (Minneapolis: Fortress, 2009), 127–63.

[5] Boyarin, *A Radical Jew,* 8–10, 32, 290 n. 10; Barclay, "Paul Among Diaspora Jews", 118; John M. G. Barclay, "'Neither Jew nor Greek': Multiculturalism and the New Perspective on Paul", in *Ethnicity and the Bible* (ed. Mark G. Brett; Leiden: Brill, 1996), 205–14; John M. G. Barclay, "Do we undermine the Law? A Study of Romans 14.1–15.6", in *Paul and the Mosaic Law* (ed. James D. G. Dunn; Grand Rapids: Eerdmans, 2001), 303–308.

to Jewish law in practice leads to a church devoid of Jews.[6] For Boyarin and Barclay, circumcision, Jewish calendar observance and dietary distinctions are fundamental boundary markers of identity for the Jewish people. The removal of the obligation of these markers opens the door to Jewish assimilation. But did Paul in fact encourage the removal of these boundary markers? Contrary to the view of Boyarin and Barclay, this monograph has found that Paul promoted Jewish continuity in his congregations. His position is reflected in his *"rule in all the churches"* that Jews were to remain practising Jews in keeping with their "calling" from God (1 Cor 7:17–20). As for Paul's example, it is reasonable to assume that he kept his own rule, even as he was "not without the law of God" (1 Cor 9:21).

---

[6] Also James D. G. Dunn, "In Search of Common Ground", in *The New Perspective on Paul: Collected Essays* (Tübingen: Mohr Siebeck, 2005), 296; Sanders, *Paul, the Law, and the Jewish People*, 178; Michael Wyschogrod, "Response to the Respondents", *Modern Theology* 2 (1995): 233; Rudolph, "Messianic Jews and Christian Theology", 58–84. History bears this out. See Margolese, *Off the Derech*, 28; Mitch L. Glaser, "A Survey of Missions to the Jews in Continental Europe 1900–1950" (Ph.D. diss., Fuller Theological Seminary, 1998), 159–61; Yaakov Ariel, *Evangelizing the Chosen People: Missions to the Jews in America, 1880–2000* (Chapel Hill: The University of North Carolina Press, 2000), 49–51; Rachel L. E. Kohn, "Ethnic Judaism and the Messianic Movement", *Jewish Journal of Sociology* 29:2 (1987): 89; Philip Cohen, *The Hebrew Christian and His National Continuity* (London: Marshall Brothers, 1909), 37. Those who argue for the theoretical possibility of Jesus-believing Jews conveying Jewish identity cross-generationally without Torah observance typically offer no socio-historical evidence to support their case.

Appendix to the Second Edition

Five Years Later:
New and Notable Publications

In his introduction to *Paul the Jew: Rereading the Apostle as a Figure of Second Temple Judaism* (2016), Gabriele Boccaccini writes:

> The New Perspective has tried hard to get rid of the most derogatory aspects of the traditional (Lutheran) reading of Paul (claiming that Judaism also should be regarded as a "respectable" religion based on grace), but has not challenged the view of Paul as the critic of Judaism and the advocate of a new supersessionist model of relations between God and humankind—God's grace "in Christ" superseded the Jewish covenant for both Jews and gentiles by creating a third separate "race". A new paradigm is emerging today with the Radical New Perspective—a paradigm that aims to fully rediscover the Jewishness of Paul. . . . Paul was a member of the early Jesus movement, and with strength and unmistakable clarity, proudly claimed his Jewishness, declaring that God also did not reject God's covenant with the Jewish people: "Has God rejected his people? By no means! I am an Israelite, a descendant of Abraham, a member of the tribe of Benjamin" (Rom. 11:1; cf. Phil. 3:5). The goal of this volume is fully to embrace the paradigm of the Radical New Perspective not as the conclusion, but as the starting point of our conversation about Paul. . . . In my opinion, the potential of such an approach has just begun to be manifested. We have still a long way to go before fully understanding all its monumental implications. . . . [T]his is the future of Pauline studies.[1]

Boccaccini is one of a growing number of scholars in the field of Second Temple Judaism and Christian Origins who are seeking to effectuate a paradigm shift through post-supersessionist interpretation of Paul.[2] Since the pub-

---

[1] Gabriele Boccaccini and Carlos A. Segovia, *Paul the Jew: Rereading the Apostle as a Figure of Second Temple Judaism* (Minneapolis: Fortress, 2016), 2–3.

[2] "Post-supersessionism designates not a single viewpoint but a loose and partly conflicting family of theological perspectives that seeks to interpret the central affirmations of Christian faith in ways that do not state or imply the abrogation or obsolescence of God's covenant with the Jewish people, that is, in ways that are not supersessionist. Positively expressed, a theology is post-supersessionist if it affirms the present validity of God's covenant with Israel as a coherent and indispensible part of the larger body of Christian teaching" (R. Kendall Soulen, "Post-supersessionism," in *A Dictionary of Jewish-Christian Relations* [ed. in Edward Kessler and Neil Wenborn; Cambridge: Cambridge University Press, 2005], 350). Cf. Joel Willitts, "Jewish Fish (ΙΧΘΥΣ) in Post-supersessionist Water: Messianic Judaism within a Post-supersessionistic Paradigm", *HTS Theological Studies* 72:4 (2016): 1–5. For a study of the origin and limitations of the English term supersessionism, see Matthew A. Tapie, *Aquinas on Israel and the Church: The Question of Supersessionism in the Theology of Thomas Aquinas* (Eugene: Pickwick, 2014). Tapie, 24, defines supersessionism as "*the Christian*

lication of *A Jew to the Jews* in 2011, a steady stream of such scholarship has advanced the conversation. The aim of this appendix is to introduce some of this recent literature.

A number of books over the past five years have endeavored to make more room in Pauline studies for the possibility of a Torah-observant Paul. These works include *"Remain in Your Calling"* (2011), *Paul's Jewish Matrix* (2011), *Paul and Judaism* (2012), *Four Views on the Apostle Paul* (2012), *Unity & Diversity in Christ* (2013), *Paul at the Crossroads of Cultures* (2013), *Por una interpretación no cristiana de Pablo de Tarso* (2013), *Paul and the Politics of Difference* (2014), *If You Call Yourself a Jew* (2014), *Paul within Judaism* (2015), *Jew Among Jews* (2015), *The So-Called Jew in Paul's Letter to the Romans* (2016), *Paul and the Gentile Problem* (2016) and *Paul the Jew* (2016).[3]

Paul within Judaism is notable because it emerged out of a collaboration of international scholars involved in the "Paul and Judaism" consultation (2010–present) at the Society of Biblical Literature. Scholars who contributed to this volume—Mark Nanos, Magnus Zetterholm, Anders Runesson, Karin Hedner-Zetterholm, Caroline Johnson Hodge, Paula Fredriksen, Neil Elliott, and Kathy Ehrensperger—sought "to describe Paul and his work from 'within Judaism,' rather than on the assumption, still current after thirty years of the 'New Perspective,' that in practice Paul left behind aspects of Jewish living

---

claim that with the advent of Christ, Jewish Law is fulfilled and obsolete, with the result that God replaces Israel with the Church."

[3] J. Brian Tucker, *"Remain in Your Calling": Paul and the Continuation of Social Identities in 1 Corinthians* (Eugene: Pickwick, 2011); Thomas G. Casey and Justin Taylor, eds., *Paul's Jewish Matrix* (Rome: Gregorian and Biblical, 2011); Reimund Bieringer and Didier Pollefeyt, eds., *Paul and Judaism: Crosscurrents in Pauline Exegesis and the Study of Jewish-Christian Relations* (London: T & T Clark, 2012); Michael F. Bird, Thomas R. Schreiner, Luke Timothy Johnson, Douglas A. Campbell and Mark D. Nanos, *Four Views on the Apostle Paul* (Grand Rapids: Zondervan, 2012); William S. Campbell, *Unity & Diversity in Christ: Interpreting Paul in Context* (Eugene: Cascade, 2013); Kathy Ehrensperger, *Paul at the Crossroads of Cultures: Theologizing in the Space Between* (London: Bloomsbury, 2013); Carlos A. Segovia, *Por una interpretación no cristiana de Pablo de Tarso: El redescubrimiento contemporáneo de un judío mesiánico* (Carlos A. Segovia, 2013), abridged version: *Pablo de Tarso Judeo o Christiano* (Madrid: Atanor Ediciones, 2013); Jae Won Lee, *Paul and the Politics of Difference: A Contextual Study of the Jewish-Gentile Difference in Galatians and Romans* (Eugene: Pickwick, 2014); Rafael Rodríguez, *If You Call Yourself a Jew: Reappraising Paul's Letter to the Roman* (Eugene: Cascade, 2014); Mark D. Nanos and Magnus Zetterholm, eds., *Paul within Judaism: Restoring the First-Century Context to the Apostle* (Minneapolis: Fortress, 2015); Kimberly Ambrose, *Jew Among Jews: Rehabilitating Paul* (Eugene: Wipf & Stock, 2015); Rafael Rodríguez and Matthew Thiessen, eds., *The So-Called Jew in Paul's Letter to the Romans* (Minneapolis: Fortress, 2016); Matthew Thiessen, *Paul and the Gentile Problem* (New York: Oxford University Press, 2016); Boccaccini and Segovia, *Paul the Jew*. See also Isaac W. Oliver, *Torah Praxis after 70 CE: Reading Matthew and Luke-Acts as Jewish Texts* (Tübingen: Mohr Siebeck, 2013).

after his discovery of Jesus as Christ (Messiah)."[4] This Fortress title has led to the growing use of the term "Paul within Judaism" to refer to the view that Paul remained a Torah-observant Jew after becoming a follower of Jesus. The earlier term coined to describe this school of thought is the Radical New Perspective, which Zetterholm popularized in *Approaches to Paul* (2009).[5]

In addition to the above works, there have been dozens of journal articles and academic essays published since 2011 that reflect a Paul within Judaism perspective. See for example Christopher Zoccali's "'Rejoice, O Gentiles, With His People': Paul's Intra-Jewish Rhetoric in Philippians 3:1–9" (2011),[6] Todd Wilson's "The Supersession and Superfluity of the Law? Another Look at Galatians" (2013)[7] and Rudolph's "Paul and the Food laws: A Reassessment of Romans 14:14, 20" (2016).[8] I have attempted to track scholarship like this and make the bibliographical information available online.[9] However, so much has come out over the past five years that it has been difficult to stay on top of it all. Moreover, there is no indication of this trend abating. Scholars are building on the research of others and this is leading to new avenues of exegetical and theological inquiry. Avant-garde books scheduled to be released over the next several years include those by Mark Nanos: *Galatians: New Testament Guides* (Sheffield, 2017), *Paul's Judaism: How to Read the Apostle's Letters from a Jewish Perspective* (Cascade, 2018), *To the Synagogues of Rome: A Jewish Commentary on Romans* (Eerdmans, 2018); Isaac Oliver and Gabriel Boccaccini, eds.: *The Early Reception of Paul the Second Temple Jew* (T & T Clark, 2017); Justin Hardin, Joel Willitts, and David Rudolph: *The Jewish New Testament: An Introduction to its Jewish Social & Conceptual Context* (Eerdmans, 2019), to mention just a few.

Another related Pauline resource in the pipeline is the *New Testament after Supersessionism* series, published by Cascade and edited by J. Brian Tucker,

---

[4] From the book summary on the back cover. Terence L. Donaldson offers a critical evaluation of the "Paul within Judaism" perspective from a "'New Perspective' Perspective" in chapter 9.

[5] Magnus Zetterholm, *Approaches to Paul: A Students Guide to Recent Scholarship* (Minneapolis; Fortress, 2009), 161–63.

[6] Christopher Zoccali, "'Rejoice, O Gentiles, With His People': Paul's Intra-Jewish Rhetoric in Philippians 3:1–9," *Criswell Theological Review* 9:1 (2011): 17–32.

[7] Todd A. Wilson, "The Supersession and Superfluity of the Law? Another Look at Galatians," in *Introduction to Messianic Judaism*, 235–44.

[8] David J. Rudolph, "Paul and the Food Laws: A Reassessment of Romans 14:14, 20," in *Paul the Jew*, 151–81. See also David J. Rudolph, "Zionism in Pauline Literature: Does Paul Eliminate Particularity for Israel and the Land in His Portrayal of Salvation Available for All the World?" in *The New Christian Zionism: Fresh Perspectives on Israel & the Land* (ed. Gerald R. McDermott; Downers Grove: InterVarsity, 2016), 167–94; David J. Rudolph, "Luke's Portrait of Paul in Acts 21:17–26," in *The Early Reception of Paul the Second Temple Jew* (ed. Isaac W. Oliver and Gabriele Boccaccini; T & T Clark, forthcoming).

[9] See www.mjstudies.com, a gateway to post-supersessionist New Testament scholarship.

Justin Hardin and David Rudolph. The NTAS series, which will bolster the case for a Paul within Judaism perspective, will include individual volumes on Romans, 1 Corinthians, 2 Corinthians, Galatians, Philippians, Ephesians and Colossians, as well as other New Testament books.[10] The purpose of the series is to read these texts from a post-supersessionist perspective given that the New Testament writers were mostly (if not all) Jesus-believing Jews who remained within the orbit of Judaism.

Alongside the Paul within Judaism reassessment in New Testament studies, there has been a burgeoning interest among theologians in how supersessionism informs the Christian canonical narrative. This wider theological reflection, taking place inside and outside of ecclesial settings, indirectly adds traction to the Paul within Judaism perspective. Books published since 2011 that have challenged traditional conceptions of the Church's relationship to Jews and Judaism include *Another Reformation* (2011), *Israel's Messiah and the People of God* (2011), *Introduction to Messianic Judaism* (2013), *Aquinas on Israel and the Church* (2014), *We the People* (2014), *Searching Her Own Mystery* (2015), *Healing the Schism* (2016), and *Azusa, Rome, and Zion* (2016).[11] Another important work—Mark Kinzer's *Jerusalem Crucified, Jerusalem Risen*—is scheduled for release in 2017.[12] Besides these books, there has been a proliferation of recent articles and essays reevaluating the supersessionist paradigm and proposing alternative approaches to Jewish presence in the body of Messiah.[13] See for example R. Kendall Soulen's "The Standard Canonical Narrative and the Problem of Supersessionism" (2013)[14] and Ger-

---

[10] Other volumes include Matthew, Mark, John, Luke-Acts, Hebrews, 1 Peter and Revelation.

[11] Peter Ochs, *Another Reformation: Postliberal Christianity and the Jews* (Grand Rapids: Baker, 2011); Mark S. Kinzer, *Israel's Messiah and the People of God: A Vision for Messianic Jewish Covenant Fidelity* (Eugene: Wipf & Stock, 2011); David J. Rudolph and Joel Willitts, eds., *Introduction to Messianic Judaism: Its Ecclesial Context and Biblical Foundations* (Grand Rapids: Zondervan, 2013); Matthew Tapie, *Aquinas on Israel and the Church* (Eugene: Cascade, 2014); Tommy Givens, *We the People: Israel and the Catholicity of Jesus* (Minneapolis: Fortress, 2014); Mark S. Kinzer, *Searching Her Own Mystery: Nostra Aetate, the Jewish People, and the Identity of the Church* (Eugene: Cascade, 2015); Jennifer M. Rosner, *Healing the Schism: Barth, Rosenzweig, and the New Jewish-Christian Encounter* (Minneapolis: Fortress, 2016); Peter Hocken, *Azusa, Rome, and Zion: Pentecostal Faith, Catholic Reform, and Jewish Roots* (Eugene: Pickwick, 2016).

[12] Mark S. Kinzer, *Jerusalem Crucified, Jerusalem Risen: N. T. Wright, the Apostolic Message, and the Jewish People* (Grand Rapids: Eerdmans, forthcoming)

[13] See www.mjstudies.com.

[14] R. Kendall Soulen, "The Standard Canonical Narrative and the Problem of Supersessionism," in *Introduction to Messianic Judaism*, 282–91.

ald McDermott's "A History of Supersessionism: Getting the Big Story Wrong" (2016).[15]

In light of the above, this new edition of *A Jew to the Jews* may be seen as part of an emerging school of thought within New Testament studies—the Paul within Judaism perspective. It is a reassessment vying for a hearing among those who were trained under older paradigms, including what is still anachronistically referred to as the New Perspective. A key text in this biblical–theological debate is 1 Cor 9:19–23 because here Paul voices his identity, calling, and ethics in relation to Jews, non-Jews and Torah-observant (expressions of) Judaism. How one reads these five verses often determines how one reads a host of other Pauline passages, and how one understands Luke's portrait of Paul the Pharisee. Therefore, the stakes are high.[16]

Over the past five years, Mark Nanos and Brian Tucker have made the most notable contributions to post-supersessionist scholarship on 1 Cor 9:19–23.[17] Nanos in particular has highlighted the ethical problems of the tradition-

---

[15] Gerald R. McDermott, "A History of Supersessionism: Getting the Big Story Wrong," in *The New Christian Zionism*, 33–44.

[16] This explains why N. T. Wright cites my monograph more than twenty-five times in *Paul and the Faithfulness of God*, Chapter 15 on "Paul and His Jewish Context" (Minneapolis: Fortress, 2013). See also Robert S. Dutch, review of David J. Rudolph, *A Jew to the Jews*, Journal for the Study of the New Testament 34:5 (August 2012): 89; Meira Z. Kensky, review of David J. Rudolph, *A Jew to the Jews*, Studies in Christian-Jewish Relations 7:1 (2012): 1–3; Joel Willitts, review of David J. Rudolph, *A Jew to the Jews*, Bulletin for Biblical Research 22:3 (2012): 451–52; Alvaro Pereira Delgado, review of David J. Rudolph, *A Jew to the Jews*, Biblica 94 (2013): 138–42; Marcin Kowalski, review of David J. Rudolph, *A Jew to the Jews*, The Biblical Annals 4 (2014): 461–65; Joseph D. Fantin, review of David J. Rudolph, *A Jew to the Jews*, Bibliotheca Sacra 171:2 (April–June 2014); Chris Miller, review of David J. Rudolph, *A Jew to the Jews*, Journal of the Evangelical Theological Society 55:2 (June 2012): 436–39; Peter J. Tomson, review of David J. Rudolph, *A Jew to the Jews*, De Stem van het Boek 2 (2012): S. 21; Brian Tucker, review of David J. Rudolph, *A Jew to the Jews*, Journal of Beliefs and Values 33:1 (April 2012): 123–27; Lionel Windsor, review of David J. Rudolph, *A Jew to the Jews*, Themelios 36:3 (November 2011): 510–11; John K. Goodrich, review of David J. Rudolph, *A Jew to the Jews*, Religious Studies Review 38:4 (December 2012): 241; Eckhard J. Schnabel, review of David J. Rudolph, *A Jew to the Jews*, Trinity Journal 34:1 (Spring 2013): 109–111; Jacob Fronczak, review of David J. Rudolph, *A Jew to the Jews*, Messiah Journal 109 (Winter 2012): 75–79.

[17] Tucker, *"Remain in Your Calling,"* 89–114. See also Karl Olav Sandnes, "A Missionary Strategy in 1 Corinthians 9.19–23?" in *Paul as Missionary: Identity, Activity, Theology, and Practice* (ed. Trevor J. Burke and Brian S. Rosner; London: T & T Clark, 2011), 128–41; Michael Barram, "Pauline Mission as Salvific Intentionality: Fostering a Missional Consciousness in 1 Corinthians 9:19–23 and 10:31—11:1," in *Paul as Missionary*, 334–46; Joel R. White, "Meals in Pagan Temples and Apostolic Finances: How Effective is Paul's Argument in 1 Corinthians 9:19–23 in the Context of 1 Corinthians 8–10?" Bulletin for Biblical Research 23:4 (2013): 531–46. Recent work on 1 Cor 9:19–23 from a more traditional perspective includes: Cavan W. Concannon, *"When You Were Gentiles": Specters of Ethnicity in Roman Corinth and Paul's Corinthian Correspondence* (New Haven: Yale University

al interpretation in "Paul's Relationship to Torah in Light of his Strategy 'to Become Everything to Everyone' (1 Corinthians 9.19–23" (2012)[18] and "Was Paul a 'Liar' for the Gospel?: The Case for a New Interpretation of Paul's 'Becoming Everything to Everyone' in 1 Cor 9:19–23" (2013).[19] Two forthcoming works that will build on Nanos, Tucker, and Rudolph are Justin Hardin's commentary on 1 Corinthians (Zondervan, 2018) and Kar Yong Lim's NTAS volume on 1 Corinthians (Cascade, 2018).

The publications surveyed in this appendix are gradually changing the landscape of New Testament studies. New questions are being asked and a new generation of scholars open to the Radical New Perspective is coming into its own. All of this is paving the way for a rethinking, reworking, and revising of existing paradigms. We can be encouraged by N. T. Wright who, though not an advocate of the Paul within Judaism perspective,[20] writes in his magnum opus *Paul and the Faithfulness of God*, "This so-called "post-supersessionist" position ... is itself well on the way to becoming a new 'consensus.'"[21]

Press, 2014); Wayne Coppins, "Juxtaposition of Freedom and Positive Servitude in 1 Corinthians 9:19 and Its Reception by Martin Luther and Gerhard Ebeling," *Lutherjahrbuch* 78 (2011): 277–98; Larry Poston, "'Shrewd as a Snake, Innocent as a Dove': The Ethics of Missionary Dissimulation and Subterfuge", *Evangelical Missions Quarterly* (October 2013): 412–19; Terry L. Wilder, "A Biblical Theology of Missions and Contextualization," *Southwestern Journal of Theology* 55:1 (Fall 2012): 1–17.

[18] Mark D. Nanos, "Paul's Relationship to Torah in Light of his Strategy 'to Become Everything to Everyone' (1 Corinthians 9.19–23)," in *Paul and Judaism*, 106–40.

[19] Mark D. Nanos, "Was Paul a 'Liar' for the Gospel?: The Case for a New Interpretation of Paul's 'Becoming Everything to Everyone' in 1 Cor 9:19–23," *Review and Expositor* 110 (Fall 2013): 591–608. Cf. Ruben Zimmerman, "Mission versus Ethics in 1 Corinthians 9: 'Implicit Ethics' as an Aid in Analyzing New Testament Texts," in *Sensitivity towards Outsiders: Exploring the Dynamic Relationship between Mission and Ethics in the New Testament and Early Christianity* (eds. Jacobus [Kobus] Kok, Tobias Nicklas, Dieter T. Roth and Christopher M. Hays; Tübingen: Mohr Siebeck, 2014), 270–89.

[20] For a post-supersessionist response to Wright's Pauline theology of Israel, see Gregory Tatum, "Law and Covenant in *Paul and the Faithfulness of God*," in *God and the Faithfulness of Paul: A Critical Examination of the Pauline Theology of N. T. Wright* (eds. Christoph Heilig, J. Thomas Hewitt and Michael F. Bird; Tübingen: Mohr Siebeck, 2016), 311–27; Paula Fredriksen, review of N. T. Wright, *Paul and the Faithfulness of God*, *The Catholic Biblical Quarterly* 77 (2015): 387–91; Givens, *We the People*, 347–414; Douglas Harink, *Paul among the Postliberals: Pauline Theology beyond Christendom and Modernity* (Grand Rapids: Brazos, 2003), 151–207; Mark Kinzer, *Jerusalem Crucified, Jerusalem Risen* (forthcoming).

[21] Wright, *Paul and the Faithfulness of God*, 1445.

Bibliography

Adams, Dwayne H. *The Sinner in Luke*. The Evangelical Theological Society Monograph Series 4. Eugene: Pickwick, 2008.

Adeyemi, Olufẹmi. "The New Covenant Torah in Jeremiah and the Law of Christ in Paul". Ph.D. diss., Dallas Theological Seminary, 2005.

Akenson, Donald H. *Saint Saul: A Skeleton Key to the Historical Jesus*. Oxford: Oxford University Press, 2000.

Allison, Dale C. "The Pauline Epistles and the Synoptic Gospels: The Pattern of the Parallels". *New Testament Studies* 28 (1982): 1–32.

—. "Paul and the Missionary Discourse". *Ephemerides Theologicae Lovanienses* 61 (1985): 369–75.

—. *Testament of Abraham*. Berlin: Walter de Gruyter, 2003.

Alon, Gedalyahu. *Jews, Judaism and the Classical World: Studies in Jewish History in the Times of the Second Temple and Talmud*. Jerusalem: The Magnes Press, 1977.

Anderson, Charles A. *Philo of Alexandria's Views of the Physical World*. WUNT 2. Tübingen: Mohr Siebeck, forthcoming.

Apisdorf, Shimon. *Kosher for the Clueless But Curious*. Baltimore: Leviathan, 2005.

Ariel, Yaakov. *Evangelizing the Chosen People: Missions to the Jews in America, 1880–2000*. Chapel Hill, N.C.: The University of North Carolina Press, 2000.

Arterbury, Andrew E. "The Ancient Custom of Hospitality: The Greek Novels and Acts 10:1–11:18". *Perspectives in Religious Studies* 29:1 (2002): 53–72.

—. "Abraham's Hospitality among Jewish and Early Christian Writers: A Tradition History of Gen 18:1–16 and Its Relevance for the Study of the New Testament". *Perspectives in Religious Studies* 30:3 (2003): 359–76.

—. *Entertaining Angels: Early Christian Hospitality in its Mediterranean Setting*. New Testament Monographs 8. Sheffield: Phoenix Press, 2005.

Back, Peter. *All Things to All Men: A Study of 1 Corinthians chapter 9:19–23*. Monograph 2. London: Red Sea Team International, 1999.

Backhaus, Knut. "'Mitteilhaber des Evangeliums' (1 Kor 9,23). Zur christologischen Grundlegung einer 'Paulus-Schule' bei Paulus". Pages 44–47 in *Christologie in der Paulus-Schule: zur Rezeptionsgeschichte des paulinischen Evangeliums*. SBS 181. Edited by Klaus Scholtissek. Stuttgart: Verlag Katholisches Bibelwerk, 2000.

Badcock, Gary D. *The Way of Life: A Theology of Christian Vocation*. Grand Rapids: Eerdmans, 1998.

Balch, David L. "'. . . you teach all the Jews . . . to forsake Moses, telling them not to . . . observe the customs' (Acts 21:21; cf. 6:14)". Pages 369–83 in *SBL 1993 Seminar Papers*. Edited by Eugene H. Lovering. Atlanta: Scholars Press, 1993.

Balserak, Jon. "'The Accommodating Act Par Excellence?': An Inquiry Into the Incarnation and Calvin's Understanding of Accommodation". *Scottish Journal of Theology* 55:4 (2002): 408–423.

Bamberger, Bernard. *Proselytism in the Talmudic Period*. Cincinnati: Hebrew Union College Press, 1939.

Bammel, Ernst. *Judaica et Paulina: Kleine Schriften II*. Mit einem Nachwort von Peter Pilhofer. WUNT 91. Tübingen: Mohr Siebeck, 1997.

Barclay, John M. G. *Obeying the Truth: A Study of Paul's Ethics in Galatians*. Edinburgh: T & T Clark, 1988.

—. "Deviance and Apostasy: Some applications of deviance theory to first-century Judaism and Christianity". Pages 114–27 in *Modelling Early Christianity: Social-Scientific Studies of the New Testament in its Context*. Edited by Philip F. Esler. London: Routledge, 1995.

—. "Paul Among Diaspora Jews: Anomaly or Apostate?" *Journal for the Study of the New Testament* 60 (1995): 89–120.

—. "'Neither Jew nor Greek': Multiculturalism and the New Perspective on Paul". Pages 197–214 in *Ethnicity and the Bible*. Biblical Interpretation Series 19. Edited by Mark G. Brett. Leiden: E. J. Brill, 1996.

—. *Jews in the Mediterranean Diaspora: From Alexander to Trajan (323 BCE – 117 CE)*. Berkeley and Los Angeles: University of California Press, 1996.

—. "Universalism and Particularism: Twin Components of Both Judaism and Early Christianity". Pages 207–24 in *The Vision for the Church: Studies in Early Christian Ecclesiology in Honour of J. P. M. Sweet*. Edited by Markus Bockmuehl and Michael B. Thompson. Edinburgh: T & T Clark, 1997.

—. "Do we undermine the Law? A Study of Romans 14.1–15.6". Pages 287–308 in *Paul and the Mosaic Law*. Edited by James D. G. Dunn. Grand Rapids: Eerdmans, 2001. Originally published in 1996 by Mohr Siebeck.

—. "Apologetics in the Jewish Diaspora". Pages 129–48 in *Jews in the Hellenistic and Roman Cities*. Edited by John R. Bartlett. London: Routledge, 2002.

—. *Pauline Churches and Diaspora Jews: Studies in the Social Formation of Christian Identity*. Tübingen: Mohr Siebeck, forthcoming.

Barnett, Paul. *The Second Epistle to the Corinthians*. Grand Rapids: Eerdmans, 1997.

Barram, Michael D. *Mission and Moral Reflection in Paul*. New York: Peter Lang, 2006.

Barreto, Eric D. *Ethnic Negotiations: The Function of Race and Ethnicity in Acts 16*. WUNT 2/294. Tübingen: Mohr Siebeck, 2010.

Barrett, C. K. "Things Sacrificed to Idols". *New Testament Studies* 11 (1965): 138–53.

—. *A Commentary on The First Epistle to the Corinthians*. Second Edition. Black's New Testament Commentaries. London: A & C Black, 1968, 1971.

—. *A Commentary on the Second Epistle to the Corinthians*. London: A & C Black, 1973.

—. *The Acts of the Apostles* II. International Critical Commentary. Edinburgh: T & T Clark, 1998.

Bartchy, S. Scott. *First-Century Slavery and 1 Corinthians 7:21*. Missoula: Society of Biblical Literature, 1973.

—. "Table Fellowship". Pages 796–800 in *Dictionary of Jesus and the Gospels*. Edited by Joel B. Green and Scot McKnight. Downers Grove: InterVarsity, 1992.

Barth, Markus. *Ephesians: Introduction, Translation, and Commentary on Chapters 1–3*. The Anchor Bible. Garden City: Doubleday, 1974.

—. "St. Paul – A Good Jew". *Horizons in Biblical Theology* 1 (1979): 7–45.

Barton, Stephen. "'All Things to All Men' (1 Corinthians 9:22): The Principle of Accommodation in the Mission of Paul". Unpublished B.A. Hons. Thesis, Macquire University, 1975.

—. "'All Things to All People': Paul and the Law in the Light of 1 Corinthians 9.19–23". Pages 271–85 in *Paul and the Mosaic Law*. Edited by James D. G. Dunn. Tübingen: Mohr Siebeck, 1996.

Bauckham, Richard. "James and the Jerusalem Church". Pages 415–80 in *The Book of Acts in its Palestinian Setting.* Edited by Richard Bauckham. Carlisle: The Paternoster Press, 1995.
—. "James and the Gentiles (Acts 15.13–21)". Pages 154–84 in *History, Literature, and Society in the Book of Acts.* Edited by Ben Witherington. Cambridge: Cambridge University Press, 1996.
—. "The Final Meeting of James and Paul: Narrative and History in Acts 21, 18–26". Pages 250–59 in *Raconter, interpréter, annoncer: Parcours de Nouveau Testament: Mélanges offerts à Daniel Marguerat pour son 60e anniversaire.* Edited by E. Steffek and Y. Bourquin. Le Monde de la Bible 47. Geneva: Labor et Fides, 2003.
—. "James, Peter, and the Gentiles". Pages 91–142 in *The Missions of James, Peter, and Paul: Tensions in Early Christianity.* Edited by Bruce Chilton and Craig Evans. Leiden: Brill, 2005.
—. "James and the Jerusalem Community". Pages 55–95 in *Jewish Believers in Jesus: The Early Centuries.* Edited by Oskar Skarsaune and Reidar Hvalvik. Peabody: Hendrickson, 2007.
—. "James and the Jerusalem Council Decision (Acts 15; 21:17–26)". In *Introduction to Messianic Judaism: Its Ecclesial Context and Biblical Foundations.* Edited by David Rudolph and Joel Willitts. Grand Rapids: Zondervan, forthcoming.
Baumgarten, Albert I. "Korban and the Pharisaic Paradosis". *Journal of the Ancient Near Eastern Society of Columbia University* 16–17 (1984/85): 5–17.
—. "The Pharisaic Paradosis". *Harvard Theological Review* 80 (1987): 63–77.
—. *The Flourishing of Jewish Sects in the Maccabean Era: An Interpretation.* Supplements to the Journal for the Study of Judaism. Leiden: Brill, 1997.
Baumgarten, Joseph M. "The Unwritten Law in the Pre-Rabbinic Period". *Journal for the Study of Judaism in the Persian, Hellenistic, and Roman Periods* 3 (1972): 7–29. Reprinted in *Studies in Qumran Law.* SJLA 24. Leiden: Brill, 1977.
—. "The Pharisaic-Saducean Controversies about Purity and the Qumran Texts". *Journal of Jewish Studies* 31 (1980): 157–70.
—. *Qumran Cave 4. XIII: The Damascus Document.* Discoveries in the Judaean Desert 18. Oxford: Clarendon, 1996.
Baur, F. C. *Paul, the Apostle of Jesus Christ, His Life and Work, His Epistles and His Doctrine: A Contribution to a Critical History of Primitive Christianity.* Translated by Allan Menzies. London: Williams & Norgate, 1876.
—. *The Church History of the First Three Centuries.* Vol. 1. Translated by Allan Menzies. London: Williams & Norgate, 1878.
Beardslee, W. A. *Human Achievement and Divine Vocation in the Message of Paul.* Studies in Biblical Theology 31. London: SCM, 1961.
Beaton, Richard. "Messiah and Justice: A Key to Matthew's Use of Isaiah 42.1–4?" *Journal for the Study of the New Testament* 75 (1999): 5–23.
—. *Isaiah's Christ in Matthew's Gospel.* SNTSMS 123. Cambridge: Cambridge University Press, 2002.
Beck, James R. and Craig L. Blomberg, eds. *Two Views on Women in Ministry.* Counterpoints Series. Grand Rapids: Zondervan, 2001.
Bell, Richard H. *The Irrevocable Call of God: An Inquiry into Paul's Theology of Israel.* WUNT 184. Tübingen: Mohr Siebeck, 2005.
Berger, David. "The Rebbe, the Jews, and the Messiah". *Commentary* 112:2 (September 2001): 23–30.
—. *The Rebbe, the Messiah and the Scandal of Orthodox Indifference.* London: The Littman Library of Jewish Civilization, 2001.
Bernheim, Pierre-Antoine. *James, Brother of Jesus.* Translated by J. Bowden. London: SCM, 1997.

Betz, H. D. *Galatians: A Commentary on Paul's Letter to the Churches of Galatia*. Hermeneia. Philadelphia: Fortress, 1979.

Bird, Michael F. "The Case of the Proselytizing Pharisees? – Matthew 23.15". *Journal for the Study of the Historical Jesus* 2:2 (2004): 117–37.

—. *Jesus and the Origins of the Gentile Mission*. Library of New Testament Studies 331. London: T & T Clark International, 2007.

—. *Crossing Over Sea and Land: Jewish Missionary Activity in the Second Temple Period*. Peabody: Hendrickson, 2010.

Black, David A. "A Note on 'the Weak' in 1 Corinthians 9:22". *Biblica* 64 (1983): 240–42.

Blass, F., A. Debrunner and Robert W. Funk, *A Greek Grammar of the New Testament and Other Early Christian Literature*. Chicago: The University of Chicago Press, 1961.

Blomberg, Craig L. *1 Corinthians*. The NIV Application Commentary. Grand Rapids: Zondervan, 1994.

—. "The Christian and the Law of Moses". Pages 397–416 in *Witness to the Gospel: The Theology of Acts*. Edited by I. Howard Marshall and David Peterson. Grand Rapids: Eerdmans, 1998.

—. *Contagious Holiness: Jesus' Meals With Sinners*. New Studies in Biblical Theology 19. Downers Grove: InterVarsity, 2005.

Bock, Darrell L. *Luke. Vol. 1. 1:1–9:50*. Baker Exegetical Commentary on the New Testament. Grand Rapids: Baker, 1994.

—. *Acts*. Baker Exegetical Commentary on the New Testament. Grand Rapids: Baker Academic, 2007.

—. "The Restoration of Israel in Luke-Acts". In *Introduction to Messianic Judaism: Its Ecclesial Context and Biblical Foundations*. Edited by David Rudolph and Joel Willitts. Grand Rapids: Zondervan, forthcoming.

Bockmuehl, Markus. *The Epistle to the Philippians*. Black's New Testament Commentary. London: A & C Black Limited, 1998.

—. *Jewish Law in Gentile Churches: Halakhah and the Beginning of Christian Public Ethics*. Edinburgh: T & T, 2000.

—. *Seeing the Word: Refocusing New Testament Study*. Grand Rapids: Baker Academic, 2006.

— and James Carleton Paget, eds. *Redemption and Resistance: The Messianic Hopes of Jews and Christians in Antiquity*. London: T & T Clark, 2007.

—. "God's Life as a Jew: Remembering the Son of God as Son of David". Pages 60–78 in *Seeking the Identity of Jesus: A Pilgrimage*. Edited by Beverly Roberts Gaventa and Richard B. Hays. Grand Rapids: Eerdmans, 2008.

—. "Jesus Christ as Son of David". In *Introduction to Messianic Judaism: Its Ecclesial Context and Biblical Foundations*. Edited by David Rudolph and Joel Willitts. Grand Rapids: Zondervan, forthcoming.

Booth, Roger P. *Jesus and the Laws of Purity: Tradition History and Legal History in Mark 7*. Sheffield: Sheffield Academic Press, 1986.

Borgen, Peder. "The Early Church and the Hellenistic Synagogue". Pages 75–97 in *Paul Preaches Circumcision and Pleases Men: And Other Essays on Christian Origins*. Trykk: Tapir, 1983. Reprinted from *Studia Theologica* 37 (1983): 55–78.

—. "Philo and the Jews in Alexandria". Pages 122–38 in *Ethnicity in Hellenistic Egypt*. Edited by Per Bilde, Troels Engberg-Pedersen, Lise Hannestad and Jan Zahle. Aarhus: Aarhus University, 1992.

—. "Proselytes, Conquest, and Mission". Pages 57–77 in *Recruitment, Conquest and Conflict: Strategies in Judaism, Early Christianity, and the Greco-Roman World*. Emory Studies in Early Christianity 6. Edited by P. Borgen, V. K. Robbins and D. B. Gowler. Atlanta: Scholars Press, 1998.

—, Kare Fuglseth and Roald Skarsten. *The Norwegian Philo Concordance Project* [database v. 1.0, Accordance edition], 2005.
Bornkamm, Günther. "The Missionary Stance of Paul in 1 Corinthians 9 and in Acts". Pages 194–207 in *Studies in Luke-Acts*. Edited by Leander E. Keck and J. Louis Martyn. Nashville: Abingdon, 1966.
—. "Das missionarische Verhalten des Paulus nach 1 Kor 9,19–23 und in der Apostelgeschichte". Pages 149–61 in *Gesammelte Aufsätze*. Vol. 4. München: Kaiser, 1966–1971.
—. *Paul*. Edited by D. M. G. Stalker. New York: Harper & Row, 1971.
Borse, U. *Der Standort des Galaterbriefes*. Bonner Biblische Beiträge. Köln: PeterHansten, 1972.
Bouwman, Gilbert. *Berufen zur Freiheit: Freiheit und Gesetz nach der Heiligen Schrift*. Düsseldorf: Patmos-Verlag, 1969.
Boyarin, Daniel. *A Radical Jew: Paul and the Politics of Identity*. Berkeley: University of California Press, 1994.
—. *Dying for God: Martyrdom and the Making of Christianity and Judaism*. Stanford: Stanford University Press, 1999.
—. *Border Lines: The Partition of Judaeo-Christianity*. Philadelphia: University of Pennsylvania Press, 2004.
Brandon, S. G. F. *The Fall of Jerusalem and the Christian Church*. London: SPCK, 1957.
Braxton, Brad R. *The Tyranny of Resolution: 1 Corinthians 7:17–24*. SBL Dissertation Series 181. Atlanta: Society of Biblical Literature, 2000.
—. *No Longer Slaves: Galatians and African American Experience*. Collegeville: The Liturgical Press, 2002.
Breuer, Edward. "Vocation and Call as Individual and Communal Imperatives". Pages 41–52 in *Revisiting the Idea of Vocation: Theological Explorations*. Washington, D.C.: The Catholic University of America Press, 2004.
Brindle, Wayne A. "'To the Jew First': Rhetoric, Strategy, History, or Theology?" *Bibliotheca Sacra* 159 (April–June 2002): 221–33.
Broadhead, Edwin K. *Jewish Ways of Following Jesus: Redrawing the Religious Map of Antiquity*. WUNT 266. Tübingen: Mohr Siebeck, 2010.
Brodie, Thomas L. "The Systematic Use of the Pentateuch in 1 Corinthians". Pages 441–57 in *The Corinthian Correspondence*. Edited by R. Bieringer. Leuven: Leuven University Press, 1996.
Bruce, F. F. *The Acts of the Apostles: The Greek Text with Introduction and Commentary*. Grand Rapids: Eerdmans, 1951.
—. *I and II Corinthians*. The New Century Bible Commentary. Grand Rapids: Eerdmans, 1971.
—. *Jesus and Christian Origins Outside the New Testament*. Grand Rapids: Eerdmans, 1974.
—. "'All Things to All Men': Diversity in Unity and Other Pauline Tensions". Pages 82–99 in *Unity and Diversity in New Testament Theology: Essays in Honor of George E. Ladd*. Edited by Robert A. Guelich. Grand Rapids: Eerdmans, 1978.
—. *The Epistle to the Galatians*: A Commentary on the Greek Text. The New International Greek Testament Commentary. Grand Rapids: Eerdmans, 1982.
—. *The Book of Acts*. Revised Edition. Grand Rapids: Eerdmans, 1988.
Brumberg-Kraus, Jonathan D. "Were the Pharisees a Conversionist Sect? Table Fellowship as a Strategy of Conversion", 2002.
Brunt, John C. "Rejected, Ignored, or Misunderstood? The Fate of Paul's Approach to the Problem of Food Offered to Idols in Early Christianity". *New Testament Studies* 31 (1985): 113–24.
Bryan, Christopher. "A Further Look at Acts 16:1–3". *Journal of Biblical Literature* 107 (1988): 292–94.

Buchanan, George Wesley. New *Testament Eschatology: Historical and Cultural Background*. Lewiston: Edwin Mellen, 1993.
Buell, Denise Kimber. "Rethinking the Relevance of Race for Early Christian Self-Definition". *Harvard Theological Review* 94:4 (2001): 449–76.
—. "Race and Universalism in Early Christianity". *Journal of Early Christian Studies* 10:4 (2002): 429–68.
— and Caroline Johnson Hodge. "The Politics of Interpretation: The Rhetoric of Race and Ethnicity in Paul". *Journal of Biblical Literature* 123:2 (2004): 235–251.
—. *Why This New Race: Ethnic Reasoning in Early Christianity*. New York: Columbia University Press, 2005.
Bultmann, Rudolf. "Die Bedeutung des geschichtlichen Jesus für die Theologie des Paulus". Pages 188–213 in *Glauben und Verstehen* I. Tübingen: Mohr Siebeck, 1933.
—. *Theology of the New Testament*. Vol. 1. New York: Scribner, 1951.
Burn, Geoffrey. "Hospitality and Incarnational Vulnerability in Luke 10.1–12". *Theology* 103:816 (2000): 445–46.
Burridge, Richard A. *Imitating Jesus: An Inclusive Approach to New Testament Ethics*. Grand Rapids: Eerdmans, 2007.
Burton, E. de W. *A Critical and Exegetical Commentary on the Epistle to the Galatians*. ICC. Edinburgh: T & T Clark, 1921.
Butarbutar, Robinson. "Resolving a Dispute, Past and Present: An Exegetical Study of Paul's Apostolic Paradigm in 1 Corinthians 9". Th.D diss. Singapore: Trinity Theological College, 1999.
Caird, George B. "'Everything to Everyone': The Theology of the Corinthian Epistles". *Interpretation* 13 (1959): 387–99.
Calvert, Nancy L. "Abraham Traditions in Middle Jewish Literature: Implications for the Interpretation of Galatians and Romans". Ph.D. diss., University of Sheffield, 1993.
Calvin, John. *The First Epistle of Paul the Apostle to the Corinthians*. Translated by John W. Fraser. London: Oliver and Boyd, 1960 (1546).
Campbell, Douglas A. "The Logic of Eschatology: The Implications of Paul's Gospel for Gender as Suggested by Galatians 3.28a in Context". Pages 58–81 in *Gospel and Gender: A Trinitarian Engagement with being Male and Female in Christ*. Edited by Douglas A. Campbell. London: T & T Clark, 2003.
—. *The Quest for Paul's Gospel: A Suggested Strategy*. London: T & T Clark, 2005.
Campbell, William S. *Paul's Gospel in an Intercultural Context*. Studies in the Intercultural History of Christianity. New York: Peter Lang, 1992.
—. "Israel". Pages 441–46 in *Dictionary of Paul and His Letters*. Edited by Gerald F. Hawthorne and Ralph P. Martin. Leicester: InterVarsity, 1993.
—. "Church as Israel, People of God". Pages 204–19 in *Dictionary of the Later New Testament and Its Developments*. Edited by Ralph P. Martin and Peter H. Davids. Leicester: InterVarsity, 1997.
—. "Significant Nuances in Contemporary Pauline Interpretation". *Irish Biblical Studies* 24 (2002): 184–99.
—. "The Crucible of Christian Identity: Paul Between Synagogue and State". The British New Testament Conference, Birmingham, 2003.
—. "'I Laid the Foundation': Paul the Architect of Christian Identity?" SBL International Meeting, Cambridge, July 2003.
—. "'All God's Beloved in Rome!' Jewish Roots and Christian Identity". Pages 67–82 in *Celebrating Romans: Template for Pauline Theology*. Edited by Sheila E. McGinn. Grand Rapids: Eerdmans, 2004.

—. "Perceptions of Compatibility between Christianity and Judaism in Pauline Interpretation". *Biblical Interpretation* 13:3 (2005): 298–316.
—. *Paul and the Creation of Christian Identity*. Edinburgh: T & T Clark, 2006.
—. "Unity and Diversity in the Church: Transformed Identities and the Peace of Christ in Ephesians". *Irish Biblical Studies* 27 (2007): 4–19.
—. "Covenant, Creation and Transformation in Paul". Paper presented at the Interdisciplinary Academic Seminar "New Perspectives on Paul and the Jews". Katholieke Universiteit Leuven, September 14–15, 2009.
—. "The Addressees of Paul's Letter to the Romans: Assemblies of God in House Churches and Synagogues?" Pages 171–95 in *Between Gospel and Election: Explorations in the Interpretation of Romans 9–11*. Edited by Florian Wilk and J. Ross Wagner. Tübingen: Mohr Siebeck, 2010.
—. "Gentile Identity and Transformation in Christ According to Paul". In *The Making of Christianity: Conflict, Contacts, and Constructions*. Edited by Magnus Zetterholm and Samuel Byrskog. Winona Lake: Eisenbrauns, forthcoming.
—. "Universality and Particularity in Paul's Understanding and Strategy of Mission". In *Paul as Missionary*. Edited by T. J. Burke and B. S. Rosner. London: T & T Clark, forthcoming.
—. "I Rate All Things as Loss: Paul's Puzzling Accounting System: Judaism as Loss or the Reevaluation of All Things in Christ". In *Celebrating Paul: Festschrift in Honor of J. A. Fitzmyer and J. Murphy-O'Connor*. Edited by Peter Spitaler. Washington, D.C.: Catholic Biblical Association of America, forthcoming.
—. "Covenantal Theology and Participation in Christ: Pauline Perspectives on Transformation". In *New Perspectives on Paul and the Jews*. Edited by R. Bieringer and D. Pollefeyt. Leuven: Peeters, forthcoming.
—. "What if God...? Changing the Perception in Rome of God's Purpose for Israel and the Church". In *Introduction to Messianic Judaism: Its Ecclesial Context and Biblical Foundations*. Edited by David Rudolph and Joel Willitts. Grand Rapids: Zondervan, forthcoming.
Capes, David B. "YHWH Texts and Monotheism in Paul's Christology". Pages 120–37 in *Early Jewish and Christian Monotheism*. JSNTSS 263. Edited by Loren T. Stuckenbruck and Wendy E. S. North. London: T & T Clark International, 2004.
Carey, Greg. *Sinners: Jesus and His Earliest Followers*. Waco: Baylor University Press, 2009.
Carleton Paget, James. "Jewish Proselytism at the Time of Christian Origins: Chimera or Reality?" *Journal for the Study of the New Testament* 62 (1996): 65–103.
—. *Jews, Christians and Jewish Christians in Antiquity*. WUNT 251. Tübingen: Mohr Siebeck, 2010.
Carras, George P. "Observant Jews in the Story of Luke and Acts". Pages 693–708 in *The Unity of Luke-Acts*. Bibliotheca Ephemeridum Theologicarum Lovaniensium. Edited by J. Verheyden. Leuven: Leuven University Press, 1999.
Carson, D. A. "Pauline Inconsistency: Reflections on 1 Corinthians 9.19–23 and Galatians 2.11–14". *Churchman* 100:1 (1986): 6–45.
—. "Mystery and Fulfillment: Toward a More Comprehensive Paradigm of Paul's Understanding of the Old and the New". Pages 393–436 in *Justification and Variegated Nomism. Vol. II. The Paradoxes of Paul*. Edited by D. A. Carson, Peter T. O'Brien and Mark A. Seifrid. WUNT 181. Tübingen: Mohr Siebeck, 2004.
Casey, M. *Aramaic Sources of Mark's Gospel*. Cambridge: Cambridge University Press, 1998.
Catchpole, David R. "Paul, James, and the Apostolic Decree". *New Testament Studies* 23 (1977): 428–44.
—. *The Quest for Q*. Edinburgh: T & T Clark, 1993.

Chadwick, Henry. "'All Things to All Men' (I Cor IX.22)". *New Testament Studies* 1 (1955): 261–75.

—. "St. Paul and Philo of Alexandria". Pages 286–307 in *History and Thought of the Early Church*. London: Variorum Reprints, 1982. Originally published in *Bulletin of the John Rylands Library* 48 (1965–66).

—. *The Enigma of St Paul*. London: University of London, The Athlone Press, 1969.

Chancey, Mark A. *The Myth of a Gentile Galilee*. Society for New Testament Studies Monograph Series 118. Cambridge: Cambridge University Press, 2003.

Chepey, Stuart D. "Nazirites in Acts and Late Second Temple Judaism: Was Luke Confused?" M. Phil. thesis. University of Oxford, May 2000.

—. "Nazirites in Late Second Temple Judaism". D. Phil. diss. University of Oxford, 2002.

—. *Nazirites in Late Second Temple Judaism: A Survey of Ancient Jewish Writings, the New Testament, Archaeological Evidence, and Other Writings from Late Antiquity*. Ancient Judaism and Early Christianity 60. Leiden: Brill, 2005.

Cheung, Alex T. *Idol Food in Corinth: Jewish Background and Pauline Legacy*. Journal for the Study of the New Testament Supplement Series 176. Sheffield: Sheffield Academic Press, 1999.

Chilton, Bruce. "The Purity of the Kingdom as Conveyed in Jesus' Meals". *Society of Biblical Literature 1992 Seminar Papers*. Edited by Eugene H. Lovering. Atlanta: Scholars, 1992.

Ciampa, Roy E. and Brian S. Rosner. *The First Letter to the Corinthians*. The Pillar New Testament Commentary. Grand Rapids: Eerdmans, 2010.

Clark, Gordon H. *First Corinthians: A Contemporary Commentary*. Nutley: Presbyterian & Reformed Publishing Company, 1975.

Cohen, Martin Samuel. *Travels on the Private Zodiac: Reflections on Jewish Life, Ritual, and Spirituality*. London Ontario: Moonstone, 1995.

Cohen, Philip. *The Hebrew Christian and His National Continuity*. London: Marshall Brothers, 1909.

Cohen, Shaye J. D. Review of Aharon Oppenheimer, *The 'Am Ha-Aretz: A Study in the Social History of the Jewish People in the Hellenistic-Roman Period*. *Journal of Biblical Literature* 97 (1978): 596–97.

—. *Josephus in Galilee and Rome. His Vita and Development as a Historian*. Columbia Studies in the Classical Tradition VIII. Leiden: Brill, 1979.

—. "Was Timothy Jewish (Acts 16:1–3)? Patristic Exegesis, Rabbinic Law, and Matrilineal Descent". *Journal of Biblical Literature* 105:2 (1986): 251–68.

—. "Respect for Judaism by Gentiles According to Josephus". *Harvard Theological Review* 80:4 (1987): 409–30.

—. "Adolph Harnack's 'The Mission and Expansion of Judaism': Christianity Succeeds Where Judaism Fails". Pages 163–69 in *The Future of Early Christianity: Essays in Honor of Helmut Koester*. Edited by Birger A. Pearson. Minneapolis: Fortress, 1991.

—. "The Place of the Rabbi in Jewish Society of the Second Century". Pages 157–73 in *The Galilee in Late Antiquity*. Edited by Lee I. Levine. New York: The Jewish Theological Seminary of America, 1992.

—. "Was Judaism in Antiquity a Missionary Religion?" Pages 14–23 in *Jewish Assimilation, Acculturation and Accommodation: Past Traditions, Current Issues and Future Prospects*. Studies in Jewish Civilization 2. Edited by Menachem Mor. New York: University Press of America, 1992.

—. *The Beginnings of Jewishness: Boundaries, Varieties, Uncertainties*. Berkeley: University of California Press, 1999.

—. *Why Aren't Jewish Women Circumcised? Gender and Covenant in Judaism*. Los Angeles: University of California Press, 2005.

Cohen-Soae, Rafael A. *Travel in Halacha*. Second Edition. Jerusalem: Bene Aharon, 2002.

Cole, R. A. *The Letter of Paul to the Galatians*. 2nd ed. TNTC 9. Grand Rapids: Eerdmans, 1989.

Collins, John J. "The Genre Apocalypse in Hellenistic Judaism". Pages 531–48 in *Apocalypticism in the Mediterranean World and the Near East. Proceedings of the International Colloquium on Apocalypticism*. Edited by David Hellholm. Tübingen: Mohr Siebeck, 1983.

—. *DIAKONIA: Reinterpreting the Ancient Sources*. Oxford: Oxford University Press, 1990.

—. *The Scepter and the Star: The Messiahs of the Dead Sea Scrolls and Other Ancient Literature*. Anchor Bible Reference Library. New York: Doubleday, 1995.

—. *Jewish Cult and Hellenistic Culture: Essays on the Jewish Encounter with Hellenism and Roman Rule*. Leiden: Brill, 2005.

Collins, Raymond F. *First Corinthians*. Sacra Pagina 7. Collegeville: Liturgical, 1999.

Conzelmann, Hans. *A Commentary on the First Epistle to the Corinthians*. Translated by J. W. Leitch. Hermeneia 36. Philadelphia: Fortress, 1975.

—. *Acts of the Apostles*. Hermeneia Series. Translated by James Limburg, A. Thomas Kraabel, and Donald H. Juel. Edited by Eldon Jay Epp with Christopher R. Matthews. Philadelphia: Fortress, 1987.

Coppins, Wayne. *The Interpretation of Freedom in the Letters of Paul: With Special Reference to the 'German' Tradition*. WUNT 2/261. Tübingen: Mohr Siebeck, 2009.

Corley, Kathleen E. "Jesus' Table Practice: Dining with 'Tax Collectors and Sinners', including Women". *Society of Biblical Literature 1993 Seminar Papers*. Edited by Eugene H. Lovering. Atlanta: Scholars, 1993.

—. *Private Women, Public Meals: Social Conflict in the Synoptic Tradition*. Peabody: Hendrickson, 1993.

Cosgrove, Charles H. *Elusive Israel: The Puzzle of Election in Romans*. Louisville: Westminster John Knox, 1997.

—. "Did Paul Value Ethnicity?" *The Catholic Biblical Quarterly* 68:2 (2006): 268–90.

Cowen, Ida. *Jews in Remote Corners of the World*. Englewood Cliffs: Prentice-Hall, 1971.

Cox, Steven. "Paul's Purificaiton Rite: Compromise or Cultural Sensitivity?" *Criswell Theological Review* 6:1 (2008): 81–96.

Craig, C. T. "The First Epistle to the Corinthians (Exegesis)". Pages 1–262 in *The Interpreter's Bible* 10. Edited by G. A. Buttrick. Nashville: Abingdon, 1953.

Cranfield, C. E. B. *A Critical and Exegetical Commentary on The Epistle to the Romans*. Vol. 1. Edinburgh: T & T Clark, 1975.

—. *A Critical and Exegetical Commentary on The Epistle to the Romans*. Vol. 2. Edinburgh: T & T Clark, 1979.

Crossley, James G. *The Date of Mark's Gospel: Insights from the Law in Earliest Christianity*. London: T & T Clark, 2004.

—. "Mark 7.1–23: Revisiting the Question of 'All Foods Clean'". Pages 8–20 in *Torah in the New Testament: Papers Delivered at the Manchester-Lausanne Seminar of June 2008*. Edited by Michael Tait and Peter Oakes. London: T & T Clark International, 2009.

—. *The New Testament and Jewish Law: A Guide for the Perplexed*. London: T & T Clark International, 2010.

Dahl, N. A. "The Future of Israel". Pages 137–58 in *Studies in Paul: Theology for the Early Christian Mission*. Minneapolis: Augsburg, 1977.

Danylak, Barry N. "The Shape of Secular Singleness and Paul's Response in 1 Corinthians 7". Ph.D. diss., University of Cambridge, forthcoming.

Darr, John A. *On Character Building: The Reader and the Rhetoric of Characterization in Luke-Acts*. Louisville: Westminster John Knox, 1992.

Das, A. Andrew. *Paul and the Jews*. Library of Pauline Studies. Peabody: Hendrickson, 2003.

—. *Solving the Romans Debate*. Minneapolis: Fortress, 2007.

Daube, David. "κερδαίνω as a Missionary Term". *Harvard Theological Review* 40 (1947): 109–20.

—. "Jewish Missionary Maxims in Paul". *Studia Theologica* 1 (1947): 158–169.

—. *The New Testament and Rabbinic Judaism*. London: Athlone, 1956. Reprinted in *New Testament Judaism: Collected Works of David Daube. Vol. 2. Studies in Comparative Legal History*. Edited by Calum Carmichael. Berkeley: The Robbins Collection, 2000.

Dauermann, Stuart. *The Rabbi as a Surrogate Priest*. Eugene: Pickwick, 2009.

Dautzenberg, Gerhard. "Der Verzicht auf das apostolische Unterhaltsrecht. Eine exegetische Untersuchung zu 1 Kor 9". *Biblica* 50 (1969): 212–32.

Davies, Eryl W. "Walking in God's Ways: The Concept of Imitatio Dei in the Old Testament". Pages 99–115 in *In Search of Wisdom: Essays in Old Testament Interpretation in Honour of Ronald E. Clements*. JSOTSS 300. Sheffield: Sheffield University Press, 1999.

Davies, Rupert. "Vocation". Pages 601–602 in *A New Dictionary of Christian Theology*. Edited by Alan Richardson and John Bowden. London: SCM, 1983.

Davies, W. D. *The Gospel and the Land: Early Christianity and Jewish Territorial Doctrine*. The Biblical Seminar 25. Sheffield: JSOT, 1974.

—. *Paul and Rabbinic Judaism: Some Rabbinic Elements in Pauline Theology*. Philadelphia: Fortress, 1980.

—. *Jewish and Pauline Studies*. Philadelphia: Fortress, 1984.

—. "Paul and the People of Israel". Pages 123–52 in *Jewish and Pauline Studies*. Philadelphia: Fortress, 1984. Reprinted from *New Testament Studies* 24 (1978): 4–39.

— and Dale C. Allison. *The Gospel According to Saint Matthew*. ICC. 3 vols. Edinburgh: T & T Clark, 1988–97.

Davila, James R. *The Provenance of the Pseudepigrapha: Jewish, Christian, or Other?* Supplements to the Journal for the Study of Judaism 105. Leiden: Brill, 2005.

Dawes, Gregory W. "'But if you can gain your freedom' (1 Corinthians 7:17–24)". *The Catholic Biblical Quarterly* 52 (1990): 681–97.

Dean, Lester. "A Response to Gerard Sloyan from Lester Dean". Pages 173–75 in *Bursting the Bonds? A Jewish-Christian Dialogue on Jesus and Paul*. Maryknoll: Orbis, 1990.

—. "Jews and Jewish Christians Must Follow Torah". Pages 176–81 in *Bursting the Bonds? A Jewish-Christian Dialogue on Jesus and Paul*. Maryknoll: Orbis, 1990.

De Boer, Willis Peter. *The Imitation of Paul: An Exegetical Study*. Kampen: J. H. Kok, 1962.

Deidun, T. J. *New Covenant Morality*. AnBib 89. Rome: Biblical Institute, 1981.

Deines, Roland. *Jüdische Steingefäße und pharisäische Frömmigkeit: Ein archäologisch-historischer Beitrag zum Verständnis von Johannes 2,6 und der jüdischen Reinheitshalacha zur Zeit Jesu*. WUNT II/52. Tübingen: Mohr Siebeck, 1993.

— and Martin Hengel. "E. P. Sanders' 'Common Judaism', Jesus, and the Pharisees: A Review Article". *Journal of Theological Studies* 46 (1995): 1–70.

—. "The Pharisees Between 'Judaisms' and 'Common Judaism'". Pages 443–504 in *Justification and Variegated Nomism: Vol. 1. The Complexities of Second Temple Judaism*. Edited by D. A. Carson, Peter T. O'Brien and Mark A. Seifrid. Tübingen: Mohr Siebeck, 2001.

Delcor, M. "La Portée chronologique de quelques interprétations du Targoum Néophyti contenues dans le cycle d'Abraham". *Journal for the Study of Judaism in the Persian, Hellenistic, and Roman Periods* 1 (1970): 105–119.

Derrett, J. Duncan M. *Law in the New Testament*. London: Darton, Longman & Todd, 1970.

Dibelius, Martin. *Studies in the Acts of the Apostles*. London: SCM, 1956.

Dickson, John P. *Mission-Commitment in Ancient Judaism and in the Pauline Communities: The Shape, Extent and Background of Early Christian Mission*. WUNT 2; Tübingen: Mohr Siebeck, 2003.

—. "Mission Commitment in Second Temple Judaism and the New Testament". In *Introduction to Messianic Judaism: Its Ecclesial Context and Biblical Foundations*. Edited by David Rudolph and Joel Willitts. Grand Rapids: Zondervan, forthcoming.

Diffenderfer, Margaret Ruth. "Conditions of Membership in the People of God: A Study Based on Acts 15 and Other Relevant Passages in Acts". Ph.D. diss., University of Durham, 1986.

Diprose, Ronald E. *Israel in the development of christian thought*. Rome: Istituto Biblico Evangelico Italiano, 2000.

—. *Israel and the Church: The Origin and Effects of Replacement Theology*. Waynesboro: Authentic Media, 2004.

Dodd, Brian J. "The Story of Christ and the Imitation of Paul in Philippians 2–3". Pages 154–161 in *Where Christology Began: Essays on Philippians 2*. Edited by Ralph P. Martin and Brian J. Dodd. Louisville: Westminster/John Knox, 1998.

—. *Paul's Paradigmatic "I": Personal Example as Literary Strategy*. JSNTSS 177. Sheffield: Sheffield Academic Press, 1999.

Dodd, C. H. "ENNOMOS KRISTOU". Pages 96–110 in *Studia Paulina in honorem J. de Zwaan*. Haarlem: Bohn, 1953.

Donahue, John R. "Tax Collectors and Sinners: An Attempt at Identification". *Catholic Biblical Quarterly* 33 (1971): 39–61.

Donaldson, Terence L. "'Riches for the Gentiles' (Rom 11:12): Israel's Rejection and Paul's Gentile Mission". *Journal of Biblical Literature* 112:1 (1993): 81–98.

—. "Israelite, Convert, Apostle to the Gentiles: The Origin of Paul's Gentile Mission". Pages 62–84 in *The Road from Damascus: The Impact of Paul's Conversion on His Life, Thought, and Ministry*. Edited by Richard N. Longenecker. Grand Rapids: Eerdmans, 1997.

—. *Paul and the Gentiles: Remapping the Apostle's Convictional World*. Minneapolis: Fortress, 1997.

—. *Judaism and the Gentiles: Jewish Patterns of Universalism [to 135 CE]* [Waco: Baylor University Press, 2007

—. *Jews and Anti-Judaism in the New Testament: Decision Points and Divergent Interpretations*. London: SPCK, 2010.

Donfried, Karl P. "Paul the Jew – But of What Sort?" Pages 11–27 in *Testimony and Interpretation: Early Christology in Its Judea-Hellenistic Milieu. Studies in Honour of Petr Pokorný*. JSNTSS 272. Edited by Jiří Mrázek and Jan Roskovec. London: T & T Clark International, 2004.

Doukhan, Jacques B. *Israel and the Church: Two Voices for the Same God*. Peabody: Hendrickson, 2002.

Drazin, Israel. "Dating Targum Onkelos by means of the Tannaitic Midrashim". *Journal of Jewish Studies* 50:2 (1999): 246–58.

Drazin, Michael. *Their Hollow Inheritance: A Comprehensive Refutation of Christian Missionaries*. Safed: G. M. Publications, 1990.

Duensing, Hugo and Aurelio de Santos Otero. "Introduction to the Apocalypse of Paul". *New Testament Apocrypha*. Edited by Wilhelm Schneemelcher. Louisville: Westminster/John Knox, 1992.

Dungan, David L. *The Sayings of Jesus in the Churches of Paul: The Use of the Synoptic Tradition in the Regulation of Early Church Life*. Oxford: Basil Blackwell, 1971.

Dunn, James D. G. *Unity and Diversity in the New Testament*. London: SCM, 1977.

—. "The Incident at Antioch (Gal. 2:11–18)". *Journal for the Study of the New Testament* 18 (1983): 3–57.

—. "Mark 2.1 – 3.6: A Bridge between Jesus and Paul on the Question of the Law". *New Testament Studies* 30 (1984): 395–415.

—. *Romans 1–8*. Word Biblical Commentary 38A. Dallas: Word, 1988.
—. *Romans 9–16*. Word Biblical Commentary 38B. Dallas: Word, 1988.
—. *Jesus, Paul and the Law: Studies in Mark and Galatians*. Louisville: Westminster/John Knox, 1990.
—. "What was the issue between Paul and 'Those of the Circumcision?'" Pages 295–318 in *Paulus und das antike Judentum*. Edited by Martin Hengel and Ulrich Heckel. Tübingen: Mohr Siebeck, 1991.
—. "Jesus, Table-Fellowship, and Qumran". Pages 254–72 in *Jesus and the Dead Sea Scrolls*. Edited by James H. Charlesworth. New York: Doubleday, 1992.
—. *The Epistle to the Galatians*. Black's New Testament Commentaries. Peabody: Hendrickson, 1993.
—. "Jesus Tradition in Paul". Pages 155–78 in *Studying the Historical Jesus: Evaluations of the State of Current Research*. Edited by Bruce Chilton and Craig Evans. Leiden: Brill, 1994.
—. "Neither Circumcision nor Uncircumcision, but . . . (Gal 5.2–12; 6.12–16; cf. 1 Cor 7.17–20)". Pages 79–122 in *La Foi Agissant par L'amour (Galates 4,12 – 6,16)*. Rome: Benedictina, 1996.
—. *The Acts of the Apostles*. Narrative Commentaries. Valley Forge: Trinity Press International, 1996.
—. "'The Law of Faith', 'the Law of the Spirit' and 'the Law of Christ'". Pages 62–82 in *Theology and Ethics in Paul and His Interpreters: Essays in Honor of Victor Paul Furnish*. Edited by Eugene H. Lovering and Jerry L. Sumney. Nashville: Abingdon, 1996.
—. "Two Covenants or One? The Interdependence of Jewish and Christian Identity". Pages 97–122 in *Geschichte – Tradition – Reflexion: Festschrift für Martin Hengel zum 70. Geburtstag*. Edited by Hubert Cancik, Hermann Lichtenberger and Peter Schäfer. Tübingen: Mohr Siebeck, 1996.
—. "Paul: Apostate or Apostle of Israel?" *ZNW* 89 (1998): 256–71.
—. *The Theology of Paul the Apostle*. Grand Rapids: Eerdmans, 1998.
—. "Who Did Paul Think He Was? A Study of Jewish-Christian Identity". *New Testament Studies* 45 (1999): 174–93.
—. "Was Judaism Particularist or Universalist?" Pages 57–73 in *Judaism in Late Antiquity*. Vol. 2. Edited by Jacob Neusner and Alan J. Avery-Peck. Leiden: Brill, 1999.
—. "The Jew Paul and His Meaning for Israel". Pages 201–15 in *A Shadow of Glory: Reading the New Testament after the Holocaust*. Edited by Tod Linafelt. New York: Routledge, 2002.
—. "Did Paul Have a Covenant Theology? Reflections on Romans 9:4 and 11:27". Pages 3–19 in *Celebrating Romans: Template for Pauline Theology*. Edited by Sheila E. McGinn. Grand Rapids: Eerdmans, 2004.
—. "Echoes of Intra-Jewish Polemic in Paul's Letter to the Galatians". Pages 221–39 in *The New Perspective on Paul: Collected Essays*. Tübingen: Mohr Siebeck, 2005.
—. "In Search of Common Ground." Pages 279–305 in *The New Perspective on Paul: Collected Essays*. Tübingen: Mohr Siebeck, 2005.
—. "Paul and the Torah: The Role and Function of the Law in the Theology of Paul the Apostle". Pages 441–61 in *The New Perspective on Paul: Collected Essays*. Tübingen: Mohr Siebeck, 2005.
—. "Philippians 3.2–14 and the New Perspective on Paul". Pages 463–84 in *The New Perspective on Paul: Collected Essays*. Tübingen: Mohr Siebeck, 2005.
Dutch, Robert S. *The Educated Elite in 1 Corinthians: Education and Community Conflict in Graeco-Roman Context*. London: T & T Clark, 2005.
Ebeling, Gerhard. *The Truth of the Gospel: An Exposition of Galatians*. Translated by David Green. Philadelphia: Fortress, 1985.

Eckstein, Hans-Joachim. *Verheißung und Gesetz. Eine exegetische Untersuchung zu Galater 2,14–4,7*. WUNT 86. Tübingen: Mohr Siebeck, 1996.
Edwards, James R. *The Hebrew Gospel and the Development of the Synoptic Tradition*. Grand Rapids: Eerdmans, 2009.
Edwards, Thomas C. *A Commentary on the First Epistle to the Corinthians*. 4th ed. London: Hodder and Stoughton, 1903.
Ehrensberger, Kathy. *That We May Be Mutually Encouraged: Feminism and the New Perspective in Pauline Studies*. New York: T & T Clark, 2004.
—. *Paul and the Dynamics of Power: Communication and Interaction in the Early Christ-Movement*. London: T & T Clark, 2007.
—. *Reading Paul in Context: Explorations in Identity Formation: Essays in Honour of William S. Campbell*. Library of New Testament Studies 428. London: T & T Clark International, 2010.
—. "'Called to be Saints' – The Identity-Shaping Dimension of Paul's Priestly Discourse in Romans". Pages 90–109 in *Reading Paul in Context: Explorations in Identity Formation: Essays in Honour of William S. Campbell*. London: T & T Clark International, 2010
Eichholz, George. "Der missionarische Kanon des Paulus. 1 Kor 9.19–23". Pages 114–20 in *Tradition and Interpretation. Studien zum Neuen Testament und zur Hermeneutik*. Theologische Bücherei 29. Munich: Chr Kaiser, 1965.
Eisenbaum, Pamela. "Paul as the New Abraham". Pages 130–45 in *Paul and Politics: Ekklesia, Israel, Imperium, Interpretation. Essays in Honor of Krister Stendahl*. Edited by Richard A. Horsley. Harrisburg: Trinity Press International, 2000.
—. "Is Paul the Father of Misogyny and Antisemitism?" *Cross Currents* 50:4 (2000–01): 506–24.
—. *Paul Was Not a Christian: The Original Message of a Misunderstood Apostle*. New York: HarperOne, 2009.
Ellicott, Charles J. *St. Paul's First Epistle to the Corinthians*. London: Longmans, Green, and Co., 1887.
Ellis, E. Earle. "Paul and His Opponents: Trends in the Research". Pages 264–98 in *Christianity, Judaism and Other Greco-Roman Cults: Studies for Morton Smith at Sixty*. Edited by Jacob Neusner. Leiden: Brill, 1975.
Ellison, H. L. "Paul and the Law – 'All Things to All Men'". Pages 195–202 in *Apostolic History and the Gospel: Biblical and Historical Essays Presented to F. F. Bruce on his 60th Birthday*. Edited by W. Ward Gasque and Ralph P. Martin. Grand Rapids: Eerdmans, 1970.
Esler, Philip F. *Community and Gospel in Luke-Acts: The Social and Political Motivations of Lucan Theology*. Cambridge: Cambridge University Press, 1987.
—. "Making and Breaking an Agreement Mediterranean Style: A New Reading of Galatians 2:1–14". *Biblical Interpretation* 3:3 (1995): 285–314.
—. *Galatians: New Testament Readings*. London: Routledge, 1998.
—. "Ancient Oleiculture and Ethnic Differentiation: The Meaning of the Olive-Tree Image in Romans 11". *Journal for the Study of the New Testament* 26:1 (2003): 103–24.
Evans, C. F. *Saint Luke*. TPI New Testament Commentaries. London: SCM, 1990.
Falk, Harvey. "Rabbi Jacob Emden's Views on Christianity". *Journal of Ecumenical Studies* 19:1 (1982): 107–109.
Fee, Gordon D. "Εἰδωλόθυτα Once Again: An Interpretation of 1 Corinthians 8–10". *Biblica* 61 (1980): 172–97.
—. *The First Epistle to the Corinthians*. NICNT. Grand Rapids: Eerdmans, 1987.
—. *Paul's Letter to the Philippians*. Grand Rapids: Eerdmans, 1995.
Feinberg, Paul D. "The Kenosis and Christology: An Exegetical-Theological Analysis of Phil 2:6–11". *Trinity Journal* 1 (1980): 21–46.

Feldman, Louis H. "Abraham the Greek Philosopher in Josephus". *Transactions and Proceedings of the American Philological Association* 99 (1968): 143–56.

—. "Hellenizations in Josephus' *Jewish Antiquities*: The Portrait of Abraham". Pages 133–53 in *Josephus, Judaism, and Christianity*. Edited by Louis H. Feldman and Gohei Hata. Leiden: Brill, 1987.

—. "Was Judaism a Missionary Religion in Ancient Times?" Pages 24–37 in *Jewish Assimilation, Acculturation and Accommodation: Past Traditions, Current Issues and Future Prospects*. Studies in Jewish Civilization 2. Edited by Menachem Mor. New York: University Press of America, 1992.

—. *Jew and Gentile in the Ancient World: Attitudes and Interactions from Alexander to Justinian*. Princeton: Princeton University Press, 1993.

—. *Josephus's Interpretation of the Bible*. Berkeley: University of California Press, 1998.

—. *Flavius Josephus, Translation and Commentary: Judean Antiquities 1–4*. Vol. 3. Edited by Steve Mason. Leiden: Brill, 2000.

Fellows, Richard G. "Was Titus Timothy?" *Journal for the Study of the New Testament* 81 (2001): 33–58.

—. "Renaming in Paul's Churches: The Case of Crispus-Sosthenes Revisited", *Tyndale Bulletin* 56:2 (2005): 111–30.

Ferguson, E. "Canon Muratori: Date and Provenance". *Studia Patristica* 17 (1982): 677–83.

Findlay, G. G. "St. Paul's First Epistle to the Corinthians", in *The Expositor's Greek Testament*. Edited by W. R. Nicoll. Grand Rapids: Eerdmans, 1961 [1900].

Finger, Reta Halteman. *Of Widows and Meals: Communal Meals in the Book of Acts*. Grand Rapids: Eerdmans, 2007.

Finsterbusch, Karin. *Die Thora als Lebensweisung für Heidenchristen: Studien zur Bedeutung der Thora für die paulinische Ethik*. Göttingen: Vandenhoeck & Ruprecht, 1996.

Fischer, John. "Paul in His Jewish Context". *The Evangelical Quarterly* 57:3 (1985): 211–36.

Fishkoff, Sue. *The Rebbe's Army: Inside the World of Chabad-Lubavitch*. New York: Schocken, 2003.

Fitzmyer, Joseph A. "A Feature of Qumran Angelology and the Angels of 1 Cor 11:10". Pages 187–204 in *Paul and Qumran*. Edited by J. Murphy-O'Connor. London: Geoffrey Chapman, 1968.

—. *The Acts of the Apostles*. The Anchor Bible 31. New York: Doubleday, 1998.

—. *First Corinthians: A New Translation with Introduction and Commentary*. The Anchor Yale Bible 32. New Haven: Yale University Press, 2008.

Fjärstedt, Biörn. *Synoptic Traditions in 1 Corinthians: Themes and Clusters of Theme Words in 1 Corinthians 1–4 and 9*. Uppsala: Theologiska Institutionen, 1974.

Forst, Binyomin. *The Laws of Kashrus: A Comprehensive Exposition of Their Underlying Concepts and Applications*. ArtScroll Halachah Series. Brooklyn: Mesorah, 2004.

Fotopoulos, John. *Food Offered to Idols in Roman Corinth: A Social-Rhetorical Reconsideration of 1 Corinthians 8–10*. WUNT 2/151. Tübingen: Mohr Siebeck, 2003.

Fraser, P. M. *Ptolemaic Alexandria*. Vol. 2. Oxford: Clarendon, 1972.

Fredriksen, Paula. "Judaism, the Circumcision of Gentiles, and Apocalyptic Hope: Another Look at Galatians 1 and 2". *Journal of Theological Studies* 42 (1991): 532–64.

—. "From Jesus to Christ: The Contribution of the Apostle Paul". Pages 77–90 in *Jews and Christians Speak of Jesus*. Edited by Arthur E. Zannoni. Minneapolis: Fortress, 1994.

—. "Torah-Observance and Christianity: The Perspective of Roman Antiquity". *Modern Theology* 11:2 (1995): 195–204.

—. "Did Jesus Oppose the Purity Laws?" *Bible Review* 11:3 (1995): 18–25, 42–47.

—. "The Holy City in Christian Thought". Pages 74–92 in *The City of the Great King: Jerusalem from David to the Present*. Edited by Nitza Rosovsky. Cambridge: Harvard University Press, 1996.
—. *Jesus of Nazareth, King of the Jews: A Jewish Life and the Emergence of Christianity*. New York: Vintage, 1999.
—. "Allegory and Reading God's Book: Paul and Augustine on the Destiny of Israel". Pages 125–49 in *Interpretation and Allegory: Antiquity to the Modern Period*. Edited by Jon Whitman. Leiden: Brill, 2000.
—. "The Birth of Christianity and the Origins of Christian Anti-Judaism". Pages 8–30 in *Jesus, Judaism and Christian Anti-Judaism: Reading the New Testament after the Holocaust*. Edited by Paula Fredriksen and Adele Reinhartz. Louisville: Westminster John Knox, 2002.
—. "Dining with the Divine". *Bible Review* (June 2002): 12, 42.
—. "What 'Parting of the Ways? Jews and Gentiles in the Ancient Mediterranean City". Pages 35–63 in *The Ways that Never Parted: Jews and Christians in Late Antiquity and the Early Middle Ages*. Edited by Adam H. Becker and Annette Yoshiko Reed. Tübingen: Mohr Siebeck, 2003.
— and Judith Lieu. "Christian Theology and Judaism". Pages 85–101 in *The First Christian Theologians: An Introduction to Theology in the Early Church*. Edited by G. R. Evans. Oxford: Blackwell, 2004.
—. "Paul, Purity and the *Ekklesia* of the Gentiles". Pages 205–17 in *The Beginnings of Christianity: A Collection of Articles*. Jerusalem: Yad Ben-Zvi, 2005.
—. "Compassion Is to Purity as Fish Is to Bicycle: Thoughts on the Construction of 'Judaism' in Current Research on the Historical Jesus". Pages 55–68 in *Apocalypticism, Anti-Semitism, and the Historical Jesus: Subtexts in Criticism*. Journal for the Study of the New Testament Supplement Series 275. Edited by J. S. Kloppenborg and J. W. Marshall. London: T & T Clark International, 2005.
—. "Mandatory Retirement: Ideas in the Study of Christian Origins Whose Time Has Come to Go". *Studies in Religion* 35:2 (2006): 231–46.
— and Oded Irshai. "Christianity Anti-Judaism: Polemics and Policies". Pages 977–1034 in *The Cambridge History of Judaism. Vol. 4: The Late Roman-Rabbinic Period*. Edited by Steven T. Katz. Cambridge: Cambridge University Press, 2006.
—. "Christians in the Roman Empire in the First Three Centuries CE". Pages 587–606 in *A Companion to the Roman Empire*. Edited by David Potter. Oxford: Blackwell, 2006.
—. *Augustine and the Jews: A Christian Defense of Jews and Judaism*. New York: Doubleday, 2008.
—. "Judaizing the Nations: The Ritual Demands of Paul's Gospel". *New Testament Studies* 56 (2010): 232–52.
Freed, Edwin D. *The Morality of Paul's Converts*. London: Equinox, 2005.
Freyne, Sean. *Galilee from Alexander the Great to Hadrian: A Study of Second Temple Judaism*. Wilmington: Michael Glazier, 1980.
—. *Jesus a Jewish Galilean: A New Reading of the Jesus-Story*. London: T & T Clark, 2004.
Friedman, Hershey H. "Placing a Stumbling Block Before the Blind Person: An In-Depth Analysis", 2002. No pages. Cited 19 December 2010. Online: http://www.jlaw.com/-Articles/placingstumbling.html.
Fung, R. Y. K. *The Epistle to the Galatians*. The New International Commentary on the New Testament. Grand Rapids: Eerdmans, 1988.
Funke, Hermann. "Antisthenes bei Paulus". *Hermes* 98 (1970): 459–71.
Furnish, Victor P. *Theology and Ethics in Paul*. New York: Abingdon, 1968.
—. *Jesus According to Paul*. Cambridge: Cambridge University Press, 1993.

Gäckle, Volker. *Die Starken und die Schwachen in Korinth und in Rom. Zu Herkunft und Funktion der Antithese in 1 Kor 8,1–11,1 und in Röm 14,1–15,13*. Tübingen: Mohr Siebeck, 2004.

Gadenz, Pablo T. *Called from the Jews and from the Gentiles: Pauline Ecclesiology in Romans 9–11*. WUNT 2/267. Tübingen: Mohr Siebeck, 2009.

Gager, John G. *Reinventing Paul*. Oxford: Oxford University Press, 2002.

—. "Did Jewish Christians See the Rise of Islam?" Pages 361–72 in *The Ways that Never Parted: Jews and Christians in Late Antiquity and the Early Middle Ages*. Edited by Adam H. Becker and Annette Yoshiko Reed. Tübingen: Mohr Siebeck, 2003.

Galloway, Lincoln E. *Freedom in the Gospel: Paul's Exemplum in 1 Cor 9 in Conversation with the Discourses of Epictetus and Philo*. Leuven: Peeters, 2004.

Gane, Roy E. "The Function of the Nazirite's Concluding Purification Offering". Pages 9–17 in *Perspectives on Purity and Purification in the Bible*. Edited by Baruch J. Schwartz, David P. Wright, Jeffrey Stackert, and Naphtali S. Meshel. London: T & T Clark International, 2008.

Ganser-Kerperin, Heiner. *Das Zeugnis des Tempels. Studien zur Bedeutung des Tempelmotivs im Lukanischen Doppelwerk*. Münster: Aschendorff, 2000.

Gardner, P. D. *The Gifts of God and the Authentication of a Christian: An Exegetical Study of 1 Corinthians 8:1–11:1*. Lanham: University Press of America, 1994.

Garland, David E. *2 Corinthians*. The New American Commentary 29. Nashville: Broadman & Holman, 1999.

—. *1 Corinthians*. Baker Exegetical Commentary on the New Testament. Grand Rapids: Baker Academic, 2003.

—. "The Dispute Over Food Sacrificed to Idols (1 Cor 8:1–11:1)." *Perspectives in Religious Studies* 30:2 (2003): 173–97.

Garlington, Donald B. "Burden Bearing and the Recovery of Offending Christians (Galatians 6:1–5)". *Trinity Journal* 12 (1991): 151–83.

Garroway, Joshua David. "Neither Jew nor Gentile, but both: Paul's 'Christians' as 'Gentile-Jews'". Ph.D. diss., Yale University, 2008.

Gasque, W. Ward. *A History of the Interpretation of the Acts of the Apostles*. Eugene, OR: Wipf and Stock, 1975.

Gaston, Lloyd. *Paul and the Torah*. Vancouver: University of British Columbia Press, 1987.

Georgi, Dieter. *The Opponents of Paul in Second Corinthians*. Edinburgh: T & T Clark, 1987. Translated from the German *Die Gegner des Paulus im 2. Korintherbrief: Studien zur Religiösen Propaganda in der Spätantike*. Neukirchen-Vluyn: Neukirchener Verlag, 1964.

Gillihan, Yonder Moynihan. "Jewish Laws on Illicit Marriage, the Defilement of Offspring, and the Holiness of the Temple: A New Halakhic Interpretation of 1 Corinthians 7:14". *Journal of Biblical Literature* 121:4 (2002): 711–44.

Gilliland, Dean S. *Pauline Theology and Mission Practice*. Eugene: Wipf and Stock, 1996.

Ginsburger, M. *Pseudo-Jonathan: Thargum Jonathan ben Usiël zum Pentateuch*. Berlin: S. Calvary, 1903.

Given, Mark D. "True Rhetoric: Ambiguity, Cunning, and Deception in Pauline Discourse". Pages 526–50 in *Society of Biblical Literature 1997 Seminar Papers*. Atlanta: Scholars, 1997.

—. *Paul's True Rhetoric: Ambiguity, Cunning, and Deception in Greece and Rome*. Emory Studies in Early Christianity. Harrisburg: Trinity Press International, 2001.

Glad, Clarence E. *Paul and Philodemus: Adaptability in Epicurean and Early Christian Psychagogy*. Leiden: Brill, 1995.

—. "Paul and Adaptability". Pages 17–41 in *Paul in the Greco-Roman World: A Handbook*. Edited by J. Paul Sampley. Harrisburg: Trinity Press International, 2003.

Glaser, Mitch L. "A Survey of Missions to the Jews in Continental Europe 1900–1950". Ph.D. diss., Fuller Theological Seminary, 1998.

Gloag, Paton J. *A Critical and Exegetical Commentary on the Acts of the Apostles* II. Minneapolis: Klock & Klock Christian, 1870.

Godet, F. L. *Commentary on the First Epistle of St. Paul to the Corinthians.* Translated by A. Cusin. Edinburgh: T & T Clark, 1886, 1898.

Gooch, Paul W. *Partial Knowledge: Philosophical Studies in Paul.* Notre Dame: University of Notre Dame Press, 1987.

Gooch, Peter D. *Dangerous Food: 1 Corinthians 8–10 in Its Context.* Ontario: Canadian Corporation for Studies in Religion/Corporation Canadienne des Sciences Religieuses by Wilfrid Laurier University Press, 1993.

Goodman, David. "Do Angels Eat?" *Journal of Jewish Studies* 37 (1986): 160–75.

Goodman, Martin. *Who Was a Jew?* Oxford: Oxford Centre for Postgraduate Hebrew Studies, 1989.

—. "Proselytising in Rabbinic Judaism". *Journal of Jewish Studies* 40 (1989): 175–85.

—. "Identity and Authority in Ancient Judaism". *Judaism* 39:2 (1990): 192–201.

—. *Mission and Conversion: Proselytizing in the Religious History of the Roman Empire.* Oxford: Clarendon Press, 1994.

—. "Jewish proselytizing in the first century". Pages 53–78 in *The Jews Among Pagans and Christians in the Roman Empire.* Edited by Judith Lieu, John North and Tessa Rajak. London: Routledge, 1994.

—. "Jews and Judaism in the Mediterranean Diaspora in the Late-Roman Period: The Limitations of Evidence". Pages 177–203 in *Ancient Judaism in its Hellenistic Context.* Supplements to the Journal for the Study of Judaism 95. Edited by Carol Bakhos. Leiden: Brill, 2005.

Gowler, David B. *Host, Guest, Enemy and Friend: Portraits of the Pharisees in Luke and Acts.* Emory Studies in Early Christianity. New York: Peter Lang, 1991.

Green, Joel B. *The Gospel of Luke.* New International Commentary on the New Testament. Grand Rapids: Eerdmans, 1997.

Greenberg, Blu. *How to Run a Traditional Jewish Household.* London: Jason Aronson, 1989.

Grosheide, F. W. *Commentary on the First Epistle to the Corinthians.* Grand Rapids: Eerdmans, 1953.

Grossfeld, Bernard. *The Targum Onqelos to Genesis: Translated, with a Critical Introduction, Apparatus, and Notes.* The Aramaic Bible 6; Edinburgh: T & T Clark, 1988.

—. "Targum Onqelos, Halakha and the Halakhic Midrashim". Pages 228–46 in *The Aramaic Bible: Targums in their Historical Context.* JSOTSS 166. Edited by D. R. G. Beattie and M. J. McNamara. Sheffield: Sheffield Academic Press, 1994.

—. *Targum Neofiti 1: An Exegetical Commentary to Genesis.* New York: Sepher-Hermon, 2000.

Guelich, Robert A. *Mark 1–8:26.* Word Biblical Commentary 34a. Dallas: Word, 1989.

Guerra, Anthony J. 'The One God Topos in Spec. Leg. 1.52'. Pages 148–57 in *Society of Biblical Literature 1990 Seminar Papers.* SBLSPS 29. Edited by David J. Lull. Atlanta: Scholars, 1990.

Gundry-Volf, Judith M. "Male and Female in Creation and New Creation: Interpretations of Galatians 3:28c in 1 Corinthians 7". Pages 95–121 in *To Tell the Mystery: Essays on New Testament Eschatology in Honor of Robert H. Gundry.* Edited by Thomas E. Schmidt and Moisés Silva. JSNTSS 100. Sheffield: Sheffield Academic Press, 1994.

—. "Christ and Gender: A Study of Difference and Equality in Gal. 3:28". Pages 439–77 in *Jesus Christus als die Mitte der Schrift.* Edited by Christof Landmesser, et al. Berlin: de Gruyter, 1997.

—. "Beyond Difference? Paul's Vision of a New Humanity in Galatians 3.28". Pages 8–36 in *Gospel and Gender: A Trinitarian Engagement with being Male and Female in Christ*. Edited by Douglas A. Campbell. London: T & T Clark, 2003.

Guttmann, Alexander. *The Struggle over Reform in Rabbinic Literature*. New York: The World Union for Progressive Judaism, 1977.

Haas, Peter. "The *Am Ha'Arets* as Literary Character". Pages 139–53 in *From Ancient Israel to Modern Judaism: Intellect in Quest of Understanding. Essays in Honor of Marvin Fox*. Vol. 2. Edited by Jacob Neusner, Ernest Frerichs and Nahum Sarna. Atlanta: Scholars, 1989.

Haber, Susan. *"They Shall Purify Themselves": Essays on Purity in Early Judaism*. Early Judaism and Its Literature 24. Edited by Adele Reinhartz. Atlanta: Society of Biblical Literature, 2008.

Hackett, Moratio B. *Commentary on Acts*. Grand Rapids: Kregel, 1992.

Haenchen, Ernst. *The Acts of the Apostles: A Commentary*. Translated by Bernard Noble and Gerald Shinn (from the 14th German edition [1965]). Oxford: Basil Blackwell, 1971.

Hafemann, Scott. "The Salvation of Israel in Romans 11:25–32: A Response to Krister Stendahl". *Ex Auditu* 4 (1988): 38–58.

—. *Paul, Moses, and the History of Israel: The Letter/Spirit Contrast and the Argument from Scripture in 2 Corinthians 3*. WUNT 81. Tübingen: Mohr Siebeck, 1995.

—. "Eschatology and Ethics: The Future of Israel and the Nations in Romans 15:1–13". *Tyndale Bulletin* 51:2 (2000): 161–92.

—. "The Role of Suffering in the Mission of Paul". Pages 165–84 in *The Mission of the Early Church to Jews and Gentiles*. Edited by Jostein Ådna and Hans Kvalbein. Tübingen: Mohr Siebeck, 2000.

—. "The Redemption of Israel for the Sake of the Gentiles (Rom 15:7–13)". In *Introduction to Messianic Judaism: Its Ecclesial Context and Biblical Foundations*. Edited by David Rudolph and Joel Willitts. Grand Rapids: Zondervan, forthcoming.

Hagner, Donald A. "Paul and Judaism: Testing the New Perspective". Pages 75–105 in *Revisiting Paul's Doctrine of Justification: A Challenge to the New Perspective*, by Peter Stuhlmacher. Downers Grove: InterVarsity, 2001.

—. "Paul as a Jewish Believer—According to His Letters". Pages 96–120 in *Jewish Believers in Jesus: The Early Centuries*. Edited by Oskar Skarsaune and Reidar Hvalvik. Peabody: Hendrickson, 2007.

Hall, Barbara. "All Things to All People: A Study of 1 Corinthians 9:19–23". Pages 137–57 in *The Conversation Continues, Studies in Paul and John*. Edited by Robert T. Fortna and Beverly R. Gaventa. Nashville: Abingdon, 1990.

Hannah, Darrell D. *The Text of 1 Corinthians in the Writings of Origen*. The New Testament in the Greek Fathers 4. Atlanta: Scholars, 1997.

—. Review of Charles A. Gieschen, *Angelomorphic Christology: Antecedents and Early Evidence*. *The Journal of Theological Studies* 51 (2000): 230–36.

Hansen, Bruce. *'All of You Are One': The Social Vision of Gal 3.28, 1 Cor 12.13 and Col 3.11*. London: T & T Clark, 2010.

Hardin, Justin K. "Decrees and Drachmas at Thessalonica: An Illegal Assembly in Jason's House (Acts 17.1–10a)". *New Testament Studies* 52 (2006): 29–49.

—. *Galatians and the Imperial Cult: A Critical Analysis of the First-Century Social Context of Paul's Letter*. WUNT II/237. Tübingen: Mohr Siebeck, 2008.

—. *1 Corinthians: A Commentary*. Regula Fidei. Grand Rapids: Zondervan, forthcoming.

—. "Equality in the Church (Gal 3:28 and Eph 2:14–18)". In *Introduction to Messianic Judaism: Its Ecclesial Context and Biblical Foundations*. Edited by David Rudolph and Joel Willitts. Grand Rapids: Zondervan, forthcoming.

Harding, Mark. "The Salvation of Israel and the Logic of Romans 11:11–36". *ABR* 46 (1998): 55–69.
Harink, Douglas. *Paul among the Postliberals: Pauline Theology Beyond Christendom and Modernity*. Grand Rapids: Brazos, 2003.
—. "Paul and Israel: An Apocalyptic Reading". Pauline Soteriology Group, Society of Biblical Literature. Philadelphia. November 2005.
—. "Jewish Priority, Election and the Gospel". In *Introduction to Messianic Judaism: Its Ecclesial Context and Biblical Foundations*. Edited by David Rudolph and Joel Willitts. Grand Rapids: Zondervan, forthcoming.
Harnack, Adolf von. *The Expansion of Christianity in the First Three Centuries*. Translated by James Moffatt. New York: Putnam's Sons, 1904.
—. *The Acts of the Apostles*. New Testament Studies 3. Translated by J. R. Wilkinson. New York: Williams & Norgate, 1909.
—. *The Date of the Acts and of the Synoptic Gospels*. New Testament Studies 4. Translated by J. R. Wilkinson. New York: Williams & Norgate, 1911.
—. "'Sanftmut, Huld und Demut' in der alten Kirche". Pages 113–29 in *Festgabe für Julius Kaftan zu seinem 70. Geburtstag*. Edited by A. Titius, F. Niebergall and G. Wobbermin. Tübingen: Mohr Siebeck, 1920.
Harrington, Hannah K. *The Impurity Systems of Qumran and the Rabbis: Biblical Foundations*. SBL Dissertation Series 143. Atlanta: Scholars, 1993.
—. "Did the Pharisees Eat Ordinary Food in a State of Ritual Purity?" *Journal for the Study of Judaism in the Persian, Hellenistic and Roman Period* 1995 (26): 42–54.
—. *The Purity Texts*. London: T & T Clark, 2004.
Harris, J. Rendel, ed. *Fragments of Philo Judaeus*. Cambridge: Cambridge University Press, 1886.
Harris, Murray J. *Jesus as God: The New Testament Use of Theos in Reference to Jesus*. Grand Rapids: Baker, 1992.
—. *Slave of Christ. A New Testament Metaphor for Total Devotion to Christ*. New Studies in Biblical Theology 8. Leicester 1999.
Harvey, Anthony E. *Jesus and the Constraints of History*. Philadelphia: The Westminster Press, 1982.
—. "Forty Strokes Save One: Social Aspects of Judaizing and Apostasy". Pages 79–96 in *Alternative Approaches to New Testament Study*. Edited by A. E. Harvey. London: SPCK, 1985.
Harvey, Graham. *The True Israel: Uses of the Names Jew, Hebrew and Israel in Ancient Jewish Literature and Early Christian Literature*. AGAJU 35. Leiden: Brill, 1996.
—. "Synagogues of the Hebrews: 'Good Jews' in the Diaspora". Pages 132–47 in *Jewish Local Patriotism and Self-Identification in the Graeco-Roman Period*. JSPSS 31. Sheffield: Sheffield Academic Press, 1998.
Hatlem, Jodie Boyer and Doug Johnson Hatlem. "Muzzling the Ox: Should Torah Be Normative for Gentile Christians?" *Studies in Christian-Jewish Relations* 5:1 (2010): 1–22.
Hawthorne, Gerald F. *Philippians*. Word Biblical Commentary 43. Waco: Word, 1983.
Hayes, Christine E. *Gentile Impurities and Jewish Identities: Intermarriage and Conversion from the Bible to the Talmud*. Oxford: Oxford University Press, 2002.
Hays, Richard B. "Christology and Ethics in Galatians: The Law of Christ". *The Catholic Biblical Quarterly* 49 (1987): 268–90.
—. *First Corinthians*. Interpretation. Louisville: John Knox, 1997.
Hayward, Robert. "Abraham as Proselytizer at Beer-Sheba in the Targums of the Pentateuch". *Journal of Jewish Studies* 49 (1998): 25–37.
Hecht, Richard D. "Scripture and Commentary in Philo [Appendix: Leviticus 19 in the Philonic Corpus]". Pages 129–64 in *Society of Biblical Literature Seminar Papers 1981*. Edited by Kent H. Richards. Atlanta: Society of Biblical Literature, 1981.

Hegermann, Harold. "The Diaspora in the Hellenistic Age". Pages 131–45 in *The Cambridge History of Judaism*. Vol. 2. Edited by W. D. Davies and L. Finkelstein. Cambridge: Cambridge University Press, 1989.

Hegg, Tim. *The Letter Writer: Paul's Background and Torah Perspective*. Tacoma: Bikurei Tziyon, 2002.

—. *Paul's Epistle to the Romans*. Vol. 1. Tacoma: TorahResource, 2005.

—. *Paul's Epistle to the Romans*. Vol. 2. Tacoma: TorahResource, 2007.

Heinrici, C. F. G. *Das erste Sendschreiben des Apostel Paulus an die Korinther*. Berlin: Hertz, 1880.

Hemer, Colin J. *The Book of Acts in the Setting of Hellenistic History*. Edited by Conrad H. Gempf. Tübingen: Mohr Siebeck, 1989.

Hengel, Martin. *Acts and the History of Earliest Christianity*. Philadelphia: Fortress Press, 1980.

—. *The Pre-Christian Paul*. Translated by John Bowden. London: SCM, 1991.

—. "The Attitude of Paul to the Law in the Unknown Years between Damascus and Antioch". Pages 25–51 in *Paul and the Mosaic Law*. Edited by James D. G. Dunn. Grand Rapids: Eerdmans, 1996.

—. "Judaism and Hellenism Revisited". Pages 6–37 in *Hellenism in the Land of Israel*. Edited by John J. Collins and Gregory E. Sterling. Christianity and Judaism in Antiquity 13. Notre Dame: University of Notre Dame Press, 2001.

Henry, Patrick. "All Things to All Persons". Pages 158–65 in *New Directions in New Testament Study*. Philadelphia: Westminster, 1979.

Héring, Jean. *The First Epistle of Saint Paul to the Corinthians*. Translated by A. W. Heathcote and P. J. Allcock. London: Epworth, 1962.

Heydenreich, August Ludwig Christian. *Commentarius in priorem divi Pauli ad Corinthios epistolam*. 2 vols. Marburgi: J. C. Krieger, 1825–1828.

Hilary, Mbachu. *Inculturation Theology of the Jerusalem Council in Acts 15: An Inspiration for the Igbo Church Today*. Frankfurt am Main: Peter Lang, 1995.

Hilgert, Earle. "The *Quaestiones*: Texts and Translations". Pages 1–15 in *Both Literal and Allegorical: Studies in Philo of Alexandria's* Questions and Answers on Genesis and Exodus. Brown Judaic Studies 232. Edited by David M. Hay. Atlanta: Scholars Press, 1991.

Hill, Craig C. *Hellenists and Hebrews: Reappraising Division within the Earliest Church*. Minneapolis: Fortress, 1992.

Himmelfarb, Martha. *A Kingdom of Priests: Ancestry and Merit in Ancient Judaism*. Philadelphia: University of Pennsylvania Press, 2006.

Hock, Ronald F. "Paul's Tentmaking and the Problem of His Social Class". *Journal of Biblical Literature* 97 (1978): 555–64.

Hodge, Caroline Johnson. "Apostle to the Gentiles: Construction of Paul's Identity". *Biblical Interpretation* 13:3 (2005): 270–88.

—. *If Sons, Then Heirs: A Study of Kinship and Ethnicity in the Letters of Paul*. Oxford: Oxford University Press, 2007.

Hodge, Charles. *An Exposition of the First Epistle to the Corinthians*. Grand Rapids: Eerdmans, 1953.

Hodgson, Peter C. *The Formation of Historical Theology: A Study of Ferdinand Christian Baur*. New York: Harper & Row, 1966.

Hoffmann, Paul. *Studien zur Theologie der Logienquelle*. Neutestamentliche Abhandlungen Neue Folge 8. Münster: Aschendorff, 1972.

Hofius, Otfried. *Der Christushymnus Philipper 2,6–11: Untersuchungen zu Gestalt und Aussage eines urchristlichen Psalms*. WUNT 17. 2nd rev. edn. Tübingen: Mohr Siebeck, 1991.

—. "The Fourth Servant Song in the New Testament Letters". Pages 16–47 in *The Suffering Servant: Isaiah 53 in Jewish and Christian Sources*. Edited by Bernd Janowski and Peter Stuhlmacher. Grand Rapids: Eerdmans, 2004.

Hogan, Pauline Nigh. *"No Longer Male and Female": Interpreting Galatians 3.28 in Early Christianity*. London: T & T Clark, 2008.

Holladay, Carl R. "Paul and His Predecessors in the Diaspora: Some Reflections on Ethnic Identity in the Fragmentary Hellenistic Jewish Authors". Pages 429–60 in *Early Christianity and Classical Culture: Comparative Studies in Honor of Abraham J. Malherbe*. Edited by John T. Fitzgerald, Thomas H. Olbright and L. Michael White. Leiden: Brill, 2003.

Hollander, Harm W. and J. Holleman. "The Relationship of Death, Sin and Law in 1 Cor 15:56". *Novum Testamentum* 35:3 (1993): 270–91.

—. "The Meaning of the Term 'Law' (NOMOS) in 1 Corinthians". *Novum Testamentum* 40 (1998): 117–135.

Holmberg, Bengt. "Jewish *Versus* Christian Identity in the Early Church". *Revue biblique* 105:3 (1998): 397–425.

Holmén, Tom. *Jesus and Jewish Covenant Thinking*. Leiden: Brill, 2001.

Holtz, Gudrund. *Damit Gott sei alles in allem: Studien zum paulinischen und frühjüdischen Universalismus*. Berlin: de Gruyter, 2007.

Holtz, Traugott. "Paul and the Oral Gospel Tradition". Pages 380–93 in *Jesus and the Oral Gospel Tradition*. Edited by Henry Wansbrough. Sheffield: Sheffield Academic Press, 1991.

Hong, I.-G. *The Law in Galatians*. JSNTSup 81. Sheffield: JSOT, 1993.

Hooker, Morna D. "Authority on Her Head: An Examination of I Cor XI.10". *New Testament Studies* 10 (1964): 410–16.

—. "Interchange in Christ". *Journal of Theological Studies* 22 (1971): 349–61.

—. "Philippians 2:6–11". Pages 151–64 in *Jesus und Paulus: Festschrift für Werner Georg Kümmel zum 70 Geburtstag*. Edited by E. Earle Ellis and Erich Grässer; Göttingen: Vandenhoeck & Ruprecht, 1975.

—. *From Adam to Christ: Essays on Paul*. Cambridge: Cambridge University Press, 1990.

—. *A Commentary on the Gospel According to St. Mark*. London: A & C Black, 1991.

—. "A Partner in the Gospel: Paul's Understanding of His Ministry". Pages 83–100 in *Theology and Ethics in Paul and His Interpreters: Essays in Honor of Victor Paul Furnish*. Edited by Eugene H. Lovering and Jerry L. Sumney. Nashville: Abingdon Press, 1996.

Hoppe, Leslie. *There Shall Be No Poor Among You: Poverty in the Bible*. Nashville: Abingdon, 2004.

Hoppe, Rudolf. "1 Cor 8.1–6 as Part of the Controversy Between Paul and the Parish in Corinth". Pages 28–39 in *Testimony and Interpretation: Early Christology in Its Judeo-Hellenistic Milieu*. London: T & T Clark International, 2004.

Horbury, William. "Land, Sanctuary and Worship". Pages 207–24 in *Early Christian Thought in its Jewish Context*. Edited by John Barclay and John Sweet. Cambridge: Cambridge University Press, 1996.

—. "The Gifts of God in Ezekiel the Tragedian". Pages 65–82 in *Messianism among Jews and Christians: Twelve Biblical and Historical Studies*. London: T & T Clark, 2003.

—. "Jerusalem in Pre-Pauline and Pauline Hope". Pages 189–26 in *Messianism Among Jews and Christians: Twelve Biblical and Historical Studies*. London: T & T Clark, 2003.

Horn, Friedrich W. "Paulus, das Nasiräat und die Nasiräer". *Novum Testamentum* 2 (1997): 117–37.

Horrell, David G. *The Social Ethos of the Corinthian Correspondence: Interests and Ideology from 1 Corinthians to 1 Clement*. Edinbugh: T & T Clark, 1996.

—. "Theological Principle or Christological Praxis? Pauline Ethics in 1 Corinthians 8.1–11.1". *Journal for the Study of the New Testament* 67 (1997): 83–114.

—. "'The Lord Commanded . . . But I Have Not Used . . .': Exegetical and Hermeneutical Reflections on 1 Cor 9.14–15". *New Testament Studies* 43 (1997): 587–603.

—. "'No Longer Jew or Greek' Paul's Corporate Christology and the Construction of Christian Community". Pages 321–44 in *Christology, Controversy and Community: New Testament Essays in Honour of David R. Catchpole*. Edited by David G. Horrell and Christopher M. Tuckett. Leiden: Brill, 2000.

—. *Solidarity and Difference: A Contemporary Reading of Paul's Ethics*. London: T & T Clark International, 2005.

Horsley, Richard A. *1 Corinthians*. Abingdon New Testament Commentaries. Nashville: Abingdon, 1998.

House, Colin. "Defilement by Association: Some Insights from the Usage of ΚΟΙΝΟΣ/ΚΟΙΝΟΩ in Acts 10 and 11". *Andrews University Seminary Studies* 21 (1983): 143–53.

Hove, Richard W. *Equality in Christ? Galatians 3:28 and the Gender Dispute*. Wheaton: Crossway, 1999.

Howard, George. *Paul: Crisis in Galatia: A Study in Early Christian Theology*. SNTSMS 35. Cambridge: Cambridge University Press, 1979.

Hübner, Hans. *Law in Paul's Thought*. Edinburgh: T & T Clark, 1984.

—. *Biblische Theologie des Neuen Testaments*. Vol. 2: *Die Theologie des Paulus und ihre neutestamentliche Wirkungsgeschichte*. Göttingen: Vandenhoeck & Ruprecht, 1993.

Humphrey, Alex. "The Implications for Today of Paul's Conduct as Recorded in Acts 21:20–26". M.Sc. thesis. Abilene Christian College, 1960.

Hurd, John C. *The Origin of 1 Corinthians*. London: SPCK, 1965. Republished by Mercer University Press, 1983.

Hurtado, Larry W. *Mark*. New International Biblical Commentary. Peabody: Hendrickson, 1989.

Huttunen, Niko. *Paul and Epictetus on Law*. London: T & T Clark International, 2009.

Instone-Brewer, David. "1 Corinthians 9.9–11: A Literal Interpretation of 'Do Not Muzzle the Ox'". *New Testament Studies* 38 (1992): 554–565.

—. *Traditions of the Rabbis From the Era of the New Testament*. Volume 1: Prayer and Agriculture. Grand Rapids: Eerdmans, 2004.

Isaac, E., trans. "1 (Ethiopic Apocalypse of) Enoch (Second Century B.C.–First Century A.D.): A New Translation and Introduction". Pages 5–89 in *The Old Testament Pseudepigrapha* I. Edited by J. H. Charlesworth. Garden City: Doubleday, 1983.

Isenberg, M. "The Sale of Sacrificial Meat". *Classical Philology* 70 (1975): 271–73.

Isenberg, Wesley, trans. *Nag Hammadi Codex*. Vol. 2. Edited by Bentley Layton. Leiden: Brill, 1989.

Jackson, F. J. Foakes and Kirsopp Lake. "The General Presentation of Paul in Acts". Pages 291–97 in *Prolegomena II: Criticism*. Volume 2 of *The Beginnings of Christianity Part I: The Acts of the Apostles*. Edited by F. J. Foakes Jackson and Kirsopp Lake. London: MacMillan, 1922.

—. "The Disciples in Jerusalem and the Rise of Gentile Christianity". Pages 300–20 in *Prolegomena I: The Jewish, Gentile and Christian Backgrounds*. Volume 1 of *The Beginnings of Christianity Part I: The Acts of the Apostles*. Edited by F. J. Foakes Jackson and Kirsopp Lake. London: MacMillan, 1939.

Jaffe, Azriela. *What Do You Mean, You Can't Eat in My Home?* New York: Schocken, 2005.

Jenkins, Claude. "Origen on 1 Corinthians". *Journal of Theological Studies* 9 (1908): 500–14.

Jeremias, J. *New Testament Theology 1: The Proclaimation of Jesus*. London: SCM, 1971.

Jervell, Jacob. *Luke and the People of God: A New Look at Luke-Acts*. Minneapolis: Augsburg, 1972.

—. *The Unknown Paul: Essays on Luke-Acts and Early Christian History*. Minneapolis: Augsburg, 1984.
—. *The Theology of the Acts of the Apostles*. Cambridge: Cambridge University Press, 1996.
—. *Die Apostelgeschichte*. Kritisch-exegetischer Kommentar über das Neue Testament. Göttingen: Vandenhoeck & Ruprecht, 1998.
Jewett, Robert. "The Redaction of 1 Corinthians and the Trajectory of the Pauline School". *Journal of the American Academy of Religion* 44:4 (1978): Supplement B.
Johnson, Alan F. *1 Corinthians*. The IVP New Testament Commentary Series. Downers Grove: InterVarsity Press, 2004.
Jones, F. S. *"Freiheit" in den Briefen des Apostels Paulus: Eine historische, exegetische und religionsgeschichtliche Studie*. Göttinger theologische Arbeiten 34. Göttingen: Vandenhoeck & Ruprecht, 1987.
—. "A Jewish Christian Reads Luke's Acts of the Apostles: The Use of the Canonical Acts in the Ancient Jewish Christian Source behind Pseudo-Clementine *Recognitions* 1.27–71". Pages 617–35 in *Society of Biblical Literature 1995 Seminar Papers*. SBL Seminar Paper Series 34. Edited by Eugene H. Lovering. Atlanta: Scholars Press, 1995.
Joseph, M. J. "A Leap into the "Slavery of Paul" from an Indian Angle". *The Indian Journal of Theology* 26:2 (1977): 73–85.
Judge, Edwin. "The Teacher as Moral Exemplar in Paul and in the Inscriptions of Ephesus". Pages 185–202 in *In the Fullness of Time: Biblical Studies in Honour of Archbishop Donald Robinson*. Edited by David Peterson and John Pryor. Homebush West, NSW: Lancer, 1992.
Kaiser, Walter C. "The Eschatologicial Hermeneutics of 'Epangelicalism': Promise Theology". *JETS* 13:2 (Spring 1970): 19–28.
Käsemann, Ernst. "A Pauline Version of 'Amor Fati'". Pages 217–35 in *New Testament Questions of Today*. Philadelphia: Fortress, 1969.
—. "The Spirit and the Letter". Pages 138–66 in *Perspectives on Paul*. London: SCM, 1971.
Kazen, Thomas. *Jesus and Purity Halakhah: Was Jesus Indifferent to Impurity?* CB New Testament Series 38. Stockholm: Almqvist & Wiksell International, 2002.
Keck, Leander E. "The Jewish Paul Among the Gentiles: Two Portrayals". Pages 461–81 in *Early Christianity and Classical Culture: Comparative Studies in Honor of Abraham J. Malherbe*. Edited by John T. Fitzgerald, Thomas H. Olbricht and L. Michael White. Leiden: Brill, 2003.
Keener, Craig S. *A Commentary on the Gospel of Matthew*. Grand Rapids: Eerdmans, 1999.
—. *1–2 Corinthians*. New Cambridge Bible Commentary. Cambridge: Cambridge University Press, 2005.
—. "Interdependence and Mutual Blessing in the Church (Rom 11, 15)". In *Introduction to Messianic Judaism: Its Ecclesial Context and Biblical Foundations*. Edited by David Rudolph and Joel Willitts. Grand Rapids: Zondervan, forthcoming.
Kelley, Robert L. "Meals with Jesus in Luke's Gospel". *Horizons in Biblical Theology* 17:2 (1995): 123–31.
Kim, Seyoon. *Paul and the New Perspective: Second Thoughts on the Origin of Paul's Gospel*. Grand Rapids: Eerdmans, 2002.
—. "Imitatio Christi (1 Corinthians 11:1): How Paul Imitates Jesus Christ in Dealing with Idol Food (1 Corinthians 8–10)". *Bulletin for Biblical Research* 13:2 (2003): 193–226.
Kinzer, Mark S. *Postmissionary Messianic Judaism: Redefining Christian Engagement with the Jewish People*. Grand Rapids: Brazos, 2005.
—. *Israel's Messiah and the People of God: A Vision for Messianic Jewish Covenantal Fidelity*. Edited by Jennifer M. Rosner. Eugene: Cascade, 2011.
Kistemaker, S. J. *1 Corinthians*. New Testament Commentary. Grand Rapids: Baker, 1993.

Klauck, Hans-Josef. *1 Korintherbrief*. Die Neue Echter Bibel 7. Würzburg: Echter Verlag, 1984.

Klawans, Jonathan. *Impurity and Sin in Ancient Judaism*. Oxford: Oxford University Press, 2000.

Klein, Michael L. *The Fragment-Targums of the Pentateuch: According to the Extant Sources*. Analecta Biblica 76. Rome: Biblical Institute Press, 1980.

Klijn, A. F. J. and G. J. Reinink. *Patristic Evidence for Jewish-Christian Sects*. Supplements to Novum Testamentum 36. Leiden: E. J. Brill, 1973.

Kloha, Jeffrey. "Idols, Eating, and Rights (1 Cor. 8:1–11:1): Faithful and Loving Witness in a Pluralistic Culture". *Concordia* (July 2004): 178–202.

Knox, Wilfred L. *St. Paul and the Church of Jerusalem*. Cambridge University Press, 1925.

—. "Abraham and the Quest for God". *Harvard Theological Review* 28:1 (1935): 55–60.

Koenig, John. *The Feast of the World's Redemption: Eucharistic Origins and Christian Mission*. Harrisburg: Trinity Press International, 2000.

—. *New Testament Hospitality: Partnership with Strangers as Promise and Mission*. Eugene: Wipf and Stock, 2001.

—. *Soul Banquets: How Meals Become Mission in the Local Congregation*. Harrisburg: Morehouse, 2007.

Koet, Bart J. "Why did Paul shave his hair (Acts 18, 18)? Nazirate and Temple in the book of Acts". Pages 129–42 in *The Centrality of Jerusalem: Historical Perspectives*. Edited by M. Poorthuis and Ch. Safrai. Kampen: Kok Pharos, 1996.

—. "As Close to the Synagogue as Can Be: Paul in Corinth (Acts 18.1–18)". Pages 397–415 in *The Corinthian Correspondence*. Edited by R. Bieringer. Leuven: Leuven University Press, 1996.

Kohn, Rachel L. E. "Ethnic Judaism and the Messianic Movement". *Jewish Journal of Sociology* 29:2 (1987): 85–96.

Kraemer, David C. *Jewish Eating and Identity Through the Ages*. London: Routledge, 2007.

Krause, Richard. "All Things to All Men: Where is the Limit? An Exegetical Study of 1 Corinthians 9:19–23". Presented to the Metro North Pastoral Conference Southeastern Wisconsin District of WELS, March 20, 1995.

Kreitzer, L. Joseph. *Jesus and God in Paul's Eschatology*. Sheffield: JSOT, 1987.

Kremer, Jacob. "Allen bin ich alles geworden, um jedenfalls einige zu retten (1 *Kor 9:22*)". Pages 13–34 in *Zielgruppen: Brennpunkte kirchlichen Lebens*. Edited by Ludwig Bertsch and Karl H. Rentmeister. Frankfurt: Verlag Knecht, 1977.

Krentz, Edgar. "Paul: All Things to All People – Flexible and Welcoming". *Currents in Theology and Mission* 24:3 (1997): 238–44.

Krinetzky, Leo. "Der Einfluss von Is 52,13–53,12 Par auf Phil 2,6–11". *TQ* 139 (1959): 157–93, 291–336.

Kruse, Colin G. *Paul, the Law and Justification*. Leicester: Apollos, 1996.

Kuck, David W. "The Freedom of Being in the World 'As If Not' (1 Cor 7:29–31)". *Currents in Theology and Mission* 28:6 (2001): 585–93.

Kurz, William S. "Kenotic Imitation of Paul and of Christ in Philippians 2 and 3". Pages 103–26 in *Discipleship in the New Testament*. Edited by Fernando F. Segovia. Philadelphia: Fortress, 1985.

Lake, Kirsopp and Henry J. Cadbury. *Acts of the Apostles: English Translation and Commentary*. Volume 4 of *The Beginnings of Christianity Part I: The Acts of the Apostles*. Edited by F. J. Foakes Jackson and Kirsopp Lake. London: MacMillan, 1933.

Lambdin, T. O., trans. *Nag Hammadi Codex 2,2–7 Vol. 1: Gospel according to Thomas, Gospel according to Philip, Hypostasis of the Archons, and indexes*. Nag Hammadi Studies 20. Edited by Bentley Layton. The Coptic Gnostic library. Leiden: Brill, 1989.

Lang, Friedrich. *Die Briefe an die Korinther*. Das Neue Testament Deutsch. Göttingen: Vandenhoeck & Ruprecht, 1986.

Langton, Daniel R. "The Myth of the 'Traditional View of Paul' and the Role of the Apostle in Modern Jewish-Christian Polemics". *Journal for the Study of the New Testament* 28:1 (2005): 69–104.

—. "Modern Jewish Identity and the Apostle Paul: Pauline Studies as an Intra-Jewish Ideological Battleground". *Journal for the Study of the New Testament* 28:2 (2005): 217–58.

—. *The Apostle Paul in the Jewish Imagination: A Study in Modern Jewish-Christian Relations*. Cambridge: Cambridge University Press, 2010.

Lapide, Pinchas and Peter Stuhlmacher. *Paul: Rabbi and Apostle*. Translated by Lawrence W. Denef. Minneapolis: Augsburg, 1984.

Laufen, Rudolf. *Die Doppelüberlieferung der Logienquelle und des Markusevangeliums*. BBB 54. Bonn: Peter Hanstein, 1980.

Le Cornu, Hilary and Joseph Shulam. *A Commentary on the Jewish Roots of Acts*. 2 vols. Jerusalem: Academon, 2003.

—. *A Commentary on the Jewish Roots of Galatians*. Jerusalem: Academon, 2005.

Levinskaya, Irina. *The Book of Acts in Its Diaspora Setting*. Vol. 5. of The Book of Acts in Its First Century Setting. Grand Rapids: Eerdmans, 1996.

Levy, B. Barry. *Targum Neophyti 1: A Textual Study* I. Studies in Judaism. New York: University Press of America, 1986.

Lichtenstein, Yechiel Tzvi. *Römerbrief*. Leipzig, 1898.

Liebman, Charles S. "Introduction". Pages xi–xviii in *Conflict and Accommodation between Jews in Israel: Religious and Secular*. Edited by Charles S. Liebman. Jerusalem: Keter Publishing House, 1990.

—. "Relations between *Dati* and *Non-Dati* Jews – Some Final Reflections". Pages 215–31 in *Conflict and Accommodation between Jews in Israel: Religious and Secular*. Edited by Charles S. Liebman. Jerusalem: Keter, 1990.

Lietzmann, H. *Die Briefe des Apostels Paulus: An die Korinther I, II*. Edited by W. G. Kümmel. 5th edition. Handbuch zum neuen Testament 9. Tübingen: Mohr Siebeck, 1949.

Lieu, Judith. *Image and Reality: The Jews in the World of the Christians in the Second Century*. Edinburgh: T & T Clark, 1996.

—. *The Gospel of Luke*. Epworth Commentaries. London: Epworth, 1997.

—. *Neither Jew Nor Gentile? Constructing Early Christianity*. London: T & T Clark, 2002.

Lightfoot, John. *A Commentary on the New Testament from the Talmud and Hebraica. Matthew – 1 Corinthians*. Vol. 4. Peabody: Hendrickson, 1979. Originally published as *Horae Hebraicae Et Talmudicae*. Oxford: Oxford University Press, 1859 [1664; Latin ed. Carpzov; Leipzig, 1675–1679].

Lincoln, Andrew T. "The Church and Israel in Ephesians 2". *The Catholic Biblical Quarterly* 49 (1987): 605–624.

Lindars, Barnabas. "All Foods Clean: Thoughts on Jesus and the Law". Pages 61–71 in *Law and Religion: Esays on the Place of the Law in Israel and Early Christianity*. Edited by Barnabas Lindars. Cambridge: James Clarke, 1988.

Lindbeck, George. "The Church as Israel: Ecclesiology and Ecumenism". Pages 78–94 in *Jews and Christians: People of God*. Edited by Carl E. Braaten and Robert W. Jenson. Grand Rapids: Eerdmans, 2003.

Lindemann, Andreas. *Der Erste Korintherbrief*. Handbuch zum Neuen Testament. Tübingen: Mohr Siebeck, 2000.

Lindsey, F. Duane. "The Call of the Servant in Isaiah 42:1–9". *Bibliotheca Sacra* 139:553 (1982): 12–31.

Loader, William R. G. *Jesus' Attitude Towards the Law: A Study of the Gospels*. WUNT 2/97. Tübingen: Mohr Siebeck, 1997.

Lodge, J. G. "All Things to All: Paul's Pastoral Strategy". *Chicago Studies* 24 (1985): 291–306.

Lohr, Joel N. "He Identified with the Lowly and Became a Slave to All: Paul's Tentmaking as a Strategy for Mission". *Currents in Theology and Mission* 34:3 (2007): 179–87.

Longenecker, Bruce W. *Eschatology and the Covenant: A Comparison of 4 Ezra and Romans 1–11*. JSNTSS 57. Sheffield: Sheffield Academic Press, 1991.

—. "Contours of Covenant Theology in the Post-Conversion Paul". Pages 125–46 in *The Road from Damascus: The Impact of Paul's Conversion on His Life, Thought, and Ministry*. Edited by Richard N. Longenecker. Grand Rapids: Eerdmans, 1997.

Longenecker, Richard N. "The Problem Practices of Acts". Pages 245–63 in *Paul: Apostle of Liberty*. New York: Harper & Row, 1964.

—. *Galatians*. WBC 41. Waco: Word, 1990.

Louw, Johannes P. and Eugene A. Nida, eds. *Greek-English Lexicon of the New Testament Based on Semantic Domains*. Second Edition. 2 vols. New York: United Bible Societies, 1989.

Lowenstein, Steven M. *The Jewish Cultural Tapestry: International Jewish Folk Traditions*. Oxford: Oxford University Press, 2000.

Lüdemann, Gerd. *Early Christianity according to the Traditions in Acts: A Commentary*. London: SCM, 1989. Originally published as *Das frühe Christentum nach den Traditionen der Apostelgeschichte. Ein Kommentar*. Göttingen: Vandenhoeck & Ruprecht, 1987.

—. *Opposition to Paul in Jewish Christianity*. Translated by M. Eugene Boring. Minneapolis: Fortress, 1989. Originally published as *Paulus, der Heidenapostel* II, *Antipaulinismus im frühen Christentum*. FRLANT 130. Göttingen: Vandenhoeck & Ruprecht, 1983.

—. *Heretics: The Other Side of Early Christianity*. Translated by John Bowden. Louisville: Westminster John Knox, 1996. Originally published as *Ketzer. Die andere Seite des frühen Christentums*. Stuttgart: Radius-Verlag, 1995.

Lumby, J. Rawson. *The Acts of the Apostles*. Cambridge: Cambridge University Press, 1904.

Maccoby, Hyam. *The Mythmaker: Paul and the Invention of Christianity*. London: Weidenfeld & Nicolson, 1986.

—. *Paul and Hellenism*. London: SCM, 1991.

—. *Ritual and Morality: The Ritual Purity System and its Place in Judaism*. Cambridge: Cambridge University Press, 1999.

Macho, Alejandro D. *Neophyti 1: Targum Palestinense MS de la Biblioteca Vaticana* I. Textos y Estudios Consejo de Recacción 7. Madrid: Consejo Superior de Investigaciones Científicas, 1968.

Mack, Burton L. *The Lost Gospel: The Book of Q and Christian Origins*. San Francisco: HarperCollins, 1993.

Maddox, R. *The Purpose of Luke-Acts*. Edinburgh: T & T Clark, 1982.

Maher, Michael. *Targum Pseudo-Jonathan: Genesis: Translated, with Introduction and Notes*. The Aramaic Bible 1B. Edinburgh: T & T Clark, 1992.

Malherbe, Abraham J. "Antisthenes and Odysseus, and Paul at War". Pages 91–119 in *Paul and the Popular Philosophers*. Minneapolis: Fortress, 1989.

Malina, Bruce J. "The Received View and What It Cannot Do: III John and Hospitality". *Semeia* 35 (1986): 171–94.

Marcus, Joel. "The Circumcision and the Uncircumcision in Rome". *New Testament Studies* 35 (1989): 67–81.

—. "The Once and Future Messiah in Early Christianity and Chabad". *New Testament Studies* 47:3 (2001): 381–401.

Marcus, Ralph. "The 'Plain Meaning' of Isaiah 42.1–4". *Harvard Theological Review* 29 (1936): 249:59.

—. *Questions and Answers on Genesis*. Cambridge: Harvard University Press, 1953.
—. *Questions and Answers on Exodus*. Cambridge: Harvard University Press, 1953.
Margolese, Faranak. *Off the Derech: Why Observant Jews Leave Judaism*. New York: Devora, 2005.
Marguerat, Daniel. "Paul and the Torah in the Acts of the Apostles". Pages 98–117 in *Torah in the New Testament: Papers Delivered at the Manchester-Lausanne Seminar of June 2008*. Edited by Michael Tait and Peter Oakes. London: T & T Clark International, 2009.
Marshall, Bruce D. "Christ and the Cultures: The Jewish People and Christian Theology". Pages 81–100 in *The Cambridge Companion to Christian Doctrine*. Edited by Colin E. Gunton. Cambridge: Cambridge University Press, 1997.
—. *Trinity and Truth*. Cambridge: Cambridge University Press, 2000.
Marshall, I. Howard. *The Gospel of Luke: A Commentary on the Greek Text*. The New International Greek Testament Commentary. Exeter: The Paternoster Press, 1978.
—. *Acts*. Tyndale New Testament Commentaries. Grand Rapids: Eerdmans, 1980.
—. "A New Understanding of the Present and the Future: Paul and Eschatology". Pages 43–61 in *The Road from Damascus: The Impact of Paul's Conversion on His Life, Thought, and Ministry*. Edited by Richard N. Longenecker. Grand Rapids: Eerdmans, 1997.
Marshall, Peter. *Enmity in Corinth: Social Conventions in Paul's Relations with the Corinthians*. WUNT 23; Tübingen: Mohr Siebeck, 1987.
Martin, Brice L. *Christ and the Law in Paul*. Leiden: E. J. Brill, 1989.
Martin, Dale B. *Slavery as Salvation: The Metaphor of Slavery in Pauline Christianity*. New Haven: Yale University Press, 1990.
Martin, Ralph P. *Carmen Christi: Philippians ii.5–11 in Recent Interpretation and in the Setting of Early Christian Worship*. Cambridge: Cambridge University Press, 1967.
—. *Philippians*. New Century Bible Commentary. Grand Rapids: Eerdmans, 1976.
—. *2 Corinthians*. Word Biblical Commentary. Waco: Word, 1986.
—. *The Epistle of Paul to the Philippians: An Introduction and Commentary*. Second Edition. Grand Rapids: Eerdmans, 1987.
Martin, Troy W. "Apostasy to Paganism: The Rhetorical Stasis of the Galatian Controversy". *Journal of Biblical Literature* 114 (1995): 437–61.
—. "Pagan and Judeo-Christian Time-Keeping Schemes in Gal 4.10 and Col 2.16". *New Testament Studies* 42 (1996): 105–19.
—. "The Covenant of Circumcision (Genesis 17:9–14) and the Situational Antitheses in Galatians 3:28". *Journal of Biblical Literature* 122:1 (2003): 111–125.
Martyn, J. Louis. *Galatians: A New Translation with Introduction and Commentary*. Anchor Bible 33A. New York: Doubleday, 1997.
—. "*Nomos* Plus Genitive Noun in Paul: The History of God's Law". Pages 575–87 in *Early Christianity and Classical Culture: Comparative Studies in Honor of Abraham J. Malherbe*. Edited by John T. Fitzgerald, Thomas H. Olbright and L. Michael White. Leiden: Brill, 2003.
Matthews, Shelly. *First Converts: Rich Pagan Women and the Rhetoric of Mission in Early Judaism and Christianity*. Stanford: Stanford University Press, 2001.
Mattill, Andrew J. "Luke as a Historian in Criticism Since 1840". Ph.D. diss., Vanderbilt University, 1959.
—. "The Purpose of Acts: Schneckenburger Reconsidered". Pages 108–22 in *Apostolic History and the Gospel*. Edited by W. Ward Gasque and Ralph P. Martin. Grand Rapids: Eerdmans, 1970.
McDermott, Gerald. "Covenant, Mission, and Relating to the Other". Paper presented at the New Frontiers in Christian-Jewish Theology Conference. New Haven, October 24, 2010.

—. "Jesus, Paul, and Israel's Covenant: Can Christians and Jews Learn from One Another?" Paper presented at the International Conference on Conversion, Covenant and Hope in the Human Future: New Frontiers in Christian and Jewish Thought. Jerusalem, February 13, 2011.

McHugh, John. "Galatians 2:11–14: Was Peter Right?" Pages 319–27 in *Paulus und das antike Judentum*. Edited by Martin Hengel and Ulrich Heckel. Tübingen: Mohr Siebeck, 1991.

McKnight, Scot. *A Light among the Gentiles: Jewish Missionary Activity in the Second Temple Period*. Minneapolis: Fortress, 1991.

McNamara, Martin. *Targum Neofiti 1: Genesis: Translated, with Apparatus and Notes*. The Aramaic Bible 1A. Edinburgh: T & T Clark, 1992.

—. "Some Targum Themes". Pages 303–56 in *Justification and Variegated Nomism: Volume 1 – The Complexities of Second Temple Judaism*. Edited by D. A. Carson, Peter T. O'Brien and Mark A. Seifrid. Tübingen: Mohr Siebeck, 2001.

Meeks, Wayne A. "The Christian Proteus". Pages 435–44 in *The Writings of St. Paul: A Norton Critical Edition*. Edited by Wayne A. Meeks. New York: W. W. Nortan & Co., 1972.

—. "Since then you would need to go out of the world: 'Group Boundaries in Pauline Christianity'". Pages 4–29 in *Critical History and Biblical Faith: New Testament Perspectives*. Edited by T. J. Ryan. Billanova: College Theology Society, 1979.

Meggitt, Justin J. "Meat Consumption and Social Conflict in Corinth". *Journal of Theological Studies* (1994): 137–41.

Melnick, Jim. "A Resurrected King Messiah: The Struggle Within Chabad and Orthodox Judaism". *Mishkan* 43 (2005): 47–62.

Menken, M. J. J. "The Quotation from Isaiah 42,1–4 in Matthew 12,18–21: Its Textual Form". *Ephemerides Theologicae Lovanienses* 75 (1999): 32–52.

Merklein, Helmut. *Der erste Brief an die Korinther*. 2 vols. Ökumenischer Taschenbuch-Kommentar. Gütersloh and Würzburg: Gütersloher Verlagshaus and Mohn and Echter Verlag, 1992/2000.

Metzger, Bruce M. *A Textual Commentary on the Greek New Testament*. Second Edition. Stuttgart: Deutsche Bibelgesellschaft, 1998.

Meyer, H. A. W. *The Acts of the Apostles* II. Critical and Exegetical Commentary on the New Testament. Edinburgh: T & T Clark, 1877.

—. *Paul's First Epistle to the Corinthians* I. Critical and Exegetical Commentary on the New Testament. Translated by William P. Dickson and Frederick Crombie. Edinburgh: T & T Clark, 1892.

Miege, Frank. "Allen alles werden: Identität und Differenz im Horizont der Liebe: Andacht über I Kor 9,19–23". Pages 309–13 in *Im Kontinuum: Annäherungen an eine relationale Erkenntnistheorie und Ontologie*. Edited by Wilfried Härle. Marburg: N.G. Elwert, 1999.

Milikowsky, Chaim. "Reflections on Hand-Washing, Hand-Purity and Holy Scripture in Rabbinic Literature". Pages 149–62 in *Purity and Holiness: The Heritage of Leviticus*. Edited by M. J. H. M. Poorthuis and J. Schwartz. Jewish and Christian Perspectives. Leiden: Brill, 2000.

Miller, Chris A. "The Relationship of Jewish and Gentile Believers to the Law between A.D. 30 and 70 in the Scripture". Ph.D. diss., Dallas Theological Seminary, 1994.

—. "Did Peter's Vision in Acts 10 Pertain to Men or the Menu?" *Bibliotheca Sacra* 159 (2002): 302–17.

Miller, Robert J., ed. *The Complete Gospels: Annotated Scholars Version*. Sonoma: Polebridge, 1992.

Minear, Paul. *Commands of Christ: Authority and Implications*. Nashville: Abingdon, 1972.

Mitchell, Margaret M. *Paul and the Rhetoric of Reconciliation: An Exegetical Investigation of the Language and Composition of 1 Corinthians*. HUT 28. Tübingen: Mohr Siebeck, 1991.

—. "'A Variable and Many-sorted Man': John Chrysostom's Treatment of Pauline Inconsistency". *Journal of Early Christian Studies* 6 (1998): 93–111.
—. "Pauline Accommodation and 'Condescension' (συγκατάβασις): 1 Cor 9:19–23 and the History of Influence". Pages 197–214 in *Paul Beyond the Judaism/Hellenism Divide*. Edited by Troels Engberg-Pedersen. Louisville: Westminster John Knox, 2001.
—. *Paul, the Corinthians and the Birth of Christian Hermeneutics*. Cambridge: Cambridge University Press, 2010.
Mitternacht, Dieter. "Foolish Galatians? – A Recipient-Oriented Assessment of Paul's Letter". Pages 408–33 in *The Galatians Debate: Contemporary Issues in Rhetorical and Historical Interpretation*. Peabody: Hendrickson, 2002.
Moffatt, James. *The First Epistle of Paul to the Corinthians*. London: Hodder and Stoughton, 1938.
Mohrlang, Roger. *Matthew and Paul: A Comparison of Ethical Perspectives*. Cambridge: Cambridge University Press, 1984.
Moo, Douglas J. *The Epistle to the Romans*. New International Commentary on the New Testament. Grand Rapids: Eerdmans, 1996.
Morissette, R. "Un Midrash sur La Mort: (1 Cor. xv, 54c à 57)". *Revue biblique* 79 (1972): 161–88.
Morris, Leon. *The First Epistle of Paul to the Corinthians: An Introduction and Commentary*. Leicester: InterVarsity, 1985.
Moshe, Beth. *Judaism's Truth Answers the Missionaries*. New York: Bloch, 1987.
Moule, C. F. D. "Obligation in the Ethic of Paul". Pages 389–406 in *Christian History and Interpretation: Studies Presented to John Knox*. Edited by W. R. Farmer, C. F. D. Moule and R. Niebuhr. Cambridge: Cambridge University Press, 1967.
Moxnes, H. "Meals and the New Community in Luke". *Svensk Exegetisk Årsbok* 51 (1986): 158–67.
Muldowney, Mary Sarah, trans. *The Work of Monks*. Pages 323–94 in *Saint Augustine: Treatises on Various Subjects*. The Fathers of the Church. Vol. 14. Edited by Roy J. Deferrari. Washington, D.C.: The Catholic University of America Press, 1952. Latin: PL 40.547–582; CSEL 41; BA 28.
Munck, Johannes. *Paul and the Salvation of Mankind*. Translated by F. Clarke. London: SCM, 1959.
Murphy-O'Connor, Jerome. "Freedom or the Ghetto". *Revue biblique* 85 (1978): 543–74.
Nanos, Mark D. *The Mystery of Romans: The Jewish Context of Paul's Letter*. Minneapolis: Fortress, 1996.
—. *The Irony of Galatians: Paul's Letter in First-Century Context*. Minneapolis: Fortress, 2002.
—. *The Galatians Debate: Contemporary Issues in Rhetorical and Historical Interpretation*. Edited by Mark D. Nanos. Peabody: Hendrickson, 2002.
—. "Intruding 'Spies' and 'Pseudo-brethren': The Jewish Intra-Group Politics of Paul's Jerusalem Meeting (Gal 2:1–10)". Pages 59–97 in *Paul and His Opponents*. Pauline Studies 2. Edited by Stanley E. Porter. Leiden: Brill, 2005.
—. "Rethinking the 'Paul and Judaism' Paradigm". Paper presented at the Yale Post-Grad Seminar, March 3, 2005.
—. "A Torah-Observant Paul? What Difference Could It Make for Christian/Jewish Relations Today?" Annual Presentation to the Christian Scholars Group on Christian-Jewish Relations, sponsored by the Center for Christian-Jewish Learning at Boston College, 4–6 June, 2005.
—. "The *Polytheist* Identity of the 'Weak', and Paul's Strategy to 'Gain' Them: A New Reading of 1 Corinthians 8:1 – 11:1". Pages 179–210 in *Paul: Jew, Greek, and Roman*. Edited by Stanley Porter. Pauline Studies 5. Leiden: Brill, 2008.

—. "The Myth of the 'Law-Free' Paul Standing between Christians and Jews". *Studies in Christian-Jewish Relations* 4:1 (2009): 1–24.

—. "Paul's Reversal of Jews Calling Gentiles 'Dogs' (Philippians 3:2): 1600 Years of an Ideological Tale Wagging an Exegetical Dog?" *Biblical Interpretation* 17.4 (2009): 448–482.

—. "Paul and Judaism". Pages 54–55 in *Codex Pauli*. Rome: Società San Paolo, 2009.

—. "Why the 'Weak' in 1 Corinthians 8–10 Were Not Christ-Believers". Pages 385–404 in *Saint Paul and Corinth: 1950 Years Since the Writing of the Epistles to the Corinthians: International Scholarly Conference Proceedings (Corinth, 23–25 September 2007)*. Vol. 2. Edited by Constantine J. Belezos, Sotirios Despotis and Christos Karakolis. Athens, Greece: Psichogios Publications S.A., 2009.

—. "Paul and Judaism: Why Not Paul's Judaism?" Pages 117–60 in *Paul Unbound: Other Perspectives on the Apostle*. Edited by Mark D. Given. Peabody: Hendrickson, 2010.

—. "'Callused', Not 'Hardened': Paul's Revelation of Temporary Protection Until All Israel Can Be Healed". Pages 52–73 in *Reading Paul in Context: Explorations in Identity Formation*. Edited by Kathy Ehrensperger and J. Brian Tucker. London: T & T Clark, 2010.

—. "'Broken Branches': A Pauline Metaphor Gone Awry? (Romans 11:11–24)". Pages 339–76 in *Between Gospel and Election: Explorations in the Interpretation of Romans 9—11*. Edited by Florian Wilk and J. Ross Wagner. Tübingen: Mohr Siebeck, 2010.

—. "Galatians". Pages 455–74 in *Blackwell's Companion to the New Testament*. Edited by David Aune. Oxford: Blackwell Publishing, 2010.

—. "Paul's Relationship to Torah in Light of His Strategy 'to Become Everything to Everyone' (1 Corinthians 9:19–22)". In *New Perspectives on Paul and the Jews*. Edited by Reimund Bieringer and Didier Pollefeyt. Leuven: Peeters, forthcoming.

—. "Paul and Judaism". In *The Jewish Annotated New Testament*. Edited by Barc Brettler and Amy Jill Levine. Oxford: Oxford University Press, forthcoming.

—. "Paul and the Jewish Tradition: The Ideology of the Shema". In *Celebrating Paul: Festschrift in Honor of J. A. Fitzmyer and J. Murphy-O'Connor*. Edited by Peter Spitaler. Washington, D.C.: Catholic Biblical Association of America, forthcoming.

Nasuti, Harry P. "The Woes of the Prophets and the Rights of the Apostle: The Internal Dynamics of 1 Corinthians 9". *The Catholic Biblical Quarterly* 50 (1988): 246–264.

Neale, David A. *None But the Sinners: Religious Categories in the Gospel of Luke*. JSNTSS 58. Sheffield: Sheffield Academic Press, 1991.

Neirynck, F. "Paul and the Sayings of Jesus". Pages 265–321 in *L'Apôtre Paul: Personnalité, Style et Conception du Ministère*. Edited by A. Vanhoye. Leuven: Leuven University, 1986.

—. "The Sayings of Jesus in 1 Corinthians". Pages 141–76 in *The Corinthian Correspondence*. Edited by R. Bieringer. Leuven: Leuven University Press, 1996.

Neller, Kenneth V. "1 Corinthians 9:19–22, A Model for Those Who Seek to Win Souls". *Restoration Quarterly* 29 (1987): 129–42.

Neufeld, Dietmar. "Jesus' Eating Transgressions and Social Impropriety in the Gospel of Mark: A Social Scientific Approach". *Biblical Theology Bulletin* 30:1 (2000): 15–26.

Neusner, Jacob. "The Fellowship (חבורה) in the Second Jewish Commonwealth". *Harvard Theological Review* 53 (1960): 125–42.

—. *Fellowship in Judaism: The First Century and Today*. London: Vallentine, Mitchell & Co., 1963.

—. *The Idea of Purity in Ancient Judaism: The Haskell Lectures, 1972–1973*. Leiden: Brill, 1973.

—. *From Politics to Piety: The Emergence of Pharisaic Judaism*. Second Edition. New York: Ktav, 1979.

—. *The Talmud of Babylonia: An American Translation* XVII. Brown Judaic Studies 72. Chico: Scholars, 1984.

—. *Judaic Law From Jesus to the Mishnah: A Systematic Reply to Professor E. P. Sanders*. Atlanta: Scholars, 1993.

— and C. Thoma. "Die Pharisäer vor und nach der Tempelzerstörung des Jahres 70 n. Chr". Pages 71–104 in *Tempelkult und Tempelzerstörung (70 n. Chr.)*. JudChr 15. Edited by S. Lauer. New York: Peter Lang, 1994.

—. *The Components of the Rabbinic Documents: From the Whole to the Parts. VII. Sifré to Deuteronomy*. South Florida Academic Commentary Series 85. Atlanta: Scholars, 1997.

—. *The Components of the Rabbinic Documents: From the Whole to the Parts IX. Genesis Rabbah Part Five*. Atlanta: Scholars, 1997.

—. "Vow-Taking, the Nazirites, and the Law: Does James' Advice to Paul Accord with Halakhah?" Pages 59–82 in *James the Just and Christian Origins*. Edited by Bruce Chilton and Craig A. Evans. Leiden: Brill, 1999.

—. *The Tosefta: Translated from the Hebrew With a New Introduction*. 2 vols. Peabody: Hendrickson, 2002.

—. "What, Exactly, is Israel's Gentile Problem? Rabbinic Perspectives on Galatians 2". Pages 275–306 in *The Missions of James, Peter, and Paul: Tensions in Early Christianity*. Edited by Bruce Chilton and Craig Evans. Leiden: Brill, 2005.

Newman, Hillel. *Proximity to Power and Jewish Sectarian Groups of the Ancient Period: A Review of Lifestyle, Values, and Halakhah in the Pharisees, Sadducees, Essenes, and Qumran*. The Brill Reference Library of Judaism 25. Edited by Ruth Ludlam. Leiden: Brill, 2006.

Newport, K. G. C. *The Sources and Sitz im Leben of Matthew 23*. JSNTSup 117. Sheffield: Sheffield Academic Press, 1995.

Newton, Derek. *Deity and Diet: The Dilemma of Sacrificial Food at Corinth*. JSNTSS 169. Sheffield: Sheffield Academic Press, 1998.

Newton, Michael. *The Concept of Purity at Qumran and in the Letters of Paul*. Cambridge: Cambridge University Press, 1985.

Neyrey, Jerome H. "The Thematic Use of Isaiah 42,1–4 in Matthew 12". *Biblica* 63 (1982): 457–73.

—. "Ceremonies in Luke-Acts: The Case of Meals and Table Fellowship". Pages 361–87 in *The Social World of Luke-Acts: Models for Interpretation*. Edited by Jerome H. Neyrey. Peabody: Hendrickson, 1991.

Nickelsburg, George W. E. "Jews and Christians in the First Century: The Struggle over Identity". Pages 613–41 in *George W. E. Nickelsburg in Perspective: An Ongoing Dialogue of Learning*. Vol. 2. Supplements to the Journal for the Study of Judaism 80. Edited by Jacob Neusner and Alan J. Avery-Peck. Leiden: Brill, 2003.

Niehoff, Maren R. "Jewish Identity and Jewish Mothers: Who Was a Jew According to Philo?" *The Studia Philonica Annual* 11 (1999): 31–54.

Nolland, John L. "A Fresh Look at Acts 15.10". *New Testament Studies* 27 (1980): 105–15.

—. *Luke 9:21–18:34*. Word Biblical Commentary 35b. Dallas: Word, 1993.

O'Brien, Peter T. *The Epistle to the Philippians: A Commentary on the Greek Text*. Grand Rapids: Eerdmans, 1991.

—. *Gospel and Mission in the Writings of Paul: An Exegetical and Theological Analysis*. Grand Rapids: Baker, 1995.

Oepke, A. *Der Brief des Paulus an die Galater*. 5th ed. THNT 9. Berlin: Evangelische Verlagsanstalt, 1984.

Ohana, M. "Prosélytisme et Targum Palestinien: Données nouvelles pour la datation de Néofiti I". *Biblica* 55 (1974): 317–32.

Oppenheimer, Aharon. *The 'Am Ha-Aretz: A Study in the Social History of the Jewish People in the Hellenistic-Roman Period*. Translated by I. H. Levine. Leiden: Brill, 1977.

Orr, William F. and James A. Walther. *1 Corinthians*. The Anchor Bible. Garden City: Doubleday, 1976.

Ottenheijm, Eric. "Impurity Between Intention and Deed: Purity Disputes in First Century Judaism and in the New Testament". Pages 129–47 in *Purity and Holiness: The Heritage of Leviticus*. Edited by M. J. H. M. Poorthuis and J. Schwartz. Jewish and Christian Perspectives. Leiden: Brill, 2000.

Parsons, Mikeal C. and Martin M. Culy, *Acts: A Handbook on the Greek Text*. Waco: Baylor University Press, 2003.

Peerbolte, L. J. Lietaert. *Paul the Missionary*. Leuven: Peeters, 2003.

Penna, Romano. *Paul the Apostle: Jew and Greek Alike*. Vol. 1. Translated by Thomas P. Wahl. Collegeville: The Liturgical Press, 1996.

Perkins, Pheme. "'To the Jews as a Jew' (1 Cor 9:20): Paul and Jewish Identity". *Studies in Christian-Jewish Relations* 4 (2009): 1–11.

Perrin, Norman. *Rediscovering the Teaching of Jesus*. New York: Harper and Row, 1967.

Pesch, Rudolf. *Die Apostelgeschichte* 2. Evangelisch-Katholischer Kommentar zum Neuen Testament. Zürich: Benziger Verlag, 1986.

Peterson, David G. *The Acts of the Apostles*. The Pillar New Testament Commentary. Grand Rapids: Eerdmans, 2009.

Petit, Françoise, ed. *Philo, Quaestiones in Genesim et in Exodum: fragmenta graeca*. PAPM 33B. Paris: Éditions du Cerf, 1978.

Phua, Richard Liong-Seng. *Idolatry and Authority: A Study of 1 Corinthians 8.1–11.1 in the Light of the Jewish Diaspora*. Library of New Testament Studies 299. London: T & T Clark, 2005.

Pickup, Martin. "Matthew's and Mark's Pharisees". Pages 67–112 in *In Quest of the Historical Pharisees*. Edited by Jacob Neusner and Bruce D. Chilton. Waco: Baylor University Press, 2007.

Piekarski, Chana, ed. *Shlichus: Meeting the Outreach Challenge. A Resource Handbook for Shluchim*. Brooklyn: Nshei Chabad, 1991.

—. *Shlichus: Outreach Insights. A Panorama of Programs and Projects*. Vol. II. Brooklyn: Nshei Chabad, 1996.

Plummer, Robert L. "Imitation of Paul and the Church's Missionary Role in 1 Corinthians". *Journal of the Evangelical Theological Society* 44:2 (2001): 219–35.

Poirier, John C. "Why Did the Pharisees Wash Their Hands?" *Journal of Jewish Studies* 47 (1996): 217–33.

— and Joseph Frankovic. "Celibacy and Charism in 1 Cor 7:5–7". *Harvard Theological Review* 89:1 (1996): 1–18.

—. "Purity Beyond the Temple in the Second Temple Era". *Journal of Biblical Literature* 122:2 (2003): 247–65.

Polhill, John B. *Acts*. The New American Commentary 26. Nashville: Broadman Press, 1992.

Porter, Stanley E. "Was Paul a Good Jew? Fundamental Issues in a Current Debate". Pages 148–74 in *Christian-Jewish Relations Through the Centuries*. Edited by Stanley E. Porter and Brook W. R. Pearson. JSNTSS 192. Sheffield: Sheffield Academic Press, 2000.

—. *Paul in Acts*. Peabody: Hendrickson, 2001. A reprint of *The Paul of Acts: Essays in Literary Criticism, Rhetoric, and Theology*. Tübingen: Mohr Siebeck, 1999.

Potok, Chaim. *The Chosen*. New York: Ballantine, 1967.

Pratt, Richard L. *I and II Corinthians*. Holman New Testament Commentary. Nashville: Broadman & Holman, 2000.

Primack, Karen, ed. *Jews in Places You Never Thought Of*. Hoboken: Ktav, 1998.

Prior, David. *The Message of 1 Corinthians: Life in the Local Church*. Leicester: Inter-Varsity, 1985.

Pritz, Ray A. *Nazarene Jewish Christianity: From the End of the New Testament Period Until Its Disappearance in the Fourth Century*. Leiden: E. J. Brill, 1988.
Rader, William. *The Church and Racial Hostility: A History of Interpretation of Ephesians 2:11–22*. Beiträge zur Geschichte der biblischen Exegese 20. Tübingen: Mohr Siebeck, 1978.
Rainbow, Paul A. "Monotheism and Christology in 1 Corinthians 8:4–6". D. Phil. diss., The Queens College, Oxford, 1987.
Räisänen, Heikki. "Galatians 2.16 and Paul's Break with Judaism". *New Testament Studies* 31 (1985): 543–53.
—. *Paul and the Law*. Second Edition. Wissenschaftliche Untersuchungen zum Neuen Testament 29. Tübingen: Mohr Siebeck, 1987.
—. *Jesus, Paul and Torah: Collected Essays*. JSNTSS 43. Translated by David E. Orton. Sheffield: JSOT, 1992.
Reed, Annette Yoshiko. "Abraham as 'Culture-Hero': *Ant.* 1.154–68 and the Greco-Roman Discourse about Astrology/Astronomy". SBL Josephus Seminar 2002.
— and Adam H. Becker. "Introduction: Traditional Models and New Directions". Pages 1–33 in *The Ways that Never Parted: Jews and Christians in Late Antiquity and the Early Middle Ages*. Edited by Adam H. Becker and Annette Yoshiko Reed. Tübingen: Mohr Siebeck, 2003.
Regev, Eyal. "Non-Priestly Purity and Its Religious Aspects According to Historical Sources and Archaeological Findings". Pages 223–44 in in *Purity and Holiness: The Heritage of Leviticus*. Edited by M. J. H. M. Poorthuis and J. Schwartz. Jewish and Christian Perspectives. Leiden: Brill, 2000.
—. "Pure Individualism: The Idea of Non-Priestly Purity in Ancient Judaism". *Journal for the Study of Judaism in the Persian, Hellenistic, and Roman Periods* 31 (2000): 176–202.
Reumann, J. "*Oikonomia* as 'Ethical Accommodation' in the Fathers, and Its Pagan Backgrounds". *StPatr* 3 (1961): 370–79.
Richardson, Alan. *History Sacred and Profane: Bampton Lectures for 1962*. London: SCM, 1964.
Richardson, Peter. *Israel in the Apostolic Church*. Society for New Testament Studies Monograph Series 10. Cambridge: Cambridge University Press, 1969.
— and Paul W. Gooch. "Accommodation Ethics". *Tyndale Bulletin* 29 (1978): 89–142.
—. "Pauline Consistency in 1 Cor 9:19–23 and Gal 2:11–14". *New Testament Studies* 26 (1980): 347–62.
—. "'I Say, Not the Lord': Personal Opinion, Apostolic Authority and the Development of Early Christian Halakhah". *Tyndale Bulletin* 31 (1980): 65–86.
—. "The Thunderbold in Q and the Wise Man in Corinth". Pages 91–111 in *From Jesus to Paul: Studies in Honour of Francis Wright Beare*. Edited by Peter Richardson and J. C. Hurd. Waterloo: Wilfrid Laurier University Press, 1984.
—. "On the Absence of 'Anti-Judaism' in 1 Corinthians". Pages 59–73 in *Anti-Judaism in Early Christianity. Vol. 1. Paul and the Gospels*. Edited by Peter Richardson. Studies in Christianity and Judaism 2. Waterloo: Wilfrid Laurier University Press, 1986.
Ridderbos, H. N. *The Epistle of Paul to the Churches of Galatia*. NICNT. Grand Rapids: Eerdmans, 1953.
Riesner, Rainer. "Paulus und die Jesus-Überlieferung". Pages 347–65 in *Evangelium, Schriftauslegung, Kirche*. Edited by J. Adna, S. J. Hafemann and O. Hofius. Göttingen: Vandenhoeck & Ruprecht, 1997.
—. "A Pre-Christian Jewish Mission?" Pages 211–50 in *The Mission of the Early Church to Jews and Gentiles*. Edited by Jostein Ådna and Hans Kvalbein. WUNT 127. Tübingen: Mohr Siebeck, 2000.

Rietveld, John N. "A Critical Examination of 1 Corinthians 9:19–23 as it Pertains to Paul's Missionary and Apologetic Strategy". M.Th. thesis. Calvin Theological Seminary, May 1983.

Robertson, Archibald and Alfred Plummer. *A Critical and Exegetical Commentary on the First Epistle of St. Paul to the Corinthians*. International Critical Commentary. 2nd ed. Edinburgh: T & T Clark, 1914.

Robinson, James M., ed. *The Nag Hammadi Library*. San Francisco: Harper, 1990.

—, Paul Hoffmann and John S. Kloppenborg, eds. *The Critical Edition of Q*. Leuven: Peeters, 2000.

Robinson, Thomas A. *Ignatius of Antioch and the Parting of the Ways: Early Jewish-Christian Relations*. Peabody: Hendrickson, 2009.

Rode, Daniel. "El Modelo de Adaptación de Pablo Según 1 Corintios 9:19–23". Pages 333–49 in *Pensar la Iglesia Hoy: Hacia una Eclesiología Adventista, Estudios teológicos presentados durante el IV Simposio Bíblico-Teológico Sudamericano en honor a Raoul Dederen*. Edited by Gerald A. Klingbeil, Martin Klingbeil and Miguel Núñez. Libertador San Martín, Entre Ríos: Editorial Universidad Adventista del Plata, 2002.

Roloff, Jürgen. *Die Apostelgeschichte*. Das Neue Testament Deutsch. Göttingen: Vandenhoeck & Ruprecht, 1981.

Rosenblum, Jordan D. *Food and Identity in Early Rabbinic Judaism*. Cambridge: Cambridge University Press, 2010.

Rosner, Brian S. *Scripture and Ethics: A Case Study of 1 Corinthians 5–7*. Biblical Studies Library. Grand Rapids: Baker, 1994.

Ross, James R. *Fragile Branches: Travels Through the Jewish Diaspora*. New York: Riverhead, 2000.

Rowland, Christopher. *Christian Origins*. London: SPCK, 1985.

Royse, James R. "The Original Structure of Philo's *Quaestiones*". *Studia philonica* 4 (1976–77): 41–78.

Rudolph, David J. "Jesus and the Food Laws: A Reassessment of Mark 7:19b". *Evangelical Quarterly* 74:4 (2002): 291–311.

—. "Paul and the Torah According to Luke". *Kesher: A Journal of Messianic Judaism* 14 (2002): 61–73.

—. "Yeshua and the Dietary Laws: A Reassessment of Mark 7:19b". *Kesher: A Journal of Messianic Judaism* 16 (2003): 97–119.

—. "Festivals in Genesis 1:14". *Tyndale Bulletin* 54:2 (2003): 23–40.

—. *Growing Your Olive Tree Marriage: A Guide for Couples from Two Traditions*. Baltimore: Lederer, 2003.

—. "Messianic Jews and Christian Theology: Restoring an Historical Voice to the Contemporary Discussion". *Pro Ecclesia* 14:1 (2005): 58–84.

—. "Divine Accommodation in Early Jewish Texts". Paper presented at the Hebrew, Jewish and Early Christian Studies Seminar. Cambridge, Cambridge University, March 7, 2005.

—. "Accommodation as *Imitatio Christi* in 1 Cor 9:19–23". Paper presented at the Oxford-Cambridge New Testament Conference. Cambridge, Cambridge University, May 27, 2005.

—. "A Jew to the Jews: Jewish Contours of Pauline Flexibility in 1 Corinthians 9:19–23". Ph.D. diss., Cambridge University, 2006.

—. Review of Kathy Ehrensperger's *Paul and the Dynamics of Power: Communication and Interaction in the Early Christ-Movement* (London: T & T Clark, 2007) in the *Journal of Beliefs and Values: Studies in Religion and Education* 2:3 (December 2007): 350–52.

—. "History of Judeo-Christian Communities in the Jewish Diaspora". Pages 136–39 in *Encyclopedia of the Jewish Diaspora: Origins, Experiences, and Culture*. Vol. 1. Edited by M. Avrum Ehrlich. Santa Barbara: ABC-CLIO, 2008.

—. "Contemporary Judeo-Christian Communities in the Jewish Diaspora". Pages 146–50 in *Encyclopedia of the Jewish Diaspora: Origins, Experiences, and Culture*. Vol. 1. Edited by M. Avrum Ehrlich. Santa Barbara: ABC-CLIO, 2008.

—. "Paul's 'Rule in All the Churches' (1 Cor 7:17–24) and Torah-Defined Ecclesiological Variegation". Paper presented at the annual meeting of the American Academy of Religion (AAR). Chicago, November 2, 2008.

—. "Guidelines for Healthy Theological Discussion". *Kesher: A Journal of Messianic Judaism* 22 (2008): 1–5.

—. "Resurrection and Jesus' Jewish Identity". Paper Presented at the Society for the Advancement of Ecclesial Theology (SAET) Symposium. Chicago, October 14, 2008.

—. "Paul's 'Rule in All the Churches' (1 Cor 7:17–24) and Torah-Defined Ecclesiological Variegation". *Studies in Christian-Jewish Relations* 5 (2010): 1–23.

—. "Jesus-Believing Jews and *Kol Yisrael*: Rethinking Long-Held Assumptions". Paper presented at the plenary session of the Society of Biblical Literature (SBL) Midwest Region Conference. Valparaiso, IN, February 12, 2010.

— and Joel Willitts, eds. *Introduction to Messianic Judaism: Its Ecclesial Context and Biblical Foundations*. Grand Rapids: Zondervan, forthcoming.

—. "Messianic Judaism in Antiquity and the Modern Era". In *Introduction to Messianic Judaism: Its Ecclesial Context and Biblical Foundations*. Edited by David J. Rudolph and Joel Willitts. Grand Rapids: Zondervan, forthcoming.

Ruef, John. *Paul's First Letter to Corinth*. Westminster Pelican Commentaries. Philadelphia: Westminster, 1977.

Ruff, Tibor. "The New Testament and the Torah". Ph.D. diss., Jewish Theological Seminary – University of Jewish Studies (Budapest), 2007.

Runesson, Anders. "Particularistic Judaism and Universalistic Christianity? Some Critical Remarks on Terminology and Theology". *Journal of Greco-Roman Christianity and Judaism* 1 (2000): 120–44.

—. "From Where to What? Common Judaism, Pharisees, and the Changing Socio-Religious Location of the Matthean Community." Pages 97–113 in *Common Judaism: Explorations in Second Temple Judaism*. Edited by Wayne McCready and Adele Reinhartz. Minneapolis: Fortress, 2008

—. "Inventing Christian Identity: Paul, Ignatius, and Theodosius I". Pages 59–92 in *Exploring Early Christian Identity*. Edited by Bengt Holmberg. Tübingen: Mohr Siebeck, 2008.

—. "Paul's Rule in All the *Ekklesiai* (1 Cor 7:17–24)". In *Introduction to Messianic Judaism: Its Ecclesial Context and Biblical Foundations*. Edited by David Rudolph and Joel Willitts. Grand Rapids: Zondervan, forthcoming.

Saillard, M. "Paul, êvangêliste. 1 Cor 9:16–19, 22–23". *Assemblées du Seigneur* 36 (1974): 34–37.

Saldarini, Anthony J. *Pharisees, Scribes and Sadducees in Palestinian Society*. Edinburgh: T & T Clark, 1988.

Salo, Kalervo. *Luke's Treatment of the Law: A Redaction-Critical Investigation*. Annales Academiae Scientiarum Fennicae Dissertationes Humanarum Litterarum 57. Helsinki: Suomalainen Tiedeakatemia, 1991.

Sandelin, Karl-Gustav. "Drawing the Line: Paul on Idol Food and Idolatry in 1 Cor 8:1–11:1". Pages 108–125 in *Neotestamentica et Philonica: Studies in Honor of Peder Borgen*. Edited by David E. Aune, Torrey Seland and Jarl Henning Ulrichsen. Leiden: Brill, 2003.

Sanders, E. P. "On the Question of Fulfilling the Law in Paul and Rabbinic Judaism". Pages 103–26 in *Donum Gentilicum: New Testament Studies in Honour of David Daube*. Edited by E. Bammel, C. K. Barrett and W. D. Davies. Oxford: At the Clarendon Press, 1978.

—. *Paul, the Law, and the Jewish People*. Philadelphia: Fortress, 1983.

—. "Testament of Abraham: A New Translation and Introduction". *The Old Testament Pseudepigrapha* I. Edited by James H. Charlesworth. New York: Doubleday, 1983.

—. *Jesus and Judaism*. Philadelphia: Fortress, 1985.

—. "Paul on the Law, His Opponents, and the Jewish People in Philippians 3 and 2 Corinthians 11". Pages 75–90 in *Anti-Judaism in Early Christianity. Vol. 1. Paul and the Gospels*. Studies in Christianity and Judaism 2. Edited by Peter Richardson. Ontario: Canadian Corporation for Studies in Religion/Corporation Canadienne des Sciences Religieuses by Wilfrid Laurier University Press, 1986.

—. *Jewish Law from Jesus to the Mishnah: Five Studies*. London: SCM, 1990.

—. "Jewish Association With Gentiles and Galatians 2:11–14". Pages 170–88 in *The Conversation Continues: Studies in Paul and John. In Honor of J. Louis Martyn*. Edited by Robert T. Fortna and Beverly R. Gaventa. Nashville: Abingdon, 1990.

—. *Judaism: Practice and Belief, 63 BCE – 66 CE*. Philadelphia: Trinity International, 1992.

Sanders, Jack T. *The Jews in Luke-Acts*. Philadelphia: Fortress, 1987.

—. "Paul Between Jews and Gentiles in Corinth". *Journal for the Study of the New Testament* 65 (1997): 67–83.

Savelle, Charles H. "A Reexamination of the Prohibitions in Acts 15". *Bibliotheca Sacra* 161 (October – December 2004): 449–68.

Schaper, Joachim L. W. "The Pharisees". Pages 402–27 in *The Cambridge History of Judaism. Vol. III. The Early Roman Period*. Edited by William Horbury, W. D. Davies and John Sturdy. Cambridge: Cambridge University Press, 1999.

Schein, Bruce E. "Our Father Abraham". Ph.D. diss., Yale University, 1973.

Schiffman, Lawrence H. "Was There a Galilean Halakhah?" Pages 143–56 in *The Galilee in Late Antiquity*. Edited by Lee I. Levine. New York: The Jewish Theological Seminary of America, 1992.

—. "Halakhic Elements in the Sapiential Texts from Qumran". Pages 89–100 in *Sapiential Perspectives: Wisdom Literature in Light of the Dead Sea Scrolls. Proceedings of the Sixth International Symposium of the Orion Center for the Study of the Dead Sea Scrolls and Associated Literature, 20–22 May, 2001*. Edited by John J. Collins, Gregory E. Sterling and Ruth A. Clements. Leiden: Brill, 2004.

Schlatter, Adolf. *Die Korintherbriefe*. Schlatters Erläuterungen zum Neuen Testament 6. Stuttgart: Calwer Berlag, 1950.

—. *The Church in the New Testament Period*. Translated by Paul P. Levertoff. London: SPCK, 1955.

—. *Das Evangelium des Lukas: aus seinen Quellen erklärt*. Second edition. Stuttgart: Calwar, 1975.

Schlier, H. *Der Brief an die Galater*. KEK 7. Göttingen: Vandenhoeck & Ruprecht, 1962.

Schlueter, Carol J. *Filling up the Measure: Polemical Hyperbole in 1 Thessalonians 2.14–16*. JSNTSS 98. Sheffield: JSOT Press, 1994.

Schmidt, Francis. *Le Testament grec d'Abraham. Introduction, edition critique des deux recensions grecques, traduction*. Tübingen: J. C. B. Mohr, 1986.

Schmithals, Walter. *Paul and James*. London: SCM, 1965.

—. *Gnosticism in Corinth: An Investigation of the Letters to the Corinthians*. Translated by J. E. Steely. Nashville: Abringdon, 1971.

Schnabel, Eckhard J. *Early Christian Mission*. 2 vols. Downers Grove: InterVarsity, 2004.

Schneider, Sebastian. *Vollendung des Auferstehens. Eine exegetische Untersuchung zu 1 Kor 15,51–52*. Noch unveröffentlichte Dissertation. Frankfurt, Phil.-Theol. Hochschule St. Georgen, 1994.

Schoeps, H. J. *Paul: The Theology of the Apostle in the Light of Jewish Religious History*. Translated by Harold Knight. Philadelphia: Westminster, 1961. Originally published as

Paulus: Die Theologie des Apostels im Lichte der jüdischen Religionsgeschichte. Tübingen: Mohr Siebeck, 1959.
Schrage, Wolfgang. *Ethik des Neuen Testaments*. Göttingen: Vandenhoeck & Ruprecht, 1982.
—. *The Ethics of the New Testament*. Edinburgh: T & T, 1988.
—. *Der erste Brief an die Korinther*. 4 vols. Evangelisch-katholischer Kommentar zum Neuen Testament. Neukirchen-Vluyn and Düsseldorf: Neukirchener Verlag and Benziger Verlag, 1991/1995/1999/2001.
Schreiner, Thomas R. *The Law and Its Fulfillment: A Pauline Theology of Law*. Grand Rapids: Baker, 1993.
—. *Romans*. Baker Exegetical Commentary on the New Testament. Grand Rapids: Baker, 1998.
—. *Paul: Apostle of God's Glory in Christ: A Pauline Theology*. Downers Grove: InterVarsity, 2001.
Schulz, Siegfried. *Q – die Spruchquelle der Evangelisten*. Zürich: Theologischer Verlag, 1972.
Schürer, Emil. *Geschichte des jüdischen Volkes im Zeitalter Jesu Christi*. 3rd–4th edn. Leipzig, 1901–1909. English translation revised and edited by G. Vermes, F. Millar, M. Black, M. Goodman and P. Vermes. *The History of the Jewish People in the Age of Jesus Christ*. 3 vols. Edinburgh: T & T Clark, 1973–87.
Schwartz, Daniel R. "Hillel and Scripture: From Authority to Exegesis". Pages 335–62 in *Hillel and Jesus: Comparative Studies of Two Major Religious Leaders*. Edited by J. H. Charlesworth and L. L. Johns. Minneapolis: Fortress, 1997.
—. "Someone who considers something to be impure – for him it is impure" (Rom 14:14): Good Manners or Law?" Paper presented at the International Symposium "Paul in His Jewish Matrix". Pontifical Gregorian University and Pontifical Biblical Institute, Rome, May 21, 2009.
Schwiebert, Jonathan. "Table Fellowship and the Translation of 1 Corinthians 5:11". *Journal of Biblical Literature* 127:1 (2008): 159–64.
Scott, J. Julius. "The Church of Jerusalem in Acts: The Final Scene (1)". Paper presented at the National Meeting of the Evangelical Theological Society. Philadelphia, November 16, 1995.
Scott, James M. "'And Then All Israel Will Be Saved' (Rom 11:26)". Pages 489–527 in *Restoration: Old Testament, Jewish, and Christian Perspectives*. Edited by James M. Scott. Leiden: Brill, 2001.
Sechrest, Love L. *A Former Jew: Paul and the Dialects of Race*. London: T & T Clark International, 2009.
Segal, Alan F. *Paul the Convert: The Apostolate and Apostasy of Saul the Pharisee*. New Haven: Yale University Press, 1990.
—. "Some Aspects of Conversion and Identity Formation in the Christian Community of Paul's Time". Pages 184–90 in *Paul and Politics: Ekklesia, Israel, Imperium, Interpretation. Essays in Honor of Krister Stendahl*. Edited by Richard A. Horsley. Harrisburg: Trinity Press International, 2000.
Seland, Torrey. "Saul of Tarsus and Early Zealotism: Reading Gal 1,13–14 in Light of Philo's Writings". *Biblica* 83 (2002): 449–71.
Sellin, Gerhard. "Hauptprobleme des Ersten Korintherbriefes". *Aufstieg und Niedergang der Römischen Welt*. II.25.4 (1987): 2940–3044.
Sellow, P. "Early Collections of Jesus' Words". Ph.D. diss., Harvard Divinity School, 1985.
Senf, Christophe. *La première Épître de Saint-Paul aux Corinthiens*. Commentaire du Nouveau Testament. Paris: Delachaux & Niestlé, 1979.
Shen, Michael Li-Tak. "Paul's Doctrine of God and the Issue of Food Offered to Idols in 1 Corinthians 8:1–11:1". Ph.D. diss., Dallas Theological Seminary, 2003.

Shin, Joyce S. "Accommodating the Other's Conscience: Saint Paul's Approach to Religious Tolerance". *Journal of the Society of Christian Ethics* 28:1 (2008): 1–23.

Shogren, Gary Steven. "'Is the kingdom of God about eating and drinking or isn't it?' (Romans 14:17)". *Novum Testamentum* 42:3 (2000): 238–56.

Shulam, Joseph and Hilary Le Cornu. *A Commentary on the Jewish Roots of Romans*. Baltimore: Lederer, 1997.

Shutt, R. J. H. "Letter of Aristeas: A New Translation and Introduction". Pages 7–34 in *The Old Testament Pseudepigrapha*. Vol. 2. Edited by James H. Charlesworth. London: Darton, Longman & Todd, 1985.

Sibinga, Joost Smit. "The Composition of 1 Cor. 9 and Its Context". *Novum Testamentum* 40 (1998): 136–63.

Sievers, Joseph. "Who Were the Pharisees?" Pages 137–55 in *Hillel and Jesus: Comparative Studies of Two Major Religious Leaders*. Edited by James H. Charlesworth and Loren L. Johns. Minneapolis: Fortress, 1997.

—. "'God's Gifts and Call Are Irrevocable': The Reception of Romans 11:29 through the Centuries and Christian Jewish Relations". Pages 127–73 in *Reading Israel in Romans: Legitimacy and Plausibility of Divergent Interpretations*. Edited by Cristina Grenholm and Daniel Patte. Harrisburg: Trinity Press International, 2000.

Sigal, Gerald. *The Jews and the Christian Missionary: A Jewish Response to Missionary Christianity*. New York: Ktav, 1981.

Sigal, Phillip. *The Halakhah of Jesus of Nazareth According to the Gospel of Matthew*. Atlanta: Society of Biblical Literature, 2007.

Silva, Moisés. *Philippians*. The Wycliffe Exegetical Commentary. Chicago: Moody, 1988.

Simon, Marcel. "The Apostolic Decree and its Setting in the Ancient Church". Pages 414–37 in *Le Christianisme Antique et son contexte religieux: Scripta Varia Volume II*. WUNT 23. Tübingen: Mohr Siebeck, 1981.

Sisson, Russell B. "The Apostle as Athlete: A Socio-Rhetorical Interpretation of 1 Corinthians 9". Ph.D. diss., Emory University, 1981.

Skarsaune, Oskar. "Jewish Believers in Jesus in Antiquity". *Mishkan* 42 (2005): 45–56.

— and Reidar Hvalvik, eds. *Jewish Believers in Jesus: The Early Centuries*. Peabody: Hendrickson, 2007.

Slee, Michelle. *The Church in Antioch in the First Century CE: Communion and Conflict*. London: Sheffield, 2003.

Sloyan, Gerard. "Did Paul Think That Jews and Jewish Christians Must Follow Torah?" Pages 170–73 in *Bursting the Bonds? A Jewish-Christian Dialogue on Jesus and Paul*. Maryknoll: Orbis, 1990.

Smallwood, Mary. "Some Notes on the Jews under Tiberius". *Latomus* 15 (1956): 314–29.

Smiles, Vincent M. "The Concept of 'Zeal' in Second-Temple Judaism and Paul's Critique of it in Romans 10:2". *The Catholic Biblical Quarterly* 2 (2002): 282–99.

Smillie, Gene R. "Isaiah 42:1–4 in Its Rhetorical Context". *Bibliotheca Sacra* 162 (2005): 50–65.

Smit, Joop. *"About the Idol Offerings": Rhetoric, Social Context, and Theology of Paul's Discourse in First Corinthians 8:1–11:1*. Leuven: Peeters, 2000.

Smith, David E. *The Canonical Function of Acts: A Comparative Analysis*. Collegeville: The Liturgical Press, 2002.

Smith, Dennis E. "The Historical Jesus at Table". Pages 466–86 in *Society of Biblical Literature 1989 Seminar Papers*. Edited by David J. Lull. Atlanta: Scholars, 1989.

Smith, Jonathan Z. "Fences and Neighbors: Some Contours of Early Judaism". Pages 1–25 in *Approaches to Ancient Judaism*. Vol. 2. Edited by William Scott Green. Chico: Scholars, 1980.

Smith, Morton. "The Reason for the Persecution of Paul and the Obscurity of Acts". Pages 261–68 in *Studies in Mysticism and Religion Presented to Gershom G. Scholem on His Seventieth Birthday by Pupils, Colleagues and Friends*. Jerusalem: The Hebrew University, 1967.

Smith, Thomas E. "The Domestication of Transcendence: Paul's Christian Halakha in 1 Corinthians 7 on Celibacy, Marriage and Divorce". Ph.D. diss., Graduate Theological Foundation, 2005.

Sohn, Seock-Tae. *The Divine Election of Israel*. Grand Rapids: Eerdmans, 1991.

Song, B. M. *The Pauline Concept of "Weakness" in 1 Corinthians and Its Usage within the Context of Paul's Resolution of the Opposition Between the Strong and the Weak in 1 Cor 8:7–13*. Washington, D.C.: The Catholic University of America, 1997.

Soulen, R. Kendall. *The God of Israel and Christian Theology*. Minneapolis: Fortress, 1996.

—. "Canonical Narrative and Gospel". In *Introduction to Messianic Judaism: Its Ecclesial Context and Biblical Foundations*. Edited by David Rudolph and Joel Willitts. Grand Rapids: Zondervan, forthcoming.

Spencer, F. Scott. *Acts*. Sheffield: Sheffield Academic Press, 1997.

Spilsbury, Paul. *The Image of the Jew in Flavius Josephus' Paraphrase of the Bible*. Texte und Studien zum antiken Judentum 69. Tübingen: Mohr Siebeck, 1998.

Stanford, W. B. *The Ulysses Theme: A Study in the Adaptability of a Traditional Hero*. 2d ed. rev. New York: Basil Blackwell & Mott, 1968.

Stanley, Christopher D. "'Neither Jew Nor Greek': Ethnic Conflict in Graeco-Roman Society". *Journal for the Study of the New Testament* 64 (1996): 101–24.

Stanton, Graham. "The Law of Christ: A Neglected Theological Gem?" Pages 169–84 in *Reading Texts, Seeking Wisdom: Scripture and Theology*. Edited by David F. Ford and Graham Stanton. London: SCM, 2003.

Stegemann, Wolfgang. *Zwischen Synagoge und Obrigkeit: Zur historischen Situation der lukanischen Christen*. Forschungen zur Religion und Literatur des Alten und Neuen Testaments. Göttingen: Vandenhoeck & Ruprecht, 1991.

Stemberger, Günter. *Pharisäer, Sadduzäer, Essener*. SBS 144. Stuttgart: Katholisches Bibelwerk, 1991.

—. *Jewish Contemporaries of Jesus: Pharisees, Sadducees, Essenes*. Translated by Allan W. Mahnke. Minneapolis: Fortress, 1995.

— and Markus Bockmuehl. *Introduction to the Talmud and Midrash*. Edinburgh: T & T Clark, 1996.

Stendahl, Kister. "The Apostle Paul and the Introspective Conscience of the West". *Harvard Theological Review* 56 (1963): 199–215.

Sterling, Gregory E. "'Thus are Israel': Jewish Self-Definition in Alexandria". *The Studia Philonica Annual* 7 (1995): 1–18.

—. "Was There a Common Ethic in Second Temple Judaism?" Pages 171–94 in *Sapiential Perspectives: Wisdom Literature in Light of the Dead Sea Scrolls. Proceedings of the Sixth International Symposium of the Orion Center for the Study of the Dead Sea Scrolls and Associated Literature, 20–22 May, 2001*. Edited by John J. Collins, Gregory E. Sterling and Ruth A. Clements. Leiden: Brill, 2004.

Stern, Lisë. *How to Keep Kosher: A Comprehensive Guide to Understanding Jewish Dietary Laws*. New York: HarperCollins, 2004.

Stern, Menachem. *Greek and Latin Authors on Jews and Judaism*. 3 vols. Jerusalem: Israel Academy of Sciences and Humanities, 1974–84.

Stolle, Volker. *Der Zeuge als Angeklagter: Untersuchungen zum Paulusbild des Lukas*. Beiträge zur Wissenschaft vom Alten und Neuen Testament. 6 Folg. Heft 2 (der ganzen Sammlung Heft 102). Stuttgart: W. Kohlhammer, 1973.

Stone, Michael E. *The Testament of Abraham: The Greek Recensions*. Missoula: Society of Biblical Literature, 1972.

Stott, John R. W. *The Message of Acts*. Downers Grove: InterVarsity Press, 1990.

Stowers, Stanley K. *A Rereading of Romans: Justice, Jews, and Gentiles*. New Haven: Yale University Press, 1994.

Strack, H. and P. Billerbeck. *Kommentar zum Neuen Testament aus Talmud and Midrash* II. München: C. H. Beck, 1924.

Stroeter, Ernst F. "Does the Jew, in Christ, Cease to Be a Jew?" *Our Hope* 2:6 (December 1895): 129–134.

Sullivan, Kevin P. *Wrestling With Angels: A Study of the Relationship between Angels and Humans in Ancient Jewish Literature and the New Testament*. Leiden: Brill, 2004.

Sumney, Jerry L. "The Place of 1 Corinthians 9:24–27 in Paul's Argument". *Journal of Biblical Literature* 119:2 (2000): 329–33.

Tannehill, Robert C. *Luke*. ANTC. Nashville: Abingdon, 1996.

Taussig, Hal. *In the Beginning Was the Meal: Social Experimentation and Early Christian Identity*. Minneapolis: Fortress, 2009.

Taylor, Justin. *Commentaire Historique (Act 18,23–28,31)*. Volume 6 of *Les Actes des Deux Apôtres*. Études Bibliques. Nouvelle Series 30. Paris: Librairie Lecoffre, 1996.

—. "The Jerusalem Decrees (Acts 15.20, 29 and 21.25) and the Incident at Antioch (Gal 2.11–14)". *New Testament Studies* 46 (2000): 372–80.

Terry, R. B. *A Discourse Analysis of First Corinthians*. Dallas: Summer Institute of Linguistics, 1995.

Theissen, Gerd. "The Strong and the Weak in Corinth: A Sociological Analysis of a Theological Quarrel". Pages 121–44 in *The Social Setting of Pauline Christianity: Essays on Corinth*. Philadelphia: Fortress, 1982. Translated from "Die Starken und Schwachen in Korinth: Soziologische Analyse eines theologischen Streites". *Evangelische Theologie* 35 (1975): 155–72.

Theobald, Michael. "'Allen bin ich alles geworden . . .' (1 Kor 9:22b) Paulus und das Problem der Inkulturation des Glaubens". *Theologische Quartalschrift* 176 (1996): 1–6.

Thielman, Frank. "The Coherence of Paul's View of the Law: The Evidence of First Corinthians". *New Testament Studies* 38 (1992): 235–53.

—. *Paul and the Law: A Contextual Approach*. DownersGrove: InterVarsity, 1994.

—. *The Law in the New Testament: The Question of Continuity*. New York: Crossroad, 1999.

Thiselton, Anthony C. *The First Epistle to the Corinthians: A Commentary on the Greek Text*. The New International Greek Testament Commentary. Grand Rapids: Eerdmans, 2000.

Thompson, Michael B. "Stumbling Blocks and Snares: The Context of Romans 14:13b". 23 May 1985. Unpublished.

—. "The Example and Teaching of Jesus in Romans 12.1–15.13". Ph.D. diss., University of Cambridge, 1988.

—. *Clothed with Christ: The Example and Teaching of Jesus in Romans 12.1–15.13*. JSNTSS 59. Sheffield: Sheffield Academic Press, 1991.

—. *The New Perspective on Paul*. Cambridge: Grove Books Limited, 2002.

Thompson, Richard P. "'Say It Ain't So, Paul!': The Accusations Against Paul in Acts 21 in Light of His Ministry in Acts 16–20". *Biblical Research* 45 (2000): 34–50.

—. "'What Do You Think You Are Doing, Paul?': Synagogues, Accusations, and Ethics in Paul's Ministry in Acts 16–21". Pages 64–78 in *Acts and Ethics*. Edited by Thomas E. Phillips. Sheffield: Sheffield Phoenix, 2005.

Thorsteinsson, Runar M. *Paul's Interlocutor in Romans 2: Function and Identity in the Context of Ancient Epistolography*. Coniectanea Biblica New Testament Series 40. Stockholm: Almqvist & Wiksell International, 2003.

Tigay, Jeffrey H. *Deuteronomy*. The JPS Torah Commentary. Philadelphia: The Jewish Publication Society, 1996.
Tinsley, E. J. *The Imitation of God in Christ*. London: SCM, 1960.
Tobin, Diane K., Gary A. Tobin and Scott Rubin, *In Every Tongue: The Racial and Ethnic Diversity of the Jewish People*. San Francisco: Institute for Jewish and Community Research, 2005.
Tomes, Roger. "Why Did Paul Get His Hair Cut? [Acts 18.18; 21.23–24]". *Luke's Literary Achievement: Collected Essays*. Edited by C. M. Tuckett. Journal for the Study of the New Testament Supplement Series. Sheffield: Sheffield Academic Press, 1995.
Tomson, Peter J. "The Names Israel and Jew in Ancient Judaism and in the New Testament". *Bijdragen* 47 (1986): 120–40, 266–89.
—. *Paul and the Jewish Law: Halakha in the Letters of the Apostle to the Gentiles*. Minneapolis: Fortress, 1990.
—. "Gamaliel's Counsel and the Apologetic Strategy of Luke-Acts". Pages 585–604 in *The Unity of Luke-Acts*. Bibliotheca Ephemeridum Theologicarum Lovaniensium. Edited by J. Verheyden. Leuven: Leuven University Press, 1999.
—. "Paul's Jewish Background in View of His Law Teaching in 1 Cor 7". Pages 251–70 in *Paul and the Mosaic Law*. Edited by James D. G. Dunn. Grand Rapids: Eerdmans, 2001. Originally published in 1996 by Mohr Siebeck.
—. *"If this be from Heaven . . .": Jesus and the New Testament Authors in their Relationship to Judaism*. Sheffield: Sheffield Academic Press, 2001.
—. "Halakhah in the New Testament: A Research Overview". Pages 135–206 in *The New Testament and Rabbinic Literature*. Supplements to the Journal for the Study of Judaism 136. Edited by Reimund Bieringer, Florentino García Martínez, Didier Pollefeyt and Peter J. Tomson. Leiden: Brill, 2010.
Toney, Carl N. *Paul's Inclusive Ethic: Resolving Community Conflicts and Promoting Mission in Romans 14–15*. WUNT 2/252. Tübingen: Mohr Siebeck, 2008.
Trobisch, David. *The First Edition of the New Testament*. Oxford: Oxford University Press, 2000.
Tucker, J. Brian. "The Role of Civic Identity on the Pauline Mission in Corinth". *Didaskalia* (Winter 2008): 71–91.
—. "'Beyond the New Perspective on Paul' and the Evangelical New Testament Scholar: Is Paul Torah-Observant in 1 Corinthians 9.20–21?" Paper presented at the annual meeting of the Evangelical Theological Society. New Orleans, November 20, 2009.
—. "The Continuation of Gentile Identity in Christ". Paper presented at the annual meeting of the Society of Biblical Literature, Special Session on Intercultural Interaction and Identity Formation in Pauline Tradition. Atlanta, November 20, 2010.
—. *You Belong to Christ: Paul and the Formation of Social Identity in 1 Corinthians 1–4*. Eugene: Pickwick, 2010.
Tuckett, Christopher M. "Paul and the Synoptic Mission Discourse?" *Ephemerides Theologicae Lovanienses* 60 (1984): 376–81.
—. *Q and the History of Early Christianity*. Peabody: Hendrickson, 1996.
Turner, Seth. "The Interim, Earthly Messianic Kingdom in Paul". *Journal for the Study of the New Testament* 25:3 (2003): 323–42.
Turner, Max. *Power from on High: The Spirit in Israel's Restoration and Witness in Luke-Acts*. JPTSS 9. Sheffield: Sheffield Academic Press, 1996.
Tyson, Joseph B. "The Gentile Mission and the Authority of Scripture in Acts". *New Testament Studies* 33 (1987): 619–31.
—. *Images of Judaism in Luke-Acts*. Columbia: University of South Carolina Press, 1992.

Uro, Risto. *Sheep among the Wolves: A Study on the Mission Instructions of Q*. Annales Academiae Scientiarum Fennicae 47. Dissertationes humanarum litterarum. Helsinki: Suomalainen Tiedeakatemia, 1987.

—. "Thomas and oral gospel tradition". Pages 8–32 in *Thomas at the Crossroads: Essays on the Gospel of Thomas*. Edinburgh: T & T Clark, 1998.

Van der Horst, Pieter W. *The Sentences of Pseudo-Phocylides: With Introduction and Commentary*. Studia in Veteris Testamenti Pseudepigrapha 4. Leiden: Brill, 1978.

Van Vorst, R. E. *The Ascents of James: History and Theology of a Jewish-Christian Community*. SBLDS 112. Atlanta: Scholars Press, 1989.

VanderKam, James C. *The Book of Jubilees*. Translated by James C. VanderKam. Lovanii: Peeters, 1989.

—. *The Book of Jubilees*. Sheffield: Sheffield Academic Press, 2001.

Verbruggen, Jan L. "Of Muzzles and Oxen: Deuteronomy 25:4 and 1 Corinthians 9:9". *Journal of the Evangelical Theological Society* 49:4 (2006): 699–711.

Vermes, Geza. *Scripture and Tradition in Judaism: Haggadic Stories*. Leiden: Brill, 1961.

Vielhauer, Philipp. "On the 'Paulinism' of Acts". Pages 33–50 in *Studies in Luke-Acts*. Edited by Leander E. Keck and J. Louis Martyn. Nashville: Abingdon, 1966.

Vlach, Michael J. *The Church as a Replacement of Israel: An Analysis of Supersessionism*. Edition Israelogie 2. Frankfurt am Main: Peter Lang, 2009.

Vlachos, Chris Alex. *The Law and the Knowledge of Good and Evil: Tha Edenic Background of the Catalytic Operation of the Law in Paul*. Eugene, OR: Pickwick, 2009.

Vollenweider, Samuel. *Freiheit als neue Schöpfung: Eine Untersuchung zur Eleutheria bei Paulus und in seiner Umwelt*. FRLANT 147. Göttingen: Vandenhoeck & Ruprecht, 1989.

Wagner, G. "Le scandale de la croix expliqué par le chant du Serviteur d'Isaïe 53. Réflexion sur Philippiens 2/6–11". *Etudes théologiques et religieuses* 61 (1986): 177–87.

Wagner, J. Ross. "The Christ, Servant of Jew and Gentile: A Fresh Approach to Romans 15:8–9". *Journal of Biblical Literature* 116:3 (1997): 473–85.

—. "The Heralds of Isaiah and the Mission of Paul: An Investigation of Paul's Use of Isaiah 51–55 in Romans". Pages 193–222 in *Jesus and the Suffering Servant: Isaiah 53 and Christian Origins*. Edited by William H. Bellinger and William R. Farmer. Harrisburg: Trinity Press International, 1998.

—. *Heralds of the Good News: Isaiah and Paul "in concert" in the Letter to the Romans*. Supplement to Novum Testamentum (NTS) 101. Leiden: Brill, 2002.

Wahlen, Clinton. "Peter's Vision and Conflicting Definitions of Purity". *New Testament Studies* 51 (2005): 505–18.

Walker, Donald D. *Paul's Offer of Leniency (2 Cor 10.1): Populist Ideology and Rhetoric in a Pauline Letter Fragment*. Tübingen: Mohr Siebeck, 2002.

Walker, William O. "Galatians 2:7b–8 as a Non-Pauline Interpolation". *The Catholic Biblical Quarterly* 65:4 (2003): 568–87.

Watson, Francis. *Paul, Judaism and the Gentiles: A Sociological Approach*. Cambridge: Cambridge University Press, 1986.

Wedderburn, Alexander J. M. "Paul and Jesus: Similarity and Continuity". Pages 117–43 in *Paul and Jesus: Collected Essays*. JSNTSS 37. Edited by A. J. M. Wedderburn. Sheffield: Sheffield Academic Press, 1989.

Wehnert, Jürgen. *Die Reinheit des christlichen Gottesvolkes aus Juden und Heiden: Studien zum historischen und theologischen Hintergrund des sogenannten Apostoldekrets*. Göttingen: Vandenhoeck & Ruprecht, 1997.

Weinstein, Sara Epstein. *Piety and Fanaticism: Rabbinic Criticism of Religious Stringency*. London: Jason Aronson, 1997.

Weiss, Johannes. *Der erste Korintherbrief*. KEK. Göttingen: Vandenhoeck & Ruprecht, 1910.

Wenham, David. "Paul's Use of the Jesus Tradition: Three Samples". Pages 7–37 in *Gospel Perspectives: The Jesus Tradition Outside the Gospels*. Vol. V. Edited by David Wenham. Eugene: Wipf and Stock, 1984.

—. *Paul: Follower of Jesus or Founder of Christianity?* Grand Rapids: Eerdmans, 1995.

Westerholm, Stephen. *Israel's Law and the Church's Faith: Paul and His Recent Interpreters*. Grand Rapids: Eerdmans, 1988.

—. "Sinai as Viewed from Damascus: Paul's Reevaluation of the Mosaic Law". Pages 147–64 in *The Road from Damascus: The Impact of Paul's Conversion on His Life, Thought, and Ministry*. Edited by Richard N. Longenecker. Grand Rapids: Eerdmans, 1997.

—. *Perspectives Old and New in Paul: The 'Lutheran' Paul and His Critics*. Grand Rapids: Eerdmans, 2004.

White, Carolline. *The Correspondence (394–419) Between Jerome and Augustine of Hippo*. Studies in Bible and Early Christianity 23. Lampeter: The Edwin Mellen Press, 1990.

Wilckens, U. "Zur Entwicklung des paulinischen Gesetzesverständnis". *New Testament Studies* 28 (1982): 154–90.

Wilder, William N. *Echoes of the Exodus Narrative in the Context and Background of Galatians 5:18*. Studies in Biblical Literature 23. New York: Peter Lang, 2001.

Wiles, Maurice F. *The Divine Apostle: The Interpretation of St. Paul's Epistles in the Early Church*. Cambridge: Cambridge University Press, 1967.

Wilk, Florian, J. Ross Wagner and Frank Schleritt, eds. *Between Gospel and Election: Explorations in the Interpretation of Romans 9–11*. WUNT 2/257. Tübingen: Mohr Siebeck, 2010.

Williams, Sam K. *Galatians*. Abingdon New Testament Commentaries. Nashville: Abingdon, 1997.

Willis, Wendell Lee. *Idol Meat in Corinth: The Pauline Argument in 1 Corinthians 8 and 10*. SBL Dissertation Series 68. Chico: Scholars Press, 1985.

—. "An Apostolic Apologia: The Form and Function of 1 Corinthians 9". *Journal for the Study of the New Testament* 24 (1985): 33–48.

Willitts, Joel. "Context Matters: Paul's Use of Leviticus 18:5 in Galatians 3:12". *Tyndale Bulletin* 54:2 (2003): 105–122.

—. "Isa 54,1 in Gal 4,24b–27: Reading Genesis in Light of Isaiah". *Zeitschrift für die Neutestamentliche Wissenschaft und die Kunde der älteren Kirche* 96:3–4 (2005): 188–210.

—. *Matthew's Messianic Shepherd-King: In Search of 'The Lost Sheep of the House of Israel'*. BZNW 147. Berlin: Walter de Gruyter, 2007.

—. "The Friendship of Matthew and Paul: A Response to a Recent Trend in the Interpretation of Matthew's Gospel". *HTS Theological Studies* 65:1 (2009): 1–8.

—. "Weighing the Words of Paul: How do we understand Paul's instructions today?" *The Covenant Companion* 3 (2009): 28–30.

— and David Rudolph, eds. *Introduction to Messianic Judaism: Its Ecclesial Context and Biblical Foundations*. Grand Rapids: Zondervan, forthcoming.

—. "Ethnic Dimensions of the New Heavens and New Earth". In *Introduction to Messianic Judaism: Its Ecclesial Context and Biblical Foundations*. Edited by David Rudolph and Joel Willitts. Grand Rapids: Zondervan, forthcoming.

Wilson, S. G. *Luke and the Law*. SNTSMS 50. Cambridge: Cambridge University Press, 1983.

Wilson, Todd A. "'Under Law' in Galatians: A Pauline Theological Abbreviation". *Journal of Theological Studies* 56:2 (2005): 362–92.

—. "The Law of Christ and the Law of Moses: Reflections on a Recent Trend in Interpretation". *Currents in Biblical Research* 5:1 (2006): 129–50.

—. *The Curse of the Law and the Crisis in Galatia: Reassessing the Purpose of Galatians*. WUNT 2/91. Tübingen: Mohr Siebeck, 2007.

—. "Peace in the Church (Rom 14)". In *Introduction to Messianic Judaism: Its Ecclesial Context and Biblical Foundations*. Edited by David Rudolph and Joel Willitts. Grand Rapids: Zondervan, forthcoming.
Winger, Michael. "The Law of Christ". *New Testament Studies* 46 (2000): 537–46.
—. "Act One: Paul Arrives in Galatia". *New Testament Studies* 48 (2002): 548–67.
Wingren, Gustaf. *Luther on Vocation*. Translated by Carl C. Rasmussen. Philadelphia: Muhlenberg, 1957.
Winston, David. "Philo's Ethical Theory". Pages 21.1:372–416 in *ANRW. Part 2, Principat, 21.1*. Edited by H. Temporini and W. Haase. Berlin: De Gruyter, 1984.
Winston, Hella. *Unchosen: The Hidden Lives of Hasidic Rebels*. Boston: Beacon, 2005.
Winter, Bruce W. *Seek the Welfare of the City: Christians as Benefactors and Citizens*. First Century Christians in the Graeco-Roman World. Grand Rapids: Eerdmans, 1994.
—. *After Paul Left Corinth: The Influence of Secular Ethics and Social Change*. Grand Rapids: Eerdmans, 2001.
Witherington III, Ben. "Not So Idle Thoughts about Eidolothuton". *Tyndale Bulletin* 44:2 (1993): 237–54.
—. *Conflict and Community in Corinth: A Socio-Rhetorical Commentary on 1 and 2 Corinthians*. Grand Rapids: Eerdmans, 1995.
—. *The Acts of the Apostles: A Socio-Rhetorical Commentary*. Grand Rapids: Eerdmans, 1998.
—. *The Gospel of Mark: A Socio-Rhetorical Commentary*. Grand Rapids: Eerdmans, 2001.
Witmer, Stephen E. *Divine Instruction in Early Christianity*. WUNT 2/246. Tübingen: Mohr Siebeck, 2008.
Witulski, Thomas. *Die Addressaten des Galaterbriefes: Untersuchungen zur Gemeinde von Antiochia ad Pisidiam*. FRLANT 193; Göttingen: Vandenhoeck & Ruprecht, 2000.
Wolff, Christian. *Der erste Brief des Paulus an die Korinther*. Vol. 2. *Auslegung der Kapitel 8–16*. THKNT 7/2. Berlin: Evangelische Verlagsanstalt, 1982.
Wright, David F. "A Race Apart? Jews, Gentiles, Christians". *Bibliotheca Sacra* 160 (April–June 2003): 131–41.
Wright, N. T. "The Messiah and the People of God: A Study in Pauline Theology with Particular Reference to the Argument of the Epistle to the Romans". D. Phil. diss., University of Oxford, 1980.
—. *The Climax of the Covenant: Christ and the Law in Pauline Theology*. London: T & T Clark, 1991.
—. "Jerusalem in the New Testament". Pages 53–77 in *Jerusalem Past and Present in the Purposes of God*. Cambridge: Tyndale House, 1992.
Wyschogrod, Michael. "A Jewish View of Christianity". Pages 104–19 in *Toward a Theological Encounter: Jewish Understandings of Christianity*. Edited by Leon Klenicki. New York: Paulist, 1991.
—. "Christianity and Mosaic Law". *Pro Ecclesia* 2:4 (1993): 451–59.
—. "Letter to a Friend". *Modern Theology* 2 (1995): 165–71.
—. "Response to the Respondents". *Modern Theology* 2 (1995): 229–41.
—. *Abraham's Promise: Judaism and Jewish-Christian Relations*. Edited by R. Kendall Soulen. Grand Rapids: Eerdmans, 2004.
Yao, Santos. "The Table Fellowship of Jesus With the Marginalized: A Radical Inclusiveness". *Journal of Asian Mission* 3:1 (2001): 25–41.
Yeo, Khiok-Khng. *Rhetorical Interaction in 1 Corinthians 8 and 10: A Formal Analysis with Preliminary Suggestions for a Chinese, Cross-Cultural Hermeneutic*. Biblical Interpretation Series 9. Leiden: Brill, 1995.
Yoder, John Howard. *The Jewish-Christian Schism Revisited*. Edited by Michael G. Cartwright and Peter Ochs. Grand Rapids: Eerdmans, 2003.

Yong, Amos. *Hospitality and the Other: Pentecost, Christian Practices, and the Neighbor*. Maryknoll: Orbis, 2008.

Young, Brad H. *Paul the Jewish Theologian: A Pharisee among Christians, Jews, and Gentiles*. Peabody: Hendrickson, 1997.

Zaas, Peter S. "Paul and the Halakhah: Dietary Laws for Gentiles in 1 Corinthians 8–10". Pages 233–45 in *Jewish Law Association Studies VII: The Paris Conference Volume*. Edited by S. M. Passamaneck and M. Finley. Atlanta: Scholars, 1994.

—. "The (Double) Vision of the Divine Picnic (Acts 10:1–11:18): The History of New Testament Kashrut III". *Jewish Law Association Studies IX: The London Conference Volume*. Edited by E. A. Goldman. Atlanta: Scholars, 1997.

Zemer, Moshe. *Evolving Halakhah: A Progressive Approach to Traditional Jewish Law*. Woodstock: Jewish Lights, 1999.

Zerwick, Max and Mary Grosvenor. *A Grammatical Analysis of the Greek New Testament*. 5th Revised Edition. Rome: Editrice Pontificio Istituto Biblico, 1996.

Zetterholm, Magnus. "A Covenant for Gentiles? Covenantal Nomism and the Incident at Antioch". Pages 168–88 in *The Ancient Synagogue From Its Origins Until 200 C.E. Papers Presented at an International Conference at Lund University, October 14–17, 2001*. Edited by Birger Olsson and Magnus Zetterholm. Stockholm: Almqvist & Wiksell International, 2003.

—. *The Formation of Christianity in Antioch: A Social-Scientific Approach to the Separation Between Judaism and Christianity*. Routledge Early Church Monographs. London: Routledge, 2003.

—. "Purity and Anger: Gentiles and Idolatry in Antioch." *Interdisciplinary Journal of Research on Religion* 1 (2005): 1–24.

—. "Paul and the Missing Messiah." Pages 33–55 in *The Messiah in Early Judaism and Christianity*. Edited by Magnus Zetterholm. Minneapolis: Fortress, 2007.

—. *Approaches to Paul: A Student's Guide to Recent Scholarship*. Minneapolis: Fortress, 2009.

—. "Jews, Christians, and Gentiles: Rethinking the Categorization within the Early Jesus Movement". Pages 242–54 in *Reading Paul in Context: Explorations in Identity Formation: Essays in Honour of William S. Campbell*. Library of New Testament Studies 428. Edited by Kathy Ehrensperger and J. Brian Tucker. London: T & T Clark International, 2010.

Zins, Robert M. "'Ennomos Christou': Believers In-lawed to Christ". *Searching Together* 16 (1987): 7–10.

Zoccali, Christopher. *Whom God Has Called: The Relationship of Church and Israel in Pauline Interpretation, 1920 to the Present*. Eugene: Pickwick, 2010.

Index of Ancient Sources

Hebrew Bible/Old Testament

Genesis
1:27–28   31
2:24   32
3   156, 158
9:3–4   42
9:4   106
12   135
17:9–14   27, 31
18   143–46
18–19   143
18:1–2   143
18:1–16   144
18:2–5   143
18:3   144
18:5   144
18:8   143
18:16–17   143
18:18   192
19:1   143
19:15   143
20   135
20:11   135
20:13   135
20:16   132

Exodus
8:10   79
9:14   79
12:14–20   38
14:4   79
14:18   79
18:11   79
19:5   54
19:5–6   79
19:6   79
21:28–29   94, 104
22:2   104

22:2–3   94
30:17–21   117
32:6   103
34:15   94
40:31   118

Leviticus
11   41–42, 72, 94
11:4   37
11:5   37
11:6   37
11:7   37
11:8   37
11:10–11   37
11:12   37
11:23   37
11:34   40
11:37   40
15:11   118
18   105
19   104–105, 107, 109
19:1–4   104
19:9–15   104, 169
19:14   104–107
19:18   82
20   105

Numbers
6:1–21   56
6:3   106
6:13–15   54
19:12   53
25:1   103
25:9   103

Deuteronomy
4:5–8   79

6:4	103	113:4–8	169
7:6	79		
9:9	192	*Isaiah*	
10:16–19	146, 169	2:2–4	79
14:2	79	11:1	169
22	104	11:2	169
25:3	155	11:4	169
26:18	79	11:10	169
27:18	105–106	30:9	161
32:17	103	35:5	169
		41:8	79
Joshua		42:1–4	169, 201
23:7	106	42:6	79
23:13–16	106	43:10	79
24:26	161	44:1–2	79
		44:8	79
Judges		44:21	79
2:3	107	49:3–6	79
		52:13–53:12	169
Ezra		60:3	79
7:12	161	61:1	169
7:14	161	61:1–2	169
7:21	161	61:6	79
7:25	161	62:12	79
9:4	82		
		Jeremiah	
Nehemiah		7:22–23	148
8:8	161		
8:18	161	*Ezekiel*	
10:29(28)	161	34	169
10:30(29)	161		
		Daniel	
Esther		1:8	126
5:5–8	126	1:12	126
6:14–7:1	126		
		Hosea	
Psalms		4:6	161
9:17	121	4:17	107
24:1	103	6:6	30, 148
25:1	37		
31:1	159	*Zechariah*	
36:31	161	8:23	79
105:34–36	107	14:16–21	7

Apocrypha

Baruch		*1 Esdras*	
4.12	161	8.19	161

8.21	161	7.12	161
8.23	161		
8.24	161	*4 Maccabees*	
		6.15	36
2 Esdras		7.6	36
7.20	161	13.22	161
Additions to Esther		*Sirach*	
14.17 C	126	9.4	152
		13.2	152
Judith		13.16	152, 191
12.7–9	127	29.1	83
12.17–19	127, 130	32.1–2	143
		32.23	82–83
1 Maccabees		41.8	161
1.11–15	81		
1.15	81	*Tobit*	
1.47	36	1.6–8	187
1.48	73	1.11	126
1.60–61	73	13.3–6	137
1.62	36	13.8(6)	121
2.46	73		
		Wisdom of Solomon	
2 Maccabees		6.18	83
6.10	73	6.23	152
9.13–17	137	8.4	152
		14.11	107
3 Maccabees		17	160
7.10	161		

Pseudepigrapha

Joseph and Aseneth		128–69	127
7.6–7	126	139	128
8.5	126	139–42	127–28
		181	128, 130
Jubilees		182–83	128
6.35	50	184	128
7.20	99	184–85	128
12.1–8	135	234	30
15.25–34	73	257	143, 192
22.16	125	275	128
23.23–24	121		
		Psalms of Solomon	
Letter of Aristeas		1.1	121
38	127	1.8	50
39	127	2.1–2	121
121–22	127		

Testament of Abraham		4.9	145
1	146	4.10	145
1.1–7	142	4.15	142, 146, 192
4.6	145	6.4	145
4.7	145–47, 192	10	146
4.7–10	142	20.15	142

New Testament

Matthew		19:17–19	82
5:17–20	72, 205	21:32	121
5:18–19	74	23:1–4	201
5:47	121, 183	23:2–3	122
6:1	197	23:4	207
6:16	197	23:5	197
9:9	181	23:15	131, 135–41, 166, 196
9:10	121	23:23	72
9:10–13	19, 209	23:23–26	198
9:13	181	23:24	40
10:5	186	26:20–29	180
10:10	180	28	139
10:10–11	185		
11:19	19, 121, 182–83, 187, 209	*Mark*	
11:28	201	2:14	181
11:28–30	201	2:15	182, 187
11:29	207	2:15–17	19, 183, 209
11:29–30	207	2:16	121
12:1–8	201	2:17	30, 181
12:9–14	201	3:17	148
14:16–21	181	5:41	148
15	185	6:37–44	181
15:1–2	50, 148, 185, 198	7	42, 47, 117, 148
15:1–20	41, 185, 201, 210	7:1–5	50, 148, 182, 198, 201
15:2	195	7:1–15	41
15:3–4	148	7:1–22	210
15:10–11	38	7:1–23	47
15:11	12, 149, 185	7:3	148, 195, 203
15:15	48	7:3–5	158
15:20	148, 185	7:5	195
15:21–28	186	7:8	41
15:32–38	181	7:9–10	148
18:6	208	7:11	148
18:11	121	7:14–15	38
18:15	165, 167, 207	7:14–19	47
18:17	183	7:15	12, 30, 38, 147–49, 170
19:6	180	7:18–23	7
19:9	180	7:19	12, 42, 47, 148–49, 170
19:17	54, 82–83	7:24–30	186

7:34	148	10:8	16, 147, 183–85, 187–90, 193
8:2–9	181	10:9	185, 189
9:42	208	10:10	189
9:42–50	147	10:11	189
10:9	180	10:16	185, 189
10:11–12	180	10:19	189
10:19	54	11:37	181
10:33	183	11:37–41	182
10:44–45	147, 181	11:37–45	200
12:28–34	147	11:42	198
12:40	197	11:46	200–201, 207
14:12–25	180	14:1	181
14:36	148	14:13	169
14:41	121, 183	14:14	169
15:22	148	14:21	169
15:34	148	15:1	121
		15:1–3	181
Luke		15:1–7	185
1:6	200	15:7	181
1:59	25	16:18	180
2:21–39	200	17:2	208
2:22	200	17:9–10	75
2:23	200	18:20	54
2:24	200	19:1–10	185
2:27	200	19:7–10	181
2:39	200	20:47	197
4:18	169	22:14–23	180
5:27	181	24:26	177
5:27–32	181		
5:29–32	19, 209	*John*	
5:30	50, 121	2:6	117
5:32	169, 181	6:5–13	181
5:33	50, 121, 183	7:10	55
7:21–22	169	7:49	50
7:29–30	181, 203	9:16	83
7:34	121, 182–83, 185, 187	17:11–12	177
7:34–36	19, 181, 209	20:28–31	177
9:1	189		
9:2	190	*Acts*	
9:6	189	2:9–11	203
9:11	188	2:11	140
9:12–17	181	2:23	160
10	188–90	2:36	177
10:1	189	4:13	50
10:1–12	185	5:34	143
10:2	189	6:1	203
10:3	189	6:5	140
10:5–8	185	6:13–14	204
10:7	180, 184, 187–89	6:14	57
10:7–8	19, 186–88, 190, 209	7:8	25, 27

Index of Ancient Sources 269

7:44	75	16	77
7:53	54	16:1	26
7:55–58	204	16:1–3	9, 23, 25–27
8:1	45	16:1–4	75
8:3	182	16:3	9, 18, 23–27, 64, 88
9:1–2	204	16:4	56, 64, 98
9:1–3	45	16:4–5	24
9:2	45	16:15	187
9:11	196	16:34	188
9:20–21	204	17	15
9:28–30	196	17:3	177
10	36–37, 47–49, 186	17:7	187
10–11	47	17:16–34	188
10:1	130	17:22	197
10:1–11:18	48	18:1–2	75
10:14	50, 182, 199	18:1–18	12
10:14–15	36	18:2	75
10:14–16	48	18:3	168
10:17	48	18:7	12, 75
10:28	48, 50, 129, 152, 199	18:7–8	187
10:28–29	48, 51	18:8	75
10:34–35	48, 51	18:11	169
10:45	27	18:12–13	204
11	37	18:13	56
11:8–18	36	18:18	9, 53, 56, 58, 67, 118, 169
11:9	49	18:24	75
11:12	49, 51	19:1	75
11:25	196	19:23	45
13:43	140	20:16	54
13:46	187	20:20–21	187
15	24, 41, 49, 56–57, 64, 84–85, 98–99, 199–200, 210	21	54, 56–57, 59–60, 63–66, 70, 72–73
15:1–2	64	21:4–5	64
15:1–16:5	90, 97	21:8	187
15:2	199	21:10–15	64
15:5	83, 199, 202	21:12–13	64
15:7	200	21:14	64
15:9	49, 51	21:16	187
15:10	199–201	21:17–26	7, 9, 13, 18, 23–24, 53–54, 57–60, 63–67, 70–73, 204, 210–11
15:10–11	25		
15:11	200		
15:19–20	49, 94	21:18–26	61
15:19–29	148	21:18–30	61
15:20	42, 46, 56, 99, 206	21:20	66, 196
15:22–16:4	57, 101	21:20–21	73, 81
15:22–16:5	97	21:20–26	60
15:23	24, 49	21:21	27, 57, 66
15:28	98	21:23	71
15:28–29	25, 94	21:23–24	53, 58, 67
15:29	42, 46, 99, 206	21:23–26	9, 70

21:23–27	67	6:14–15	17, 154–55
21:24	53–56, 60, 64, 68, 70–72, 160, 210	7	82
		7:9	156
21:25	24, 46, 56, 90, 94, 97–99, 206	7:11	156
21:26	53, 55	7:22	161
21:39	7, 34, 89, 196	7:25	161
22:3	7, 34, 45, 89, 143, 196, 198, 202–203	8:3–4	176
		8:7	161
22:12	66, 200	8:30	76
23:6	50, 55, 64–65, 130, 137, 196, 202	9–11	91
		9:1–4	1
23:31	75	9:3–5	169
24:5	45, 204	9:4–5	46, 80
24:14	45	9:5	169, 177
24:14–18	57, 64–65	9:24	76
24:18	210	10:2	55
24:22	45	10:10–12	31
24:23	75	10:12	63
25:8	57, 64–65	11:1	6, 177
26:4–5	196	11:12–15	82
26:5	55, 130, 137, 198	11:13	32, 34, 41, 89
26:11	204	11:25–27	82
26:23	177	11:28–29	80
28:17	57, 64–65	11:29	46, 80
28:22	45	12:1–15:13	207–208
28:30–31	188	12:13–14	191
		12:16	151, 169
Romans		13:9	82, 105
1:1	76	14	3, 8–9, 11, 35, 38–39, 41, 43, 89, 149
1:3	177		
1:3–4	177	14–15	16, 43
1:4	204	14:1–6	3–4, 6
1:16	187	14:1–15:1	174
1:18–3:20	91	14:1–15:6	211
2:12	155, 159	14:2	36–37, 42–43
2:17–29	74	14:3–4	35
2:25	74, 81	14:4–12	43
2:25–27	73, 81	14:10	35
2:25–29	6	14:13	35, 107
2:26	54	14:13–23	43
3:1–2	46, 80	14:14	6–8, 36–41, 94, 149
3:7–8	69, 114	14:15	36
3:30	73, 81	14:17	36–37
4:7	159	14:20	7–8, 36–37, 41–43, 149
4:9–12	81	14:21	36, 43
4:11–12	32, 73–74, 81	15:1	177
4:12	55	15:1–3	16, 169, 175, 179
4:15	155	15:1–13	87
4:16	74, 81	15:3	43, 169
5:6	168	15:7	35, 43, 169, 175, 179

15:7–9	43	7:2–6	86
15:7–13	43	7:2–8	85
15:8	73, 81, 169	7:5–7	87
15:9–12	43	7:7	86–87
15:12	169, 177	7:9	86
15:25	65	7:10	164
15:27	82	7:10–11	180
		7:10–16	85

1 Corinthians

1–4	17, 75	7:12–13	100
1:1	76	7:16	142, 163
1:9	76	7:17	76, 78–83, 87–88, 98–99, 163
1:12	75, 175	7:17–20	13, 19, 28, 75–76, 83–84, 98, 162, 205, 210, 212
1:18	167	7:17–24	13, 23, 33, 75–79, 81, 84–85, 87–88, 163, 205
1:18–25	17	7:17–27	83, 86
1:22	34, 154	7:18	76–77, 80–82, 84–85, 98, 100, 162
1:22–24	75		
1:23	159	7:18–20	83–84
1:24	34	7:19	6–7, 9, 16, 28, 30, 32, 78, 82–85, 88, 98, 162, 170
1:26	76		
1:26–29	168	7:19–20	79
2:1–5	17	7:20	76, 78–82, 98
2:16	175	7:21	84–85, 88
3:4–5	75	7:21–22	76
3:5–7	29, 45, 88	7:21–23	150
3:22	75	7:22	175
3:23	175	7:23	84
4:6	75	7:24	76, 79
4:10	168	7:27	85–86, 88
4:12	168	7:28	86
4:16–17	35	7:29–31	86
4:17	75	7:32–34	16
5	208	7:32–35	88
5–7	160	7:35	88
5–10	99	7:36	86
5:6–8	193	7:36–37	86
5:6–11	193	7:39	86
5:7	75	8	11, 14, 90–92, 108, 115,
5:9	90, 151–52	8–10	11–12, 16, 19, 43, 91–92, 100, 163, 174, 193, 209
5:9–10	142		
5:9–11	100	8:1	10
5:11	151–52, 193	8:1–13	104, 108
6:9–11	99	8:1–10:22	93
6:12	63	8:1–11:1	10, 14, 17, 19, 90–98, 100–101, 107–108, 111, 116, 120, 147, 151, 156, 158–60, 173, 193, 204
6:15	175		
7	28, 73, 77, 83, 86, 88, 98, 163, 204		
7–11	190	8:1–11:34	142
7:1	10, 85	8:4	103
7:1–39	85		

8:4–8	10		152, 159–60, 162–63, 166–71, 173–74, 176, 178, 182, 190, 192–94, 205, 208–11
8:6	103		
8:7	168		
8:7–8	10	9:20	2–3, 5–9, 11, 13–14, 16–17, 59, 150, 153–58, 161–62, 165, 170, 187, 194, 196, 201–204, 209
8:7–10	174		
8:7–11	167		
8:7–13	43		
8:9	92, 104, 108	9:20–21	1, 6, 12, 17, 75, 111–13, 151–52, 155, 163
8:9–10	168		
8:9–12	10	9:20–22	174
8:9–13	174	9:21	11, 19, 147, 149–50, 154, 156, 159–65, 170, 190, 204–207, 210, 212
8:10	92–93		
8:12–13	175		
8:13	91, 104, 107–108, 147, 174, 208	9:21–22	177
		9:22	6, 15, 111, 131, 133, 150, 163, 167, 168, 169, 174, 193
9	27, 59, 71, 90–91, 107–108, 115, 132, 150, 154, 174, 180, 188–90, 192–93, 205, 210		
		9:23	70, 112, 167
		9:24–27	108, 174
9–10	160	9:27	16, 112, 190
9:1	108, 150, 181, 189	10	11, 14, 90–92, 108, 115, 174
9:1–18	16, 150	10:1–13	167
9:1–23	43	10:1–22	90
9:2	189	10:1–11:1	108
9:3	107	10:7	103
9:4	189, 193	10:8	103
9:5	75, 189	10:13	92
9:6	189	10:14–22	43
9:7	189, 194	10:18	8, 75, 119, 202–203
9:8–9	115, 154, 161–62, 205	10:19–20	10, 94
9:9	194	10:20	103
9:9–11	205	10:21	93
9:10	194	10:22	92
9:11	189	10:23–30	11
9:12	108, 189	10:23–33	147
9:13	119, 189, 194, 203	10:23–11:1	93
9:14	19, 75, 115, 163–64, 180, 184, 187–89, 205, 209	10:25	10–11, 93–94
		10:25–27	43
9:14–15	161, 205	10:25–30	205–206
9:16	189	10:26	94, 103
9:17	189	10:27	10–11, 16, 19, 93, 95–96, 101, 183–84, 188–90, 193, 209
9:18	189–90		
9:19	16, 108, 150–51, 158, 169–70, 174, 181	10:27–28	95
		10:27–29	10, 101
9:19–22	142, 151, 153, 162, 165–68, 173–74, 207	10:27–30	188
		10:28	95, 190
9:19–23	1–11, 13–19, 21, 23, 27, 30, 35, 43–44, 49, 53, 59, 66–68, 72–73, 75, 88, 90, 108–16, 118–20, 123, 130–32, 135, 137, 142–43, 147, 149–50,	10:28–29	43, 96
		10:28–11:1	43
		10:29	96
		10:29–30	96
		10:30	94

10:31	43, 174, 193	3	29
10:31–33	147, 175	3:6–11	29, 45
10:31–11:1	142, 193	3:8	29
10:32	4, 8, 33–34, 75, 104, 108, 154, 159, 174	3:9	29
		3:11	29
10:32–33	16, 120, 151, 159–60, 173–74, 176, 207	3:16	4
		4	69, 114
10:32–11:1	19, 173, 176, 205, 209, 174–75	4:1–2	13
10:33		4:2	69, 114
10:33–11:1	174	4:3	114
11	180	4:4	114
11:1	12, 14, 16, 35, 43, 91, 147–49, 164–65, 169, 173–76, 179, 181, 193, 205, 208	5:9	16
		5:16	179
		5:17	28
		5:21	176
11:1–16	31	6:10	168–69, 178
11:2	174	8:9	168–69, 175–76, 178–79
11:2–3	174	10:1	179, 207
11:2–16	86	10:5	70
11:11–15	43	10:7	175
11:14	31	11	204
11:20–32	193	11:7	169
11:23	180	11:22	6, 177
11:23–25	180	11:24	155, 187, 204
11:33–34	193	11:30	168
12–14	91	12:5	168
12:4–5	76	12:9–10	168
12:13	8–9, 30, 34, 75, 154	12:11	29, 45
12:27	175	12:16	69, 114
12:28–31	76	13:4	168
14	160	13:9	168
14:34	31		
14:37	82	*Galatians*	
15:3	180	1:10	6, 151
15:5	75	1:11–12	179
15:21–22	156	1:13	4, 44–45, 114, 182
15:22	177	1:13–14	6, 8, 44–45, 55, 89
15:23	175	1:14	45, 50, 137, 158, 195–96
15:35–44	88	1:15	76
15:44–49	156	1:23	182
15:45	177	2	47, 50, 53, 99
15:51–52	156	2:1–10	75
15:56	156–58	2:3	27, 32, 34, 89
16:1	75	2:6	99
16:3	75	2:7	73, 75
16:8	75	2:7–9	73, 81
16:10	75	2:11	60
16:12	75	2:11–14	3–6, 46, 49, 59, 66, 68, 99, 102, 123, 126, 128–29, 187, 196, 198–99
2 Corinthians			
1:19	204		

2:11–18	129–30, 187, 196	4:32–5:1	175
2:12	32, 34, 46–47, 89	5:1–2	179
2:13	69	5:22–24	31
2:14	9, 32, 34, 46–47, 50–53, 89	5:25	179
2:14–15	6	6:2	82
2:15	3, 8, 31, 50, 121, 160, 178, 183		

Philippians

2:15–20	7	2:5–8	175–76, 180
2:16	72	2:5–11	179
2:18	114	2:7	176–77
2:20	178, 204	2:9–11	177
3	30	2:12	167
3:10	155	3	204
3:13	155	3:2–11	1, 6
3:13–14	176	3:2–14	45
3:23	155	3:3	73, 81
3:23–26	17	3:5	25, 45, 88, 130, 137, 157, 170, 194, 196, 203
3:28	4–9, 28, 30–32, 75, 85, 88		
4:4	155	3:5–8	6, 45, 198, 202
4:4–5	17, 176–77, 180	3:7	45
4:5	155	3:8	7, 44–45, 89
4:9	78	3:9	45
4:12	7, 178		
4:12–14	191	*Colossians*	
4:14	146	2:14	98
4:21	155, 158	3:11	30, 73, 75, 81
5	77	3:18	31
5:2–12	28	4:10	82
5:3	13, 23, 72–74, 81, 84, 154	4:11	73, 81
5:6	6–7, 28, 30, 32, 78, 84, 88	4:10–11	32, 34, 89
5:13–6:10	163		
5:14	105	*1 Thessalonians*	
5:18	155	1:9	99
5:19–21	99	2:3	13
5:23	99	2:14–16	52
5:25	55		
6:1	206	*1 Timothy*	
6:1–2	207	2:12	31
6:1–5	163, 206–207	6:14	82
6:2	163–65, 206–207		
6:5	207	*2 Timothy*	
6:12–16	28	1:5	26, 75
6:13	54	2:8	177
6:15	4, 6–7, 28, 30, 32, 78, 84, 88	3:15	26

Ephesians

Titus

1:20–21	177	1:14	82
2:11	33–34, 73, 81, 89		
2:11–22	33	*Hebrews*	
2:15	33, 82, 98	1:3–4	177

13:2	146	*2 John*	
13:3	146	10–11	181
James		*Revelation*	
2:10	72, 74, 83, 154	1:4–8	177
		2:14–15	97
1 Peter		2:19–20	97
2:5	79	12:17	82
2:9	79	14:12	82
3:1	165	22:16	177

NT Apocrypha

Gospel of Thomas
14   185

Philo

Abr.		156	187
56	79		
98	79	*Mos.*	
107–108	142, 144, 191	1.149	79, 137
107–115	142, 146	2.27	134
113	143	2.36	134
115	142, 144, 191	2.43–44	134
118	142, 144, 191		
		Plant.	
Cher.		54–60	79
15	132, 135		
		Praem.	
Decal.		114	79
52	134	152	134
76–79	134		
81	134	*Prob.*	
		26	129
Ebr.		141	129
177	129		
217–19	129	*Prov.*	
		2.58	129
Ios.			
34	112	*QE*	
85–87	137	2.42	79
Legat.		*QG*	
3	79	4	134

4.8–10	142
4.10	146
4.45	135
4.69	131–35
4.204	135

Spec.
1.1–10	73
1.51	134
1.97	79
1.153	187
1.186	181
1.247–54	118
1.307–308	169
1.309	134
1.319–23	134, 141
2.163–67	79
2.168	79
4.73–74	169

Virt.
90–91	169
102	134
175	134
178	134
179	134
181–82	134

Josephus

Ag. Ap.
2.144	181
2.149	199
2.175	181
2.187	181, 199
2.210	153
2.227–28	199

Ant.
1.14	181, 199
1.161–68	135
1.196–200	142–43, 146
4.231–37	169
4.233	205
4.276	106
4.309	199
5.132	199
8.21	199
8.115–17	137
8.120	83
8.395	83
11.121	161
11.124	161
11.130	161
12.145	54
12.240–41	81
13.257–58	73
13.288–99	119, 125
13.296–99	158, 195, 198–99
13.298	119
13.318	73
13.400–15	119
13.408	198
13.408–409	199
13.423	199
14.245	187
14.261	100
17.41	198, 203
17.159	83
18.21	124
18.345	199
20.17–96	137
20.23	186
20.38–46	181
20.201	181, 198

J. W.
1.108–12	199
1.110	181, 198, 203
1.229	54
2.119	181
2.129–31	124
2.138	124
2.142	139
2.143	124
2.162	198
2.262	199
7.45	137

Life
191	198
198	198

Dead Sea Scrolls

1Q28^a		*4Q271*	
2.3–10	124	3.7–15	105–106
1Q33		*4Q285*	
7.4–6	124	8.9	105
1QH^a		*4Q367*	
7.15	105, 107	2.13	104
1QS		*4Q372*	
2.12–17	105	8.7	105
5.13	124		
6.17–21	124	*4Q415*	
7.2–21	124	11.6–7	105–106
8.22–24	124		
		4Q418	
4Q266 fr. 5		167.6–7	105
1.15	139		
		4Q430	
4Q269		1.3	105, 107
9.1–3	105		
9.4–8	105	*11Q14*	
		2.13	105
4Q270			
5.14–17	105	*CD*	
5.17–21	105	15.14–15	124

Targumic Texts

Tg. Onq.		*Tg. Ps.–J.*	
Gen 12.5	135	Deut 27.18	106
Frg. Tg.			
Lev 19.14	106		

Mishnah

Avodah Zarah		*Hullin*	
2.3	36	2.8	95
4.4–5	103	7	38

Yadayim
4.6–7   119

Yoma
8.5–6   102

Zevahim
1.1   95

Tosefta

Avodah Zarah
5.5   103

Berakhot
2.21   143, 192
4.1   103

Hullin
2.18   95

Sotah
22b   201

Babylonian Talmud

Bava Metzi'a
86b   192

Derekh Eretz Rabbah
7.7   143, 191

Hullin
96–100   38

Nedarim
62b   106

81b   106

Pesahim
22b   106
50b–51a   106

Qiddushin
66a   125

Yoma
82a   102

Jerusalem Talmud

Berakhot
8   106
12a   106
67a   201

Sotah
5.5   197

Midrash

Gen. Rab.
48.14   143, 192

Exod. Rab.
42.5   143
47.5   192

Lev. Rab.
34.8   192

Num. Rab.
10.5   144
10.6   192

Eccl. Rab.
3.14   192

Pesiq. Rab Kah.
4.7   39

Sifre
Deut 32.2   135

Early Christian Literature

1 Clement
16.17   207

Aristides
Apol. 2.1   33

Augustine
Epist.
40.4   193
82   193

Op. mon.
11(12)   160, 163, 205

Chrysostom
Hom.
1 Cor 9.13   69

Sac.
1.8   69

Clement of Alexandria
Strom.
6.5.41   33

Didache
13.1–2   185

Irenaeus
Haer.
1.6.3   97
1.24.5   97
1.28.2   97

Jerome
Comm.
Isa. 9.1   200

Epist.
82   60
112   59–60

John of Damascus
De Fide
3.17   178

C. Jacob.
52.41–43   178

Justin Martyr
Dial.
122.5   139

Origen
Fr. 1 Cor.
43.513.14   153

Classical Authors

Antisthenes
Scholium on Od.
1.1   111

Cassius Dio
Hist.
57.18.5a   137

Cicero
Off.
3.50–53   135

Verr.
2.1.39.101   121

Dio Chrysostom
Or.
4.98   121
14.14   121

Diodorus Siculus
Bib. Hist.
34.1.2   127

Lucian
Men.
11   121

Philostratus
Vit. Apoll.
5.33   127

Plutarch
Alc.
23.4–6   112

Mor.
96F–97   121
236C   112

Tacitus
Hist.
5.5.2   127

Theophrastus
Char.
6   121

Virgil
Georg.
4.407–13   112

Index of Modern Authors

Adams, Dwayne H. 121–22, 169, 188, 208
Adna, J. 181
Akenson, Donald H. 84
Allcock, P. J. 76
Allison, Dale C. 137, 145, 188–89
Alon, Gedalyahu 116–19
Apisdorf, Shimon 130
Ariel, Yaakov 212
Arterbury, Andrew E. 129, 144, 146–47, 190
Aune, David E. 93

Back, Peter 59
Badcock, Gary D. 77
Bakhos, Carol 26
Balch, David L. 57
Bamberger, Bernard 139
Bammel, Ernst 72, 164
Barclay, John M. G. 6, 87, 89, 115, 129–30, 155, 211–12
Barnett, Paul 204
Barrett, C. K. 6, 10–11, 23, 27, 59, 65, 70–71, 79–80, 92, 96–97, 101, 108–9, 114, 151, 166–67, 173, 204, 210
Bartchy, Scott 85, 121, 182, 191
Barth, Karl 78
Barth, Markus 33
Barton, Stephen 112, 167–68, 173–74
Bauckham, Richard 47–48, 51, 56, 61–62, 97, 125
Bauer, Bruno 65
Baumgarten, Albert I. 118, 124–25, 195
Baumgarten, Joseph M. 105, 119, 195
Baur, F. C. 64–66, 69
Beardslee, W. A. 77
Beare, F. W. 179
Beaton, Richard 201, 207
Beck, James R. 31
Bernheim, Pierre-Antoine 47

Bertram, G. 54
Betz, H. D. 46–47, 146, 155, 179
Bieringer, Reimund 12, 14, 83, 161
Bilde, Per 80
Billerbeck, P. 53
Binyamin A. S. 52
Bird, Michael F. 80, 122, 136–37, 139
Black, David A. 167
Blass, F. 55
Blomberg, Craig L. 31, 58–59, 61, 96, 153, 167
Bock, Darrell L. 58
Bockmuehl, Markus 17, 24, 47, 83, 118, 143, 158, 177–78, 181, 210–211
Booth, Roger P. 30
Borgen, Peder 80, 136
Boring, M. Eugene 58
Bornkamm, Günther 26–27, 59, 98, 151, 192, 205
Borse, U. 155
Bourquin, Y. 61
Bouwman, Gilbert 64, 163
Bowden, John 47, 67, 77
Boyarin, Daniel 28, 30–31, 211–12
Brandon, S. G. F. 60
Braxton, Brad R. 76, 79–81, 87, 211
Brett, Mark G. 211
Breuer, Edward 79
Brodie, Thomas L. 161
Bruce, F. F. 24–25, 28, 36, 48, 55, 58, 70, 72, 96, 111, 157, 181, 185, 206
Brumberg-Kraus, Jonathan D. 140–141, 202
Brunt, John C. 97–98
Bryan, Christopher 25–27
Buchanan, George W. 87
Buell, Denise K. 32
Bultmann, Rudolf 131, 179
Burn, Geoffrey 185
Burridge, Richard A. 183

Burton, E. de W. 155
Butarbutar, Robinson 91, 166
Buttrick, G. 96

Cadbury, Henry J. 58
Calvert, Nancy L. 146
Calvin, John 77, 154
Campbell, Douglas A. 30–31
Campbell, William S. 29, 33, 35, 46, 75, 78, 178, 211
Carleton Paget, James 136, 139–40
Carmichael, Calum 136
Carras, George P. 57, 200
Carson, D. A. 5, 71, 89, 120, 164–65, 167
Cartwright, Michael G. 87
Casey, M. 42
Catchpole, David R. 7, 97, 184
Chadwick, Henry 15, 111, 130–134, 193
Chancey, Mark A. 186
Charlesworth, James H. 124, 128, 145, 194–95
Chepey, Stuart D. 53, 55–56, 67, 118
Cheung, Alex T. 92–97, 99–100, 104, 107–8
Chilton, Bruce D. 38, 47–48, 53, 117, 180, 186
Ciampa, Roy E. 8–9, 59, 76, 82–83, 86, 88, 153
Clarke, F. 60
Cohen, Martin Samuel 191
Cohen, Philip 212
Cohen, Shaye J. D. 26, 74, 81, 122, 137–38, 199
Collins, John J. 104–5, 127, 145
Collins, Raymond F. 28, 79, 83, 86, 98, 154, 156, 173
Conzelmann, Hans 28, 65, 75, 79–80, 92, 95, 97–98, 108, 153, 162, 164, 166, 192
Coppins, Wayne 150, 162
Corley, Kathleen E. 121
Cosgrove, Charles H. 1, 30, 47
Cowen, Ida 203
Craig, C. T. 96
Cranfield, C. E. B. 42, 80, 154
Crombie, Frederick 59
Crossley, James G. 36, 42, 47, 51, 117–18, 127, 130, 183, 187, 205
Culy, Martin M. 55

Dahl, N. A. 179
Das, A. Andrew 36
Daube, David 72, 130–131, 135–37, 142, 165–67, 192
Dauermann, Stuart 80
Davies, Rupert 77
Davies, W. D. 55, 58, 84, 87, 137, 169
Davila, James R. 145
Dawes, Gregory W. 76, 79, 85, 88
De Boer, Willis P. 173, 175
Dean, Lester 204
Deidun, T. J. 161
Deines, Roland 117–18, 120, 195
Deming, Will 86
Dibelius, Martin 48
Dickson, John P. 100, 136–37, 140, 142, 173, 183
Dickson, William P. 59
Dietmar Neufeld 121
Diffenderfer, Margaret 57
Diprose, Ronald E. 34
Dodd, Brian J. 111, 175, 179
Dodd, C. H. 164
Donaldson, Terence L. 141
Drazin, Michael 13
Dungan, David L. 205
Dunn, James D. G. 2, 6, 10–11, 24, 28, 30, 44–45, 50–53, 58, 61–62, 73–74, 81, 89, 96, 112, 121–22, 124, 129–30, 155, 157, 161, 164, 169, 180, 183, 186–87, 195–96, 198–99, 211–12
Dutch, Robert S. 108

Ebeling, Gerhard 12, 47, 167
Edwards, Thomas C. 159
Ehrensperger, Kathy 32, 35, 37, 42, 44, 211
Eisenbaum, Pamela 30–32, 120, 211
Ellicott, Charles J. 58, 153
Ellison, H. L. 55, 81
Emden, Jacob 77
Emerson, R. W. 70
Engberg-Pedersen, Troels 113
Esler, Philip F. 6, 46, 66, 125, 128–30, 200
Evans, Craig A. 47, 53, 180, 183–84

Falk, Harvey 77

Fee, Gordon D. 10, 12, 59, 76, 80, 86, 92, 101, 109, 150, 153, 166–67, 173–74, 205
Feldman, Louis H. 106, 136, 140
Fellows, Richard G. 27, 75
Findlay, G. G. 153
Finger, Reta H. 191
Finley, M. 100
Fishkoff, Sue 141–42, 197
Fitzgerald, John T. 74, 161
Fitzmyer, Joseph A. 46, 58, 76
Fjärstedt, Biörn 188–89
Ford, David F. 163
Forst, Binyomin 39
Fortna, Robert T. 5, 102
Fotopoulos, John 91–95, 99–100, 173
Frankovic, Joseph 87
Fraser, John W. 154
Fredriksen, Paula 30, 35, 211
Freed, Edwin D. 153
Friedlaender, Graetz 139
Friedman, Hershey H. 106
Fuglseth, Kare 132
Fung, R. Y. K. 46
Furnish, Victor P. 153, 164, 179, 190, 207
Furstenberg, Yair 38

Galloway, Lincoln E. 150
Gane, Roy E. 54
Ganser-Kerperin, Heiner 56
Gardner, P. D. 151, 153, 160, 166–67, 174
Garland, David E. 85–86, 91, 95–97, 100, 108, 155, 162, 165, 167–68, 173–76, 178, 204
Garlington, Donald B. 163, 206–7
Gasque, Ward W. 55, 60
Gaston, Lloyd 154
Gaventa, Beverly R. 5, 102, 178
Gempf, Conrad H. 24
Georgi, Dieter 136
Given, Mark D. 14, 16, 114, 151–52
Glad, Clarence E. 110, 113, 115, 151–52, 160, 164–65, 167, 191, 207–8
Glaser, Mitch L. 212
Gloag, Paton J. 58
Godet, F. L. 59, 153–54, 167
Goldman, E. A. 48
Gooch, Paul W. 3, 59, 89, 120, 150, 166, 176, 182–84, 186, 208
Gooch, Peter D. 92, 100, 204

Goodman, David 144
Goodman, Martin 26, 136–41, 166
Gowler, David B. 55
Graetz, H. 139
Green, David 12
Green, Joel B. 117, 121
Greenberg, Blu 130
Grenholm, Cristina 80
Grosheide, F. W. 59
Grosvenor, Mary 55
Guelich, Robert A. 111, 182
Guhrt, J. 104
Gundry-Volf, Judith M. 31–32, 80, 178
Guttmann, Alexander 52

Haas, Peter 122
Haase, W. 80
Hackett, Moratio B. 58
Haenchen, Ernst 26, 65–67
Hafemann, Scott 29, 87, 169
Hall, Barbara 5–6, 163, 173–74, 205
Hannah, Darrell D. 153
Hansen, Bruce 75
Hanstein, Peter 184
Hardin, Justin K. 78, 211
Harink, Douglas 84, 87, 211
Harnack, Adolf von 33, 63, 80–83, 138, 207
Harrington, Hannah K. 49, 117–18, 120, 123–25
Harris, J. Rendel 132–33
Harvey, Anthony E. 156, 204–5
Hatlem, Doug J. 205
Hatlem, Jodie Boyer 205
Hay, David M. 132
Hayes, Christine E. 49, 125, 164
Hays, Richard B. 7, 59, 80, 96, 108, 160, 164–65, 167–68, 173–74, 178
Heath, J. M. F. 158
Heathcote, A. W. 76
Hecht, Richard D. 105
Heckel, Ulrich 49
Heinrici, G. 153
Hellholm, David 145
Hemer, Colin J. 23–24, 58, 66
Hengel, Martin 49, 58, 73, 195
Héring, Jean 76
Heydenreich, August L. C. 150, 158–59, 194
Hilary, Mbachu 199

Hilgert, Earle 132
Hill, Craig C. 58, 68
Himmelfarb, Martha 79
Hodge, Caroline J. 29, 32, 47, 113, 154, 211
Hodge, Charles 59, 154
Hoffmann, Paul 184
Hogan, Pauline Nigh 31
Holladay, Carl R. 74, 81
Hollander, Harm W. 156
Holleman, J. 156
Holmberg, Bengt 84
Holmén, Tom 148
Holtz, Gudrun 85
Holtz, Traugott 180
Hong, I.-G. 155, 157
Hooker, Morna D. 122, 153, 176–79
Hoppe, Leslie 103
Horbury, William 87, 117, 132
Horn, Friedrich W. 58
Horrell, David G. 7–8, 12, 14, 28, 46–47, 89, 91–92, 164–65, 167, 173–76, 205
Horsley, Richard A. 30, 153, 173, 180
House, Colin 36–37
Hove, Richard W. 32
Howard, George 87
Hübner, Hans 154
Humphrey, Alex 60
Hurd, John C. 92, 97, 173, 204, 207
Hurtado, Larry W. 183
Huttunen, Niko 83, 110
Hvalvik, Reidar 97

Instone-Brewer, David 104, 205
Isenberg, M. 94

Jackson, F. J. Foakes 58, 63–64
Jellinek, A. 139
Jenkins, Claude 153
Jervell, Jacob 55, 57
Jewett, Robert 90
Johns, Loren L. 194–95
Johnson, Alan F. 77–79
Jones, F. S. 96, 150
Joseph, M. J. 166

Keck, Leander E. 27
Keener, Craig S. 40, 165–66
Kelley, Robert L. 191

Kim, Seyoon 11–12, 14, 147–49, 165, 169–70, 173–74, 176, 180, 208
Kinzer, Mark S. 17, 33, 37, 42, 48, 84, 87, 204, 211
Kistemaker, S. J. 59, 154, 167
Klawans, Jonathan 30, 125, 181
Klingbeil, Gerald A. 7
Kloppenborg, John S. 184
Knight, Harold 166
Knox, Wilfred L. 13, 57, 84
Koenig, John 188, 193
Koet, Bart J. 12, 56, 75, 118
Kohn, Rachel L. E. 212
Kraemer, David C. 130
Kratz, R. 54
Krause, Richard 59
Kreitzer, L. Joseph 87
Krentz, Edgar 162
Kruse, Colin G. 87
Kuck, David W. 86
Kurz, William S. 173

Ladd, George E. 111
Lake, Kirsopp 58, 63–64
Lambdin, T. O. 185
Lang, Friedrich 59
Lauer, S. 195
Laufen, Rudolf 184
Layton, Bentley 185
Le Cornu, Hilary 67, 191, 211
Leitch, J. W. 28
Levertoff, Paul P. 57
Levine, L. 186
Levinskaya, Irina 24, 26, 138–39
Lichtenstein, Yechiel Tzvi 37
Liddell, H. 198
Liebman, Charles S. 196
Lietzmann, H. 108, 167
Lieu, Judith 33, 138, 185
Lightfoot, John 157, 194–95
Limburg, James 65
Linafelt, Tod 2
Lincoln, Andrew T. 33
Lindars, Barnabas 49
Lindemann, Andreas 28
Loader, William R. G. 182
Longenecker, Bruce W. 1
Longenecker, Richard N. 1, 58, 155–56, 169
Louw, Johannes P. 54

Lovering, Eugene H. 38, 57, 121, 153, 164
Lowenstein, Steven M. 203
Lüdemann, Gerd 23, 58, 66–67
Ludlam, Ruth 199
Lull, David J. 121
Lumby, J. Rawson 58
Luther, Martin 25, 77–79

Maccoby, Hyam 117
Mack, Burton L. 184
Maddox, R. 58
Magnus Zetterholm 46, 84, 103, 129, 211
Mahnke, Allan W. 195
Malherbe, Abraham J. 74, 111–12, 161
Marcus, Joel 33, 74
Marcus, Ralph 132–34
Margolese, Faranak 197, 207, 212
Marguerat, Daniel 61, 200
Marshall, Bruce D. 178
Marshall, I. Howard 58, 68, 169, 184, 190
Marshall, Peter 110–113
Martin, Brice L. 58
Martin, Dale B. 112–13, 168
Martin, Ralph P. 55, 60, 175, 179, 207
Martin, Troy W. 31
Martyn, J. Louis 27–28, 30, 33, 89, 102, 155, 161, 163–65
Mason, Steve 106
Mattill, Andrew J. 60–62
McHugh, John 49
McKnight, Scot 121, 136–37, 140
Meeks, Wayne A. 29, 202
Meggitt, Justin J. 100
Menzies, Allan 64
Merk, Otto 179
Merklein, Helmut 92
Metzger, Bruce M. 153
Meyer, H. A. W. 58, 153, 167
Milikowsky, Chaim 117
Miller, Chris A. 27, 48, 55–57, 72
Miller, Robert J. 184
Minear, Paul 188
Mitchell, Margaret M. 91–92, 112–15, 151, 153
Mitternacht, Dieter 74
Moffatt, James 33, 59, 167
Mohrlang, Roger 201
Moo, Douglas J. 154, 161
Mor, Menachem 137, 140

Morris, Leon 9, 59, 167
Moshe, Beth 13
Moule, C. F. D. 154
Muldowney, Mary S. 77, 160, 163
Munck, Johannes 60, 139
Murphy-O'Connor, Jerome 46, 92

Nanos, Mark D. 14–15, 17, 30–31, 35–36, 38, 45–47, 51, 75–76, 84, 87, 100, 129, 154, 167, 211
Neale, David A. 122
Neirynck, F. 189
Neller, Kenneth V. 151, 153, 166–68, 173–74, 207
Neufeld, Dietmar 121, 191
Neusner, Jacob 48, 53, 65, 67, 102, 116–20, 122–23, 143, 192, 195, 198
Newman, Hillel 199
Newport, K. G. C. 201
Newton, Derek 96, 119, 173
Neyrey, Jerome H. 123
Nicoll, W. R. 153
Nida, Eugene A. 54
Niehoff, Maren R. 26
Noble, Bernard 26
Nolland, John L. 186

Oakes, Peter 47, 200
O'Brien, Peter T. 150, 166–67, 173
Ochs, Peter 87
Oepke, A. 155
Olsson, Birger 129
Oppenheimer, Aharon 122
Orr, William F. 76, 173
Orton, David E. 48
Ottenheijm, Eric 38, 120, 149
Overbeck, Franz 65

Parsons, Mikeal C. 55
Passamaneck, S. M. 100
Patte, Daniel 80
Pearson, Birger A. 138
Pearson, Brook W. R. 44
Peder Borgen 80, 102, 132, 136
Peerbolte, L. J. Lietaert 195
Perrin, Norman 122
Pesch, Rudolf 58
Peterson, David 58
Petit, Françoise 132–33, 135
Phua, Richard L. 158–59, 194

Pickup, Martin 48
Piekarski, Chana 142
Plummer, Alfred 59, 153, 167
Plummer, Robert L. 173–74
Poirier, John C. 87, 118, 182
Polhill, John B. 58
Pollefeyt, Didier 14
Poorthuis, M. 38, 56, 118
Porter, Stanley E. 14, 44, 58, 61–62, 68, 71–72, 75
Potok, Chaim 52
Primack, Karen 203
Prior, David 59

Rader, William 33
Räisänen, Heikki 2, 48, 58, 64, 72, 154
Rasmussen, Carl C. 79
Regev, Eyal 118, 187, 196
Richards, Kent H. 105
Richardson, Alan 77
Richardson, Peter 3, 34, 49, 59, 66, 68, 89, 120, 158–59, 163, 166, 176, 182–84, 186, 194, 204, 207
Ridderbos, H. N. 155
Riesner, Rainer 136, 181
Rietveld, John N. 59, 150
Robertson, Archibald 59, 153, 167
Rode, Daniel 7, 166, 173
Roloff, Jürgen 58, 68
Rosenblum, Jordan D. 40, 191
Rosner, Brian S. 8–9, 59, 86, 104
Ross, James R. 203
Rowland, Christopher 58
Royse, James R. 134
Rubin, Scott 203
Rudolph, David J. 17, 33, 35, 42, 47, 75, 148, 212
Ruef, John 95
Runesson, Anders 84, 211
Ryan, T. J. 202

Safrai, Ch. 56
Saldarini, Anthony J. 194–96, 199
Salo, Kalervo 182
Sampley, J. Paul 110
Sandelin, Karl-Gustav 93
Sanders, Jack 55
Schaper, Joachim L. W. 117–19, 199
Schick, Moses 52
Schiffman, Lawrence H. 105, 186

Schlatter, Adolf 57, 75
Schlier, H. 155
Schlueter, Carol J. 52
Schmidt, F. 145
Schmithals, Walter 58, 68, 90
Schnabel, Eckhard J. 47, 165, 186, 190
Schneider, Sebastian 156
Schoeps, H. J. 166, 192
Scholem, Gershom G. 71
Schrage, Wolfgang 8, 75, 78–79, 92, 150, 153, 160, 163–64, 166–67, 173–74, 179, 192
Schreiner, Thomas R. 58, 161
Schulz, Siegfried 179, 184
Schürer, Emil 202
Schwartz, Baruch J. 54
Schwartz, Daniel R. 40, 195
Schwartz, J. 38, 118
Schwegler, Albert 65
Schwiebert, Jonathan 193
Scott, R. 198
Sechrest, Love L. 33, 89, 203, 211
Segal, Alan F. 140
Segovia, Fernando F. 173
Seland, Torrey 55
Sellin, Gerhard 90
Sellow, P. 184
Shen, Michael Li-Tak 108, 173, 204
Shinn, Gerald 26
Shogren, Gary S. 36–37
Shulam, Joseph 67, 191
Shutt, R. J. H. 128
Sibinga, Joost Smit 91
Sievers, Joseph 80, 194
Sigal, Gerald 13
Simon, Marcel 98
Skarsaune, Oskar 47, 97
Skarsten, Roald 132
Slee, Michelle 46
Sloyan, Gerard 157, 194, 204
Smiles, Vincent M. 55
Smit, Joop 92, 97, 103
Smith, Dennis E. 121–22
Smith, Morton 71
Soulen, R. Kendall 25, 34–35, 178
Spencer, F. Scott 24–25
Spitaler, Peter 46
Stalker, D. 98
Stanford, W. B. 111
Stanley, Christopher D. 32

Stanton, Graham 163, 165
Steely, J. E. 90
Steffek, E. 61
Stegemann, Wolfgang 56
Stemberger, Günter 143, 195, 198
Sterling, Gregory E. 104–5, 181
Stern, Menachem 127
Stolle, Volker 53
Stone, Michael E. 145
Stott, John R. W. 58
Stowers, Stanley K. 159–60
Strack, H. 53
Stroeter, Ernst F. 77
Sullivan, Kevin P. 146
Sumney, Jerry L. 153, 164, 174
Sweet, John 87

Tait, Michael 47, 200
Taylor, Justin 46, 58, 99
Temporini, H. 80
Terry, R. B. 98
Thackeray, H. St. J. 106
Theissen, Gerd 92, 168
Thielman, Frank 16, 58, 82–83, 154, 161–62, 167
Thiselton, Anthony C. 8–9, 28, 59, 78, 86, 150, 153, 160, 164, 166, 168, 173
Thompson, Michael B. 179, 207–8
Tigay, Jeffrey H. 106
Tobin, Diane K. 203
Tobin, Gary A. 203
Tomes, Roger 58, 65
Tomson, Peter J. 13–14, 17, 26, 28, 36, 42, 49, 73, 75, 83–84, 94–98, 103–4, 129, 143, 151, 153, 205, 211
Toney, Carl N. 16, 43
Trobisch, David 62–63, 68
Tucker, J. Brian 17, 34–35, 75, 84, 178, 193, 211
Tuckett, Christopher M. 7, 58, 183–84, 189
Turner, Seth 87
Tyson, Joseph B. 48

Uro, Risto 184

Van der Horst, Pieter W. 105
Vanhoye, A. 189
Verheyden, J. 57, 143
Vermes, Geza 202

Vlach, Michael J. 33
Vlachos, Chris A. 156–58
Vollenweider, Samuel 112, 165, 192

Wahlen, Clinton 36–37, 48
Walker, Donald D. 207
Walker, William O. 73
Walther, James A. 76, 173
Wansbrough, Henry 180
Watson, Francis 13, 36, 154
Wedderburn, Alexander 183
Weinstein, Sara E. 197
Weiss, Johannes 90–92, 181
Wenham, David 179–80, 190, 207
Westerholm, Stephen 154, 156
Whitaker, G. H. 135
White, Carolline 193
Wilder, William N. 155
Wiles, Maurice F. 49
Wilkinson, J. R. 63
Williams, Sam K. 47
Willis, Wendell 91, 108, 174
Willitts, Joel 76–77, 211
Wilson, Todd A. 58, 68, 155, 163–65, 211
Wimbush, Vincent L. 86
Winger, Michael 160–161, 164
Wingren, Gustaf 79
Winston, David 80
Winston, Hella 197
Winter, Bruce W. 24, 80–81, 84, 100, 193
Witherington III, Ben 24, 37, 58, 68, 92, 95, 108, 160, 164, 167
Wolff, Christian 173
Wright, David F. 33
Wright, N. T. 103, 169
Wyschogrod, Michael 25, 56, 200, 212

Yeo, Khiok-Khng 90–92
Yoder, John Howard 87
Young, Brad H. 159

Zaas, Peter S. 48, 100
Zeller, Eduard 65
Zemer, Moshe 102
Zerwick, Max 55
Zetterholm, Magnus 47–48, 87, 95, 100, 103, 128–29, 211
Ziesler, J. A. 36
Zoccali, Christopher 29, 33, 44, 46, 21

Subject Index

Abraham 4, 52, 135, 142–46, 192
Adiaphora 44
Angels 106–7, 142–44, 146, 192
Anti-Circumcision Language 30
Antioch 3, 46, 58, 87, 95, 99–100, 129–30, 187–88, 196, 199
Apostasy 6, 57, 62, 72, 140, 204
Apostolic Decree 25–27, 43, 49, 56–57, 60, 64, 90, 97–101, 108, 148
Aquilla 75
Assimilation 80–81, 115, 137, 140
Association 16, 37, 41–43, 48, 50, 89, 95, 115, 121, 149, 151–52, 160, 165, 170, 187, 191, 204, 206–7
Augustine 60, 76–77, 160, 162–63, 193, 205

Banquet 96, 127–28, 169, 193
Barnabas 47, 101, 115, 188
Basilidians 97
Blessings 28, 31–32, 82, 85–87, 98, 105, 178, 182, 201
Blind 104–6, 134, 169, 208
Blood 42, 56
Boundaries 2, 34, 64, 74, 88, 108, 121–22, 137, 145, 206
Boundary Markers 202, 212
Burdens 120, 163, 197–201, 206–7

Calling 1, 53, 55, 57, 59, 61, 63, 65, 67, 69, 71, 73, 75–88, 98, 122, 162, 169, 178, 212
Case Law 104, 109
Celibacy 85–88
Cephas 46–47, 50–52, 75, 89, 115
Chabad 141–42
Chameleon 6, 112, 114, 191
Children 9, 27, 106, 111, 142
Christology 3, 7, 78, 86–87, 163–64, 175, 177–79, 208

Christ's Law 1, 11–12, 16, 19, 111, 116, 147, 149–50, 163–65, 170, 204, 206–8
Circumcision 4–5, 9, 23–28, 30–33, 46, 49, 53–54, 64–66, 73–75, 77–81, 83–86, 88, 98, 162, 197, 199–200, 212
Clean 36–37, 39–41, 43–44, 89, 123, 149, 185, 190
Commandments 1, 9, 16, 25, 28, 33, 35, 41, 43, 54, 72, 74, 77–78, 82–87, 98–99, 104, 106–8, 117, 120, 129, 148, 156, 162, 170, 180, 187, 201
Commensality 16, 116, 123–24, 142, 187, 190, 193, 206, 208–9
Common Judaism 44–45, 73, 89, 120, 122, 195, 197
Conciliation 9, 61, 68, 71
Condescension 113, 115, 151, 153
Conscience 4, 10, 39, 41, 63, 69, 94–96, 114, 147, 206
Conservative Jews 158
Consistency 49, 55, 59, 66, 68, 70, 72, 157, 159, 169
Contact 36–38, 40–41, 48, 95, 99–101, 120, 140
Contamination 36, 38, 40
Conversion 26, 44, 49, 134, 137–41, 199, 202
Converts 47, 134–39, 141–42, 153–54, 165–66, 196
Corinth 4, 12, 29, 75–76, 78, 87, 90, 92, 96–103, 109–13, 152, 154, 156, 161, 163, 167–68, 175, 190, 193
Covenant 1, 5, 9, 24–27, 29, 35, 37, 42, 44–46, 50, 54–55, 73–74, 81–82, 103, 129, 169, 193
Culture 1, 27, 37, 87, 99, 101, 110, 180, 191, 203–4
Cunning 13, 16, 69, 114

Subject Index

Customs 6, 9, 41, 50, 53, 57, 65, 73, 81, 122, 143, 152, 180–181, 188, 191–92, 195, 198, 204
Cynics 113

Decalogue 100, 105
Deception 13, 16, 25, 62, 69, 114, 152, 210–211
Defilement 36–38, 41–42, 126, 185, 187
Dejudaisation 81
Devout Jews 196
Diaspora Jews 24, 26–27, 37, 53, 61, 74, 81, 105, 107, 137–39, 141, 149, 153, 187, 195–96, 203–4, 206
Dietary Laws 3, 10, 38–39, 41–42, 44, 47–49, 51–52, 94, 100, 102–3, 106, 109, 114, 126–28, 130, 148–49, 154, 182, 184–85, 187, 198, 204, 206
Differentiation 32, 35, 56, 129, 149, 178
Dining 94, 101, 117, 121, 124, 126, 128, 182, 191
Discontinuity 45, 59, 149
Displacement 211
Diversity 44, 62, 111, 116, 129, 149, 157, 178, 187, 202–3
Dominical Commands 19, 115, 164, 180, 184, 187–88, 209
Duplicitous 17
Duties 24, 57, 77, 84, 135, 138

Ecclesiology 4–5, 8, 29, 33–35, 45–46, 49, 57, 61–62, 65, 75, 87–88, 97–99, 102, 148, 152, 162–63, 182–83, 205, 211–12
Ekklesia 174
Election 1, 76, 79–80
Enslaved Leader 112
Epictetus 83, 110, 150
Epicureanism 113
Epispasm 80–81
Equality 32, 63, 176, 191
Equivocation 64
Erasure 2, 4–7, 27–28, 30, 32–34, 52, 89, 203, 211
Eschatology 5, 36, 86–87, 169, 178
Essenes 119–20, 122, 124, 195, 199
Ethics 86–87, 104–5, 107, 109, 111, 114, 142, 152–53, 162, 164, 168, 179, 208
Ethnicity 5–7, 9, 29, 32, 78, 158, 211
Eutychianism 178

Exclusivism 202
Exemplar 208
Exemption 24–25, 40–42, 49, 64, 94, 148, 199
Expediency 5, 9, 23–24

Faith 26, 28, 35–36, 41, 44, 49, 57, 59, 68, 71, 73, 77–78, 83–84, 133, 164–65, 167, 179, 204
Falsehood 69, 114
Festivals 37–38, 52, 64, 134
Food 4, 10–11, 16, 19, 32, 36–44, 46–47, 49–51, 53–54, 90–97, 99–104, 107–9, 115–19, 121–28, 130, 141–45, 147–49, 157, 173, 181–83, 185–88, 190–194, 196, 198, 202–6, 208–9
Food Laws 3, 10, 36, 38–39, 41–42, 44, 47–49, 51–52, 66, 94, 100, 102–3, 106, 109, 114, 126–28, 130, 148–49, 154, 182, 184–85, 187, 198, 204, 206
Foolhardiness 12
Foreskin 73–75, 79–81, 83–84, 86, 88
Former Gentiles 33–34
Former Jews 2, 4–7, 27–28, 30, 32–34, 52, 89, 203, 211
Forty Lashes 204
Freedom 3, 8, 11, 15, 35, 46, 63–64, 76, 78–79, 85, 88, 96, 134, 150–151, 162–63, 197, 205
Frum Jews 197
Fulfillment 5, 58, 104, 178

Galilee 186, 199, 203
Gamaliel 143, 203
Gentile Identity 31, 34, 74, 81, 84, 87
Gentiles 3, 5, 8, 11–13, 17, 24–30, 32–37, 41–43, 45–53, 55–57, 63, 65, 71–73, 75, 77–79, 81–86, 89, 94–96, 98–103, 106, 109, 115–16, 120–122, 125–31, 134–41, 145, 148–49, 152, 154, 159–60, 162, 169–70, 177–78, 183–84, 186–88, 190, 194, 197, 199–202, 204–6, 210–211
Gentile Sinners 19, 31, 50, 125, 140, 160, 183, 190, 202, 206, 208–9
Gentilise 80–81, 88, 163
Genus Tertium 33
Gnosticism 90, 97
God-Fearers 48, 75, 139, 145, 153
God's Law 116, 161–62, 170

Gospel 12–13, 24, 26, 31, 40, 42, 46–47, 50, 55, 57–58, 60, 66, 70–71, 73, 77, 108, 112, 114, 117, 121–22, 124–25, 128, 130, 148, 150, 152–53, 166–68, 173, 176–78, 180–185, 187–90, 193, 198, 200, 204, 206, 210
Grace 25, 154, 201
Guests 16, 47, 55, 95, 101, 116, 128, 142–47, 152, 169, 188, 191–95
Gymnasium 81

Halakhah 13, 17, 38, 40–42, 47, 53, 77, 82–83, 94, 99–100, 103, 105, 119–20, 123, 148, 152, 158, 186, 196–97, 199, 206–7, 209
Halakhic Flexibility 17, 206
Haredim 196–97
Hasidim 141
Hillel 38, 120, 122, 143, 192, 194–95
Historical Reliability of Acts 9, 23–24, 58–59, 66–67
Holiness 37–38, 43–44, 68, 81, 116–18, 120, 122, 144
Holy Nation 79–80
Hospitality 19, 141–46, 152, 169, 181, 186–88, 190–194, 196, 204, 209
Host 55, 116, 130, 142–43, 145–47, 152, 157, 186, 188, 190–194, 204
Household 10, 12, 16, 37, 43, 46, 48, 52, 75, 95–96, 101, 116–17, 122–23, 129, 141, 144, 152, 182, 185–87, 193, 195, 206
Hyperbole 29–30, 32, 51–52, 89, 152
Hyper-Literal Interpretation 15, 194
Hypocrisy 46, 50–51, 59–60, 69–71, 84, 95, 131, 133, 138

Identification 146, 152, 167, 169, 175
Identity 1, 3, 6–8, 26, 28–29, 34–35, 40, 44, 74, 78–79, 84, 130, 135, 144, 151, 168, 177–78, 191, 212
Idolatry 10–11, 15, 17, 36–37, 42, 46, 56, 90–103, 106–9, 115, 125–26, 128, 130, 159, 173, 190, 194, 204
Idol-Food 2, 10–12, 43, 46, 90–101, 103–4, 107–9, 126–27, 160, 167–68, 204, 208
Imitatio Christi 12, 14, 19, 35, 147–49, 164, 168–69, 173–76, 178–86, 188, 190, 192, 194, 196, 198, 200, 202, 204, 206, 208
Imitation 15–16, 19, 117–18, 131, 133, 142, 147, 151, 165, 173–76, 179–81, 185, 192–93, 209
Imperial Cult 78, 93
Impurity 30, 36–42, 48–49, 67, 117–18, 120–121, 123, 125, 129–30, 149, 181
Inconsistency 5, 12, 15, 64, 71, 90–91, 97, 164–65, 167
Indeterminate Food 94, 101–3, 108–9, 190
Indifference 9, 25–26, 28, 41, 47, 59, 72, 87, 96–97, 99, 103, 206, 211
Intention 38, 69, 109, 120, 149, 155
Interchange 176–79, 182
Interim Ethic 87
Intermarriage 26, 49, 85–88, 129
Intra-Jewish Polemic 51–52, 89, 185–87, 196, 201, 208
Invitations 130, 169
Irrelevance 28
Isaiah 169, 200–201
Israel 2, 4, 8, 29–30, 33–35, 37–38, 41, 44–45, 47–49, 71, 74–75, 79–81, 87, 106–7, 117, 119, 127–28, 131, 134, 138, 141–42, 158, 177–78, 181, 194–96, 202–4
Israel's Calling 79, 82

James 2, 6, 9, 11, 24, 28, 30, 45–48, 51, 53–62, 64, 66–73, 89, 97, 100, 112, 124, 129, 157, 161, 164, 169, 180, 183, 210–212
Jerome 59–60, 193, 200
Jerusalem 3, 9, 13, 35, 49, 53, 56–57, 60–69, 71, 75, 81, 84, 87, 98, 101, 116–17, 127, 139, 188, 191, 196, 200, 210
Jerusalem Collection 60–61, 65, 188
Jerusalem Congregation 13, 25, 55, 57, 60–62, 67–72, 84, 97, 101, 200
Jerusalem Council 24, 27, 42, 46, 49, 56, 64, 84, 98–99, 101, 199–200
Jesus 11–12, 19, 26, 28, 30, 34, 38, 40–42, 47–49, 61, 80–83, 87, 97, 101–2, 117, 121–24, 129, 138–39, 147–49, 157, 163, 169–70, 177–83, 185–91, 193–96, 198–201, 204–10

Jesus-Believing Gentiles 30, 34–35, 40–42, 44, 49, 56, 83, 199
Jesus-Believing Jews 1, 19, 24, 27, 30, 33–35, 41, 43–44, 47, 49, 54, 64, 66, 71–72, 75, 79–80, 82–83, 148, 157, 194, 200, 212
Jesus-Believing Nazirites 56, 65
Jesus-Believing Pharisees 199
Jesus' Command 163, 182, 189, 205
Jesus' Halakhah 38, 40, 47, 117, 120–121, 140, 148–49, 181–83, 186–87, 191, 205
Jesus Tradition 178–80, 182, 184, 189–90, 207–8
Jew-Gentile Distinction 1, 4, 7–8, 11–12, 30–35, 41–44, 56, 73–75, 79, 81, 83–87, 98, 128–30, 136, 157, 163, 183, 194, 205, 211
Jewish Apostasy 4, 44, 89
Jewish Assimilation 211
Jewish Calling 79–80, 82, 85
Jewish Continuity 212
Jewish Flesh 45, 177
Jewish Flexibility 206, 210
Jewish Goyim 52
Jewish Greek 30, 32, 82, 104, 148
Jewish Hospitality 143, 146, 152, 187, 192
Jewish Law 2, 9, 11–15, 36–38, 40, 42, 49, 54, 56–57, 60–61, 63, 65–66, 70–71, 76, 82–83, 94, 96–97, 101–2, 104, 111–12, 116–17, 127–30, 141, 148–49, 151, 153–54, 157, 161, 170, 187, 195, 197–98, 205–6, 210–211
Jewish Messiah 177
Jewishness 7–8, 17, 23, 25, 27, 29–33, 35, 37, 39, 41, 43, 45–47, 49, 51, 53, 55, 57, 59, 61, 63, 65, 67, 69, 71, 73–75, 77, 79–81, 83, 85, 87–88, 90, 101, 103, 105, 142, 178
Jewish Particularity 28
Jewish Proselytizing 57, 116, 130, 132–38, 140, 165, 169
Jewish Sinners 120, 125, 140, 206
Jewish Tradition 1, 10, 37, 50, 101, 103, 200
John 5–6, 50, 55, 58, 83, 102, 155, 177–78, 181, 211
Josephus 37, 54, 73, 81, 83, 100, 106, 119, 125, 135, 137, 139–40, 142–44, 146, 153, 158, 161, 169, 181, 186–87, 195, 198–99, 203, 205
Judaism 1–3, 6, 8–10, 13–14, 26, 30, 37, 44–46, 50–51, 64–65, 70–72, 75, 82, 90, 101, 104–5, 114, 116–21, 127, 129–32, 134, 136–42, 154, 165–66, 195–96, 204–5
Justification 30, 32, 87

Kingdom 38, 79, 117, 185–86, 188
Kinship 29, 182, 201
Kosher Food 38–39, 130, 141, 186

Lapsed Paul 59
Law 1–5, 7, 9, 11–14, 16–17, 19, 25, 27, 30, 33, 35–37, 40–45, 47–49, 53–58, 60–68, 70–75, 77, 81–84, 87, 94, 103, 105–6, 110–112, 115–17, 119, 121–23, 127–30, 134–35, 148–65, 167, 170, 174, 177, 182–83, 186–87, 190–191, 194–206, 209–12
Lawless 15, 121, 127, 159–60, 165, 205, 207–8
Law Observance 1, 14, 16, 41, 54–57, 62–63, 65, 67, 71–72, 74, 81–83, 129, 157, 194, 196, 198, 201, 208, 210
Lenient Halakhah 119–20, 130, 186, 206
Less Strict Jews 50, 120
Letter of Aristeas 30, 127–28, 192, 210
Liberal Jew 10, 101
Life of Apollonius 127
Lifestyle Adaptability 15–16
Lightfoot-Sloyan Hypothesis 194–95
Love Command 11–12, 149, 164
Lukan James 57
Lukan Paul 27, 64, 66–67, 71
Lukan Peter 50
Luke 9, 12, 16, 19, 24–27, 47, 50, 53–58, 60–62, 64–70, 72–73, 75, 94, 97–98, 101, 117, 121–23, 143, 147, 160, 169, 177, 180–191, 193, 196–201, 203–4, 208–10
Luther 25, 77–79, 179

Macellum 93–94, 99–103, 109
Mainstream Jews 101, 103, 116, 119, 181, 201, 208
Male-Female Distinction 31
Mark 7, 12, 14, 16–17, 19, 30–32, 38, 41–42, 45–48, 50, 54, 75–76, 84, 114,

117, 121, 147–49, 158, 170, 180–183, 186–87, 195, 197–98, 201, 203, 208–11
Market 43, 93–94, 100, 103, 134, 141
Marriage 79, 85–86
Mashal 12, 48, 148–49, 192
Masquerade 6, 114
Matrilineal Descent 26
Matthew 40, 48, 82, 131, 137–40, 157, 180, 185, 197, 201, 207
Meals 10–11, 36–37, 40–41, 43, 47, 50, 93, 95, 99–104, 116–18, 123–26, 128–30, 142, 182, 191, 193, 195, 198, 205–6
Menu 47–49, 130, 191
Messiah 77, 86–87, 99, 169, 177, 193, 201, 207–8
Messianic Halakhah 206
Messianic Jews 35, 212
Metonymy 73, 75, 80–81
Mikvaot 186
Missiology 1, 43, 48, 60, 80, 99, 122, 137, 139–41, 145, 150, 166, 169, 173, 182–83, 188, 193
Mission Discourse 188
Mixtures 36–41, 44, 89, 94, 130, 186, 206
Mosaic Law 1–2, 11–12, 28, 36, 38, 41, 48–49, 52, 56, 58–59, 66–67, 72, 82–83, 108, 110, 112, 127–28, 148–51, 153, 156–58, 160–162, 164–65, 170, 195, 199–200, 204–5, 209–11
Moses 1, 11–12, 29, 36, 54, 57–58, 60–61, 77, 79, 82–83, 115, 134, 137, 148–49, 159, 161–65, 170, 192, 195, 199, 205–6
Motive 27, 65, 86

Narrow Interpretation 197–98, 200–201
Nations 30, 35, 37, 48, 81–82, 87, 107, 127–28, 139, 157, 178, 203
Nazarene Sect 45, 200, 206
Nazirite Vow 9, 53–56, 62–65, 67, 106, 118, 169
New Covenant 63
New Creation 4–5, 7–8, 28, 33, 178
New Israel 47
Noachide Laws 83, 99, 200
Nomistic Language 11–12, 16, 82, 110, 205

Non-Jews 15, 36, 42, 48, 52, 83, 125, 148, 187, 200
Nothing 1, 7–8, 10, 28–30, 37–39, 41, 43, 53, 68, 83–85, 94, 98–99, 161–62, 168, 202, 210
Nullification 38–40, 148, 170

Obedience 13, 28, 57, 61, 70–71, 80, 83–84, 155, 162
Obligations 1, 24–25, 72–73, 75, 77, 131, 162, 200, 212
Observant Jews 1–2, 25, 50, 53–57, 62, 65, 67–68, 71, 83, 101, 122, 124, 129, 141, 158, 161, 186, 195–97, 200, 202–3, 210
Obsolete Identity 8
Occasional Conformity 2, 13, 35, 71, 88
Occupational Callings 78
Odysseus 111
Offence 4, 16, 33–34, 61
Old Israel 4
Oneness 31, 47
One New Man 33
Ontological Categories 37–38
Open Table-Fellowship 19, 123–24, 142, 147, 173, 182, 206, 209–10
Operational Flexibility 141
Opponents 62, 65, 68, 75, 113, 136, 199, 204
Opportunism 6
Ordinances 33, 37, 81–82, 134
Ordinary Jews 17, 19, 50, 117–18, 123, 138, 141–42, 157, 181–82, 185, 187, 190, 194–95, 202–4, 208–9
Orthodox Jews 39, 52, 130
Outreach 130–131, 136, 141–42, 160, 165, 196
Outsiders 52–53, 127, 160, 195, 208

Pagans 48, 93, 95, 97, 125, 138, 159, 193
Pars-Pro-Toto Language 73–74, 81
Particularity 78, 178
Passover 75, 193
Paternalism 35
Patrons 112, 158, 168
Paul 1–19, 23–105, 107–16, 118, 120–123, 129–31, 136–37, 139–40, 142–43, 147–70, 173

Subject Index

Pauline Accommodation 15, 17, 50, 68, 110, 113, 115, 131–32, 143, 147, 149, 151, 153, 169, 176, 192–93, 205–6
Pauline Authorship 73
Pauline Deception 114
Paulinism 15
Paul's Apostasy 6
Paul's Commands 80, 101, 103
Paul's Ecclesiology 5
Paul's Eschatology 86–87
Paul's Ethics 7, 78, 109, 147, 155, 173
Paul's Expediency 23
Paul's Flexibility 68
Paul's Freedom 150–151
Paul's Gospel 30, 33, 75, 169, 177
Paul's Halakhah 42, 83
Paul's Hyperbole 32
Paul's Identification 55, 175
Paul's Identity 1
Paul's Imitation of Christ 16, 164–65, 170, 175–76, 209
Paul's Inconsistency 50, 63, 73
Paul's Jewishness 1–2, 9, 14, 24, 28, 64, 66, 73, 83, 98, 111–15, 152, 210–211
Paul's Messianism 87, 169
Paul's Mission 83, 193
Paul's Opponents 110
Paul's Purification 210
Paul's Relativising 29
Paul's Rule 19, 33, 98, 162, 205
Paul's Self-Enslavement 107, 111–12
Paul's Torah Observance 56, 206
Paul's Un-Jewishness 8, 70, 83
Paul's Vow 56
Paul the Pharisee 39, 50, 55, 120, 166, 187, 196, 202
Pentateuch 38, 157, 161
Pentecost 54, 67, 75
Perichoresis 178
Peter 3, 25, 32, 36, 47–51, 53, 60, 65, 89, 150, 182, 188, 199–201
Peter's Vision 36–37, 47–49
Pharisaic Accommodation 116, 119–20, 124
Pharisaic Halakhah 25, 39–40, 44–45, 52, 89, 117–20, 122–25, 135, 137–38, 140, 143, 148, 157–58, 170, 185, 194–95, 197–203, 206, 209–10
Pharisaic Proselytizing 136–39, 141–42, 166, 202

Pharisees 19, 40, 45, 50–51, 55, 61, 64–65, 99, 116–25, 129, 135, 137–42, 148, 157–59, 166, 169, 181–83, 185–87, 190, 194–203, 207–9
Philo 73, 79, 100, 105, 112, 118, 129, 131–35, 137, 139–44, 146, 169, 181, 187, 191
Pious Fraud 13, 59, 64, 66, 73, 211
Pious Jews 1, 56, 67, 116–17, 123, 127–28, 130, 197
Polytheistic Gentiles 10, 14, 129, 167, 187
Pork 38–39, 43, 102, 141, 206
Potentially Defiled 36
Practising Jews 9, 19, 45, 57, 84, 162, 205, 210, 212
Pretence 68–69
Priests 62, 79–80, 116–19, 128, 202–3
Prioritization 47
Priscilla 75
Prohibited Foods 36, 93–94, 130
Proselytes 47, 134–39, 141–42, 153–54, 165–66, 196
Proselytizing Pharisees 136–37, 139
Psychagogy 113
Punctiliousness 45, 198
Purity Laws 9, 12, 30, 35–38, 40, 42, 44, 46–49, 53–54, 67, 100, 103, 117–19, 121–25, 129–30, 140–141, 147–49, 182, 186, 195–96, 198, 202

Qumran Halakhah 79, 105–7, 116, 119, 123–24, 129, 199
Qumran Jews 50, 120, 123–25, 195

Rabban Gamaliel 77
Rabbi Jacob Emden 77
Rabbinic Judaism 26, 38–40, 52, 55, 67, 72, 80, 84, 95, 102–4, 106, 109, 120, 122, 192, 197–98
Reassessment 13–15, 17–18, 21, 209
Reform Rabbis 52
Regulations 37, 98, 195, 199
Relativization 29, 78, 148
Religious Jews 181, 197, 208
Relinquishing Rights 115, 150–151, 205
Renegade Jews 127–28
Renunciation 11, 99, 151, 176
Replacement 33, 83
Repudiation 12, 203
Requirements 61, 82, 118, 150, 197

Respective Callings 83
Responsibilities 11, 24, 43, 84, 98, 105, 205
Restrictions 49, 72, 78, 108, 128, 130
Restrictive Clause 16, 19, 154, 156, 160, 162–63, 190, 201, 203, 209–10
Revalorization 32, 178
Rhetorical Adaptability 15–17
Rhetorical Strategy 17, 29–30, 45, 70, 74, 88, 91–92, 110, 112–14, 138
Righteousness 45, 121–22, 181, 198
Ritual 25, 30, 54, 63, 74, 78, 97, 103, 108, 117, 130, 148, 180, 191, 200
Ritual Purity 9, 41–42, 46, 50–51, 53–54, 57, 65, 67, 116–19, 122–24, 127, 141, 148, 157, 182, 185–87, 195–96, 198, 202
Rome 28, 33–34, 37–40, 42–43, 55, 74–75, 84, 107, 161
Rubbish Language 44–46
Rule in All the Churches 12–13, 75, 80–81, 83–84, 87–88, 98–99, 149, 162–63, 190–192, 205, 210, 212
Rulings 12, 40, 98–99, 102–3, 122, 149
Rumours 53–54, 57, 60, 68, 71

Sabbath 37, 52, 68, 83, 121, 141–42, 201
Sacrifices 9–10, 30, 53–54, 57, 60, 65, 67, 93–96, 102, 117–18, 203
Sadducean Halakhah 119–20, 194–96, 199
Salvation 25–26, 28, 43, 76, 78, 86, 112, 134, 167–68
Samaritans 153
Sarah 132–33, 135
Saturnilians 97
Scrupulous Jews 37, 39–41, 50, 116, 122, 129–30, 158, 197–98
Second Temple Judaism 11, 19, 44, 51, 53, 55, 74, 79, 82, 87, 104, 108, 116, 118, 120, 123, 125, 127–28, 131, 136–39, 143, 147, 149, 157, 161, 173, 182, 194, 210–211
Sectarian Jews 44–45, 50, 116, 119, 122, 124–25, 141–42, 183, 195, 198–99, 202, 209
Self-Contradiction 63
Self-Enslavement 151
Self-Humbling 112, 177
Semitic Idiom 148

Septuagint 82, 104, 140
Servanthood 29, 76–77, 79–80, 108, 111, 118, 144, 147, 169, 177
Servant Nation 79
Servile Flatterer 110
Shammai 120, 122
Shellfish 38, 43, 51, 102
Shema 103
Shlichim 141–42
Shoulder-Pharisee 201
Simpletons 12, 26, 154
Sin 30, 54, 86, 103, 122, 125, 133, 154, 156–57, 159, 177, 181
Sinai 29
Sinners 19, 42, 45, 50, 69, 120–123, 147, 159–60, 164–67, 169–70, 181–83, 185, 187–88, 190, 205–9
Situation-Callings 76, 79
Skandalon 104, 106–9
Slaves 16, 85, 88, 108, 112, 121, 150, 166, 168, 174, 176–77, 181
Solidarity 191
Son of David 177
Son of God 168, 177, 204
Sophistic Deception 114
Soteriology 88, 111–14, 131, 133–35, 167, 169, 174, 181
Spiritual Contamination 41, 94
Spiritual Immaturity 35
Spiritual Israel 8
Standards 11, 15, 42, 45, 50, 57, 71–72, 89, 101, 116, 121–25, 157, 159, 168, 195, 197
Strangers 146, 188, 191
Strict Jews 17, 19, 50, 120, 130, 141, 158–59, 181, 186, 190, 194–95, 197–99, 201–3, 206, 208–9
Stringent Interpretations 40, 119, 125, 197
Stumbling Blocks 10, 12, 25, 35, 41, 43–44, 93, 104–9, 120, 126, 147, 167–68, 208
Subidentity 153, 170, 194, 202–3
Supererogatory Commandments 118
Supersessionism 33
Synagogue Discipline 156
Synagogues 12, 56, 68, 75, 102, 131, 134, 140, 156, 187, 204

Table-Fellowship 17, 19, 35–36, 41–44, 93, 95, 116–18, 121–30, 140–142,

145–47, 152, 157, 164, 166, 169, 182–83, 185–88, 190–191, 193–96, 198, 202, 204, 206, 209–10
Taboos 48, 129
Tarsus 196
Tax Collectors 121, 169, 181–82, 185, 188
Temple 9–10, 53–57, 59–62, 66–67, 93, 95, 116, 118, 182, 203, 210
Tendenz 24, 210
Tertium Genus 34
Tertium Quid 178
Testimony 53, 63–65, 69, 74, 154, 210
Theatres 37, 101, 133
Third Race 4–5, 7–8, 33–34, 211
Timothy 9, 24–27, 75, 77
Timothy's Circumcision 23–25, 27, 88
Tithed Food 50, 117–18, 122–23, 130, 140–141, 196, 198, 202
Titus 27, 32
Torah 5, 14–15, 36–37, 41, 47–49, 54, 56, 61, 64, 66, 71–72, 77, 84, 101, 104–5, 117, 120, 125–26, 128–30, 134, 138, 142, 148, 153–54, 157–58, 161–62, 194, 196–98, 200–202, 205–6, 208, 210
Torah-Observant Jews 1–2, 7–13, 18–19, 23–25, 35–36, 38–39, 43, 52–59, 62, 64–66, 68–70, 72–74, 84, 114, 116, 118, 127–28, 142, 149, 153–54, 158–60, 170, 181, 185–87, 194, 196–97, 200–201, 204–7, 210, 212
Torah-Observant Paul 2, 4, 12–15, 17–19, 23, 33, 44, 53–54, 60, 68, 73, 75, 87–88, 90, 108–10, 114, 150, 153–54, 162, 169–70, 173, 209
Tradition 14, 23, 37, 41, 50, 54, 66, 104, 109, 115, 129, 134–35, 148, 157–58, 180, 182–85, 187, 193, 195–96, 199–201, 210
Transcendence 4–5, 7
Transference 5
Transgressors 124, 159, 207
Traps 61, 104, 107
Treasured Possession 79
Tribes 45, 127–28
Trickery 13, 55, 59, 69, 73, 211
Trivialization 29
Troublemaker 204
True Israel 4

True Jews 52, 197
True Rhetoric 16, 114, 151, 160, 191
Trustworthiness of Acts 23–24

Ultra-Orthodox Jews 38–39, 141
Uncircumcision 4–5, 28, 30, 33, 73–74, 84, 162
Unclean Food 36–41, 43–44, 46–47, 49–51, 53, 89, 94, 102, 123, 126, 149, 182, 185–86, 190, 204, 206
Under the Law 19, 67, 115, 153–55, 157–58, 170, 190, 194, 196–99, 201, 208–9
Unimportance 28
Unity 34, 62, 72, 90–91, 107, 111, 182, 191
Unity With Distinction 32, 85
Un-Jewish 10, 101, 103, 109
Unleavened Bread 38, 54, 192
Unsubstantiated Rumours 204

Valentinians 97
Vegetables 37, 44, 126, 130
Versatility 131, 133
Very Strict Jews 186, 196–97
Vocational Callings 77–79
Vows 9, 53, 67–68, 118

Weak 10, 35, 37, 39, 43, 104, 109, 167, 174, 208
Welcoming 35, 141–42, 162
Wickedness 122, 126, 159
Wine 36, 43, 106, 118, 125–26, 191
Without the Law 159–60, 204
Women 31, 81, 85–86, 102, 111, 117, 121, 132, 176–77
Worship 52, 87, 95

Yeshiva 38, 52
Yeshua 84
YHWH 177
Yoke 77, 199–201, 207
Yom Kippur 102

Zealous for Torah 9, 45, 50, 54–55, 70–72, 100, 139, 141, 158, 196, 210

www.ingramcontent.com/pod-product-compliance
Lightning Source LLC
Chambersburg PA
CBHW060508300426
44112CB00017B/2592